New Zealand
Wines
2021

Michael Cooper's Buyer's Guide

upstart press

A catalogue record for this book is available from the National Library of New Zealand

ISBN 978-1-988516-86-8

An Upstart Press Book
Published in 2020 by Upstart Press Ltd
Level 6, BDO Tower, 19–21 Como St, Takapuna
Auckland, New Zealand

Designed by www.cvdgraphics.nz
Printed by Opus Group Pty Ltd

Front cover photograph: iStock

Reviews of the latest editions

'Want to find a good New Zealand wine? You'd be hard-pressed to go past *New Zealand Wines 2020: Michael Cooper's Buyer's Guide*.' – Emma Jenkins, *Winestate*

'For anybody who is interested in New Zealand wine, it doesn't come any better. A great book – it always is.' – Leighton Smith

'Michael has a lovely, laid-back tasting notes style that doesn't scream at you. A very reliable taster.' – Caro's Wine Merchants

'So when Cooper says a wine is great – and great value – you sit up and listen.' – Josie Steenhart, *Stuff*

'[Michael Cooper is] New Zealand's leading consumer advocate in wine.' – Allan Scott, *Marlborough Man*

'The softcover book that first made its presence felt in 1992 has become somewhat of a bible for wine lovers here at home and, more recently via his website, overseas.' – Tessa Nicholson, *New Zealand Winegrower*

'. . . the Gandalf of New Zealand wine critics, Michael Cooper . . .' – Yvonne Lorkin, Canvas, *New Zealand Herald*

'Michael is deeply entrenched in the landscape of New Zealand wine. . . . We consider his extensive knowledge and long experience vital as a benchmark tool when reflecting on our wines.' – Dry River

Michael Cooper is New Zealand's most acclaimed wine writer, with 45 books and several major literary awards to his credit, including the Montana Medal for the supreme work of non-fiction at the 2003 Montana New Zealand Book Awards for the first edition of his magnum opus, *Wine Atlas of New Zealand*. In the 2004 New Year Honours, Michael was appointed an Officer of the New Zealand Order of Merit for services to wine writing.

Author of the country's biggest-selling wine book, the annual *New Zealand Wines: Michael Cooper's Buyer's Guide*, now in its 29th edition, he was awarded the Sir George Fistonich Medal in recognition of services to New Zealand wine in 2009. The award is made each year at the country's largest wine competition, the New Zealand International Wine Show, to a 'living legend' of New Zealand wine. The weekly wine columnist for the *New Zealand Listener*, he has also been the New Zealand editor of Australia's *Winestate* magazine for many years, and he writes regular wine features for *North & South* magazine.

In 1977 he obtained a Master of Arts degree from the University of Auckland with a thesis entitled 'The Wine Lobby: Pressure Group Politics and the New Zealand Wine Industry'. He was marketing manager for Babich Wines from 1980 to 1990, and since 1991 has been a full-time wine writer.

Cooper's other major works include *100 Must-Try New Zealand Wines* (2011); the much-extended second edition of *Wine Atlas of New Zealand* (2008); *Classic Wines of New Zealand* (second edition 2005); *The Wines and Vineyards of New Zealand* (published in five editions from 1984 to 1996); and *Pocket Guide to Wines of New Zealand* (second edition 2000). He is the New Zealand consultant for Hugh Johnson's annual, best-selling *Pocket Wine Book*.

Michael's comprehensive, frequently updated website, *MichaelCooper.co.nz*, was launched in 2011.

Contents

The Winemaking Regions of New Zealand

Area in producing vines 2020 (percentage of national producing vineyard area)

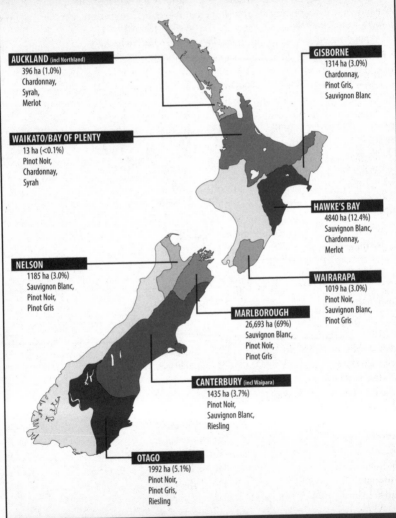

AUCKLAND (incl Northland)
396 ha (1.0%)
Chardonnay,
Syrah,
Merlot

WAIKATO/BAY OF PLENTY
13 ha (<0.1%)
Pinot Noir,
Chardonnay,
Syrah

NELSON
1185 ha (3.0%)
Sauvignon Blanc,
Pinot Noir,
Pinot Gris

GISBORNE
1314 ha (3.0%)
Chardonnay,
Pinot Gris,
Sauvignon Blanc

HAWKE'S BAY
4840 ha (12.4%)
Sauvignon Blanc,
Chardonnay,
Merlot

WAIRARAPA
1019 ha (3.0%)
Pinot Noir,
Sauvignon Blanc,
Pinot Gris

MARLBOROUGH
26,693 ha (69%)
Sauvignon Blanc,
Pinot Noir,
Pinot Gris

CANTERBURY (incl Waipara)
1435 ha (3.7%)
Pinot Noir,
Sauvignon Blanc,
Riesling

OTAGO
1992 ha (5.1%)
Pinot Noir,
Pinot Gris,
Riesling

These figures (rounded to the closest percentages) are from New Zealand Winegrowers' *Vineyard Register Report 2017–2020*. During the period 2017 to 2020, the total area of producing vines was predicted to expand from 36,943 to 38,886 hectares – a rise of just over 5 per cent.

Preface

Things are rosy in the wine industry – at least on the surface. The quality of New Zealand wine has certainly never been better, reflecting the advancing maturity of the country's vines and winegrowers.

Covid-19 presented a stiff challenge. The vast majority of the 2020 grape crop was still on the vines when the Government announced New Zealand would go into lockdown on 26 March. However, the industry was quickly told it could operate as an 'essential service', enabling the vintage to go ahead under Alert Level 4 restrictions, and no cases were reported of virus transmission in the vineyards or wineries.

From the start, the prospects of top-flight wine from 2020 looked good. Dryness was a key factor. From late December to mid-April, Marlborough – where nearly 78 per cent of the national grape crop was harvested – recorded less than a quarter of its normal rainfall. 'For overall fruit quality, this is one of the best vintages I have experienced,' enthused Ivan Sutherland, co-founder of Dog Point Vineyard.

2020 was a bumper vintage – 11 per cent heavier than 2019 and above the previous record, set in 2014. However, the industry needed a big harvest, says Philip Gregan, CEO of New Zealand Winegrowers. 'New Zealand wine stocks are estimated to have been at record low levels going into vintage 2020.'

Some large wine producers are thriving. Delegat Group (which owns the Oyster Bay and Delegat brands, plus Barossa Valley Estate in Australia) achieved record sales in the year to 30 June – up by 9 per cent to 3.3 million cases. Profit after tax for the year rose 37 per cent to $64.1 million.

Forsyth Barr, an investment firm, believes that Delegat's success reflects its high degree of exposure to 'off-premise' consumption (via supermarket sales). 'The economic backdrop remains uncertain, with expectations that global wine consumption declines in the near term due to the disruption of the food service [especially restaurants] channel, more than offsetting an increase in at-home consumption.'

Even the spectacular growth in wine exports (worth over $1.8 billion in 2019) is arousing concern. Shipments in bulk now account for over 40 per cent of all wine leaving New Zealand, growing at more than double the rate of bottled wine exports.

Blair Gibbs, of Winelord, in Nelson, distinguishes between 'good' and 'bad' bulk exports. 'Good bulk belongs to a company with capability to transfer the wine to one of its offshore partners, package it under one of their own brands and proceed to distribute it in their local market. Bad bulk is … sold at a commodity price to any national or international buyer, to be blended (?), packaged in the destination market and sold at discounted prices.'

Many wine producers are struggling to survive. A senior figure in the Central Otago wine scene expects 'a lot of failure down here of wineries… Central Otago Pinot Noir is all premium priced in export markets and predominantly consumed on-premise. But the wines that are seeing growth in sales are 100 per cent grocery and in the $10–$15 range. None of this is Central Otago Pinot Noir. The ones you really feel most for are those that recently spent millions of dollars on new cellar door and lodge facilities.'

Grasshopper Rock, an acclaimed producer of Central Otago Pinot Noir, is candid about its current challenges. 'In the year of our smallest harvest since 2007, we were also dealing with a substantial drop in sales through restaurant and retail channels. With Covid-19, borders closed and restaurants struggling globally, we made the decision to sell much of our fruit.'

The good news is that online retail sales are booming. Wineries are using Facebook Live and Instagram Live to expand their audiences, and using Zoom to run live interactive tasting sessions.

Overseas wines, which dominate the sub-$10 category, control over 40 per cent of the total market for wine in New Zealand. As Daniel Schwarzenbach, of Blackenbrook Vineyard, in Nelson, has observed: 'The biggest challenge for the whole industry is going to be selling the beautiful wines we are making this year.'

Now is a great time to go out of your way to support local winegrowers.

— *Michael Cooper*

Vintage Charts 2010–2020

WHITES	Auckland	Gisborne	Hawke's Bay	Wairarapa	Nelson	Marlborough	Canterbury	Otago
2020	6	6	6	6	5–6	6–7	6–7	4
2019	7	7	7	6	6	5	6	6
2018	3–4	4	4	4	3–4	4	4	4
2017	3	4	4	3	3	2–5	3–4	5
2016	3	4	4	5	3	4–5	5–6	5
2015	5	5	5	5	4	6	6	4
2014	6	6	5–6	5–6	5–6	5	3–5	5
2013	7	7	7	6	5	6–7	6–7	5–6
2012	3–4	2	3–4	3–4	4	4–5	4–5	4–6
2011	3	3	4	4	4	4	4	3
2010	7	6–7	7	6	7	7	6	6

REDS	Auckland	Gisborne	Hawke's Bay	Wairarapa	Nelson	Marlborough	Canterbury	Otago
2020	7	6	7	6	5–6	6–7	6–7	4
2019	7	7	7	6	6	7	6	5
2018	3–4	4	4	4	3	3	4	4
2017	2	3	3	3	3	3–5	3–4	5
2016	3	4	4	5	3	5	5–6	5
2015	4	4	5	5	4	5	6	4
2014	5–6	5–6	5–6	5–6	5–6	5	3–5	5
2013	6–7	7	6–7	6	6	6–7	6–7	5–6
2012	3–5	2	3	3–4	4	4–5	4–5	4–6
2011	2	2	3–4	4	3	4	4	3
2010	7	6	6	5	6	6–7	5	5–6

7 = Outstanding 6 = Excellent 5 = Above average 4 = Average 3 = Below average 2 = Poor 1 = Bad

2020 Vintage Report

From the start, the prospects for superb wine from the 2020 vintage looked strong. 'We know parts of the country have been in drought and the pastoral farmers don't like that,' observed Philip Gregan, CEO of New Zealand Winegrowers, on 23 May, 'but for us in the wine industry, these conditions are absolutely tailor-made for producing great wine.'

'For overall fruit quality, this is one of the best vintages I've experienced,' enthused industry veteran Ivan Sutherland, of Dog Point Vineyard in Marlborough. In Hawke's Bay, Nicholas Buck, CEO of Te Mata Estate, declared 2020 was 'probably the greatest vintage' in his career, 'even better than 2019.'

With a total of 457,000 tonnes of grapes harvested, it was a bumper crop – 11 per cent bigger than 2019 and nearly 3 per cent above the previous record, set in 2014. Sauvignon Blanc dominated the harvest (73.8 per cent), followed by Pinot Noir (7.7 per cent), Pinot Gris (6.5 per cent), Chardonnay (6.2 per cent), Merlot (2.5 per cent) and Riesling (1 per cent). Almost 65 per cent of the country's entire grape crop was of a single grape variety from a single region – Marlborough Sauvignon Blanc.

Spring began with average September temperatures around most of the country. October was wetter than usual in most east coast regions, with normal temperatures in the North Island and upper South Island, but colder than usual from central Canterbury to Otago.

Then in late spring, temperatures soared. November proved to be the country's hottest ever, coupled with below-average rain in east coast wine regions. By the end of spring, NIWA reported that the warmth in the North Island had 'dried out the ground'.

Summer started in December as 'a tale of two islands' – warmer than average in most of the North Island, but cooler than usual in the south. In early to mid-January, NIWA reported 'a broad swathe of the upper North Island, stretching from Cape Reinga to Coromandel and Waikato, along with parts of Hawke's Bay and Wairarapa, were experiencing very dry conditions.'

February was a mixed bag: although wet in the south, extremely dry, warm weather in the upper South Island and North Island intensified the drought. In early autumn, on 12 March the entire North Island and parts of the South Island (including Tasman, Marlborough and North Canterbury) were declared officially to be in drought.

March temperatures were average across most of the North Island, but cooler than normal in the eastern and lower South Island. In April – the key harvest month – conditions stayed favourable for winegrowing, with mild temperatures, low rainfall and dry soils in most regions in the North Island and upper South Island.

Auckland (and Northland)

Expect some fine wines from the north this year. Villa Maria, based at Mangere, praised 2020 as 'one of the best we have seen in Auckland, with near-perfect warm and dry conditions for ripening fruit without disease pressure'.

In Auckland, growers harvested 1249 tonnes of grapes – 21 per cent less than in 2019 and just 0.3 per cent of the national crop. Chardonnay was the principal variety (401 tonnes), followed by Pinot Gris (237 tonnes), Syrah (152 tonnes) and Merlot (141 tonnes).

Northland growers harvested just 269 tonnes of grapes – 16 per cent less than in 2019 and less than 0.1 per cent of the national crop. Syrah topped the charts with 49 tonnes picked, just ahead of Pinot Gris (48 tonnes) and Chardonnay (41 tonnes).

In spring, September was wetter and warmer than usual, followed by a warm October with average rainfall. November was drier than usual, with temperatures well above average.

Mudbrick, on Waiheke Island, reported 'a difficult start to the season', with some hail damage, 'and all blocks being battered by constant windy wet weather in the spring.' However, Villa Maria, at Mangere, reported 'an excellent start to the season, with uniform bud-burst and flowering'.

At the start of summer, December was warmer and drier than normal, in both Auckland and Northland. The pattern of above-average temperatures continued into January, with well below average rainfall. On 22 January, NIWA reported 'widespread extreme dryness, from northern Waikato up to Northland, reflecting too many dry westerly winds and not enough rain'. Northland kiwi were observed struggling to feed on hard-baked soils, unable to probe the ground for bugs.

On 12 February, an official drought was declared in all areas north of Auckland's harbour bridge. During the last month of summer, the weather stayed warm and much drier than normal.

Autumn opened with a dry March and average temperatures. Obsidian, on Waiheke Island, reported on 9 March that 'picking commenced on 24 February due to veraison [the onset of ripening] occurring roughly two weeks earlier than previous vintages. The season has been exceptionally dry, with a record-breaking 47 days without rain. As a result, there is an abundance of exceptionally high quality, deliciously ripe fruit across all varieties.'

In April, the weather in Auckland stayed much drier than usual, with average temperatures.

On 15 April, Kumeu River reported an early vintage, 'dry but not particularly warm. Everything looks great.' Mudbrick enthused: 'The reds this year have been mind-blowing! Fruit was in perfect condition, with concentration not seen on Waiheke since 2013. The Bordeaux varieties (Malbec, Merlot, Cabernet Sauvignon and Petit Verdot) are black, with intense perfume and structure.'

Gisborne

Unlike Auckland, Gisborne's growers picked a significantly larger grape crop than in 2019 – up by 17 per cent. At 18,959 tonnes, Gisborne produced 4.3 per cent of the country's harvest in 2020, with Chardonnay (8770 tonnes) the principal variety, followed by Sauvignon Blanc (4376 tonnes) and Pinot Gris (4322 tonnes.)

In spring, September was dry, with average temperatures. October saw normal warmth and higher than usual rainfall, followed by a hot (2.1°C above normal), slightly drier than usual November. Villa Maria reported that 'warm and settled weather over the late spring flowering period produced healthy yields'.

Overall, summer was warm and dry. A warm, slightly wet December was followed by a warm, dry January (with half the normal rainfall) and a dry, hot February (with temperatures averaging 1.9°C above average).

Autumn began with a cool, dry March. On 11 March, James Millton reported the '2020 vintage is amazing, such good conditions… Today we harvested the Clos de Ste Anne Viognier and, again, I am amazed with the quality.'

After a warm, far drier than usual April, Villa Maria reported its 'earliest Gisborne vintage to date. Excellent Pinot Gris and Gewürztraminer wines have been produced, but undoubtedly the shining stars from our Gisborne vineyards are once again Chardonnay and Albariño.'

Hawke's Bay

Lovers of red wine and Chardonnay should expect some striking Hawke's Bay wines from 2020. 'The Hawke's Bay 2019–20 growing season was slightly cooler than the last four seasons… but still above the long-term average,' noted Nick Picone, group chief winemaker for Villa Maria. He described 2020 as 'considerably drier to the point of drought, reminding me of another great Hawke's Bay vintage – 2013'.

At 43,247 tonnes of grapes, the Hawke's Bay crop was 16 per cent heavier than in 2019, accounting for 9.8 per cent of the national harvest. Sauvignon Blanc (12,422 tonnes) was the variety most commonly harvested, followed by Merlot (10,525 tonnes), Chardonnay (6987 tonnes), Pinot Gris (6058 tonnes), Pinot Noir (2070 tonnes) and Syrah (2057 tonnes).

In spring, a warm September with above-average rainfall was followed by a wetter than usual October with normal temperatures. November, however, was drier and much hotter than usual, with temperatures at Napier Aero averaging 2.1°C above normal.

Villa Maria reported that 'with a few hurdles in spring, including frost and hailstorms, Hawke's Bay was off to a nervous start. Unfortunately, the hail did impact some of our growers…' Other reports surfaced that some early-budding varieties in the Bridge Pa Triangle sub-region were wiped out by October hail.

Summer proved favourably warm and dry. December saw average rainfall and well above average temperatures, followed by a slightly warmer than average, dry January. In February, the NIWA station at Napier Aero recorded far less than usual rainfall and average temperatures 2.1°C above normal.

In autumn, a dry, slightly cooler than average March was followed by a warm, notably dry April. On 9 April, Nicholas Buck, CEO of Te Mata Estate, described 2020 as 'probably the greatest vintage' in his experience, 'with an early start and early finish. Even better than 2019.'

There were some cautionary notes. Rob MacCulloch, at a large contract winery, reported a 'heavy' Merlot crop, and that the drought caused some vineyards to have 'pretty stressed vines and fruit, with low sugars and plummeting acids'.

However, on 4 May, Bilancia reported that the growing season had been 'textbook perfect, dry (but we can work with that) and warm (but not too hot, so great flavour development).' After picking Chardonnay from its *la collina* vineyard on 2 March, two weeks earlier than usual, Bilancia winemaker Warren Gibson stated it was 'the best Chardonnay I have seen in all my vintages in Hawke's Bay'. The first Syrah from *la collina* was harvested on 28 March, 'in beautiful condition; perfect flavour and ripeness'.

Wairarapa

Roger Parkinson, of Nga Waka winery, summarised Martinborough's vintage in June 2020. 'Temperature records show a pretty typical year with … no extended or extreme hot spells. The real story of the growing season is the rainfall and the extended dry period from late December until mid-March… Quality is outstanding, with bright, concentrated flavours in the white varieties and rosé, and remarkable colour, texture and depth of flavour in the Pinot Noir.'

At 4472 tonnes, the Wairarapa region's grape crop was slightly bigger than 2019 (up two per cent), constituting just one per cent of the country's total harvest. Pinot Noir (2067 tonnes) and Sauvignon Blanc (1771 tonnes) dominated, followed distantly by Pinot Gris (279 tonnes) and Chardonnay (200 tonnes).

Spring began with a cool, dry September, followed by a cool, wet October and dry, warm November (temperatures at Martinborough were 2.2°C above average). 'The season began with a wonderful flowering,' reported the regional organisation, Wairarapa Wine, 'producing even berry and bunch size not seen for some time.'

Summer started with a warm, dry December and a dry January with average temperatures. In February, the rainfall stayed well below normal and temperatures soared – 2.2°C above average in Martinborough.

In autumn, the weather proved variable. Masterton, in the northern Wairarapa, received 303 per cent of its normal rainfall in March, but very little rain in April. At Martinborough, temperatures were above average in both March and April.

'2020 was an incredible vintage,' says Dry River. Wairarapa Wine described 2020 as 'one of the most favourable Pinot Noir seasons in many years. The resulting wines show deep colour, pure varietal flavours and great tannin structure.'

Nelson

After a cool, dry season, Nelson winegrowers harvested 11,572 tonnes of grapes (6 per cent less than in 2019), accounting for 2.6 per cent of the total New Zealand harvest. Sauvignon Blanc dominated the crop (7868 tonnes), followed distantly by Pinot Gris (1224 tonnes), Pinot Noir (1040 tonnes) and Chardonnay (750 tonnes).

Spring had a wetter than normal start during September and October, with average warmth. However, in November, temperatures climbed to an average of 1.0°C above normal, with slightly below-average rainfall.

In summer, a warm but wet December was followed by warm, dry conditions in January and February. 'We had a nice, gentle incline clicking up through the warm summer months,' reported Kina Cliffs, 'watching the regular sunshine and low rainfall create beautifully ripe and healthy grapes with lovely flavour.'

In autumn, a cool, dry March was followed by a similarly dry April, with average warmth. Seifried reported 'another early and very condensed vintage' with 'beautiful, clean fruit.'

Blackenbrook enthused that 'the quality of the fruit we have harvested is right up with the very best we have ever had…'

Marlborough

'For overall fruit quality, this is one of the best vintages I have experienced,' enthused Ivan Sutherland, co-founder of Dog Point Vineyard, on 20 April 2020. At 343,036 tonnes of grapes (12 per cent more than in 2019), the Marlborough crop accounted for a whopping 77.7 per cent of the national harvest.

Sauvignon Blanc (295,301 tonnes) was by far the most common variety, trailed distantly by Pinot Noir (20,027 tonnes), Pinot Gris (13,494 tonnes), Chardonnay (9793 tonnes) and Riesling (2246 tonnes). Rob Agnew, of Plant & Food Research (Marlborough), noted that temperatures over the growing season were cooler than in 2019 and 2018, but still well above the long-term average.

Dryness was a crucial factor. From 21 December to 18 April, Marlborough recorded less than a quarter of its normal rainfall. 'But despite the very dry conditions, vines fared far better than in the summer of 2019, which saw crippling water stress in some vineyards,' reported Agnew. 'The main difference was a big dump of rain between 16 and 20 December 2019, which ensured plants, soils and waterways were more resilient to the subsequent dry patch.'

Due to the dry weather, the individual berries were much smaller than average, and bunch numbers were down too. However, Agnew also observed that 'warm weather in late November and early December 2019 saw excellent flowering for Sauvignon Blanc, so berry numbers were well up on average, resulting in final yields being average, or close to it'.

In spring, September brought normal temperatures and above-average rainfall, followed by a cool, dry October. November, however, was drier than usual and markedly warmer – temperatures at Blenheim Aero were 1.7°C above normal. Villa Maria reported 'an excellent berry set'.

Summer started with a cool, damp December, followed by a cool, very dry January. Bush fires in Australia 'influenced the weather for the month of January quite substantially,' according to Hans Herzog Estate, 'with the smog cooling down temperatures quite a bit'. February, however, was a lot warmer and drier than normal, with temperatures at Blenheim Aero 1.6°C above the long-term average.

In early autumn, March was cooler and much drier than usual – allowing the grapes to ripen without major disease pressures – and April was favourably warm and dry. On 22 April, Jules Taylor reported: 'The continual mild, dry conditions meant that the fruit harvested was in perfect condition.'

'Overall, the quality is good,' declared John Forrest on 15 April. 'It's been a disease-free harvest.' Hans Herzog was highly enthusiastic. 'All the late-ripening varieties loved the dry and beautiful Indian summer and performed extremely well with great physiological ripeness... The dryness made for small berries with less – but extremely concentrated – juice.'

Canterbury

'2020 looks set to be recognised as an exceptional year,' declared Pegasus Bay, after the earliest-ever vintage at Waipara. At 9861 tonnes, North Canterbury's grape crop was 19 per cent heavier than in 2019, accounting for 2.1 per cent of the national harvest. In volume terms, Sauvignon Blanc was the principal variety (3733 tonnes), followed by Pinot Gris (1986 tonnes), Pinot Noir (1933 tonnes) and Riesling (1508 tonnes).

In spring, a warm, dry September and cool October were followed by a hot November (The Bone Line reported its hottest November on record). 'The shoots got away to a good start and were untouched by frost,' reported Pegasus Bay. 'Weather over flowering was warm and still, leading to a plentiful set and a potentially bumper crop. Accordingly, we thinned the crop heavily.'

Summer began with dry, slightly warmer than normal conditions in December and January, followed by a dry, much warmer than average February. 'Summer was hot and dry,' declared Pegasus Bay, 'giving us optimally ripened grapes in beautiful condition.'

In early autumn, March was 'cold', reported The Bone Line, 'giving the vines a break and slowing ripening.' March saw 'well above normal' rainfall in North Canterbury, according to NIWA, with heavy rain during 28–30 March. April, however, brought a return to dry weather, with above-average temperatures.

'North Canterbury had its earliest-ever harvest,' observed Black Estate, at Waipara. 'The fruit is absolutely beautiful and delicious... We are seeing really clean, gorgeous little bunches.' Mountford Estate declared: 'The quality of the 2020 vintage wine will be superb. I can guarantee this.'

'The wines have a real vibrancy and true concentration,' reported The Bone Line, which was 'truly excited' about its Sauvignon Blanc and Pinot Noir, and praised its Chardonnay and Riesling as 'really great'.

Otago

'You certainly won't hear anyone in Central Otago pronouncing this as the "vintage of the century",' declared Misha's Vineyard on 22 April. 'Overall it has been a cool and wet season.'

At 8515 tonnes of grapes, Central Otago's crop was 28 per cent less than 2019, accounting for just 1.9 per cent of the national harvest. At 114 tonnes, the harvest in the Waitaki Valley, North Otago, was tiny – but still 180 per cent heavier than in 2019. Pinot Noir dominated the crop in Central Otago, with 6469 tonnes, followed by Pinot Gris (1084 tonnes), Riesling (350 tonnes), Sauvignon Blanc (262 tonnes) and Chardonnay (244 tonnes).

In spring, a dry, warm September and cool, damp October were followed by a warm November – temperatures at Cromwell were 1.6°C above average. Grasshopper Rock, at Alexandra, reported 'an average spring season', with 'some hard early frosts and a surprise hail storm [on 16 November], but nothing to impact on quality'.

Summer opened with a cold, windy, wet December (causing 'some unevenness in fruit set,' noted Terra Sancta, at Bannockburn), followed by a dry January with average temperatures and wet, moderately warm February. On 10 March, Ceres, at Bannockburn, said the harvest was running 10 days to two weeks late.

In autumn, March temperatures at Cromwell plunged to 1.7°C below normal, followed by a colder than usual April. On 21 April, Maori Point, at Tarras, reported its crop levels were down by 20 to 40 per cent. Winemaker Matt Evans noted: 'There is much more *millerandage* [bunches with berries varying greatly in size and maturity] than we normally see.'

However, in terms of quality, Misha's Vineyard reported that 'achieving sugar ripeness with lower yields was relatively easy and the cooler temperatures saw higher acidity retained'. Chard Farm was decidedly upbeat, declaring 2020 to be 'an excellent vintage. The reduced crops produced some exciting wines. We brought in very clean, aromatic fruit, similar to 2017, with good acids, sugars and concentration.'

Best Buys of the Year

Best White Wine Buy of the Year

Stoneleigh Latitude Marlborough Sauvignon Blanc 2020
★★★★★, $17–$20

'Marlborough in a glass', I jotted down, after tasting this great-value wine. Estate-grown in Pernod Ricard NZ's vineyards in the 'Golden Mile', which lines Rapaura Road, on the north side of the Wairau Valley, it was deliberately crafted as a 'full-on' style with 'big aromatics' – and delivers the goods.

Harvested from mature, 15 to 31-year-old vines, mostly in the original Stoneleigh Vineyard, it was mainly tank-fermented, but 25 per cent of the blend was fermented in seasoned oak cuves, to add 'palate weight and texture'. Bright, light lemon/green, it is mouthfilling and vibrantly fruity, with deep, ripe tropical-fruit flavours, finely balanced acidity, and a rich, basically dry (4.9 grams/litre of residual sugar) finish. Already delicious, this punchy, youthful, very harmonious wine is likely to be at its best from mid-2021 onwards.

A big seller in Sweden, Canada and Australia, it's also distributed widely in New Zealand, through supermarkets, fine-wine stores and restaurants. Looking for a five-star Sauvignon Blanc at a three-star price? Here it is.

Best Rosé Wine Buy of the Year

Momo Organic Marlborough Rosé 2020
★★★★☆, $18

Certified organic, this is a delicious, distinctive marriage of Pinot Gris, Sémillon and Pinot Noir, cool-fermented in stainless steel tanks and matured briefly on its yeast lees. A bright pink, finely poised wine, it has lively peach, strawberry and watermelon flavours, showing excellent delicacy and depth, and a dry finish. From Seresin Estate, it offers delicious drinking for the summer of 2020–21.

Best Red Wine Buy of the Year

Villa Maria Cellar Selection Hawke's Bay Merlot 2019
★★★★☆, $15–$18

Offering outstanding value, this Gimblett Gravels red was matured for a year in French oak barriques (15 per cent new). Deeply coloured, with a fragrant, berryish, spicy bouquet, it is mouthfilling and supple, with concentrated, ripe blackcurrant, plum and spice flavours, oak complexity, and a long, very harmonious finish.

Vino Fino, a prominent, specialist wine retailer in Christchurch, praises Villa Maria Cellar Selection Hawke's Bay Merlot 2019 as 'the best value red in New Zealand' – and I agree. Well worth cellaring, it's already a delicious mouthful.

Other shortlisted wines

Whites
Askerne Hawke's Bay Sauvignon Blanc 2019 ★★★★☆ $20
Church Road Hawke's Bay Pinot Gris 2020 ★★★★☆ $20
Eradus Awatere Valley Marlborough Pinot Gris 2020 ★★★★ $15
Eradus Awatere Valley Marlborough Sauvignon Blanc 2020 ★★★★ $17
Giesen New Zealand Riesling 2019 ★★★★☆ $15
Hunter's Marlborough Chardonnay 2019 ★★★★☆ $23
Hunter's Marlborough Pinot Gris 2020 ★★★★☆ $19
Main Divide North Canterbury Gewürztraminer 2019 ★★★★☆ $21
Mount Riley Limited Release Marlborough Sauvignon Blanc 2020 ★★★★ $17
Mount Riley Marlborough Gewürztraminer 2020 ★★★★ $15
Nga Waka Martinborough Sauvignon Blanc 2020 ★★★★☆ $19
Old Coach Road Nelson Sauvignon Blanc 2020 ★★★☆ $14
Seifried Nelson Gewürztraminer 2020 ★★★★☆ $19
Stoneleigh Wild Valley Marlborough Sauvignon Blanc 2020 ★★★★☆ $18
Sugar Loaf Marlborough Sauvignon Blanc 2020 ★★★★☆ $20
Thornbury Marlborough Sauvignon Blanc 2020 ★★★★ $16
Two Rivers Convergence Marlborough Sauvignon Blanc 2020 ★★★★★ $24
Vidal Reserve Hawke's Bay Chardonnay 2018 ★★★★☆ $20
Villa Maria Cellar Selection Gisborne Albariño 2020 ★★★★☆ $18
Villa Maria Private Bin Marlborough Sauvignon Blanc 2020 ★★★★ $15
Yealands Reserve Awatere Valley Marlborough Sauvignon Blanc 2020 ★★★★☆ $19

Rosés
Yealands Marlborough Rosé 2020 ★★★★ $15

Reds
Alexander Dusty Road Martinborough Pinot Noir 2019 ★★★★★ $27
Brookfields Back Block Hawke's Bay Syrah 2019 ★★★★☆ $21
Brookfields Ohiti Estate Cabernet Sauvignon 2018 ★★★★☆ $21
Church Road Hawke's Bay Merlot/Cabernet Sauvignon 2018 ★★★★☆ $20
Church Road McDonald Series Hawke's Bay Merlot 2016 ★★★★★ $28
Church Road McDonald Series Hawke's Bay Syrah 2019 ★★★★★ $28.
Clos Henri Petit Clos Marlborough Pinot Noir 2019 ★★★★☆ $27
Esk Valley Gimblett Gravels Merlot/Cabernet Sauvignon/Malbec 2018 ★★★★☆ $20
Jackson Estate Homestead Marlborough Pinot Noir 2019 ★★★★ $23
Luna Martinborough Pinot Noir 2018 ★★★★ $24
Mission Barrique Reserve Hawke's Bay Cabernet Sauvignon 2018 ★★★★★ $30
Mount Riley Marlborough Pinot Noir 2019 ★★★★ $20
Mountford Liaison North Canterbury Pinot Noir 2016 ★★★★★ $28
Omeo Hidden Valley Single Vineyard Central Otago Pinot Noir 2017 ★★★★★ $30
Satyr by Sileni Estates Foothills Pinot Noir 2019 ★★★★ $16
Seifried Nelson Pinot Noir 2019 ★★★★ $19
Stables Ngatarawa Reserve Hawke's Bay Syrah 2019 ★★★★ $16
Stoneleigh Rapaura Series Marlborough Pinot Noir 2019 ★★★★☆ $25
Te Mata Estate Vineyards Hawke's Bay Merlot/Cabernet Sauvignon 2019 ★★★★☆ $22
Thornbury Central Otago Pinot Noir 2019 ★★★★☆ $26
Villa Maria Private Bin Organic Hawke's Bay Merlot 2019 ★★★★ $15
Yealands Marlborough Pinot Noir 2019 ★★★★ $19

Classic Wines of New Zealand

A large crop of 28 new Potential Classics, 25 new Classics and 7 new Super Classics are the features of this year's closely revised list of New Zealand wine classics.

What is a New Zealand wine classic? It is a wine that in quality terms consistently ranks in the very forefront of its class. To qualify for selection, each label must have achieved an outstanding level of quality for at least three vintages; there are no flashes in the pan here.

By identifying New Zealand wine classics, my aim is to transcend the inconsistencies of individual vintages and wine competition results, and to highlight consistency of excellence. When introducing the elite category of Super Classics, I restricted entry to wines which have achieved brilliance in at least five vintages (compared to three for Classic status). The Super Classics are all highly prestigious wines, with a proven ability to mature well (even the Sauvignon Blancs, compared to other examples of the variety).

The Potential Classics are the pool from which future Classics will emerge. These are wines of outstanding quality which look likely, if their current standards are maintained or improved, to qualify after another vintage or two for elevation to Classic status. All the additions and elevations on this year's list are identified by an asterisk.

Some wines on the classics list are not reviewed every year. If a wine is not currently on sale, this generally reflects a lack of favourable weather in recent vintages.

Super Classics

Branded and Other White Wines
Dog Point Vineyard Section 94

Chardonnay
Ata Rangi Craighall; Church Road Grand Reserve Hawke's Bay; Church Road Tom; Clearview Reserve; Clos de Ste Anne Naboth's Vineyard; Dry River; ***Esk Valley Winemakers Reserve Hawke's Bay; Fromm Clayvin Vineyard Marlborough; Kumeu River Estate; Kumeu River Hunting Hill; Kumeu River Mate's Vineyard; Neudorf Moutere; ***Pegasus Bay; Sacred Hill Riflemans; ***Seresin Reserve; Te Mata Elston; ***Vidal Legacy Reserve Hawke's Bay; Villa Maria Reserve Barrique Fermented Gisborne; Villa Maria Keltern

Gewürztraminer
Dry River Lovat Vineyard; Johanneshof Marlborough; Lawson's Dry Hills Marlborough

Pinot Gris
Dry River

Riesling
Dry River Craighall Vineyard; Dry River Craighall Vineyard Selection; Felton Road Bannockburn; Pegasus Bay

Sauvignon Blanc
Cloudy Bay New Zealand; Cloudy Bay Te Koko; Saint Clair Wairau Reserve; Seresin Marlborough; Te Mata Cape Crest

Viognier
Te Mata Zara

Sweet Whites
Forrest Estate Botrytised Riesling; Framingham Noble Riesling; Villa Maria Reserve Noble Riesling

Bottle-fermented Sparklings
Deutz Marlborough Cuvée Blanc de Blancs; Nautilus Cuvée Marlborough

Rosé
***Terra Sancta Bannockburn

Branded and Other Red Wines
Craggy Range Le Sol; Esk Valley Heipipi The Terraces; Puriri Hills Harmonie Du Soir; Stonyridge Larose; Te Mata Coleraine

Cabernet Sauvignon-predominant Reds
Esk Valley Winemakers Reserve Gimblett Gravels Cabernet Sauvignon/Merlot/Malbec/Cabernet Franc; Te Mata Awatea Cabernets/Merlot; Villa Maria Reserve Gimblett Gravels Cabernet Sauvignon/Merlot

Merlot
Church Road Tom Merlot/Cabernet; Villa Maria Reserve Hawke's Bay

Pinot Noir
Ata Rangi; Burn Cottage Burn Cottage Vineyard; Dry River; Felton Road Bannockburn; Felton Road Block 3; Felton Road Block 5; ***Felton Road Cornish Point; Fromm Clayvin Vineyard Marlborough; Neudorf Moutere; Pegasus Bay; Pegasus Bay Prima Donna; Quartz Reef Bendigo Estate Single Ferment; Rippon Tinker's Field Mature Vine; Valli Gibbston Vineyard; Villa Maria Reserve Marlborough

Syrah
Esk Valley Winemakers Reserve Gimblett Gravels; Passage Rock Reserve; Stonecroft Gimblett Gravels Reserve; Te Mata Estate Bullnose; Trinity Hill Homage Gimblett Gravels Hawke's Bay

Classics

Albariño
**Villa Maria Single Vineyard Braided Gravels Hawke's Bay

Chardonnay
Babich Irongate; Cloudy Bay; Dog Point Vineyard; Felton Road Bannockburn; Felton Road Block 2; Greenhough Hope Vineyard; **Greystone Erin's Reserve Waipara Valley; Greywacke Marlborough; Mahi Twin Valleys Vineyard; Mission Jewelstone; Nautilus Marlborough; Pyramid Valley Vineyards Lion's Tooth Canterbury; Te Whau Vineyard Waiheke

Island; Villa Maria Reserve Hawke's Bay; Villa Maria Reserve Marlborough; **Villa Maria Single Vineyard Taylors Pass

Chenin Blanc
Millton Te Arai Vineyard

Gewürztraminer
Greystone Waipara Valley; Lawson's Dry Hills The Pioneer Marlborough; Pegasus Bay; Spy Valley Envoy Johnson Vineyard Marlborough; **Stonecroft Old Vine

Pinot Gris
Greystone Waipara; **Greywacke Marlborough; Neudorf Moutere; Villa Maria Single Vineyard Seddon

Riesling
Felton Road Dry; Framingham Classic; Misha's Vineyard Limelight; Misha's Vineyard Lyric; Rippon

Sauvignon Blanc
Auntsfield Single Vineyard Southern Valleys; Brancott Estate Letter Series 'B' Brancott Marlborough; Clos Henri Marlborough; Dog Point Vineyard Marlborough; Greywacke Wild; Greywacke Marlborough; Lawson's Dry Hills Marlborough; Pegasus Bay Sauvignon/Sémillon; Staete Landt Annabel Marlborough; Villa Maria Reserve Clifford Bay; Villa Maria Reserve Wairau Valley

Viognier
Clos de Ste Anne Les Arbres

Sweet Whites
**Mondillo Central Otago Nina; Pegasus Bay Encore Noble Riesling

Bottle-fermented Sparklings
**Cloudy Bay Pelorus NV; Deutz Marlborough Prestige Cuvee; **Hunter's Miru Miru Reserve; Quartz Reef Méthode Traditionnelle [Vintage]

Branded and Other Red Wines
Alpha Domus AD The Aviator; Babich The Patriarch; **Clearview The Basket Press; Craggy Range Aroha; Craggy Range Sophia; **Elephant Hill Hawke's Bay Hieronymus; Gillman; Mission Jewelstone Gimblett Gravels Antoine; Newton/Forrest Cornerstone; Puriri Hills Pope; Sacred Hill Brokenstone; Sacred Hill Helmsman; Te Whau The Point; Trinity Hill The Gimblett

Cabernet Sauvignon-predominant Reds
Babich Irongate Cabernet/Merlot/Franc; Brookfields Reserve Vintage ['Gold Label'] Cabernet/Merlot; Vidal Legacy Gimblett Gravels Cabernet Sauvignon/Merlot

Merlot-predominant Reds
**Elephant Hill Reserve Hawke's Bay Merlot/Cabernet Franc/Cabernet

Pinot Noir
Akarua Central Otago; **Akitu A1 Central Otago; **Amisfield RKV Reserve Central Otago; Bannock Brae Central Otago; Carrick Bannockburn Central Otago; **Cloudy Bay Te Wahi Central Otago; Doctor's Flat Central Otago; Dog Point Vineyard Marlborough; **Felton Road Calvert; **Fromm Cuvee 'H' Marlborough; Gibbston Valley Le Maitre; Fromm Fromm Vineyard; Gibbston Valley Reserve; Grasshopper Rock Earnscleugh Vineyard; Greenhough Hope Vineyard; **Greywacke Marlborough; **Misha's Vineyard The

High Note Central Otago; **Nga Waka Martinborough Lease Block; Palliser Estate; Pisa Range Estate Black Poplar Block; Prophet's Rock Home Vineyard Central Otago; Quartz Reef Bendigo Estate Single Vineyard; Rippon 'Rippon' Mature Vine Central Otago; **Rockburn Central Otago; **Tarras Vineyards The Canyon Single Vineyard Central Otago; **Terra Sancta Jackson's Block Bannockburn; **Terra Sancta Slapjack Block Bannockburn; Two Paddocks Central Otago; Valli Bannockburn Vineyard Central Otago; Valli Bendigo Vineyard Central Otago; Villa Maria Single Vineyard Southern Clays Marlborough

Syrah

Brookfields Hillside; Church Road Grand Reserve Hawke's Bay; Craggy Range Gimblett Gravels Vineyard; **Elephant Hill Airavata Hawke's Bay; **Elephant Hill Reserve Hawke's Bay; La Collina; Mission Jewelstone Hawke's Bay; Sacred Hill Deerstalkers Hawke's Bay; Stonyridge Pilgrim Syrah/Mourvedre/Grenache; Vidal Legacy Hawke's Bay; Villa Maria Reserve Hawke's Bay

Tempranillo

Hans Herzog Marlborough

Potential Classics

Albariño

Nautilus Marlborough

Chardonnay

Alpha Domus AD Hawke's Bay; Auntsfield Cob Cottage Southern Valleys Marlborough; Auntsfield Single Vineyard Southern Valleys Marlborough; Bilancia Hawke's Bay; Boneline, The, Sharkstone Waipara; *Brookfields Marshall Bank; Carrick Cairnmuir Terraces EBM; *Clearview Endeavour Hawke's Bay; Collaboration Aurulent Hawke's Bay; Elephant Hill Reserve Hawke's Bay; *Elephant Hill Salomé Hawke's Bay; *Greystone Organic Waipara Valley North Canterbury; Kumeu River Coddington; *Matawhero Irwin Gisborne; Mills Reef Elspeth Gimblett Gravels; Pegasus Bay Virtuoso; Pyramid Valley Vineyards Fields of Fire; Spy Valley Envoy Marlborough; *Stonecroft Old Vine Gimblett Gravels

Hawke's Bay; *Tony Bish Skeetfield Hawke's Bay; Trinity Hill Gimblett Gravels [Black Label]; *Vavasour Anna's Vineyard Awatere Valley Marlborough; *Vidal Soler Hawke's Bay; Villa Maria Single Vineyard Ihumatao

Chenin Blanc

Astrolabe Wrekin Vineyard; Clos de Ste Anne La Bas

Gewürztraminer

Villa Maria Single Vineyard Ihumatao

Grüner Veltliner

*Lime Rock Central Hawke's Bay

Muscat

Pegasus Bay

Pinot Blanc

*Greenhough Hope Vineyard Nelson

Pinot Gris

Georges Road Selection; Hans Herzog Marlborough; Misha's Vineyard Dress Circle; *Ostler Waitaki Valley North Otago; *Prophet's Rock Central Otago; *Quartz Reef Bendigo Estate Single Vineyard Central Otago; Spy Valley Envoy Marlborough; *Vavasour Awatere Valley Marlborough

Riesling

Greystone Waipara Valley; Greywacke Marlborough; *Maude Mt Maude Vineyard East Block Wanaka; *Maude Mt Maude Vineyard Wanaka Dry; *Mount Edward Central Otago; Pegasus Bay Bel Canto Dry; Prophet's Rock Central Otago Dry; Saint Clair Pioneer Block 9 Big John

Sauvignon Blanc

*Brancott Estate Chosen Rows Marlborough; Church Road Grand Reserve; Churton Best End Marlborough; Churton Marlborough; Clos Marguerite Marlborough; Fairbourne Marlborough; Folium Reserve Marlborough; Hans Herzog Sur Lie; *Jules Taylor OTQ Limited Release Single Vineyard Marlborough; Lawson's Dry Hills Reserve; Mahi Marlborough; *Nautilus The Paper Nautilus Marlborough; Spy Valley Envoy Johnson Vineyard; Villa Maria Single Vineyard Taylors Pass Marlborough; Whitehaven Greg Awatere Vineyard Single Vineyard

Sweet White Wines

*Churton Marlborough Petit Manseng; Esk Valley Late Harvest Chenin Blanc; Felton Road Block 1 Riesling; Framingham Select Riesling;

Pegasus Bay Aria Late Harvest Riesling; Pegasus Bay Finale Noble Barrique Matured Sauvignon Blanc/Sémillon; Riverby Estate Marlborough Noble Riesling; Seifried Winemaker's Collection Sweet Agnes Nelson Riesling

Bottle-fermented Sparklings

*Cloudy Bay Pelorus Rose; Daniel Le Brun Blanc de Blancs Méthode Traditionnelle; Daniel Le Brun Vintage Méthode Traditionnelle; *Gibbston Valley NV Méthode Traditionnelle; Nautilus Cuvée Marlborough Vintage Rosé

Branded and Other Red Wines

Clearview Enigma; Clearview Old Olive Block; Frenchman's Hill Estate Blood Creek 8; Obsidian Reserve The Obsidian; Passage Rock Magnus

Cabernet Sauvignon-predominant Reds

Awaroa Requiem Waiheke Island Cabernet/Merlot/Malbec; Church Road McDonald Series Cabernet Sauvignon; Mills Reef Elspeth Cabernet/Merlot; Mills Reef Elspeth Cabernet Sauvignon; Stonecroft Gimblett Gravels Cabernet Sauvignon

Malbec

Stonyridge Luna Negra Waiheke Island

Merlot

Church Road McDonald Series Hawke's Bay; Hans Herzog Spirit of Marlborough Merlot/Cabernet Sauvignon

Montepulciano

Hans Herzog Marlborough

Pinot Noir

Akarua The Siren Bannockburn; Alexander Martinborough; Amisfield Central Otago; Auntsfield Single Vineyard Southern Valleys Marlborough; *Aurum Mathilde Organic Central Otago; Black Estate Damsteep North Canterbury; *Burn Cottage Moonlight Race Central Otago; Burn Cottage Valli Vineyard Gibbston; Carrick Excelsior Central Otago; Coal Pit Tiwha Central Otago; Craggy Range Te Muna Road Vineyard Martinborough; Folding Hill Bendigo Central Otago; Folium Reserve Marlborough; Gibbston Valley China Terrace Bendigo; Gibbston Valley School House Central Otago; Greystone Thomas Brothers; Greystone Waipara Valley Canterbury; Lowburn Ferry Home Block; *Martinborough Vineyard Home Block; Mondillo Bella Reserve; Mondillo Central Otago; Mount Edward Central Otago; Mt Difficulty Bannockburn; Mt Difficulty Single Vineyard Long Gully; Peregrine Central Otago; Rippon Emma's Block; Rockburn The Art Central Otago; Rock Ferry Trig Hill Vineyard; Spy Valley Envoy Johnson Vineyard Waihopai Valley; Te Kairanga John Martin Martinborough; Two Paddocks Proprietor's Reserve The Fusilier Bannockburn Vineyard; Two Paddocks Proprietor's Reserve The Last Chance Earnscleugh Vineyard; Urlar Select Parcels; Valli Burn Cottage Central Otago; Villa Maria Single Vineyard Taylors Pass Marlborough; Whitehaven Greg Southern Valleys Single Vineyard; Wooing Tree Sandstorm Reserve Single Vineyard

Syrah

*Ash Ridge Doppio Chave; Church Road McDonald Series; Church Road Tom; Clos de Ste Anne The Crucible; Fromm Syrah Fromm Vineyard; Man O' War Dreadnought; Mission Huchet; Passage Rock Waiheke Island; *Smith & Sheth Cru Omahu; Trinity Hill Gimblett Gravels Hawke's Bay

Cellar Sense

Most wine in New Zealand is young and consumed on the day it is bought. Several producers, such as Pegasus Bay, Puriri Hills and Hans Herzog, regularly offer bottle-aged vintages for sale, but around the country, barely 1 per cent of the wine we buy is cellared for even a year.

So it's great news that more and more wineries are releasing or rereleasing mature, bottle-aged wines, up to a decade old, including Pinot Noirs, Cabernet Sauvignons, Merlots, Chardonnays, Rieslings – even barrel-fermented Sauvignon Blancs. Age has not wearied most of these beauties, proving the country's finest wines can mature well for a decade or longer.

Sauvignon Blanc, which accounts for over 70 per cent by volume of all New Zealand wine, is not usually seen as a variety that needs time to develop. A decade or two ago, Marlborough winemakers often stated that the region's Sauvignon Blancs 'should be picked, pressed and pissed by Christmas'.

Today, most Sauvignon Blancs develop soundly for a couple of years, but the popularity of New Zealand Pinot Noir has done far more to persuade consumers around the world that this country's wine can mature gracefully – as it must, if New Zealand is to be accepted as a serious wine producer.

'To gain true international recognition, an industry has to be capable of making wines that improve with age – that's the ultimate quality factor,' stresses John Buck, co-founder of Te Mata Estate, acclaimed for its long-lived Hawke's Bay Cabernet/Merlots. 'People need to be able to put wine into their cellars with confidence and know that when they pull them out they will be a damn sight better than when they put them in.'

But do all winemakers share that view? Geoff Kelly, a Wellington-based critic, believes too much emphasis is placed on young wines in New Zealand, partly because many wine judges are winemakers. 'Generalising, winemakers ... speak most highly of fresh and fruity smells and flavours in wine. How else can they sell their young wines? Consequently, it is quite rare to find New Zealand winemakers who really enjoy old wines or attend tastings of them.'

If you are keen to build up a cellar of distinguished Chardonnays, Rieslings, Pinot Noirs, Syrahs or Cabernet/Merlots, how do you decide what to buy? Confidence comes from 'vertical' tastings, where several vintages of a wine are tasted side by side. Vertical tastings, staged more and more frequently in New Zealand, let you assess the overall quality of a wine, the evolution of its style, the impact of vintage variation and its maturation potential.

To sum up, I suggest drinking most New Zealand Sauvignon Blancs at nine months to two years old. Screwcaps preserve the wines' freshness markedly better than corks did. Most fine-quality Chardonnays are at their best at three to five years old; top Rieslings at three to seven years old.

Middle-tier Pinot Noirs, Merlots and Syrahs typically drink well for five years; outstanding examples can flourish for much longer. New Zealand's top Cabernet/ Merlot blends from Hawke's Bay and Waiheke Island are still the safest bet for long-term cellaring over decades.

Cellaring Guidelines

Grape variety	Best age to open
White	
Sauvignon Blanc	
(non-wooded)	6–24 months
(wooded)	1–3 years
Arneis	1–3 years
Albariño	1–4 years
Gewürztraminer	1–4 years
Grüner Veltliner	1–4 years
Viognier	1–4 years
Pinot Gris	1–4 years
Sémillon	1–4 years
Chenin Blanc	2–5 years
Chardonnay	2–5 years
Riesling	2–7+ years
Red	
Pinotage	1–3 years
Malbec	1–5 years
Cabernet Franc	2–5 years
Montepulciano	2–5 years
Merlot	2–5+ years
Pinot Noir	2–5+ years
Syrah	2–5+ years
Tempranillo	2–5+ years
Cabernet Sauvignon	3–7+ years
Cabernet/Merlot	3–7+ years
Other	
Sweet whites	2–5 years
Bottle-fermented sparklings	
(vintage-dated)	3–5+ years

How to Use this Book

It is essential to read this brief section to understand how the book works. Feel free to skip any of the other preliminary pages, but not these.

The majority of wines have been listed in the book according to their principal grape variety, as shown on the front label. Oyster Bay Marlborough Sauvignon Blanc, for instance, can be located simply by turning to the Sauvignon Blanc section. Wines with front labels that do not refer clearly to a grape variety or blend of grapes, such as Craggy Range Les Beaux Cailloux, can be found in the Branded and Other Wines sections for white and red wines.

Most entries are firstly identified by their producer's name. Wines not usually called by their producer's name, such as Church Road Hawke's Bay Merlot/Cabernet Sauvignon (from Pernod Ricard NZ), or Maui Waipara Pinot Noir (from Tiki), are listed under their most common name.

The star ratings for quality reflect my own opinions, formed where possible by tasting a wine over several vintages, and often a particular vintage several times. *The star ratings are therefore a guide to each wine's overall standard in recent vintages*, rather than simply the quality of the latest release. However, to enhance the usefulness of the book, in the body of the text I have also given a *quality rating for the latest vintage of each wine*; sometimes for more than one vintage. (Since 2010 wineries have been able to buy stickers to attach to their bottles, based on these ratings.)

I hope the star ratings give interesting food for thought and succeed in introducing you to a galaxy of little-known but worthwhile wines. It pays to remember, however, that wine-tasting is a business fraught with subjectivity. You should always treat the views expressed in these pages for what they are – one person's opinion. The quality ratings are:

★★★★★	Outstanding quality (gold medal standard)
★★★★☆	Excellent quality, verging on outstanding
★★★★	Excellent quality (silver medal standard)
★★★☆	Very good quality
★★★	Good quality (bronze medal standard)
★★☆	Average quality
★★	Plain
★	Poor
No star	To be avoided

These quality ratings are based on comparative assessments of New Zealand wines against one another. A five-star Merlot/Cabernet Sauvignon, for instance, is an outstanding-quality red judged by the standards of other Merlot/Cabernet Sauvignon blends made in New Zealand. It is not judged by the standards of overseas reds of a similar style (for instance Bordeaux), because the book is focused solely on New

Zealand wines and their relative merits. (Some familiar New Zealand wine brands in recent years have included varying proportions of overseas wine. To be featured in this book, they must still include at least some New Zealand wine in the blend.)

Where brackets enclose the star rating on the right-hand side of the page, for example (★★★), this indicates the assessment is only tentative, because I have tasted very few vintages of the wine. A dash is used in the relatively few cases where a wine's quality has oscillated over and above normal vintage variations (for example ★–★★★).

Super Classic wines, Classic wines and Potential Classic wines (see page 20) are highlighted in the text by the following symbols:

Super Classic	Classic	Potential Classic

Each wine has also been given a dryness-sweetness, price and value-for-money rating. The precise levels of sweetness indicated by the four ratings are:

DRY	Less than 5 grams/litre of residual sugar
MED/DRY	5–14 grams/litre of residual sugar
MED	15–49 grams/litre of residual sugar
SW	50 and over grams/litre of residual sugar

Less than 5 grams of residual sugar per litre is virtually imperceptible to most palates – the wine tastes fully dry. With between 5 and 14 grams, a wine has a hint of sweetness, although a high level of acidity (as in Rieslings or even Marlborough Sauvignon Blancs, which often have 4 to 6 grams per litre of residual sugar) reduces the perception of sweetness. Where a wine harbours over 15 grams, the sweetness is clearly in evidence.

At above 50 grams per litre, most wines are unabashedly sweet, although high levels of acidity can still disguise the degree of sweetness. Most wines that harbour more than 50 grams per litre of sugar are packaged in half bottles, made to be served with dessert, and can be located in the Sweet White Wines section. However, a growing number of low-alcohol, sweet but not super-sweet, mouth-wateringly crisp Rieslings, not designed as dessert wines and usually packaged in 750-ml bottles, can also be found in the Riesling section.

Prices shown are based on the average price in a supermarket or wine shop (as indicated by the producer), except where most of the wine is sold directly to consumers from the winery, either over the vineyard counter or via mail order or the Internet.

The art of wine buying involves more than discovering top-quality wines. The real challenge – and the greatest satisfaction – lies in identifying wines at varying quality levels that deliver outstanding value for money. The symbols I have used are self-explanatory:

–V	=	Below average value
AV	=	Average value
V+	=	Above average value

The ratings discussed thus far are all my own. Many of the wine producers themselves, however, have also contributed individual vintage ratings of their own top wines over the past decade and the 'When to drink' recommendations. (The symbol **WR** indicates Winemaker's Rating, and the symbol **NM** alongside a vintage means the wine was not made that year.) Only the producers have such detailed knowledge of the relative quality of all their recent vintages (although in some cases, when the information was not forthcoming, I have rated a vintage myself). The key point you must note is that *each producer has rated each vintage of each wine against his or her highest quality aspirations for that particular label, not against any absolute standard.* Thus, a 7 out of 7 score merely indicates that the producer considers that particular vintage to be an outstanding example of that particular wine; not that it is the best-quality wine he or she makes.

The 'When to drink' (**Drink**) recommendations (which I find myself referring to constantly) are largely self-explanatory. The **P** symbol for PEAKED means that a particular vintage is already at, or has passed, its peak; no further benefits are expected from aging.

Here is an example of how the ratings work:

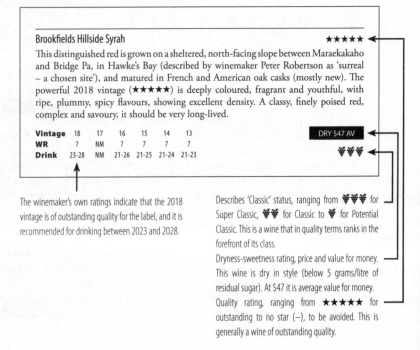

Brookfields Hillside Syrah   ★★★★★

This distinguished red is grown on a sheltered, north-facing slope between Maraekakaho and Bridge Pa, in Hawke's Bay (described by winemaker Peter Robertson as 'surreal – a chosen site'), and matured in French and American oak casks (mostly new). The powerful 2018 vintage (★★★★★) is deeply coloured, fragrant and youthful, with ripe, plummy, spicy flavours, showing excellent density. A classy, finely poised red, complex and savoury, it should be very long-lived.

Vintage	18	17	16	15	14	13
WR	7	NM	7	7	7	7
Drink	23-28	NM	21-26	21-25	21-24	21-23

DRY $47 AV

❦❦❦

The winemaker's own ratings indicate that the 2018 vintage is of outstanding quality for the label, and it is recommended for drinking between 2023 and 2028.

Describes 'Classic' status, ranging from ❦❦❦ for Super Classic, ❦❦ for Classic to ❦ for Potential Classic. This is a wine that in quality terms ranks in the forefront of its class.

Dryness-sweetness rating, price and value for money. This wine is dry in style (below 5 grams/litre of residual sugar). At $47 it is average value for money.

Quality rating, ranging from ★★★★★ for outstanding to no star (−), to be avoided. This is generally a wine of outstanding quality.

White Wines

Albariño

Called Albariño in Spain and Alvarinho in Portugal, this fashionable variety produces appetisingly crisp wines described by Riversun Nurseries at Gisborne as possessing 'distinctive aromatic, peachy characteristics, similar to Viognier'. Coopers Creek's 2011 bottling was the first true example of Albariño from New Zealand or Australia. With its loose clusters, thick skins and good resistance to rain, Albariño could thrive in this country's wetter regions. New Zealand's 38 hectares of bearing Albariño vines in 2020 were mostly in Gisborne (20 hectares) and Hawke's Bay (7 hectares), but there are also pockets in Marlborough (4 hectares), Nelson (3 hectares) and Auckland (2 hectares). Of all white-wine varieties to emerge in New Zealand over the past decade, Albariño is one of the most exciting.

Astrolabe Kekerengu Coast Sleepers Vineyard Marlborough Albariño ★★★★

Grown at Kekerengu, the 2019 vintage (★★★★) was hand-harvested and fermented and matured for five months in an even split of tanks and old French oak barrels. It has strong, very lively, citrusy, slightly appley flavours, fresh acidity, and a dry (2 grams/litre of residual sugar) finish. Full of youthful vigour, it's well worth cellaring to 2022+.

DRY $27 –V

Babich Family Estates Single Vineyard Marlborough Albariño ★★★★

Certified organic, the highly attractive 2019 vintage (★★★★☆) was estate-grown in the Headwaters Vineyard, near Renwick, in the Wairau Valley, tank-fermented and lees-aged for seven months. A dry style (3.7 grams/litre of residual sugar), it is fresh and mouthfilling, with strong, lively fruit flavours, a slightly salty streak, finely balanced acidity, and a lengthy finish. Offering great drinkability, it's a drink-now or cellaring proposition.

DRY $25 AV

Coopers Creek Select Vineyards Bell-Ringer Gisborne Albariño ★★★★

Fresh, lively and full-bodied, the 2019 vintage (★★★★☆) is a partly barrel-fermented, finely balanced wine with strong, citrusy, peachy, spicy flavours and a dry finish. Offering great drinkability, it's a drink-now or cellaring proposition.

Vintage	19	18	17
WR	7	6	5
Drink	20-21	P	P

DRY $22 V+

Forrest Marlborough Albariño ★★★★

The 2018 vintage (★★★★) is drinking well now. Partly (10 per cent) handled in old oak casks, it is fresh and full-bodied, with strong, peachy, spicy, slightly gingery flavours, and a dryish (5 grams/litre of residual sugar), crisp finish.

MED/DRY $25 AV

Hunting Lodge, The, Marlborough Albariño   ★★★★☆

Albariño, according to The Hunting Lodge, 'offers the best parts of a Riesling and Viognier, but with none of their hang-ups'. The attractive 2018 vintage (★★★★☆) is a single-vineyard wine, grown and hand-picked in the Awatere Valley. It was mostly fermented and lees-aged for four months in tanks, but 10 per cent was handled in seasoned oak barriques. Invitingly scented, it is mouthfilling, fresh and vibrantly fruity, with strong, peachy flavours to the fore, hints of spices, apples and ginger, and a dryish (5.3 grams/litre of residual sugar), appetisingly crisp finish.

MED/DRY $26 AV

Left Field Gisborne Albariño   ★★★★☆

Offering great value, the 2019 vintage (★★★★☆) was handled mostly in stainless steel tanks; 15 per cent of the blend was fermented in seasoned French oak puncheons. Bright, light lemon/green, it is scented and mouthfilling, with ripe tropical-fruit flavours, showing good concentration, a distinct touch of complexity, and a crisp, dry (3 grams/litre of residual sugar), long finish. (From Te Awa.)

Vintage	19	18
WR	7	6
Drink	20-24	20-23

DRY $19 V+

Linden Estate Hawke's Bay Albariño   (★★★☆)

The distinctive 2019 vintage (★★★☆) was estate-grown in the Esk Valley, hand-harvested and matured for three to four months on its yeast lees in barrels. Bright, light yellow/green, with a slightly honeyed bouquet, it's a medium to full-bodied wine with peachy, spicy flavours, fresh acidity and good depth. A slightly Gewürztraminer-like wine, it's already drinking well.

MED/DRY $25 –V

Mahurangi River Winery Matakana Albariño   ★★★★

Grown north of Auckland, the 2016 vintage (★★★★) was fermented in a concrete egg. Full-bodied, with good concentration of citrusy, slightly peachy and spicy flavours, showing a touch of complexity, and a dry, harmonious, lingering finish, it's a good, all-purpose wine. (2016 is the last vintage of this label.)

Vintage	16	15	14
WR	7	6	7
Drink	P	P	P

DRY $29 –V

Mount Riley Marlborough Albariño   (★★★★)

Offering great value, the 2020 vintage (★★★★) is a freshly scented, lively wine with strong, citrusy, slightly appley and spicy flavours. Full-bodied, it is finely balanced, with crisp but not high acidity, lots of youthful vigour and a basically dry finish. Best drinking mid-2021+.

DRY $15 V+

Nautilus Marlborough Albariño ★★★★★

This consistently classy, single-vineyard wine is handled without oak. Attractively scented, the 2019 vintage (★★★★★) is full-bodied, with strong, vibrant, citrusy, peachy, spicy flavours, a slightly salty streak, fresh acidity, and a finely balanced, persistent, dry (4 grams/litre of residual sugar) finish. A great all-purpose wine. The 2020 vintage (★★★★☆) is still very youthful. Mouthfilling, it is bright, light yellow/green, with vibrant, ripe stone-fruit and spice flavours, showing a distinct touch of complexity, fresh acidity, and a dry (3 grams/litre of residual sugar), very harmonious finish. Best drinking 2022+.

DRY $29 V+

Redmetal Vineyards Bridge Pa Triangle Block Five Hawke's Bay Albariño ★★★★★

An emerging star. The delicious 2020 vintage (★★★★★) was fermented and matured on its yeast lees for three months in stainless steel tanks, then bottled young. Invitingly scented, it is mouthfilling and vibrantly fruity, with intense, yet delicate, citrusy, gently spicy flavours, a hint of pineapple, and a dry (3 grams/litre of residual sugar), long finish. Full of youthful vigour, it's an instantly appealing wine; drink now or cellar.

Vintage	20	19	18
WR	7	NM	6
Drink	21-24	NM	20-24

DRY $28 V+

Sileni Grand Reserve Advocate Hawke's Bay Albariño ★★★★☆

The powerful 2018 vintage (★★★★☆) was estate-grown in the Bridge Pa Triangle. Bright, light yellow/green, it is full-bodied, with concentrated, peachy, spicy flavours, and a dry (1.9 grams/litre of residual sugar), crisp, long finish.

DRY $25 V+

Smith & Sheth Cru Heretaunga Albariño ★★★★★

The youthful 2019 vintage (★★★★☆) is a single-vineyard wine, hand-harvested in the Bridge Pa Triangle, Hawke's Bay. Fermented and matured for 10 months in seasoned oak barriques, it has a fragrant, complex bouquet. Weighty, with strong stone-fruit, pear and spice flavours, a hint of toasty oak and a long, crisp, dry finish, it's well worth cellaring to at least mid-2021+.

DRY $32 AV

Stanley Estates Single Vineyard Awatere Valley Marlborough Albariño ★★★★

The 2017 vintage (★★★★) was mostly handled in stainless steel tanks (60 per cent), but 40 per cent of the blend was fermented with indigenous yeasts in seasoned oak barrels and oak-aged for 10 months. Fresh and full-bodied, it is vibrantly fruity, with good intensity of citrusy, tangy flavours, dry (2.9 grams/litre of residual sugar) and crisp.

Vintage	17	16
WR	6	5
Drink	20-23	20-22

DRY $23 AV

Terrace Edge North Canterbury Albariño   ★★★★☆

Full of youthful vigour, the punchy 2020 vintage (★★★★☆) was fermented in seasoned oak casks. Certified organic, it is a pale straw, mouthfilling wine with a strong surge of peachy, citrusy, spicy flavours, and an off-dry (9 grams/litre of residual sugar), appetisingly crisp finish. Best drinking 2022+.

Vintage	20
WR	7
Drink	21-27

 MED/DRY $27 AV

Tohu Single Vineyard Whenua Matua Upper Moutere Nelson Albariño   (★★★★)

Drinking well now, the 2018 vintage (★★★★) is a characterful, medium-bodied wine, with very good depth of stone-fruit and spice flavours, slightly toasty notes adding complexity, and a crisp, dryish finish.

 MED/DRY $28 –V

Torlesse Waipara Albariño   (★★★☆)

Still on sale, the 2017 vintage (★★★☆) was fermented in old oak barrels and made in a medium-dry (9 grams/litre of residual sugar) style. Bright yellow/pale gold, it is fleshy, with very good depth of ripe tropical-fruit flavours, a subtle oak influence, and balanced acidity. Ready.

 MED/DRY $25 –V

Villa Maria Cellar Selection Gisborne Albariño   ★★★★☆

Bargain-priced, the 2020 vintage (★★★★☆) is already delicious. Bright, light lemon/green, it is full-bodied, with strong, lively, peachy, slightly spicy flavours, and a dry (4 grams/litre of residual sugar), crisp finish. Well worth discovering.

Vintage	20	19	18	17
WR	7	7	6	7
Drink	20-23	20-22	20-22	P

DRY $18 V+

Villa Maria Single Vineyard Braided Gravels Hawke's Bay Albariño   ★★★★★

Already drinking well, but full of youthful vigour, the outstanding 2019 vintage (★★★★★) was hand-harvested and fermented in a concrete egg-shaped tank. Highly scented, it is vibrant and sweet-fruited, with mouthfilling body and a powerful surge of ripe stone-fruit and spice flavours, intense, dry and lingering. Best drinking mid-2021+.

Vintage	19	18
WR	7	7
Drink	20-23	20-22

DRY $30 AV

Waimea Nelson Albariño   ★★★☆

Still on sale, the 2017 vintage (★★★★) is a punchy, medium-bodied wine, clearly varietal, with firm acid spine, a slightly salty streak, and strong, peachy, citrusy, spicy flavours.

 DRY $20 AV

Arneis

Still fairly rare here, with 20 hectares of bearing vines in 2020, Arneis (pronounced 'Are-nay-iss') is a traditional grape of Piedmont, in north-west Italy, where it yields soft, early-maturing wines with slightly herbaceous aromas and almond flavours. The word 'Arneis' means 'little rascal', which reflects its tricky character in the vineyard; a vigorous variety, it needs careful tending. First planted in New Zealand in 1998 at the Clevedon Hills vineyard in South Auckland, its potential has been explored by numerous producers, but after peaking at 40 hectares in 2016, plantings are now declining. Coopers Creek released the country's first varietal Arneis from the 2006 vintage. Most of the remaining vines in 2020 were clustered in Gisborne (10 hectares) and Hawke's Bay (9 hectares).

Coopers Creek SV Gisborne Arneis The Little Rascal ★★★★☆

Still on sale, the well-priced 2017 vintage (★★★★☆) is a fleshy, weighty wine, with strong, vibrant, peachy, slightly spicy flavours. Scented, with excellent intensity and harmony, it's an ideal, all-purpose, dryish wine, offering delicious drinking.

MED/DRY $22 V+

Deep Down Marlborough Arneis (★★★★★)

Certified organic, the impressive, very age-worthy 2019 vintage (★★★★★) is a single-vineyard wine, fermented with indigenous yeasts in a mix of seasoned French oak puncheons (75 per cent) and tanks (25 per cent). Light lemon/green, it is strongly scented, mouthfilling and vibrantly fruity, with concentrated, citrusy, spicy flavours, firm acid spine, and a finely textured, dry (4 grams/litre of residual sugar), lasting finish.

DRY $35 AV

Hans Herzog Marlborough Arneis ★★★★

Certified organic, the 2017 vintage (★★★☆) is an unoaked wine, fleshy and dry. Pale straw, it is full-bodied and fleshy, although not highly aromatic, with peachy, slightly spicy flavours, showing very good depth, a touch of complexity, and a rounded finish.

DRY $44 –V

Maison Noire Hawke's Bay Arneis (★★★★)

Well worth trying, the 2020 vintage (★★★★) is a hand-picked, single-vineyard wine, full-bodied and vivacious, with strong, citrusy, appley, slightly spicy flavours, a sliver of sweetness (10 grams/litre of residual sugar), fresh acidity, and loads of drink-young appeal.

MED/DRY $22 V+

Branded and Other White Wines

Dog Point Vineyard Section 94, Craggy Range Les Beaux Cailloux, Vergence White by Pegasus Bay – in this section you'll find all the white wines that don't feature varietal names. Lower-priced branded white wines can give winemakers an outlet for grapes like Chenin Blanc, Sémillon and Riesling that otherwise can be hard to sell. They can also be an outlet for coarser, less delicate juice ('pressings'). Some of the branded whites are quaffers, but others are highly distinguished.

Akitu Central Otago Pinot Noir Blanc (★★★★)

The distinctive 2019 vintage (★★★★) is from Hawkesbury Estates, at Wanaka. Matured for five months on its light yeast lees in tanks, it is faintly pink, mouthfilling and dry, with vibrant, youthful, peachy, spicy flavours, showing good intensity. Best drinking 2021.

DRY $45 –V

Beautiful Chaos Marlborough Natural White (★★★★)

From Seresin, the 2019 vintage (★★★★) is a blend of Sauvignon Blanc (75 per cent) and Chardonnay (25 per cent), estate-grown and hand-harvested in the Omaka Valley, fermented on skins in amphorae (clay pots), and bottled without fining or filtering. Straw-hued, it is distinctive, with ripe, non-herbaceous flavours, gentle tannins, and a fully dry (1 gram/litre of residual sugar) finish. 'Made in a minimalist, mindful way', it's certified organic.

DRY $30 –V

Brennan Gibbston Central Otago Orange (★★★★★)

A memorable mouthful, the 2017 vintage (★★★★★) is a blend of Pinot Gris (73 per cent), Muscat (15 per cent) and Riesling (12 per cent), made 'following ancient winemaking traditions', including fermentation on skins for two months in old French oak barriques. It is highly aromatic and full-bodied, with an orange/slight amber hue, deep, peachy, spicy flavours, showing excellent complexity, gentle tannins, and loads of interest.

DRY $50 AV

Brennan Gibbston Central Otago Trio ★★★★

The 2018 vintage (★★★★☆) is a blend of three aromatic varieties – Gewürztraminer (45 per cent), Riesling (45 per cent) and Muscat (10 per cent). Bright, light lemon/green, with a perfumed, gently spicy bouquet, it is full-bodied and vibrantly fruity, with a splash of sweetness and excellent depth of stone-fruit and spice flavours, finely balanced and lingering. It's drinking well now.

MED/DRY $33 –V

Carrick Central Otago Electric No 1 (★★★★☆)

Still on sale, the 2017 vintage (★★★★☆) was estate-grown at Bannockburn and matured for eight months in seasoned oak barrels. Named after a dredge, it is a field blend of 'all white varieties grown at Carrick', especially Pinot Gris (40 per cent of the blend), and was designed to be a 'dry wine, textural rather than varietal'. Mouthfilling and vibrantly fruity, it has strong, citrusy fruit flavours to the fore, fresh acidity, a subtle seasoning of oak adding complexity, and obvious potential. Certified organic.

DRY $36 –V

Craggy Range Les Beaux Cailloux   ★★★★★

After the impressive 2009–2011 vintages, this prestigious Gimblett Gravels, Hawke's Bay Chardonnay was discontinued, due to the removal of virus-infected vines, but it resumed production in 2016. Les Beaux Cailloux means 'the beautiful pebbles'. The 2011 vintage sold at $63, but the price has surged to $150 for the 2017 vintage (★★★★★). Still youthful, it is weighty and tightly structured, with a lovely sense of delicacy and harmony. Matured for 10 months in French oak barriques (38 per cent new), it is full-bodied, very savoury and complex, with grapefruit-like flavours, enriched with biscuity oak, and a well-rounded finish. Best drinking 2022+.

DRY $150 –V

Dog Point Vineyard Section 94   ★★★★★

This ranks among the country's greatest oak-aged Sauvignon Blancs. Looking for 'texture, rather than rich aromatics', Dog Point fermented and lees-aged the 2016 vintage (★★★★★) for 18 months in seasoned French oak casks. Hand-harvested in the Dog Point Vineyard (for which 'Section 94' was the original survey title), at the confluence of the Brancott and Omaka valleys, and fermented with indigenous yeasts, it is a powerful, tightly structured wine, full of potential. It has highly concentrated, citrusy, gently herbaceous flavours, showing excellent vigour and complexity, balanced acidity, and a fully dry, lasting finish. (The very classy 2013 vintage (★★★★★), held back to acquire bottle-age, was released in 2019. Proving the ageability of well-crafted Marlborough Sauvignon Blanc, it is still very vigorous, with light colour, a real sense of youthful drive, and lovely depth and harmony.)

Vintage	16	15	14	13	12
WR	7	7	7	7	5
Drink	20-28	20-24	20-24	20-22	P

DRY $40 AV

🍇🍇🍇

Hunting Lodge, The, White Mischief Crowd Blend   ★★★★

The distinctive 2019 vintage (★★★★) was made from Pinot Gris, Albariño and Riesling, grown in Marlborough, and mostly handled in tanks; 10 per cent of the blend was fermented in seasoned French oak barriques. Bright, light lemon/green, it is medium-bodied, with vibrant stone-fruit and spice flavours, showing good delicacy, a distinct touch of complexity, and a dryish (9.5 grams/litre of residual sugar), appetisingly crisp finish.

MED/DRY $30 –V

Judge Rock The Alibi Central Otago Blanc de Noir   (★★★★)

Faintly pink, the 2019 vintage (★★★★) of this white wine was made from mature Pinot Noir vines, grown at Alexandra. Offering very easy drinking, it is vibrantly fruity, with strong, fresh, peachy, slightly strawberryish and spicy flavours, and an off-dry (12 grams/litre of residual sugar) finish.

MED/DRY $30 –V

Lawson's Dry Hills Marlborough Ranu   ★★★★

The lively, very youthful 2020 vintage (★★★★) is a co-fermented blend of equal portions of Pinot Gris, Riesling and Gewürztraminer, fermented in old oak casks. A fresh, medium-bodied wine, it is vigorous, with strong, citrusy, appley flavours and a finely poised, dryish finish. Best drinking 2022+.

Vintage	20
WR	6
Drink	20-25

MED/DRY $30 –V

Marsden Bay of Islands Fumé Blanc   (★★★☆)

The age-worthy 2019 vintage (★★★☆) of this 'Northland Sav' was fermented and matured for six months in seasoned French oak barriques. Bright, light lemon/green, it is a fresh and lively, medium-bodied wine, with ripely herbaceous flavours, a hint of toasty oak, crisp acidity, and very good depth. Best drinking mid-2021+.

DRY $30 –V

Millton Gisborne Les Trois Enfants   (★★★★☆)

Still on sale and full of personality, the 2017 vintage (★★★★☆) is a blend of Gewürztraminer, Riesling and Muscat, co-fermented in tanks and large oak barrels. Weighty, with a spicy, vaguely honeyed bouquet, it is a strongly Gewürztraminer-influenced style, with concentrated, peachy, spicy, slightly honeyed flavours, and a firm, dryish (7.4 grams/litre of residual sugar) finish. Certified organic.

MED/DRY $24 V+

Paper Road Wairarapa CPR Field Blend   (★★★★)

From Borthwick Vineyard at Gladstone, in the northern Wairarapa, the 2019 vintage (★★★★) is a blend of Pinot Gris (48 per cent), Riesling (35 per cent) and Chardonnay (17 per cent). Fresh and full-bodied, it is vibrantly fruity, with strong, peachy, slightly spicy flavours and a crisp, dryish finish. A very lively and harmonious wine, enjoyable young, it offers good drinking now to 2022.

DRY $22 V+

Prophet's Rock Cuvée aux Antipodes Blanc   (★★★★★)

Already delicious, the 2018 vintage (★★★★★) is a single-vineyard Chardonnay, grown at Pisa, in Central Otago, and fermented and matured for 17 months in oak barrels (15 per cent new). Bright, light yellow/green, it is weighty and rich, with concentrated stone-fruit flavours, hints of toast and butterscotch, refined acidity and a long finish. A very harmonious wine, it's a drink-now or cellaring proposition.

DRY $98 –V

Providore Luminaire Central Otago Blanc de Noir   (★★★★)

Very pale pink, the distinctive 2018 vintage (★★★★) was made from Pinot Noir grapes, removed immediately from their skins. Veering towards rosé, it's a gentle, mouthfilling wine with good weight, peach, strawberry and spice flavours, a vague suggestion of sweetness, and a smooth finish.

MED/DRY $25 AV

Pyramid Valley North Canterbury Orange   (★★★★☆)

The copper-coloured 2018 vintage (★★★★☆) was hand-picked in the Porter Vineyard, at Waipara, tank-fermented, lees-aged for six months in seasoned French oak demi-muids, and bottled unfined and unfiltered. The label makes no mention of grape varieties, but Pinot Gris would be my first guess. Full-bodied, it's a complex wine, with gentle tannins, strong strawberry, watermelon and peach flavours, and hints of spices, apricots and oranges. A very harmonious wine, it's full of personality.

DRY $35 –V

Seresin Chiaroscuro   ★★★★☆

The 2018 vintage (★★★★) of this Marlborough white is a blend of Riesling (55 per cent), Pinot Gris (37 per cent) and Gewürztraminer (8 per cent), hand-picked and co-fermented in puncheons and barriques. Bright, light lemon/green, it is a fresh, medium-bodied wine with peachy, citrusy, spicy flavours, showing a distinct touch of complexity, and a crisp, dry finish. Drink now or cellar.

Vintage	12
WR	6
Drink	P

DRY $30 –V

Sileni Estate Selection Hawke's Bay Alba   ★★★★

Still on sale, the 2016 vintage (★★★★) is an unusual blend of Pinot Gris, Sauvignon Blanc, Albariño, Muscat and Chardonnay, barrel-aged for five months. Weighty, fleshy and dry (2.9 grams/litre of residual sugar), it's an aromatic wine, with peach, pear and spice flavours, showing excellent complexity and depth.

Vintage	16	15
WR	6	7
Drink	20-25	20-25

DRY $33 –V

Vergence White by Pegasus Bay Mk 1   ★★★★☆

The non-vintage wine (★★★★☆) on sale in late 2020 is based on Sémillon from the 2018 vintage, matured in large old barrels for 18 months, then blended with Muscat, Riesling, Sauvignon Blanc, Gewürztraminer and Chardonnay. Estate-grown at Waipara, in North Canterbury, it is a bright, light yellow/green, concentrated, vigorous wine, poised and youthful, with strong, ripe, peachy, spicy flavours, showing excellent complexity. It needs time; best drinking 2022+.

DRY $27 AV

Waiheke Road Hawke's Bay Raumati

Probably in full stride, the 2017 vintage (★★★☆) is a rare blend of Chenin Blanc (50 per cent), Albariño (25 per cent) and Verdelho (25 per cent), partly oak-aged. Pale straw, it is medium-bodied, with lively, peachy, slightly spicy flavours, showing good complexity and depth. (From Awaroa Winery.)

DRY $45 –V

Wooing Tree Blondie   ★★★☆

This 'blanc de noir' – a white (or rather faintly pink) Central Otago wine – is estate-grown at Cromwell. It is made from hand-picked Pinot Noir grapes; the juice is held briefly in contact with the skins and then fermented in tanks. Offering very easy drinking, it is typically fresh and smooth, in a dryish style with vibrant, peachy, spicy flavours, showing very good delicacy and depth.

MED/DRY $28 –V

Yealands Estate Single Vineyard Awatere Valley Marlborough PGR   ★★★★

Worth cellaring, the 2019 vintage (★★★★) is an estate-grown blend of three aromatic varieties – Pinot Gris (55 per cent), Riesling (29.5 per cent) and Gewürztraminer (15.5 per cent). It has a scented bouquet, leading into a fresh, full-bodied wine with an array of fruit flavours – citrus fruits, pears and lychees – gentle spicy notes, and a finely balanced, crisp, dry (3 grams/litre of residual sugar) finish. Best drinking 2021+.

DRY $25 AV

Breidecker

A nondescript crossing of Müller-Thurgau and the white hybrid Seibel 7053, Breidecker is rarely seen in New Zealand. There were 32 hectares of bearing vines recorded in 2003, but less than 1 hectare in 2020 (0.4 hectares in Central Otago). Its early-ripening ability is an advantage in cooler regions, but Breidecker typically yields light, fresh quaffing wines, best drunk young.

Black Ridge Central Otago Breidecker (★★★★★)

Still on sale, the 2016 vintage (★★★★★) is the best Breidecker I've tasted – and there were quite a few in New Zealand about 30 years ago. Weighty, fleshy, soft and gently aromatic, it has generous, vibrant, citrusy, peachy flavours, a slightly spicy, earthy streak, a splash of sweetness (16 grams/litre of residual sugar), and finely balanced acidity. Drink now.

MED $22 V+

Chardonnay

Do you drink Chardonnay? Sauvignon Blanc is our biggest-selling white-wine variety by far, and Pinot Gris is riding high, but neither of these popular grapes produces New Zealand's greatest dry whites. Chardonnay wears that crown. It's less fashionable than 20 or 30 years ago, but Chardonnay is our most prestigious white-wine variety. No other dry whites can command such lofty prices; many New Zealand Chardonnays are on the shelves at $50 or more. And although it has lost ground to Sauvignon Blanc and Pinot Gris, Chardonnay is still a big seller. Winegrowers are currently reporting a surge in sales, suggesting that Chardonnay is coming back into fashion. However, New Zealand Chardonnay has yet to make the huge international impact of our Sauvignon Blanc. Our top Chardonnays are classy, but so are those from a host of other countries in the Old and New Worlds.

In 2019, Chardonnay accounted for 1.9 per cent by volume of New Zealand's wine exports (far behind Sauvignon Blanc, with 85.8 per cent). There's an enormous range to choose from. Most wineries – especially in the North Island and upper South Island – make at least one Chardonnay; many produce several and the big wineries produce dozens. The hallmark of New Zealand Chardonnays is their delicious varietal intensity – the leading labels show notably concentrated aromas and flavours, threaded with fresh, appetising acidity.

The price of New Zealand Chardonnay ranges from under $10 to over $150. The quality differences are equally wide, although not always in relation to their prices. Lower-priced wines are typically fermented in stainless steel tanks and bottled young with little or no oak influence; these wines rely on fresh, lemony, uncluttered fruit flavours for their appeal. Chardonnays labelled as 'unoaked' were briefly popular a few years ago, as winemakers with an eye on overseas markets worked hard to showcase New Zealand's fresh, vibrant fruit characters. But without oak flavours to add richness and complexity, Chardonnay handled entirely in stainless steel tanks can be plain – even boring.

The key to the style is to use well-ripened, intensely flavoured grapes. Mid-price wines may be fermented in tanks and matured in oak casks, which adds to their complexity and richness, or fermented and/or matured in a mix of tanks and barrels (or handled entirely in tanks, with oak chips or staves suspended in the wine). The top labels are fully fermented and matured in oak barrels (normally French barriques, with varying proportions of new casks); there may also be extended aging on (and regular stirring of) yeast lees and varying proportions of a secondary, softening malolactic fermentation. The best of these display the arresting subtlety and depth of flavour for which Chardonnay is so highly prized. Chardonnay plantings have been far outstripped in recent years by Sauvignon Blanc, as wine producers respond to overseas demand, and in 2020 it constituted 8.4 per cent of the national bearing vineyard.

The variety is spread throughout the wine regions, particularly Marlborough (where 34 per cent of the vines are concentrated), Hawke's Bay (32 per cent) and Gisborne (20 per cent). Gisborne is renowned for its softly mouthfilling, ripe, peachy Chardonnays, which offer very seductive drinking in their youth; Hawke's Bay yields sturdy wines with rich grapefruit and stone-fruit flavours, power and longevity; and Marlborough's Chardonnays are slightly leaner in a cool-climate, appetisingly crisp style. Chardonnay has often been dubbed 'the red-wine drinker's white wine'. Chardonnays are usually (although not always, especially cheap models) fully dry, as are all reds with any aspirations to quality. Chardonnay's typically mouthfilling body and multi-faceted flavours are another obvious red-wine parallel. Broaching a top New Zealand Chardonnay at less than two years old can be unrewarding – the finest of the 2016s will offer excellent drinking during 2021. If you must drink Chardonnay when it is only a year old, it makes sense to buy one of the cheaper, less complex wines specifically designed to be enjoyable in their youth.

144 Islands Northland Chardonnay   (★★★★☆)

Grown at Mangawhai Heads, the 2017 vintage (★★★★☆) is an elegant, single-vineyard wine. Hand-picked, it was fermented and matured for 11 months in French oak casks (25 per cent new). Fresh and full-bodied, with an oaky, buttery fragrance, it has generous, peachy, slightly toasty flavours, showing good complexity, balanced acidity, and a long, tightly structured finish. Best drinking 2021+.

DRY $35 –V

747 Estate Gisborne Chardonnay   (★★★☆)

Labelled as a 'Chablis style', the 2017 vintage (★★★☆) was made by Denis Irwin, formerly of Matawhero fame, who died in April 2020. Medium-bodied, it is a fruity, flavoursome, finely balanced wine, enjoyable young but only moderately complex.

DRY $24 AV

Aitken's Folly Riverbank Road Wanaka Central Otago Chardonnay   ★★★★

Still on sale, the distinctive 2016 vintage (★★★★☆) is based solely on Chardonnay clone 548. Estate-grown at Wanaka, it was fermented and matured for a year in French oak casks (30 per cent new). Bright, light yellow, it has strong, citrusy aromas and flavours, showing very good complexity, and a crisp, long finish. Ready.

DRY $28 AV

Alchemy Hawke's Bay Chardonnay   ★★★★☆

Offering very good value, the 2016 vintage (★★★★☆) is a single-vineyard wine, hand-harvested at Puketapu, in the Dartmoor Valley, and fermented and matured in French oak barrels (35 per cent new). Fragrant, rich and lively, it is a weighty, finely textured wine, with strong, ripe stone-fruit flavours, well seasoned with toasty oak, balanced acidity, and good complexity. It's drinking well now.

DRY $29 V+

Alexander Martinborough Chardonnay   ★★★★☆

Labelled as a 'Chablis style', the 2018 vintage (★★★★☆) is a single-vineyard wine, hand-picked and fermented and matured in two-year-old French oak casks. The bouquet is fragrant and complex; the palate is full-bodied and dry, with strong, citrusy, peachy flavours, balanced acidity, and very good complexity. A stylish wine with obvious potential, it should be at its best 2021+.

DRY $29 V+

Allan Scott [Black Label] Marlborough Chardonnay   (★★★★)

Unfolding well, the 2018 vintage (★★★★) is a rich, smooth wine, hand-picked in the Wairau Valley and fermented and aged for eight months in French oak puncheons. Mouthfilling, it has strong, ripe stone-fruit flavours, gently seasoned with toasty oak, a hint of butterscotch and a slightly creamy texture. Good value.

DRY $22 V+

Allan Scott Eli Marlborough Chardonnay   (★★★★☆)

Still available, the debut 2016 vintage (★★★★☆) is rare – just one barrel was produced. Fermented with indigenous yeasts and given 'lots' of lees-stirring, it's a weighty, harmonious wine, concentrated and finely textured, with deep, citrusy, peachy flavours, biscuity and well-rounded.

DRY $100 –V

Allan Scott Generations Marlborough Chardonnay   ★★★★

The 2016 vintage (★★★★☆) is a powerful style, estate-grown in the Wallops Vineyard, in the Wairau Valley, and fermented and matured for 12 months in French oak puncheons (80 per cent new). Given a full, softening malolactic fermentation, it is weighty, rich and lively, with substantial body, concentrated grapefruit and peach flavours, and toasty, buttery notes adding an upfront appeal. Ready.

DRY $31 –V

Allan Scott Marlborough Chardonnay   ★★★☆

Priced right, the fresh, vibrantly fruity 2018 vintage (★★★☆) was fermented in French oak puncheons and wood-aged for eight months. Light lemon/green, with a citrusy bouquet, it has lively grapefruit and peach flavours, slightly biscuity notes adding complexity, balanced acidity and good depth.

DRY $18 V+

Alpha Domus AD Hawke's Bay Chardonnay   ★★★★★

The powerful, savoury 2016 vintage (★★★★★) was estate-grown in the Bridge Pa Triangle and fermented and matured for a year in French oak casks. A classic regional style, it is ripely fragrant and full-bodied, with generous, citrusy, peachy flavours, seasoned with biscuity oak, excellent complexity, and a tightly structured, long finish.

DRY $38 AV

Anchorage Family Estate Nelson Chardonnay   ★★☆

A 'lightly oaked' style, the 2019 vintage (★★☆) was lees-aged and went through a full, softening malolactic fermentation. Pale straw, it is an uncomplicated, pleasantly fruity wine, with fresh acidity and drink-young appeal.

DRY $16 AV

Aotea by Seifried Nelson Chardonnay   (★★★★☆)

The 2019 vintage (★★★★☆) is an elegant, youthful wine, fermented and lees-aged for a year in French oak barriques (partly new). Bright, light yellow/green, with a fresh, citrusy, slightly biscuity bouquet, it is mouthfilling and creamy-textured, with ripe grapefruit and peach flavours, showing excellent intensity and complexity. Best drinking 2022+.

DRY $39 –V

Aronui Nelson Chardonnay   ★★★★

Drinking well now, the 2016 vintage (★★★★) was hand-picked and barrel-fermented. It is mouthfilling, with vibrant, citrusy, peachy flavours, showing very good depth, and slightly biscuity and buttery notes adding complexity. (From Kono, also owner of the Tohu brand.)

DRY $22 V+

Ash Ridge Estate Hawke's Bay Chardonnay   ★★★★

The 2018 vintage (★★★★) was estate-grown in the Bridge Pa Triangle and fermented in French oak barrels (10 per cent new). Bright, light lemon/green, with a smoky fragrance, it has ripe stone-fruit flavours, finely integrated toasty oak, and very good complexity and depth. It's drinking well now.

DRY $22 V+

Ash Ridge Premium Bridge Pa Triangle Hawke's Bay Chardonnay   ★★★★

Crafted in a 'bold' style, the 2017 vintage (★★★★) was made using 'high-impact' French oak barrels and 'lots' of malolactic fermentation. Bright, light lemon/green, it is rich and rounded, with balanced acidity and strong, peachy, toasty, buttery flavours. Best drinking 2021.

DRY $32 –V

Ash Ridge Reserve Hawke's Bay Chardonnay   ★★★★☆

Estate-grown in the Bridge Pa Triangle, the 2017 vintage (★★★★☆) was fermented and matured in French oak casks (40 per cent new). Designed for cellaring, it is bright, light lemon/green, with a fragrant, complex, slightly smoky bouquet. An elegant, medium to full-bodied, tightly structured wine, it has generous, peachy, citrusy, slightly nutty flavours, fresh acidity, and a long, savoury finish. Best drinking 2021+.

DRY $42 –V

Ashwell Martinborough Chardonnay   ★★★★

The youthful, complex 2019 vintage (★★★★☆) was grown on the Martinborough Terrace, barrique-fermented and oak-aged for a year. Well worth cellaring, it is a bright, light lemon/green wine, mouthfilling and dry, with concentrated, ripe stone-fruit and toasty oak flavours, fresh acidity, and good complexity. Best drinking 2022+.

Vintage	19	18	17
WR	5	5	5
Drink	20-27	20-26	20-25

DRY $28 AV

Askerne Hawke's Bay Chardonnay   ★★★★

Priced right, the 2019 vintage (★★★★) was estate-grown and fermented and matured for 10 months in oak barrels (20 per cent new). Bright, light yellow/green, it is full-bodied and sweet-fruited, with generous, ripe stone-fruit flavours, oak-derived complexity and a smooth finish. Already highly approachable, it should break into full stride mid-2021+.

DRY $24 V+

Askerne Reserve Hawke's Bay Chardonnay   ★★★★☆

The powerful 2018 vintage (★★★★☆) was fermented and matured in French oak barrels (35 per cent new). Bright, light yellow/green, it is mouthfilling and sweet-fruited, with strong, ripe stone-fruit flavours, seasoned with toasty oak, excellent complexity and a rich, smooth finish. Best drinking 2021+.

> DRY $32 AV

Askerne The Archer Hawke's Bay Chardonnay   (★★★★★)

Launched from the 2018 vintage (★★★★★), this is Askerne's new top-tier Chardonnay. A powerful, very age-worthy wine, it was fully barrel-fermented (45 per cent new oak). Bright, light yellow/green, it has a fragrant, slightly smoky bouquet. Full-bodied, it is highly concentrated, with deep grapefruit, peach and spice flavours, complex, savoury, rich and long. Best drinking 2022+.

> DRY $50 AV

Astrolabe Marlborough Chardonnay   ★★★★☆

The 2019 vintage (★★★★☆) was hand-harvested at three sites in the Awatere Valley, lower Wairau Valley and the Southern Valleys, and fermented and matured for 10 months in French oak barriques and puncheons. Bright, light lemon/green, it is a subtle, mouthfilling wine, with ripe stone-fruit flavours, slightly biscuity and creamy notes adding complexity, and a finely textured, smooth, very harmonious finish. Drink now or cellar.

Vintage	19	18
WR	6	6
Drink	21-25	20-26

> DRY $30 AV

Astrolabe The Farm Marlborough Chardonnay   (★★★★★)

The stylish 2019 vintage (★★★★★) was estate-grown at Astrolabe Farm, at Grovetown, in the lower Wairau Valley, hand-harvested and fermented and matured for 10 months in French oak puncheons. Bright, light lemon/green, it is a highly fragrant, medium to full-bodied wine, concentrated and youthful, with ripe stone-fruit flavours, a subtle seasoning of biscuity oak, and a very harmonious, creamy-textured finish. Already delicious, it's well worth cellaring to 2022+.

Vintage	19
WR	6
Drink	20-28

> DRY $45 AV

Astrolabe Wrekin Marlborough Chardonnay   (★★★★★)

The very harmonious, youthful 2019 vintage (★★★★★) was grown in the Wrekin Vineyard, in the Southern Valleys. Hand-harvested and fermented and matured for 10 months in French oak puncheons, it is bright, light lemon/green, with fresh, generous, citrusy, peachy flavours, biscuity notes adding complexity, and a creamy-textured, long finish. Showing obvious potential, it should be at its best 2022+.

Vintage	19
WR	6
Drink	20-28

> DRY $45 AV

Ata Rangi Craighall Martinborough Chardonnay   ★★★★★

This memorable wine has richness, complexity and downright drinkability. From a company-owned block of low-yielding Mendoza-clone vines in the Craighall Vineyard, planted in 1983, it is hand-picked, whole-bunch pressed and fermented with indigenous yeasts in French oak barriques (around 25 per cent new). The 2017 vintage (★★★★★) is bright, light lemon/green, with a fragrant, slightly creamy bouquet. A refined, subtle wine, it is full-bodied, with fresh, youthful, peachy, citrusy, slightly biscuity flavours, showing excellent delicacy and depth, finely integrated oak, balanced acidity and a long finish. Best drinking 2021+.

Vintage	17	16	15	14	13
WR	7	7	7	7	7
Drink	20-25	20-24	20-23	20-22	20-21

 DRY $55 AV

Ataahua Waipara Chardonnay   ★★★★

The distinctive, pale gold 2018 vintage (★★★★) was fermented with indigenous yeasts in seasoned oak barrels. A 'full-on' style, it is weighty and sweet-fruited, with strong, ripe stone-fruit flavours, vaguely honeyed notes, fresh acidity, and lots of drink-young appeal.

Vintage	18	17
WR	6	7
Drink	20-25	20-27

 DRY $30 -V

Auntsfield Cob Cottage Southern Valleys Marlborough Chardonnay   ★★★★★

This single 'block' – rather than just single 'vineyard' – wine is estate-grown on the south side of the Wairau Valley. The outstanding 2016 vintage (★★★★★), matured for 11 months in French oak casks (20 per cent new), is a weighty wine, slightly creamy-textured, with deep citrus and stone-fruit flavours, and very finely integrated, biscuity oak. Combining power and elegance, it is highly concentrated, vibrant and 'complete'.

Vintage	16
WR	7
Drink	20-28

 DRY $48 AV

Auntsfield Single Vineyard Southern Valleys Marlborough Chardonnay   ★★★★★

This consistently rewarding wine is estate-grown on the south side of the Wairau Valley, hand-harvested and fermented and matured in French oak barrels (18 per cent new in 2017). The elegant, still youthful 2017 vintage (★★★★☆) is fragrant and full-bodied, with vibrant, citrusy, peachy, slightly biscuity flavours, fresh acidity, very good intensity and a fully dry, tightly structured finish. Retasted in mid-2020, it is still unfolding; best drinking 2022+.

DRY $36 AV

Aurum Organic Central Otago Chardonnay ★★★★☆

The impressive 2018 vintage (★★★★★) was estate-grown, hand-harvested, and fermented and matured for a year in French oak barrels (18 per cent new). Bright, light lemon/green, it is highly refined, with fresh, vibrant stone-fruit flavours, showing excellent ripeness, delicacy and depth, mealy and toasty notes adding complexity, balanced acidity, and a seamless, lingering finish. Still youthful, it should be at its best 2022+. Certified organic.

Vintage	18
WR	6
Drink	20-30

 DRY $45 –V

Awatere River by Louis Vavasour Marlborough Chardonnay ★★★★

The 2018 vintage (★★★★☆) was fermented, partly with indigenous yeasts, in French oak barrels. Straw-hued, it is weighty and generous, with rich stone-fruit flavours, balanced acidity, and a rounded finish. Drink now to 2022.

Vintage	15
WR	6
Drink	20-21

 DRY $30 –V

Babich Black Label Hawke's Bay Chardonnay ★★★★

The Black Label range is aimed primarily at the restaurant trade. Finely balanced for current consumption, the 2018 vintage (★★★★) is a fragrant, vibrantly fruity wine with generous, ripe stone-fruit flavours to the fore, a subtle seasoning of oak adding complexity, slightly buttery notes, and a well-rounded finish.

 DRY $23 V+

Babich Family Estates Headwaters Organic Marlborough Chardonnay ★★★★☆

Estate-grown near Renwick, in the Wairau Valley, the classy 2017 vintage (★★★★☆) is great value. Fermented and matured for eight months in French oak barriques, it is fragrant and vibrantly fruity, with strong, citrusy, peachy flavours, fresh acidity, slightly buttery and nutty notes, and excellent depth, vigour, complexity and harmony.

 DRY $25 V+

Babich Hawke's Bay Chardonnay ★★★☆

Enjoyable young, the 2018 vintage (★★★☆) is an unoaked style, fresh, full-bodied and vibrantly fruity, with ripe stone-fruit flavours to the fore, good mouthfeel and texture, and a rounded finish.

 DRY $20 AV

Babich Irongate Chardonnay ★★★★★

Babich's flagship Chardonnay. A stylish wine, Irongate was traditionally markedly leaner and tighter than other top Hawke's Bay Chardonnays, while performing well in the cellar, but the latest releases have more drink-young appeal. It is based on hand-picked fruit from the shingly Irongate Vineyard in Gimblett Road, fully barrel-fermented (about 20 per cent new), and lees-matured for up to 10 months. Fragrant and finely textured, the 2018 vintage (★★★★★) is a weighty wine, with deep peach and grapefruit flavours, mealy notes adding complexity, and a seamless, lingering finish. Fresh, youthful and finely poised, it's already enjoyable, but likely to be at its best 2022+.

Vintage	18	17	16	15	14	13
WR	6	6	7	7	6	7
Drink	20-28	20-27	20-27	20-26	20-25	20-25

Baby Doll Hawke's Bay Chardonnay   (★★★☆)

Enjoyable young, the 2019 vintage (★★★☆) is a lively, fruit-driven style, with good depth of ripe stone-fruit flavours, a hint of toastiness and a rounded, creamy-smooth finish. (From Yealands.)

DRY $18 V+

Big Sky Chardonnay   (★★★★)

The 2019 vintage (★★★★) was grown at Gladstone, in the northern Wairarapa, fermented with indigenous yeasts in a 50:50 split of new oak puncheons and seasoned barriques, and wood-matured for six months. Bright, light lemon/green, with a creamy, buttery bouquet, it is full-bodied, with generous, peachy, slightly toasty flavours, fresh acidity and a smooth finish. Enjoyable young, it should be at its best mid-2021+.

DRY $38 –V

Bilancia Hawke's Bay Chardonnay   ★★★★★

The tightly structured, elegant 2017 vintage (★★★★☆) was estate-grown on the lower terraces of *la collina* Vineyard, hand-picked and fermented and matured for 16 months in French oak puncheons. Fragrant, it is a youthful wine, still very fresh and vibrant, with concentrated, grapefruit-like flavours, mealy notes, a subtle seasoning of oak and a lingering finish. Best drinking 2022+.

DRY $30 V+

Bilancia Tiratore Chardonnay   (★★★★★)

The youthful but already very expressive 2018 vintage (★★★★★) is Bilancia's first 'single vineyard, flagship Chardonnay' from the *la collina* Vineyard, in Hawke's Bay. The goal is a 'tighter, food-friendly wine that will age gracefully'. Bright, light yellow, it is a powerful, weighty, bold wine, with deep, vibrant stone-fruit flavours, showing an almost honeyed richness, nutty notes adding complexity, a slightly oily texture, and a very harmonious, well-rounded finish. Best drinking 2022+.

DRY $90 AV

Black Barn Vineyards Barrel Fermented Hawke's Bay Chardonnay   ★★★★★

The classy, youthful 2019 vintage (★★★★★) was hand-harvested at Havelock North and in the Tuki Tuki Valley, and fermented and matured for 11 months in oak barrels (20 per cent new). Bright, light yellow/green, it is fragrant and mouthfilling, with strong peach and grapefruit flavours, mealy and biscuity notes adding complexity, and a finely poised, lasting finish. Best drinking 2022+.

DRY $39 AV

Black Cottage Reserve Marlborough Chardonnay   ★★★☆

Priced right, the 2017 vintage (★★★☆) was hand-picked in the Wairau Valley (mostly) and the Southern Valleys, and oak-aged. It has fresh, vibrant, grapefruit-like flavours, savoury notes adding complexity, and a creamy-smooth finish.

DRY $20 AV

Black Estate Home Chardonnay Young Vines   (★★★★)

Certified organic, the vigorous 2019 vintage (★★★★) was hand-harvested from vines planted at Waipara in 2011, barrel-fermented with indigenous yeasts, and bottled unfined and unfiltered. Pale gold, it is very age-worthy, with mouthfilling body, strong, peachy, citrusy flavours, oak complexity, and lively acidity. Best drinking 2022+.

DRY $40 –V

Black Estate Home North Canterbury Chardonnay   ★★★★☆

The 2019 vintage (★★★★☆) is from the Home Vineyard at Omihi, Waipara. Hand-picked from vines planted in 2011 and 1994, and fermented with indigenous yeasts in French oak barrels, it was bottled unfined and unfiltered. Light gold, it is powerful, with concentrated stone-fruit flavours, a hint of spice, balanced acidity and a long, crisp finish. Best drinking 2022+. Certified organic.

DRY $45 –V

Blackenbrook Family Reserve Nelson Chardonnay   ★★★★☆

The powerful 2019 vintage (★★★★☆) was estate-grown, hand-harvested and matured for a year in American (60 per cent) and French oak barrels (80 per cent new). Bright, light yellow/green, it is mouthfilling and weighty, in a strongly oak-influenced style with concentrated, peachy, nutty, toasty flavours, balanced acidity and a slightly creamy texture. Still very youthful, it should be at its best 2022+.

Vintage	14
WR	7
Drink	20-25

DRY $43 –V

Blackenbrook Nelson Chardonnay ★★★★

Estate-grown, the attractive 2019 vintage (★★★★) was hand-harvested and matured for a year in seasoned American (90 per cent) and French (10 per cent) oak casks. Full-bodied, fresh and lively, it has strong peach and grapefruit flavours, with biscuity oak adding complexity, and lots of drink-young appeal. Best drinking mid-2021+.

Vintage	19	18
WR	6	6
Drink	21-25	20-24

DRY $25 AV

Blank Canvas Escaroth Marlborough Chardonnay (★★★★☆)

The very age-worthy 2019 vintage (★★★★☆) is a single-vineyard wine, grown at Taylors Pass, in the Southern Valleys. Hand-picked, it was fermented with indigenous yeasts in French oak barriques and puncheons (30 per cent new). Bright, light lemon/green, it has a fragrant, youthful, complex, slightly smoky bouquet. Weighty, with generous, grapefruit-like flavours, a subtle seasoning of oak, excellent complexity, balanced acidity and a tight-knit finish, it should be at its best 2022+.

DRY $45 –V

Blank Canvas Reed Marlborough Chardonnay (★★★★★)

Slightly more extroverted at this stage than its Escaroth stablemate, the classy 2019 vintage (★★★★★) is a single-vineyard, Waihopai Valley wine, hand-picked and fermented with indigenous yeasts in French oak puncheons (40 per cent new). Bright, light lemon/green, it is mouthfilling and savoury, with concentrated, citrusy, peachy flavours, finely integrated oak and impressive complexity. A powerful, distinctive wine with obvious potential, it's best cellared to 2022+.

DRY $45 AV

Boneline, The, Barebone Waipara Chardonnay ★★★★☆

The powerful, distinctive 2018 vintage (★★★★☆) is a youthful wine, made with 'minimal use of old oak barrels'. Bright, light lemon/green, it is weighty, with concentrated, ripe stone-fruit flavours to the fore, considerable complexity, finely balanced acidity, and a dry, lengthy finish.

DRY $30 AV

Boneline, The, Sharkstone Waipara Chardonnay ★★★★★

An emerging classic from North Canterbury. Already delicious, the striking 2018 vintage (★★★★★) was estate-grown, hand-picked from mature vines and fermented with indigenous yeasts in French oak barrels. Bright, light lemon/green, it is fragrant, tightly structured and intense, with searching, grapefruit-like flavours, gentle biscuity and buttery notes adding complexity, and a long, seamless finish. A notably elegant, distinctly cool-climate style, it's a very 'complete' wine, set to unfold gracefully for a decade.

DRY $45 AV

Brancott Estate Identity Wairau Valley Marlborough Chardonnay   (★★★☆)

Drinking well young, the debut 2018 vintage (★★★☆) was grown in the Renwick and Brancott districts, and partly oak-fermented (17 per cent of the blend was fermented in French oak foudres). Mouthfilling, it has good depth of fresh, ripe, peachy flavours, showing a touch of complexity, and a harmonious, slightly creamy-textured finish.

DRY $22 AV

Brancott Estate Letter Series 'O' Marlborough Chardonnay   ★★★★☆

Named after the company's Omaka Vineyard, this typically powerful, high-flavoured wine is hand-picked at sites on the south side of the Wairau Valley, fermented with indigenous yeasts in French oak barriques (about 40 per cent new), and given a full, softening malolactic fermentation. An upfront style, the 2017 vintage (★★★★☆) has a fragrant, smoky bouquet, mouthfilling body and strong, ripe, peachy, slightly toasty flavours. Weighty and youthful, it should be at its best during 2020–21.

DRY $25 V+

Brennan Gibbston Central Otago Chardonnay   ★★★★

Full of youthful drive, the 2018 vintage (★★★★☆) of this tightly structured, estate-grown wine was barrel-fermented and lees-aged. Bright, light yellow/green, it is full-bodied, with ripe stone-fruit and toasty oak flavours, showing impressive complexity and depth, fresh acidity, and a finely balanced, lengthy finish. Best drinking 2021+.

DRY $33 –V

Brick Bay Matakana Chardonnay   ★★★★☆

The 2017 vintage (★★★★) was estate-grown and barrel-fermented. Mouthfilling, fresh and lively, it has ripe, citrusy, peachy, nutty flavours, complex and savoury, finely balanced acidity, and a lingering finish.

DRY $44 –V

Brightwater Vineyards Lord Rutherford Barrique Nelson Chardonnay   ★★★★★

This classy, single-vineyard, estate-grown wine is hand-picked and fermented and matured for up to a year in French oak barriques (25 per cent new in 2016). The 2016 vintage (★★★★★) is a refined, vibrant, tightly structured wine, mouthfilling, with concentrated, citrusy, peachy, slightly toasty flavours, creamy notes, excellent complexity, and a lingering finish. Best drinking 2021+.

DRY $40 AV

Vintage	16
WR	7
Drink	20-22

Brightwater Vineyards Nelson Chardonnay   ★★★★

The attractive 2016 vintage (★★★★) was estate-grown, fermented and matured for 10 months in French oak barrels (20 per cent new), and given a full, softening malolactic fermentation. It is fragrant, mouthfilling and lively, with considerable complexity, balanced acidity, and good intensity of lemony, peachy, slightly toasty and buttery flavours.

DRY $28 AV

Bronte Nelson Chardonnay ★★★☆

From Rimu Grove, the 2016 vintage (★★★☆) was grown at Moutere and French oak-aged. Full-bodied and vibrant, with a fragrant, citrusy, peachy bouquet, it has ripe-fruit flavours to the fore, fresh acidity, and good depth.

Vintage	16	15
WR	6	7
Drink	20-27	20-26

 DRY $24 AV

Brookfields Bergman Chardonnay ★★★★

Named after the Ingrid Bergman roses in the estate garden, this wine is grown alongside the winery at Meeanee, in Hawke's Bay. The 2019 vintage (★★★★) was almost entirely fermented and matured for nine months in American and French oak barrels (10 per cent new). Bright, light lemon/green, it is mouthfilling and sweet-fruited, with strong, ripe, peachy, slightly toasty and creamy flavours, showing good vigour and concentration, and a well-rounded finish. Drink now to 2022. Fine value.

Vintage	19
WR	7
Drink	20-24

 DRY $21 V+

Brookfields Marshall Bank Chardonnay ★★★★★

Brookfields' top Chardonnay is named after proprietor Peter Robertson's grandfather's property in Otago. Grown in a vineyard adjacent to the winery at Meeanee and fermented and matured (with weekly stirring of its yeast lees) in French oak barriques (partly new), it is a powerful, classy, concentrated Hawke's Bay wine. The weighty, fleshy 2019 vintage (★★★★★) is a classic regional style, with deep stone-fruit and toasty oak flavours, showing excellent complexity and harmony, and a dry, long finish. Already drinking well, it should be at its best 2022+.

Vintage	19	18
WR	7	7
Drink	22-27	21-26

DRY $35 AV

Bushmere Estate Classic Gisborne Chardonnay ★★★★

The youthful 2018 vintage (★★★★) was grown in the Central Valley and French oak-matured for 18 months. Bright, light lemon/green, with a fragrant, slightly biscuity bouquet, it is fresh and lively, in an elegant style with ripe, citrusy, peachy flavours, gently seasoned with oak, balanced acidity, and a dry finish. Best drinking mid-2021+.

 DRY $25 AV

Carrick Bannockburn Central Otago Chardonnay   ★★★★☆

Certified organic, the 2017 vintage (★★★★) was hand-picked, barrel-fermented with indigenous yeasts and bottled unfined and unfiltered. Full-bodied, with strong, peachy, toasty, slightly buttery flavours, and a crisp, dry finish, it's a vigorous wine, drinking well now.

Vintage	17	16	15	14
WR	7	6	5	6
Drink	20-24	20-23	20-21	20-21

DRY $39 –V

Carrick Cairnmuir Terraces EBM Chardonnay   ★★★★★

From a region producing increasingly fine, often underrated Chardonnays, this is one of the best. EBM means 'extended barrel maturation'. Estate-grown at Bannockburn, the stylish 2016 vintage (★★★★★) was fermented and matured for 18 months in French oak barrels (10 per cent new). Full-bodied and vibrantly fruity, with strong, citrusy, slightly peachy flavours, gently seasoned with oak, excellent complexity, and a tight, persistent finish, it's breaking into full stride now. Certified organic.

Vintage	16	15	14	13
WR	7	5	6	7
Drink	20-26	20-22	20-21	P

DRY $47 AV

Catalina Sounds Single Vineyard Sound of White Marlborough Chardonnay   (★★★★☆)

The elegant 2017 vintage (★★★★☆) was estate-grown and hand-harvested in the Waihopai Valley, and fermented and matured in French oak puncheons. Fragrant, fresh and full-bodied, it is vibrantly fruity, with vigorous grapefruit and peach flavours, biscuity, mealy notes adding complexity, and a long, creamy-textured finish. Best drinking 2021+.

DRY $35 –V

Chard Farm Closeburn Central Otago Chardonnay   ★★★★

The 2018 vintage (★★★★) is an unoaked style, matured on its yeast lees in stainless steel tanks. Bright, light yellow/green, it is weighty, with strong, citrusy, slightly appley aromas and flavours, a creamy texture, and a dry, smooth finish. It's drinking well now.

Vintage	18
WR	5
Drink	20-23

DRY $31 –V

Chard Farm Judge & Jury Central Otago Chardonnay   ★★★★☆

Already drinking well, the 2019 vintage (★★★★☆) was 'made with minimal oak' to showcase its fruit characters – 43 per cent of the blend was handled in tanks and 57 per cent in seasoned oak barrels. Pale yellow/green, it is mouthfilling and vibrantly fruity, with strong, youthful, peachy, citrusy flavours, gently mealy, biscuity notes, fresh acidity, and a faintly buttery, very harmonious finish. Best drinking mid-2021+.

Vintage	19
WR	7
Drink	21-27

DRY $39 –V

Church Road 1 Single Vineyard Tuki Tuki Chardonnay   (★★★★★)

Already very expressive, the 2018 vintage (★★★★★) is a pale gold Hawke's Bay wine, hand-picked and fermented and matured for 11 months in French oak casks (21 per cent new). Fragrant, with a distinct whiff of 'struck match', it is highly concentrated, with fresh acidity, lively stone-fruit flavours, balanced toasty oak and impressive complexity. Best drinking 2022+.

DRY $70 AV

Church Road Grand Reserve Hawke's Bay Chardonnay   ★★★★★

This very classy wine sits above the McDonald Series (but below Tom and 1 Single Vineyard) in the Church Road hierarchy. Still very youthful, the 2019 vintage (★★★★★) is a powerful wine, grown mostly in the Tuki Tuki Valley and fermented with indigenous yeasts in French oak barrels (30 per cent new). Fragrant, with a complex, slightly smoky bouquet, it has rich, vigorous, stone-fruit and toasty oak flavours, threaded with fresh acidity, and a lasting finish. Best drinking mid-2022+.

DRY $40 AV

Church Road Hawke's Bay Chardonnay   ★★★★

This mouthfilling, rich wine is made by Pernod Ricard NZ at Church Road winery in Hawke's Bay. Described by winemaker Chris Scott as 'unashamedly just a little bit old school', it is typically fleshy and smooth, with ripe stone-fruit flavours, showing good complexity and depth. The 2019 vintage (★★★★) is a youthful, great-value wine, fermented and aged for 11 months in French and Hungarian oak casks (35 per cent new). Bright, light yellow/green, with a fragrant, savoury bouquet, it is full-bodied, fresh and dry, with generous, ripe stone-fruit flavours and biscuity oak adding complexity. Best drinking mid-2021+.

DRY $20 V+

Church Road McDonald Series Hawke's Bay Chardonnay   ★★★★★

Typically a great buy, with greater richness and complexity than most $27 Chardonnays. Fresh and youthful, the 2019 vintage (★★★★☆) is a mouthfilling, sweet-fruited wine, hand-picked, mostly in the Tuki Tuki Valley, and fermented and matured for 11 months in French oak barrels (19 per cent new). Bright, light yellow/green, it has generous, ripe stone-fruit flavours, toasty and mealy notes adding complexity, balanced acidity and good potential. Best drinking 2022+.

DRY $27 V+

Church Road Tom Chardonnay ★★★★★

This is the pinnacle of Church Road's Hawke's Bay Chardonnays – as its price conveys. The 2019 vintage (★★★★★), grown entirely in the Tuki Tuki Valley, is the first to include fruit (28 per cent of the blend) from the company's Terraces Vineyard, sited further inland than its Tuki Tuki Vineyard (72 per cent). Hand-picked, it was fermented and matured for 11 months on its full yeast lees in French oak barriques (31 per cent new). Still a baby, it has a highly fragrant, smoky bouquet, leading into a mouthfilling, weighty wine with lush, vigorous stone-fruit and nutty oak flavours, showing notable intensity, and a long, dry finish. Best drinking 2024+.

 DRY $150 –V

Clearview Beachhead Hawke's Bay Chardonnay ★★★★☆

This Hawke's Bay winery has a reputation for powerful Chardonnays, and top vintages of this good-value label are no exception. Estate-grown and hand-harvested on the coast at Te Awanga, the 2018 vintage (★★★★☆) was fermented and matured for eight months in French oak barrels. Pale gold, it is weighty, with fresh acidity and loads of citrusy, peachy, toasty, slightly buttery flavour. Drink now or cellar to 2022.

Vintage	18	17	16	15
WR	5	5	5	7
Drink	20-22	20-22	20-21	20-21

DRY $29 V+

Clearview Endeavour Hawke's Bay Chardonnay ★★★★★

One of New Zealand's highest-priced Chardonnays, this wine is estate-grown at Te Awanga, hand-picked from (Mendoza-clone) vines planted in 1989, fermented with indigenous yeasts and matured for an unusually long period in barrels. It typically makes a very bold statement. The 2018 vintage (★★★★★) is a powerful, yet refined wine. Bright, light yellow/green, it is sturdy, with concentrated, youthful flavours of stone-fruit, seasoned with biscuity oak, impressive complexity, slightly smoky notes, and a long, very harmonious finish. Already drinking well, it's a very age-worthy wine; best drinking 2022+.

 DRY $175 –V

Clearview Reserve Hawke's Bay Chardonnay ★★★★★

For his premium Chardonnay label, winemaker Tim Turvey aims for a 'big, grunty, upfront' style – and hits the target with ease. It's typically a hedonist's delight – an arrestingly bold, intense, savoury, mealy, complex wine with layers of flavour. The 2018 vintage (★★★★★) was hand-picked from mature vines at Te Awanga and fermented and matured in 'predominantly new' French oak casks. Already open and expressive, it's a classic regional style, full-bodied, with concentrated, ripe stone-fruit flavours, threaded with fresh acidity, and toasty, buttery notes adding richness and complexity. An extroverted style, it's a drink-now or cellaring proposition.

Vintage	18	17	16	15	14	13
WR	5	5	6	7	7	7
Drink	20-28	20-27	20-26	20-25	20-25	20-23

DRY $45 AV

Clearview Three Rows Hawke's Bay Chardonnay   ★★★★★

From '3 rows on the Clearview Estate Main Block' at Te Awanga, the tight, elegant 2019 vintage (★★★★★) was barrel-fermented and lees-aged for 10 months. Light lemon/green, it is mouthfilling and vigorous, with intense, citrusy, peachy flavours, savoury notes adding complexity, and a fragrant, slightly smoky bouquet. A classy young wine, it's well worth cellaring to 2023+. The 2018 vintage (★★★★★) was tasted in mid-2020. Full of youthful drive, it is full-bodied, with tight, grapefruit-like flavours, complex, savoury and long, finely integrated oak, and a distinct hint of gunflint. Best drinking 2022+.

Clearview White Caps Hawke's Bay Chardonnay   ★★★★

Very much a 'style' wine, the 2019 vintage (★★★★) is designed to go 'back to the excesses of the 1980s', with 'loads of oak and buttery toast'. Bright yellow/green, it is a mouthfilling wine, with bold, ripe, peachy, toasty flavours. An extroverted style, it's already drinking well.

Clos de Ste Anne Chardonnay Naboth's Vineyard   ★★★★★

Once described by co-founder James Millton as 'a stiletto, not a slipper', Millton's Chardonnay is based on ungrafted, unirrigated vines, over 25 years old, in the steep, north-east-facing Naboth's Vineyard in the Poverty Bay foothills. Grown biodynamically and hand-harvested, it is fermented with indigenous yeasts in mostly second-fill French oak barriques, and has usually not been put through malolactic fermentation, 'to leave a pure, crisp mineral flavour'. Top vintages are powerful, notably stylish and complete. The 2018 vintage (★★★★☆) is a pale straw, tightly structured, medium to full-bodied wine, with vigorous, youthful stone-fruit flavours, showing very good complexity, and obvious potential.

Cloudy Bay New Zealand Chardonnay   ★★★★★

A powerful Marlborough wine with impressively concentrated, savoury, lemony, mealy flavours and a proven ability to mature well over the long haul. The grapes are sourced from numerous company-owned and growers' vineyards at Brancott, Fairhall, Benmorven and in the Central Wairau Valley. The wine is fermented with indigenous yeasts in French oak barriques (15 per cent new in 2018), lees-aged in barrels, and most goes through a softening malolactic fermentation. The 2018 vintage (★★★★☆) is still unfolding. Bright, light lemon/green, it is fresh and full-bodied, with good intensity of vibrant, peachy, citrusy flavours, gentle biscuity notes adding complexity, and good acid spine. Best drinking 2022+.

Vintage	18	17	16	15	14
WR	7	7	7	7	7
Drink	20-27	20-26	20-25	20-24	P

Collaboration Aurulent Hawke's Bay Chardonnay   ★★★★★

The refined 2018 vintage (★★★★★) was fermented and matured for 11 months in French oak casks (22 per cent new). Bright, light yellow/green, it has a fresh, smoky fragrance. Mouthfilling, it is vibrantly fruity, with strong, youthful, grapefruit-like flavours, hints of biscuity oak, excellent complexity, and a long, slightly creamy finish. Best drinking 2021+.

Vintage	18	17	16	15	14	13
WR	6	6	6	7	7	7
Drink	20-25	20-24	20-23	20-23	20-22	20-21

DRY $37 AV

Collaboration Impression White Hawke's Bay Chardonnay   ★★★★

The 2018 vintage (★★★★☆) was matured for eight months in seasoned French oak barrels and given a full, softening malolactic fermentation. Bright yellow, with a fragrant, slightly buttery bouquet, it is a sweet-fruited, well-rounded wine, with generous stone-fruit flavours, gentle, nutty oak characters adding complexity, and loads of drink-young appeal.

DRY $27 AV

Coniglio Hawke's Bay Chardonnay   ★★★★☆

The 2015 vintage (★★★★☆), still available, was estate-grown in the inland, elevated Riverview Vineyard, hand-harvested, fermented with indigenous yeasts and barrel-aged for 18 months. Full-bodied, with concentrated, peachy, toasty flavours, it has very good vigour and complexity, fresh acidity, and a long finish.

Vintage	15
WR	7
Drink	20-25

DRY $90 –V

Coopers Creek Gisborne Chardonnay   ★★★☆

Enjoyable young, the 2018 vintage (★★★☆) was fermented and aged for 10 months in seasoned oak barrels. Bright, light yellow/green, it is an upfront style, with plenty of ripe, peachy, slightly toasty flavour, and a well-rounded finish.

DRY $18 V+

Coopers Creek Select Vineyards Big + Buttery Gisborne Chardonnay   ★★★★

For those who want to 'relive the 80s', the 2018 vintage (★★★★) is a bold style, fermented and aged for 11 months in American oak barrels (33 per cent new). Bright, light yellow/green, with a fragrant, toasty bouquet, it is mouthfilling, with balanced acidity, and strong, youthful, peachy, toasty flavours. Best drinking 2021+.

DRY $25 AV

Coopers Creek Select Vineyards Limeworks Hawke's Bay Chardonnay ★★★★

If you like toasty, creamy, full-flavoured Chardonnays, try this. Grown in the Havelock North hills, the 2018 vintage (★★★★) was fermented and matured for 10 months in American oak casks (30 per cent new), and given a full, softening malolactic fermentation. Fragrant and full-bodied, it has generous stone-fruit flavours, strongly seasoned with toasty oak, and good complexity.

DRY $25 AV

Coopers Creek Select Vineyards Plainsman Hawke's Bay Chardonnay ★★★★

The subtle, creamy-textured 2018 vintage (★★★★) was fermented and matured for 10 months in barrels, but with no use of new oak. Fresh and full-bodied, it has very good depth of ripe, peachy, slightly yeasty flavours, considerable complexity, balanced acidity, and lots of drink-young charm.

DRY $22 V+

Coopers Creek Swamp Reserve Chardonnay ★★★★☆

Based on the winery's best Hawke's Bay grapes, this seductive Chardonnay has a finely judged balance of rich, citrusy, peachy fruit flavours and toasty oak. Hand-picked in the company's Middle Road Vineyard at Havelock North, it is fermented and matured in French oak barriques (30 per cent new in 2018), and given a full, softening malolactic fermentation. The 2018 vintage (★★★★★) is a very classy, harmonious wine. Full-bodied, it has concentrated, peachy, slightly spicy flavours, gentle biscuity and smoky notes adding complexity, and a finely balanced, lasting finish. Best drinking 2022+.

DRY $39 –V

Craft Farm Home Vineyard Hawke's Bay Chardonnay ★★★★☆

The 2017 vintage (★★★★☆) was estate-grown at Puketapu and barrel-fermented with indigenous yeasts. Medium to full-bodied, with a fragrant, complex bouquet, it has rich, ripe stone-fruit flavours to the fore, and a tightly structured, long finish. It's drinking well now.

DRY $35 –V

Craggy Range Gimblett Gravels Vineyard Hawke's Bay Chardonnay ★★★★★

This stylish wine is typically mouthfilling and savoury, with complexity from fermentation and maturation in French oak barriques (19 per cent new in 2018). The 2018 vintage (★★★★★), barrel-aged for 10 months, shows lovely freshness and harmony, with a slightly smoky bouquet. Bright, light lemon/green, it is mouthfilling, vibrant and youthful, with finely balanced acidity, deep stone-fruit flavours, mealy, biscuity notes adding complexity, and a lingering finish. Best drinking 2021+.

DRY $40 AV

Craggy Range Kidnappers Vineyard Hawke's Bay Chardonnay ★★★★

Grown near the coast, at Te Awanga, the 2018 vintage (★★★★) was handled for 10 months in French oak puncheons (10 per cent new). Fresh and vibrant, it is medium to full-bodied, with vigorous, citrusy, peachy flavours, a gentle seasoning of biscuity oak, and a crisp, dry, lingering finish. Best drinking 2021+.

DRY $30 –V

Crazy by Nature Gisborne Shotberry Chardonnay ★★★☆

From Millton, this is an unoaked style. The 2017 vintage (★★★★) was blended with Viognier (7 per cent) and Marsanne (4 per cent) to 'extend the palate weight', and tank-fermented. It is full-bodied and sweet-fruited, with ripe, citrusy, peachy flavours, good acid balance, a touch of complexity, and excellent depth and harmony. Certified organic.

DRY $21 AV

Dashwood by Vavasour Marlborough Chardonnay ★★★☆

Enjoyable young, the 2018 vintage (★★★☆) offers great value. It is fragrant, with good weight and depth of fresh, ripe, peachy flavours, slightly toasty and buttery notes, and a creamy-smooth finish.

DRY $16 V+

De La Terre Hawke's Bay Barrique Ferment Chardonnay ★★★★☆

The very powerful 2018 vintage (★★★★☆) was estate-grown at Havelock North and fermented in French oak casks (28 per cent new). Bright, light yellow/green, it is robust (14.8 per cent alcohol), with strong stone-fruit flavours, a hint of honey, and fresh acidity. Full of personality, it's a drink-now or cellaring proposition.

DRY $30 AV

De La Terre Reserve Hawke's Bay Chardonnay ★★★★★

Delicious now, the 2016 vintage (★★★★★) was estate-grown at Havelock North and fermented in French oak barrels (50 per cent new). Bright, light lemon/green, it is richly fragrant and full-bodied, with intense peach and grapefruit flavours, showing impressive vigour and complexity, fresh acidity, and strong personality.

Vintage	16	15	14	13
WR	6	6	7	6
Drink	20-28	20-22	20-23	20-22

DRY $40 AV

Deep Down Marlborough Chardonnay (★★★★☆)

Already very approachable, the youthful, harmonious 2019 vintage (★★★★☆) was grown in the Wrekin Vineyard and fermented and matured in French oak puncheons (15 per cent new). Bright, light yellow/green, it is full-bodied, with a fragrant, buttery bouquet and strong, citrusy, peachy flavours, showing excellent delicacy and length. Best drinking 2022+. Certified organic.

DRY $45 –V

Delegat Crownthorpe Terraces Chardonnay ★★★★

From one vintage to the next, this is a great buy. The 2018 vintage (★★★★) was estate-grown at the company's cool, elevated, inland site at Crownthorpe, in Hawke's Bay, and fully fermented and matured for a year in French oak barriques (new and one year old). An elegant, youthful wine, it is full-bodied, with strong, ripe, peachy, citrusy, slightly biscuity flavours, fresh acidity, good complexity, and a finely poised, lengthy finish. Best drinking 2021+.

DRY $20 V+

Deliverance Waipara Chardonnay (★★★★)

This good-value wine is from Muddy Water (owned by Greystone). The 2019 vintage (★★★★), delicious young, was fermented initially in tanks, then finished its fermentation in French oak barrels. Bright, light lemon/green, it is a fragrant, full-bodied wine, with fresh acidity and generous, vibrant, peachy, slightly toasty and buttery flavours, showing considerable complexity. Drink now or cellar.

Vintage	18
WR	6
Drink	20-23

DRY $23 V+

Delta Hatters Hill Marlborough Chardonnay ★★★★☆

Already drinking well, the 2019 vintage (★★★★☆) was grown principally in the Ure Valley, south of the Awatere Valley, and fermented and matured for 10 months in French oak barriques. Fresh and elegant, it has excellent weight and vibrancy, with strong, peachy, citrusy flavours, gentle biscuity and toasty notes adding complexity, balanced acidity, and a well-rounded, harmonious finish.

Vintage	19	18
WR	6	5
Drink	21-24	20-23

DRY $27 V+

Delta Marlborough Chardonnay ★★★★

Instantly likeable, the 2019 vintage (★★★★) was grown in the lower Wairau Valley and mostly handled in tanks; 25 per cent of the blend was fermented in seasoned French oak barrels. Light lemon/green, it is vibrantly fruity and very finely balanced, with generous, ripe stone-fruit flavours to the fore, a distinct touch of complexity, fresh acidity, and a dry, harmonious finish.

DRY $20 V+

Dog Point Vineyard Marlborough Chardonnay ★★★★★

This classy wine is estate-grown and hand-harvested on the south side of the Wairau Valley, fermented and matured for 18 months in French oak barriques (10 per cent new in 2018), and given a full, softening malolactic fermentation. The 2018 vintage (★★★★★) is bright, light yellow/green, with a fragrant, slightly smoky bouquet. Tightly structured, with a real sense of youthful vigour, it has intense stone-fruit flavours, finely integrated oak, fresh acidity, and impressive complexity. Best drinking 2023+. Certified organic.

Vintage	18	17	16	15	14	13
WR	6	7	7	7	7	7
Drink	20-30	20-29	20-28	20-27	20-26	20-21

DRY $40 AV

Domain Road Defiance Vineyard Central Otago Chardonnay ★★★★☆

Offering good value, the 2017 vintage (★★★★☆) of this Bannockburn wine was fermented and matured for 10 months in French oak barriques (35 per cent new). Light lemon/green, with a fresh, complex, citrusy, slightly smoky bouquet, it is elegant and youthful, with grapefruit-evoking flavours, showing good complexity, savoury, biscuity notes and a lengthy finish. Best drinking 2021+.

 DRY $28 V+

Vintage	17	16
WR	6	6
Drink	20-23	20-22

Dry River Martinborough Chardonnay ★★★★★

Elegance, restraint and subtle power are the key qualities of this classic wine. It's not a bold, upfront style, but tight, savoury and seamless, with rich grapefruit and nut flavours that build in the bottle for several years. Based on low-cropping 20 and 30-year-old vines in the Craighall and Dry River Estate vineyards, it is hand-harvested, whole-bunch pressed and fermented in French oak hogsheads (with a low proportion of new casks). The proportion of the blend that goes through a softening malolactic fermentation does not usually exceed 15 per cent. The 2018 vintage (★★★★★) is a highly refined, age-worthy wine. Full-bodied, with generous stone-fruit flavours, mealy and biscuity notes adding complexity, and fresh acidity, it shows excellent delicacy, depth and harmony. Made with a restrained winemaking touch, it should be at its best 2021+.

DRY $65 AV

Vintage	18	17	16	15	14	13	12
WR	5	5	7	7	7	7	5
Drink	20-26	20-25	20-25	20-25	20-24	20-23	20-22

Dunnolly Estate Reserve Waipara Valley Chardonnay ★★★★

Showing obvious potential, the refined 2017 vintage (★★★★☆) was matured for nine months in French oak barriques (30 per cent new). Fresh and mouthfilling, it has excellent depth and delicacy of grapefruit, peach and pear flavours, with a cool-climate thread, and a lingering finish.

DRY $32 –V

Durvillea Marlborough Chardonnay ★★★☆

Offering good value, the 2019 vintage (★★★★) is a regional blend, grown in the Wairau Valley (72 per cent) and the Awatere Valley (28 per cent). Hand-harvested and barrel-matured for seven months, it is a characterful wine, bright, light lemon/green, with ripe, peachy, citrusy flavours, gently seasoned with oak, moderate acidity, considerable complexity, and a slightly creamy finish. Drink now or cellar.

DRY $20 AV

Vintage	19
WR	6
Drink	20-22

Elephant Hill Hawke's Bay Chardonnay ★★★★☆

The fragrant, youthful 2018 vintage (★★★★☆) was estate-grown at Te Awanga and in the Bridge Pa Triangle, and fermented and matured for a year in French oak casks (25 per cent new). Bright, light lemon/green, it is full-bodied, with generous, ripe stone-fruit flavours, gently seasoned with toasty oak, good complexity and a finely balanced, dry, persistent finish.

 DRY $34 AV

Elephant Hill Reserve Hawke's Bay Chardonnay ★★★★★

The rich, tightly structured 2017 vintage (★★★★★) was estate-grown at Te Awanga (principally) and in the Bridge Pa Triangle, fermented with indigenous yeasts and matured for a year in French oak barrels (26 per cent new). Bright, light lemon/green, it is full-bodied, with concentrated, ripe stone-fruit flavours, biscuity, mealy notes adding complexity, and a crisp, sustained finish. A refined, tight-knit, still youthful wine, it's well worth cellaring.

 DRY $54 AV

Elephant Hill Salomé Hawke's Bay Chardonnay ★★★★★

The classy 2018 vintage (★★★★★) was estate-grown at Te Awanga and in the Bridge Pa Triangle, and fermented and matured for 15 months in French oak casks (28 per cent new). Bright, light lemon/green, with a fragrant, youthful bouquet, it is mouthfilling and vibrantly fruity, with ripe stone-fruit flavours, showing excellent delicacy and depth, finely integrated oak, fresh acidity, and a poised, tightly structured, long finish. A classic cellaring style, it should break into full stride 2022+.

 DRY $75 AV

Esk Valley Hawke's Bay Chardonnay ★★★★

Top vintages can offer irresistible value. Retasted in mid-2020, the 2018 vintage (★★★★☆) was predominantly (92 per cent) fermented in French oak barriques (12 per cent new); 8 per cent of the blend was cool-fermented in tanks. Weighty, with a fragrant, complex bouquet, it is vibantly fruity, with generous, ripe stone-fruit flavours to the fore, slightly spicy and smoky notes adding complexity, and obvious potential. Best drinking 2021+.

Vintage	18	17	16	15	14	13
WR	6	5	7	7	6	6
Drink	20-22	20-21	P	P	P	P

DRY $20 V+

Esk Valley Winemakers Reserve Hawke's Bay Chardonnay ★★★★★

Often one of the region's most distinguished Chardonnays. The 2018 vintage (★★★★★) is a single-vineyard wine, hand-picked at Bay View and fermented with indigenous yeasts in French oak barriques (40 per cent new). Bright, light yellow/green, with a smoky bouquet, it is a medium to full-bodied wine, full of youthful vigour, with deep stone-fruit flavours, mealy and biscuity notes adding complexity, lively acidity and a tightly structured, long finish. Best drinking 2022+.

Vintage	19	18	17	16	15	14	13
WR	7	7	7	7	7	7	7
Drink	20-25	20-25	20-25	20-23	20-25	20-24	20-23

DRY $32 V+

Falconhead Hawke's Bay Chardonnay ★★★

The good-value 2017 vintage (★★★☆) was fully barrel-fermented and oak-aged for a year. Drinking well now, it is fresh and mouthfilling, with peachy, slightly toasty flavours, showing considerable complexity, balanced acidity and good depth.

DRY $17 AV

Family Company, The, Gisborne Chardonnay (★★★★)

The 2018 vintage (★★★★) was hand-picked in the Kawatiri Vineyard at Hexton and fermented in French oak casks (30 per cent new). Retasted in early 2020, it is a bright yellow, mouthfilling wine with rich, peachy, slightly toasty flavours, showing good complexity, and a dry, lingering finish. Drink now or cellar. (From Longbush.)

DRY $28 AV

Felton Road Bannockburn Central Otago Chardonnay ★★★★★

This classy, distinctive wine is grown at Bannockburn and matured in French oak barriques, with restrained use of new oak. Bright, light lemon/green, the 2019 vintage (★★★★★) was estate-grown in The Elms and Cornish Point vineyards, and barrel-aged for 13 months (10 per cent new). Highly refined, it is a youthful, sweet-fruited, harmonious wine, with deep, delicate, peachy, citrusy, slightly biscuity flavours, slightly smoky notes adding complexity, and a well-rounded finish.

Vintage	19	18	17	16	15	14	13	12
WR	7	7	7	7	7	7	7	7
Drink	20-33	20-32	20-32	20-30	20-29	20-28	20-24	20-26

DRY $50 AV

Felton Road Block 2 Central Otago Chardonnay ★★★★★

This typically outstanding wine is grown in a 'special part of The Elms Vineyard in front of the winery', which has the oldest vines. The very youthful 2019 vintage (★★★★☆) was matured for 16 months in seasoned French oak barrels (avoiding the use of new oak), and bottled unfined and unfiltered. Bright, light lemon/green, it is a Chablis-like wine, with strong, citrusy, slightly appley and peachy flavours, showing excellent delicacy, a gentle oak seasoning, firm acid spine, and a long finish.

Vintage	19	18	17
WR	7	7	7
Drink	20-35	20-34	20-33

DRY $66 AV

Felton Road Block 6 Central Otago Chardonnay   ★★★★★

Estate-grown in The Elms Vineyard at Bannockburn, the 2019 vintage (★★★★★) was matured for 16 months in seasoned French oak casks, and bottled unfined and unfiltered. Bright, light lemon/green, it is mouthfilling and savoury, with generous, ripe stone-fruit flavours, slightly toasty and smoky notes adding complexity, finely balanced acidity, and a long finish. Best drinking 2023+.

Vintage	19	18	17
WR	7	7	7
Drink	20-35	20-34	20-33

DRY $66 AV

Forrest John Forrest Collection Wairau Valley Marlborough Chardonnay   ★★★★★

Tasted in August 2018, the 2011 vintage (★★★★★) was seemingly in full stride. Grown at three sites, it is weighty and rounded, with concentrated peach and grapefruit flavours, biscuity notes adding complexity, balanced acidity and a rich, harmonious finish. From a much cooler season, the 2012 vintage (★★★★☆) is slightly more austere, with mouthfilling body, strong, citrusy flavours, showing good complexity, and a crisp, tightly structured finish. Likely to be very long-lived, the impressive 2013 vintage (★★★★★) is fragrant, youthful and finely balanced, with concentrated, peachy, citrusy flavours, slightly toasty, savoury and creamy, and a lasting finish.

DRY $45 AV

Framingham Marlborough Chardonnay   ★★★★

The 2019 vintage (★★★★) was partly barrel-fermented. Bright, light lemon/green, with a creamy bouquet, it is weighty, with generous, peachy, citrusy, slightly spicy flavours, and a smooth finish. Delicious young.

DRY $30 –V

Fromm Clayvin Vineyard Marlborough Chardonnay   ★★★★★

Fromm's finest Chardonnay is grown on the southern flanks of the Wairau Valley, where the clay soils, says winemaker Hätsch Kalberer, give 'a less fruity, more minerally and tighter character'. Fermented with indigenous yeasts in French oak barriques, with little or no use of new wood, it is barrel-aged for well over a year. It is a rare wine – only three barrels were produced in 2016 – and top vintages mature well for a decade. The 2016 vintage (★★★★★) is highly refined. Light lemon/green, it is vigorous and youthful, with deep grapefruit and nut flavours, complex and savoury, gentle acidity, and a highly fragrant bouquet. A very 'complete' wine with a long finish, it should be at its best 2021+.

DRY $65 AV

❦ ❦ ❦

Gibbston Valley 95 China Terrace Central Otago Chardonnay   ★★★★★

A wine to ponder over, the classy 2019 vintage (★★★★★) is a single-vineyard Bendigo wine, estate-grown at 320 metres above sea level, and hand-picked solely from highly regarded clone 95 vines. Fermented with indigenous yeasts in French oak barriques and puncheons (25 per cent new), and barrel-aged for 11 months, it is a highly refined wine, bright, light yellow/green, with deep, ripe, peachy, biscuity flavours, showing excellent complexity and harmony, balanced acidity, and a long finish. Well worth cellaring.

DRY $55 AV

Gibbston Valley China Terrace Bendigo Single Vineyard Chardonnay   ★★★★☆

Here's more evidence that Central Otago has great Chardonnay potential. The 2019 vintage (★★★★☆) was estate-grown, at 320 metres above sea level, and fermented and matured for 10 months in French oak barriques and puncheons (20 per cent new). Bright, light lemon/green, with a fragrant, citrusy bouquet, it is a very fresh and vibrant, slightly Chablis-like wine, with citrusy, gently biscuity flavours, showing very good complexity, and finely balanced acidity. A classy young wine, it should be at its best 2022+.

DRY $42 –V

Giesen Hawke's Bay Chardonnay   ★★☆

Enjoyable young, the 2019 vintage (★★☆) was handled in a mix of tanks, French oak barrels and German oak fuders. Bright, light lemon/green, it is fresh, fruity and simple, with lively, ripe, peachy flavours, and a smooth finish. Priced right.

Vintage	14
WR	4
Drink	P

DRY $15 AV

Giesen The Fuder Series Single Vineyard Clayvin Marlborough Chardonnay   (★★★★★)

Certified organic, the 2015 vintage (★★★★★) was hand-harvested from mature vines in the Clayvin Vineyard and fermented and matured in large (1000-litre-capacity) German oak fuders. Pale yellow, with a fragrant, highly complex bouquet, it is a powerful, full-bodied wine, with concentrated citrus and stone-fruit flavours, fresh acidity, a minerally streak, gently nutty notes adding complexity, and a real sense of youthful drive and depth. Best drinking 2021+.

DRY $50 AV

Golden Queen Chardonnay   (★★★☆)

From Brunton Estate, the 2018 vintage (★★★☆) was French oak-aged for nine months. Bright yellow, it's a lush, upfront style, full-bodied, toasty, buttery and slightly honeyed, with a creamy texture.

DRY $20 AV

Greenhough Hope Vineyard Nelson Chardonnay ★★★★★

This consistently impressive wine is estate-grown at Hope, in Nelson, hand-picked, barrel-fermented with indigenous yeasts and matured in French oak barriques (25 per cent new in 2017). The 2017 vintage (★★★★☆) is a bright, light yellow/green, mouthfilling wine with rich stone-fruit flavours, slightly buttery notes, fresh acidity, and very good vigour and potential. Best drinking 2021+. Certified organic.

DRY $36 AV

Greenhough Nelson Chardonnay ★★★★

This consistently enjoyable wine is designed to express a 'fresh, taut' style, with background oak providing 'some subtle, savoury complexities'. Lemon-scented, the 2017 vintage (★★★★) was grown at Hope, in the Morison and Greenhough vineyards, barrel-fermented (16 per cent new) and oak-aged for 10 months. Fresh and citrusy, with peachy, biscuity notes adding complexity and a slightly minerally thread, it's drinking well now.

Vintage	17	16	15
WR	7	5	6
Drink	20-22	P	P

DRY $28 AV

Greyrock Hawke's Bay Chardonnay ★★★

The easy-drinking 2018 vintage (★★☆) has lively, citrusy, peachy flavours in an uncomplicated, fruit-driven style, with a fresh, smooth (4 grams/litre of residual sugar) finish. (From Sileni.)

DRY $19 AV

Greyrock Te Koru Hawke's Bay Chardonnay (★★★★)

The elegant 2018 vintage (★★★★) is a medium-bodied style, with strong, vibrant, peachy, citrusy flavours, a touch of complexity, fresh acidity, and good drive and length. Best drinking 2021+.

DRY $20 V+

Greystone Erin's Reserve Waipara Valley Chardonnay ★★★★★

Greystone views Chardonnay as 'the finest white wine variety'. Grown on steep, north-facing limestone slopes, this wine is hand-harvested, fermented with indigenous yeasts, given a full, softening malolactic fermentation, and matured in French oak casks (40 per cent new in 2018). The 2018 vintage (★★★★★) is a lovely young wine. Bright, light yellow/green, with a fragrant, complex bouquet, it is mouthfilling, with concentrated, vibrant, savoury, peachy, citrusy flavours, showing excellent complexity, that build to a poised, lasting finish. Likely to be long-lived, it should break into full stride 2023+.

Vintage	18
WR	7
Drink	20-29

DRY $99 –V

Greystone Organic Waipara Valley North Canterbury Chardonnay ★★★★★

Already very expressive, the distinctive 2018 vintage (★★★★★) of this organically certified wine was hand-harvested, barrel-fermented and matured for 11 months in French oak barriques (15 per cent new). Bright, light yellow, it is weighty and fleshy, with concentrated, ripe, peachy, slightly citrusy flavours, fresh acidity and a very finely textured, long finish. Best drinking 2021+.

Vintage	18
WR	7
Drink	20-28

DRY $42 AV

Greywacke Marlborough Chardonnay ★★★★★

The vigorous, youthful 2017 vintage (★★★★★) is bright, light yellow/green, with a fragrant, complex bouquet. Mouthfilling, it has deep, vibrant grapefruit and peach flavours, finely integrated oak, slightly smoky notes, and a long, savoury, harmonious finish. Best drinking 2022+. Retasted in mid to late 2019, the 2016 vintage (★★★★☆) is an elegant, tightly structured, very age-worthy wine, hand-harvested and oak-aged for 18 months (French barriques, 12 per cent new). Mouthfilling, with a complex, slightly smoky bouquet, it has ripe, peachy, slightly toasty flavours, strong and youthful. Best drinking 2021+.

Vintage	17	16	15	14	13	12
WR	5	6	6	6	6	5
Drink	20-29	20-28	20-27	20-26	20-25	P

DRY $42 AV

Grove Mill Wairau Valley Marlborough Chardonnay ★★★★

Bargain-priced, the full-flavoured 2018 vintage (★★★★) was matured for 10 months in French oak casks (20 per cent new). Bright, light yellow/green, with a fragrant, slightly toasty and smoky bouquet, it is mouthfilling, with peachy, toasty flavours, showing good complexity, finely balanced acidity and very good depth. Drink now or cellar.

Vintage	18
WR	6
Drink	20-25

DRY $20 V+

Haha Hawke's Bay Chardonnay ★★★☆

Offering fine value, the 2019 vintage (★★★☆) was grown in the Bridge Pa Triangle and Gimblett Gravels, barrel-fermented and given a full, softening malolactic fermentation. Creamy-textured, it has fresh, ripe grapefruit and peach flavours, slightly toasty notes adding complexity, and a dry, well-rounded finish. Enjoyable young.

DRY $18 V+

Haha Marlborough Chardonnay ★★★☆

The 2017 vintage (★★★☆) is a fully barrel-fermented wine, balanced for early enjoyment. Fresh and full-bodied, it's a lively, 'fruit-driven' style with good flavour depth, and a well-rounded finish. Bargain-priced.

Vintage	17	16	15	14	13
WR	7	7	7	7	7
Drink	20-21	P	P	P	P

DRY $18 V+

Hancock & Sons Bridge Pa Hawke's Bay Chardonnay   (★★★★)

The distinctive 2018 vintage (★★★★) from winemaker John Hancock and his son, Willy, was hand-harvested in a single vineyard and principally handled in tanks; a quarter to a third of the blend was fermented in French oak barrels (mostly seasoned). Bright, light lemon/green, it is fragrant, with very good weight and depth of grapefruit and peach-like flavours, a subtle seasoning of nutty oak, and impressive vigour, delicacy and harmony. An elegant, 'fruit-driven' style, it should be at its best 2021+.

Vintage	18
WR	5
Drink	20-23

DRY $25 AV

Hans Herzog Marlborough Chardonnay   ★★★★★

At its best, this is a notably powerful wine with layers of peach, grapefruit and nut flavours. The age-worthy 2017 vintage (★★★★★) was estate-grown in the Wairau Valley, hand-picked, fermented with indigenous yeasts in a French oak puncheon, barrel-aged for 22 months, and bottled unfined and unfiltered. A pale gold, sturdy wine, it is very fleshy and harmonious, with concentrated, ripe stone-fruit flavours, finely integrated oak adding complexity, and an enticing fragrance. Best drinking 2021+. Certified organic.

DRY $44 AV

Hihi Classic Gisborne Chardonnay   (★★★★)

The age-worthy 2018 vintage (★★★★) was hand-harvested in the EIT Vineyard, fermented in French and Hungarian oak casks (one to three years old), and barrel-aged for 10 months. Medium to full-bodied, it is vibrantly fruity, with ripe, citrusy, peachy flavours, showing considerable complexity, and a smooth, slightly creamy finish. Best drinking 2021+.

DRY $25 AV

Hopesgrove Single Vineyard Hawke's Bay Chardonnay   ★★★★★

Tasted in mid-2019, the rich 2016 vintage (★★★★☆) was estate-grown, hand-harvested and barrel-aged for nine months (30 per cent new). Bright, light lemon/green, it is mouthfilling, with finely balanced acidity and generous, peachy, slightly buttery and toasty flavours, showing good complexity. The 2015 vintage (★★★★★), also tasted in mid-2019, is a classic regional style, maturing very gracefully. Full-bodied, it is rich but elegant, with deep, concentrated, peachy, slightly toasty flavours, showing excellent complexity, and a fragrant, complex bouquet. Delicious drinking now onwards.

Vintage	16	15
WR	6	5
Drink	20-22	20-20

DRY $35 AV

Huntaway Reserve Gisborne Chardonnay   ★★★☆

Ready to roll, the easy-drinking 2017 vintage (★★★☆) is weighty, ripe and rounded. It has generous, peachy, slightly toasty flavours, showing a touch of complexity, and a smooth finish. (From Lion.)

DRY $22 AV

Hunter's Marlborough Chardonnay ★★★★

This wine has traditionally placed its accent on vibrant fruit flavours, overlaid with very subtle wood-aging characters. The impressive 2019 vintage (★★★★☆), grown in the Rapaura, Renwick and Omaka districts, was fermented with indigenous yeasts and lees-aged for 10 months in French oak puncheons (15 per cent new). A refined, generous wine, it is full-bodied, fresh and lively, with strong, ripe stone-fruit flavours, showing good complexity, and a tightly structured, long finish. A top vintage of this label, it's very age-worthy; best drinking 2023+. Great value.

Vintage	19	18	17	16	15	14	13
WR	7	6	5	7	7	7	6
Drink	20-27	20-26	20-25	20-21	P	P	P

DRY $23 V+

Hunter's Offshoot Marlborough Chardonnay ★★★★☆

Estate-grown at Rapaura, the youthful 2018 vintage (★★★★☆) was hand-picked from mature vines, fermented with indigenous yeasts in large (900-litre) oak barrels, and wood-aged for a year. Bright, light lemon/green, it is a vibrant, medium-bodied wine, crisp and tightly structured, with strong, peachy, biscuity flavours, showing very good vigour and complexity, and a persistent finish. Best drinking 2022+.

DRY $35 –V

Hunting Lodge, The, Expressions Lustrous Hawke's Bay Chardonnay (★★★★)

Grown principally in the Bridge Pa Triangle, the youthful 2018 vintage (★★★★) was fermented and lees-aged for nine months in French oak barriques (15 per cent new). Bright, light lemon/green, it is vibrantly fruity, with fresh stone-fruit flavours, finely integrated oak adding complexity, slightly creamy notes, and a crisp finish. Showing good vigour and harmony, it's a drink-now or cellaring proposition.

DRY $24 V+

Hunting Lodge, The, Hawke's Bay Chardonnay ★★★★☆

The elegant, youthful 2019 vintage (★★★★☆) was fermented and aged on its yeast lees for nine months in French oak barriques (35 per cent new). Bright, light lemon/green, it is full-bodied and vibrantly fruity, with ripe stone-fruit flavours, hints of grapefruit and spices, mealy and toasty notes adding complexity, lively acidity and a lingering finish. Well worth cellaring to 2022+.

DRY $30 AV

Hunting Lodge, The, Home Block Waimauku Chardonnay ★★★★★

From the old site of Matua Valley, in West Auckland, the 2019 vintage (★★★★★) was harvested from 11-year-old vines, hand-picked, and fermented and lees-aged for nine months in French oak barriques (30 per cent new). Bright, light lemon/green, it is mouthfilling, youthful and tightly structured, with strong, ripe grapefruit and stone-fruit flavours, mealy notes, finely integrated oak, fresh acidity, and a sustained finish. A highly refined, complex wine, it's still unfolding; best drinking 2023+.

DRY $64 AV

Jackson Estate Shelter Belt Single Vineyard Marlborough Chardonnay   ★★★★

Offering fine value, the 2017 vintage (★★★★☆) was estate-grown in the Wairau Valley and partly (25 per cent) handled in tanks; the majority (75 per cent) was fermented and matured for nine months in oak barrels (25 per cent new). It has a fragrant, slightly creamy bouquet, leading into an elegant, sweet-fruited wine with vibrant, citrusy, peachy flavours, biscuity, savoury notes adding complexity, and a very harmonious, lingering finish.

Vintage	17	16
WR	5	5
Drink	20-27	20-26

DRY $24 V+

Johanneshof Marlborough Chardonnay   (★★★☆)

The 2018 vintage (★★★☆) is the first Chardonnay from Johanneshof in nearly 20 years – the fruit was until recently all reserved for the company's sparkling Blanc de Blancs. Bright, light lemon/green, it was hand-picked and French oak-aged for eight months. Fresh, lively and youthful, it has strong, citrusy, slightly appley flavours, a subtle oak influence, some peachy, toasty notes, and appetising acidity. Best drinking mid-2021+.

DRY $32 –V

Johner Wairarapa Chardonnay   ★★★☆

The 2018 vintage (★★★★) was fermented and lees-matured for a year in French oak casks (20 per cent new). Bright, light yellow/green, it is a mouthfilling, generous, slightly creamy wine with ripe, peachy, slightly toasty and biscuity flavours, showing excellent complexity and depth. Best drinking 2021+.

Vintage	18
WR	6
Drink	20-23

DRY $26 –V

Jules Taylor Marlborough Chardonnay   ★★★★

The 2019 vintage (★★★★) was grown at two sites in the Southern Valleys. Partly barrel-fermented and fully barrel-aged, it is a bright, light lemon/green wine, mouthfilling and vibrant, with fresh, ripe, citrusy, peachy flavours, full of youthful vigour, slightly toasty notes adding complexity, and a creamy-smooth finish. Best drinking mid-2021+.

Vintage	19	18	17	16	15
WR	5	5	6	6	6
Drink	20-24	20-23	20-22	20-21	P

DRY $25 AV

Jules Taylor OTQ Limited Release Single Vineyard Marlborough Chardonnay ★★★★★

The powerful 2018 vintage (★★★★★) was grown in the Meadowbank Vineyard, on the south side of the Wairau Valley, and fermented with indigenous yeasts in French oak barriques (partly new). Bright, light lemon/green, with a fragrant, smoky bouquet, it has strong personality, with mouthfilling body, concentrated, vigorous, slightly toasty flavours, showing excellent complexity, finely balanced acidity, and a dry, lasting finish. Already delicious, it should be at its best 2021+.

Vintage	18	
WR	6	DRY $40 AV
Drink	20-23	

Junction Corner Post Central Hawke's Bay Chardonnay (★★★★)

The lively, youthful 2018 vintage (★★★★) was hand-picked on the Takapau Plains and fermented and matured for 18 months in French oak casks (45 per cent new). Bright, light yellow/green, with a citrusy, biscuity, slightly buttery bouquet, it is mouthfilling, with crisp, vibrant, grapefruit-like flavours that linger well. Best drinking mid-2021+.

DRY $29 AV

Kahurangi Estate Nelson Chardonnay (★★★★)

Enjoyable now, the 2018 vintage (★★★★) has plenty of youthful impact. Bright, light lemon/green, it is a fruit-driven style, with a subtle seasoning of oak and strong, vibrant, peachy flavours, fresh, crisp and lingering.

DRY $25 AV

Kahurangi Mt Arthur Reserve Nelson Chardonnay ★★★★

Made in a bold, upfront style, the 2019 vintage (★★★★) was matured for 10 months in 'a mix of new French and American oak barriques'. Pale straw, with a rich, creamy bouquet, it has strong, peachy, toasty flavours, fresh acidity, and a smooth finish. Best drinking mid-2021+.

DRY $28 AV

Kaimira Estate Brightwater Chardonnay ★★★★

Certified organic, the 2017 vintage (★★★★) was estate-grown at Brightwater, in Nelson, and fermented with indigenous yeasts in French oak barrels (20 per cent new). Light lemon/green, it is an elegant, lemon-scented, full-bodied wine, with strong, vibrant grapefruit and peach flavours, a subtle seasoning of oak, and fresh acidity. It's drinking well now.

Vintage	17	16	15	
WR	6	6	6	DRY $25 AV
Drink	20-24	20-22	P	

Karikari Estate Northland Calypso Chardonnay   ★★★★

Grown on the Karikari Peninsula, in the Far North, the youthful 2019 vintage (★★★★) is a bright, light yellow/green wine, tank-fermented, with some oak influence. Enjoyable from the start, it is fresh, fruity and full-bodied, with generous, ripe, peachy, slightly buttery flavours, balanced acidity, and a lingering finish. Best drinking mid-2021+.

 DRY $27 AV

Kelly Washington Rapaura Marlborough Chardonnay   (★★★★)

Still unfolding, the 2018 vintage (★★★★) is a single-vineyard wine, hand-picked from 25-year-old vines at Rapaura, in the Wairau Valley, and fermented and matured in French oak barrels (partly new). Bright, light lemon/green, it is medium to full-bodied, with strong, vibrant, peachy, toasty flavours, dry and crisp. Open mid-2021+. Certified organic.

 DRY $50 –V

Kidnapper Cliffs Hawke's Bay Chardonnay   ★★★★★

From Te Awa, the classy 2014 vintage (★★★★★) was estate-grown, mostly in the Bridge Pa Triangle, hand-picked, fermented with indigenous yeasts in French oak hogsheads (40 per cent new), and barrel-aged for 10 months. It has a fragrant, complex bouquet, with a distinct whiff of 'struck match'. Mouthfilling, with concentrated peach and grapefruit flavours, a subtle seasoning of oak, and very impressive vibrancy, poise and length, it's an elegant, tightly structured wine, likely to be at its best 2021+.

Vintage	14	13
WR	7	6
Drink	20-21	P

 DRY $55 AV

Kim Crawford New Zealand Chardonnay   ★★★☆

The easy-drinking 2017 vintage (★★★☆), grown in Marlborough and Hawke's Bay, is 'uncluttered by oak'. Light lemon/green, it is mouthfilling, fleshy and smooth, with good depth of fresh, ripe, peachy, citrusy flavours, balanced acidity, and lots of drink-young appeal. Priced right.

 DRY $17 V+

Kina Beach Vineyard Nelson Reserve Chardonnay   ★★★★☆

Currently on sale, the 2015 vintage (★★★★☆) was barrel-fermented with indigenous yeasts. Still youthful, it is bright, light yellow/green, with a fragrant, citrusy bouquet. Mouthfilling, it is an elegant wine, crisp and lively, with a subtle oak influence, and a lingering finish. Best drinking 2021+.

Vintage	16
WR	6
Drink	20-24

DRY $38 –V

Koha Marlborough Chardonnay   (★★☆)

The easy-drinking 2018 vintage (★★☆) is a 'lightly oaked' style. Light lemon/green, it is fresh, fruity and uncomplicated, with ripe, peachy, slightly appley flavours, showing decent depth, and a smooth finish. (From te Pā.)

DRY $19 –V

Kono Nelson Chardonnay   (★★★☆)

The 2018 vintage (★★★☆) was estate-grown at Upper Moutere, hand-harvested and fermented in French oak casks (partly new). Bright, light lemon/green, with a distinctly buttery bouquet, it is mouthfilling and soft, with good depth of peachy, biscuity flavours, showing a touch of complexity, and a smooth finish. Enjoyable young.

DRY $20 AV

Kōparepare Marlborough Chardonnay   (★★★☆)

Tasted in mid-2019, the 2016 vintage (★★★☆) offers very good value. Made by Whitehaven, it is sold through fishing clubs in support of LegaSea and its commitment to restore inshore fisheries to abundance. Bright, light yellow/green, it is full-bodied, with fresh, generous, peachy flavours, slightly buttery and toasty notes, and a dry, smooth finish. Ready.

DRY $16 V+

Kumeu River Coddington Chardonnay   ★★★★★

This typically powerful, rich wine is grown in the Coddington Vineyard, between Huapai and Waimauku. The grapes, cultivated on a clay hillside, achieve an advanced level of ripeness (described by Kumeu River as 'flamboyant, unctuous, peachy'). Mouthfilling, complex and slightly nutty, it's typically a lusher, softer wine than its Hunting Hill stablemate (below). The 2019 vintage (★★★★★) was hand-picked, fermented with indigenous yeasts in French oak barriques and wood-matured for 11 months. Showing the weighty, concentrated, sweet-fruited style typical of the site, it is a powerful, rich and youthful wine with deep, ripe, citrusy, peachy flavours, mealy and biscuity notes adding complexity, finely balanced acidity, and a very harmonious, long, dry finish. A top vintage, it should be at its best 2023+.

Vintage	19	18	17	16	15	14	13	12
WR	7	5	6	7	7	7	7	5
Drink	21-27	20-26	20-23	20-22	20-22	20-21	P	P

DRY $55 AV

Kumeu River Estate Chardonnay   ★★★★★

This wine ranks fifth in the company's hierarchy of six Chardonnays, after four single-vineyard labels, but is still outstanding. Grown at Kumeu, in West Auckland, it is powerful, with rich, beautifully interwoven flavours and a seductively creamy texture, but also has good acid spine. The key to its quality lies in the vineyards, says winemaker Michael Brajkovich: 'We manage to get the grapes very ripe.' Grown in several blocks around Kumeu, hand-picked, fermented with indigenous yeasts and lees-aged (with weekly or twice-weekly lees-stirring) in Burgundy oak barriques (typically 25 per cent new), the wine normally undergoes a full, softening malolactic fermentation. The 2019 vintage (★★★★★) has a real sense of youthful drive and potential.

Bright, light lemon/green, it's an elegant, full-bodied wine with strong, ripe, citrusy, peachy flavours, finely integrated oak, mealy and savoury notes adding complexity, and a dry, long finish. Best drinking 2022+.

Vintage	19	18	17	16	15	14	13
WR	7	5	6	6	7	7	7
Drink	21-27	20-26	20-22	20-21	P	P	P

DRY $32 V+

Kumeu River Hunting Hill Chardonnay ★★★★★

This outstanding single-vineyard wine – my favourite in the Kumeu River range – is grown on slopes above Mate's Vineyard, directly over the road from the winery at Kumeu (originally planted in 1982, the site was replanted in 2000). A notably elegant wine, in its youth it is generally less lush than its Coddington stablemate (above), but with good acidity and citrusy, complex flavours that build well across the palate. Bright, light lemon/green, the 2019 vintage (★★★★★) was hand-picked, fermented with indigenous yeasts in French oak barriques and wood-aged for 11 months. Richly fragrant, it is weighty but not heavy, with vibrant, ripe stone-fruit and spice flavours, and finely integrated oak. A very generous and harmonious wine, with a long finish, it's already delicious; best drinking 2023+.

Vintage	19	18	17	16	15	14	13
WR	7	5	6	7	7	7	7
Drink	21-29	20-26	20-24	20-23	20-22	20-21	P

DRY $70 AV

Kumeu River Mate's Vineyard Kumeu Chardonnay ★★★★★

This extremely classy, single-vineyard wine is Kumeu River's flagship. It is made entirely from the best of the fruit harvested from Mate's Vineyard, planted in 1990 on the site of the original Kumeu River vineyard purchased by Mate Brajkovich in 1944. Similar to Kumeu River Estate Chardonnay, but more opulent and concentrated, it offers the same rich, harmonious flavours, typically with a stronger seasoning of new French oak (about 30 per cent). The 2019 vintage (★★★★★) was hand-picked, barrel-fermented and oak-aged for 11 months. Bright, light lemon/green, it is a seamless wine, fleshy and sweet-fruited, with strong, ripe peach and grapefruit flavours, mealy and biscuity notes adding complexity, and a very harmonious, well-rounded finish. Already delicious, it should be at its best 2023+.

Vintage	19	18	17	16	15	14	13
WR	7	5	6	7	7	7	7
Drink	21-29	20-26	20-23	20-23	20-22	20-21	P

DRY $80 AV

Kumeu River Rays Road Chardonnay ★★★★☆

Estate-grown, the 2019 vintage (★★★★) is from an elevated (180 metres above sea level), north-facing site in Hawke's Bay. Hand-picked, it was fermented with indigenous yeasts in a mix of stainless steel tanks (20 per cent) and seasoned French oak barrels (80 per cent). Bright, light lemon/green, it is a very youthful, vigorous wine, with strong, lemony, appley flavours, threaded with crisp acidity, a subtle seasoning of oak, and obvious cellaring potential. Best drinking 2022+.

Vintage	19
WR	7
Drink	21-27

DRY $40 -V

Kumeu Village Hand Harvested Chardonnay ★★★★

Kumeu River's lower-tier, drink-young wine is hand-picked from heavier-bearing Chardonnay clones than the Mendoza commonly used for the top wines, and is typically fermented with indigenous yeasts in tanks and seasoned French oak casks. The 2019 vintage (★★★★), grown in Kumeu and Hawke's Bay, was 20 per cent barrel-fermented. Bright, light lemon/green, it is fresh, lively and mouthfilling, with vigorous, citrusy, peachy flavours, mealy, savoury notes adding complexity, balanced acidity, and good immediacy. Fine value.

DRY $18 V+

Lake Chalice The Falcon Marlborough Chardonnay ★★★☆

Buoyantly fruity, the 2018 vintage (★★★☆) is a partly barrel-fermented wine, grown principally in the Falcon Vineyard, in the central Wairau Valley, and lees-aged for 10 months. Medium-bodied, it has fresh, citrusy, peachy fruit flavours to the fore, a hint of biscuity oak, moderate complexity and lively acidity. Best drinking 2021+.

DRY $19 V+

Lake Chalice The Raptor Marlborough Chardonnay ★★★★☆

Drinking well in its youth, the 2019 vintage (★★★★) was grown mostly in the central Wairau Valley and barrel-fermented with indigenous yeasts. Light yellow/green, it is full-bodied, with generous, ripe stone-fruit flavours, oak complexity, balanced acidity, and good harmony.

DRY $23 V+

Landing, The, Bay of Islands Boathouse Chardonnay (★★★★☆)

Well worth cellaring, the vigorous 2019 vintage (★★★★☆) was estate-grown, hand-harvested and fermented and matured for 11 months in French oak barriques (10 per cent new). Bright, light lemon/green, with a fragrant, slightly biscuity bouquet, it is mouthfilling, with ripe stone-fruit flavours, strong and vibrant, and good complexity. Best drinking 2023+.

DRY $27 V+

Landing, The, Bay of Islands Chardonnay ★★★★☆

Estate-grown at a coastal site in the northern Bay of Islands, the bright, light yellow 2017 vintage (★★★★☆) was matured for a year in French oak barriques. Drinking well now, it is a weighty, fleshy wine, with concentrated, ripe stone-fruit flavours, seasoned with toasty oak, excellent complexity and harmony, and a long finish.

DRY $40 –V

Vintage	17	16	15	14	13
WR	4	4	5	5	6
Drink	20-21	P	P	P	P

Last Shepherd, The, Gisborne Chardonnay ★★★★

The 2017 vintage (★★★★) is mouthfilling, with generous, ripe, peachy flavours, balanced acidity, slightly buttery notes, considerable complexity, and a smooth finish. A distinctly regional style, it's ready to roll.

DRY $25 AV

Lawson's Dry Hills Marlborough Chardonnay   ★★★☆

The 2020 vintage (★★★☆) is a fresh, vibrantly fruity wine (8 per cent of the blend was fermented in old barrels). Light lemon/green, it is full-bodied, with ripe, peachy, citrusy flavours to the fore, a slightly creamy texture, and lots of drink-young appeal.

Vintage	20
WR	6
Drink	20-25

DRY $20 AV

Lawson's Dry Hills Reserve Marlborough Chardonnay   ★★★★☆

Offering great value, the 2019 vintage (★★★★★) was estate-grown in the Chaytors Road Vineyard, near the coast in the Wairau Valley, and fermented with indigenous yeasts in French oak barriques (25 per cent new). A stylish, harmonious young wine, it is full-bodied, rich and rounded, with generous, ripe, peachy, slightly spicy and toasty flavours, dry, complex and long. Already delicious, it is very age-worthy and likely to be at its best 2022+.

Vintage	19	18	17	16	15	14	13
WR	7	7	6	7	7	6	6
Drink	20-27	20-25	20-25	20-25	20-22	P	P

DRY $28 V+

Le Pont Grand Vin Blanc Chardonnay   ★★★★☆

Grown in Gisborne, the bold 2017 vintage (★★★★☆) was fermented and matured in French and Hungarian oak barrels (20 per cent new). Bright, light lemon/green, it is mouthfilling, with rich, ripe stone-fruit flavours, strongly seasoned with toasty, nutty oak, fresh acidity and a slightly buttery finish. The 2018 vintage (★★★★☆) was grown in the Matawhero district and barrel-aged for 14 months. Bright yellow, it is a powerful, weighty wine, with peachy, toasty aromas and flavours, showing good complexity and harmony. (From Poverty Bay Wine.)

DRY $40 –V

Left Field Hawke's Bay Chardonnay   ★★★★

From Te Awa, the 2018 vintage (★★★☆) is a 'fruit-driven' style of Chardonnay, full-bodied, with strong, peachy, citrusy flavours, a subtle seasoning of oak, and appealing freshness and harmony. Good value.

DRY $18 V+

Leveret Estate Hawke's Bay Chardonnay   ★★★★

Offering good value, the 2019 vintage (★★★★) is an attractive young wine, estate-grown in the cool, elevated Riverview Vineyard. Mouthfilling and vibrantly fruity, it has ripe stone-fruit flavours, gently seasoned with toasty oak, fresh acidity and considerable complexity. Finely balanced, it's already enjoyable, but best cellared to mid-2021+.

Vintage	19
WR	7
Drink	21-27

DRY $22 V+

Leveret Estate Reserve Hawke's Bay Chardonnay   ★★★★☆

Still unfolding, the good-value 2018 vintage (★★★★☆) was estate-grown at the cool, inland Riverview Vineyard and fermented and matured in French oak casks. Bright, light lemon/green, it is full-bodied and lively, with strong, ripe stone-fruit flavours, well seasoned with biscuity, toasty oak, fresh acidity, and excellent vigour, concentration and complexity. Best drinking 2022+.

Linden Estate Esk Valley Hawke's Bay Chardonnay   ★★★★

Showing good personality, the 2018 vintage (★★★★) is a sturdy, high-flavoured wine with a slightly biscuity bouquet. Mouthfilling, it has ripe stone-fruit flavours to the fore, considerable complexity, and a soft, creamy-textured finish.

Linden Estate Reserve Hawke's Bay Chardonnay   ★★★★☆

Still on sale, the classy 2016 vintage (★★★★★) was hand-harvested in the Esk Valley and fermented with indigenous yeasts in French oak barriques. A classic regional style, it is a mouthfilling, slightly buttery wine with rich grapefruit and peach flavours, showing excellent delicacy and complexity, gentle acidity and a long, harmonious finish. A top vintage of this label, it's drinking well now.

Vintage	16	15
WR	7	6
Drink	20-21	P

Lost Garden by Trinity Hill Hawke's Bay Chardonnay   (★★★★)

The 2019 vintage (★★★★) was made 'for the now and for the moment'. Lush, but not flabby, it is a pale lemon/green, fleshy, vibrantly fruity wine, not highly complex, but offering generous, ripe stone-fruit flavours, with a slightly creamy texture, gentle acidity, and a well-rounded finish. Best drinking 2021–22.

Luna Eclipse Martinborough Chardonnay   ★★★★☆

Hand-picked on the Martinborough Terrace, the generous 2018 vintage (★★★★☆) was fermented and matured for 11 months in French oak casks, and bottled unfined and unfiltered. Bright, light yellow/green, it is mouthfilling and sweet-fruited, with concentrated, youthful, peachy, citrusy flavours, gently seasoned with toasty oak, balanced acidity, and very good complexity. Best drinking 2021+.

LV by Louis Vavasour Marlborough Chardonnay   (★★★★☆)

The powerful, bold 2016 vintage (★★★★☆) is mouthfilling and rich, with deep, ripe stone-fruit and toasty oak flavours, and a well-rounded, harmonious finish. Showing very good complexity, it's drinking well now. (From Awatere River Wine Co.)

DRY $49 –V

Mahi Alchemy Single Vineyard Marlborough Chardonnay   ★★★★☆

Well worth cellaring, the lively 2018 vintage (★★★★☆) was grown at Rapaura, hand-harvested and fermented and matured for 15 months in French oak barriques. Bright, light yellow/green, with a slightly smoky bouquet, it has excellent intensity of crisp, citrusy, slightly biscuity flavours, finely integrated oak, and a long, tightly structured finish. Best drinking 2022+.

Vintage	18
WR	6
Drink	20-27

 DRY $39 –V

Mahi Marlborough Chardonnay   ★★★★☆

The 2018 vintage (★★★★) was hand-harvested at three sites in the Wairau Valley, fermented with indigenous yeasts in French oak barriques and wood-aged for 11 months. Still unfolding, it is bright, light yellow/green, with strong stone-fruit flavours, oak complexity, slightly smoky notes, and a fresh, crisp finish. Best drinking mid-2021+.

Vintage	18	17	16	15	14	13
WR	6	6	6	6	6	6
Drink	20-25	20-24	20-24	20-21	20-21	P

 DRY $34 AV

Mahi Single Vineyard Twin Valleys Marlborough Chardonnay   ★★★★★

Hand-picked in the Twin Valleys Vineyard, at the junction of the Wairau and Waihopai valleys, the refined 2017 vintage (★★★★★) was fermented with indigenous yeasts and matured in French oak barriques. Maturing very gracefully, it is a bright, light yellow/green, full-bodied, complex wine, with vigorous, citrusy, peachy flavours, enriched with biscuity oak, and a lasting finish. Best drinking 2022+.

Vintage	17	16
WR	6	6
Drink	20-27	20-24

 DRY $39 AV

Main Divide South Island Chardonnay   ★★★☆

The 2019 vintage (★★★) is bright, light gold, with a slightly honeyed bouquet. Mouthfilling, it is ripe and peachy, in an uncomplicated but full-flavoured style. (From Pegasus Bay.)

 DRY $21 AV

Maison Noire Hawke's Bay Chardonnay   ★★★★

The generous, very harmonious 2019 vintage (★★★★☆) offers top value. Barrel-fermented, it is a bright, light lemon/green, mouthfilling wine, with strong, vibrant stone-fruit flavours, slightly biscuity notes adding complexity, and a finely poised finish. Showing obvious potential, it should be at its best 2022+.

DRY $25 AV

Man O' War Valhalla Waiheke Island Chardonnay   ★★★★★

Made from 'our finest barrels of Chardonnay', this tightly structured wine is estate-grown at the remote, eastern end of Waiheke Island. Hand-harvested and fermented with indigenous yeasts in French oak puncheons (36 per cent new), the 2019 vintage (★★★★★) is a pale yellow, powerful, weighty wine with rich, ripe stone-fruit and nutty oak flavours, balanced acidity and a long, dry finish. Still very youthful, with a commanding presence, it's well worth cellaring to 2023+.

 DRY $49 AV

Vintage	19
WR	7
Drink	20-27

Man O' War Waiheke Island Chardonnay   (★★★☆)

Still unfolding, the 2018 vintage (★★★☆) was handled in French oak puncheons (18 per cent new). Bright, light yellow/green, it is mouthfilling, with fresh acidity and very good depth of ripe, peachy, slightly toasty flavours, showing considerable complexity. Best drinking mid-2021+.

 DRY $34 –V

Man O' War Waiheke Island Valkyrie Chardonnay   (★★★★☆)

The 2017 vintage (★★★★☆) has a complex, fragrant bouquet. Full-bodied, it has concentrated, ripe, peachy flavours, slightly toasty and smoky notes, fresh acidity, and a long finish. It's drinking well now.

 DRY $38 –V

Marsden Bay of Islands Black Rocks Chardonnay   ★★★★

Grown at Kerikeri, this Northland wine is impressive in favourably dry seasons – sturdy, with concentrated, ripe sweet-fruit flavours, well seasoned with toasty oak, in a typically lush, upfront, creamy-smooth style. The very age-worthy 2019 vintage (★★★★☆) was fermented and matured for a year in French oak barriques (30 per cent new). Light lemon/green, with a slightly creamy bouquet, it is youthful, fresh and lively, with mouthfilling body and strong, peachy, nutty flavours, showing good complexity. Currently slightly oaky, but well worth cellaring, it should be at its best 2022+.

 DRY $40 –V

Vintage	19	18	17	16
WR	7	4	5	6
Drink	20-24	20-22	20-22	20-23

Martinborough Vineyard Home Block Chardonnay   ★★★★★

The refined 2018 vintage (★★★★★) was fermented and matured for a year in French oak casks (23 per cent new). Bright, light lemon/green, it is fresh, youthful and weighty, with generous, ripe stone-fruit flavours, finely integrated nutty oak, excellent complexity, and a rich, well-rounded finish. Well worth cellaring, it should be at its best 2021+.

DRY $39 AV

Vintage	18	17
WR	7	7
Drink	20-28	20-28

Matahiwi Estate Hawke's Bay Chardonnay   (★★★☆)

The easy-drinking 2019 vintage (★★★☆) is a single-vineyard wine, partly barrel-matured. Fresh, lively and youthful, it is full-bodied, with good depth of ripe stone-fruit flavours, a touch of complexity, and a dry, slightly creamy finish. Best drinking mid-2021+.

Vintage	19	DRY $23 AV
WR	6	
Drink	20-26	

Matahiwi Estate Holly Hawke's Bay Chardonnay   ★★★★

Made in an upfront style, the 2019 vintage (★★★★) was barrel-fermented. Bright yellow/green, with a complex bouquet, it is full-bodied, with strong, ripe stone-fruit and biscuity oak flavours, and a slightly creamy texture. Drink now or cellar.

Vintage	18	DRY $30 –V
WR	6	
Drink	20-24	

Matakana Estate Terroir Edition Chardonnay   ★★★★☆

Drinking well now, but still very age-worthy, the 2016 vintage (★★★★☆) was grown at Matakana, north of Auckland, fermented with indigenous yeasts and barrel-matured for nearly a year. Light gold/green, it is full-bodied, with strong, ripe stone-fruit flavours, showing good complexity, and a rich, harmonious, well-rounded finish.

DRY $36 –V

Matawhero Church House Barrel Fermented Gisborne Chardonnay   ★★★★☆

Already very expressive, the 2019 vintage (★★★★☆) was grown in the Tietjen Vineyard, in the Hexton hills, partly hand-harvested, and fermented in tanks and American and European oak barrels. Fragrant, with a slightly buttery bouquet, it is mouthfilling and sweet-fruited, with generous, ripe stone-fruit flavours, well seasoned with toasty oak, balanced acidity, and a dry, smooth finish. A high-flavoured style, with loads of drink-young appeal, it should break into full stride mid-2021+.

DRY $30 AV

Matawhero Irwin Gisborne Chardonnay   ★★★★★

An extroverted, 'full-on' style, the golden 2018 vintage (★★★★★) was harvested from vines planted in 2013 in the Tietjen Vineyard and fermented and lees-aged for nine months in American and Hungarian oak barriques (30 per cent new). A highly distinctive wine with a fragrant, complex bouquet, it is powerful and lush, with notably concentrated, ripe, peachy, mealy, toasty flavours, finely balanced acidity, and a lasting finish. Already a memorable mouthful, it's a drink-now or cellaring proposition.

DRY $60 AV

Matawhero Single Vineyard Gisborne Chardonnay   ★★★★

The softly mouthfilling 2019 vintage (★★★★), grown in the Tietjen Vineyard, is already drinking well. Bright, light yellow/green, it has strong, ripe stone-fruit flavours, slightly spicy notes, gentle acidity, and a rich, creamy-smooth finish.

DRY $23 V+

Matt Connell Wines Lowburn Single Vineyard Chardonnay   (★★★★☆)

The 2017 vintage (★★★★☆), enjoyable young, was hand-picked in Central Otago and fermented in French oak barriques (10 per cent new). Fragrant, mouthfilling and rich, it has generous, citrusy, peachy flavours, a hint of butterscotch, savoury, mealy notes adding complexity, and a well-rounded finish.

DRY $38 –V

Maude Central Otago Chardonnay   (★★★★☆)

The creamy-textured 2019 vintage (★★★★☆) was fermented and lees-aged for eight months in French oak casks (10 per cent new). Fragrant, with a citrusy, slightly biscuity bouquet, it has good weight, with citrusy, peachy, mealy flavours, showing impressive depth, a subtle seasoning of oak, and a very smooth, harmonious finish. Best drinking mid-2021+.

DRY $30 AV

Maude Mt Maude Vineyard Wanaka Chardonnay Reserve   ★★★★☆

This classy Central Otago wine is hand-harvested from estate-grown vines, planted in 1994, and fermented and matured in French oak puncheons (15 per cent new in 2018). The refined 2018 vintage (★★★★★) is already delicious. Bright, light lemon/green, with a fragrant, slightly creamy bouquet, it is mouthfilling, vibrantly fruity and youthful, with deep, peachy, citrusy flavours, finely integrated oak, excellent complexity, and a lasting, very harmonious finish.

DRY $38 –V

Maui Hawke's Bay Chardonnay   (★★★☆)

The 2017 vintage (★★★☆) is a 'fruit-driven' style, tank-fermented, with some oak handling. Full-bodied, with a fresh, slightly buttery bouquet, it has grapefruit and peach flavours, showing good depth, and a slightly spicy, smooth finish. Very user-friendly. (From Tiki.)

Vintage	17
WR	7
Drink	P

DRY $19 V+

Maui Waipara Chardonnay   (★★☆)

The 2017 vintage (★★☆) is full-bodied, with peachy, vaguely honeyed flavours, crisp acidity and a rustic streak. Ready.

DRY $18 –V

ME by Matahiwi Estate Hawke's Bay Chardonnay

Enjoyable young, the 2019 vintage (★★★☆) is a 'fruit-driven' style, handled in tanks and barrels. Bright, light yellow/green, it is vibrantly fruity, with fresh, ripe, peachy flavours, a touch of complexity, balanced acidity, and lots of drink-young appeal.

Vintage	19	DRY $20 AV
WR	6	
Drink	20-24	

Milcrest Nelson Reserve Chardonnay

The 2016 vintage (★★★★) is an estate-grown, single-vineyard wine, fermented and matured for 11 months in French (97 per cent) and American (3 per cent) oak barriques. Full-bodied, with a fragrant, slightly buttery bouquet, it has good concentration of peachy, slightly toasty flavours and a well-rounded, harmonious finish.

DRY $44 –V

Mills Reef Bespoke Hawke's Bay Chardonnay

A tribute to the 'famous old-school style' of Chardonnay, with 'lashings of toasty oak', this wine is handled in a combination of French and American oak casks, and given a full, softening malolactic fermentation. The 2017 vintage (★★★★) is full-bodied, with ripe, peachy, buttery, toasty flavours, in a generous, well-rounded style, for drinking now.

DRY $35 –V

Mills Reef Elspeth Hawke's Bay Chardonnay

Past vintages under the top Elspeth label flowed from the Gimblett Gravels, but the stylish 2019 (★★★★☆) was hand-picked in the cool, elevated Riverview Vineyard. Fermented and matured for a year in French oak casks (32 per cent new), it is mouthfilling, with vibrant, peachy, citrusy flavours, showing good delicacy, well-integrated oak, fresh acidity, and a tightly structured finish. Best drinking 2022+.

Vintage	19	DRY $45 AV
WR	7	
Drink	21-31	🍇

Mills Reef Estate Hawke's Bay Chardonnay

The 2020 vintage (★★★) is an easy-drinking wine, full-bodied, with vibrant, peachy fruit flavours to the fore, slightly toasty notes, fresh acidity and lots of drink-young appeal.

Vintage	19	DRY $19 AV
WR	6	
Drink	21-23	

Mills Reef Reserve Hawke's Bay Chardonnay ★★★★

The generous 2019 vintage (★★★★) was barrel-fermented. Bright, light lemon/green, it is full-bodied and vibrantly fruity, with ripe, peachy, slightly toasty flavours, showing very good depth and harmony. Best drinking 2022+.

Vintage	19	18	17	16	15	14	13
WR	7	7	7	6	7	7	7
Drink	21-25	20-22	20-21	P	P	P	P

DRY $25 AV

Millton Opou Vineyard Gisborne Chardonnay ★★★★☆

Certified organic, the 2018 vintage (★★★★☆) is already delicious. Hand-picked and fermented with indigenous yeasts in small French oak barrels (10 per cent new), it is a fleshy, sweet-fruited wine, lively, rich and rounded, with excellent complexity, harmony and length. Drink now or cellar.

Vintage	18	17	16	15	14
WR	5	5	5	6	6
Drink	20-27	20-26	20-25	20-25	20-24

DRY $34 AV

Mission Barrique Reserve Hawke's Bay Chardonnay ★★★★☆

For Mission's classy, upper-tier Chardonnay, the style goal is a wine that 'emphasises fruit characters rather than oak, but offers some of the benefits of fermentation and maturation in wood'. The 2019 vintage (★★★★) was fermented in a mix of tanks and barrels, then fully matured for nine months in French oak casks. Still very youthful, it is a highly fragrant, mouthfilling wine, with strong, vibrant stone-fruit flavours, slightly buttery notes and fresh acidity. It has obvious cellaring potential; best drinking 2022+.

DRY $29 V+

Mission Hawke's Bay Chardonnay ★★★☆

The good-value 2019 vintage (★★★☆) is enjoyable young. A 'fruit-driven' Chardonnay style, it is fresh and full-bodied, with ripe, peachy, citrusy flavours to the fore, gentle biscuity notes, balanced acidity, and very good depth.

DRY $18 V+

Mission Jewelstone Hawke's Bay Chardonnay ★★★★★

Classy stuff. Made in a bolder, more upfront style than some past releases, the 2018 vintage (★★★★☆) was grown at Taradale and in the Gimblett Gravels, partly hand-harvested and fully barrel-fermented (33 per cent new). Pale gold, it is a powerful, fleshy wine, with deep stone-fruit and toasty oak flavours. Best drinking mid-2021+.

Vintage	18	17	16	15	14	13	12
WR	5	7	7	7	7	6	5
Drink	20-25	20-24	20-23	20-22	20-21	P	P

DRY $40 AV

Mission Vineyard Selection Hawke's Bay Chardonnay ★★★☆

The 2017 vintage (★★★★) is a single-vineyard wine, grown at Te Awanga and partly barrel-fermented. Offering very good value, it is mouthfilling, with strong, fresh, peachy, citrusy, slightly toasty flavours, good complexity and lots of current-drinking appeal.

 DRY $19 V+

Momo Organic Marlborough Chardonnay ★★★☆

Certified organic, the 2018 vintage (★★★☆) was grown at sites in the Omaka Valley and the western Wairau Valley, partly hand-picked, fermented in tanks and barrels, then fully matured in old oak barrels. Pale gold, it has good depth of citrusy, peachy fruit flavours, a distinct touch of complexity, fresh acidity, and a dry finish. It's drinking well now.

 DRY $20 AV

Montana NZ Collection Big & Buttery Gisborne Chardonnay (★★★☆)

The pale gold 2018 vintage (★★★☆) is not as 'big and buttery' as its label suggests. Medium to full-bodied, it has plenty of ripe, peachy, slightly toasty flavour, with fresh acidity keeping things lively, and considerable complexity. It's drinking well now.

 DRY $20 AV

Montana Reserve Gisborne Chardonnay ★★★☆

The 2017 vintage (★★★☆) is bargain-priced. Full-bodied, it has generous, ripe, peachy flavours, slightly smoky notes adding a touch of complexity, and a smooth, very harmonious finish.

 DRY $17 V+

Montford Estate Marlborough Chardonnay (★★★★)

The youthful, vibrantly fruity 2019 vintage (★★★★) has a fresh, slightly buttery bouquet, leading into a mouthfilling wine with strong, peachy flavours, finely balanced oak and acidity, and a lengthy finish. Best drinking 2022+. (From te Pā.)

 DRY $20 V+

Morton Estate [Black Label] Gisborne Chardonnay ★★★★

This label was for decades indivisibly associated with the Hawke's Bay region, but since 2016 it has been grown in Gisborne. The 2018 vintage (★★★★) is an extroverted style, fresh and full-bodied, with generous, ripe, peachy flavours, seasoned with toasty oak, balanced acidity, and a slightly buttery finish. (From Lion.)

 DRY $20 V+

Mount Brown Estates North Canterbury Chardonnay ★★★☆

Oak-aged for nearly a year, the 2018 vintage (★★★) is a youthful wine, medium to full-bodied, with fresh, citrusy, peachy, gently toasty flavours. Priced right.

Vintage	18
WR	4
Drink	20-24

DRY $16 V+

Mount Edward Central Otago Chardonnay   ★★★★

Certified organic, the 2018 vintage (★★★★☆) was grown in the Morrison Vineyard, at Pisa, and fermented and lees-aged for nearly a year in seasoned French oak casks. Bright, light yellow/green, it has a fragrant, slightly buttery bouquet, leading into a mouthfilling, fleshy wine with generous, peachy flavours, showing very good complexity, a slightly creamy texture, and a long, harmonious finish. Drink now or cellar.

 DRY $31 –V

Mount Riley 17 Valley Marlborough Chardonnay   ★★★★☆

The very harmonious 2019 vintage (★★★★☆) was hand-picked and fermented and matured in French oak barriques (30 per cent new). Fragrant, with a slightly creamy, biscuity bouquet, it is mouthfilling and vibrant, with youthful grapefruit and peach flavours, showing excellent delicacy, a subtle seasoning of oak adding complexity, and obvious potential. Best drinking 2022+.

Vintage	14	13	12
WR	7	7	7
Drink	20-21	P	P

 DRY $28 V+

Mount Riley Marlborough Chardonnay   ★★★☆

Skilfully balanced, the 2017 vintage (★★★☆) was fermented in stainless steel tanks (30 per cent) and French oak barriques (70 per cent). It has a fragrant, slightly buttery bouquet, leading into a full-bodied palate with generous, peachy, citrusy, slightly toasty flavours, balanced acidity, and a dry finish. Bargain-priced.

 DRY $16 V+

Moutere Hills Nelson Chardonnay   ★★★★☆

The powerful 2019 vintage (★★★★☆) was estate-grown, hand-picked and fermented and matured for 11 months in French oak barrels. Bright yellow/green, it is mouthfilling and rich, with strong, peachy, slightly toasty and buttery flavours, fresh acidity and good potential; best drinking 2022+.

 DRY $35 –V

Moutere Hills Sarau Reserve Nelson Chardonnay   ★★★★★

The lush 2018 vintage (★★★★☆) was estate-grown, hand-harvested and fermented and matured for 11 months in French oak barriques. Bright, light yellow/green, it is full-bodied, with ripe stone-fruit flavours, seasoned with biscuit oak, balanced acidity, creamy notes, and a very harmonious finish. Drink now or cellar.

Vintage	18	17
WR	7	6
Drink	20-25	20-26

 DRY $55 AV

Mt Beautiful North Canterbury Chardonnay ★★★★

Estate-grown at Cheviot, north of Waipara, the 2017 vintage (★★★★) is fragrant and full-bodied, with citrusy, peachy, biscuity flavours, finely integrated oak, good complexity, fresh acidity, and a long finish. Best drinking 2021+.

Vintage	17	16	15	14
WR	6	7	6	5
Drink	20-24	20-25	20-21	P

DRY $27 AV

Mt Difficulty McFelin Ridge Lowburn Valley Chardonnay (★★★★☆)

The vibrant 2018 vintage (★★★★☆) is a single-vineyard wine, grown at around 300 metres above sea level and fermented and matured for 11 months in French oak casks (18 per cent new). Bright, light lemon/green, with a fragrant, gently biscuity bouquet, it's distinctly cool-climate style, with excellent intensity of grapefruit-evoking flavours, a subtle oak influence, balanced acidity, good complexity, and a long finish. Elegant and age-worthy, it's well worth cellaring.

Vintage	18
WR	6
Drink	20-26

DRY $37 –V

Mt Difficulty Packspur Lowburn Valley Chardonnay (★★★★★)

The very classy 2018 vintage (★★★★★) is from the oldest vineyard site at Lowburn, in Central Otago, planted in 1992 at 360 to 380 metres above sea level. Fermented and matured for 11 months in French oak casks (12 per cent new), it is elegant and weighty, with deep, vibrant, citrusy, peachy, slightly creamy flavours, a subtle seasoning of oak, and a Chablis-like elegance and length. Already delicious, it's well worth cellaring.

DRY $47 AV

Muddy Water Waipara Chardonnay ★★★★★

Certified organic, the refined 2018 vintage (★★★★☆) was hand-picked from vines planted in 1993. Fermented with indigenous yeasts in French oak puncheons (15 per cent new) and wood-aged for 11 months, it is bright, light lemon/green, with fragrant, lemony scents. An elegant, cool-climate style, it is citrusy and slightly peachy, with gentle, biscuity, mealy notes, finely integrated oak, good complexity, and a very harmonious, long finish. Best drinking 2022+.

Vintage	18
WR	7
Drink	20-30

DRY $39 AV

Nanny Goat Vineyard Central Otago Chardonnay ★★★☆

A distinctly cool-climate style, the 2018 vintage (★★★★) is a single-vineyard wine, hand-picked near Cromwell and fermented and matured in French oak casks (10 per cent new). Fresh and crisp, it has grapefruit-like flavours, gently seasoned with oak, firm acid spine, and a lingering finish. Well worth cellaring, it should be at its best 2021+.

DRY $35 –V

Nautilus Marlborough Chardonnay ★★★★★

Delicious from the start, the 2019 vintage (★★★★★) was fermented and lees-stirred in oak casks (25 per cent new). Bright, light lemon/green, it is mouthfilling, generous and very harmonious, in a sweet-fruited, softly mouthfilling style with ripe stone-fruit flavours, integrated oak, balanced acidity and a long finish. Best drinking 2022+.

Vintage	19	18	17	16	15
WR	7	7	7	7	7
Drink	20-25	20-24	20-23	20-21	P

DRY $35 AV

Neck of the Woods Dartmoor Hawke's Bay Chardonnay ★★★★

The 2018 vintage (★★★★) was hand-picked in the Dartmoor Valley, and fermented and matured for 11 months in French oak barrels (25 per cent new). Pale gold, with a toasty bouquet, it's an upfront style, with strong, peachy, oaky, slightly creamy flavours, showing considerable complexity, fresh acidity, and lots of drink-young appeal.

DRY $32 –V

Neudorf Moutere Chardonnay ★★★★★

Superbly rich but not overblown, with arrestingly intense flavours enlivened with fine acidity, this multi-faceted Nelson wine enjoys a reputation second to none among New Zealand Chardonnays. Grown in clay soils threaded with gravel at Upper Moutere, it is hand-harvested from mature vines, fermented with indigenous yeasts, and lees-aged, with regular stirring, for a year in French oak barriques (15 per cent new in 2018). Bright, light lemon/green, the very elegant 2018 vintage (★★★★★) is a weighty, vibrant, tightly structured wine, with rich stone-fruit and grapefruit flavours, mealy and oaky notes adding complexity, and a long, very harmonious finish. Powerful, yet graceful, it should be at its best for drinking 2022+. Certified organic.

Vintage	18	17	16	15	14	13
WR	6	6	6	7	6	6
Drink	20-25	20-24	20-23	20-22	20-21	P

DRY $79 AV

Neudorf Rosie's Block Chardonnay ★★★★☆

Retasted in early 2020, the stylish 2018 vintage (★★★★☆) of this Nelson wine was grown mostly at Upper Moutere (including Neudorf's own Rosie's Block), fermented with indigenous yeasts and lees-aged for 10 months in French oak casks (15 per cent new). Light lemon/green, it is a very lively, full-bodied wine, with concentrated peach and grapefruit flavours, integrated oak, savoury, mealy notes, fresh acidity and a lengthy, very harmonious finish. Best drinking 2021+.

DRY $33 AV

Nga Waka Home Block Martinborough Chardonnay   ★★★★☆

This single-vineyard wine is from vines planted in 1988. At its best, it is an authoritative wine, weighty and concentrated, with strong personality. Already highly expressive, the 2018 vintage (★★★★★) was fermented and matured for 10 months in French oak casks (30 per cent new), and given a full, softening malolactic fermentation. Pale gold, it is a powerful, lush, weighty style with concentrated, peachy, toasty flavours, showing very good complexity, and a rounded finish.

Vintage	18	17	16	15	14	13
WR	6	6	6	6	7	7
Drink	20-22	20-22	20-22	20-21	P	P

 DRY $40 –V

Nga Waka Martinborough Chardonnay   ★★★★

This is a consistently rewarding wine. The pale gold 2018 vintage (★★★★☆) was fermented and matured for 10 months in French oak casks (20 per cent new). Already drinking well, it's a powerful, upfront style, with mouthfilling body, generous, peachy, slightly buttery and toasty flavours, showing good complexity, and a creamy-smooth finish.

Vintage	18	17	16	15
WR	6	6	6	6
Drink	20-22	20-22	P	P

 DRY $30 –V

Nockie's Palette Hawke's Bay Chardonnay   ★★★★★

The bold, almost brash 2018 vintage (★★★★☆) was made for Nockie's Palette (in Central Otago) by Clearview Estate, at Te Awanga, in Hawke's Bay. Bright, light yellow/green, it is a powerful wine, crafted in a very upfront style, with concentrated, ripe stone-fruit flavours, buttery and toasty notes adding complexity, balanced acidity, and loads of drink-young appeal.

 DRY $46 AV

Novum Marlborough Chardonnay   ★★★★☆

An obvious candidate for cellaring, the bright, light lemon/green 2019 vintage (★★★★☆) was hand-harvested and fermented and matured in French oak barriques (10 per cent new). Made in a restrained, subtle style, reminiscent of Chablis, it is fresh, full-bodied and dry, with delicate, citrusy, slightly appley and biscuity flavours, lively acidity and a lingering finish. Open mid-2022+.

 DRY $47 –V

Oak Estate 1000 Vines Reserve Hawke's Bay Chardonnay   (★★★★☆)

Full of youthful vigour, the 2018 vintage (★★★★☆) was hand-picked in the Bridge Pa Triangle and fermented and matured in French oak barrels. Bright, light lemon/green, it is full-bodied, with rich stone-fruit flavours, seasoned with nutty oak, excellent complexity, fresh acidity, and a tightly structured finish. Best drinking 2022+.

DRY $45 –V

Oak Estate Home Block Hawke's Bay Chardonnay   (★★★★)

Drinking well in its youth, the 2018 vintage (★★★★) is a single-vineyard wine, grown in the Bridge Pa Triangle and barrel-fermented. Light yellow, it is mouthfilling, with ripe, peachy flavours, fresh and generous, a gentle seasoning of toasty oak, balanced acidity, and a slightly creamy texture. Drink now to 2021.

DRY $28 AV

Obsidian Reserve Waiheke Island Chardonnay   ★★★★☆

The 2018 vintage (★★★★☆) is a fresh, generous, very age-worthy wine, fermented with indigenous yeasts in French oak barrels (40 per cent new) and wood-aged for 10 months. Weighty and sweet-fruited, with concentrated stone-fruit flavours, balanced acidity, good complexity and a slightly creamy texture, it should be at its best 2021+.

DRY $48 –V

Odyssey Gisborne Chardonnay   ★★★☆

The 2018 vintage (★★★☆) is a single-vineyard wine, fermented and matured in seasoned oak casks. Bright, light yellow, it is full-bodied, with strong, peachy, toasty, buttery aromas and flavours. If you prefer a 'full-on' Chardonnay style, try this.

DRY $20 AV

Odyssey Hera Chardonnay   (★★★★★)

Rich and tightly structured, the powerfu, lush 2018 vintage (★★★★★) was grown in Gisborne, hand-picked and fermented with indigenous yeasts in French oak puncheons (50 per cent new). Bright yellow, it is a stylish wine, still youthful, with concentrated grapefruit and peach flavours, showing impressive complexity, and a lasting finish. Best drinking mid-2021+.

DRY $65 AV

Odyssey Reserve Iliad Gisborne Chardonnay   ★★★★☆

Well worth cellaring, the 2018 vintage (★★★★☆) is a single-vineyard wine, hand-harvested and fermented with indigenous yeasts in French oak barriques (30 per cent new). Pale straw, it is fragrant and mouthfilling, with generous stone-fruit and toasty oak flavours, showing good complexity. A 'full-on' style, it's already approachable, but likely to be at its best 2021+.

DRY $32 AV

Ohinemuri Estate Opou Reserve Poverty Bay Chardonnay   ★★★★

The 2017 vintage (★★★★) is a single-vineyard wine, grown at Opou, in Gisborne, and fermented and lees-aged for nine months in French oak barriques (20 per cent new). It is mouthfilling and sweet-fruited, with fresh, generous, peachy, slightly toasty flavours, and a well-rounded finish.

DRY $25 AV

Old Coach Road Nelson Chardonnay   ★★★

The easy-drinking 2018 vintage (★★☆) was mostly oak-aged (70 per cent of the blend spent several months in French oak). Light straw, with a creamy bouquet, it is full-bodied, with peachy, slightly spicy and honeyed flavours. Drink young.

DRY $15 V+

Old Coach Road Unoaked Nelson Chardonnay ★★☆

Priced right, the 2019 vintage (★★☆) from Seifried is a no-fuss wine, bright, light lemon/green, with fresh, citrusy, peachy aromas and flavours, slightly creamy notes, and a crisp, dry finish.

Vintage	19
WR	5
Drink	20-22

DRY $14 AV

Old House Vineyards One Tree Nelson Chardonnay ★★★★

The 2018 vintage (★★★★) was estate-grown and hand-picked at Upper Moutere, fermented with indigenous yeasts and matured for 11 months in French oak barrels. Light yellow/green, with a creamy bouquet, it is full-bodied, with generous, youthful, citrusy, peachy flavours, mealy and biscuity notes adding complexity, balanced acidity, and good potential; best drinking 2021+.

Vintage	18	17
WR	7	6
Drink	20-30	20-30

DRY $35 –V

On Giants' Shoulders Martinborough Chardonnay ★★★★☆

The richly flavoured, youthful 2018 vintage (★★★★☆) was fermented and matured for 11 months in French oak barrels (25 per cent new). Bright, light lemon/green, it is an elegant, medium to full-bodied wine, with generous, ripe, peachy, slightly mealy flavours, showing very good delicacy and complexity. Well worth cellaring, it should break into full stride 2022+.

DRY $40 –V

Oyster Bay Marlborough Chardonnay ★★★★

This huge-selling, moderately priced wine is designed to showcase Marlborough's incisive fruit flavours. About half the blend is handled solely in tanks; the other half is fermented, lees-stirred and matured for nine months in oak barrels, predominantly French. It typically offers strong, ripe, citrusy, peachy flavours, threaded with appetising acidity. The 2018 vintage (★★★★), grown in the Wairau and Awatere valleys, is an excellent example of the 'fruit-driven' style of Chardonnay. Bright, light lemon/green, it is a medium to full-bodied wine, with fresh, vibrant fruit flavours, finely integrated oak adding complexity, balanced acidity and loads of drink-young appeal.

DRY $20 V+

Pā Road Marlborough Chardonnay ★★★☆

Offering good value, the bright, light lemon/green 2019 vintage (★★★☆) is an easy-drinking style, full-bodied, with vibrant, citrusy, slightly peachy flavours, toasty notes adding a touch of complexity, and good depth. (From te Pā.)

DRY $18 V+

Paddy Borthwick Wairarapa Chardonnay

Estate-grown at Gladstone, in the northern Wairarapa, the 2019 vintage (★★★★☆) is an attractive wine, already drinking well but worth cellaring to 2022+. Bright, light lemon/green, it is weighty, youthful and sweet-fruited, with strong, citrusy, peachy flavours, biscuity and buttery notes adding complexity, and a smooth, very harmonious finish.

DRY $25 AV

Palliser Estate Martinborough Chardonnay

The classy 2019 vintage (★★★★★) is bright, light yellow/green, with an invitingly fragrant, complex, slightly smoky bouquet. Mouthfilling, vigorous and savoury, it is youthful, with concentrated, ripe stone-fruit flavours, finely integrated toasty oak adding complexity, and a long, finely poised finish. Best drinking 2023+.

DRY $44 –V

Palliser Estate Om Santi Vineyard Martinborough Chardonnay

The pale yellow 2018 vintage (★★★★★) is from Palliser's original vineyard (replanted in 2005). Hand-picked, it was barrel-fermented with indigenous yeasts, French oak-aged for 14 months, and bottled unfined and unfiltered. Weighty and rich, it is an elegant wine, with deep, ripe, peachy, citrusy flavours, savoury and toasty notes, and a fragrant, complex bouquet. Still youthful, it's well worth cellaring.

DRY $55 AV

Palliser Estate The Great Riddler Martinborough Chardonnay

Produced in honour of Richard Riddiford (1950–2016), the company's founding managing director, the 2016 vintage (★★★★★) is rare – only 500 bottles exist. Grown in the original Om Santi Vineyard, it was fermented with indigenous yeasts in French oak barriques (20 per cent new), oak-aged for 18 months, given a full, softening malolactic fermentation, and bottled unfiltered. Bright, light lemon/green, it is a full-bodied, slightly creamy wine with concentrated, peachy, slightly toasty flavours, showing excellent vigour, delicacy, harmony and length. Best drinking 2021+.

DRY $85 AV

Paritua Hawke's Bay Chardonnay

The classy 2018 vintage (★★★★★) was fermented and matured for 11 months in French oak casks (40 per cent new). Bright, light lemon/green, it is full-bodied, refined, vibrant and youthful, with strong citrus and stone-fruit flavours, finely integrated oak, excellent complexity, fresh acidity, and a very harmonious, lingering finish. Showing obvious potential, it's well worth cellaring to 2022+.

DRY $35 AV

Vintage	18
WR	6
Drink	20-23

Paritua Stone Paddock Hawke's Bay Chardonnay   (★★★★)

Delicious young, the 2018 vintage (★★★★) is a vibrantly fruity, tank-fermented style. Bright, light lemon/green, it is full-bodied and sweet-fruited, with ripe, citrusy, peachy flavours, finely balanced acidity, and excellent poise, freshness and depth. Drink now to 2021.

Vintage	18
WR	6
Drink	20-23

DRY $22 V+

Pask Declaration Gimblett Gravels Chardonnay   ★★★★☆

The winery's top Chardonnay is estate-grown in the Gimblett Gravels, Hawke's Bay. The 2016 vintage (★★★★☆) was fermented and matured for 11 months in French oak puncheons (67 per cent new). Retasted in mid-2020, it is bright, light yellow/green, with a fragrant, complex bouquet. An elegant, tightly structured wine, it is medium to full-bodied, with very good intensity of crisp, ripe, citrusy, peachy, slightly toasty flavours, still fresh and youthful. Best drinking 2021+. The classy, youthful 2019 vintage (★★★★★) was handled in French oak casks (50 per cent new). Bright, light lemon/green, it is a refined, subtle wine, weighty and harmonious, with rich grapefruit and biscuity oak flavours, showing excellent delicacy and depth, and a long, dry finish. Best drinking 2023+.

Vintage	19
WR	7
Drink	21-31

DRY $50 –V

Pask Gimblett Gravels Chardonnay   ★★★★

This second-tier Hawke's Bay Chardonnay is designed to highlight its vibrant fruit characters, with a subtle wood influence. The elegant 2018 vintage (★★★★) was matured for nine months in French oak puncheons. Light lemon/green, with a hint of straw, it has a fragrant, fresh, slightly biscuity bouquet. Vibrant, with strong, delicate, citrusy, peachy flavours, gently seasoned with oak, it's a tightly structured wine with good complexity, worth cellaring. Best drinking mid-2020+. Bright, light lemon/green, the 2019 vintage (★★★★) is full-bodied, with fresh, vibrant stone-fruit flavours to the fore, finely integrated oak, balanced acidity, and a slightly creamy, harmonious finish. Best drinking 2022+.

DRY $22 V+

Pask Instinct Liquid Gold Hawke's Bay Chardonnay   (★★☆)

The very easy-drinking 2018 vintage (★★☆) was hand-picked and fermented in an even split of tanks and seasoned oak barrels. Bright, light yellow/green, it is medium-bodied, with vibrant, citrusy, peachy flavours to the fore and a smooth finish.

DRY $17 –V

Pask Small Batch Wild Yeast Gimblett Gravels
Hawke's Bay Chardonnay   ★★★★

The very age-worthy, youthful 2019 vintage (★★★★☆) was fermented with indigenous yeasts and lees-aged for a year in French oak barrels (20 per cent new). Pale lemon/green, with a fresh, elegant bouquet, it has vibrant, citrusy, peachy, mealy flavours, showing excellent ripeness, delicacy and depth, and a finely poised finish. Best drinking 2022+.

DRY $25 AV

Passage Rock Reserve Waiheke Island Chardonnay   ★★★★☆

Bright yellow/pale gold, the 2018 vintage (★★★★☆) was hand-harvested and fermented and matured in large French oak casks. Fresh and mouthfilling, it has strong, ripe stone-fruit and toasty oak flavours, showing very good complexity. Already very expressive, it's a drink-now or cellaring proposition.

Vintage	18
WR	5
Drink	20-22

DRY $50 –V

Peacock Sky Waiheke Island Chardonnay   ★★★☆

The 2018 vintage (★★★☆) was hand-harvested and French oak-aged for six months. Bright, light yellow, it is fresh and full-bodied, with lively, ripe, peachy, slightly toasty flavours, showing moderate complexity, and a smooth finish. Very easy drinking.

DRY $42 –V

Pegasus Bay Chardonnay   ★★★★★

Strapping yet delicate, richly flavoured yet subtle, this sophisticated North Canterbury wine is one of the country's best Chardonnays grown south of Marlborough. Muscular and taut, it typically offers a seamless array of fresh, crisp, citrusy, biscuity, complex flavours and great concentration and length. Estate-grown at Waipara, it is based on ungrafted, Mendoza-clone vines (about 30 years old), hand-picked and given lengthy oak aging (the 2018 vintage was fermented and lees-aged for a year in French oak puncheons, 30 per cent new). The 2018 vintage (★★★★★) is bright, light yellow/green, with a rich, smoky, fragrant bouquet. Weighty, concentrated and youthful, it is powerful, with deep stone-fruit flavours, finely integrated oak, impressive complexity and a long finish. Best drinking 2022+.

Vintage	18	17	16	15	14	13	12
WR	5	6	6	6	5	7	6
Drink	20-29	20-29	20-28	20-27	20-23	20-23	20-24

DRY $43 AV

🍇🍇🍇

Pegasus Bay Virtuoso Chardonnay   ★★★★★

Blended from the 'best barrels', this wine is hand-harvested from the company's mature, Mendoza-clone vines at Waipara. Fermented with indigenous yeasts, it is lees-aged for a year in French oak puncheons (30 per cent new in 2016), matured in tanks on light lees for several more months before bottling, and then bottle-aged for a year prior to its release. The

2016 vintage (★★★★★) has a fragrant, complex, inviting bouquet. Light lemon/green, it is full-bodied, rich and rounded, with deep stone-fruit and nut flavours, slightly smoky notes, excellent complexity, balanced acidity, and a seamless finish. Drink now or cellar.

Vintage	16	15
WR	6	6
Drink	20-29	20-28

DRY $60 AV

Pencarrow Martinborough Chardonnay   ★★★★

This is Palliser Estate's second-tier Chardonnay. Bright, light yellow/green, the 2019 vintage (★★★★) is a moderately complex style, citrusy and slightly creamy, with fresh acidity, very good flavour depth, and a long finish. Weighty and sweet-fruited, with lots of youthful vigour, it should be at its best mid-2021+.

DRY $26 AV

Petane Puriri Block Hawke's Bay Chardonnay   ★★★★

Well worth cellaring, the 2019 vintage (★★★★) was grown at Eskdale and fermented in oak barrels (20 per cent new). An elegant wine, it is fresh and full-bodied, with vibrant, ripe, citrusy, peachy flavours, gently seasoned with oak. Enjoyable young, it should break into full stride from 2022 onwards.

DRY $30 –V

Pirinoa Road Hawke's Bay Chardonnay   (★★★★)

Enjoyable young, the 2018 vintage (★★★★) was French oak-aged. Bright, light lemon/green, it is weighty and rounded, with strong, ripe, citrusy, peachy flavours, gentle biscuity notes adding considerable complexity, finely balanced acidity and a very harmonious, lingering finish. Drink now to 2022. (From Snapper Rock.)

DRY $23 V+

Pukeora Estate Ruahine Range Chardonnay   ★★★☆

Grown on limestone slopes in Central Hawke's Bay, the 2017 vintage (★★★☆) was hand-picked and fermented and matured for 11 months in French oak barrels (25 per cent new). Light gold, it is full-bodied, with firm acid spine and strong, grapefruit-like flavours, showing considerable complexity.

DRY $27 –V

Pyramid Valley Field of Fire Chardonnay   ★★★★★

The very youthful 2018 vintage (★★★★★) was estate-grown on an elevated, south-east-facing slope at Waikari, in North Canterbury. Bright, light yellow/green, with a fresh, citrusy fragrance, it is mouthfilling, with intense, lemony, slightly appley flavours, crisp, tightly structured and long. A Chablis-like wine with a real sense of youthful vigour and drive, it's well worth cellaring to 2023+.

DRY $125 –V

Pyramid Valley Marlborough Chardonnay ★★★★☆

Already delicious, the 2018 vintage (★★★★★) was hand-harvested from mature vines at Dog Point Vineyard, in the Southern Valleys, and fermented and matured in demi-muids (large French oak casks, holding 450 to 600 litres). Bright, light lemon/green, it is mouthfilling and fragrant, with very generous, ripe stone-fruit flavours, showing good complexity, and a rich, smooth finish.

DRY $40 –V

Pyramid Valley North Canterbury Chardonnay (★★★★)

Still very youthful, the vigorous 2018 vintage (★★★★) is bright yellow, with a citrusy bouquet. It has lively, grapefruit-like flavours, showing good intensity, gently biscuity notes, and a crisp, tightly structured finish. Open mid-2021+.

DRY $40 –V

Pyramid Valley Vineyards Lion's Tooth Chardonnay ★★★★★

Estate-grown on an east-facing slope at Waikari, in North Canterbury, the 2018 vintage (★★★★★) is a powerful (14.5 per cent alcohol), very youthful wine, with obvious potential. Light gold, it is sturdy, with concentrated, ripe stone-fruit flavours, gently seasoned with oak, steely acidity, and highly impressive intensity, structure and complexity. Best drinking 2023+.

DRY $125 –V

Quarter Acre Hawke's Bay Chardonnay ★★★★★

Instantly inviting, the 2018 vintage (★★★★★) is a multi-site blend, hand-picked and fermented and lees-aged for nine months in French oak casks. Bright, light lemon/green, it has a highly fragrant, complex bouquet, leading into a full-bodied, sweet-fruited wine with concentrated, vibrant stone-fruit flavours, showing excellent complexity, depth and harmony. A classic Hawke's Bay style, it's a drink-now or cellaring proposition.

DRY $35 AV

Quartz Reef Bendigo Estate Single Vineyard Central Otago Chardonnay (★★★★☆)

Certified organic and biodynamic, the debut 2018 vintage (★★★★☆) was estate-grown, hand-harvested and fermented with indigenous yeasts in French oak casks. Bright, light lemon/green, with a highly fragrant, mealy, slightly biscuity bouquet, it is mouthfilling and smooth, with fresh, ripe, generous stone-fruit flavours, finely integrated oak, balanced acidity and excellent complexity. A very harmonious wine, it should be at its best 2021+.

DRY $37 –V

Ra Nui Marlborough Wairau Valley Chardonnay ★★★★

The very harmonious 2016 vintage (★★★★) was fermented and matured in French oak casks (20 per cent new). Bright, light yellow/green, it is mouthfilling, with good concentration of peachy, citrusy, slightly buttery flavours, balanced acidity and a smooth finish.

DRY $35 –V

Radburnd Hawke's Bay Chardonnay   (★★★★★)

From winemaker Kate Radburnd, best known for her long spell at Pask (1990–2017), the classy, youthful 2018 vintage (★★★★★) was grown at Mangatahi and Bridge Pa, hand-picked and fermented and matured for 11 months in French oak puncheons and barriques (new and seasoned). Full of potential, it is mouthfilling and highly concentrated, with deep, citrusy, peachy flavours, woven with fresh acidity, finely integrated oak, and impressive vigour, complexity and length. A top debut, it's well worth cellaring to 2022+.

DRY $85 AV

Rapaura Springs Bouldevines Vineyard Omaka Valley
Marlborough Chardonnay   (★★★★★)

The classy young 2019 vintage (★★★★★) was grown on stony soils at the entrance to the Omaka Valley and handled in French oak casks (47 per cent new). Bright, light lemon/green, with a fragrant, complex, slightly smoky bouquet, it is a powerful wine, mouthfilling and youthful, with vibrant stone-fruit and biscuity oak flavours, a slightly creamy texture and a very long, harmonious finish. Best drinking 2022+.

Vintage	19
WR	7
Drink	20-25

DRY $37 AV

Rapaura Springs Reserve Marlborough Chardonnay   ★★★★

Enjoyable young, the 2018 vintage (★★★★) is a vibrantly fruity wine, grown in the Southern Valleys and partly barrel-fermented. Bright, light yellow/green, it has rich, peachy, slightly toasty flavours, fresh acidity, and a finely balanced finish. Drink now or cellar.

Vintage	18	17	16	15
WR	5	6	6	7
Drink	20-24	20-25	20-23	20-24

DRY $29 AV

Rapaura Springs The Oaks Vineyard Omaka Valley
Marlborough Chardonnay   (★★★★☆)

The youthful 2018 vintage (★★★★☆) was hand-picked and fermented in French oak barriques and puncheons (40 per cent new). Bright, light lemon/green, with a fragrant, toasty bouquet, it is mouthfilling and creamy-textured, with concentrated, vibrant grapefruit and peach flavours, and a finely balanced, lingering finish. Best drinking mid-2021+.

DRY $37 –V

Renato Nelson Chardonnay ★★★★

The mouthfilling, generous 2018 vintage (★★★★) was estate-grown on the coast, at Kina, and fermented and matured for nine months in French oak barriques (20 per cent new). Bright, light lemon/green, it is full-bodied, with strong, ripe stone-fruit flavours, seasoned with toasty oak, balanced acidity, and good complexity.

Vintage	19	18	17	16	15	14
WR	7	6	7	6	6	6
Drink	22-25	20-24	20-23	20-22	20-22	20-21

DRY $26 AV

Rimu Grove Nelson Chardonnay ★★★★☆

This wine is typically full of personality. Estate-grown near the coast in the Moutere hills and fermented and lees-matured for 11 months in French oak casks, the bright, light yellow/green 2019 vintage (★★★★☆) has a fragrant, slightly oaky bouquet, leading into a full-bodied, youthful wine with fresh acidity and strong, ripe, peachy, nutty flavours, showing very good complexity. Best drinking 2022+.

Vintage	19	18	17	16	15	14	13
WR	7	7	6	7	7	7	7
Drink	20-35	20-32	20-30	20-30	20-30	20-25	20-28

DRY $52 –V

Riverby Estate Marlborough Chardonnay ★★★★

Enjoyable now, but worth cellaring, the 2018 vintage (★★★★) was fermented in French oak casks (25 per cent new). Bright, light yellow/green, it is full-bodied, with ripe, peachy, slightly buttery flavours, finely integrated oak, and very good harmony and depth.

Vintage	18
WR	7
Drink	21-30

DRY $28 AV

Riverview Hawke's Bay Chardonnay (★★★★☆)

Still on sale, the vigorous 2015 vintage (★★★★☆) was estate-grown at a cool, elevated, inland site and fermented and matured in French oak casks (50 per cent new). An elegant, tightly structured wine, it has very good intensity of grapefruit and peach flavours, barrel-ferment complexity, fresh acidity and a lengthy finish. (From The Wine Portfolio.)

DRY $26 V+

Roaring Meg Central Otago Chardonnay (★★★☆)

From Mt Difficulty, the very easy-drinking 2018 vintage (★★★☆) was handled in stainless steel tanks, concrete eggs and oak barrels. Bright, light lemon/green, it is full-bodied, with fresh, citrusy fruit flavours to the fore, good depth, creamy notes, and a smooth finish.

DRY $30 –V

Rock Ferry 3rd Rock Marlborough Chardonnay

(★★★★☆)

Certified organic, the 2018 vintage (★★★★☆) was estate-grown at Rapaura and matured for 11 months in one barrique and one puncheon. It has a fragrant, slightly biscuity and creamy bouquet. Mouthfilling and fresh, it is still youthful, with good concentration of citrusy, peachy flavours, mealy, nutty notes adding complexity, balanced acidity, and obvious cellaring potential. Best drinking 2021+.

DRY $45 –V

Rock Ferry The Corners Vineyard Marlborough Chardonnay

★★★★★

The highly distinctive 2018 vintage (★★★★★) was fermented in a concrete egg, rather than oak barrels. Bright yellow/slight green, it is mouthfilling, crisp and concentrated, with fresh, lively, citrusy, peachy flavours, showing impressive intensity and complexity, and a dry, long finish. Best drinking 2021+. Certified organic.

DRY $55 AV

Rogue Vine The Debonair Rogue Bay of Islands Chardonnay

★★★★

From a Kerikeri-based company, the 2019 vintage (★★★★) was French oak-aged. Already drinking well, it is mouthfilling, with a creamy bouquet and ripe stone-fruit flavours, rich and rounded.

DRY $28 AV

Rongopai Hawke's Bay Chardonnay

★★☆

The 2017 vintage (★★★) is a 'fruit-driven' style, handled entirely in stainless steel tanks. Fresh and lively, with peachy, slightly spicy flavours, showing a touch of complexity, it offers good, easy drinking. (From Babich.)

DRY $19 –V

Ruru Central Otago Chardonnay

★★★☆

Enjoyable young, the 2019 vintage (★★★★) was grown at Alexandra and partly barrel-fermented. Bright, light yellow, it's an upfront style, mouthfilling, fresh and buttery, with ripe, peachy, slightly toasty flavours, balanced acidity, and good intensity. Drink now or cellar. (From Immigrant's Vineyard.)

DRY $24 AV

Sacred Hill Hawke's Bay Chardonnay

★★★

Lemon-scented, the 2018 vintage (★★★) is a vibrantly fruity wine, estate-grown in the Riflemans Vineyard. Citrusy and peachy, with fresh acidity, it has moderate complexity, and good drink-young appeal.

DRY $17 AV

Sacred Hill Reserve Hawke's Bay Chardonnay ★★★★

Finely balanced for early enjoyment, the 2018 vintage (★★★★) is a vibrantly fruity wine, fermented and lees-aged in an even split of tanks and French oak barriques (25 per cent new). It is fragrant and harmonious, with fresh, generous stone-fruit flavours to the fore, lively acidity, and slightly toasty, buttery notes adding complexity.

DRY $22 V+

Vintage	16	15
WR	7	5
Drink	P	P

Sacred Hill Riflemans Chardonnay ★★★★★

Sacred Hill's flagship Chardonnay is one of New Zealand's greatest – powerful yet elegant, with striking intensity and outstanding cellaring potential. Grown in the cool, inland, elevated (100 metres above sea level) Riflemans Vineyard in the Dartmoor Valley of Hawke's Bay, it is hand-picked from mature, own-rooted, Mendoza-clone vines and fermented with indigenous yeasts in French oak barriques (80 per cent new in 2019). The 2019 vintage (★★★★★) is bright, light lemon/green, with a fragrant, complex, slightly smoky bouquet. Mouthfilling, vibrant and concentrated, it is highly refined, with deep, very youthful stone-fruit and toasty oak flavours, poised, rich and very harmonious. Best drinking 2022+.

DRY $70 AV

Sacred Hill Single Vineyard Hawke's Bay Chardonnay (★★★☆)

Enjoyable young, the 2018 vintage (★★★☆) was grown in the Riflemans Vineyard and fermented and lees-aged for 10 months in French oak barriques (30 per cent new). Made in an upfront style, it is fresh and full-bodied, with a slightly smoky bouquet, peachy, slightly toasty flavours, good vigour, and a crisp, dry finish.

DRY $25 –V

Sacred Hill Wine Thief Hawke's Bay Chardonnay ★★★★☆

Designed as a 'richer and toastier' style than the flagship Riflemans Chardonnay (above), this wine is grown in the same vineyard, hand-picked and fermented with indigenous yeasts in French oak barriques (50 per cent new in 2019). The 2019 vintage (★★★★☆) is a youthful, tightly structured wine, mouthfilling and vibrant, with concentrated, ripe stone-fruit flavours, a strong, toasty oak influence, good complexity, slightly smoky notes, fresh acidity and a lengthy finish. Best drinking 2022+.

DRY $35 –V

Saint Clair Omaka Reserve Marlborough Chardonnay ★★★★☆

This is typically a fat, creamy wine, weighty and rich, made in a bold, upfront style. Grown in the Southern Valleys – mostly in the company's vineyard in the Omaka Valley – it is hand-picked, fermented and lees-aged for 10 months in American oak casks, and given a full, softening malolactic fermentation. The 2018 vintage (★★★★☆) is a youthful, full-bodied wine, with strong, peachy, slightly toasty flavours, fresh acidity, and a lingering, creamy-textured, very harmonious finish. Best drinking 2021+.

Vintage	18	17	16	15	14	13
WR	6	6	7	7	7	7
Drink	20-22	20-21	P	P	P	P

DRY $40 –V

Saint Clair Origin Marlborough Chardonnay (★★★★)

Skilfully crafted, the 2017 vintage (★★★★) of this 'fruit-driven' Chardonnay was grown in the Wairau Valley and fermented in a mix of tanks and French and American oak barrels. Mouthfilling, it is vibrantly fruity, with very good depth of grapefruit and peach flavours, finely balanced acidity, slightly toasty, buttery notes adding complexity, and a fresh, dry finish.

DRY $22 V+

Saint Clair Pioneer Block 10 Twin Hills Marlborough Chardonnay ★★★★★

Already delicious, the 2018 vintage (★★★★★) was grown mostly in the company's Omaka Valley vineyard. Fermented and lees-aged for 10 months in French and American oak casks (50 per cent new), it is mouthfilling and fleshy, with peachy, slightly biscuity flavours, showing excellent complexity and richness, balanced acidity, and a long, rounded finish. Best drinking 2021+.

DRY $33 V+

Sanctuary Marlborough Chardonnay ★★★

The attractive, easy-drinking 2018 vintage (★★★) was handled in an even split of tanks and old French oak barriques. Full-bodied, it has vibrant, citrusy, slightly appley flavours to the fore, fresh acidity and a smooth finish. (From Grove Mill.)

DRY $20 –V

Satyr by Sileni Estates Kereru Hawke's Bay Chardonnay ★★★☆

The 2019 vintage (★★★☆) was hand-picked and barrel-fermented. Bright, light lemon/green, it is lively, with generous, vibrant, peachy flavours, showing moderate complexity, fresh acidity, and lots of drink-young appeal. Good value.

DRY $15 V+

Scout Lowburn Central Otago Chardonnay (★★★★)

The debut 2019 vintage (★★★★) was grown at two Lowburn sites, hand-picked and fermented with indigenous yeasts in French oak barriques (20 per cent new). Bright, light lemon/green, it is fresh and lively, with citrusy, appley, biscuity flavours, showing good delicacy, balanced acidity, and a very harmonious finish. Best drinking mid-2021+.

DRY $34 –V

Scout Southern Valleys Marlborough Chardonnay   (★★★★☆)

Already enjoyable, the 2019 vintage (★★★★☆) is a single-vineyard wine, grown in the Southern Valleys, hand-picked, fermented with indigenous yeasts in French oak casks (20 per cent new), and bottled unfined and unfiltered. Pale lemon/green, it is a weighty, sweet-fruited, smooth wine, with a slightly creamy bouquet and strong, peachy, citrusy, biscuity flavours, lively and persistent.

DRY $34 AV

Seifried Nelson Chardonnay   ★★★

The attractive 2019 vintage (★★★☆) was tank-fermented, lees-aged for over a year in French oak barriques (one to three years old), and given a full, softening malolactic fermentation. Bright, light yellow/green, with a slightly toasty bouquet, it has very good depth of peachy, slightly creamy flavours and a smooth, very harmonious finish. Enjoyable young, it offers fine value.

Vintage	19	18	17	16	15	14	13
WR	6	6	6	6	6	6	6
Drink	20-28	20-28	20-27	20-26	20-25	20-24	20-21

DRY $19 AV

Seifried Winemaker's Collection Nelson Barrique Fermented Chardonnay   ★★★★

This is typically a bold style, concentrated and creamy, with loads of flavour. The powerful 2017 vintage (★★★★☆) was fermented and matured for a year in French oak barriques. It is mouthfilling, with strong stone-fruit and spice flavours, toasty oak, good complexity, fresh acidity and obvious potential; best drinking 2021+.

DRY $26 AV

Seresin Chardonnay Reserve   ★★★★★

Finesse is the keynote quality of this organically certified Marlborough wine. Estate-grown in the Raupo Creek Vineyard, in the Omaka Valley, the 2016 vintage (★★★★★) was hand-picked, fermented with indigenous yeasts and lees-aged for 11 months in French oak barriques (15 per cent new), then blended and matured for a further six months in old French oak puncheons. Weighty and complex, it's a powerful wine, with deep, still youthful, citrusy, peachy flavours and a very harmonious finish. Drink now or cellar.

DRY $45 AV

Seresin Marlborough Chardonnay   ★★★★☆

This stylish, BioGro-certified wine is designed to 'focus on the textural element of the palate rather than emphasising primary fruit characters'. It is typically a full-bodied and complex wine with good mouthfeel, ripe melon/citrus characters shining through, subtle toasty oak and fresh acidity. The 2018 vintage (★★★★☆) was estate-grown in the Raupo Creek Vineyard, in the Omaka Valley, hand-picked, and the majority of the blend (75 per cent) was fermented with indigenous yeasts and lees-aged for 10 months in French oak puncheons (10 per cent new).

Bright, light yellow/green, it is fragrant, fresh and full-bodied, with ripe, citrusy, slightly peachy flavours, gently seasoned with oak, balanced acidity, and a finely balanced finish. Best drinking 2022+. Good value.

Settler Crownthorpe Hawke's Bay Chardonnay   (★★★☆)

Still on sale, the 2016 vintage (★★★☆) was estate-grown at a cool, elevated site in inland Hawke's Bay, barrel-fermented and oak-aged for nine months. Fresh and mouthfilling, it has good vigour and depth of flavour, a touch of complexity, and a crisp finish. Ready.

Sileni Cellar Selection Hawke's Bay Chardonnay   ★★★☆

The 2019 vintage (★★★★) is the best yet. Made in a 'lightly oaked' style, it is an instantly appealing wine, mouthfilling and sweet-fruited, with very satisfying weight and depth of ripe, peachy flavours, hints of toast and butterscotch, and fresh, balanced acidity. Best drinking mid-2021+.

Sileni Grand Reserve Lodge Hawke's Bay Chardonnay   ★★★★☆

Fresh, youthful and finely balanced, the 2018 vintage (★★★★☆) was fermented and lees-aged for 10 months in French oak barriques. Fragrant, with concentrated, ripe stone-fruit flavours, buttery and toasty notes adding complexity, and good acid spine, it has obvious cellaring potential. Best drinking mid-2021+.

Sileni Reserve Oaked Hawke's Bay Chardonnay   (★★★☆)

The 2018 vintage (★★★☆) is a fresh and lively, medium-bodied wine, with peachy, toasty, slightly buttery flavours. A moderately complex style with balanced acidity and good depth, it's a drink-now or cellaring proposition.

Smith & Sheth Cru Heretaunga Chardonnay   ★★★★★

Described by the producer as 'almost Chablis-like in style', the 2018 vintage (★★★★☆) was hand-picked from mature vines in the Bridge Pa Triangle and at Mangatahi. Fermented and lees-aged for 10 months in French oak barriques (19 per cent new), it is a very age-worthy wine, medium to full-bodied, with strong, crisp, citrusy flavours, peachy notes, a subtle seasoning of oak, and a slightly buttery finish. Best drinking 2022+.

DRY $40 AV

Smith & Sheth Cru Howell Vineyard Chardonnay   ★★★★★

From 20-year-old vines in the Bridge Pa Triangle, Hawke's Bay, the highly refined 2018 vintage (★★★★★) was hand-picked and fermented and matured for 10 months in French oak barriques (67 per cent new). Bright, light lemon/green, it is weighty, fleshy and rounded, with rich, ripe stone-fruit and toasty oak flavours, savoury and complex, fine acidity and a long, seamless finish. Already delicious, it should be at its best 2022+.

DRY $60 AV

Smith & Sheth Cru Mangatahi Chardonnay ★★★★★

The youthful 2018 vintage (★★★★★) was hand-picked from mature vines in the elevated, inland district of Mangatahi, in Hawke's Bay, and fermented and aged for 10 months in French oak barriques (50 per cent new). Bright, light yellow/green, with a highly fragrant, slightly smoky bouquet, it has a real sense of youthful vigour. A powerful, weighty wine with concentrated, peachy, toasty, complex flavours, it needs time; open 2022+.

DRY $60 AV

Snapper Rock Hawke's Bay Chardonnay (★★★☆)

Priced right, the 2018 vintage (★★★☆) is enjoyable young. Bright, light yellow, it is mouthfilling, with ripe stone-fruit flavours, hints of butter and honey, moderate complexity, and very good depth. Drink now to 2021.

DRY $17 V+

Soho Carter Waiheke Island Chardonnay ★★★★☆

This estate-grown, single-vineyard wine is hand-harvested at Onetangi and fermented and matured in French oak barriques. The 2017 vintage (★★★★☆) has excellent poise and depth. Mouthfilling, with strong, fresh, peachy, slightly nutty flavours and finely balanced acidity, it's drinking well now.

DRY $40 –V

Soljans Estate Fifth Generation Series Kumeu Chardonnay (★★★★★)

The highly impressive 2016 vintage (★★★★★) was estate-grown and hand-picked at Kumeu, in West Auckland, and matured for 18 months in French oak barriques. Full-bodied, rich and smooth, it's a powerful style with concentrated, complex stone-fruit flavours, gentle acidity, and a finely textured, very harmonious, lasting finish. Already delicious, it's likely to be at its best 2021+.

DRY $48 AV

Spade Oak The Prospect Ormond Gisborne Chardonnay ★★★★☆

The attractive 2018 vintage (★★★★☆), harvested from young vines, was fermented and matured for 10 months in French oak barrels (15 per cent new). Despite a label reference to 'lashings of toasty vanillin oak', it's a harmonious wine, fresh and full-bodied, with generous, ripe stone-fruit flavours, enriched but not dominated by oak, balanced acidity, very good complexity, and a lengthy finish. Drink now or cellar.

DRY $28 V+

Spade Oak Vigneron Gisborne Chardonnay ★★★★☆

Retasted in 2020, the 2015 vintage (★★★★★) is probably in full stride. A single-vineyard wine, it was fermented and matured for 10 months in oak barrels (25 per cent new). Bright yellow/green, it is a classy, weighty wine with deep stone-fruit flavours, slightly buttery and toasty notes adding complexity, balanced acidity, and a finely poised, very harmonious finish. The 2018 vintage (★★★★☆) is bright, light yellow, with substantial body and loads of peachy, buttery, slightly creamy flavour, showing excellent complexity. Drink now or cellar.

DRY $30 AV

Spade Oak Vineyard V Gisborne Chardonnay ★★★

The 'V' on the label of the 2018 vintage (★★★) is a reference to the winemaker, Steve Voysey, an industry veteran. Drinking well now, it is fresh and lively, with a touch of complexity and plenty of ripe, peachy, slightly toasty flavour.

DRY $19 AV

Spinyback Nelson Chardonnay ★★★

From Waimea Estates, the 2018 vintage (★★★) is enjoyable now. Mouthfilling, with a fragrant, citrusy bouquet, gentle acidity and good depth of peachy, citrusy, slightly buttery flavours, it's priced sharply.

DRY $15 V+

Spring Creek Estate Marlborough Chardonnay (★★★)

Priced right, the 2018 vintage (★★★) is drinking well now. Bright, light yellow/green, it is a 'fruit-driven', uncomplicated wine, lemon-scented, with satisfying depth of fresh, ripe, citrusy flavours, balanced acidity and a dry finish. (From Hunter's.)

DRY $17 AV

Spy Valley Envoy Johnson Vineyard Marlborough Chardonnay ★★★★★

This elegant, tightly structured wine is estate-grown in the Waihopai Valley, hand-harvested, fermented with indigenous yeasts and lees-aged in French oak barriques (mostly seasoned) for up to 20 months. Currently on sale, the 2015 vintage (★★★★☆) is bright, light yellow/green, with vigorous, citrusy, peachy, slightly toasty flavours, showing very good intensity. Still youthful, it should be at its best 2022+.

Vintage	15	14	13	12
WR	6	6	6	6
Drink	20-23	20-22	20-21	P

DRY $35 AV

Spy Valley Marlborough Chardonnay ★★★★

The elegant, still youthful 2017 vintage (★★★★) was estate-grown at two sites – in the Johnson Vineyard, in the lower Waihopai Valley, and the Outpost Vineyard, in the Omaka Valley. Hand-harvested and matured for 11 months in French oak barrels, it is a fresh, medium-bodied wine, bright, light lemon/green, with vibrant, peachy, mealy flavours, a subtle seasoning of biscuity oak, lively acidity, and very good complexity and depth. Best drinking mid-2021+.

DRY $25 AV

Stables Reserve Ngatarawa Hawke's Bay Chardonnay ★★★

The 2018 vintage (★★★) is a partly barrel-fermented wine, vibrant and full-bodied, with fresh, peachy, slightly toasty flavours, showing a touch of complexity, balanced acidity, and a slightly creamy finish.

DRY $20 –V

Staete Landt Josephine Marlborough Chardonnay   ★★★★☆

This single-vineyard wine is estate-grown at Rapaura, in the Wairau Valley. The 2018 vintage (★★★★) was hand-harvested and fermented and matured in French oak barriques. Bright, light yellow/green, it is medium to full-bodied, with strong, vibrant, peachy, slightly citrusy flavours, gently seasoned with biscuity oak, and a crisp, tightly structured finish. Still developing, it should be at its best mid-2021+.

DRY $28 V+

Starborough Marlborough Chardonnay   ★★★★☆

The powerful 2019 vintage (★★★★☆) is a single-vineyard, Awatere Valley wine, handled in French oak casks (40 per cent new). Bright, light yellow/green, it has a fragrant, ripe, slightly buttery bouquet. An extroverted wine, already drinking well, it is mouthfilling, with concentrated, peachy, slightly toasty flavours. Drink now or cellar.

DRY $28 V+

State of Flux Yealands Estate Awatere Valley Marlborough Chardonnay   (★★★★)

Labelled as a 'Chablis-style', the 2018 vintage (★★★★) was grown at an inland site, hand-harvested from mature vines, and fermented and matured for 11 months in an egg-shaped concrete vessel. Bright, light lemon/green, it has a citrusy bouquet, leading into a medium to full-bodied wine with strong, grapefruit-like flavours, slightly buttery notes, and very good delicacy, vigour and length.

DRY $40 –V

Stone Bridge Gisborne Chardonnay   ★★★★

Still on sale and drinking well now, the 2015 vintage (★★★★) was hand-harvested and fermented and matured for over a year in French oak barrels (25 per cent new). Bright, light gold, it is mouthfilling and fleshy, with generous, ripe, peachy, toasty flavours and a smooth, slightly buttery finish.

DRY $25 AV

Stonecroft Gimblett Gravels Hawke's Bay Chardonnay   ★★★★☆

Certified organic, the 2019 vintage (★★★★☆) is a single-vineyard wine, estate-grown at Roys Hill. Fermented and matured for six months in seasoned French oak barrels, it was given a full, softening malolactic fermentation. Bright, light yellow/green, it is fresh, full-bodied, sweet-fruited and generous, with concentrated stone-fruit flavours, well-integrated oak and a well-rounded finish. Still youthful but already drinking well, it should be at its best 2021+.

Vintage	19	18	17	16	15	14	13
WR	7	7	6	5	6	6	6
Drink	20-26	20-26	20-24	20-22	20-22	20-21	P

DRY $27 V+

Stonecroft Old Vine Gimblett Gravels Hawke's Bay Chardonnay   ★★★★★

The impressive 2019 vintage (★★★★★) is a rare wine – only three barrels were made. From vines planted in Mere Road in 1992, it was hand-picked, fermented and matured for 10 months in French oak casks (35 per cent new), and given a full, softening malolactic fermentation.

Bright, light lemon/green, it is mouthfilling and sweet-fruited, with concentrated, ripe stone-fruit flavours, showing excellent complexity, a slightly creamy texture and a rich, harmonious finish. Already delicious, it should be at its best 2022+.

Vintage	19
WR	7
Drink	21-27

 DRY $45 AV

Stoneleigh Latitude Marlborough Chardonnay ★★★★

Grown at Rapaura, the 2019 vintage (★★★★) offers fine value. Bright, light yellow/green, it is full-bodied and sweet-fruited, with a slightly smoky bouquet, good concentration of vibrant, ripe stone-fruit flavours, finely integrated oak, and some aging potential. Best drinking mid-2021+.

 DRY $22 V+

Stoneleigh Marlborough Chardonnay ★★★

Offering very easy-drinking, the 2019 vintage (★★★) is vibrantly fruity, with good depth of ripe, peachy flavours, a touch of complexity and a smooth finish. Best drinking mid-2021+.

DRY $14 V+

Stoneleigh Rapaura Series Single Vineyard Marlborough Chardonnay ★★★★☆

This single-vineyard wine is fermented and matured in new and one-year-old French oak casks. The 2018 vintage (★★★★☆) is bright, light lemon/green, with a fragrant, smoky bouquet. Mouthfilling, with a strong sense of youthful drive, it has strong, ripe stone-fruit and toast flavours, showing good vigour and complexity, and a tight finish. Best drinking 2021+.

 DRY $25 V+

Stoneleigh Wild Valley Marlborough Chardonnay ★★★☆

Offering fine value, the 2019 vintage (★★★★) was fermented with indigenous ('wild') yeasts. Bright, light yellow/green, it is mouthfilling, with ripe, peachy flavours, showing very good vigour and depth, a distinct touch of complexity, and a finely poised finish. Best drinking mid-2021+.

 DRY $19 V+

Sugar Loaf Marlborough Chardonnay ★★★★☆

The classy 2017 vintage (★★★★☆) was estate-grown at Rapaura, hand-harvested and fermented in French oak casks (25 per cent new). Fragrant and smooth, with grapefruit-like flavours to the fore, peachy, nutty notes and a well-rounded finish, it's a restrained, delicate, finely poised wine, showing excellent complexity and harmony.

 DRY $28 V+

Summerhouse Marlborough Chardonnay ★★★☆

Enjoyable young, the 2019 vintage (★★★☆) is bright, light lemon/green, with a freshly scented bouquet. Mouthfilling, it is lively, with very good depth of citrusy, peachy flavours, showing a distinct touch of complexity.

Vintage	19
WR	5
Drink	20-25

 DRY $19 V+

Tatty Bogler Waitaki Valley North Otago Chardonnay ★★★★☆

The very elegant, subtle 2018 vintage (★★★★★) was matured for 10 months in old oak barrels. Showing good cellaring potential, it is mouthfilling, fresh and youthful, with vibrant, citrusy, peachy flavours, finely integrated oak and a lasting finish. Best drinking 2022+. (From Forrest Estate.)

 DRY $35 –V

Te Awa Single Estate Hawke's Bay Chardonnay ★★★★☆

The youthful 2019 vintage (★★★★☆) was fermented and matured in French oak hogsheads (35 per cent new). Bright, light yellow/green, with a fresh, slightly smoky bouquet, it is mouthfilling, with vibrant stone-fruit flavours, gently seasoned with toasty oak, and a crisp, finely poised finish. Best drinking 2022+.

Vintage	19	18	17	16	15	14
WR	6	7	7	7	7	6
Drink	21-25	20-29	20-28	20-25	20-25	20-24

 DRY $25 V+

Te Awanga Estate Hawke's Bay Chardonnay ★★★★

The 2018 vintage (★★★★) was partly hand-picked and partly barrel-fermented. Enjoyable young, it is fresh and lively, with very good depth of citrusy, slightly peachy flavours, a restrained oak influence, appetising acidity, and a lengthy finish.

 DRY $25 AV

Te Awanga Estate One Off Underground Organic Hawke's Bay Chardonnay (★★★★☆)

Certified organic, the 2018 vintage (★★★★☆) was grown at Maraekakaho. A distinctive wine, it is weighty, fleshy, vibrantly fruity and smooth, with generous, ripe stone-fruit flavours, showing good complexity and harmony, a slightly creamy texture and a welcoming fragrance. Drink now or cellar.

DRY $35 –V

Te Kairanga John Martin Martinborough Chardonnay   ★★★★☆

Made from the 'best vineyard parcels', this wine is fermented and matured in French oak puncheons (27 per cent new in 2018). The 2018 vintage (★★★★☆) has strong, ripe stone-fruit flavours, gently seasoned with toasty oak, and excellent delicacy, harmony and depth. Best drinking 2021+.

Vintage	18	17
WR	7	6
Drink	20-27	20-25

 DRY $40 –V

Te Kairanga Martinborough Chardonnay   ★★★★

The stylish, very harmonious 2018 vintage (★★★★) was fermented and matured in French oak puncheons (19 per cent new). Fresh, mouthfilling and finely balanced, it has strong, ripe stone-fruit flavours, gently seasoned with toasty oak, good complexity, and lots of drink-young appeal.

 DRY $25 AV

Te Mata Elston Chardonnay   ★★★★★

One of New Zealand's most illustrious Chardonnays, Elston is a stylish, intense, slowly evolving Hawke's Bay wine. At around four years old, it is notably complete, showing concentration and finesse. The grapes are grown and hand-picked principally at two sites in the Te Mata hills in Havelock North, and the wine is fully fermented in French oak barriques (35 per cent), with full malolactic fermentation. The 2018 vintage (★★★★★) is weighty, rich and rounded. Light lemon/green, it is highly fragrant and finely poised, with deep, ripe grapefruit and peach flavours, integrated oak and fresh acidity. Powerful yet subtle, it should break into full stride 2022+.

Vintage	18	17
WR	7	6
Drink	20-23	20-22

 DRY $40 AV

🍇🍇🍇

Te Mata Estate Vineyards Hawke's Bay Chardonnay   ★★★★

This good-value, consistently attractive wine is sourced from the company's vineyards at Woodthorpe Terraces, in the Dartmoor Valley, the Bridge Pa Triangle and at Havelock North. Fermented and lees-aged in an even split of tanks and seasoned French oak barrels, it is typically a harmonious wine with fresh, ripe grapefruit characters to the fore, a gentle seasoning of biscuity oak, very good depth and a touch of complexity. The 2018 vintage (★★★★) is fresh, full-bodied and youthful, with strong grapefruit and stone-fruit flavours, showing a distinct touch of complexity, a slightly creamy texture and a persistent finish. Best drinking 2021+.

Vintage	18	17	16	15
WR	7	6	6	6
Drink	20-22	20-21	P	P

DRY $22 V+

te Pā Marlborough Chardonnay   ★★★★☆

The 2019 vintage (★★★★☆) was fermented and matured in French oak barrels (40 per cent new). It is fragrant, mouthfilling and lively, with concentrated, peachy, citrusy flavours, slightly smoky notes, a hint of toasty oak and good complexity. Best drinking 2022+. Fine value.

DRY $25 V+

te Pā The Reserve Collection St Leonard's Marlborough Chardonnay   ★★★★★

The impressive 2018 vintage (★★★★★) is a single-vineyard wine, grown in the central Wairau Valley, hand-picked, barrel-fermented (50 per cent new oak), and bottled unfined and unfiltered. It has light lemon/green, not entirely clear, colour. Weighty and rich, it is still youthful, with concentrated, ripe, peachy, citrusy flavours, showing excellent delicacy, biscuity and mealy notes adding complexity, gentle acidity, and a very harmonious, rounded finish. Best drinking 2022+.

DRY $60 AV

Te Whau Vineyard Waiheke Island Chardonnay   ★★★★★

For its vintage-to-vintage consistency, this was Te Whau's finest wine, full of personality, but the 2017 vintage (★★★★☆) is the last. An elegant wine, it has ripe, peachy flavours, a hint of pear, a subtle seasoning of oak, excellent delicacy, balanced acidity and a lasting finish. Best drinking 2021+.

DRY $95 –V

Terra Sancta Riverblock Bannockburn Central Otago Chardonnay   ★★★★☆

The stylish, youthful 2018 vintage (★★★★☆) is well worth cellaring. Estate-grown, hand-harvested and fermented in French oak puncheons (25 per cent new), it has a citrusy, slightly creamy bouquet. Mouthfilling, it is vibrantly fruity, with strong, grapefruit-like flavours, gentle biscuity notes, balanced acidity, and a very harmonious, lingering finish.

Vintage	18	17	16	15	14
WR	6	6	7	7	7
Drink	20-27	20-26	20-23	20-21	20-22

DRY $31 AV

Testify Te Awanga Hawke's Bay Chardonnay   (★★★★★)

The classy, youthful 2018 vintage (★★★★★) was grown near the coast, at Te Awanga, and fermented in new French oak casks. Bright, light lemon/green, with a fragrant, gently smoky bouquet, it is mouthfilling and lively, with concentrated, ripe, peachy flavours, finely integrated oak, impressive complexity, fresh acidity and a lengthy finish. Best drinking 2022+. (From Decibel.)

DRY $44 AV

Thomas Waiheke Island Chardonnay

The powerful 2018 vintage (★★★★☆) was barrel-fermented and lees-aged for over a year. Straw/pale gold, it is mouthfilling and concentrated, with fresh acidity, ripe stone-fruit flavours and biscuity, smoky notes adding complexity. Still youthful, it's worth cellaring to 2022+.

`DRY $46 –V`

Thornbury Gisborne Chardonnay

Offering great value, the 2018 vintage (★★★☆) is a softly mouthfilling wine, with very satisfying depth of fresh, ripe, peachy, slightly toasty flavour, gentle acidity, a slightly creamy texture, and a smooth finish. A typical regional style, it's enjoyable young. (From Villa Maria.)

Vintage	18
WR	6
Drink	20-22

`DRY $16 V+`

Three Paddles Martinborough Chardonnay

From Nga Waka, the 2018 vintage (★★★☆) is a lightly oaked, 'fruit-driven' style, enjoyable young. Vibrantly fruity, it has ripe stone-fruit flavours to the fore, with a hint of toasty oak, balanced acidity, and a smooth finish.

Vintage	18
WR	6
Drink	20-21

`DRY $18 AV`

Tiki Hawke's Bay Chardonnay ★★★

Drinking well now, the 2017 vintage (★★★☆) is vibrantly fruity, with good depth of fresh, ripe grapefruit-like flavours, slightly buttery and toasty notes, and a well-rounded finish.

Vintage	17
WR	6
Drink	20-21

`DRY $20 –V`

Tiki Koro Hawke's Bay Chardonnay

Rich but elegant, the 2018 vintage (★★★★★) was hand-picked and fermented and lees-aged in French oak casks (55 per cent new). It is a full-bodied, very age-worthy wine, with deep, vibrant stone-fruit flavours, finely balanced acidity, and excellent complexity and length. Best drinking 2021+.

Vintage	18
WR	6
Drink	20-22

`DRY $35 AV`

Tiki Single Vineyard Hawke's Bay Chardonnay

The 2018 vintage (★★★★) is a single-vineyard wine, fermented and matured for 10 months in French oak barriques. Enjoyable young, it is an upfront style, full-bodied, with ripe stone-fruit, toast and butterscotch flavours, rich and rounded.

Vintage	18
WR	6
Drink	P

DRY $25 AV

Tohu Gisborne Chardonnay

The 2018 vintage (★★★☆) is an easy-drinking, 'fruit-driven' style, tank-fermented with the use of oak. It is full-bodied, fresh and vibrant, with ripe, peachy, slightly toasty flavours, and a creamy-smooth finish. Enjoyable young.

DRY $20 AV

Tohu Hemi Reserve Marlborough Chardonnay

The 2016 vintage (★★★★) was hand-harvested from estate-grown vines in the Awatere Valley and fermented in old French oak barriques. An elegant wine with fresh, citrusy scents, it has vibrant, grapefruit-like flavours, a slightly minerally streak, good complexity and a lingering finish. Best drinking 2021+.

DRY $38 –V

Tohu Single Vineyard Whenua Awa Awatere Valley Marlborough Chardonnay

The elegant 2017 vintage (★★★★★) is a distinctly cool-climate wine, grown in the upper Awatere Valley and French oak-aged. Bright, light lemon/green, with a fragrant, fresh, slightly smoky bouquet, it is vigorous, with intense, peachy, citrusy flavours, oak complexity, and a finely balanced, long finish. Best drinking 2021+.

DRY $36 AV

Tohu Single Vineyard Whenua Matua Upper Moutere Nelson Chardonnay

Well worth cellaring, the 2017 vintage (★★★★☆) is a fresh, elegant, vigorous wine with strong, citrusy, peachy flavours, toasty and smoky notes adding complexity, appetising acidity and a poised, slightly creamy finish. Best drinking 2021+.

DRY $30 AV

Toi Toi Gisborne Chardonnay ★★★

Offering easy, early drinking, the 2019 vintage (★★★) is mouthfilling and vibrantly fruity, with fresh, peachy, slightly spicy flavours to the fore, just a hint of oak and a smooth finish. Still youthful, it should be at its best during 2021.

DRY $17 AV

Toi Toi Reserve Gisborne Chardonnay ★★★★

The 2018 vintage (★★★★☆) is a sturdy, sweet-fruited wine, in the classic regional style. Pale gold, it has concentrated, ripe, peachy flavours, with toasty and buttery notes adding richness and complexity, and finely balanced acidity. Made in a generous, 'full-on' style, it's a drink-now or cellaring proposition.

DRY $29 AV

Tony Bish Fat and Sassy Hawke's Bay Chardonnay (★★★★)

'All curves and lusciousness with exceptional sass', the 2019 vintage (★★★★) was made with use of barrel fermentation and a softening malolactic fermentation. Bright, light yellow/green, it is a generous, upfront style, fruity and creamy-textured, with mouthfilling body and ripe, peachy flavours, very smooth and harmonious. Drink young.

Vintage	19
WR	6
Drink	20-21

DRY $22 V+

Tony Bish Golden Egg Hawke's Bay Chardonnay ★★★★★

The distinctive, very age-worthy 2018 vintage (★★★★★) was hand-picked at Te Awanga and handled in concrete egg-shaped fermenters, which 'create natural convection currents, holding the yeast lees in suspension'. Bright, light yellow/green, it is a very elegant style, subtle and satisfying, with concentrated, citrusy, peachy flavours, showing good complexity, balanced acidity, and a lasting finish. Best drinking 2022+.

Vintage	18
WR	7
Drink	20-24

DRY $40 AV

Tony Bish Heartwood Hawke's Bay Chardonnay ★★★★☆

Still very youthful, the 2019 vintage (★★★★☆) was hand-picked and fermented and matured in French oak barriques (30 per cent new). Bright, light yellow/green, with a fragrant, slightly oaky bouquet, it is mouthfilling, with strong, fresh stone-fruit flavours, showing good concentration, balanced acidity, and very good delicacy and length. Well worth cellaring.

Vintage	19
WR	6
Drink	20-23

DRY $35 –V

Tony Bish Skeetfield Hawke's Bay Chardonnay   ★★★★★

Still unfolding, the pale gold 2018 vintage (★★★★★) is based on mature, Mendoza-clone vines in the Skeetfield Vineyard at Ohiti. Hand-harvested, it was fermented and matured for a year in French oak barriques (60 per cent new). Highly fragrant, it is a full-bodied, powerful but not heavy wine, savoury and complex, with concentrated, ripe stone-fruit flavours, integrated toasty oak, fresh acidity, and a very long finish. Best drinking 2022+.

Vintage	18
WR	7
Drink	20-26

 DRY $60 AV

Tony Bish Zen Hawke's Bay Chardonnay   ★★★★★

This powerful, distinctive wine is made in an 'ovum' – an egg-shaped French oak barrel which creates unique convection currents, keeping the wine's yeast lees in suspension. Harvested from mature vines in the Skeetfield Vineyard, at Fernhill, it is fermented with indigenous yeasts, and bottled unfined and unfiltered. The second 2018 vintage (★★★★★) is a bright, light yellow/green, sturdy, rich wine, with notably concentrated stone-fruit flavours, finely poised acidity, and highly impressive complexity and harmony. Well worth cellaring, it's already delicious.

Vintage	18
WR	7
Drink	20-25

 DRY $140 –V

Trinity Hill 125 Gimblett Single Vineyard Gimblett Gravels Chardonnay   (★★★★★)

A delicious, notably 'complete' wine, the debut 2018 vintage (★★★★★) was hand-harvested from clone 95 vines in the Tin Shed Vineyard, which has 'unusually deep silt over gravel', and fermented and lees-aged for 17 months in a new French oak puncheon. It has an invitingly fragrant, complex bouquet, leading into a lovely young wine with concentrated, peachy, mealy, slightly biscuity flavours, showing notable depth, texture and refinement. Best drinking 2022+.

 DRY $80 AV

Trinity Hill Gimblett Gravels Chardonnay   ★★★★★

The winery's flagship 'black label' Chardonnay from Hawke's Bay is typically intense and finely structured. Grown in the Gimblett Gravels and fermented and matured for a year in French oak puncheons (30 per cent new), the 2017 vintage (★★★★★) is maturing very gracefully. Bright, light yellow/green, it is fragrant, rich and youthful, in a tight, elegant style, with balanced acidity, vibrant, peachy, slightly toasty flavours, showing excellent complexity and concentration, and a long, harmonious finish.

 DRY $40 AV

TW Estate Gisborne Chardonnay   ★★★☆

Gisborne in a glass, the generous 2018 vintage (★★★☆) was handled without oak. Full-bodied, it is sweet-fruited and vibrant, with fresh, ripe, peachy flavours, showing good depth, and a smooth finish.

DRY $17 V+

TW Platinum Chardonnay (★★★★☆)

Labelled as a 'decadent' style, the 2017 vintage (★★★★☆) was estate-grown in Gisborne and barrel-aged for 18 months. Bright, light yellow/green, with a creamy, toasty bouquet, it is full-bodied, with rich stone-fruit flavours, strongly seasoned with oak, balanced acidity, and excellent complexity.

DRY $48 –V

TW Reserve Gisborne Chardonnay ★★★★☆

The 2018 vintage (★★★★☆) was harvested from estate-grown, mature vines on the Golden Slope and fermented and matured for 10 months in oak barrels. Mouthfilling and sweet-fruited, it shows good complexity, with generous, peachy, slightly spicy and toasty flavours, creamy notes, gentle acidity and a lingering finish. Best drinking 2021+.

DRY $28 V+

Twin Totara Kumeu Vineyard Chardonnay (★★★★☆)

Offering good value, the 2018 vintage (★★★★☆) was estate-grown in West Auckland. Fragrant and refined, it is mouthfilling, vibrant and youthful, with excellent depth of ripe grapefruit and peach flavours, finely integrated biscuit oak, balanced acidity and obvious potential for cellaring. Best drinking 2022+.

DRY $25 V+

Two Rivers Clos Des Pierres Marlborough Chardonnay ★★★★☆

From two sites, in the Wairau Valley and Southern Valleys, the 2018 vintage (★★★★☆) was fermented and matured for 11 months in French oak barrels, a new French oak cuve and a concrete egg tank. It has a slightly smoky bouquet, leading into a full-bodied wine with very good intensity of youthful, peachy, citrusy flavours, crisp and long. A lively wine, it should be at its best 2021+.

Vintage	18	17
WR	7	7
Drink	20-24	20-23

DRY $36 –V

Unison Maestro Hawke's Bay Chardonnay (★★★★☆)

Still unfolding, the 2018 vintage (★★★★☆) was grown in the Ohiti Valley and fermented and matured for 10 months in French oak barrels. Fresh and elegant, it is medium to full-bodied, with strong, ripe stone-fruit flavours, gentle toasty notes, lively acidity and excellent complexity. A vigorous young wine, it should be at its best 2021+.

DRY $32 AV

Vavasour Anna's Vineyard Awatere Valley Marlborough Chardonnay ★★★★★

From a site within the original, terraced vineyard in the lower Awatere Valley, the 2017 vintage (★★★★★) was fermented with indigenous yeasts and matured for 11 months in French oak barriques. A lovely wine, it is lemon-scented and tightly structured, with layers of citrusy, peachy, slightly biscuity flavours, showing excellent vibrancy, delicacy and depth. Full of vigour and potential, it should break into full stride from 2021 onwards.

Vintage	17
WR	7
Drink	20-28

DRY $40 AV

Vavasour Awatere Valley Marlborough Chardonnay ★★★★☆

This typically rich, creamy-textured wine is grown in the Awatere Valley, given a full, softening malolactic fermentation and lees-aged in French oak barrels (18 per cent new in 2018). The delicious 2018 vintage (★★★★★) was oak-aged for nine months. Bright yellow/green, it is weighty and vibrantly fruity, with generous, ripe, peachy flavours, biscuity notes adding complexity, fresh acidity, and a finely balanced finish. Best drinking 2021+.

Vintage	18	17
WR	7	6
Drink	20-25	20-25

DRY $30 AV

Vidal Anthony Joseph Vidal 1888 Hawke's Bay Chardonnay ★★★★★

'The absolute pinnacle of Vidal Estate', the 2016 vintage is extremely rare. Only 61 cases were made of the debut 2014 vintage (★★★★★), released in 2017, and the wine was not produced in 2015, 2017 or 2018. Hand-picked in the Kokako Vineyard, in the Ohiti Valley, the 2016 vintage (★★★★★), released in 2019, was fermented and lees-aged for a year in French oak casks (33 per cent new). From a warm growing season, it has a highly fragrant, complex bouquet, with a hint of gunflint. Bright, light yellow/green, it is very intense and vibrant, with deep, youthful, grapefruit-like flavours, a subtle seasoning of oak, appetising acidity, and a lasting finish. Likely to be a 10-year wine, it's well worth cellaring to 2022+.

Vintage	16
WR	7
Drink	20-26

DRY $120 –V

Vidal Hawke's Bay Chardonnay ★★★☆

Offering great value and already drinking well, the 2019 vintage (★★★★) was fermented and lees-stirred in a mix of tanks and seasoned French oak barriques. Bright, light lemon/green, it is an elegant wine, very fresh and vibrant, with peachy, citrusy flavours to the fore, a subtle seasoning of oak adding complexity, and lots of youthful impact.

Vintage	19	18	17	16
WR	7	7	6	6
Drink	20-23	20-23	20-21	P

DRY $16 V+

Vidal Legacy Hawke's Bay Chardonnay ★★★★★

Still extremely youthful, the 2019 vintage (★★★★★) was hand-harvested in the Keltern and Kokako vineyards and fermented and matured for 10 months in French oak barriques (70 per cent new). Bright, light lemon/green, with a fragrant, smoky bouquet, it is weighty, vigorous and finely structured, with intense, well-ripened stone-fruit flavours, biscuity, savoury notes adding complexity, and a long, dry finish. Best drinking 2023+.

Vintage	19	18
WR	7	7
Drink	20-27	20-26

 DRY $60 AV

Vidal Reserve Hawke's Bay Chardonnay ★★★★

This middle-tier label is a consistently good buy, and the latest release offers irresistible value. The 2018 vintage (★★★★☆) was fermented and matured for 10 months in French oak casks (15 per cent new). Already delicious, it is bright, light lemon/green, with a slightly smoky fragrance. Mouthfilling, fresh and generous, it has citrusy, peachy, slightly toasty flavours, showing excellent richness, delicacy and complexity. Best drinking 2021+.

Vintage	19	18	17	16	15
WR	7	7	7	7	7
Drink	20-24	20-25	20-21	20-21	P

 DRY $20 V+

Vidal Soler Hawke's Bay Chardonnay ★★★★★

The Soler range is positioned above Reserve and below Legacy in the Vidal range. Grown at three sites, including the famous Keltern Vineyard, the notably refined 2019 vintage (★★★★★) was fermented and matured for 10 months in French oak barriques (33 per cent new). Already highly approachable, it has a fragrant, slightly smoky bouquet. Full-bodied, it has strong, ripe stone-fruit flavours, biscuity, mealy notes adding complexity, finely balanced acidity, and a very harmonious, lasting finish. Best drinking 2022+.

Vintage	19	18	17
WR	7	7	7
Drink	20-27	20-26	20-24

 DRY $35 AV

Villa Maria Cellar Selection Hawke's Bay Chardonnay ★★★★

Typically a great buy. The youthful, vibrant 2019 vintage (★★★☆) was fermented and matured for 11 months in French oak barriques (10 per cent new). Full-bodied, it has very good depth of ripe stone-fruit flavours, slightly toasty notes adding considerable complexity, and a dry, harmonious finish.

Vintage	19	18	17	16
WR	7	6	7	7
Drink	20-24	20-22	20-22	20-21

 DRY $18 V+

Villa Maria Cellar Selection Marlborough Chardonnay ★★★★

Typically a stylish, great-value wine. The 2017 vintage (★★★★), grown in the Wairau and Awatere valleys, was partly hand-picked, fully fermented in oak barriques (partly with indigenous yeasts), and barrel-matured for nine months. An elegant, vibrantly fruity wine, it has citrusy, peachy flavours, woven with fresh acidity, biscuity and buttery notes adding complexity, and good length.

DRY $18 V+

Vintage	18	17	16	15
WR	6	6	6	6
Drink	20-22	20-22	P	P

Villa Maria Keltern Hawke's Bay Chardonnay ★★★★★

Grown at a cool, inland site on the western edge of the Bridge Pa Triangle, this arresting wine is hand-harvested, fermented with indigenous yeasts and lees-aged in French oak barriques (40 per cent new in 2019). The 2019 vintage (★★★★★) is bright, light lemon/green, with a fragrant, slightly smoky bouquet. A very graceful, youthful, tightly structured wine, it is mouthfilling, with concentrated, vibrant, complex flavours that build to a powerful, very harmonious finish. Best drinking 2023+.

DRY $80 AV

Villa Maria Platinum Selection Sur Lie Hawke's Bay Chardonnay (★★★★★)

Offering outstanding value, the very elegant, youthful 2018 vintage (★★★★★) was grown mostly in the Keltern Vineyard, barrel-fermented and aged 'sur lie' (on its yeast lees). Fresh and finely poised, it is sweet-fruited and tightly structured, with citrusy, peachy, mealy flavours, a subtle seasoning of oak, balanced acidity, and a lengthy, very harmonious finish. Best drinking 2022+.

DRY $25 V+

Vintage	18
WR	7
Drink	20-23

Villa Maria Private Bin East Coast Chardonnay ★★★

The 2019 vintage (★★★) was handled in stainless steel tanks and seasoned oak barrels. Full-bodied, it is fresh and lively, with good depth of citrusy, peachy flavours, and a crisp, dry (2 grams/litre of residual sugar) finish. Enjoyable young.

DRY $15 V+

Vintage	19	18	17
WR	6	6	6
Drink	20-23	20-22	20-21

Villa Maria Reserve Barrique Fermented Gisborne Chardonnay ★★★★★

This wine has for many years been acclaimed as one of the region's finest Chardonnays. The 2019 vintage (★★★★★) was estate-grown in the McDiarmid Hill Vineyard and fermented with indigenous yeasts in French oak barriques (52 per cent new). Barrel-aged for 11 months, it is an extroverted, but very age-worthy, wine. Bright, light yellow/green, with a fragrant, smoky bouquet, it is powerful, with deep stone-fruit flavours, showing very good complexity, a strong, toasty oak influence, fresh acidity and a tightly structured finish. It needs time; best drinking 2022+.

Vintage	19	18	17	16	15	14	13
WR	7	7	6	7	7	7	7
Drink	20-26	20-25	20-24	20-24	20-23	20-22	20-21

DRY $40 AV

Villa Maria Reserve Hawke's Bay Chardonnay ★★★★★

The very stylish 2019 vintage (★★★★★) was fermented with indigenous yeasts in French oak barriques (38 per cent new), and barrel-aged for 11 months. Bright, light lemon/green, it has a fragrant, slightly creamy and smoky bouquet. Mouthfilling, rich, ripe and rounded, it has deep stone-fruit flavours, enriched with toasty oak, and a long, very harmonious finish. Best drinking 2023+.

Vintage	19	18	17	16	15	14	13
WR	7	7	6	7	7	7	7
Drink	20-26	20-25	20-24	20-24	20-23	20-22	20-21

DRY $40 AV

Villa Maria Reserve Marlborough Chardonnay ★★★★★

This distinguished, concentrated, finely structured wine is hand-harvested in the warmest sites supplying Chardonnay grapes to Villa Maria, in the Awatere and Wairau valleys. The 2018 vintage (★★★★☆) is still extremely youthful. Full-bodied, it has strong stone-fruit and spice flavours, a subtle seasoning of French oak, balanced acidity, and a finely textured, lingering finish. Best drinking 2022+. (The 2001 vintage, tasted in mid-2018, was a revelation – still drinking extremely well at 17 years old.)

Vintage	18	17	16	15	14	13
WR	7	7	7	7	7	7
Drink	20-25	20-25	20-22	20-22	20-22	P

DRY $35 AV

Villa Maria Single Vineyard Ihumatao Chardonnay ★★★★★

This impressive wine is estate-grown at Mangere, in South Auckland. The 2019 vintage (★★★★★) was hand-picked, fermented with indigenous yeasts in French oak barriques (30 per cent new), and oak-aged for 11 months. Bright, light lemon/green, it has a fragrant, citrusy bouquet. A very elegant wine, it has deep, citrusy, peachy flavours, gently seasoned with oak, slightly buttery notes adding complexity, balanced acidity, and a persistent finish. Still very youthful, it's well worth cellaring to 2023+.

Vintage	19	18	17	16	15	14	13
WR	7	7	7	7	NM	7	7
Drink	20-26	20-25	20-24	20-22	NM	20-22	20-21

DRY $50 AV

Villa Maria Single Vineyard Taylors Pass Chardonnay ★★★★★

Grown in the company's Taylors Pass Vineyard in Marlborough's Awatere Valley, this wine is hand-picked, fermented and matured in French oak barriques (25 per cent new in 2018). The classy, age-worthy 2018 vintage (★★★★★) has a scented, citrusy bouquet, leading into a mouthfilling, vibrantly fruity wine with citrusy, slightly peachy and biscuity flavours, a subtle seasoning of oak, and a long, very harmonious finish. Best drinking 2022+.

Vintage	18	17	16	15	14	13
WR	7	7	7	7	7	7
Drink	20-25	20-25	20-22	20-22	20-22	P

DRY $35 AV

Volcanic Hills Hawke's Bay Chardonnay ★★★★

The 2018 vintage (★★★★) was grown in the elevated, relatively cool Crownthorpe district and fermented in oak casks (25 per cent new). Bright yellow/green, with a toasty, slightly creamy bouquet, it is sweet-fruited, with generous stone-fruit flavours, balanced acidity, and lots of drink-young appeal.

DRY $29 AV

Waimea Nelson Chardonnay ★★★★

Offering good value, the 2017 vintage (★★★★) was hand-picked and fermented and lees-aged for 11 months in French oak puncheons (45 per cent new). Mouthfilling, with strong, vibrant, peachy, slightly toasty flavours, showing very good balance and depth, and fresh acidity, it should be at its best 2021+.

DRY $22 V+

Wairau River Reserve Marlborough Chardonnay ★★★★☆

The 2017 vintage (★★★★☆) is a single-vineyard wine, estate-grown at Rapaura, hand-harvested and fermented and matured for 10 months in oak barrels. Full-bodied, with a fresh, slightly smoky bouquet, it has vibrant peach and grapefruit flavours, finely integrated oak, good delicacy and vigour, and obvious cellaring potential. Best drinking 2021+.

DRY $30 AV

Watermark Basketweave Hawke's Bay Chardonnay (★★★★)

Enjoyable young, the bright, light lemon/green 2019 vintage (★★★★) was hand-harvested and fermented in a mix of tanks (65 per cent) and oak barrels (35 per cent). Fresh and lively, it is medium to full-bodied, with generous, slightly creamy flavours, showing a distinct touch of complexity, fresh acidity, and a very harmonious finish. (From Hopesgrove.)

DRY $25 AV

West Brook Barrique Fermented Chardonnay ★★★★

Drinking well now, the 2017 vintage (★★★★) was grown in Marlborough and French oak-matured. Light gold, it is mouthfilling, with loads of peachy, nutty, toasty flavour, woven with fresh acidity, and good complexity.

Vintage	15
WR	5
Drink	P

DRY $29 AV

West Brook Waimauku Chardonnay ★★★★☆

Set for a long life, the 2016 vintage (★★★★★) was hand-picked at Waimauku, in West Auckland, and barrel-fermented. Highly refined, it is a bright, light lemon/green, full-bodied wine, with ripe stone-fruit flavours, showing excellent delicacy and depth, mealy notes, and finely integrated oak. Subtle and savoury, with balanced acidity and a long, tight finish, it should break into full stride 2022+.

Vintage	16	15
WR	6	6
Drink	21-26	20-24

DRY $44 –V

Whistling Buoy Kokolo Vineyard Canterbury Chardonnay ★★★★

From vines planted in 2001 on Banks Peninsula, at the head of Lyttelton Harbour, the 2015 vintage (★★★★☆), tasted in 2020, is drinking well now. Fermented and matured for over a year in seasoned French oak barrels, it is bright yellow/green, with mouthfilling body (14.5 per cent alcohol), deep, citrusy flavours, finely integrated oak, very good complexity and a crisp, tightly structured, sustained finish. The 2016 vintage (★★★★) is also tight and lively, in a distinctly cool-climate style. Fermented and matured for a year in seasoned French oak casks, it is bright, light yellow/green, with vigorous, grapefruit-like flavours, firm acidity and very good intensity. Drink now to 2022.

DRY $36 –V

Whitehaven Marlborough Chardonnay ★★★★☆

The 2019 vintage (★★★★) was hand-harvested, fermented and matured in French oak puncheons (35 per cent new), and given a full, softening malolactic fermentation. Bright, light lemon/green, with a creamy bouquet, it is mouthfilling, with generous, vibrant, peachy, citrusy flavours, well-integrated oak, good complexity, gentle acidity, and a dry, smooth finish. Best drinking 2022+.

DRY $28 V+

Wild Earth Central Otago Chardonnay ★★★★☆

The 2019 vintage (★★★★☆) is a very refreshing Chardonnay, reminiscent of Chablis. A single-vineyard wine, grown at Bendigo, it was hand-picked and fermented and matured for 10 months in French oak casks (15 per cent new). Bright, light lemon/green, it is elegant and vibrantly fruity, with youthful, lemony, appley flavours to the fore, a gentle seasoning of biscuity oak, balanced acidity and a sustained finish. Best drinking 2022+.

DRY $32 AV

Wither Hills Cellar Selection Marlborough Barrel Fermented Chardonnay   (★★★★☆)

Drinking well now, the 2018 vintage (★★★★☆) was grown in the Taylor River Vineyard. Pale straw, it is mouthfilling and fleshy, with generous, ripe stone-fruit flavours, a gentle seasoning of toasty, biscuity oak adding complexity, and a very harmonious, smooth finish. It's a rare wine – only 980 bottles were produced.

DRY $26 V+

Wither Hills Cellar Selection Marlborough Unoaked Chardonnay   (★★★★)

Only 1050 bottles were made of the 2018 vintage (★★★★). Fresh and dry, it is medium to full-bodied, with citrusy, slightly peachy and mealy flavours, finely balanced acidity, a distinct touch of complexity, and very good texture, harmony and depth.

DRY $26 AV

Wither Hills Marlborough Chardonnay   ★★★☆

Enjoyable young, the 2018 vintage (★★★☆) is fresh and full-bodied, with good depth of peachy, slightly toasty flavours and a smooth, dry, creamy-textured finish. Priced right.

DRY $18 V+

Wither Hills Single Vineyard Benmorven Marlborough Chardonnay   ★★★★☆

Hand-harvested and barrel-fermented, the delicious 2018 vintage (★★★★☆) offers fine value. A youthful, sweet-fruited wine, it has good intensity of ripe, peachy, slightly toasty flavours, fresh acidity, oak-derived complexity and a slightly creamy finish. Best drinking 2021+.

DRY $26 V+

Wrights Reserve Organic Gisborne Chardonnay   ★★★★☆

Certified organic, the attractive 2018 vintage (★★★★☆) was grown in the Ormond Valley, matured for a year in new French oak casks, and given a full, softening malolactic fermentation. Pale straw, it is mouthfilling, savoury, ripe and rounded, with good complexity, and a creamy-smooth finish. Best drinking 2021+.

DRY $38 –V

Zephyr Marlborough Chardonnay   ★★★★★

The 2019 vintage (★★★★☆) is a single-vineyard wine, grown at Dillons Point, in the lower Wairau Valley. Hand-picked from mature (25-year-old) vines, it was fermented and matured in large French oak casks. Refined and very youthful, it has concentrated, peachy, citrusy, slightly toasty flavours, fresh acidity and a finely balanced, dry finish. Still unfolding, it's well worth cellaring to 2022+. The 2018 vintage (★★★★★) is highly fragrant. Grown in the same vineyard at Dillons Point, it is weighty, concentrated and finely textured, with ripe, peachy, gently biscuity flavours, complex, very generous and harmonious. Drink now onwards.

DRY $33 V+

Chenin Blanc

Today's Chenin Blancs are far riper, rounder and more enjoyable to drink than the austere, acidic wines of the 1980s, when Chenin Blanc was far more extensively planted in New Zealand. Yet this classic grape variety is still struggling for an identity. A few years ago, several labels were discontinued, not for their lack of quality or value, but lack of buyer interest. The good news, however, is that a wave of impressive new Chenin Blancs has recently hit the shelves.

A good New Zealand Chenin Blanc is fresh and buoyantly fruity, with melon and pineapple-evoking flavours and a crisp finish. In the cooler parts of the country, the variety's naturally high acidity (an asset in the warmer viticultural regions of South Africa, the United States and Australia) can be a distinct handicap. But when the grapes achieve full ripeness here, this classic grape of Vouvray, in the Loire Valley, yields sturdy wines that are satisfying in their youth yet can mature for many years, gradually unfolding a delicious, honeyed richness.

Only three wineries have consistently made impressive Chenin Blancs over the past decade — Millton, Margrain and Esk Valley — but others, such as Astrolabe, are adding new interest. Many growers, put off by the variety's late-ripening nature and the susceptibility of its tight bunches to botrytis rot, have uprooted their vines. Plantings plummeted from 372 hectares in 1983 to 23 hectares of bearing vines in 2020.

Chenin Blanc is now the country's thirteenth most widely planted white-wine variety, with plantings concentrated in Hawke's Bay, Gisborne and Central Otago. In the future, winemakers who plant Chenin Blanc in warm, sunny vineyard sites with devigorating soils, where the variety's vigorous growth can be controlled and yields reduced, can be expected to produce the ripest, most concentrated wines. New Zealand winemakers have yet to fully explore the potential of Chenin Blanc.

Astrolabe Marlborough Chenin Blanc Demi-Sec ★★★★

The 2019 vintage (★★★★☆) was grown in the Wrekin Vineyard, in the Southern Valleys, and handled without oak. Full of drink-young charm, it is attractively scented, fresh and very vibrant, in a medium to full-bodied style, with ripe peach and pear flavours, gentle sweetness (12 grams/litre of residual sugar), and balanced acidity. Still youthful, it's well worth cellaring.

Vintage	19		MED/DRY $25 AV
WR	6		
Drink	20-30		

Astrolabe Vineyards Wrekin Vineyard Chenin Blanc ★★★★★

The 2019 vintage (★★★★★) has a powerful presence. A single-vineyard wine, hand-harvested in the Southern Valleys, it was partly (40 per cent) fermented with indigenous yeasts in seasoned French oak puncheons. Richly scented, it is full-bodied, with deep, vibrant, peachy, slightly spicy flavours, and a long, dry (2.3 grams/litre of residual sugar) finish. Still very youthful, it should be at its best 2023+.

Vintage	19	18	DRY $35 V+
WR	6	6	
Drink	20-30	20-30	

Black Estate North Canterbury Home Chenin Blanc ★★★★☆

Certified organic, the 2018 vintage (★★★★☆) was estate-grown at Omihi, hand-picked, barrel-fermented with indigenous yeasts, and bottled unfined and unfiltered. Light gold, it is a mouthfilling, energetic wine with a strong surge of ripe, peachy, slightly spicy flavours, a subtle seasoning of oak adding complexity, and a crisp, bone-dry, lasting finish. Best drinking 2022+. The youthful 2019 vintage (★★★★☆) was also hand-harvested, barrel-fermented, and bottled unfined and unfiltered. Pale gold, it has strong personality, with good intensity of peachy, slightly citrusy and spicy flavours, a subtle oak influence and fresh, appetising acidity. Best drinking 2022+. Certified organic.

DRY $45 –V

Clos de Ste Anne La Bas Gisborne Chenin Blanc ★★★★★

Certified biodynamic, the 2018 vintage (★★★★☆) is from a section of the vineyard 'down there' (La Bas). Grown in Millton's Clos de Ste Anne hillside vineyard at Manutuke, in Gisborne, and fermented with indigenous yeasts, it was matured for nine months in large, 600-litre oak barrels ('demi-muids'). Pale gold, it is medium-bodied, with concentrated, vigorous, peachy, vaguely toasty flavours, showing good complexity, a strong sense of youthful drive, and a dry, harmonious finish. Best drinking 2022+.

DRY $90 AV

Easthope Two Terraces Vineyard Hawke's Bay Chenin Blanc (★★★★☆)

Well worth cellaring, the 2019 vintage (★★★★☆) was hand-picked at Maraekakaho and fermented and matured in a concrete, egg-shaped tank. Bright, light lemon/green, it is mouthfilling and vibrant, with good concentration of ripe tropical-fruit flavours, savoury notes adding complexity, moderate acidity and a dry, long finish. Best drinking 2022+.

DRY $35 –V

Esk Valley Winemakers Reserve Hawke's Bay Chenin Blanc ★★★★★

Already delicious, the 2019 vintage (★★★★★) was hand-picked at Maraekakaho, fermented in a mix of tanks (44 per cent) and large (600-litre) French oak barrels (56 per cent), and matured on its yeast lees for 10 months. Bright, light lemon/green, it is full-bodied and fresh, with vibrant, ripe tropical-fruit flavours, a subtle seasoning of oak, finely balanced acidity, excellent complexity, and a powerful, dryish (5 grams/litre of residual sugar), very harmonious finish. Drink now or cellar.

Vintage	19
WR	7
Drink	20-30

MED/DRY $35 AV

Forrest Marlborough Chenin Blanc ★★★★☆

The 2018 vintage (★★★★☆) was handled in a 50:50 split of tanks and barrels. Very harmonious, it is fresh, lively and youthful, with ripe, citrusy, peachy flavours, showing a touch of complexity, balanced acidity, and an off-dry (7.5 grams/litre of residual sugar) finish. Best drinking 2021+.

MED/DRY $25 V+

Giunta Hawke's Bay Chenin Blanc   (★★★★)

Pronounced 'June-TAH', the attractive 2019 vintage (★★★★) is a single-vineyard wine, grown at Maraekakaho. Bright, light lemon/green, it is a fresh and lively, medium to full-bodied wine, with crisp peach and pineapple flavours, showing good intensity, and an off-dry, finely balanced finish. Best drinking 2021+. (From Decibel.)

MED/DRY $26 –V

Maison Noire Home Block Hawke's Bay Chenin Blanc   ★★★★★

The classy 2019 vintage (★★★★★) is a distinctive, single-vineyard wine, hand-picked at Waimarama. Light lemon/green, it is powerful and full-bodied, in a dry style with vibrant, peachy, citrusy, slightly biscuity flavours, oak complexity, balanced acidity and a finely poised, persistent finish. Still very youthful, it should be at its best mid-2021+.

DRY $30 AV

Matawhero Church House Single Vineyard Gisborne Chenin Blanc   ★★★★

The 2018 vintage (★★★★☆) was harvested from young vines at Patutahi. A vigorous, very harmonious wine, it's already delicious. Bright, light lemon/green, it is mouthfilling, with good intensity of fresh, ripe tropical-fruit flavours, fractional sweetness (5 grams/litre of residual sugar) balanced by appetising acidity, and strong personality.

MED/DRY $25 AV

Millton Te Arai Vineyard Gisborne Chenin Blanc   ★★★★★

Certified organic, this Gisborne wine is one of New Zealand's best-known Chenin Blancs. It's a richly varietal wine with concentrated, fresh, vibrant fruit flavours to the fore in some vintages and nectareous scents and flavours in others. The grapes are hand-picked at up to four stages of ripening, culminating in some years ('It's in the lap of the gods,' says James Millton) in a final harvest of botrytis-affected fruit. Fermentation is in tanks and large 600-litre French oak casks, used in the Loire for Chenin Blanc. Bright, light lemon/green, the 2018 vintage (★★★★★) is a fresh, medium-bodied wine, with excellent intensity of crisp, peachy, vaguely honeyed flavours, good complexity, and a slightly sweet (8 grams/litre of residual sugar), appetisingly crisp finish. Finely poised, with strong personality, it's already delicious, but well worth cellaring to 2023+.

MED/DRY $35 AV

Mount Edward Central Otago Chenin Blanc   ★★★★☆

Certified organic, the distinctive 2018 vintage (★★★★★) is a tightly structured, dry style, grown in the Morrison Vineyard at Lowburn. Matured in a mix of stainless steel barrels (60 per cent) and oak casks (40 per cent), it is invitingly scented, with concentrated, youthful, vibrantly fruity flavours, showing impressive ripeness and vigour, good acid spine and obvious potential; best drinking 2022+.

DRY $29 AV

Moutere Hills Nelson Chenin Blanc   ★★★★

The 2019 vintage (★★★★) is a youthful, vigorous wine, hand-picked from 26-year-old vines and matured for 11 months in old French oak barrels. Medium-bodied, it has good intensity of peachy, slightly appley flavours, with a subtle seasoning of oak adding complexity, and a crisp, tightly structured finish. Best drinking 2022+.

Vintage	19	18
WR	7	6
Drink	20-27	20-26

DRY $35 –V

Mt Difficulty Long Gully Bannockburn Chenin Blanc   ★★★★☆

Showing obvious potential for cellaring, the 2018 vintage (★★★★☆) is a single-vineyard wine, made in a medium style (21 grams/litre of residual sugar) with finely balanced acidity. Light lemon/green, it is freshly scented and vibrantly fruity, with strong, peachy, citrusy flavours, showing excellent vigour, delicacy and length. Best drinking 2021+.

MED $34 –V

Queensberry Gardens Central Otago Chenin Blanc   ★★★★

Well worth cellaring, the 2018 vintage (★★★★) was estate-grown at Queensberry – midway between Cromwell and Wanaka – and lees-aged in old barrels. It is a medium-bodied, vibrantly fruity wine, with vigorous, peachy, citrusy, appley flavours, showing very good varietal character, and a dryish (9 grams/litre of residual sugar), lengthy finish. Best drinking 2021+.

MED/DRY $28 –V

Fiano

A traditional low-yielding variety of Campania, in south-west Italy, Fiano is also grown in Sicily, Argentina and Australia. Only 1 hectare is planted in New Zealand, according to New Zealand Winegrowers' *Vineyard Register Report 2017–2020*, but its age-worthy wines have been praised by UK writer Oz Clarke as 'exciting' and 'distinctive'.

Jenny Dobson Hawke's Bay Fiano   (★★★★★)

Well worth discovering, the 2017 vintage (★★★★★) is from vines in the Bridge Pa Triangle that were previously allocated to the Bushhawk Vineyard label. Fermented and lees-aged in stainless steel tanks and barrels, it's a distinctive wine with satisfying body, concentrated, peachy, slightly spicy flavours, and a long, dry, finely balanced finish.

DRY $35 AV

Gewürztraminer

Only a trickle of Gewürztraminer is exported (0.05 per cent of our total wine shipments in 2019), and the majority of New Zealand bottlings lack the power and richness of the great Alsace model. Yet this classic grape is starting to get the respect it deserves from grape-growers and winemakers here. If you haven't yet discovered the delights of this pungently perfumed, spicy variety, give yourself a treat.

For most of the 1990s, Gewürztraminer's popularity was on the wane. Between 1983 and 1996, New Zealand's plantings of Gewürztraminer dropped by almost two-thirds. A key problem is that Gewürztraminer is a temperamental performer in the vineyard, being particularly vulnerable to adverse weather at flowering, which can decimate grape yields. Now there is proof of a renewal of interest: the area of bearing vines has surged from 85 hectares in 1998 to 227 hectares in 2020. Most of the plantings are in Marlborough (37 per cent of the national total), Hawke's Bay (19 per cent) and Gisborne (17 per cent), but there are also significant pockets in Nelson, Canterbury and Otago.

Gewürztraminer is a high-impact wine, brimming with scents and flavours. 'Spicy' is the most common adjective used to pinpoint its distinctive, heady aromas and flavours; tasters also find nuances of gingerbread, freshly ground black pepper, cinnamon, cloves, mint, lychees and mangoes. Once you've tasted one or two Gewürztraminers, you won't have any trouble recognising it in a blind tasting – it's one of the most forthright, distinctive white-wine varieties of all.

Askerne Hawke's Bay Gewürztraminer ★★★★☆

Delicious young, the 2019 vintage (★★★★☆) is a perfumed and mouthfilling, off-dry style (12 grams/litre of residual sugar), with peach, lychee and spice flavours, fresh and rich, a hint of ginger, fresh acidity, and a long, spicy, well-rounded finish.

MED/DRY $24 V+

Askerne Reserve Hawke's Bay Gewürztraminer (★★★★★)

Exotically perfumed, the powerful, very youthful 2019 vintage (★★★★☆) was handled entirely in tanks. Bright, light lemon/green, it is a mouthfilling, distinctly medium style (20 grams/litre of residual sugar), with strong, finely balanced peach, pear and spice flavours, and a lengthy, well-spiced finish.

MED $32 AV

Ataahua Waipara Gewürztraminer ★★★★★

Highly perfumed, the 2019 vintage (★★★★★) of this North Canterbury wine is a fresh, weighty, youthful wine, tank-fermented and briefly lees-aged. Made in a dryish style, it has concentrated, ripe peach, lychee and spice flavours, a hint of ginger, a touch of complexity, and lovely depth and harmony. Best drinking mid-2021+.

MED/DRY $26 V+

Blackenbrook Vineyard Nelson Gewürztraminer ★★★★

A consistently attractive wine. Estate-grown and hand-picked, the 2019 vintage (★★★★☆) was mostly handled in tanks, but 9 per cent of the blend was matured in old barrels. Light lemon/green, it is gently perfumed and mouthfilling, with peach, pear, lychee and ginger flavours, showing excellent delicacy and freshness, and a distinctly spicy, off-dry (6 grams/litre of residual sugar) finish. Best drinking 2021+.

MED/DRY $25 AV

Vintage	19	18	17	16
WR	7	6	7	5
Drink	20-23	20-22	20-21	P

Bladen Tilly Vineyard Marlborough Gewürztraminer   ★★★★☆

Richly perfumed, the 2019 vintage (★★★★☆) was estate-grown and hand-picked in the Wairau Valley. Softly mouthfilling, it is weighty, with ripe stone-fruit and spice flavours, showing excellent delicacy, gentle acidity, a slightly oily texture, and an off-dry (13 grams/litre of residual sugar) finish.

MED/DRY $29 AV

Brennan Gibbston Central Otago Gewürztraminer   (★★★★☆)

Finely poised and youthful, the 2018 vintage (★★★★☆) is an estate-grown wine with an invitingly perfumed, floral, spicy bouquet. Mouthfilling and fresh, it is strongly varietal, with rich, yet delicate, peachy, spicy flavours, a slightly oily texture, and obvious potential. Best drinking 2021+.

MED/DRY $40 –V

Cicada Marlborough Gewürztraminer   ★★★★

Perfumed and youthful, the 2018 vintage (★★★★) is mouthfilling, with very good depth of fresh peach, spice, lychee and ginger flavours, and a dryish (5 grams/litre of residual sugar), finely balanced finish. Best 2021+. (From Riverby Estate.)

Vintage	18	17
WR	7	7
Drink	20-26	20-25

MED/DRY $24 AV

Dry River Lovat Vineyard Gewürztraminer   ★★★★★

From mature vines in Martinborough, the 2019 vintage (★★★★★) is an arresting wine. Powerful and weighty (14.5 per cent alcohol), it is bright, light yellow/green, with notably rich stone-fruit and spice flavours, a hint of ginger, unusual complexity, a slightly oily texture, and an off-dry (15 grams/litre of residual sugar), finely balanced, lasting finish. Already delicious, it's well worth cellaring to 2023+.

Vintage	19	18	17	16	15	14	13
WR	7	6	6	6	6	6	6
Drink	20-31	20-30	20-29	20-28	20-27	20-26	20-25

MED/DRY $55 AV

Falconhead Hawke's Bay Gewürztraminer   ★★★

Retasted in mid to late 2020, the easy-drinking 2019 vintage (★★★☆) was mostly handled in tanks (5 per cent of the blend was barrel-fermented). Light gold, with a fragrant, spicy bouquet, it is mouthfilling, with good depth of spicy, peachy, slightly gingery flavours, slightly sweet (9 grams/litre of residual sugar) and smooth. It's enjoyable now.

Vintage	19
WR	7
Drink	20-24

MED/DRY $16 V+

Gibbston Valley Le Maitre Central Otago Gewürztraminer   (★★★★☆)

The rare 2019 vintage (★★★★☆) was hand-harvested from 37-year-old vines in the home block at Gibbston. Fermented in old oak barrels, it is a bright, light lemon/green, exotically perfumed wine, mouthfilling and rounded, with strong yet delicate pear, lychee and spice flavours, showing good complexity, and a dry (3 grams/litre of residual sugar) finish. Best drinking 2022+. Certified organic.

 DRY $42 –V

Greystone Waipara Valley North Canterbury Gewürztraminer   ★★★★★

An emerging star. Certified organic, the delicious 2018 vintage (★★★★★) was estate-grown and hand-harvested, and part of the blend was fermented and matured for five months in oak barrels. It is highly perfumed and softly mouthfilling, with fresh, deep stone-fruit and spice flavours, gentle sweetness (18 grams/litre of residual sugar) and a rich, well-rounded finish.

 MED $33 AV

Hans Herzog Marlborough Gewürztraminer   (★★★★☆)

Certified organic, the 2017 vintage (★★★★☆) was estate-grown in the Wairau Valley, hand-picked, fermented with indigenous yeasts and matured for nine months in French oak puncheons. Deep amber, it's a distinctive, 'full-on' style with concentrated spice and apricot flavours, and a firm, bone-dry finish.

 DRY $39 –V

Hunter's Marlborough Gewürztraminer   ★★★★

Estate-grown at Rapaura, on the north side of the Wairau Valley, the 2020 vintage (★★★★☆) is an exotically perfumed, mouthfilling, fleshy wine, strongly varietal, with lively peach, pear and spice flavours, and a long, dryish (6 grams/litre of residual sugar), well-rounded finish. Best drinking 2022+.

Vintage	20
WR	7
Drink	20-30

DRY $25 AV

Johanneshof Marlborough Gewürztraminer   ★★★★★

This beauty is one of the country's greatest Gewürztraminers. Hand-harvested in the Wairau Valley, the 2019 vintage (★★★★★) is bright, light yellow, with an exotic, richly perfumed bouquet. Still very youthful, it is mouthfilling, with rich stone-fruit, ginger and spice flavours, showing lovely delicacy and depth, fresh acidity and an off-dry (12 grams/litre of residual sugar), very harmonious finish. Best drinking 2023+.

 MED/DRY $31 AV

Lawson's Dry Hills Marlborough Gewürztraminer ★★★★★

One of the country's most impressive Gewürztraminers. Grown in the Home Block and nearby Woodward Vineyard, at the foot of the Wither Hills, it is typically harvested at about 24 brix and mostly fermented in stainless steel tanks; a small part of the blend (5 to 10 per cent) is given 'the full treatment', with a high-solids, indigenous yeast ferment in seasoned French oak barriques, malolactic fermentation and lees-stirring. Still unfolding, the 2018 vintage (★★★★☆) is perfumed and weighty, with vibrant pear, lychee and spice flavours, a touch of complexity, gentle sweetness (6.7 grams/litre of residual sugar), and excellent delicacy, harmony and length; best drinking mid-2021+. The 2019 vintage (★★★★☆) is a mouthfilling, youthful wine, bright, light lemon/green, with delicate peach, pear and spice flavours, fresh acidity, and a finely textured, off-dry (6 grams/litre of residual sugar), lingering finish. Still opening out, it needs time; best drinking 2022+.

Vintage	19	18	17	16	15	14	13	12
WR	7	6	7	7	7	6	7	7
Drink	20-25	20-24	20-25	20-24	20-24	20-22	P	P

Lawson's Dry Hills The Pioneer Marlborough Gewürztraminer ★★★★★

The 2019 vintage (★★★★★) is an Alsace-style wine, estate-grown in the Home Block and fermented with indigenous yeasts in seasoned French oak barriques. From vines nearly 40 years old, 'with trunks as thick as thighs', it is bright, light lemon/green, with a youthful, highly perfumed bouquet. Mouthfilling, with vibrant peach, pear and spice flavours, showing unusual complexity, and a slightly sweet, rounded finish, it needs time; open 2022+.

MED $30 AV

Loveblock Marlborough Gewürztraminer (★★★★★)

Estate-grown in the lower Awatere Valley, the intensely varietal 2018 vintage (★★★★★) offers great value. Bright yellow/green, it is perfumed, weighty and rich, with concentrated, ripe, peachy, spicy flavours, a slightly oily texture, balanced acidity and a smooth, gently sweet, lasting finish.

MED $22 V+

Main Divide North Canterbury Gewürztraminer ★★★★☆

Offering great value, the youthful 2019 vintage (★★★★☆) from Pegasus Bay was fermented with indigenous yeasts in old oak puncheons and then barrel-aged for three months. Bright, light yellow/green, it is fragrant, with rich, peachy, well-spiced flavours, a slightly oily texture, good complexity, and a long, slightly sweet (12 grams/litre of residual sugar), distinctly spicy finish. Best drinking 2022+.

Misha's Vineyard The Gallery Central Otago Gewürztraminer ★★★★★

The delicious 2019 vintage (★★★★★) was estate-grown at Bendigo and 50 per cent of the blend was fermented with indigenous yeasts in old French oak barrels. Bright, light yellow/green, it is fleshy and highly perfumed, with concentrated, ripe, peachy, spicy flavours, a hint of ginger, and an off-dry (11 grams/litre of residual sugar), smooth finish. A powerful, finely poised, youthful wine, it should break into full stride 2022+.

 MED/DRY $32 AV

Mission Hawke's Bay Gewürztraminer ★★★★

Enjoyable young, the 2020 vintage (★★★☆) is a weighty, softly textured wine with a perfumed bouquet and moderately rich stone-fruit and spice flavours, slightly sweet and smooth. Good value.

MED/DRY $16 V+

Mount Riley Marlborough Gewürztraminer ★★★★

This label offers great value. Perfumed and full-bodied, the 2019 vintage (★★★★) is a single-vineyard wine, grown in the Southern Valleys and principally handled in tanks; 10 per cent of the blend was barrel-fermented. Enjoyable from the start, it is invitingly scented, with vibrant peach, lychee and spice flavours, showing a distinct touch of complexity, slight sweetness, and excellent depth and harmony. The 2020 vintage (★★★★) is instantly appealing. Grown in the Omaka Valley and partly (10 per cent) barrel-fermented, it is a strongly varietal, mouthfilling wine, fresh, lively and poised, with peachy, citrusy, spicy flavours, a hint of apricots, gentle acidity and an off-dry (7.5 grams/litre of residual sugar) finish.

 MED/DRY $15 V+

Mt Difficulty Growers Series Station Block Pisa Range Gewürztraminer (★★★★)

Still on sale, the 2016 vintage (★★★★) was grown at Pisa, in the Cromwell Basin. Drinking well now, it is perfumed and mouthfilling, with concentrated, peachy, spicy, slightly gingery flavours, showing some bottle-aged complexity, and a vaguely honeyed, gently sweet (32 grams/litre of residual sugar) finish.

 MED $27 –V

Ohinemuri Estate Matawhero Gewürztraminer ★★★☆

Still available, the 2015 vintage (★★★★) was grown in Gisborne and mostly handled in tanks; 10 per cent of the blend was fermented and matured for four months in oak barrels. Mouthfilling, slightly sweet (15 grams/litre of residual sugar) and smooth, with peachy, gently spicy flavours, it's a finely balanced, strongly varietal wine, enticingly perfumed.

MED $24 –V

Old Coach Road Nelson Gewürztraminer ★★★☆

Bargain-priced, the 2020 vintage (★★★☆) is an attractively perfumed, very fresh and lively wine, medium-bodied, with vibrant peach, pear, lychee and spice flavours, and a slightly sweet (14 grams/litre of residual sugar) finish. Best drinking mid-2021+. (From Seifried Estate.)

Vintage	20
WR	6
Drink	20-25

 MED/DRY $14 V+

Pegasus Bay Gewürztraminer ★★★★★

Estate-grown at Waipara, in North Canterbury, the delicious 2018 vintage (★★★★★) was handled for six months in old oak puncheons. Bright, light lemon/green, it is a powerful, youthful wine, weighty and rich, with concentrated, peachy, spicy, slightly gingery flavours, a vague hint of honey, and a complex, perfumed bouquet. Made in an off-dry style (14 grams/litre of residual sugar), it's full of personality.

Vintage	18	17	16	15	14	13
WR	6	NM	5	NM	7	7
Drink	20-22	NM	20-22	NM	20-22	20-21

 MED/DRY $30 AV

Petane Hawke's Bay Gewürztraminer (★★★★☆)

Weighty and more complex than most Gewürztraminers, the 2018 vintage (★★★★☆) was hand-harvested at Eskdale and Havelock North, and partly barrel-fermented. Light lemon/green, with a fragrant, gently spicy bouquet, it is full-bodied and concentrated, with strong, ripe pear, lychee and spice flavours, a hint of ginger, and a dryish finish. A subtle, distinctive wine, it's worth discovering.

 MED/DRY $27 AV

Queensberry The Lazy Dog Blown Away Central Otago Gewürztraminer (★★★★☆)

The attractive 2018 vintage (★★★★☆) was estate-grown at Queensberry – midway between Cromwell and Wanaka – and fermented and lees-aged in 'pre-loved' barrels. Mouthfilling and finely balanced, it is clearly varietal, with strong pear and lychee flavours, a hint of apricot and distinctly spicy notes. A very harmonious wine with a touch of complexity and a dryish finish (9 grams/litre of residual sugar), it should reward cellaring.

 MED/DRY $29 AV

Ruru Central Otago Gewürztraminer ★★★★

Drinking well in its youth, the 2019 vintage (★★★★) was grown in the Immigrant's Vineyard, at Alexandra. Pale lemon/green, it is perfumed and full-bodied, with fresh, vibrant lychee and spice flavours, a gentle splash of sweetness (9 grams/litre of residual sugar), and a smooth finish. Best drinking mid-2021+.

Vintage	19	18	17	16	15
WR	6	6	7	NM	6
Drink	20-29	20-27	20-26	NM	20-24

 MED/DRY $27 –V

Seifried Nelson Gewürztraminer ★★★★☆

Typically a floral, well-spiced wine, offering top value. The 2020 vintage (★★★★☆) is a pungently perfumed, distinctly medium style (26 grams/litre of residual sugar). Medium to full-bodied, it has fresh, strong, peachy, spicy flavours, a hint of apricot, gentle acidity, and excellent delicacy and harmony. Drink now or cellar. A great buy.

Vintage	19	18	17	16	15	14	13
WR	7	7	6	6	6	6	6
Drink	20-24	20-23	20-21	P	P	P	P

MED/DRY $19 V+

Shangri-La Nelson Gewürztraminer (★★★★)

From Blackenbrook, the perfumed 2020 vintage (★★★★) was estate-grown and hand-picked. Pale, it is softly mouthfilling, with pear, lychee and spice flavours, a hint of apricot, fresh acidity, very good delicacy and depth, and an off-dry (6 grams/litre of residual sugar) finish. Best drinking mid-2021+.

MED/DRY $25 AV

Soljans Estate Gisborne Gewürztraminer (★★★☆)

Highly perfumed, the 2019 vintage (★★★☆) is a very easy-drinking wine, fresh, medium-bodied and vibrantly fruity, with plenty of peachy, spicy flavour, a sliver of sweetness, and balanced acidity. Drink now or cellar.

MED/DRY $20 AV

Spy Valley Envoy Johnson Vineyard Marlborough Gewürztraminer ★★★★★

Estate-grown in the lower Waihopai Valley, hand-harvested from mature vines and fermented in small oak vessels, the 2018 vintage (★★★★★) is an arresting wine. It is powerful (15 per cent alcohol), with lovely depth of citrus-fruit, peach, pear and spice flavours, showing notable delicacy, richness and harmony. A sweetish style (68 grams/litre of residual sugar) with a rich, oily texture, it's hard to resist.

Vintage	18	17	16	15	14	13
WR	7	6	7	7	6	7
Drink	20-25	20-23	20-22	P	P	P

SW $33 AV

Spy Valley Marlborough Gewürztraminer ★★★★☆

Estate-grown in the Waihopai Valley, the 2020 vintage (★★★★☆) was fermented and lees-aged in tanks. It is a powerful, fleshy wine, with vibrant, ripe flavours of pears and spices, showing excellent delicacy and depth, gentle acidity, and an off-dry (6 grams/litre of residual sugar), smooth finish. Well worth cellaring, it should break into full stride 2022+.

MED/DRY $25 V+

Stables Ngatarawa Gewürztraminer (★★★☆)

The 2018 vintage (★★★☆) of this modestly priced Hawke's Bay wine has a spicy, vaguely honeyed bouquet, leading into a mouthfilling, exuberantly fruity wine with lots of peachy, spicy flavour. Fine value.

MED/DRY $13 V+

Stonecroft Gimblett Gravels Hawke's Bay Gewürztraminer   ★★★★☆

Certified organic, the powerful 2019 vintage (★★★★★) was estate-grown in the Roys Hill Vineyard, hand-picked and tank-fermented. Bright, light lemon/green, it is highly perfumed and weighty, with concentrated, youthful peach, pear, lychee and spice flavours, and a dryish (6 grams/litre of residual sugar) finish. A very age-worthy wine, it's well worth cellaring to 2022+.

Vintage	19	18	17
WR	5	6	5
Drink	20-26	20-25	20-24

MED/DRY $27 AV

Stonecroft Old Vine Gewürztraminer   ★★★★★

The Gewürztraminers from this tiny Hawke's Bay winery are among the finest in the country. This 'Old Vine' wine is made entirely from grapes hand-picked from the original Mere Road plantings of 1983. Certified organic, the 2019 vintage (★★★★★) is rare – only 30 cases were produced. Straw-hued, with a hint of gold, it has an enveloping, highly perfumed, spicy bouquet. A powerful wine (15 per cent alcohol), it is youthful, with highly concentrated, peachy, spicy flavours, a hint of apricot, and a slightly sweet (9 grams/litre of residual sugar), lasting finish. Best drinking 2022+.

Vintage	19
WR	5
Drink	21-27

MED/DRY $45 AV

Villa Maria Private Bin East Coast Gewürztraminer   ★★★☆

This regional blend, grown at sites stretching from Auckland to Waipara, typically offers very good value. The 2020 vintage (★★★☆) is pale, fresh and full-bodied, with very good depth of pear, lychee and spice flavours, and a smooth, off-dry (7.5 grams/litre of residual sugar) finish. Offering very easy drinking, it's bargain-priced.

Vintage	20	19	18	17	16
WR	6	6	7	6	7
Drink	20-24	20-23	20-22	P	P

MED/DRY $15 V+

Villa Maria Single Vineyard Ihumatao Gewürztraminer   ★★★★★

Estate-grown at Mangere, in South Auckland, the 2017 vintage (★★★★☆) was hand-picked and predominantly (80 per cent) fermented in seasoned French oak puncheons. Mouthfilling and fleshy, it is strongly varietal, with vibrant pear, lychee and spice flavours, showing good complexity, gentle acidity, an off-dry finish (10.8 grams/litre of residual sugar), and an enticingly perfumed bouquet. Drink now or cellar.

Vintage	17
WR	7
Drink	20-23

MED/DRY $30 AV

Waimea Nelson Gewürztraminer ★★★★

The attractive 2019 vintage (★★★★) is a perfumed wine, fresh and mouthfilling. Strongly varietal, it has generous pear, lychee and spice flavours, showing good delicacy, and an off-dry (13 grams/litre of residual sugar) finish. Best drinking 2021+.

MED/DRY $22 V+

Waipara Hills Waipara Valley Gewürztraminer (★★★☆)

The 2018 vintage (★★★☆) is highly perfumed. Mouthfilling, it is dryish (7 grams/litre of residual sugar), with plenty of peachy, spicy flavour, in a strongly varietal style. Ready.

MED/DRY $21 AV

Whitehaven Marlborough Gewürztraminer ★★★★☆

Offering fine value, the 2018 vintage (★★★★☆) has a fragrant, well-spiced bouquet. It is weighty and fleshy, with strong, peachy, spicy, slightly gingery flavours, and a slightly sweet (11 grams/litre of residual sugar), soft finish. Delicious young, it's full of personality.

MED/DRY $23 V+

Zephyr Marlborough Gewürztraminer ★★★★☆

Well worth cellaring, the 2019 vintage (★★★★★) is a single-vineyard wine, grown at Dillons Point, in the lower Wairau Valley. Richly perfumed, it is full-bodied, with fresh, concentrated, peachy, citrusy, spicy flavours, showing excellent vibrancy and delicacy, a touch of complexity, gentle acidity, and a long, off-dry, finely poised finish. A harmonious wine with obvious potential, it should be at its best 2021+.

MED/DRY $28 AV

Grüner Veltliner

Grüner Veltliner, Austria's favourite white-wine variety, is currently stirring up interest in New Zealand, especially in the south. 'Grü-Vee' is a fairly late ripener in Austria, where it yields medium-bodied wines, fruity, crisp and dry, with a spicy, slightly musky aroma. Most are drunk young, but the finest wines, with an Alsace-like substance and perfume, are more age-worthy. Coopers Creek produced New Zealand's first Grüner Veltliner from the 2008 vintage. Of the country's 46 hectares of bearing Grüner Veltliner vines in 2020, most were clustered in Marlborough (31 hectares), with Nelson (8 hectares) a distant second.

Bannock Brae Marlene's Central Otago Grüner Veltliner ★★★★☆

The impressive 2017 vintage (★★★★★) is highly scented, mouthfilling and dry. Bright, light lemon/green, it has concentrated stone-fruit, peach, ginger and spice flavours, slightly toasty notes, and excellent vigour and complexity.

Vintage	17	16	15	14
WR	6	7	7	6
Drink	20-23	20-22	20-21	P

DRY $25 V+

Blank Canvas Marlborough Grüner Veltliner ★★★★★

Currently on sale and drinking well, the 2015 vintage (★★★★★) is a single-vineyard wine, grown at Rapaura. Hand-picked, it was partly handled in tanks, but 60 per cent of the blend was fermented in French oak puncheons (20 per cent new). Bright, light lemon/green, it is highly fragrant, with substantial body and strong, peachy, slightly spicy, vaguely toasty flavours, complex, dry (2 grams/litre of residual sugar), rounded and long.

DRY $28 V+

Hans Herzog Marlborough Grüner Veltliner ★★★★☆

Still on sale, the distinctive 2014 vintage (★★★★☆) was estate-grown in the Wairau Valley, and fermented and matured for a year in French oak puncheons. A light gold, mouthfilling wine, it has generous, peachy, citrusy flavours, showing good complexity, and a fully dry finish. Ready. Certified organic.

DRY $44 –V

Hunter's Marlborough Grüner Veltliner (★★★★)

The 2018 vintage (★★★★) is a single-vineyard, Awatere Valley wine, hand-picked and fermented and lees-aged for 10 months in seasoned oak puncheons. Mouthfilling and dry (2 grams/litre of residual sugar), with strong, peachy, slightly spicy flavours, fresh, balanced acidity and good complexity, it's drinking well now.

DRY $25 AV

Jules Taylor Marlborough Grüner Veltliner   ★★★★☆

Grüner Veltliner is described by winemaker Jules Taylor as 'the illegitimate lovechild of Pinot Gris and Riesling'. Still very youthful, the 2020 vintage (★★★★☆) was grown in the Wairau Valley. Pale lemon/green, it has vibrant, citrusy, spicy flavours, very good delicacy, a touch of complexity, and a dry (1.5 grams/litre of residual sugar), lingering finish. Best drinking 2022+.

Vintage	20	DRY $25 V+
WR	5	
Drink	20-24	

Lime Rock Grüner Veltliner   ★★★★★

This Central Hawke's Bay wine is estate-grown, hand-harvested and typically partly barrel-fermented. The impressive 2019 vintage (★★★★★) is rare – only 70 cases were produced. Bright, light lemon/green, it is highly aromatic, mouthfilling, fresh and concentrated, with slightly toasty notes adding complexity, and a dry (4 grams/litre of residual sugar) finish. Weighty, vigorous and lingering, it shows strong personality.

Vintage	19	DRY $39 AV
WR	7	
Drink	20-24	

Mount Edward Central Otago Grüner Veltliner   ★★★★☆

Certified organic, the 2016 vintage (★★★★★) was grown in the Morrison Vineyard, at Pisa. Richly scented, it is mouthfilling and vibrantly fruity, with intense, peachy, citrusy, spicy flavours, showing a distinct touch of complexity, and a finely poised, dryish finish. (Retasted in early 2020, it is still lively, maturing very gracefully and probably approaching its peak.)

MED/DRY $29 AV

Nautilus Marlborough Grüner Veltliner   ★★★★☆

The 2019 vintage (★★★★☆) is full of promise. Handled with a small amount of barrel fermentation, it is fresh and mouthfilling, with strong, peachy, spicy flavours, a vaguely salty streak, balanced acidity, and a dry (3 grams/litre of residual sugar), lingering finish. Best drinking 2021+.

Vintage	19	DRY $30 –V
WR	7	
Drink	20-24	

Quartz Reef Bendigo Estate Single Vineyard
Central Otago Grüner Veltliner   (★★★★★)

Full of personality, the 2019 vintage (★★★★★) is one of the finest Grüner Veltliners to date in New Zealand. From vines planted in 2008, it was estate-grown, hand-harvested, fermented with indigenous yeasts and lees-aged for eight months. Freshly scented, it is mouthfilling, with vibrant, ripe, peachy, spicy flavours, showing notable intensity, moderate acidity, and a dry (2.6 grams/litre of residual sugar), lasting finish. Certified organic and biodynamic, it's already delicious, but worth cellaring.

DRY $37 AV

Riverby Estate Marlborough Grüner Veltliner   ★★★★

The vigorous young 2019 vintage (★★★★) was hand-picked at Rapaura, in the Wairau Valley. It is medium to full-bodied, with good intensity of peachy, slightly spicy flavours, and a dry (4 grams/litre of residual sugar) finish. Best drinking 2022+.

Vintage	19
WR	6
Drink	20-28

Rock Ferry The Corners Vineyard Marlborough Grüner Veltliner   ★★★★★

Certified organic, the 2018 vintage (★★★★★) was estate-grown at Rapaura and handled in stainless steel tanks (70 per cent) and seasoned oak barrels (30 per cent). A classy wine, it is aromatic and medium-bodied, with intense, pure, citrusy, slightly spicy flavours, showing good complexity, and a dry (3.5 grams/litre of residual sugar), persistent finish.

Saint Clair Origin Marlborough Grüner Veltliner   ★★★☆

The easy-drinking 2018 vintage (★★★☆) was partly fermented in old oak barrels. Light lemon/green, it is medium-bodied, with good depth of peachy, slightly spicy and gingery flavours, fresh and smooth.

Seifried Nelson Grüner Veltliner   ★★★☆

The 2018 vintage (★★★★) is a good buy. Fragrant and full-bodied, it has plenty of personality, with peachy, slightly spicy flavours, showing excellent vigour and depth, slightly toasty notes, and a dry (2.9 grams/litre of residual sugar) finish.

Waimea Nelson Grüner Veltliner   ★★★★

Grown on the Waimea Plains, the 2018 vintage (★★★★☆) is punchy, crisp and lively, with strong, citrusy, peachy flavours, hints of spices and ginger, and a dry (3.9 grams/litre of residual sugar) finish.

Wither Hills Cellar Selection Marlborough Grüner Veltliner   (★★★★☆)

The distinctive 2018 vintage (★★★★☆) was estate-grown at Rarangi, near the coast. Highly fragrant, it is full-bodied and dryish, with vibrant, youthful, peachy, citrusy, slightly spicy flavours, finely balanced and lingering. Best drinking 2021+.

MED/DRY $25 V+

Marsanne

Cultivated extensively in the northern Rhône Valley of France, where it is often blended with Roussanne, Marsanne yields powerful, sturdy wines with rich pear, spice and nut flavours. Although grown in Victoria since the 1860s, it is extremely rare in New Zealand, with 1 hectare of bearing vines in 2020, clustered mostly in Gisborne.

Hunting Lodge, The, New Zealand Marsanne/Viognier ★★★★

The 2017 vintage (★★★★) was hand-harvested in Gisborne and Hawke's Bay and a small part of the blend (10 per cent) was barrel-fermented. It is full-bodied and fleshy, with fresh, ripe stone-fruit flavours to the fore, good vigour, and a tight, dry (2 grams/litre of residual sugar) finish. Best drinking 2021+.

DRY $25 AV

Trinity Hill Gimblett Gravels Marsanne/Viognier ★★★★☆

The 2016 vintage (★★★★☆) is a weighty, softly seductive blend of Marsanne (51 per cent) and Viognier (49 per cent), hand-picked and fermented and matured for 14 months in seasoned French oak puncheons. It has an inviting floral, ripely scented bouquet. Mouthfilling, it has fresh, peachy, slightly buttery flavours, showing good richness, very gentle acidity, and a smooth (5 grams/litre of residual sugar), persistent finish.

MED/DRY $35 –V

Vintage	16	15	14
WR	6	6	6
Drink	20-21	P	P

Muscat

Muscat vines grow all over the Mediterranean, but Muscat is rarely seen in New Zealand as a varietal wine, because it ripens late in the season, without the lushness and intensity achieved in warmer regions. Of the country's 25 hectares of bearing Muscat vines in 2020, 22 hectares were clustered in Gisborne. Most of the grapes are used to add an inviting, musky perfume to low-priced sparklings, modelled on the Asti Spumantes of northern Italy.

Brennan Gibbston Central Otago Muscat   (★★★★)

Described on the label as a 'playful' wine, the 2018 vintage (★★★★) is clearly varietal, perfumed and full-bodied, with strong, vibrant, peachy, appley flavours, a splash of sweetness, and lively acidity. Ready.

MED $50 –V

Pegasus Bay Muscat   ★★★★★

This rare, estate-grown, North Canterbury wine is made in a sturdy Alsace style, hand-picked ultra-ripe at Waipara, tank-fermented and matured for six months in old oak puncheons. The powerful 2017 vintage (★★★★★) is highly perfumed, weighty and fleshy, with concentrated, peachy, slightly spicy flavours, showing a distinct touch of complexity, and a smooth, slightly sweet (18 grams/litre of residual sugar) finish. Delicious.

Vintage	17	16
WR	7	5
Drink	20-25	20-24

MED $31 AV

Pinot Blanc

If you love Chardonnay, try Pinot Blanc. A white mutation of Pinot Noir, Pinot Blanc is highly regarded in Italy and California for its generous extract and moderate acidity, although in Alsace and Germany the more aromatic Pinot Gris finds greater favour. With its fullness of weight and subtle aromatics, Pinot Blanc can easily be mistaken for Chardonnay in a blind tasting. The variety is still rare in New Zealand, but in 2020 there were 10 hectares of bearing vines, mostly in Marlborough and Central Otago.

Blackenbrook Pinot Blanc Nelson ★★★★☆

The 2020 vintage (★★★★☆) is from second-crop vines, estate-grown and hand-picked at Tasman. Handled without oak, it is invitingly scented and mouthfilling, with vibrant peach, pear, lychee and spice flavours, a hint of apricot, excellent delicacy and depth, and an off-dry (9 grams/litre of residual sugar) finish. A powerful wine, it should be long-lived; best drinking 2022+.

Vintage	20	19
WR	7	7
Drink	20-25	20-23

 MED/DRY $28 AV

Gibbston Valley Red Shed Bendigo Single Vineyard
Central Otago Pinot Blanc ★★★★☆

The 2018 vintage (★★★★☆) was estate-grown and hand-picked at Bendigo, fermented with indigenous yeasts in old French barriques, and lees-aged in oak for 10 months. Bright, light lemon/green, with a creamy bouquet, it is weighty and vibrant, with generous, youthful, peachy, slightly spicy flavours, showing good complexity, balanced acidity, and a finely textured, dry, smooth finish. Drink now or cellar.

 DRY $39 –V

Greenhough Hope Vineyard Nelson Pinot Blanc ★★★★★

Certified organic, the classy 2016 vintage (★★★★★) was estate-grown, hand-picked, and fermented and aged for 18 months in seasoned French oak puncheons. Highly refined, with a fragrant bouquet, it is full-bodied, with rich, vibrant stone-fruit flavours, gently seasoned with oak, moderate acidity, and a dry, very harmonious finish.

Vintage	16	15
WR	6	6
Drink	20-21	P

 DRY $36 AV

Kelly Washington Rapaura Marlborough Pinot Blanc (★★★★★)

From Auckland-based Tamra Kelly (formerly chief winemaker at Yealands Estate), the impressive 2018 vintage (★★★★★) was hand-picked and barrel-aged. Bright yellow/green, it is a fragrant, softly mouthfilling, slightly Chardonnay-like wine, with excellent complexity and deliciously rich, peachy, slightly buttery flavours. Certified organic.

 DRY $35 AV

Mount Edward Central Otago Pinot Blanc   (★★★★☆)

The subtle 2018 vintage (★★★★☆) was hand-picked in the Morrison Vineyard at Lowburn and fermented and matured in stainless steel barrels. Full-bodied, it is weighty and finely textured, with ripe stone-fruit flavours, showing good complexity, and a dryish, very harmonious finish. Drink now or cellar.

MED/DRY $29 AV

Mt Rosa Central Otago Pinot Blanc   (★★★★)

Attractively scented, the 2018 vintage (★★★★) was grown at Gibbston and handled in an even split of tanks and old French oak casks. Worth cellaring, it is full-bodied, with vibrantly fruity, pear-like flavours, showing a touch of complexity and very good depth, and a dry (1–2 grams/litre of residual sugar) finish. Best drinking 2021+.

DRY $40 –V

Rock Ferry Orchard Vineyard Marlborough Pinot Blanc Egg Ferment   ★★★★☆

Certified organic, the youthful 2017 vintage (★★★★) is a single-vineyard wine, hand-picked at Rapaura, in the Wairau Valley, and fermented in a concrete egg. Mouthfilling, it is vibrantly fruity, with pear, peach and spice flavours, fresh acidity, and a dryish (5.2 grams/litre of residual sugar) finish. Well worth cellaring, it should be at its best 2021+.

MED/DRY $30 –V

Saint Clair Pioneer Block 28 Waihopai Marlborough Pinot Blanc   (★★★★)

Still unfolding, the 2018 vintage (★★★★) was tank-fermented and made in a dryish (4.8 grams/litre of residual sugar) style. Bright lemon/green, it is a fresh, medium to full-bodied wine, with very good depth of peachy, citrusy, spicy flavours, balanced acidity, and a slightly creamy texture. Best drinking mid-2021+.

DRY $29 –V

Tohu Single Vineyard Whenua Awa Upper Awatere Marlborough Pinot Blanc   (★★★★☆)

A drink-now or cellaring proposition, the 2018 vintage (★★★★☆) is a vibrantly fruity, partly barrel-fermented wine. Full-bodied and dry, with a fragrant, creamy bouquet, it has fresh, peachy, slightly toasty flavours, balanced acidity and excellent depth.

DRY $36 –V

Pinot Gris

New Zealanders' love affair with Pinot Gris shows no signs of abating, and the wines are also starting to win an international reputation. The variety has recently spread like wildfire – from 130 hectares of bearing vines in 2000 to 2519 hectares in 2020 – and it accounts for 6.5 per cent of the total producing vineyard area. New Zealand's third most extensively planted white-wine variety, with plantings almost quadruple those of Riesling, Pinot Gris is trailing only Sauvignon Blanc and Chardonnay.

A mutation of Pinot Noir, Pinot Gris has skin colours ranging from blue-grey to reddish-pink, sturdy extract and a fairly subtle, spicy aroma. It is not a difficult variety to cultivate, adapting well to most soils, and ripens with fairly low acidity to high sugar levels. In Alsace, the best Pinot Gris are matured in large casks, but the wood is old, so as not to interfere with the grape's subtle flavour.

What does Pinot Gris taste like? Imagine a wine that couples the satisfying weight and roundness of Chardonnay with some of the aromatic spiciness of Gewürztraminer. A popular and versatile wine, Pinot Gris is well worth getting to know.

In terms of style and quality, however, New Zealand Pinot Gris vary widely. Many of the wines lack the enticing perfume, mouthfilling body, flavour richness and softness of the benchmark wines from Alsace. These lesser wines, typically made from heavily cropped vines, are much leaner and crisper – more in the tradition of cheap Italian Pinot Grigio.

Popular in Germany, Alsace and Italy, Pinot Gris is now playing an important role here too. Well over half of the country's plantings are concentrated in Marlborough (45 per cent) and Hawke's Bay (19 per cent), but there are also significant pockets of Pinot Gris in Gisborne, Otago, Canterbury, Nelson, Wairarapa and Auckland.

12,000 Miles Wairarapa Pinot Gris ★★★☆

From Gladstone Vineyard, the 2018 vintage (★★★☆) was grown in the northern Wairarapa, briefly lees-aged and handled without oak. Attractively scented, it is medium to full-bodied, vibrantly fruity and smooth, with plenty of peachy, slightly spicy flavour, finely balanced for early drinking.

MED/DRY $20 AV

Allan Scott Marlborough Pinot Gris ★★★☆

Enjoyable young, the 2019 vintage (★★★☆) is a mouthfilling, off-dry wine (8 grams/litre of residual sugar), vibrantly fruity and smooth, with good depth of pear, peach and spice flavours and a scented bouquet.

MED/DRY $18 V+

Anchorage Family Estate Nelson Pinot Gris ★★★

Offering very easy drinking, the 2020 vintage (★★★☆) is an invitingly scented, vibrant, medium-bodied wine with youthful pear, lychee and spice flavours, balanced acidity, and a gentle splash of sweetness. Showing good depth, it's enjoyable young.

MED $17 AV

Anna's Way Marlborough Pinot Gris ★★★☆

The 2018 vintage (★★★☆) is lively and mouthfilling, with satisfying depth of peachy, citrusy, slightly spicy flavours, and a smooth, dry (2.1 grams/litre of residual sugar) finish. (From Awatere River Wine Co.)

DRY $17 V+

Archangel Central Otago Pinot Gris ★★★★

The attractively scented 2018 vintage (★★★★) is a full-bodied, off-dry style. It has pear and lychee aromas and flavours, showing excellent delicacy and harmony, hints of lemons, apples and spices, and obvious potential.

 MED/DRY $25 AV

Ash Ridge Hawke's Bay Estate Pinot Gris ★★★★

The 2018 vintage (★★★★) is a bright, light yellow/green wine, fragrant and full-bodied, with ripe, peachy, spicy flavours, showing good concentration, a touch of complexity, and a dryish finish.

 MED/DRY $22 V+

Askerne Hawke's Bay Pinot Gris ★★★★

Still unfolding, the 2019 vintage (★★★★) is a youthful wine, mostly handled in tanks; 12.5 per cent of the blend was barrel-fermented and briefly oak-aged. Bright, light lemon/green, it is weighty and fleshy, with strong, ripe pear-like flavours, gentle spicy notes, and a dryish finish. Best drinking mid-2021+.

 MED/DRY $23 AV

Astrolabe Kekerengu Coast Pinot Gris ★★★★

The 2018 vintage (★★★★) is a single-vineyard Marlborough wine, hand-picked at Kekerengu. Full of youthful vigour, it is fresh and vibrant, with generous, peachy, slightly spicy flavours, dry (2.5 grams/litre of residual sugar) and smooth.

 DRY $27 –V

Astrolabe Marlborough Pinot Gris ★★★★

The 2019 vintage (★★★★☆) was grown principally (60 per cent) in the Awatere Valley, but also in the Wairau Valley and at Kekerengu. Mostly hand-harvested, it is a bright, light lemon/green, full-bodied wine, with good intensity of vibrant, citrusy, peachy, slightly spicy flavours, a touch of complexity, and a lingering, basically dry (4 grams/litre of residual sugar) finish. Drink now or cellar.

Vintage	19	18	17
WR	7	6	6
Drink	20-30	20-23	20-22

DRY $25 AV

Ata Rangi Lismore Pinot Gris ★★★★☆

Grown in the Lismore Vineyard in Martinborough, 400 metres from the Ata Rangi winery, the impressive 2018 vintage (★★★★★) was handled in old, large oak barrels. It is highly fragrant and mouthfilling, with excellent depth of vibrant pear and spice flavours, showing good complexity, and a very harmonious, dry (4.5 grams/litre of residual sugar) finish. A distinctive wine with good aging potential, it should be at its best 2021+.

Vintage	18
WR	7
Drink	20-25

DRY $28 AV

Aurum Organic Central Otago Pinot Gris   ★★★★☆

Certified organic, the youthful 2018 vintage (★★★★☆) was estate-grown and hand-harvested at Lowburn, tank-fermented with indigenous yeasts, and matured on its yeast lees for eight months. Light lemon/green, it is full-bodied, with fresh, lively pear and spice flavours, a sliver of sweetness (8 grams/litre of residual sugar), and excellent delicacy, vigour and depth. Best drinking 2021+.

Vintage	18	MED/DRY $28 AV
WR	6	
Drink	20-27	

Awatere River by Louis Vavasour Marlborough Pinot Gris   ★★★★

The youthful 2019 vintage (★★★☆) is a very fresh and lively wine, pale lemon/green, with good depth of citrusy, slightly appley and spicy flavours, and a basically dry finish. Best drinking 2021+.

DRY $20 V+

Baby Doll Marlborough Pinot Gris   (★★★☆)

The 2020 vintage (★★★☆) is full-bodied, with very good depth of fresh pear and spice flavours, lively acidity, and a finely balanced, dryish finish. Best drinking mid-2021+. Priced right. (From Yealands.)

Vintage	20	MED/DRY $18 V+
WR	7	
Drink	20-23	

Bald Hills Kirameki Bannockburn Central Otago Pinot Gris   ★★★★

Delicious now, the 2018 vintage (★★★★☆) is a full-bodied wine, hand-picked and made with a small percentage of barrel fermentation. Attractively scented, it is vibrantly fruity, with strong pear, peach and spice flavours, a sliver of sweetness (8 grams/litre of residual sugar), and a finely balanced, lingering finish.

MED/DRY $30 –V*

Bellbird Spring Waipara Valley Block Eight Pinot Gris   ★★★★

Still on sale, the 2015 vintage (★★★★) is a medium style, barrel-matured for five months. It is a straw-hued, full-bodied wine, with generous, peachy, slightly spicy and gingery flavours, showing good complexity, and a gently sweet, well-rounded finish. Ready.

MED $32 –V

Bellbird Spring Waipara Valley Dry Pinot Gris   ★★★★

The 2017 vintage (★★★☆) was fermented in old oak barrels. It is a distinctive, medium to full-bodied wine with a restrained bouquet, peachy, slightly yeasty and nutty flavours, showing considerable complexity, and a dry finish.

DRY $32 –V

Black Cottage Marlborough Pinot Gris   ★★★☆

The 2020 vintage (★★★☆) is a lively, medium-bodied wine, grown in the Wairau Valley and fermented and lees-aged in tanks. Bright, light lemon/green, it is a fully dry style (2 grams/litre of residual sugar) with youthful, peachy, slightly citrusy and spicy flavours, showing good vigour and depth. Best drinking mid-2021+. (From Two Rivers.)

DRY $18 V+

Blackenbrook Nelson Pinot Gris   ★★★★☆

Estate-grown and hand-picked from mature vines, the powerful 2020 vintage (★★★★☆) was handled in a mix of tanks (90 per cent) and old oak barrels (10 per cent). Pale lemon/green, it is fleshy, with strong, vibrant pear, lychee and spice flavours, fresh acidity, slight sweetness (6 grams/litre of residual sugar), and a distinctly spicy finish. Best drinking 2022+.

Vintage	20	19	18
WR	7	7	5
Drink	20-25	20-23	20-22

MED/DRY $25 V+

Bladen Marlborough Pinot Gris   (★★★★)

Hand-picked from 'some of the oldest Pinot Gris vines in Marlborough', the 2019 vintage (★★★★) is a fragrant, dry wine (3.7 grams/litre of residual sugar), estate-grown in the Wairau Valley. Light lemon/green, it is full-bodied and fresh, with moderately concentrated, vibrant pear, lychee and spice flavours, showing very good delicacy and varietal character. Still very youthful, it should be at its best 2021+.

DRY $27 –V

Boatshed Bay Marlborough Pinot Gris   ★★★★

Delicious young, the 2018 vintage (★★★★) is a fleshy, medium-dry style (7.6 grams/litre of residual sugar) from Grove Mill. Mouthfilling and vibrantly fruity, it has strongly varietal pear and peach flavours, showing excellent delicacy and depth.

MED/DRY $18 V+

Brancott Estate Identity Awatere Valley Marlborough Pinot Gris   (★★★★)

The Identity range is designed to celebrate Marlborough's sub-regional styles. The 'generous, optimistic' 2018 vintage (★★★★) has mouthfilling body, vibrant pear and spice flavours, gentle sweetness (8.8 grams/litre of residual sugar), and excellent delicacy and length.

MED/DRY $22 V+

Brennan Gibbston Central Otago Pinot Grigio   (★★★★)

Estate-grown, the 2018 vintage (★★★★) is a freshly aromatic wine, full-bodied, crisp and lively, with strong peach, pear and spice flavours, appetising acidity, and a dryish, finely balanced finish. Drink now or cellar.

DRY $27 –V

Brennan Gibbston Central Otago Pinot Gris (★★★★)

The 2018 vintage (★★★★) is full-bodied, with strong stone-fruit and spice flavours, fresh, balanced acidity, a touch of oak-derived complexity, and an off-dry finish. Best drinking 2021+.

MED/DRY $35 –V

Brick Bay Matakana Pinot Gris ★★★★

At its best, this estate-grown wine is weighty, rich and smooth. Hand-picked and lees-aged, it is made in an off-dry style. The 2019 vintage (★★★☆) is attractively scented, mouthfilling and slightly sweet (12 grams/litre of residual sugar), with concentrated, ripe stone-fruit, pear and spice flavours, and a deliciously well-rounded finish. Drink now or cellar.

MED/DRY $54 –V

Brightwater Vineyards Nelson Pinot Gris ★★★★

The 2018 vintage (★★★★) is a fragrant, medium to full-bodied wine, made in an off-dry style (15 grams/litre of residual sugar). Bright, light lemon/green, it is finely poised, with strong peach, pear and spice flavours, gentle acidity, and a smooth finish. Already delicious.

Vintage	18	17	16
WR	6	6	6
Drink	20-21	P	P

MED $22 V+

Bronte Nelson Pinot Gris ★★★★

Rimu Grove's second-tier label. Hand-picked in the Moutere hills and mostly handled in tanks (10 per cent oak-aged), the 2019 vintage (★★★★) is an off-dry style (7 grams/litre of residual sugar), with mouthfilling body and vibrant peach, pear and spice flavours, showing excellent delicacy and depth. A very harmonious wine, it's a drink-now or cellaring proposition.

Vintage	19	18	17
WR	7	6	6
Drink	20-27	20-24	20-23

MED/DRY $25 AV

Brookfields Robertson Hawke's Bay Pinot Gris ★★★★

This label originated in the early 1980s. Handled without oak, the 2020 vintage (★★★★) was tank-fermented and lees-aged. Full-bodied and basically dry (4 grams/litre of residual sugar), it is attractively scented, with vibrant, ripe pear, lychee and spice flavours, a touch of complexity, and a lively, harmonious finish. Best drinking mid-2021+.

Vintage	20
WR	7
Drink	20-25

DRY $21 V+

Camshorn Waipara Pinot Gris (★★★★)

Delicious young, the 2019 vintage (★★★★) is an invitingly scented, mouthfilling wine, with vibrant, peachy, gently spicy flavours, a sliver of sweetness, and a finely poised, very harmonious finish. Fine value.

MED/DRY $18 V+

Catalina Sounds Marlborough Pinot Gris ★★★★

Grown at two sites in the Waihopai Valley, the stylish 2018 vintage (★★★★☆) was mostly estate-grown (in the Sound of White Vineyard), and partly (15 per cent) barrel-fermented. Very pale straw, it is ripely scented, mouthfilling and dry, with concentrated, peachy, citrusy, spicy flavours, showing good complexity, a slightly oily texture, and a lingering finish.

DRY $25 AV

Caythorpe Family Estate Marlborough Pinot Gris (★★★☆)

The very easy-drinking 2020 vintage (★★★☆) is a fresh, medium-bodied wine, with good depth of peachy, citrusy, slightly spicy flavours, balanced acidity, and a dryish (5 grams/litre of residual sugar) finish. Drink now or cellar.

MED/DRY $20 AV

Ceres Swansong Bannockburn Central Otago Pinot Gris ★★★★

Invitingly scented, the 2018 vintage (★★★★☆) is a single-vineyard wine, full-bodied and fleshy. It has concentrated, ripe stone-fruit flavours, with gentle spicy notes and an off-dry, creamy-textured finish. Drink now or cellar.

MED/DRY $28 –V

Chard Farm Sur Lie Central Otago Pinot Gris ★★★★☆

Well worth cellaring, the elegant 2019 vintage (★★★★) was hand-picked in the Cromwell Basin and fermented and lees-aged in tanks. Bright, light lemon/green, it is vibrantly fruity and tightly structured, with fresh peach, pear and spice flavours, showing very good delicacy and depth, and a dry finish. Best drinking mid-2021+.

Vintage	19
WR	5
Drink	21-23

DRY $26 AV

Church Road Gwen Hawke's Bay Pinot Gris ★★★★

Aiming for a 'dry, mineral style', the lively 2019 vintage (★★★★) was estate-grown at Matapiro and hand-picked relatively early. Medium to full-bodied, it has fresh acidity and good concentration of peachy, slightly spicy flavours. Best drinking 2021+.

DRY $27 –V

Church Road Hawke's Bay Pinot Gris ★★★★☆

Estate-grown in Pernod Ricard NZ's relatively cool, elevated, inland site at Matapiro, this is a consistently impressive and enjoyable, weighty, Alsace-style wine, bargain-priced. Already delicious, the 2020 vintage (★★★★☆) was harvested with some berry shrivel. Sturdy (14.5 per cent alcohol), it is fleshy, with good intensity of vibrant pear, lychee and spice flavours, a slightly sweet, harmonious finish and a ripely scented bouquet. Best drinking 2022+.

MED $20 V+

Church Road McDonald Series Hawke's Bay Pinot Gris ★★★★★

Pale gold, the 2019 vintage (★★★★★) is a powerful, sturdy wine, estate-grown at Matapiro, harvested relatively late with some berry shrivel, and fermented and lees-aged in French oak cuves. It has concentrated stone-fruit and spice flavours, balanced acidity, hints of apricot and honey, gentle sweetness, and a rich, very harmonious finish.

MED $27 V+

Clark Estate Blackbirch Marlborough Pinot Gris (★★★★)

The 2018 vintage (★★★★) is a lively Awatere Valley wine. Invitingly scented, it is mouthfilling, with ripe stone-fruit flavours, showing good vigour and intensity, fresh acidity, and a dryish (5 grams/litre of residual sugar), finely balanced finish. Best drinking 2021+.

MED/DRY $19 V+

Clericus Wild Pinot Gris (★★★★☆)

Showing plenty of personality, the 2016 vintage (★★★★☆) of this Awatere Valley wine was made with use of indigenous yeasts and oak. Medium to full-bodied, it has concentrated stone-fruit and spice flavours, hints of ginger and honey, good complexity, and a gently sweet (15 grams/litre of residual sugar), finely balanced finish. (From Clark Estate.)

MED $29 AV

Coopers Creek Kumeu Pinot Gris ★★★

The 2017 vintage (★★★☆) of this West Auckland wine is less aromatic than southern Pinot Gris, but offers plenty of body and flavour. Fleshy, it has fresh, generous stone-fruit flavours, with hints of honey and spice, and a tight, dryish finish. Priced right.

MED/DRY $18 AV

Coopers Creek Select Vineyards The Pointer Marlborough Pinot Gris ★★★★

The Alsace-style 2017 vintage (★★★★) is full-bodied and generous. A strongly varietal wine, it has very good weight and depth of peachy, slightly spicy flavours, and a slightly sweet, rounded, very harmonious finish.

MED/DRY $23 AV

Crater Rim, The, Waipara Valley Pinot Gris ★★★★

The 2018 vintage (★★★★) is a sturdy, single-vineyard wine, fermented with indigenous yeasts in seasoned French oak barriques. Light gold, it is mouthfilling and slightly sweet, with a touch of tannin, strong, peachy, spicy flavours, oak complexity, and plenty of drink-young appeal.

MED/DRY $22 V+

Dancing Petrel Northland Pinot Gris (★★★★)

Grown on Paewhenua Island, in the Far North, the 2019 vintage (★★★★) was hand-picked and tank-fermented. It has fresh, gently spicy aromas, leading into a mouthfilling, lively wine with strong, youthful pear, lychee and spice flavours, good weight and a finely textured, dryish finish. Best drinking 2021+.

DRY $20 V+

Dashwood by Vavasour New Zealand Pinot Gris ★★★☆

This is a consistently good buy. The 2019 vintage (★★★☆) doesn't claim on the label to be of Marlborough origin. Full-bodied, fresh and vibrantly fruity, it has plenty of ripe, peachy, slightly spicy flavour, and a dryish (5.3 grams/litre of residual sugar) finish.

MED/DRY $16 V+

Delta Marlborough Pinot Gris ★★★☆

Offering very easy drinking, the 2019 vintage (★★★☆) is an attractively scented wine. Medium-bodied, it is strongly varietal, with vibrant pear and spice flavours, showing good depth, and a slightly off-dry (4.5 grams/litre of residual sugar) finish.

MED/DRY $20 AV

Domain Road Defiance Bannockburn Central Otago Pinot Gris ★★★★

Well worth cellaring, the 2019 vintage (★★★★☆) of this single-vineyard wine was mostly handled in tanks; 22 per cent of the blend was fermented in seasoned French oak barriques. Light lemon/green, it is mouthfilling, with vibrant, peachy, citrusy, slightly spicy flavours, showing good intensity and drive, a slightly minerally streak, and an off-dry (10 grams/litre of residual sugar), crisp finish. Best drinking 2021+.

Vintage	19	18
WR	7	6
Drink	20-22	20-21

MED/DRY $27 –V

Dragon Bones Waitaki Valley North Otago Pinot Gris ★★★★☆

The 2016 vintage (★★★★) from Lone Hill Vineyards is still youthful. Bright, light lemon/green, it is fragrant and weighty, with fresh, vigorous stone-fruit and spice flavours, gentle sweetness (18 grams/litre of residual sugar), and finely balanced acidity. It should be long-lived; best drinking 2021+.

MED $21 V+

Dry River Martinborough Pinot Gris ★★★★★

From the first vintage in 1986, for many years Dry River towered over other New Zealand Pinot Gris, by virtue of its exceptional body, flavour richness and longevity. A sturdy Martinborough wine, it has peachy, spicy characters that can develop great subtlety and richness with maturity (at around five years old for top vintages, which also hold well for a decade). It is grown in the estate and nearby Craighall vineyards, where the majority of the vines are over 25 years old. In the past, it was not wood-aged, but the 2017 (★★★★★) was 15 per cent barrel-fermented and 30 per cent of the 2018 vintage (★★★★★) spent 10 months in old oak hogsheads. The striking 2019 vintage (★★★★★) is mostly from vines planted in 1979. Richly scented, it is notably weighty and sweet-fruited, with highly concentrated peach, pear and spice flavours, a slightly oily texture, and a long, off-dry (16 grams/litre of residual sugar) finish. Combining power, delicacy, depth and harmony, it is clearly a top vintage, already drinking well but best cellared to 2022+. Benchmark stuff.

Vintage	19	18	17	16	15	14	13	12
WR	7	7	7	7	7	7	6	7
Drink	20-31	20-30	20-29	20-28	20-27	20-26	20-25	20-22

MED $65 AV

Dunnolly North Canterbury Pinot Gris (★★★★)

Offering fine value, the 2017 vintage (★★★★) was grown at three sites and matured on its yeast lees. Light yellow/green, it is mouthfilling, fresh and vibrant, with peachy, spicy flavours, showing a touch of complexity and good richness, and a basically dry (4.8 grams/litre of residual sugar) finish.

DRY $19 V+

Durvillea D Marlborough Pinot Gris ★★★☆

Retasted in August 2020, the bargain-priced 2019 vintage (★★★☆) was mostly (62 per cent) grown in the Awatere Valley, but also in the Southern Valleys and at Kekerengu. Pale and fragrant, it is full-bodied, with good depth of pear and peach flavours, gentle spicy notes, and a dry (3.9 grams/litre of residual sugar), smooth finish. It's drinking well now. (From Astrolabe.)

DRY $15 V+

Elder, The, Martinborough Pinot Gris ★★★★★

The 2018 vintage (★★★★★) is a distinctive wine, estate-grown and hand-picked at Te Muna, tank-fermented and partly matured for eight months in seasoned French oak barrels. Scented, mouthfilling and vibrantly fruity, it has strong pear, lychee and spice flavours, lees-aging notes adding complexity, balanced acidity, and a long finish. Still youthful and tightly structured, it should be at its best 2021+.

DRY $42 AV

Eradus Awatere Valley Marlborough Pinot Gris ★★★★

The finely balanced 2020 vintage (★★★★) is a top buy. Bright, light lemon/green, it is attractively scented and mouthfilling, with strong, vibrant pear and spice flavours, fresh acidity, and a dry finish. Drink now or cellar.

DRY $15 V+

Esk Valley Hawke's Bay Pinot Gris ★★★★☆

Retasted in mid-2020, the pale straw 2019 vintage (★★★★★) was grown at Maraekakaho and partly (15 per cent) barrel-fermented. Invitingly scented, it is full-bodied and fleshy, with generous, vibrant, pear-like flavours, hints of lychees and spices, a distinct touch of complexity, a slightly oily texture, and a basically dry (4.7 grams/litre of residual sugar), lingering finish. Unfolding very gracefully, it offers excellent value. The 2020 vintage (★★★★) is pale straw, with fresh pear and spice aromas and flavours, showing a distinct touch of barrel-ferment complexity, and a dryish finish. Still unfolding, it should be at its best mid-2021+.

DRY $19 V+

Vintage	20	19	18	17
WR	7	7	6	6
Drink	20-25	20-24	20-23	P

Falconhead Hawke's Bay Pinot Gris ★★★☆

Priced sharply and enjoyable young, the 2020 vintage (★★★☆) is a full-bodied, dryish wine (6 grams/litre of residual sugar), slightly Gewürztraminer-like, with fresh acidity and generous, peachy, well-spiced flavours. Drink now to 2022. (From The Wine Portfolio.)

Vintage	20	MED/DRY $16 V+
WR	7	
Drink	20-22	

Flaxmore Moutere Nelson Pinot Gris ★★★★

Estate-grown, hand-picked and tank-fermented in the Moutere hills, the 2019 vintage (★★★★☆) is a mouthfilling, dryish wine with good weight and a distinct touch of complexity. Showing plenty of character, it has pear, citrus, lychee and spice flavours, a real sense of youthful vigour, savoury notes and a long finish. Best drinking 2022+.

 MED/DRY $22 V+

Forrest Marlborough Pinot Gris ★★★☆

Enjoyable young, the 2018 vintage (★★★☆) was mostly tank-fermented; 5 per cent of the blend was handled in old oak casks. Mouthfilling, it has fresh, peachy, citrusy, slightly spicy flavours, showing very good depth, and an off-dry (5.9 grams/litre of residual sugar) finish.

MED/DRY $22 AV

Framingham Marlborough Pinot Gris ★★★★☆

Delicious young, the 2019 vintage (★★★★☆) was hand-harvested in the Wairau Valley. It is ripely scented and fleshy, with strong pear, peach and spice flavours, showing a distinct touch of complexity, balanced acidity, and an off-dry (10 grams/litre of residual sugar), smooth finish. A very harmonious, Alsace-style wine, it's a drink-now or cellaring proposition.

 MED/DRY $25 V+

Gale Force Marlborough Pinot Gris (★★☆)

Still on sale, the low-priced 2017 vintage (★★☆) was grown in the Awatere Valley. Light and crisp, with citrusy aromas, it has lemony, slightly appley flavours and a fully dry finish. Verging on three stars, it offers fine value. (From Clark Estate.)

DRY $12 V+

Georges Road Selection Waipara Pinot Gris ★★★★★

Full of personality, the 2017 vintage (★★★★★) was estate-grown, hand-picked and fermented with indigenous yeasts in seasoned oak barrels. Light yellow/green, it is mouthfilling, with stone-fruit and spice flavours, a vague hint of honey, and excellent complexity and richness. Made in a dry style (4 grams/litre of residual sugar), it's drinking well now.

 DRY $26 V+

Gibbston Valley GV Collection Central Otago Pinot Gris ★★★★☆

Drinking well now, the 2018 vintage (★★★★☆) was grown at two sites at Bendigo, hand-picked and partly (25 per cent) barrel-fermented. Bright, light yellow/green, it is mouthfilling and lively, with strong, peachy, spicy flavours, showing a distinct touch of complexity, and a dryish (5 grams/litre of residual sugar), lingering finish.

MED/DRY $28 AV

Gibbston Valley School House Central Otago Pinot Gris ★★★★★

The highly refined 2019 vintage (★★★★★) was hand-picked at an elevated Bendigo site (350 to 400 metres above sea level), and fermented and lees-aged for 10 months in stainless steel barriques (40 per cent) and French acacia puncheons (60 per cent). Bright, light lemon/green, it is richly scented, with strong, vibrant, peachy flavours, hints of apricot and spices, excellent delicacy, and a long, off-dry (9 grams/litre of residual sugar) finish. Best drinking 2022+. Certified organic.

MED/DRY $39 AV

Gladstone Vineyard Pinot Gris ★★★★☆

The 2018 vintage (★★★★) was estate-grown in the northern Wairarapa and handled with some fermentation on skins, barrel fermentation and lees-aging. It is mouthfilling and smooth, with generous, peachy, spicy, slightly gingery flavours, showing some complexity, and a dry finish.

DRY $27 AV

Greyrock Hawke's Bay Pinot Gris (★★☆)

The easy-drinking 2018 vintage (★★☆) is light and lively, in a medium-bodied style with fresh peach, pear and spice flavours, and an off-dry (6.5 grams/litre of residual sugar) finish. (From Sileni.)

MED/DRY $19 –V

Greyrock Te Koru Hawke's Bay Pinot Gris (★★★☆)

Fresh and lively, the 2019 vintage (★★★☆) is full-bodied, with good vigour and depth of peach, pear and spice flavours, dry (4.6 grams/litre of residual sugar) and harmonious. (From Sileni.)

DRY $20 AV

Greystone Organic Waipara Valley North Canterbury Pinot Gris ★★★★★

At its best, this is one of the finest Pinot Gris in the country. The 2019 vintage (★★★★★) was handled mostly in tanks (10 per cent was barrel-aged), and lees-aged for five months. Full of youthful vigour, it is a distinctly Alsace-style wine – sturdy, vibrantly fruity and rich. Pale straw, it is mouthfilling, with strong, pure peach, pear and spice flavours, a sliver of sweetness (7 grams/litre of residual sugar), and a well-rounded, lingering finish. Open mid-2021+. Certified organic.

Vintage	19
WR	6
Drink	20-26

MED/DRY $26 V+

Greystone Sand Dollar Waipara Pinot Gris

Certified organic, the fragrant, very lively 2018 vintage (★★★★☆) was mostly tank-fermented, with a small portion handled in old oak barrels. Full-bodied, with rich peach, pear and lychee flavours, showing good complexity, and a long, dry (3.9 grams/litre of residual sugar), gently spicy finish, it shows obvious potential; best drinking 2021+.

DRY $28 AV

Greywacke Marlborough Pinot Gris

Grown principally in the Southern Valleys, but also at Rapaura, the 2017 vintage (★★★★★) was hand-picked, fermented in a mix of old oak barrels (mostly) and tanks, blended, and then lees-aged for six months in old barrels. Attractively scented, it is a very Alsace-style wine, sturdy and rich, with deep peach, pear and spice flavours, showing good complexity, and an off-dry (10 grams/litre of residual sugar), very harmonious finish. Already a lovely mouthful, it's also well worth cellaring. Still unfolding, the 2018 vintage (★★★★☆) is ripely scented and weighty, with concentrated stone-fruit and spice flavours, gentle sweetness, fresh acidity and obvious potential for cellaring; open 2022+.

Vintage	18	17	16	15	14	13
WR	6	6	6	6	6	6
Drink	20-26	20-25	20-24	20-23	20-22	20-22

MED/DRY $31 AV

Grove Mill Wairau Valley Marlborough Pinot Gris

The youthful 2019 vintage (★★★☆) is a freshly aromatic, mouthfilling wine with ripe, peachy, spicy flavours, a sliver of sweetness, balanced acidity, and an easy-drinking charm.

MED/DRY $19 V+

Haha Hawke's Bay Pinot Gris

Offering good value, the 2020 vintage (★★★☆) was tank-fermented and lees-aged. Bright, light lemon/green, it is mouthfilling, with good depth of ripe, peachy, gently spicy flavours, gentle acidity, and an off-dry (5.6 grams/litre of residual sugar), well-rounded finish.

MED/DRY $18 V+

Hans Herzog Marlborough Pinot Gris

Prepare for something different! Estate-grown on the northern side of the Wairau Valley, the 2017 vintage (★★★★★) is a thought-provoking wine, like its predecessors. Apricot-coloured, from long skin contact with the juice, it was partly oak-aged (20 per cent of the blend was handled in French oak puncheons). Ripely perfumed, it is weighty, sweet-fruited and bone-dry, with powerful peach, strawberry and apricot flavours, a touch of tannin, and loads of personality. Certified organic.

DRY $39 AV

Hawkshead Central Otago Pinot Gris   ★★★★★

Fragrant, fresh and full-bodied, the 2019 vintage (★★★★☆) was hand-harvested at Gibbston (75 per cent) and Lowburn (25 per cent), and mostly handled in tanks; 15 per cent of the blend was fermented in seasoned oak barrels. Matured on its yeast lees for five months, it's a weighty wine with strong, ripe stone-fruit flavours, showing good vigour and a distinct touch of complexity, fresh acidity, and a dry (2 grams/litre of residual sugar), lengthy finish. Best drinking 2021+.

DRY $29 V+

Huntaway Reserve Gisborne Pinot Gris   ★★★☆

The 2018 vintage (★★★☆) is full-bodied, with ripe stone-fruit flavours, showing very good freshness and depth, and a finely balanced, dryish, smooth finish.

MED/DRY $22 AV

Hunter's Marlborough Pinot Gris   ★★★★☆

The very age-worthy 2020 vintage (★★★★☆) was grown at Rapaura and mostly handled in tanks, but 15 per cent of the blend was fermented in old oak barrels. Made in a dryish style (6 grams/litre of residual sugar), it is fleshy and tightly structured, with ripe stone-fruit and spice flavours, showing excellent complexity, depth and harmony.

MED/DRY $19 V+

Hunting Lodge, The, Expressions Plush Marlborough Pinot Gris   ★★★★

Freshly scented, the 2019 vintage (★★★★) is instantly appealing, with a gentle splash of sweetness and strong, vibrant, peachy, slightly spicy flavours. Drink now.

MED/DRY $22 V+

Hunting Lodge, The, Marlborough Pinot Gris   ★★★★☆

The 2019 vintage (★★★★☆) is attractively scented and full-bodied, with strong pear and lychee flavours, hints of peaches and spices, good delicacy and a dryish, lingering finish. A lively, youthful wine with good potential, it should be at its best 2021+.

MED/DRY $26 AV

Invivo Marlborough Pinot Gris   ★★★

The 2020 vintage (★★★☆) is a very easy-drinking wine. Pale lemon/green, it is mouthfilling, with fresh, vibrant, citrusy flavours, hints of pears and spices, good varietal character and depth, and a dryish (5 grams/litre of residual sugar) finish. Enjoyable young.

MED/DRY $19 AV

Johanneshof Marlborough Pinot Gris   ★★★★

The powerful 2018 vintage (★★★★☆) is weighty and fleshy, with generous stone-fruit and spice flavours, a touch of complexity and a slightly sweet, smooth finish. Full of personality, it's drinking well now.

MED/DRY $29 –V

Johner Estate Limestone Pinot Gris   (★★★★)

The 2019 vintage (★★★★) was grown in Hawke's Bay. Made in a basically dry style (4 grams/litre of residual sugar), it has fresh, strong pear, lychee and spice flavours, crisp acidity, and very good vigour and depth. Best drinking 2021+.

Vintage	19
WR	7
Drink	20-23

DRY $26 –V

Jules Taylor Marlborough Pinot Gris   ★★★★☆

Grown at three sites in the Awatere and Wairau valleys, the youthful 2020 vintage (★★★★☆) was mostly handled in tanks; a small percentage of the blend was oak-aged. It is highly aromatic, with fresh pear, lychee and spice flavours, showing excellent delicacy and depth, and a dry (3.7 grams/litre of residual sugar) finish. Best drinking mid-2021+.

Vintage	20
WR	6
Drink	20-23

DRY $25 V+

Junction Red Card Central Hawke's Bay Pinot Gris   (★★★★)

Drinking well now, the 2018 vintage (★★★★) is a powerful, hand-picked wine, aromatic and full-bodied. Bright, light lemon/green, it is weighty, with strong, peachy, slightly spicy flavours. Fine value.

MED/DRY $16 V+

Kahurangi Nelson Pinot Gris   (★★★)

Still very youthful, the easy-drinking 2020 vintage (★★★) is a fresh, full-bodied wine, with lively pear, lychee and spice flavours, and an off-dry finish. Open mid-2021+.

MED/DRY $17 AV

Kono Nelson Pinot Gris   (★★★☆)

Offering good value, the 2018 vintage (★★★☆) is freshly scented, vibrant and mouthfilling, with lively pear/spice flavours, balanced acidity, and a dryish finish. Enjoyable young.

MED/DRY $18 V+

Kumeu River Estate Pinot Gris   ★★★★

This consistently attractive wine is grown at Kumeu, in West Auckland, aged on its yeast lees, but not oak-matured. Pale lemon/green, the distinctive 2019 vintage (★★★★☆) is a weighty, basically dry wine (4.6 grams/litre of residual sugar), with strong, vibrant stone-fruit, pear and spice flavours, showing a distinct touch of complexity, and balanced acidity. A top vintage of this label, it's a drink-now or cellaring proposition.

DRY $27 –V

Lake Chalice The Falcon Marlborough Pinot Gris ★★★☆

Freshly scented, the 2019 vintage (★★★☆) is a lively, medium-bodied wine with good depth of vibrant pear, lychee and spice flavours, a hint of ginger, balanced acidity, and a dry (4 grams/litre of residual sugar) finish.

Landing, The, Bay of Islands Pinot Gris ★★★★

Showing very good depth and drive, the 2019 vintage (★★★★) of this Northland wine was hand-picked and made in an off-dry style (7 grams/litre of residual sugar). Pale straw, it is a lively, medium-bodied wine with clear-cut varietal characteristics, fresh acidity and strong pear and spice flavours. Best drinking 2021+.

MED/DRY $27 –V

Lawson's Dry Hills Marlborough Pinot Gris ★★★★

The very pale pink 2020 vintage (★★★★) is an off-dry style (6 grams/litre of residual sugar). It has very good depth of ripe, strawberryish, spicy flavours, a hint of apricot, a touch of complexity, and a finely balanced finish. Still very youthful, it's well worth cellaring to at least mid-2021+. Retasted in mid-2020, the 2019 vintage (★★★★) is drinking well now. Straw-hued, it's a slightly Gewürztraminer-like wine, with strong, peachy, spicy, slightly gingery flavours, showing considerable complexity, and a lengthy, dryish (5 grams/litre of residual sugar) finish.

Vintage	20	19
WR	7	6
Drink	20-23	20-21

MED/DRY $20 V+

Lawson's Dry Hills Reserve Marlborough Pinot Gris ★★★★☆

The finely textured 2018 vintage (★★★★☆) was mostly estate-grown in the Waihopai Valley and 10 per cent of the blend was fermented with indigenous yeasts in old French oak casks. It is mouthfilling, with concentrated, ripe peach, pear and spice flavours, showing a distinct touch of complexity, and a smooth, dryish (5 grams/litre of residual sugar) finish. The 2019 vintage (★★★★☆) is a pale gold, fleshy wine with strong, ripe stone-fruit and spice flavours, balanced acidity, and a rich, basically dry finish. Already very expressive, it should be drinking well now to 2022.

Vintage	18
WR	6
Drink	20-21

DRY $25 V+

Lawson's Dry Hills The Pioneer Marlborough Pinot Gris ★★★★☆

Retasted in mid-2020, the 2016 vintage (★★★★★) has flourished with bottle-age. Hand-picked in the Waihopai Valley, it was fermented with indigenous yeasts in old French oak barriques. Pale gold, it is fleshy, with concentrated, ripe stone-fruit flavours, hints of pears and spices, a distinct touch of complexity, and an off-dry (14 grams/litre of residual sugar) finish. A powerful wine, it's drinking well now.

Vintage	16	15
WR	7	7
Drink	20-25	P

MED/DRY $30 –V

Left Field Hawke's Bay Pinot Gris ★★★★

Offering good value, the easy-drinking 2020 vintage (★★★★) is an attractively scented, mouthfilling wine, with very good intensity of peach, pear and spice flavours, and a dryish (5.6 grams/litre of residual sugar) finish. (From Te Awa.)

Vintage	20	19	18	17
WR	7	7	5	5
Drink	20-23	20-21	P	P

MED/DRY $18 V+

Leveret Estate Marlborough Pinot Gris (★★★★)

The 2019 vintage (★★★★) is fresh and full-bodied, with very good varietal character, delicacy and depth of peach, pear and spice flavours. Made in an off-dry style (8 grams/litre of residual sugar), it has gentle acidity and a very harmonious finish.

MED/DRY $22 V+

Lime Rock Central Hawke's Bay Pinot Gris ★★★★

Estate-grown near Waipawa, the bright, light lemon/green 2019 vintage (★★★★) was fermented in a mix of tanks and old oak barriques. Made in a dry style, it is fresh and full-bodied, with ripe pear, lychee and spice flavours, balanced acidity, and a smooth finish. Best drinking 2021+.

DRY $24 AV

Loveblock Marlborough Pinot Gris ★★★★☆

Certified organic, the 2019 vintage (★★★★) was estate-grown in the Awatere Valley. Full-bodied, it is youthful, with strong pear and spice flavours, fresh acidity, and a dryish, persistent finish.

MED/DRY $22 V+

Luna Martinborough Pinot Gris ★★★★

The 2019 vintage (★★★★) was grown at Blue Rock Vineyard and partly barrel-fermented. Very faintly pink, it is mouthfilling and vibrantly fruity, with peachy, spicy flavours, showing very good complexity and depth, and a dry (2 grams/litre of residual sugar), smooth finish. Best drinking 2021+.

DRY $24 AV

Mahi Marlborough Pinot Gris ★★★★

The attractively scented 2019 vintage (★★★★) is a single-vineyard wine, hand-picked near Ward, in the Awatere Valley, and mostly handled in tanks; 10 per cent of the blend was fermented in seasoned French oak casks. Light lemon/green, it is mouthfilling, with fresh, youthful pear and spice flavours, showing a touch of complexity, and a fully dry finish. Worth cellaring.

Vintage	20	19	18	17	16
WR	7	7	6	6	6
Drink	20-26	20-22	20-22	20-21	P

 DRY $24 AV

Main Divide North Canterbury Pinot Gris ★★★★

From Pegasus Bay, this is a consistently good buy. Tank-fermented and lees-aged, the 2018 vintage (★★★★) is full-bodied, with good concentration of peachy, slightly spicy, vaguely honeyed flavours, gentle sweetness (10 grams/litre of residual sugar) and balanced acidity. Best drinking 2021+.

 MED/DRY $21 V+

Man O' War Exiled Waiheke and Ponui Islands Pinot Gris ★★★★

The youthful 2019 vintage (★★★★☆) was estate-grown on Waiheke and Ponui islands and handled without oak. Light yellow/green, it is mouthfilling and fleshy, with good intensity of fresh, lively peach, pear and spice flavours, a distinct splash of sweetness (27 grams/litre of residual sugar), fresh acidity, and a finely poised finish. Best drinking mid-2021+.

Vintage	19
WR	7
Drink	20-27

 MED $30 –V

Man O' War Waiheke and Ponui Islands Pinot Gris ★★★☆

Estate-grown on Waiheke and Ponui islands, the youthful 2019 vintage (★★★☆) was handled in tanks and made in an off-dry style. Pale gold, it is medium-bodied, with fresh, lively pear and spice flavours, gentle sweetness (15 grams/litre of residual sugar), and a crisp finish. Best drinking mid-2021+.

 MED $20 AV

Maori Point Grand Reserve Central Otago Pinot Gris (★★★★☆)

Still on sale, the 2013 vintage (★★★★☆) was fermented with indigenous yeasts and lees-stirred in French oak barrels (50 per cent new), and ensconced in a heavy, punted bottle. Last tasted in 2018, it is a sturdy, fleshy wine with rich stone-fruit flavours to the fore, oak-derived complexity, balanced acidity, and a long, bone-dry finish.

DRY $75 –V

Map Maker Marlborough Pinot Gris ★★★☆

From Staete Landt, the well-priced 2017 vintage (★★★☆) was estate-grown at Rapaura, in the Wairau Valley, hand-picked, and part of the blend was fermented in old French oak puncheons. It is a medium to full-bodied wine with vibrant, delicate pear and spice flavours, showing a touch of complexity, and a finely textured, dry (3.3 grams/litre of residual sugar) finish.

DRY $19 V+

Marsden Bay of Islands Pinot Gris ★★★★

In favourable seasons, this Kerikeri, Northland winery produces an impressive Pinot Gris. The 2020 vintage (★★★★) is a pale straw, attractively scented wine, full-bodied, with peach, pear and spice flavours, fresh and strong, and an off-dry finish. Well worth cellaring.

MED/DRY $31 –V

Martinborough Vineyard Te Tera Martinborough Pinot Gris ★★★★

Offering good value, the 2019 vintage (★★★★) is an attractively scented wine, fleshy and sweet-fruited. Bright, light lemon/green, it is weighty, with generous, ripe, peachy, slightly spicy flavours, and a dry (3.3 grams/litre of residual sugar), slightly creamy finish.

Vintage	19
WR	7
Drink	20-23

DRY $20 V+

Matahiwi Estate Wairarapa Pinot Gris (★★★☆)

Offering easy drinking, the 2020 vintage (★★★☆) is a very pale pink wine, medium-bodied, with good depth of fresh, peachy flavours, hints of strawberries and spices, and a dryish (6 grams/litre of residual sugar) finish. Best drinking mid-2021+.

Vintage	20
WR	5
Drink	20-23

MED/DRY $23 –V

Matawhero Single Vineyard Gisborne Pinot Gris ★★★☆

Still unfolding, the 2019 vintage (★★★☆), grown at Patutahi, is a freshly scented wine, medium-bodied, with good depth of pear, lychee and spice flavours, lively acidity, and an off-dry (5 grams/litre of residual sugar) finish.

MED/DRY $23 –V

Maude Central Otago Pinot Gris ★★★★☆

Attractively scented, the 2019 vintage (★★★★☆) is a regional blend, fermented in a mix of tanks (60 per cent) and seasoned French oak barriques (40 per cent). Mouthfilling and vibrantly fruity, it is full of youthful vigour, with strong, yet delicate, pear, lychee and spice flavours, a distinct touch of complexity, and a crisp, finely balanced, dry finish. Best drinking mid-2021+.

DRY $27 AV

Maui Marlborough Pinot Gris   ★★★☆

The easy-drinking 2017 vintage (★★★☆) was estate-grown in the upper Wairau Valley. It is full-bodied, with good depth of ripe, peachy flavours, a hint of sweetness, and a smooth, very harmonious finish. Ready. (From Tiki.)

MED/DRY $18 V+

ME by Matahiwi Estate Wairarapa Pinot Gris   (★★★☆)

Enjoyable young, the 2020 vintage (★★★☆) is a pale pink, fresh, medium-bodied wine, with plenty of peachy, spicy, strawberryish flavour, a hint of apricot, and a slightly sweet (6 grams/litre of residual sugar) finish.

Vintage	20
WR	5
Drink	20-23

MED/DRY $20 AV

Mills Reef Estate Hawke's Bay Pinot Gris   ★★★☆

Enjoyable young, the 2020 vintage (★★★) is a pale straw, easy-drinking wine with good depth of peach and pear flavours, hints of spices and ginger, and an off-dry (6 grams/litre of residual sugar) finish.

Vintage	20
WR	7
Drink	21-23

MED/DRY $19 V+

Mills Reef Reserve Hawke's Bay Pinot Gris   ★★★★

The attractive 2020 vintage (★★★★) is invitingly scented and full-bodied, with strong, ripe peach, pear, lychee and spice flavours, balanced acidity, and a very harmonious, basically dry (4 grams/litre of residual sugar) finish. Best drinking mid-2021+.

Vintage	20	19	18	17
WR	7	7	7	6
Drink	21-23	20-22	20-21	P

DRY $25 AV

Mischief Waipara Pinot Gris   (★★★★)

From a company based at Amberley, in North Canterbury, the 2018 vintage (★★★★) is enjoyable young. Full-bodied, it has ripe, peachy, vaguely honeyed flavours, a gentle splash of sweetness (8 grams/litre of residual sugar), and a welcoming fragrance.

MED/DRY $22 V+

Misha's Vineyard Dress Circle Central Otago Pinot Gris ★★★★★

The refined 2019 vintage (★★★★★) was estate-grown at Bendigo and 42 per cent of the blend was fermented with indigenous yeasts in old French oak hogsheads. Made in an off-dry style (6.3 grams/litre of residual sugar), it is highly scented and strongly varietal. Mouthfilling, it has rich, vibrant pear, lychee and spice flavours, a very subtle oak influence, fresh, balanced acidity and a very harmonious finish. Best drinking 2021+.

Vintage	19	18	17	16	15	14	13
WR	6	7	6	7	7	6	6
Drink	20-29	20-29	20-27	20-28	20-27	20-26	20-25

 MED/DRY $28 V+

Mission Marlborough Pinot Gris ★★★

Enjoyable young, the 2019 vintage (★★★) is an attractively scented, mouthfilling wine with vibrant, ripe, peachy flavours, and an off-dry (7 grams/litre of residual sugar), distinctly spicy finish.

MED/DRY $18 AV

Momo Organic Marlborough Pinot Gris (★★★★)

From Seresin, the 2020 vintage (★★★★) is certified organic. Bright, light lemon/green, it is a youthful, tightly structured wine, with fresh, peachy, slightly spicy flavours, showing good concentration, a touch of complexity and a dry finish. Best drinking mid-2021+.

DRY $20 V+

Montana Reserve Hawke's Bay Pinot Gris ★★★☆

Offering good value, the 2018 vintage (★★★☆) is a medium to full-bodied wine, drinking well in its youth. It has good depth of ripe, peachy, slightly spicy flavours, and a slightly sweet, well-rounded finish.

MED/DRY $17 V+

Montford Estate Marlborough Pinot Gris (★★★☆)

The vibrant, finely balanced 2019 vintage (★★★☆) was grown in the Wairau and Awatere valleys. Bright, light lemon/green, it is medium to full-bodied, with good depth of fresh, lively pear and spice flavours, dry (4 grams/litre of residual sugar) and crisp. (From te Pā.)

DRY $20 AV

Morepork Vineyard Northland Pinot Gris ★★★★☆

Estate-grown and hand-harvested at a very small, single-variety vineyard in Kerikeri, the very youthful 2020 vintage (★★★★☆) is richly scented and mouthfilling, with strong, ripe pear, lychee and spice flavours, showing very good delicacy, fresh acidity, and a long, basically dry (4 grams/litre of residual sugar), finely poised finish. Best drinking 2022+.

Vintage	20	19	18	17
WR	7	7	5	7
Drink	20-22	20-21	P	P

DRY $24 V+

Mount Brown Estates Grand Reserve North Canterbury Pinot Gris   ★★★★☆

Attractively scented, the strongly varietal 2019 vintage (★★★★☆) is already drinking well. Mouthfilling and vibrantly fruity, it has stone-fruit, pear and spice flavours, showing excellent delicacy and depth, slight sweetness (11 grams/litre of residual sugar), and a finely poised, lingering finish. Offering good value, it should be at its best 2021+.

Vintage	18
WR	6
Drink	20-24

 MED/DRY $22 V+

Mount Brown Estates North Canterbury Pinot Gris   ★★★☆

Offering great value, the 2020 vintage (★★★☆) was made with some use of oak (15 per cent of the blend was handled in old barriques). Softly mouthfilling, it is clearly varietal, with good depth of ripe peach, pear and spice flavours, fresh, balanced acidity, and an off-dry (7 grams/litre of residual sugar) finish. Enjoyable young, it offers very easy drinking.

Vintage	20
WR	7
Drink	20-24

MED/DRY $16 V+

Mount Edward Central Otago Pinot Gris   (★★★★☆)

The 2019 vintage (★★★★☆) is a single-vineyard wine, hand-harvested at Gibbston and fermented in tanks (60 per cent) and old oak casks (40 per cent). Bright, light lemon/green, it is full-bodied, with concentrated, peachy, slightly spicy flavours, showing a distinct touch of complexity, and a dryish, lively finish. Best drinking 2021+.

 MED/DRY $29 AV

Mount Riley Marlborough Pinot Gris   ★★★★

Priced sharply, the bright, light lemon/green 2020 vintage (★★★☆) is a youthful, easy-drinking style, fresh and lively, with mouthfilling body and good depth of pear and spice flavours, slightly sweet and smooth. Best drinking mid-2021+.

 MED/DRY $15 V+

Moutere Hills Nelson Pinot Gris   ★★★☆

Attractively scented, the 2019 vintage (★★★★) is a single-vineyard wine, mostly handled in tanks; 10 per cent of the blend was barrel-fermented. Bright, light yellow/green, it is medium to full-bodied, with very good vigour and depth of pear, lychee and spice flavours, fresh acidity, and a dryish (5 grams/litre of residual sugar), finely balanced finish. Best drinking 2021+.

MED/DRY $25 –V

Mt Beautiful North Canterbury Pinot Gris   ★★★★

Estate-grown at Cheviot, north of Waipara, the 2018 vintage (★★★★) is sturdy, with generous stone-fruit and spice flavours, showing a distinct touch of complexity, and a dry finish.

 DRY $24 AV

Mt Difficulty Bannockburn Pinot Gris   ★★★★☆

Grown and hand-picked at Bannockburn, in Central Otago, the 2018 vintage (★★★★☆) is a fleshy, dry wine (4 grams/litre of residual sugar). It is weighty and vibrantly fruity, with concentrated, ripe stone-fruit flavours, hints of ginger and spice, a touch of complexity, and a finely textured finish.

 DRY $26 AV

Mt Rosa Central Otago Pinot Gris   ★★★★☆

From a Gibbston-based producer, the 2018 vintage (★★★★) is fragrant, with a slightly creamy bouquet. Full-bodied and fleshy, it has very good depth of peachy, slightly spicy flavours and an off-dry, well-rounded finish.

 MED/DRY $30 –V

Mud House Single Vineyard Home Block Waipara Valley Pinot Gris   (★★★★☆)

The classy 2018 vintage (★★★★☆) is mouthfilling, with fresh, generous stone-fruit flavours, gentle spicy notes, good acidity and an off-dry, lingering finish.

 MED/DRY $26 AV

Mud House Sub Region Series Grovetown Marlborough Pinot Gris   ★★★★

The 2018 vintage (★★★★) was grown at Grovetown, north of Blenheim, in the Wairau Valley (and so is a district, rather than sub-regional, wine). It is scented, with generous, peachy, distinctly spicy, slightly gingery flavours. Forward in its appeal, it's a rather Gewürztraminer-like wine, ready to roll.

MED/DRY $20 V+

Nautilus Marlborough Pinot Gris   ★★★★☆

Still unfolding, the 2020 vintage (★★★★) was mostly tank-fermented (5 per cent of the blend was fermented in old oak casks). Mouthfilling, it is vibrantly fruity and dry (4 grams/litre of residual sugar), with youthful stone-fruit, lychee and spice flavours, showing very good drive, delicacy and harmony. Best drinking mid-2021+.

Vintage	20	19
WR	7	7
Drink	20-25	20-24

DRY $29 AV

Neck of the Woods Central Otago Pinot Gris   (★★★★)

The 2019 vintage (★★★★) was hand-harvested at Lowburn and Pisa, in the Cromwell Basin, and mostly (80 per cent) handled in old oak barrels. Freshly scented, it is full-bodied and vibrantly fruity, with lively pear, lychee and spice flavours, showing a touch of complexity, and a dry (1.5 grams/litre of residual sugar), crisp finish. Best drinking 2021+.

 DRY $28 –V

Neudorf Moutere Pinot Gris   ★★★★★

The youthful 2019 vintage (★★★★☆) is an estate-grown Nelson wine, fermented with indigenous yeasts (30 per cent in old oak barrels). Bright, light lemon/green, it is fresh and vibrant, with peach, pear and spice flavours, showing a touch of complexity, excellent delicacy and length, and an off-dry (6 grams/litre of residual sugar) finish. Best drinking 2022+.

MED/DRY $33 AV

Nikau Point Reserve Marlborough Pinot Gris   ★★☆

Estate-grown, the 2019 vintage (★★★) is enjoyable young. Freshly scented, with mouthfilling body, it has plenty of ripe, peachy, slightly spicy and gingery flavour, and a basically dry (4.8 grams/litre of residual sugar) finish.

DRY $16 AV

Nikau Point Select Hawke's Bay Pinot Gris   ★★☆

The 2020 vintage (★★☆) is a very easy-drinking style, full-bodied, with decent depth of peachy, spicy flavours, a hint of apricot, and an off-dry (7 grams/litre of residual sugar) finish.

MED/DRY $14 AV

Vintage	20
WR	6
Drink	20-22

Nobody's Hero Marlborough Pinot Gris   ★★★☆

From Framingham, the easy-drinking 2019 vintage (★★★☆) is a mouthfilling wine with vibrant, peachy, distinctly spicy flavours, a sliver of sweetness, balanced acidity and a smooth finish. Enjoyable young.

MED/DRY $20 AV

O:TU Marlborough Pinot Gris   ★★★☆

Offering very easy, enjoyable drinking, the 2020 vintage (★★★☆) is a lively, aromatic wine with vibrant peach, pear and spice flavours, a sliver of sweetness (7 grams/litre of residual sugar), balanced acidity and good depth.

MED/DRY $20 AV

Obsidian Estate Waiheke Island Pinot Gris   ★★★★

Faintly pink, the 2019 vintage (★★★★) is a youthful, single-vineyard wine, weighty and smooth. Attractively scented, it is full-bodied and strongly varietal, with pear, apple and spice flavours, showing very good freshness, delicacy and depth, and a dry (3.5 grams/litre of residual sugar) finish. Best drinking 2021+.

DRY $31 –V

Ohau Wines Selected Vines Pinot Gris   (★★★★)

Estate-grown in the Horowhenua, the 2019 vintage (★★★★) was partly oak-aged and made in a medium style (18 grams/litre of residual sugar). Pale straw, it is a vibrantly fruity, gently sweet wine, with mouthfilling body and very good depth of fresh peach, pear and spice flavours, finely balanced for early drinking.

MED $32 –V

Ohinemuri Limestone Pinot Gris   (★★★☆)

Still on sale, the 2016 vintage (★★★☆) was grown in Central Hawke's Bay and mostly handled in tanks, with 10 per cent barrel fermentation. Full-bodied, it has good depth of peachy, slightly spicy flavours and an off-dry (8 grams/litre of residual sugar) finish.

MED/DRY $27 –V

Old Coach Road Nelson Pinot Gris   ★★★

From Seifried, the fresh, lively 2020 vintage (★★★) is medium-bodied, with gentle pear, apple and spice flavours, fractional sweetness (6 grams/litre of residual sugar), balanced acidity and lots of drink-young charm. Priced right.

Vintage	20
WR	6
Drink	20-22

MED/DRY $14 V+

Opawa Marlborough Pinot Gris   ★★★☆

This wine is made in a 'lighter, crisper' style than its Nautilus Estate stablemate. Tank-fermented and briefly lees-aged, the 2019 vintage (★★★☆) is light yellow/green, fresh and full-bodied, with good depth of peachy, spicy, vaguely honeyed flavours, showing a touch of complexity, and a crisp, dry (3 grams/litre of residual sugar) finish. A slightly Gewürztraminer-like wine, it's already enjoyable.

DRY $22 AV

Ostler Lakeside Waitaki Valley Pinot Gris   ★★★★☆

Grown at Lake Waitaki, the youthful 2018 vintage (★★★★☆) was partly fermented in old oak barriques. Bright, light lemon/green, it is floral and weighty, with strong peach, pear and spice flavours, showing a distinct touch of complexity, gentle sweetness (14 grams/litre of residual sugar) balanced by fresh acidity, and obvious cellaring potential. Best drinking 2022+.

MED/DRY $30 –V

Ostler Waitaki Valley North Otago Pinot Gris   ★★★★★

Delicious now, the 2018 vintage (★★★★★) is part of Ostler's 'Grower Selection'. Full-bodied, it is concentrated, with vibrant, pure, pear-like flavours, hints of peaches and spices, a sliver of sweetness (8 grams/litre of residual sugar), lively acidity, and lovely depth, vibrancy and harmony. Fine value.

MED/DRY $25 V+

Oyster Bay Hawke's Bay Pinot Gris ★★★☆

Grown mostly at Crownthorpe, a relatively cool, elevated, inland district, this is a good, all-purpose wine, modelled on dry Italian Pinot Grigio rather than the richer, sweeter Pinot Gris of Alsace. Handled without oak, the 2019 vintage (★★★☆) is enjoyable young. Fragrant, it is medium to full-bodied, with fresh, lively peach, pear and spice flavours, and a smooth finish.

 DRY $20 AV

Paddy Borthwick Wairarapa Pinot Gris ★★★★

Estate-grown at Gladstone, the 2018 vintage (★★★★) is a full-bodied, partly barrel-fermented wine, with strong, vibrant pear, lychee and spice flavours, and a lingering, dry finish. Showing good varietal character and a distinct touch of complexity, it should be at its best 2021+.

 DRY $24 AV

Palliser Estate Martinborough Pinot Gris ★★★★

The 2019 vintage (★★★★☆) is an Alsace-style Pinot Gris, estate-grown and partly hand-harvested. Well worth cellaring, it is weighty and vibrantly fruity, with strong, ripe pear, peach and spice flavours, finely balanced acidity and a slightly sweet (8 grams/litre of residual sugar), harmonious finish. Best drinking 2022+.

 MED/DRY $31 –V

Pask Instinct Sun Kissed Hawke's Bay Pinot Gris ★★★☆

Offering good value, the 2020 vintage (★★★☆) is a mouthfilling, dry style (2 grams/litre of residual sugar), fresh and lively, with ripe peach, pear and spice flavours and a well-rounded finish. Enjoyable young.

 DRY $17 V+

Pencarrow Martinborough Pinot Gris ★★★☆

From Palliser Estate, the 2020 vintage (★★★☆) is pale, with fresh pear and spice aromas. A lively, medium-bodied wine, it has good depth of youthful pear, peach and spice flavours, a hint of sweetness and a finely balanced finish. Offering very easy drinking, it should be at its best mid-2021+.

 MED/DRY $23 –V

Peregrine Central Otago Pinot Gris ★★★★☆

Certified organic, the distinctive, lively 2019 vintage (★★★★☆) was estate-grown at Bendigo, Pisa and Gibbston, and handled with a small portion (20 per cent) of barrel fermentation. Bright, light lemon/green, it is finely scented and mouthfilling, with concentrated, peachy, slightly spicy flavours, and a basically dry (4 grams/litre of residual sugar) finish. Best drinking mid-2021+.

DRY $29 AV

Peregrine Saddleback Central Otago Pinot Gris ★★★★☆

The 2019 vintage (★★★★) was blended from estate-grown grapes, hand-harvested at Bendigo, Pisa and Gibbston. Light lemon/green, it is full-bodied, with lively peach, pear and spice flavours, showing good varietal character, and a fresh, finely balanced, basically dry (4.5 grams/litre of residual sugar) finish. Enjoyable young.

DRY $20 V+

Petane Hau Hau Block Hawke's Bay Pinot Gris ★★★★

Invitingly scented, the 2019 vintage (★★★★) was hand-harvested at Eskdale in two picks, mid and late season. Light yellow/green, it is a fresh, medium-bodied wine with strong peach, lychee and spice flavours, a sliver of sweetness, balanced acidity and lots of youthful vigour. Best drinking mid 2021+.

MED/DRY $27 –V

Prophet's Rock Central Otago Pinot Gris ★★★★★

Estate-grown and hand-picked at two Bendigo sites, in the Cromwell Basin, the bright, light lemon/green 2018 vintage (★★★★★) is delicious now. Fermented with indigenous yeasts, it is an Alsace-style wine, finely scented and full-bodied, with rich stone-fruit and spice flavours, showing a distinct touch of complexity, gentle sweetness, fresh acidity and notable depth, harmony and length. Drink now or cellar.

Vintage	18	17	16	15
WR	6	7	7	6
Drink	20-29	20-29	20-28	20-22

 MED/DRY $36 AV

Quartz Reef Bendigo Estate Single Vineyard Central Otago Pinot Gris ★★★★★

Certified organic and biodynamic, the 2019 vintage (★★★★★) was estate-grown at Bendigo, hand-picked and fermented and lees-aged in tanks. A top example of fully dry Pinot Gris (below 1 gram/litre of residual sugar), it is richly scented, full-bodied and finely textured, with excellent weight and depth of fresh pear, lychee and spice flavours, very pure, delicate and lingering. Best drinking 2022+. Tasted in early 2020, the 2018 vintage (★★★★★) is strongly scented, fleshy and dry (2 grams/litre of residual sugar), with generous, ripe stone-fruit and pear flavours, gentle acidity, a slightly oily texture and a well-rounded finish. A very harmonious wine with great drinkability, it's a drink now or cellaring proposition.

Vintage	19	18	17
WR	6	6	6
Drink	20-23	20-22	20-22

 DRY $33 AV

Ra Nui Wairau Valley Marlborough Pinot Gris ★★★★

The 2018 vintage (★★★★) was 20 per cent oak-fermented. Drinking well now, it is medium to full-bodied, with fresh, strong, peachy, slightly spicy flavours, lively acidity and an off-dry (6 grams/litre of residual sugar), finely balanced finish.

MED/DRY $25 AV

Rapaura Springs Reserve Marlborough Pinot Gris ★★★★

The 2019 vintage (★★★☆) was mostly handled in tanks; 5 per cent of the blend was fermented in old barrels. Light lemon/green, it is full-bodied, with vibrant, peachy flavours, hints of spices and ginger, a touch of complexity, and a dryish (6.5 grams/litre of residual sugar) finish.

 MED/DRY $19 V+

Vintage	19	18	17	16
WR	6	7	6	7
Drink	20-22	20-23	P	P

Renato Nelson Pinot Gris ★★★★

Drinking well in its youth, the 2019 vintage (★★★☆) is a blend of grapes from Upper Moutere and Kina, on the coast. Full-bodied, it has strong, peachy, spicy flavours, with a hint of strawberry, and an off-dry (9 grams/litre of residual sugar) finish.

 MED/DRY $20 V+

Vintage	19	18	17	16	15	14
WR	6	6	7	6	7	7
Drink	20-22	20-23	20-22	P	20-21	20-21

Rimu Grove Nelson Pinot Gris ★★★★★

The classy 2019 vintage (★★★★★) was grown in the Moutere hills and mostly handled in tanks; 15 per cent of the blend was French oak-aged. Bright, light lemon/green, it is a mouthfilling, fleshy wine, finely poised, with peach and pear flavours, showing excellent delicacy and richness, and an off-dry (8 grams/litre of residual sugar), long finish. Best drinking 2022+.

 MED/DRY $32 AV

Vintage	19
WR	7
Drink	20-35

Riverby Estate Marlborough Pinot Gris ★★★☆

The youthful, finely balanced 2019 vintage (★★★★) was handled in tanks. Bright, light lemon/green, it is a scented, medium-bodied wine with vibrant, peachy flavours, a sliver of sweetness (5 grams/litre of residual sugar), fresh acidity and a tightly structured, persistent finish. Best drinking mid-2021+.

 MED/DRY $22 AV

Vintage	19	18
WR	6	7
Drink	20-28	20-24

Rock Ferry 3rd Rock Marlborough Pinot Gris ★★★★☆

Certified organic, the 2018 vintage (★★★★☆) is an estate-grown wine, fleshy and full-bodied, with good complexity and a slightly creamy texture. Vibrantly fruity, it has strong, ripe stone-fruit flavours to the fore, balanced acidity and a dryish, long finish.

MED/DRY $27 AV

Rock Ferry Orchard Vineyard Pinot Gris on Skins   (★★★★☆)

Definitely a 'food' wine, the 2017 vintage (★★★★☆) was grown in Marlborough and oak-aged for nine months. Made in a dry style (3.5 grams/litre of residual sugar), it is straw-coloured, with a hint of orange. Full-bodied, it is concentrated, with strong, peachy, spicy flavours, a hint of oranges, a touch of tannin adding slight austerity, and loads of personality.

DRY $39 –V

Rock Ferry Trig Hill Vineyard Central Otago Pinot Gris   ★★★★★

Still on sale, the powerful, ageworthy 2016 vintage (★★★★☆) was estate-grown at Bendigo and partly (18 per cent) handled in seasoned oak puncheons. Ripely scented, it is sturdy and fleshy, with ripe, peachy, citrusy, spicy flavours, showing a distinct touch of complexity, and a dry (4.5 grams/litre of residual sugar), smooth finish. Best drinking 2021+. Certified organic.

DRY $33 AV

Rogue Vine Original Rogue Bay of Islands Pinot Gris   ★★★★

The youthful 2020 vintage (★★★★) is from 'rogue' (unintentional) plantings at Kerikeri, in Northland. Pale, fresh and full-bodied, it has good concentration of ripe stone-fruit, pear and spice flavours, fresh acidity, and an off-dry (7 grams/litre of residual sugar), smooth finish. Best drinking 2022+.

MED/DRY $25 AV

Ruru Central Otago Pinot Gris   ★★★☆

Grown in the Immigrant's Vineyard at Alexandra, the 2018 vintage (★★★★) was hand-picked and mostly fermented in tanks; 25 per cent of the blend was fermented in a new French oak barrel. It is a vibrantly fruity, full-bodied wine with good flavour intensity and a dryish (5.8 grams/litre of residual sugar), crisp, finely balanced finish.

MED/DRY $22 AV

Russian Jack Marlborough Pinot Gris   ★★★★

Priced sharply, the 2019 vintage (★★★★) is fresh and mouthfilling, with good concentration of peach, pear and spice flavours, dryish and smooth. A strongly varietal, invitingly scented wine, it's delicious from the start.

MED/DRY $19 V+

Saint Clair Origin Marlborough Pinot Gris   (★★★☆)

The 2017 vintage (★★★☆) is a fragrant, mouthfilling, dryish wine (4.6 grams/litre of residual sugar). Vibrantly fruity, it has peachy, slightly spicy flavours, showing very good depth, and a rounded finish.

DRY $22 AV

Saint Clair Pioneer Block 5 Bull Block Marlborough Pinot Gris   ★★★★

Full of personality, the 2016 vintage (★★★★☆) was grown in the Omaka Valley. Mouthfilling, rich and smooth, it has strong pear and peach flavours, a gentle splash of sweetness (10.6 grams/litre of residual sugar), and a very harmonious finish.

MED/DRY $27 –V

Sanctuary New Zealand Pinot Gris   ★★★☆

The 2018 vintage (★★★☆) is not identified by region, but offers good value. Fragrant, it is medium to full-bodied, with very good depth of fresh peach, pear and spice flavours, slight sweetness (7.1 grams/litre of residual sugar), and a smooth, harmonious finish. (From Foley Family Wines.)

MED/DRY $18 V+

Saveé Sea Marlborough Pinot Gris   (★★☆)

Priced right, the 2017 vintage (★★☆) is a fresh, medium-bodied wine, vibrantly fruity, with gentle, pear-like flavours and an off-dry finish. Pleasant, easy drinking. (From Awatere River Wine Co.)

MED/DRY $14 AV

Seifried Nelson Pinot Gris   ★★★

The very easy-drinking 2020 vintage (★★★☆) is a pale straw, medium-bodied wine with plenty of peachy, spicy flavour, a hint of apricot, fresh acidity and an off-dry (9 grams/litre of residual sugar) finish. A slightly Gewürztraminer-like wine, it's enjoyable from the start.

Vintage	20
WR	6
Drink	20-23

MED/DRY $19 AV

Selaks The Taste Collection Hawke's Bay Luscious Pinot Gris   (★★★☆)

The debut 2017 vintage (★★★☆) struck me more as a gently sweet, rather than truly 'luscious', wine. Fragrant and fresh, it has pear, lychee and spice flavours, showing good vigour and depth.

MED/DRY $22 AV

Seresin Marlborough Pinot Gris   ★★★★

Certified organic, this is one of the region's most distinctive Pinot Gris. The 2019 vintage (★★★★) was estate-grown and hand-picked in the Raupo Creek Vineyard, in the Omaka Valley. Partly oak-aged, it is a bright, light lemon/green, attractively scented wine, medium-bodied, with fresh, peachy, citrusy, slightly spicy flavours, showing a distinct touch of complexity, good delicacy and a finely balanced, dry (1.5 grams/litre of residual sugar), lingering finish. Best drinking mid-2021+.

DRY $25 AV

Sherwood Estate Stoney Range Waipara Valley Pinot Gris   ★★★☆

Offering good value, the 2019 vintage (★★★☆) was grown in North Canterbury and partly barrel-fermented. Full-bodied, it has very good depth of peachy, citrusy, slightly spicy flavours and a crisp, off-dry, finely balanced finish. Best drinking 2021+.

MED/DRY $17 V+

Sileni Cellar Selection Hawke's Bay Pinot Gris   ★★★

The smooth, easy-drinking 2019 vintage (★★★) is fresh and full-bodied, with lively, peachy, spicy flavours, and fractional sweetness (4.5 grams/litre of residual sugar) adding to its drink-young charm. A good, all-purpose wine.

DRY $20 –V

Sileni Estate Selection Priestess Hawke's Bay Pinot Gris   ★★★★

Drinking well now, the 2018 vintage (★★★★) is a full-bodied wine with concentrated stone-fruit and spice flavours, a hint of ginger, a distinct touch of barrel-ferment complexity (50 per cent), and a basically dry (4 grams/litre of residual sugar) finish.

DRY $22 V+

Snapper Rock Coastal New Zealand Pinot Gris   (★★★☆)

Bargain-priced, the 2019 vintage (★★★☆) is a single-vineyard wine, grown at Waipara. An easy-drinking, medium-bodied style, it is freshly scented, with good depth of vibrant fruit flavours, lively acidity and an off-dry (5 grams/litre of residual sugar) finish.

MED/DRY $15 V+

Soljans Estate Kumeu Pinot Gris   ★★★☆

Drinking well in its youth, the 2019 vintage (★★★★) was estate-grown and hand-picked at Kumeu, in West Auckland. Pale straw, it is weighty and fleshy, with strong stone-fruit and spice flavours and a dryish (6.5 grams/litre of residual sugar), smooth finish.

MED/DRY $20 AV

Southern Cross Hawke's Bay Pinot Gris   (★★★)

Priced right, the 2019 vintage (★★★) is freshly scented and full-bodied. Bright, light lemon/green, it is clearly varietal, with balanced acidity, good depth of pear and spice flavours, and an off-dry (5.5 grams/litre of residual sugar) finish. (From The Wine Portfolio.)

MED/DRY $16 V+

Spinyback Nelson Pinot Gris   ★★★

From Waimea Estate, the sharply priced 2018 vintage (★★★) is an aromatic, buoyantly fruity wine, medium-bodied, with citrusy, appley flavours, a hint of passionfruit, and a dryish finish. Good, easy drinking.

MED/DRY $15 V+

Spy Valley Envoy Johnson Vineyard Waihopai Valley Marlborough Pinot Gris ★★★★★

Estate-grown in the lower Waihopai Valley, the 2017 vintage (★★★★☆) was harvested from vines planted in 1999 and barrel-aged for 10 months. A medium-bodied wine, it has concentrated, fresh, peachy, spicy flavours, showing good complexity, and abundant sweetness (76 grams/litre of residual sugar). Well worth cellaring.

Vintage	17	16
WR	6	6
Drink	20-23	20-22

 SW $32 AV

Spy Valley Single Estate Marlborough Pinot Gris ★★★★☆

Drinking well now, the 2018 vintage (★★★★☆) was hand-picked at 23.7 to 26.3 brix in the Southern Valleys and fermented in tanks and old oak vessels. Bright, light yellow/green, it is fragrant and weighty, with rich, ripe stone-fruit flavours, a hint of ginger, a distinct touch of complexity, gentle acidity, and an off-dry (9.4 grams/litre of residual sugar), very harmonious finish.

 MED/DRY $25 V+

Stables Ngatarawa Pinot Gris ★★★

From Mission, the 2019 vintage (★★★), grown in Hawke's Bay, offers good value. Enjoyable young, it is mouthfilling, fresh and slightly creamy, with peachy, strongly spicy flavours, showing good depth, and a dryish finish.

 MED/DRY $13 V+

Stables Ngatarawa Reserve Hawke's Bay Pinot Gris ★★★☆

The 2019 vintage (★★★) is a pale straw wine, fresh and mouthfilling, with plenty of peachy, spicy flavour. Slightly Gewürztraminer-like, with an off-dry finish, it's enjoyable young.

 MED/DRY $16 V+

Staete Landt State of Bliss Marlborough Pinot Gris ★★★★☆

The 2017 vintage (★★★★☆) is a 'serious' style of Pinot Gris, estate-grown, hand-picked and fermented in old French oak puncheons. It is fragrant and weighty, with strong peach, pear and spice flavours, oak complexity and a long, dry (3.2 grams/litre of residual sugar) finish. Best drinking 2021+.

Vintage	17
WR	6
Drink	20-23

 DRY $25 V+

Stanley Estate Single Vineyard Awatere Valley Marlborough Pinot Gris ★★★

The 2019 vintage (★★☆) is a bright, light lemon/green, tightly structured wine with peachy, spicy, off-dry flavours and crisp acidity, but it lacks a bit of fragrance and finesse.

 MED/DRY $20 –V

Starborough Family Estate Marlborough Pinot Gris   ★★★★

The attractive 2020 vintage (★★★★) was grown in the Wairau (70 per cent) and Awatere (30 per cent) valleys, and mostly handled in tanks; 15 per cent of the blend was fermented in old oak barrels. Bright, light lemon/green, it is mouthfilling and vibrantly fruity, with strong, peachy, slightly spicy flavours, a hint of apricot, fresh acidity and a finely balanced, dryish (6 grams/litre of residual sugar) finish. Drink now or cellar.

 MED/DRY $20 V+

Stoneleigh Marlborough Pinot Gris   ★★★☆

The easy-drinking 2020 vintage (★★★☆) is full-bodied, with fresh, lively pear, lychee and spice flavours, showing good varietal character, a gentle splash of sweetness, balanced acidity, and a smooth finish. Priced right.

 MED/DRY $18 V+

Stoneleigh Wild Valley Marlborough Pinot Gris   ★★★★

Showing plenty of personality, the 2020 vintage (★★★★☆) was fermented with indigenous ('wild') yeasts. Bright, light lemon/green, it is an off-dry style, with fresh, strong pear and spice flavours, showing good vigour and complexity, and a finely balanced finish. Priced sharply.

 MED/DRY $20 V+

Sugar Loaf Marlborough Pinot Gris   (★★★★)

The 2018 vintage (★★★★) was handled in tanks (75 per cent) and old French oak (25 per cent). Full-bodied, it is fresh and vibrantly fruity, with ripe, peachy flavours to the fore, citrusy, appley, spicy notes, balanced acidity, and a tightly structured, dryish (6 grams/litre of residual sugar), lingering finish.

 MED/DRY $20 V+

Summerhouse Marlborough Pinot Gris   ★★★★

The 2020 vintage (★★★☆) is an easy-drinking style, with fresh, spicy aromas. It has good depth of lively, peachy, spicy flavours, with a hint of ginger, and an off-dry (6.2 grams/litre of residual sugar) finish. Open mid-2021+.

Vintage	20	19	18	17
WR	6	6	7	7
Drink	20-25	20-22	20-23	20-22

MED/DRY $19 V+

Tarras Vineyards Central Otago Pinot Gris   ★★★★☆

Grown in the Alexandra sub-region of Central Otago, the 2019 vintage (★★★★☆) is an attractively scented, mouthfilling and vibrantly fruity wine, with very good intensity of peach, pear and spice flavours, a touch of complexity and a dryish, crisp, lingering finish. Best drinking mid-2021+.

 MED/DRY $24 AV

Tatty Bogler Waitaki Valley North Otago Pinot Gris   ★★★★

Clearly a top vintage, the 2019 vintage (★★★★★) is an Alsace-style wine, produced in a full-bodied, vigorous, off-dry style. Weighty, with strong, vibrant stone-fruit flavours, gentle spicy notes, fresh acidity and a very harmonious finish, it's already delicious, but likely to be long-lived. Best drinking mid-2021+.

MED/DRY $25 AV

Te Awanga Estate Hawke's Bay Pinot Gris   (★★★★)

The characterful 2019 vintage (★★★★) is a faintly pink/orange wine, fresh and full-bodied. Drinking well in its youth, it has generous, ripe, peachy, spicy flavours, a hint of apricot and a dry, well-rounded finish.

DRY $20 V+

Te Kairanga Martinborough Pinot Gris   ★★★★

Well worth cellaring, the refined 2019 vintage (★★★★☆) was fermented in tanks (75 per cent) and old French oak puncheons (25 per cent). Light lemon/green, with fragrant, fresh, pear-like aromas, it is mouthfilling and vibrant, with peach, pear and spice flavours, showing excellent delicacy and depth, a distinct touch of complexity, and a dry finish (3 grams/litre of residual sugar).

DRY $25 AV

te Pā Marlborough Pinot Gris   ★★★★

Offering good value, the 2019 vintage (★★★★) was grown in the Awatere (68 per cent) and Wairau (32 per cent) valleys, and partly (20 per cent) barrel-fermented. Light lemon/green, it is mouthfilling and vibrantly fruity, with very good depth of youthful, peachy, slightly spicy flavours, hints of pears and ginger, balanced acidity, and a dryish (4.5 grams/litre of residual sugar) finish.

DRY $19 V+

Terra Sancta Lola's Block Bannockburn Central Otago Pinot Gris   ★★★★☆

The highly refined 2018 vintage (★★★★★) was hand-harvested and matured for 10 months in old, neutral French oak puncheons. Currently delicious, it is weighty, with excellent delicacy and depth of peach, pear and lychee flavours, a subtle suggestion of oak adding complexity, balanced acidity and a finely textured, dryish (5 grams/litre of residual sugar), lasting finish. Drink now to 2023. The vigorous, light lemon/green 2019 vintage (★★★★) is fresh and full-bodied, with youthful lemon, apple and lychee flavours, showing a distinct touch of complexity, and a crisp, dryish finish. Best drinking mid-2021+.

Vintage	18	17	16
WR	7	7	6
Drink	20-26	20-23	20-21

MED/DRY $29 AV

Terra Sancta Mysterious Diggings Bannockburn Central Otago Pinot Gris   ★★★★

Estate-grown, hand-picked and partly (10 per cent) barrel-fermented, the light lemon/green 2019 vintage (★★★★) is a youthful, full-bodied wine, with vibrant peach, pear and spice flavours, showing very good depth, and a dryish (5 grams/litre of residual sugar), finely poised finish. Best drinking 2021+.

Vintage	19	18	17
WR	6	6	7
Drink	20-22	20-21	20-22

MED/DRY $24 AV

Terrace Edge North Canterbury Pinot Gris   ★★★★☆

Certified organic, the 2019 vintage (★★★★☆) is a characterful Waipara wine, predominantly (60 per cent) fermented in old barrels; the rest was handled in tanks. Invitingly scented, it is fleshy, with good intensity of stone-fruit and spice flavours, a hint of toastiness and an off-dry (8 grams/litre of residual sugar) finish. Still youthful, it should break into full stride mid-2021+.

Vintage	19
WR	7
Drink	21-26

MED/DRY $25 V+

Theory & Practice Hawke's Bay Pinot Gris   ★★★★

Grown at two coastal sites, the 2018 vintage (★★★★) was fermented in tanks (mostly) and large German oak fuders. It is fresh and lively, with mouthfilling body, generous, peachy, slightly spicy flavours, a touch of complexity and an off-dry, well-rounded finish.

MED/DRY $25 AV

Thomas Legacy Waiheke Island Pinot Gris   (★★★★☆)

The rare (450 bottles only) 2018 vintage (★★★★☆) was estate-grown and hand-picked at Batch Winery. It is a finely balanced, medium-bodied style, with fresh, concentrated pear, peach and spice flavours, showing excellent delicacy and depth, and a slightly sweet (20 grams/litre of residual sugar), long finish.

MED $76 –V

Thornbury Waipara Pinot Gris   ★★★☆

The 2020 vintage (★★★☆), grown in North Canterbury, was tank-fermented and lees-aged. It is very pale straw, with scented, pear-like aromas. Fresh and vibrantly fruity, it has good depth of youthful pear, peach and spice flavours, and an off-dry (5.7 grams/litre of residual sugar) finish. A good buy. (From Villa Maria.)

Vintage	20	19	18	17	16
WR	5	6	5	4	7
Drink	20-22	20-21	20-21	P	P

MED/DRY $16 V+

Tiki Estate Waipara Pinot Gris   (★★★☆)

The lively 2019 vintage (★★★☆) is fresh and mouthfilling, with youthful, peachy, slightly spicy flavours, showing good depth, and an off-dry (6.5 grams/litre of residual sugar) finish. Best drinking 2021+.

Vintage	19	MED/DRY $20 AV
WR	6	
Drink	20-21	

Tohu Awatere Valley Marlborough Pinot Gris   ★★★☆

The 2019 vintage (★★★☆) is full-bodied and clearly varietal, with peach, pear and spice aromas, fresh, moderately concentrated flavours and a smooth, dryish (5 grams/litre of residual sugar) finish. Priced right.

Vintage	19	MED/DRY $18 V+
WR	7	
Drink	20-24	

Tohu Nelson Pinot Gris   (★★★☆)

The 2018 vintage (★★★☆) is a mouthfilling, fully dry wine (1.5 grams/litre of residual sugar), with very good depth of fresh, pear-like flavours, slightly spicy notes and a finely balanced, smooth finish.

DRY $18 V+

Toi Toi Brookdale Reserve Marlborough Pinot Gris   ★★★★

The 2019 vintage (★★★★) is an attractively scented, full-bodied, vibrant wine, with fresh, youthful pear and lychee flavours, showing clear-cut varietal characteristics, and a slightly sweet, very harmonious finish. Best drinking mid-2021+.

MED/DRY $22 V+

Toi Toi Marlborough Pinot Gris   ★★★☆

The 2018 vintage (★★★☆) is a fresh, mouthfilling wine, grown in the Omaka Valley. It has pear and lemon flavours, showing very good delicacy and vibrancy, balanced acidity and a smooth, off-dry (7.7 grams/litre of residual sugar) finish.

Vintage	18	MED/DRY $17 V+
WR	7	
Drink	P	

Trinity Hill Hawke's Bay Pinot Gris   ★★★☆

The 2020 vintage (★★★☆) is a single-vineyard wine. Pale/lemon, it is medium-bodied, fresh and lively, with very youthful, peachy, slightly spicy flavours and an off-dry, smooth finish. Best drinking 2022+.

MED/DRY $23 –V

Two Sisters Central Otago Pinot Gris

★★★★☆

The youthful 2019 vintage (★★★★☆) is a single-vineyard wine, hand-harvested at Lowburn, in the Cromwell Basin, and fermented with indigenous yeasts. Well worth cellaring, it is a bright, light lemon/green, full-bodied wine, with vibrant, dry peach, pear and spice flavours, showing excellent delicacy, purity and length. Best drinking 2021+.

 DRY $30 –V

Unison Bumble Bee Hawke's Bay Pinot Gris

(★★★★)

The fleshy, youthful 2019 vintage (★★★★) was hand-picked, tank-fermented and lees-stirred for three months. Full-bodied, it has fresh, strong peach, pear, lychee and spice flavours, finely balanced acidity and a fully dry finish. Best drinking mid 2021+.

 DRY $24 AV

Urlar Gladstone Pinot Gris

★★★★

Certified organic, the light gold 2018 vintage (★★★★☆) was estate-grown and hand-picked in the northern Wairarapa, and fermented and aged in old oak barrels. Showing strong personality, it is a fresh, medium-bodied wine with concentrated, peachy, vaguely honeyed flavours, considerable complexity, and a long, basically dry finish. Drink now or cellar.

Vintage	17
WR	6
Drink	19-23

 DRY $29 –V

Valli Gibbston Vineyard Central Otago Pinot Gris

★★★★☆

Still unfolding, the 2019 vintage (★★★★☆) was estate-grown, hand-picked and handled without oak. Bright, light lemon/green, it is a refined, very youthful wine with vibrant, citrusy, slightly appley and peachy flavours, fresh acidity, and a long, dry (3 grams/litre of residual sugar) finish. Best drinking 2022+.

Vintage	19	18	17	16
WR	5	7	7	7
Drink	22-32	20-26	20-25	20-24

 DRY $30 –V

Vavasour Awatere Valley Marlborough Pinot Gris

★★★★★

A consistently impressive wine, bargain-priced. Partly (10 per cent) fermented and matured for four months in seasoned French oak casks, the 2019 vintage (★★★★★) has a fresh, fragrant bouquet. Very finely balanced, with peachy, slightly spicy flavours, showing lovely delicacy and depth, it's an off-dry style (7 grams/litre of residual sugar), already delicious.

MED/DRY $23 V+

Vidal Hawke's Bay Pinot Gris ★★★★

Offering fine value, the 2020 vintage (★★★★) was grown mostly at Maraekakaho, in the Bridge Pa Triangle. Made in a dry style (4 grams/litre of residual sugar), it is freshly scented and mouthfilling, with strong, vibrant, pear-like flavours, gentle spicy notes, and excellent delicacy and length.

DRY $16 V+

Vintage	20	19	18	17
WR	6	7	6	6
Drink	20-22	20-21	P	P

Vidal Reserve Hawke's Bay Pinot Gris ★★★★

Showing good intensity, the 2019 vintage (★★★★) is a single-vineyard wine, matured for 10 months on its yeast lees in tanks. Full-bodied, it has vibrant pear, peach and spice flavours, attractive delicacy, and a basically dry (4 grams/litre of residual sugar), lengthy finish.

DRY $20 V+

Vintage	20	19
WR	6	7
Drink	20-22	20-21

Villa Maria Cellar Selection Marlborough Pinot Gris ★★★★

The 2020 vintage (★★★★) is a mouthfilling, fleshy, dryish wine (5.8 grams/litre of residual sugar), with very good depth of ripe stone-fruit flavours, hints of pears and spices, and a finely balanced, very harmonious finish. Best drinking mid-2021+. Fine value.

MED/DRY $15 V+

Vintage	20
WR	7
Drink	20-22

Villa Maria Platinum Selection Sur Lie Marlborough Pinot Gris (★★★★★)

The delicious, youthful 2019 vintage (★★★★★) was grown mostly in the Awatere Valley and partly barrel-fermented. Richly scented, it is fleshy and vibrant, with intensely varietal flavours of pears, peaches and lychees, showing excellent delicacy and depth, and a dryish finish.

MED/DRY $25 V+

Villa Maria Private Bin East Coast Pinot Gris ★★★★

The very easy-drinking, great-value 2020 vintage (★★★★) is full of youthful vigour. Bright, light lemon/green, it is vibrantly fruity, with strong peach, pear and spice flavours, a sliver of sweetness (5.5 grams/litre of residual sugar), and a finely poised, lingering finish.

MED/DRY $13 V+

Vintage	20	19	18	17	16
WR	7	7	7	7	6
Drink	20-23	20-22	20-21	P	P

Villa Maria Single Vineyard Seddon Marlborough Pinot Gris ★★★★★

One of the country's top Pinot Gris, this Awatere Valley wine is estate-grown, hand-harvested and barrel-fermented (90 per cent in seasoned oak barrels in 2019). The light yellow/green 2019 vintage (★★★★☆) is a mouthfilling, fleshy wine, with strong, yet delicate, stone-fruit and spice flavours, fresh acidity, and a finely poised, dryish (5 grams/litre of residual sugar) finish.

Vintage	19	18	17	16
WR	6	7	6	7
Drink	20-25	20-22	P	P

MED/DRY $30 AV

Volcanic Hills Marlborough Pinot Gris (★★★☆)

Grown in the Awatere Valley, the 2019 vintage (★★★☆) is a fresh, full-bodied wine with ripe peach and pear flavours, hints of spices and ginger, and a dryish finish. Enjoyable young.

MED/DRY $23 –V

Waimea Nelson Pinot Gris ★★★☆

The 2019 vintage (★★★☆) is already drinking well. Bright, light lemon/green, it is mouthfilling, with good depth of fresh, peachy, gently spicy flavours, a hint of ginger, and an off-dry finish.

MED/DRY $18 V+

West Brook Waimauku Pinot Gris ★★★☆

The 2018 vintage (★★★★) is a fresh and lively, medium-bodied wine, with peach, pear, lychee and spice flavours, showing very good delicacy, vibrancy and depth. Made in an off-dry style, it should be at its best mid-2021+.

Vintage	16
WR	5
Drink	19-22

MED/DRY $25 –V

Whitehaven Marlborough Pinot Gris ★★★★

The fragrant 2018 vintage (★★★★) is vibrantly fruity, with very good depth of peachy, slightly spicy and gingery flavours, and an off-dry (5.3 grams/litre of residual sugar), smooth, very harmonious finish. Best drinking 2021+.

MED/DRY $22 V+

Wild Earth Central Otago Pinot Gris ★★★★☆

Still unfolding, the 2019 vintage (★★★★) is a 3:1 blend of Gibbston and Lowburn grapes, partly (25 per cent) fermented in old French oak barrels. Pale lemon/green, it has strong, pear-like aromas and flavours, peachy and spicy notes, a distinct touch of complexity and a long, lively finish. Best drinking mid-2021+.

MED/DRY $28 AV

Wither Hills Cellar Selection Marlborough Pinot Gris   (★★★★☆)

The vigorous 2018 vintage (★★★★☆) is a single-vineyard, Awatere Valley wine. Mouthfilling and vibrant, with rich pear, peach and spice flavours, showing good delicacy, it is youthful, with a dryish finish. Best drinking 2021+.

 MED/DRY $26 AV

Wither Hills Marlborough Pinot Gris   ★★★☆

Fragrant and full-bodied, the 2019 vintage (★★★★) has generous pear and spice flavours, a sliver of sweetness and finely balanced acidity. An Alsace-style Pinot Gris, with very good weight, depth and harmony, it's delicious young,

 MED/DRY $18 V+

Woven Stone Ohau Single Vineyard Pinot Gris   (★★★☆)

From Ohau, in the Horowhenua, the 2019 vintage (★★★☆) is a faintly pink wine. Fresh and gently spicy, it is an easy-drinking style, with peachy, strawberryish flavours, a distinct touch of tannin, good depth and an off-dry (9.8 grams/litre of residual sugar) finish.

 MED/DRY $17 V+

Yealands Estate Single Vineyard Marlborough Pinot Gris   ★★★★

Estate-grown in the Seaview Vineyard, in the lower Awatere Valley, the 2019 vintage (★★★★) was partly barrel-fermented. Bright, light lemon/green, it is mouthfilling, with vibrant peach, pear and spice flavours, showing very good depth, a touch of complexity, and a dry (3.4 grams/litre of residual sugar) finish. Best drinking 2021+.

 DRY $25 AV

Vintage	19
WR	6
Drink	20-24

Yealands Reserve Awatere Valley Marlborough Pinot Gris   (★★★★)

Already very open and expressive, the 2019 vintage (★★★★) was estate-grown in the Awatere Valley. It is invitingly scented and mouthfilling, with vibrant, peachy, spicy, slightly gingery flavours, balanced acidity and a smooth, dry (3 grams/litre of residual sugar) finish.

DRY $19 V+

Riesling

Riesling isn't yet one of New Zealand's great successes in overseas markets and most New Zealand wine lovers also ignore Riesling. The favourite white-wine variety of many winemakers especially those in the South Island — Riesling barely registers on the wine sales charts in supermarkets, generating about 1 per cent of the dollar turnover.

Around the world, Riesling has traditionally been regarded as Chardonnay's great rival in the white-wine quality stakes, well ahead of Sauvignon Blanc. So why are wine lovers here slow to appreciate Riesling's stature?

Riesling is usually made in a slightly sweet style, to balance the grape's natural high acidity, but this obvious touch of sweetness runs counter to the fashion for dry wines. And fine Riesling demands time (at the very least, three years) to unfold its full potential; drunk in its infancy, as it so often is, it lacks the toasty, minerally, honeyed richness that is the real glory of Riesling.

After being overhauled by Pinot Gris in 2007, Riesling ranks as New Zealand's fourth most extensively planted white-wine variety. However, between 2007 and 2020, its total area of bearing vines contracted from 868 to 665 hectares.

The great grape of Germany, Riesling is a classic cool-climate variety, particularly well suited to the cooler growing temperatures and lower humidity of the South Island. Its two strongholds are Marlborough (where 40 per cent of the vines are clustered) and Canterbury (36 per cent), but the grape is also widely planted in Otago, Nelson and Wairarapa.

Riesling styles vary markedly around the world. Most Marlborough wines are medium to full-bodied (11 to 13 per cent alcohol), with just a touch of sweetness. However, a new breed of Riesling has emerged in the past decade – lighter (only 7.5 to 10 per cent alcohol) and markedly sweeter. These refreshingly light, sweet Rieslings offer a more vivid contrast in style to New Zealand's other major white wines, and are much closer in style to the classic German model.

Anchorage Family Estate Nelson Riesling ★★★☆

Light and lively, the 2019 vintage (★★★☆) is a dryish style (5 grams/litre of residual sugar), with very good depth of lemony, appley flavours, fresh, crisp and full of youthful vigour.

MED/DRY $18 V+

Astrolabe Farm Marlborough Dry Riesling ★★★★

Grown at Grovetown, in the Wairau Valley, the 2018 vintage (★★★★) is a single-vineyard wine, partly hand-picked. A fresh, medium-bodied wine, it has citrusy, slightly appley flavours, showing very good vigour and depth, and a slightly off-dry (5.3 grams/litre of residual sugar), crisp finish. Drink now or cellar.

Vintage	18
WR	6
Drink	20-31

MED/DRY $27 –V

Ataahua Waipara Riesling ★★★★☆

Instantly appealing, the 2018 vintage (★★★★☆) is a rich, medium style (44 grams/litre of residual sugar). Attractively scented, it has strong, citrusy, peachy, slightly appley flavours, showing good delicacy, and a lovely balance of sweetness and mouth-watering acidity. Drink now or cellar.

Vintage	18	17
WR	7	6
Drink	20-25	20-25

MED $26 AV

Aurum Central Otago Dry Riesling ★★★★☆

The 2018 vintage (★★★★☆) was hand-harvested from 20-year-old vines. It is mouthfilling and fresh, with strong, peachy, citrusy flavours, a sliver of sweetness (8 grams/litre of residual sugar) and firm acid spine. Showing excellent weight, intensity and length, it's well worth cellaring.

Vintage	18	17
WR	6	6
Drink	20-30	20-27

 MED/DRY $28 AV

Bald Hills Last Light Bannockburn Central Otago Single Vineyard Riesling ★★★★☆

The richly scented 2018 vintage (★★★★★) has a strong sense of youthful drive. Light lemon/green, it is medium-bodied, with penetrating, yet delicate, citrusy, appley flavours, some peachy notes, appetising acidity, and a distinctly off-dry (25 grams/litre of residual sugar), lasting finish. Already delicious, it's well worth cellaring to 2022+. The 2017 vintage (★★★★) is an attractively scented, medium-bodied wine with citrusy flavours, a hint of passionfruit and very good depth. Slightly sweet (21 grams/litre of residual sugar), with some toasty, bottle-aged notes emerging, it's drinking well now.

 MED $30 –V

Bannock Brae Central Otago Dry Riesling ★★★★☆

Grown in the Cromwell Basin, the characterful 2017 vintage (★★★★☆) reflects 'traditional practices of German winemakers 200 years ago', including fermentation in old oak barrels. It is lively and minerally, with strong lemon/lime flavours, showing excellent delicacy and complexity, and a crisp, dry (4.6 grams/litre of residual sugar) but not austere finish.

 DRY $25 V+

Black Barn Single Vineyard Hawke's Bay Riesling (★★★★☆)

Unfolding well, the 2019 vintage (★★★★☆) is a 'Mosel style' wine, harvested from 25-year-old vines at Havelock North. Light-bodied, it is vivacious, with a delicious interplay of sweetness (45 grams/litre of residual sugar) and acidity, good intensity of citrusy, appley flavours, and complex, bottle-aged notes starting to emerge.

 MED $39 –V

Black Estate Damsteep North Canterbury Riesling ★★★★

Certified organic, the 2019 vintage (★★★★) is a dry style (1.8 grams/litre of residual sugar), given an extended period of lees-aging in stainless steel tanks and some old barrels. Pale straw, with yeasty aromas, it is full-bodied, with generous, ripe stone-fruit and spice flavours, a hint of ginger, and good complexity and harmony. A distinctive wine, it's already quite expressive and likely to be at its best 2021+.

DRY $30 –V

Black Stilt Waitaki Valley Riesling ★★★★

Still on sale, the 2016 vintage (★★★★) is a fragrant, full-bodied wine from North Otago. It is slightly sweet (15 grams/litre of residual sugar), with strong, citrusy, appley flavours, youthful vigour, balanced acidity, and good harmony.

MED $22 V+

Bladen Eight Rows Marlborough Riesling (★★★★)

From eight rows of mature vines, the fragrant 2019 vintage (★★★★) is a single-vineyard, hand-harvested wine, grown in the Wairau Valley. Bright, light lemon/green, it is medium-bodied, with lemony, appley flavours, showing excellent vigour and depth, a gentle splash of sweetness (16 grams/litre of residual sugar), and a finely poised finish. Best drinking 2021+.

MED $25 AV

Blank Canvas Marlborough Riesling (★★★★)

The 2018 vintage (★★★★) is a single-vineyard, Awatere Valley wine, light-bodied (8.6 per cent alcohol) and gently sweet (23 grams/litre of residual sugar), with mouth-watering acidity. It has strong, lemony, appley flavours, showing very good delicacy and harmony, and obvious cellaring potential; open 2021+.

Vintage	18
WR	5
Drink	20-25

MED $28 –V

Boneline, The, Hellblock Waipara Riesling ★★★★☆

The highly appealing 2018 vintage (★★★★☆) is a medium style (21 grams/litre of residual sugar). Bright, light lemon/green, it is medium-bodied, with good intensity of citrusy, limey flavours, showing excellent freshness and vigour, and a finely balanced, lingering finish. Best drinking 2021+.

MED $32 –V

Boneline, The, Waipara Dry Riesling (★★★★)

Almost dry (6 grams/litre of residual sugar) but not austere, the 2017 vintage (★★★★) is a light lemon/green, fragrant, medium-bodied wine. Showing good concentration, it has citrusy, slightly appley flavours, balanced acidity, a touch of bottle-aged complexity, and good harmony. Drink now or cellar.

MED/DRY $28 –V

Brennan Gibbston Central Otago Riesling (★★★★☆)

The powerful 2018 vintage (★★★★☆) is full-bodied, with fresh grapefruit and peach flavours, showing good ripeness and richness. Bright, light lemon/green, with gentle sweetness and lively acidity, it's a generous, finely balanced wine, well worth cellaring.

MED/DRY $33 –V

Brightwater Vineyards Nelson Natural Light Riesling   (★★★★)

Freshly scented, the 2019 vintage (★★★★) is light in terms of alcohol (9 per cent), but there's no shortage of flavour. Bright, light lemon/green, it is tightly structured, with vibrant, lemony, appley flavours, showing good intensity, and a slightly sweet (10 grams/litre of residual sugar), mouth-wateringly crisp finish. Best drinking 2021+.

Vintage	19
WR	6
Drink	20-23

 MED/DRY $22 V+

Brightwater Vineyards Nelson Riesling   ★★★★☆

Estate-grown and hand-picked on the Waimea Plains, the 2017 vintage (★★★★☆) is an off-dry style (10 grams/litre of residual sugar). A finely poised, medium-bodied wine, it has strong, fresh, lively, lemony flavours, hints of limes and apricots, good acid spine, and a long finish. Already enjoyable, it should be at its best 2021+.

Vintage	17
WR	6
Drink	20-22

 MED/DRY $22 V+

Burn Cottage Central Otago Riesling/Grüner Veltliner   ★★★★☆

Certified organic, the 2017 vintage (★★★★★) is an estate-grown, hand-picked blend of Riesling (67 per cent) and Grüner Veltliner (33 per cent), fermented and matured for 11 months in stainless steel barrels and old oak barriques. Bright, light yellow/green, it is mouthfilling, with highly concentrated, peachy, slightly spicy and toasty flavours, showing good complexity, and a finely balanced, dryish (10 grams/litre of residual sugar) finish. Full of personality.

MED/DRY $55 –V

Carrick Central Otago Dry Riesling   ★★★★☆

Certified organic, the 2017 vintage (★★★★☆) is a bone-dry wine, hand-picked and fermented with indigenous yeasts in old French oak barrels. It is fresh, medium-bodied and vibrantly fruity, with good intensity of lemony, appley flavours, a minerally streak, good acid spine and obvious potential; open 2021+.

Vintage	17
WR	6
Drink	20-26

 DRY $27 AV

Caythorpe Family Estate Marlborough Riesling   ★★★☆

The youthful 2020 vintage (★★★☆) is a single-vineyard, Wairau Valley wine. Fresh and lively, it is medium-bodied, with citrusy, limey flavours, and an off-dry (7 grams/litre of residual sugar) finish. Balanced for easy drinking, it should be at its best 2022+.

MED/DRY $20 AV

Ceres Black Rabbit Vineyard Central Otago Riesling   ★★★★☆

Grown at Bannockburn, the 2018 vintage (★★★★☆) is attractively scented, with a Mosel-like balance and lightness (10.5 per cent alcohol). Bright, light lemon/green, it is vivacious, with strong lemon/lime flavours, gentle sweetness (34 grams/litre of residual sugar), and fresh acidity. Already delicious, it's age-worthy too.

Clark Estate Block 8 Marlborough Riesling   ★★★★

The 2017 vintage (★★★★☆) is an elegant, Mosel-style wine, offering good value. Grown in the upper Awatere Valley, it is fresh, light (8 per cent alcohol) and lively, with strong, citrusy, slightly appley flavours, a distinct splash of sweetness (42 grams/litre of residual sugar), firm acid spine, and obvious cellaring potential. Best drinking 2021+.

Clark Estate Classic Marlborough Riesling   (★★★★)

Delicious young, the 2018 vintage (★★★★) is an attractively scented wine, grown in the upper Awatere Valley. Pale straw, it is fresh, medium-bodied and crisp, with a gentle splash of sweetness and generous, ripe, peachy flavours, showing good vigour and depth. Balanced for easy drinking, it should also reward cellaring.

Coopers Creek Marlborough Riesling   ★★★☆

Finely balanced for early enjoyment, the 2018 vintage (★★★☆) is a fresh, medium-bodied wine with vibrant, lemony, appley flavours, showing good depth, a gentle splash of sweetness and lively acidity. Drink now or cellar.

MED/DRY $18 V+

Crater Rim, The, Waipara Riesling   ★★★★☆

Tasted in mid-2018, the 2012 to 2014 vintages, all from a single vineyard, showed impressive quality and value. The 2014 vintage (★★★★☆) is a medium style (30 grams/litre of residual sugar), with strong, ripe, peachy, slightly spicy flavours, building bottle-aged complexity. The 2013 vintage (★★★★☆) has excellent drive and depth, with peachy, spicy flavours, low alcohol (9.5 per cent), gentle sweetness, and lovely harmony. Maturing well, the 2012 vintage (★★★★) is slightly more restrained, with a pale lemon/green hue, good weight, a splash of sweetness, and strong, lemony, appley flavours.

Dashwood by Vavasour Marlborough Riesling   ★★★★

The 2019 vintage (★★★★) offers top value. Light-bodied, it is attractively scented, with vibrant, citrusy, slightly appley flavours, gentle sweetness (19 grams/litre of residual sugar), appetising acidity, and very good delicacy, depth and harmony. Already enjoyable, it should be at its best 2021+.

Vintage	19
WR	7
Drink	20-25

Doctors', The Marlborough Riesling ★★★★

Light and lively, the 2019 vintage (★★★★) is already very enjoyable. Crafted in a low-alcohol style (9 per cent), it is strongly varietal, with fresh, citrusy, appley flavours, a distinct splash of sweetness (37 grams/litre of residual sugar), and finely balanced acidity. Good summertime sipping. (From Forrest Estate.)

MED $22 V+

Domain Road Duffers Creek Bannockburn Central Otago Riesling ★★★★☆

Drinking well now, the 2017 vintage (★★★★☆) is a medium style, hand-picked at two sites. It is invitingly scented, with strong, vibrant, citrusy, slightly appley flavours, a gentle splash of sweetness (14.7 grams/litre of residual sugar), appetising acidity, and a long finish. Full of youthful vigour, it should be at its best 2021+.

MED/DRY $25 V+

Domain Road The Water Race Bannockburn Central Otago Dry Riesling ★★★★

Highly scented, the 2017 vintage (★★★★☆) is a vigorous, youthful wine, dryish (5.5 grams/ litre of residual sugar) rather than bone-dry. Bright, light lemon/green, it is medium-bodied, with penetrating, vibrant, citrusy flavours, firm acid spine and obvious potential; open 2021+.

MED/DRY $25 AV

Dragon Bones Waitaki Valley North Otago Riesling (★★★★★)

From Lone Hill Vineyard, the 2016 vintage (★★★★★) is a delicious wine, bargain-priced. Described as a 'spatlese trocken style', it is a single-vineyard, hand-picked wine, with a bright light lemon/green hue and highly scented bouquet. Full of personality, it has intense, peachy, lemony flavours, gentle sweetness (7 grams/litre of residual sugar), crisp acidity, slightly toasty, bottle-aged notes adding complexity, and a poised, long finish. Great value.

MED/DRY $22 V+

Dry River Craighall Vineyard Martinborough Riesling ★★★★★

One of the finest Rieslings in the country, this is typically a wine of exceptional purity, delicacy and depth, with a proven ability to flourish in the cellar for many years. The grapes are sourced from a small block of mature vines, mostly over 20 years old, in the Craighall Vineyard, with yields limited to an average of 6 tonnes per hectare, and the wine is stop-fermented just short of dryness – the 2019 vintage (★★★★★) has 7 grams/litre of residual sugar. Bright, light lemon/green, it has a real sense of youthful drive and vigour. Approachable now, but well worth cellaring to at least 2024, it has intense, citrusy flavours to the fore, lively acidity, hints of peaches and spices, and a dryish, lasting finish.

MED/DRY $55 AV

Dry River Craighall Vineyard Selection Martinborough Riesling   ★★★★★

This consistently classy wine is late-harvested to 'produce a Riesling with low alcohol, high residual sugar and high acidity, in order to create a tension between these components'. The gently botrytis-affected 2018 vintage (★★★★★) is a lovely mouthful. Bright, light gold, it has a fragrant, slightly honeyed bouquet, concentrated, ripe, peachy flavours, abundant sweetness (120 grams/litre of residual sugar), and a crisp, lasting finish. Drink now or cellar.

SW $69 –V

Esk Valley Marlborough Riesling   ★★★★

The 2019 vintage (★★★★) is a tightly structured wine, bright, light lemon/green, with lemony, appley flavours, showing very good vigour and depth, and an off-dry, crisp finish. Still unfolding, it should break into full stride 2022+.

Vintage	18	17	MED/DRY $20 V+
WR	6	6	
Drink	20-25	20-23	

Felton Road Bannockburn Central Otago Riesling   ★★★★★

Estate-grown in The Elms Vineyard, this gently sweet style has deep flavours woven with fresh acidity. It offers more drink-young appeal than its Dry Riesling stablemate, but invites long-term cellaring. Hand-picked and tank-fermented with indigenous yeasts, it is bottled with a high level of residual sugar (56 grams/litre in 2020). Vivacious and finely poised, the 2020 vintage (★★★★★) shows notable vigour, delicacy and intensity. Bright, light lemon/green, it has incisive lemon, apple and lime flavours, fresh acidity, and obvious potential; best drinking 2025+.

Vintage	20	19	18	SW $41 AV
WR	7	7	7	
Drink	20-40	20-39	20-38	

Felton Road Dry Riesling   ★★★★★

Estate-grown in schisty soils at Bannockburn, in Central Otago, this wine is hand-picked in The Elms Vineyard and fermented with indigenous yeasts. The 2020 vintage (★★★★★) is an immaculate, full-bodied wine, bright, light lemon/green, with deep, peachy, citrusy, limey flavours, and a finely poised, basically dry (6 grams/litre of residual sugar), lasting finish. Already very harmonious, it should break into full stride 2025+.

Vintage	20	19	18	MED/DRY $41 AV
WR	7	7	7	
Drink	20-35	20-34	20-33	

Forrest Marlborough Riesling ★★★★

Drinking well now, the 2017 vintage (★★★★) is light to medium-bodied (10.5 per cent alcohol), with fresh, strong, citrusy flavours, a splash of sweetness (8 grams/litre of residual sugar), and very good depth and harmony.

MED/DRY $20 V+

Framingham Classic Marlborough Riesling ★★★★★

Top vintages of this Marlborough wine are strikingly aromatic, richly flavoured and zesty. The classy, very age-worthy 2019 vintage (★★★★★) was harvested from 'some of Marlborough's oldest Riesling vines'. Bright, light yellow/green, it is a medium-dry style (14 grams/litre of residual sugar), with penetrating, peachy, citrusy, limey flavours, threaded with lively acidity, and lovely depth, vigour and harmony. Best drinking 2022+.

MED/DRY $30 AV

Framingham Jack Frost Marlborough Riesling (★★★★)

In a growing season when 'your organic Riesling vineyard gets frosted for the first time in 35 years, what do you do?', Framingham checked with mates next door, to see what else was available. The 2016 vintage (★★★★) is mouthfilling, ripe and rounded, with gentle sweetness, moderate acidity, and strong, peachy, vaguely honeyed flavours.

MED $20 V+

Georges Road Block Three Waipara Riesling ★★★★☆

The 2017 vintage (★★★★☆) was estate-grown in North Canterbury, hand-picked, fermented with indigenous yeasts and lees-aged. A tightly structured, medium-bodied wine, it is highly scented, with strong, peachy, citrusy, slightly spicy and gingery flavours, crisp, lively acidity, and an off-dry (8 grams/litre of residual sugar), lasting finish. It should be long-lived.

MED/DRY $25 V+

Gibbston Valley GV Collection Central Otago Riesling ★★★★

Retasted in 2020, the 2018 vintage (★★★★) was grown at Bendigo and Pisa, hand-picked and cool-fermented in tanks. It is a medium-bodied, vibrantly fruity wine, with strong, lemony, limey, slightly appley flavours, gentle sweetness (9.5 grams/litre of residual sugar), appetising acidity, and slightly toasty, bottle-aged notes emerging. It's drinking well now.

MED/DRY $28 –V

Gibbston Valley La Maitre Central Otago Riesling (★★★★★)

The vigorous 2019 vintage (★★★★★) was hand-harvested from mature vines (up to 37 years old) in the home vineyard at Gibbston. Bright, light lemon/green, it is intense and youthful, with gently sweet (16 grams/litre of residual sugar), citrusy, appley flavours, crisp and lasting. Likely to be long-lived, it should be at its best 2023+. Certified organic.

MED $42 AV

Gibbston Valley Red Shed Central Otago Riesling ★★★★★

The 2019 vintage (★★★★★) is a single-vineyard Bendigo wine, hand-harvested and partly (15 per cent) fermented in old French oak casks. Bright, light lemon/green, it is finely balanced, with strong, fresh, citrusy flavours, gentle sweetness (7 grams/litre of residual sugar), good complexity, and a crisp, long finish. Best drinking 2023+.

MED/DRY $39 AV

Giesen Gemstone Limited Release Marlborough Riesling ★★★★☆

Full of interest, the 2018 vintage (★★★★) is a single-vineyard, Awatere Valley wine, fermented in a mix of large granite tanks (made from a 'giant slab of volcanic rock'), seasoned French oak puncheons, and stainless steel tanks. Fragrant and light-bodied, it has citrusy, slightly appley flavours, gentle sweetness (39 grams/litre of residual sugar), balanced acidity, a distinct touch of complexity, and notable harmony. Already enjoyable, it's well worth trying.

MED $20 V+

Giesen New Zealand Riesling ★★★★☆

Offering great value, the 2019 vintage (★★★★☆) was grown in Marlborough and Waipara, North Canterbury. Light lemon/green, it is attractively scented, light (9.5 per cent alcohol) and vivacious, in an easy-drinking, gently sweet style (42 grams/litre of residual sugar). Lemony, appley and peachy, with very good delicacy, harmony and depth, it's already delicious.

MED $15 V+

Greenhough Apple Valley Nelson Riesling ★★★★★

Instantly appealing, the 2019 vintage (★★★★★) was grown and hand-picked at Upper Moutere. Light-bodied (9.5 per cent alcohol) and gently sweet, it is attractively scented, with intense peach, lemon and apple flavours, showing excellent freshness, delicacy and harmony.

MED $22 V+

Greenhough Hope Vineyard Nelson Riesling ★★★★☆

This wine is hand-harvested from vines that average over 20 years old. Certified organic, the 2015 vintage (★★★★☆) was handled entirely in tanks. An attractively scented, medium-bodied wine, it has strong, vigorous, citrusy, limey flavours, a minerally streak, a touch of complexity, and a dryish (6 grams/litre of residual sugar), crisp finish. Best drinking 2021+.

Vintage	15	14	13
WR	7	7	6
Drink	20-23	20-21	P

MED/DRY $26 AV

Greystone Waipara Valley North Canterbury Riesling   ★★★★★

Greystone sees this wine as 'the truest expression of the variety for us'. Certified organic, the youthful 2018 vintage (★★★★☆) was hand-picked, with some botrytis ('noble rot') influence. Fragrant, with a slightly honeyed bouquet, it is full-bodied and gently sweet (23 grams/litre of residual sugar), with vibrant, ripe, citrusy, peachy flavours, rich and rounded.

Vintage	18
WR	7
Drink	20-30

 MED $27 V+

Greywacke Marlborough Riesling   ★★★★★

The 2018 vintage (★★★★★) is a single-vineyard wine, grown at Fairhall. Hand-harvested, it was 50 per cent fermented in old oak barriques and fully oak-matured. Scented and rich, it is a full-bodied, medium style (19 grams/litre of residual sugar), with generous, ripe, peachy, citrusy flavours, balanced acidity, and excellent delicacy and length. Well worth cellaring, it's already delicious.

Vintage	18	17	16	15	14	13
WR	6	6	6	5	5	6
Drink	20-27	20-26	20-25	20-24	20-23	20-23

 MED $31 AV

Grove Mill Wairau Valley Marlborough Riesling   ★★★☆

Still on sale, the 2016 vintage (★★★☆) is full-bodied, with gentle sweetness (6 grams/litre of residual sugar) and plenty of citrusy, peachy, slightly spicy flavour.

Vintage	16
WR	6
Drink	20-26

 MED/DRY $20 AV

Hans Herzog Marlborough Riesling   ★★★★★

Still on sale, the fragrant 2014 vintage (★★★★★) was estate-grown in the Wairau Valley and matured for nine months in French oak puncheons. Bright, light yellow, it is a powerful, full-bodied style, delicious now, with deep, vibrant grapefruit-like flavours, and a fully dry finish. Certified organic.

DRY $49 AV

Hawkshead Central Otago Riesling   ★★★★☆

The 2019 vintage (★★★★) was grown at Lowburn, in the Cromwell Basin. Bright, light lemon/green, it is full-bodied and fleshy, with strong, ripe, citrusy, peachy flavours, and a dryish (5 grams/litre of residual sugar) finish. Still youthful, it's well worth cellaring.

 MED/DRY $29 AV

Hunter's Marlborough Riesling ★★★★

This wine is consistently good and bargain-priced. Grown at Rapaura, the 2019 vintage (★★★★) is a scented, medium-bodied wine with strong, fresh lemon/lime flavours, dryish, poised and lingering. Still very youthful, the pale lemon/green 2020 vintage (★★★★) is scented and dryish (6 grams/litre of residual sugar), with vibrant, citrusy, appley flavours that linger well. Best drinking 2022+.

MED/DRY $19 V+

Jackson Estate Homestead Marlborough Dry Riesling ★★★★

Still on sale, the 2016 vintage (★★★★☆), partly barrel-aged, is a very good buy. Bright, light yellow/green, it has a lemony, slightly toasty, inviting fragrance. Medium-bodied, it has strong, citrusy, slightly peachy flavours, bottle-aged complexity, and a crisp, dry (3.8 grams/litre of residual sugar), long finish.

Vintage	16
WR	6
Drink	20-26

DRY $20 V+

Johanneshof Marlborough Riesling ★★★★☆

Already drinking well, the hand-picked 2019 vintage (★★★★☆) is a very user-friendly wine. Ripely scented, it has good vigour and concentration, with generous, peachy, slightly spicy, vaguely honeyed flavours, fresh acidity, and an off-dry (14 grams/litre of residual sugar) finish.

MED/DRY $25 V+

Julicher Martinborough Riesling ★★★★

Estate-grown at Te Muna, the 2018 vintage (★★★★) is ripely scented, with slightly toasty, bottle-aged notes emerging. Bright, light lemon/green, it is a gently sweet style, with strong, ripe, peachy flavours, a hint of passionfruit, and good acid spine. Drinking well now, it should also reward cellaring.

MED/DRY $26 –V

Junction Runaway Central Hawke's Bay Riesling (★★★★)

Hand-picked on the Takapau Plains, the 2018 vintage (★★★★) is a bright, lemon/green wine, scented and lively. Medium-bodied, it has good intensity of citrusy, limey flavours, and a crisp, medium-dry finish. Best drinking mid-2021+.

MED/DRY $22 V+

Kahurangi Estate Mt Arthur Reserve Nelson Riesling ★★★★☆

Offering good value, the vigorous 2019 vintage (★★★★☆) is bright, light lemon/green, with penetrating, lemony, limey flavours, ripe, peachy notes, and a crisp, off-dry finish. Best drinking 2022+.

MED/DRY $21 V+

Lake Chalice The Falcon Marlborough Riesling   ★★★☆

Still very youthful, the 2019 vintage (★★★☆) is a single-vineyard wine with a scented, slightly appley bouquet. Medium-bodied, it is finely balanced, with citrusy, appley flavours, showing very good depth, slight sweetness, and firm acid spine. Best drinking 2021+.

Lawson's Dry Hills Marlborough Riesling   ★★★★

The youthful 2018 vintage (★★★★) is a single-vineyard wine, grown in the Waihopai Valley. Light lemon/green, it is medium-bodied, with strong, citrusy, slightly spicy flavours, and an off-dry (8 grams/litre of residual sugar), crisp finish. Best drinking 2022+. Retasted in mid-2020, the 2017 vintage (★★★★) has good intensity of lemon, lime and apple flavours, a touch of bottle-aged complexity, and a crisp, dryish finish.

Vintage	18	17	16	15	14
WR	6	7	6	7	6
Drink	20-30	20-28	20-24	20-22	P

Loveblock Marlborough Riesling   (★★★★)

A full-bodied, medium-sweet style, the 2018 vintage (★★★★) was estate-grown in the lower Awatere Valley. It has a slightly honeyed bouquet, with generous, ripe stone-fruit flavours and a distinct splash of sweetness (43 grams/litre of residual sugar), balanced by appetising acidity. Drink now or cellar.

Luna Martinborough Riesling   ★★★☆

'Created for youthful drinking', the hand-picked 2019 vintage (★★★☆) is light and lively, with very good depth of citrusy, slightly appley flavours, and a slightly sweet (7 grams/litre of residual sugar), crisp finish. Enjoyable young.

Main Divide North Canterbury Riesling   ★★★★

Currently delicious, the 2016 vintage (★★★★) of this good-value Waipara wine is a distinctly medium style. Bright, light yellow/green, it has generous, citrusy, peachy, slightly spicy flavours, a hint of honey, fresh acidity, and excellent immediacy and harmony. (From Pegasus Bay.)

Maori Point Single Vineyard Central Otago Riesling   ★★★★☆

Full of potential, the lively 2019 vintage (★★★★★) is an estate-grown, hand-harvested wine, already delicious. Bright, light lemon/green, it is medium-bodied, with fresh, concentrated, citrusy, appley flavours, showing a distinct touch of complexity, gentle sweetness, appetising acidity, and a finely poised, long finish. Best drinking 2022+.

Vintage	19	18
WR	7	6
Drink	20-24	20-22

MED/DRY $29 AV

Martinborough Vineyard Manu Martinborough Riesling ★★★★☆

The 2018 vintage (★★★★★) is already delicious, but well worth cellaring. Finely scented, it has intense, lemony, appley flavours, gentle sweetness (23 grams/litre of residual sugar), fresh acidity, and lovely vibrancy, depth and harmony.

 MED $28 AV

Maude Mt Maude Vineyard East Block Wanaka Riesling ★★★★★

From vines planted in 1994 on a steep, north-facing slope at Wanaka, in Central Otago, the 2019 vintage (★★★★★) is light and racy, with an attractively scented bouquet. Bright, light lemon/green, it is a Mosel-like wine, with intense lemon/apple flavours, gentle sweetness (41 grams/litre of residual sugar), lively acidity, and a long finish. Best drinking 2022+.

Vintage	19	18	17	16	15
WR	7	7	7	7	5
Drink	20-29	20-26	20-26	20-26	20-22

 MED $32 AV

Maude Mt Maude Vineyard Wanaka Dry Riesling ★★★★★

Hand-harvested from vines planted in Central Otago in 1994, the racy 2019 vintage (★★★★★) is very youthful and intense. Full of potential, it is a medium-bodied wine, with strong lemon/lime flavours, showing excellent delicacy and vigour, fractional sweetness (6 grams/litre of residual sugar), and a crisp, lasting finish.

Vintage	19	18	17	16	15
WR	7	7	6	7	5
Drink	20-29	20-26	20-26	20-29	20-25

 MED/DRY $32 AV

Millton Opou Vineyard Riesling ★★★★☆

Typically scented, with rich, lemony, often honeyed flavours, this is the country's northernmost fine-quality Riesling. Harvested from Gisborne vines of varying ages – the oldest planted in 1981 – it is gently sweet, in a less racy style than South Island wines. The grapes, grown in the Opou Vineyard at Manutuke, are hand-picked over a month at three stages of ripening, usually culminating in a final pick of botrytis-affected fruit. Still on sale, the 2015 vintage (★★★★☆) is a low-alcohol (8.5 per cent), gently sweet wine (36 grams/litre of residual sugar). Light and tangy, it has intense, vibrant lemon/lime flavours, appetising acidity, and excellent poise and vigour. Certified organic.

Vintage	15	14	13	12
WR	6	6	7	6
Drink	20-25	20-25	20-22	P

MED $28 AV

Misha's Vineyard Limelight Riesling ★★★★★

This single-vineyard wine is estate-grown and hand-harvested at Bendigo, in Central Otago. Still unfolding, the bright, light lemon/green, youthful 2017 vintage (★★★★☆) is a medium style (27 grams/litre of residual sugar), with complexity gained by fermenting 26 per cent of the blend with indigenous yeasts in old French oak barrels. From a very cool growing season, it is crisp and light-bodied (9 per cent alcohol by volume), with strong, lemony, limey, slightly appley flavours, showing a distinct touch of complexity, firm acid spine, and a lingering finish. Best drinking 2022+.

MED $30 AV

Misha's Vineyard Lyric Central Otago Riesling ★★★★★

This is the sort of 'dry' Riesling New Zealand needs a lot more of. Estate-grown and hand-harvested at Bendigo, the classy, distinctive 2019 vintage (★★★★★) is fractionally off-dry (4 grams/litre of residual sugar). It was mostly handled in tanks, but 25 per cent of the blend was fermented with indigenous yeasts in old French oak barrels. Bright, light lemon/green, it is medium to full-bodied, with deep, citrusy, limey flavours, dry but not austere, very good complexity, and a finely structured, long finish. Already approachable, it should be at its best for drinking 2023+. (Note: this wine was not produced in 2017 or 2018.)

DRY $30 AV

Mission Hawke's Bay Riesling ★★★☆

Priced right, the lively, medium-bodied 2019 vintage (★★★☆) has good depth of citrusy, slightly appley flavours, a sliver of sweetness (6.5 grams/litre of residual sugar), fresh but not high acidity, and very good vigour and harmony. Best drinking 2022+.

MED/DRY $16 V+

Mondillo Central Otago Riesling ★★★★☆

Estate-grown at Bendigo, the 2020 vintage (★★★★☆) is a lively, very youthful wine with strong, peachy, citrusy, appley flavours, a gentle splash of sweetness (13 grams/litre of residual sugar), tangy acidity, and a lasting finish. A very harmonious wine with obvious potential, it's well worth cellaring to 2023+.

MED/DRY $28 AV

Mount Brown Estates North Canterbury Riesling ★★★☆

Delicious young, the 2019 vintage (★★★★) is a distinctly medium style (30 grams/litre of residual sugar). Attractively scented, it is light-bodied, with fresh, peachy, slightly limey flavours, crisp acidity, and a finely poised, lengthy finish. Great value.

Vintage	19
WR	6
Drink	20-27

MED $16 V+

Mount Edward Central Otago Riesling

★★★★★

Certified organic, the classy 2018 vintage (★★★★★) was fermented with indigenous yeasts in stainless steel barrels and tanks, and matured for three months on its yeast lees. Bright, light yellow/green, it is a highly scented, fleshy, full-bodied wine, with rich, ripe, peachy, slightly limey flavours, woven with fresh acidity, and a dryish (8 grams/litre of residual sugar), very harmonious finish. Drink now or cellar.

 MED/DRY $27 V+

Mount Riley Marlborough Riesling

★★★☆

Already very approachable, the sharply priced 2020 vintage (★★★☆) is a light lemon/green, medium-bodied wine, with fresh, lemony, appley flavours, a sliver of sweetness, lively acidity, and very good balance and depth. Best drinking 2022+.

 MED/DRY $15 V+

Moutere Hills Single Vineyard Nelson Riesling

★★★★

Showing plenty of personality, the 2019 vintage (★★★★☆) was estate-grown at Upper Moutere. Bright, light yellow/green, it is invitingly scented, with strong, lemony, appley flavours, slightly toasty, bottle-aged notes emerging, a gentle splash of sweetness (20 grams/litre of residual sugar), and a crisp, finely balanced, lengthy finish. Drink now or cellar.

 MED $29 –V

Mt Beautiful North Canterbury Riesling

★★★★☆

Estate-grown at Cheviot, the 2017 vintage (★★★★★) has a strong presence. Already very expressive, it is a highly scented, medium-bodied wine, with concentrated, citrusy, appley flavours, showing excellent drive and immediacy, gentle sweetness, a touch of complexity, and a long, minerally finish.

Vintage	17	16	15
WR	5	7	7
Drink	20-23	20-25	20-25

 MED/DRY $28 AV

Mt Difficulty Bannockburn Central Otago Dry Riesling

★★★★☆

Estate-grown, the 2018 vintage (★★★★☆) is a mouthfilling, bone-dry wine, but not at all austere. Fleshy, with generous, ripe grapefruit and lime flavours, it's a distinctive wine, fresh and finely balanced. Very age-worthy, it's already drinking well.

Vintage	18
WR	6
Drink	20-28

DRY $27 V+

Mt Difficulty Packspur Lowburn Valley Riesling ★★★★☆

Currently delicious, the 2017 vintage (★★★★★) is a single-vineyard, Central Otago wine, from an elevated site (360 to 380 metres above sea level), planted in 1992. Bright, light yellow/green, it is mouthfilling and fleshy, with highly concentrated, peachy, citrusy flavours, woven with fresh acidity, gentle sweetness (29 grams/litre of residual sugar), and a long, very harmonious finish. Drink now or cellar.

MED $39 –V

Mt Difficulty Target Bannockburn Medium Riesling ★★★★☆

From Central Otago, the 2017 vintage (★★★★☆) is drinking well now. Made in a medium style (37 grams/litre of residual sugar), it is attractively scented and lively, with very good intensity of lemony, slightly appley and peachy flavours, balanced acidity, and excellent vibrancy and harmony.

Vintage	17
WR	6
Drink	20-28

MED $26 AV

Mud House The Mound Vineyard Waipara Valley Riesling ★★★★

Made in a 'medium-sweet' style, the 2018 vintage (★★★★) is a single-vineyard wine, estate-grown in North Canterbury. It is light (8.5 per cent alcohol) and lively, with crisp, lemony, appley flavours, showing good intensity, and firm acid spine. Best drinking 2021+.

MED $23 AV

Mud House Waipara Valley Riesling ★★★☆

Priced sharply, the 2018 vintage (★★★☆) is a medium style. Enjoyable young, it is bright, light lemon/green, with good depth of citrusy, peachy, gently sweet flavours, in a fresh, medium-bodied style, balanced for smooth, easy drinking.

MED $15 V+

Old Coach Road Nelson Riesling ★★★

From Seifried, the 2018 vintage (★★★) is priced very sharply. Bright, light yellow/green, it has good depth of lemony, slightly spicy flavours, a hint of honey, gentle sweetness (16 grams/litre of residual sugar), and plenty of drink-young charm.

MED $14 V+

Omeo Blackman's Gully Single Vineyard Central Otago Riesling ★★★★

The 2019 vintage (★★★☆), grown at Alexandra, is a bright, light lemon/green wine, fresh and youthful, with good depth of peachy, slightly spicy flavours, a hint of ginger, and a slightly sweet (8 grams/litre of residual sugar), crisp finish. Drink now or cellar.

Vintage	19	18	17
WR	6	7	6
Drink	20-27	20-26	20-25

MED/DRY $23 AV

Paddy Borthwick Wairarapa Riesling ★★★★

The attractive 2018 vintage (★★★★) is a single-vineyard wine, scented and full-bodied, with lively acidity, good intensity of citrusy, limey flavours, and an appetisingly crisp, dry (3 grams/litre of residual sugar) finish. Drink now or cellar.

DRY $22 V+

Palliser Estate Martinborough Riesling ★★★★

The 2019 vintage (★★★★☆) is full of youthful vigour. Bright, light lemon/green, it is medium to full-bodied, with fresh, concentrated, peachy, lemony, limey flavours, gentle sweetness (11 grams/litre of residual sugar), balanced acidity, and obvious potential. Best drinking 2022+.

MED/DRY $26 –V

Pegasus Bay Bel Canto Riesling Dry ★★★★★

Bel Canto means 'Beautiful Singing'. Based on the estate's mature, ungrafted vines at Waipara, in North Canterbury, late-harvested with 'a good portion of noble botrytis', the 2017 vintage (★★★★★) is a very powerful, weighty wine (14.5 per cent alcohol), with concentrated, peachy flavours, hints of oranges and honey, good delicacy, and a dry (5.2 grams/litre of residual sugar), lasting finish. It should be long-lived; open 2021+. The 2019 vintage (★★★★★) is bright, light yellow/green, with a gently honeyed bouquet. Still youthful, it is mouthfilling, with intense, ripe, grapefruit-like flavours, a hint of marmalade, and a crisp, dryish, lasting finish. Best drinking 2023+.

MED/DRY $37 AV

Pegasus Bay Riesling Aged Release ★★★★★

This 'Aged Release' label is a re-release of the Waipara Valley, North Canterbury classic when it is 10 years old. The 2010 vintage (★★★★★), currently on sale, should flourish for 20 years. Bright, light yellow/green, it is rich and vigorous, with concentrated, lemony, limey flavours, slightly honeyed notes, and a crisp, gently sweet (28 grams/litre of residual sugar), tightly structured finish. Best drinking 2023+.

MED $40 AV

Pegasus Bay Waipara Valley North Canterbury Riesling ★★★★★

Classy stuff. Estate-grown at Waipara, in North Canterbury, in top vintages it is richly fragrant and thrillingly intense, with flavours of citrus fruits and honey, complex and luscious. Based on mature vines and stop-fermented in a distinctly medium style, it breaks into full stride at about three years old and can mature well for over a decade. The 2017 vintage (★★★★★) is bright, light yellow/green, with a gently honeyed bouquet. Concentrated, with gentle sweetness (21 grams/litre of residual sugar), it has lush stone-fruit flavours, a hint of honey, and good acid spine. Best drinking 2021+.

Vintage	17	16	15
WR	6	5	6
Drink	20-33	20-32	20-32

MED $30 AV

Prophet's Rock Central Otago Dry Riesling ★★★★✦

Estate-grown and hand-picked at Bendigo, in the Cromwell Basin, the 2017 vintage (★★★★☆) was fermented with indigenous yeasts in old oak barrels. Light lemon/green, it is a youthful, tightly structured wine, with strong, citrusy, limey flavours, and a crisp, dryish (6.7 grams/litre of residual sugar), persistent finish. Best drinking 2021+.

MED/DRY $40 AV

Rimu Grove Nelson Riesling ★★★✦

The vigorous 2019 vintage (★★★★) is a light-bodied style (10 per cent alcohol), with very good intensity of lemony, appley flavours, hints of pears and spices, and a finely poised, slightly sweet (15 grams/litre of residual sugar), crisp finish. Best drinking 2022+.

Vintage	19	18	17	16	15	14	13
WR	7	6	6	6	7	6	7
Drink	20-30	20-30	20-30	20-27	20-26	20-25	20-21

MED $32 –V

Riverby Estate Marlborough Riesling ★★★☆

Still youthful, the 2018 vintage (★★★☆) is a single-vineyard wine, grown at Rapaura. Medium-bodied, it has good depth of citrusy, slightly appley flavours, and a crisp, dryish (5 grams/litre of residual sugar) finish. Unfolding well, the 2017 vintage (★★★★) is medium-bodied, with strong, lemony flavours, slightly toasty, bottle-aged notes adding complexity, balanced acidity and a finely balanced (6 grams/litre of residual sugar), lengthy finish.

Vintage	18	17
WR	7	7
Drink	20-28	20-30

MED/DRY $22 AV

Riverby Estate Sali's Block Marlborough Riesling ★★★☆

Estate-grown at Rapaura, the bright, light lemon/green 2019 vintage (★★★☆) is a fresh, medium-bodied wine, with good depth of ripe, peachy, slightly spicy flavours, and an off-dry (11 grams/litre of residual sugar) finish. Still youthful, it should be at its best 2022+.

Vintage	19	18	17
WR	7	6	7
Drink	20-28	20-23	20-25

MED/DRY $22 AV

Rock Ferry Trig Hill Vineyard Central Otago Riesling ★★★★☆

Currently on sale, the 2015 vintage (★★★★★) is a bright, light lemon/green, richly scented wine, with a powerful presence. Mouthfilling, vigorous and dry (3.5 grams/litre of residual sugar), it has concentrated lemon, apple and spice flavours, developing bottle-aged complexity and a long, tightly structured finish. Certified organic.

DRY $33 –V

Ruru Central Otago Riesling   (★★★★)

Already drinking well, the 2019 vintage (★★★★) is a fresh, single-vineyard wine, hand-harvested at Alexandra. Bright, light lemon/green, it is a fleshy, off-dry style (8 grams/litre of residual sugar), with generous, ripe, peachy, slightly spicy flavours. A very harmonious wine, it should be at its best mid-2021+.

MED/DRY $24 AV

Saint Clair Pioneer Block 9 Big John Marlborough Riesling   ★★★★★

Light and lively, the 2018 vintage (★★★★) was grown in the lower Brancott Valley and stop-fermented to make a medium-sweet style. Pale, it has strong, citrusy, peachy, slightly limey flavours and a sweetish (45 grams/litre of residual sugar), appetisingly crisp, very harmonious finish. Best drinking 2021+.

MED $27 V+

Saving Grace Dry Riesling   (★★★★★)

From Waipara Hills, the 2018 vintage (★★★★★) is a shining example of deliciously drinkable, yet basically dry (5 grams/litre of residual sugar) Riesling. Estate-grown at Waipara, in North Canterbury, it was hand-picked, fermented with indigenous yeasts and lees-aged for six months. It has a fragrant, citrusy, appley, inviting bouquet. Finely poised, with rich fruit flavours, a slightly minerally thread, and a real sense of youthful drive, it's a drink-now or cellaring proposition.

MED/DRY $28 V+

Scout Glasnevin Waipara Riesling   (★★★★★)

Well worth discovering, the classy 2019 vintage (★★★★★) was hand-picked from 'some of the oldest Riesling vines planted in Waipara'. Fermented with indigenous yeasts in tanks (85 per cent) and old French oak barriques (15 per cent), and matured on its yeast lees for 10 months, it is tightly structured, with excellent intensity of peachy, lemony flavours. Finely balanced, it is fractionally sweet (7 grams/litre of residual sugar), with a real sense of youthful drive and strong personality.

MED/DRY $26 V+

Seifried Nelson Riesling   ★★★★

From a pioneer of Riesling in New Zealand, the 2019 vintage (★★★★) is typically good value. Well worth cellaring, it is full-bodied, crisp and dry (3.8 grams/litre of residual sugar), with vigorous, citrusy, slightly appley flavours, showing very good depth. Open 2021+.

MED/DRY $18 V+

Seresin Dry Marlborough Riesling   (★★★★★)

Certified organic, the youthful 2018 vintage (★★★★★) was estate-grown and hand-harvested in the Omaka Valley, and matured for six months in oak barrels (6 per cent new). Bright, light yellow/green, it is highly fragrant, tightly structured and dry (2.5 grams/litre of residual sugar), with intense, lemony, limey flavours, showing good complexity, and a lasting finish. Best drinking 2022+.

DRY $25 V+

Seresin Memento Marlborough Riesling   (★★★★★)

Now on sale, the vivacious 2016 vintage (★★★★★) is a medium style, estate-grown in the Omaka Valley and handled without oak. Bright, light lemon/green, it is currently delicious, with strong, citrusy flavours, a gentle splash of sweetness (19 grams/litre of residual sugar), fresh acidity, and complex, toasty, bottle-aged notes emerging. Certified organic.

 MED $25 V+

Sherwood Estate Stoney Range Waipara Valley Riesling   (★★★☆)

Priced sharply, the 2019 vintage (★★★☆) is a distinctly medium style (19 grams/litre of residual sugar). It has punchy, citrusy flavours, slightly spicy and gingery notes emerging, and a crisp, tangy finish. Best drinking 2021+.

 MED $17 V+

Soho Maren Marlborough Riesling   ★★★★

Very 'open' and expressive, the 2017 vintage (★★★★☆) is a freshly scented, medium-bodied wine with incisive, citrusy, slightly peachy and gingery flavours, gentle sweetness (12.9 grams/litre of residual sugar), and firm acid spine. Drink now or cellar.

MED/DRY $25 AV

Spinyback Nelson Riesling   ★★★

Invitingly scented, the 2017 vintage (★★★☆) is a slightly sweet style, with good depth of citrusy, gently spicy flavours, finely balanced for easy drinking. (From Waimea Estates.)

MED/DRY $15 V+

Spring Creek Estate Marlborough Riesling   (★★★)

Estate-grown at Rapaura, the 2019 vintage (★★★☆) is a fresh, appetisingly crisp, medium-bodied wine. Still very youthful, it has a sliver of sweetness, and good depth of vibrant, lemony, appley flavours. Best drinking mid-2021+. (From Hunter's.)

MED/DRY $17 AV

Spy Valley Envoy Johnson Vineyard Waihopai Valley
Marlborough Dry Riesling   ★★★★★

Estate-grown and hand-picked from the oldest vines, the 2017 vintage (★★★★★) was initially fermented in old oak barrels, then transferred to stainless steel tanks. Finely scented, it is intense, with tightly structured, citrusy, slightly peachy and toasty flavours that build across the palate to a crisp, dry (4.5 grams/litre of residual sugar), harmonious finish. A distinctive, classy wine, it's a drink-now or cellaring proposition.

Vintage	17	16
WR	6	6
Drink	20-27	20-26

DRY $33 AV

Spy Valley Single Vineyard Marlborough Riesling ★★★★

The 2016 vintage (★★★★☆) is a full-bodied, dryish style (6 grams/litre of residual sugar), fermented in tanks and barrels. Retasted in mid-2020, it is a bright, light yellow/green, attractively scented wine, with very good intensity of citrusy, limey, vaguely honeyed flavours, slightly toasty, bottle-aged notes adding complexity, and a crisp, long finish. Drink now or cellar.

 MED/DRY $25 AV

Stoneleigh Marlborough Riesling ★★★☆

Priced sharply, the youthful 2020 vintage (★★★☆) is a pale lemon/green, medium-bodied wine, with strong, lemony, limey flavours, showing good varietal character, and a crisp, off-dry finish. Best drinking 2022+.

 MED/DRY $15 V+

Sugar Loaf Marlborough Riesling (★★★★☆)

Delicious young, the 2018 vintage (★★★★☆) from this Rapaura-based producer is a regional blend. Attractively scented, it is light and lively, with gentle sweetness (28 grams/litre of residual sugar), finely balanced acidity and strong, yet delicate, peachy, lemony, appley flavours. Already very harmonious, it's a drink-now or cellaring proposition, offering excellent value.

 MED $20 V+

Te Kairanga Martinborough Riesling ★★★★

Estate-grown, the 2018 vintage (★★★★) is a finely poised wine. It has fresh lemon/lime flavours, a gentle splash of sweetness (8.6 grams/litre of residual sugar), balanced acidity, and excellent depth. Best drinking 2021+.

Vintage	18
WR	6
Drink	20-25

MED/DRY $25 AV

Terra Sancta Miro's Block Old Vine Bannockburn Riesling ★★★★☆

From seven rows of vines, the 2018 vintage (★★★★☆) is a highly scented, medium-bodied wine, handled in seasoned French oak barriques. It has strong, peachy, lemony, appley flavours, a touch of sweetness (15 grams/litre of residual sugar), lively acidity, and a finely balanced finish. Still youthful, it should be at its best 2021+.

Vintage	18
WR	7
Drink	20-28

 MED/DRY $26 AV

Terrace Edge Classic Waipara Riesling ★★★★

Already enjoyable, the distinctive 2019 vintage (★★★★☆) was hand-picked and made in a medium-dry style (12 grams/litre of residual sugar). Bright, light lemon/green, it is mouthfilling, fresh and youthful, with ripe flavours of peaches, lemons and apples, showing excellent depth and harmony. Best drinking 2022+. Certified organic.

Vintage	19	MED/DRY $24 AV
WR	7	
Drink	21-30	

Terrace Edge Liquid Geography North Canterbury Riesling ★★★★☆

Already very expressive, the 2019 vintage (★★★★★) is a classy young wine, hand-harvested (with 5 per cent botrytised fruit) and fermented in a mix of stainless steel tanks (40 per cent) and seasoned French oak barrels (60 per cent). Bright, light lemon/green, it is vibrantly fruity and gently sweet, with concentrated, ripe, peachy, slightly spicy flavours, very finely balanced for early drinking. Certified organic. The 2020 vintage (★★★★☆), also certified organic, is a medium style (28 grams/litre of residual sugar), handled without oak. Bright, light yellow/green, it has rich, ripe, peachy, slightly appley and spicy flavours, with a vague suggestion of honey, and a finely poised finish. Open 2022+.

Vintage	20	MED $24 V+
WR	7	
Drink	21-30	

Thomas Martinborough Riesling (★★★★☆)

From Batch Winery, based on Waiheke Island, the 2018 vintage (★★★★☆) is well worth cellaring. Medium-bodied, it has strong, vibrant flavours of peaches and grapefruit, a gentle splash of sweetness (14 grams/litre of residual sugar), good acid spine, and excellent drive, harmony and length.

MED/DRY $38 –V

Three Miners Central Otago Riesling (★★★★)

Invitingly scented, the 2017 vintage (★★★★) is a lively, light-bodied, estate-grown wine, hand-picked at Earnscleugh, near Alexandra. It has citrusy, slightly appley flavours, showing excellent delicacy and depth, and a slightly sweet, finely balanced finish. Drink now or cellar.

MED/DRY $23 AV

Tohu Single Vineyard Marlborough Riesling ★★★★

Estate-grown in the upper Awatere Valley, the vigorous 2017 vintage (★★★★) is a dryish style (7 grams/litre of residual sugar). Fresh and youthful, it has strong, lemony, appley, slightly peachy flavours, threaded with crisp acidity, and obvious potential; open 2021+.

MED/DRY $22 V+

Tohu Single Vineyard Whenua Awa Awatere Valley Marlborough Riesling   (★★★★)

Attractively scented and lively, the 2018 vintage (★★★★) is a fresh, generous, estate-grown wine, already drinking well. It has peachy, slightly gingery flavours, with a sliver of sweetness balanced by appetising acidity, and excellent vibrancy, harmony and depth. Best drinking 2022+.

MED/DRY $28 –V

Toi Toi Reserve Marlborough Riesling   (★★★★)

The 2018 vintage (★★★★) is already drinking well. Bright, light yellow/green, it is fresh and crisp, with strong, ripe peach, lemon and passionfruit flavours, a hint of apricot, and a dryish finish.

MED/DRY $28 –V

Two Paddocks Central Otago Riesling   ★★★★

Estate-grown in the Red Bank Vineyard at Earnscleugh, near Alexandra, the 2018 vintage (★★★★☆) is a weighty, fleshy, full-bodied Riesling. Ripely scented, it is a powerful, youthful wine, with concentrated, citrusy, peachy flavours, a sliver of sweetness (8 grams/litre of residual sugar), and lively acidity. Already very approachable, it should be at its best 2022+. Certified organic.

MED/DRY $33 –V

Two Paddocks Picnic Central Otago Riesling   ★★★★

Certified organic, the 2018 vintage (★★★★) was estate-grown and hand-picked in the Red Bank Vineyard, at Earnscleugh, near Alexandra. Made in an off-dry style (12 grams/litre of residual sugar), it is ripely scented and fleshy, with fresh, generous stone-fruit flavours, balanced acidity, and lots of drink-young charm.

MED/DRY $28 –V

Urlar Gladstone Riesling   ★★★★☆

Certified organic, the vigorous 2018 vintage (★★★★☆) was estate-grown and hand-picked in the northern Wairarapa. Bright, light yellow/green, it is a dry style (less than 5 grams/litre of residual sugar), with good intensity of citrusy flavours, a hint of passionfruit, slightly toasty notes, and firm acid spine. Best drinking mid-2021+.

DRY $25 V+

Valli Waitaki North Otago Riesling   ★★★★☆

The arresting 2018 vintage (★★★★★) is delicious young. Notably fragrant, vibrant and intense, it has excellent weight and depth of citrusy, appley, peachy flavours, gentle sweetness (14.4 grams/litre of residual sugar), and a racy, very harmonious finish. Best drinking 2021+.

Vintage	18	MED/DRY $30 –V
WR	7	
Drink	20-33	

Villa Maria Private Bin Marlborough Riesling ★★★★

Bargain-priced, the very youthful 2020 vintage (★★★☆) was made in a slightly sweet style (10 grams/litre of residual sugar). Pale lemon/green, it is a fresh and lively, medium-bodied wine, with very good vigour and depth of lemon, apple and lime flavours. Best drinking 2022+.

Vintage	20	19	18
WR	6	6	5
Drink	20-25	20-22	20-22

 MED/DRY $15 V+

Waipara Hills Waipara Valley Riesling ★★★★

Finely balanced for early enjoyment, the 2018 vintage (★★★★) is medium-bodied, fresh and lively. It has vibrant, citrusy, peachy flavours, a gentle splash of sweetness, appetising acidity, and excellent depth and harmony.

 MED/DRY $22 V+

West Brook Marlborough Riesling ★★★★☆

Still unfolding, the vigorous 2018 vintage (★★★★☆) is a bright, light lemon/green, strongly scented wine, medium-bodied, with very good intensity of peachy, citrusy flavours, a touch of bottle-aged complexity, gentle sweetness (16 grams/litre of residual sugar), and lively acidity. Best drinking mid-2021+.

Vintage	18
WR	6
Drink	21-28

 MED $25 V+

Whitehaven Marlborough Riesling ★★★★

The 2018 vintage (★★★★) is a highly aromatic, very finely balanced wine, with lots of youthful impact. Bright, light lemon/green, it has strong, citrusy, slightly spicy flavours, gentle sweetness (10.7 grams/litre of residual sugar), and a moderately crisp finish. Enjoyable young, it should break into full stride 2021+.

 MED/DRY $22 V+

Wild Earth Central Otago Riesling ★★★★☆

Full of youthful impact, the 2018 vintage (★★★★☆) is a single-vineyard wine, hand-picked at Bendigo. Bright, light lemon/green, it is scented and vibrantly fruity, with very good intensity of ripe, peachy, limey flavour and a crisp, off-dry, lingering finish. Drink now or cellar.

MED/DRY $27 AV

Wither Hills Marlborough Riesling ★★★★

Instantly appealing, the 2018 vintage (★★★★) is scented and vibrantly fruity. Light lemon/green, it is medium-bodied, with very good depth of fresh lemon/lime flavours, a sliver of sweetness, appetising acidity, and excellent delicacy and harmony. Well worth cellaring, it offers good value.

 MED/DRY $18 V+

Yealands Marlborough Riesling (★★★★)

Priced sharply, the 2019 vintage (★★★★) is a fresh, lively, medium-bodied wine with very good depth of citrusy, slightly peachy and spicy flavours, and a slightly sweet (12.5 grams/litre of residual sugar), very harmonious finish.

Vintage	19
WR	7
Drink	20-28

MED/DRY $16 V+

Yealands Single Vineyard Late Pick Awatere
Valley Marlborough Riesling (★★★★☆)

Already drinking well, the 2019 vintage (★★★★☆) has a scented, slightly honeyed bouquet. Light lemon/green, it has rich, peachy, slightly spicy and honeyed flavours, fresh and youthful, and a very harmonious, smooth finish. Drink now or cellar.

MED/DRY $30 –V

Zephyr Marlborough Riesling (★★★★)

Still youthful, the 2019 (★★★★) is a single-vineyard wine, grown at Dillons Point, in the lower Wairau Valley. Fresh and medium-bodied, it has very good depth of citrusy, appley flavours, and an off-dry (7 grams/litre of residual sugar), appetisingly crisp finish. Best drinking 2022+.

MED/DRY $24 AV

Sauvignon Blanc

Sauvignon Blanc is New Zealand's major calling card in the wine markets of the world, often — but not always, due to the rising challenge from Chile – winning trophies at big competitions in the UK. For countless wine lovers overseas, New Zealand 'is' Sauvignon Blanc, almost invariably from Marlborough. The rise to international stardom of New Zealand Sauvignon Blanc was remarkably swift. Government Viticulturist Romeo Bragato imported the first Sauvignon Blanc vines from Italy in 1906, but it was not until 1974 that Matua Valley marketed New Zealand's first varietal Sauvignon Blanc, grown in West Auckland. Montana first planted Sauvignon Blanc vines in Marlborough in 1975; its first bottling of Marlborough Sauvignon Blanc flowed in 1979. In 2019, 85.8 per cent by volume of New Zealand's wine exports were based on Sauvignon Blanc.

Sauvignon Blanc is by far New Zealand's most extensively planted variety, in 2020 comprising 61 per cent of the bearing national vineyard. Almost 90 per cent of the vines were concentrated in Marlborough, with further significant plantings in Hawke's Bay, Nelson, Canterbury and Wairarapa.

Between 2005 and 2020, the area of bearing Sauvignon Blanc vines surged from 7277 hectares to 23,799 hectares. The flavour of New Zealand Sauvignon Blanc varies according to fruit ripeness. At the herbaceous, under-ripe end of the spectrum, vegetal and fresh-cut grass aromas hold sway; riper wines show capsicum, gooseberry and melon-like characters; very ripe fruit displays tropical-fruit flavours.

Intensely herbaceous Sauvignon Blancs are not hard to make in the viticulturally cool climate of the South Island and the lower North Island (Wairarapa). 'The challenge faced by New Zealand winemakers is to keep those herbaceous characters in check,' says Kevin Judd, of Greywacke Vineyards, formerly chief winemaker at Cloudy Bay. 'It would be foolish to suggest that these herbaceous notes detract from the wines; in fact I am sure that this fresh edge and intense varietal aroma are the reason for its international popularity. The better of these wines have these herbaceous characters in context and in balance with the more tropical-fruit characters associated with riper fruit.'

There are two key styles of Sauvignon Blanc produced in New Zealand. Wines handled entirely in stainless steel tanks – by far the most common – place their accent squarely on their fresh, direct fruit flavours. Alternatively, many top labels are handled principally in tanks, but 5 to 15 per cent of the blend is barrel-fermented, adding a touch of complexity without subduing the wine's fresh, punchy fruit aromas and flavours.

Another major style difference is regionally based: the crisp, incisively flavoured wines of Marlborough contrast with the softer, less pungently herbaceous Hawke's Bay style. These are wines to drink young (traditionally within 18 months of the vintage) while they are irresistibly fresh, aromatic and tangy, although the oak-matured, more complex wines can mature well for several years. The swing since the 2001 vintage from corks to screwcaps has also boosted the longevity of the wines. Rather than running out of steam, many are still highly enjoyable at two years old.

Allan Scott Marlborough Sauvignon Blanc ★★★★

Offering good value, the 2019 vintage (★★★★) is a mouthfilling, fresh, sweet-fruited wine, drinking well in its youth. Bright, light lemon/green, it is aromatic, with strong, ripely herbaceous flavours, dry (3 grams/litre of residual sugar) and crisp.

DRY $18 V+

Allan Scott Organic Nelson Sauvignon Blanc (★★★☆)

Certified organic, the 2019 vintage (★★★☆) is a crisp, medium-bodied wine, with strong herbaceous and tropical-fruit flavours, threaded with fresh, tangy acidity, and a dry (3.8 grams/litre of residual sugar) finish.

DRY $18 V+

Anchorage Family Estate Nelson Sauvignon Blanc

The 2020 vintage (★★★) is a fresh, medium-bodied wine, strongly varietal, with tropical-fruit and herbaceous flavours, and a crisp, lively finish. Enjoyable young.

DRY $17 AV

Anchorage Reserve Nelson Sauvignon Blanc

The 2020 vintage (★★★★) is bright, light yellow/green, fresh and full-bodied, with finely balanced acidity, and strong, ripe tropical-fruit flavours that linger well. Best drinking 2021+.

DRY $19 V+

Anna's Way Marlborough Sauvignon Blanc ★★★☆

The 2020 vintage (★★★☆) was grown at three sites in the Awatere Valley. Pale lemon/green, it is a vivid sub-regional style, with strong, clearly herbaceous flavours, very fresh and lively.

DRY $17 V+

Aotea by Seifried Nelson Sauvignon Blanc ★★★★★

The 2020 vintage (★★★★★) is based on 'the very best fruit harvested from our family vineyard'. An intensely varietal wine, it is highly aromatic, with penetrating tropical-fruit and herbaceous flavours, firm acid spine, and a long, basically dry (4.3 grams/litre of residual sugar) finish. Still very youthful, it should be at its best mid-2021+.

Vintage	20	19	18
WR	7	7	7
Drink	20-22	20-21	P

DRY $29 V+

Ashwell Martinborough Sauvignon Blanc ★★★☆

Estate-grown on the Martinborough Terraces, the 2019 vintage (★★★★) is ripely scented, with strong tropical-fruit flavours, showing good freshness and vigour, finely balanced acidity, and a lengthy finish.

DRY $20 AV

Askerne Hawke's Bay Sauvignon Blanc ★★★★

The 2019 vintage (★★★★☆) proves that Hawke's Bay can make delicious Sauvignon Blanc. A distinctive wine, it is fleshy and lively, with concentrated passionfruit/lime flavours, a touch of complexity, and a finely balanced, dry, lasting finish.

DRY $20 V+

Askerne Hawke's Bay Sauvignon Blanc/Sauvignon Gris/Sémillon ★★★★☆

Still youthful, the 2019 vintage (★★★★☆) is a characterful wine, blended from Sauvignon Blanc (77 per cent), Sémillon (13 per cent) and Sauvignon Gris (10 per cent). Although mostly handled in tanks, 40 per cent was fermented and matured for eight months in oak barrels (21 per cent new). Bright, light lemon/green, it is ripely fragrant, full-bodied and sweet-fruited, with ripe tropical-fruit flavours and finely integrated oak adding complexity. Best drinking mid-2021+.

DRY $23 V+

Astrolabe Awatere Valley Marlborough Sauvignon Blanc ★★★★☆

The 2020 vintage (★★★★☆) is a bright, light lemon/green, full-bodied wine, with generous tropical-fruit and herbaceous flavours, vigorous, finely balanced, bone-dry and lingering. Best drinking mid-2021+.

Vintage	20	DRY $27 AV
WR	6	
Drink	20-23	

Astrolabe Marlborough Sauvignon Blanc ★★★★☆

The 2020 vintage (★★★★☆) is a regional blend, grown mostly (56 per cent) in the Awatere Valley, with smaller parcels from Kekerengu, the Wairau Valley and the Southern Valleys. Bright, light lemon/green, it is fresh and full-bodied, with tropical-fruit and herbaceous flavours, showing very good intensity, and a fully dry finish.

Vintage	20	DRY $25 V+
WR	6	
Drink	20-23	

Astrolabe Valleys Kekerengu Coast Marlborough Sauvignon Blanc ★★★★☆

Grown at Kekerengu, south of the Awatere Valley, the distinctive 2019 vintage (★★★★★) was mostly handled in tanks, but 20 per cent of the blend was fermented in old oak casks. Well worth discovering, it is a highly individual wine, light lemon/green, mouthfilling and lively, with delicate, ripely herbaceous flavours, crisp and long. Finely poised, with a real sense of youthful drive, it should be at its best mid-2021+.

Vintage	19	18	DRY $27 AV
WR	6	6	
Drink	20-26	20-24	

Ata Rangi Martinborough Raranga Sauvignon Blanc ★★★★

The lively 2018 vintage (★★★★) was hand-picked and 45 per cent barrel-fermented. Bright, light lemon/green, it is medium to full-bodied, with strong, ripely herbaceous flavours, a distinct touch of complexity, and a tightly structured finish.

Vintage	18	DRY $24 AV
WR	6	
Drink	20-23	

Auntsfield Single Vineyard Southern Valleys
Marlborough Sauvignon Blanc ★★★★★

Estate-grown on the south side of the Wairau Valley, on the site where the region's first wines were made in the 1870s, the 2018 vintage (★★★★★) was mostly handled in tanks; 5 per cent was fermented in old French oak casks. It is mouthfilling and dry (2.9 grams/litre of residual sugar), with excellent weight and depth of ripely herbaceous grapefruit/lime flavours. A powerful, finely poised wine with a long finish, it should age well.

Vintage	18	17
WR	6	6
Drink	20-22	20-21

Awatere River Marlborough Sauvignon Blanc ★★★★

Offering good value, the 2020 vintage (★★★★) was grown at three sites in the Awatere Valley and partly hand-picked. Light lemon/green, it is fresh and strongly varietal, with punchy, vigorous, slightly citrusy and grassy flavours, dry and crisp.

Baby Doll Marlborough Sauvignon Blanc ★★★☆

Already drinking well, the 2020 vintage (★★★★) is a very good buy. Bright, light lemon/green, it is highly aromatic, mouthfilling and smooth, with good intensity of herbaceous flavours, some tropical-fruit notes, fresh acidity, and a dry (3.8 grams/litre of residual sugar), lingering finish. (From Yealands.)

Vintage	20
WR	7
Drink	20-22

Bel Echo by Clos Henri Marlborough Sauvignon Blanc ★★★★★

This well-priced, distinctive wine is grown in the more clay-based soils at Clos Henri (the top wine, sold as 'Clos Henri', is from the stoniest blocks), hand-harvested, tank-fermented and matured on its yeast lees. Bright, light lemon/green, the delicious 2018 vintage (★★★★★) is ripely scented and mouthfilling, with deep tropical-fruit flavours, enlivened by fresh acidity, and a dry finish. Full-bodied, generous and harmonious, it's certified organic.

Vintage	18	17
WR	6	6
Drink	20-25	20-24

DRY $27 V+

Black Cottage Marlborough Sauvignon Blanc ★★★★

From Two Rivers, the 2020 vintage (★★★★) is an aromatic, punchy wine, grown in the Wairau and Awatere valleys. Tank-fermented, it is intensely varietal, with good intensity of fresh, ripe passionfruit/lime flavours, and a dry (3 grams/litre of residual sugar), appetisingly crisp finish.

Vintage	20	19	18
WR	7	6	6
Drink	20-21	P	P

 DRY $18 V+

Blackenbrook Nelson Sauvignon Blanc ★★★★

Estate-grown at Tasman, the 2020 vintage (★★★★☆) was hand-harvested and fermented in tanks (mostly) and old oak barrels (3 per cent). Pale lemon/green, it is very aromatic and punchy, with lively, youthful, ripely herbaceous flavours, showing excellent delicacy, a touch of complexity, and a crisp, dry (3 grams/litre of residual sugar), lingering finish.

Vintage	20	19	18
WR	6	6	6
Drink	20-21	P	P

 DRY $21 V+

Blank Canvas Marlborough Sauvignon Blanc ★★★★☆

The impressive 2019 vintage (★★★★★) is a single-vineyard wine, grown at Dillons Point. Weighty and finely textured, it is refined, with incisive, very pure, ripely herbaceous flavours, a slightly salty streak, appetising acidity, and a dry (2 grams/litre of residual sugar), harmonious, lasting finish.

DRY $28 AV

Blind River Awatere Valley Marlborough Sauvignon Blanc ★★★★★

This classy, single-vineyard wine is partly (10 per cent) barrel-fermented. The 2020 vintage (★★★★★) is very fresh and lively, with mouthfilling body, melon, passionfruit and green-capsicum flavours, showing excellent intensity, a touch of complexity, and a long, dry finish. Good buying.

Vintage	20
WR	7
Drink	21-25

 DRY $25 V+

Blind River Tekau Awatere Valley Marlborough Sauvignon Blanc ★★★★★

The delicious 2018 vintage (★★★★★) is a distinctive, single-vineyard wine, fermented with indigenous yeasts in French oak barrels (partly new). Light gold, it is weighty, fleshy and dry (1.5 grams/litre of residual sugar), with concentrated tropical-fruit flavours, slightly toasty notes adding complexity, and a rich, rounded finish. It's drinking well now.

Vintage	18
WR	7
Drink	20-25

 DRY $30 AV

Boneline, The, Waipara Sauvignon Blanc ★★★★☆

The distinctive 2018 vintage (★★★★☆) is a clearly varietal but not pungent wine, grown in North Canterbury. Bright, light lemon/green, it is weighty and mouthfilling, with fresh, ripely herbaceous flavours, showing excellent vigour, a minerally streak, and a well-rounded, dryish (7 grams/litre of residual sugar), very finely textured finish.

MED/DRY $25 V+

Brancott Estate Chosen Rows Marlborough Sauvignon Blanc ★★★★★

From the company that planted the region's first Sauvignon Blanc vines in 1975, Chosen Rows is promoted as 'the ultimate expression of Marlborough Sauvignon Blanc'. The goal is to create 'an age-worthy wine with great palate weight and texture... a sophisticated, thought-provoking wine'. The third, 2015 vintage (★★★★★) was released in late 2019. Fermented and matured mostly in large oak cuves (19 per cent of the blend was handled in one-year-old French oak puncheons), it is a powerful, very weighty wine, bright, light yellow/green, with deep, ripe passionfruit/lime flavours, gently seasoned with toasty oak, finely balanced acidity, and a very long finish. Best drinking 2021+.

Vintage	13	12	11	10
WR	7	NM	NM	7
Drink	P	NM	NM	

DRY $80 –V

Brancott Estate Letter Series 'B' Brancott Marlborough Sauvignon Blanc ★★★★★

This wine is promoted by Pernod Ricard NZ as 'our finest expression of Marlborough's most famous variety' – and lives up to its billing. 'Palate weight, concentration and longevity' are the goals. It has traditionally been grown in the company's sweeping Brancott Vineyard, on the south, slightly cooler side of the Wairau Valley, and a significant portion (14 per cent in 2018) is fermented and lees-aged in large French oak vessels, to add 'some toast and spice as well as palate richness'. The delicious 2018 vintage (★★★★★) has rich, ripe tropical-fruit aromas, leading into a fleshy, sweet-fruited wine with strong passionfruit/lime flavours, showing considerable complexity, and a dry, very harmonious finish.

DRY $25 V+

Brancott Estate Marlborough Sauvignon Blanc ★★★☆

This famous wine is promoted as 'the original Marlborough Sauvignon Blanc', since it is descended directly from the pioneering label, Montana Marlborough Sauvignon Blanc, launched in 1979. It is usually aromatic and medium-bodied, with strong, freshly herbaceous flavours of melons and green capsicums, lively and balanced for early drinking.

DRY $17 V+

Brick Bay Marlborough Sauvignon Blanc (★★★★)

Drinking well now, the 2019 vintage (★★★★) is a fresh, lively wine. It was mostly handled in tanks, but part of the blend was fermented in old oak barrels. Crisp and dry (3.6 grams/litre of residual sugar), it is mouthfilling, with good intensity of ripe passionfruit and lime flavours.

DRY $44 –V

Brightwater Vineyards Lord Rutherford Nelson Sauvignon Blanc   ★★★★☆

Grown at Hope, on the Waimea Plains, the distinctive 2019 vintage (★★★★★) is a single-vineyard wine, from mature vines. Handled without oak, it is full-bodied, with highly concentrated, ripe flavours of passionfruit and pineapple, balanced acidity, and a dry (4 grams/litre of residual sugar), sustained finish. Drink now to 2021.

Vintage	19
WR	6
Drink	20-22

 DRY $25 V+

Brightwater Vineyards Nelson Sauvignon Blanc   ★★★★

Grown at Hope, on the Waimea Plains, and briefly lees-aged, this is a consistently attractive wine, fresh and punchy. The 2019 vintage (★★★★☆) is mouthfilling and dry (3 grams/litre of residual sugar), with very good vigour and intensity of ripe tropical-fruit flavours.

Vintage	19	18
WR	6	5
Drink	20-21	P

 DRY $20 V+

Camshorn Waipara Sauvignon Blanc   (★★★★)

Drinking well now, the 2019 vintage (★★★★) is a very fresh and punchy, strongly varietal wine. Light lemon/green, it is highly aromatic, with penetrating tropical-fruit and herbaceous flavours, crisp and finely balanced.

 DRY $18 V+

Catalina Sounds Sound of White Marlborough Sauvignon Blanc   ★★★★☆

Still on sale, the complex 2017 vintage (★★★★★) was estate-grown in the Sound of White Vineyard, in the upper Waihopai Valley, and fermented in large French oak foudres. Mouthfilling, it has concentrated, ripely herbaceous flavours, gently seasoned with oak, excellent delicacy and complexity, and a well-rounded, long finish. A savoury and subtle, finely textured, very harmonious wine, it's now at its peak.

DRY $32 –V

Caythorpe Family Estate Marlborough Sauvignon Blanc   ★★★☆

Grown in the 'heart of the Wairau Plains', the 2020 vintage (★★★) is a single-vineyard, estate-grown wine. Pale lemon/green, it is aromatic, fresh and lively, with ripe passionfruit, lime and herb flavours, showing good intensity, and a dry, crisp finish.

 DRY $20 AV

Church Road Grand Reserve Barrel Fermented
Hawke's Bay Sauvignon Blanc ★★★★★

Full of personality, the 2019 vintage (★★★★★) of this oak-aged wine is already delicious. Estate-grown mostly in the Redstone Vineyard, in the Bridge Pa Triangle, with some fruit from Matapiro, it was hand-harvested and fermented with indigenous yeasts in French oak barrels (20 per cent new). Bright, light yellow/green, it is mouthfilling, with concentrated, ripe tropical-fruit flavours, fresh and vigorous, slightly toasty notes, balanced acidity, and excellent depth and complexity. Best drinking 2022+.

 DRY $40 AV

Church Road McDonald Series Hawke's Bay Barrel Fermented
Sauvignon Blanc ★★★★☆

Currently on sale, the 2018 vintage (★★★★☆) is a weighty, complex, non-herbaceous style of Sauvignon Blanc, partly (33 per cent) fermented with indigenous yeasts in old oak barriques. Bright, light yellow/green, it is mouthfilling and concentrated, with youthful, ripe tropical-fruit flavours, integrated oak, fresh acidity, and obvious potential. Best drinking mid-2021+.

 DRY $27 AV

Churton Best End Marlborough Sauvignon Blanc ★★★★★

This is Churton's 'single block, organic Sauvignon Blanc'. From a north-facing slope, 185 metres above sea level, in the Waihopai Valley, the 2017 vintage (★★★★★) was fermented and lees-aged for a year in French oak puncheons (20 per cent new), and bottled unfined and unfiltered. Weighty and tightly structured, it has vigorous, intense, ripely herbaceous flavours, showing good complexity, a minerally streak, very finely integrated oak, and a sustained, dry (1.4 grams/litre of residual sugar) finish. Best drinking 2021+. Certified organic.

Vintage	17	16	15	14	13
WR	6	NM	7	NM	7
Drink	20-25	NM	20-28	NM	20-28

 DRY $47 AV

Churton Marlborough Sauvignon Blanc ★★★★★

This producer aims for a style that 'combines the renowned flavour and aromatic intensity of Marlborough fruit with the finesse and complexity of fine European wines'. Estate-grown on an elevated site in the Waihopai Valley, it is hand-harvested and a small part of the blend (15 per cent in 2017) is fermented and lees-aged in seasoned and new French oak puncheons. The most recent vintage I have tasted is the 2017 (★★★★★). Certified organic, it is a fleshy, distinctive wine, fragrant and mouthfilling, with intense, ripely herbaceous flavours, subtle, biscuity notes adding complexity, and a lingering, fully dry, finely textured finish.

Vintage	17	16	15	14	13
WR	5	6	7	5	7
Drink	20-22	20-25	20-28	20-20	20-25

 DRY $27 V+

Clos Henri Marlborough Sauvignon Blanc   ★★★★★

The Clos Henri Vineyard near Renwick is owned by Henri Bourgeois, a leading, family-owned producer in the Loire Valley, who feels this wine expresses 'a unique terroir... and French winemaking approach'. A sophisticated and distinctive Sauvignon Blanc, in top years it's a joy to drink. Certified organic, the powerful 2018 vintage (★★★★★) was hand-picked and mostly fermented and matured on its yeast lees in tanks; 10 per cent was fermented and aged in French oak barrels. Bright, light yellow/green, it is weighty and concentrated, with generous, ripe tropical-fruit flavours, showing good complexity, and a long, dry finish. It's delicious now.

Vintage	18	17	16	15	14	13	12
WR	7	4	7	7	6	7	7
Drink	20-26	20-21	20-25	20-22	20-21	20-21	P

DRY $34 AV

Clos Henri Petit Clos Marlborough Sauvignon Blanc   ★★★★

From this Wairau Valley estate's youngest vines, the bright yellow/green 2018 vintage (★★★★) is a good buy. Certified organic, it has a fresh, ripe bouquet, leading into a mouthfilling, sweet-fruited wine with generous tropical-fruit flavours, crisp, dry and lively. Retasted in August 2020, it's a distinctive wine, drinking well now.

Vintage	19	18
WR	6	4
Drink	20-23	P

DRY $21 V+

Clos Marguerite Marlborough Sauvignon Blanc   ★★★★★

Estate-grown at Seaview, in the Awatere Valley, this wine is consistently classy. The 2019 vintage (★★★★★) was mostly lees-aged for six months in tanks; 10 per cent of the blend was barrel-fermented. Bright, light lemon/green, it is aromatic, mouthfilling and vibrantly fruity, with impressive weight and intensity of ripely herbaceous flavours, showing a distinct touch of complexity, good acid spine, and a dry (3.5 grams/litre of residual sugar), persistent finish. Youthful, with excellent freshness, vigour and depth, it should offer top drinking during 2021.

DRY $30 AV

Cloudy Bay New Zealand Sauvignon Blanc   ★★★★★

New Zealand's most internationally acclaimed wine is sought after from Sydney to New York and London. Its irresistibly aromatic and zesty style and intense flavours stem from 'the fruit characters that are in the grapes when they arrive at the winery'. It is sourced from company-owned and several long-term contract growers' vineyards in the Rapaura, Fairhall, Renwick and Brancott districts of the Wairau Valley, Marlborough. The wine is mostly cool-fermented with cultured and indigenous yeasts in stainless steel tanks and aged on its yeast lees, and a small percentage of the blend (4 per cent in 2020) is fermented at warmer temperatures in old French barriques and large-format oak vats. Bright, light lemon/green, the 2020 vintage (★★★★★) is delicious from the start. A very classy, weighty wine, it is ripely scented, with deep tropical-fruit flavours, gentle herbaceous notes, a distinct touch of complexity, and a finely textured, dry (2.4 grams/litre of residual sugar), long finish. A top vintage of this regional classic, it should break into full stride mid-2021+.

DRY $37 AV

Cloudy Bay Te Koko Sauvignon Blanc ★★★★★

Te Koko o Kupe ('The Oyster Dredge of Kupe') is the original name for Cloudy Bay; it is also the name of the Marlborough winery's intriguing oak-aged Sauvignon Blanc. Highly refined, the 2016 vintage (★★★★★) was grown in the Wairau Valley, fermented in French oak barrels (only 8 per cent new, to ensure a subtle oak influence), and matured in wood on its yeast lees for 15 months. Retasted in mid-2020, it is a bright, light yellow/green, fleshy wine, with generous, ripe tropical-fruit flavours, a hint of nutty oak, and excellent complexity and harmony. Rich and savoury, it's delicious now, but also worth cellaring to 2022.

Vintage	16	15
WR	7	7
Drink	20-26	20-25

DRY $60 AV

Coal Pit Central Otago Sauvignon Blanc ★★★☆

The youthful 2019 vintage (★★★☆) is a single-vineyard wine, hand-picked from mature, 25-year-old vines at Gibbston. Bright, light lemon/green, it is aromatic, crisp and freshly herbaceous, in a medium-bodied, strongly varietal style, with appetising acidity, and punchy melon and green-capsicum flavours. Best drinking 2021+.

DRY $27 –V

Crater Rim, The, Waipara Valley Sauvignon Blanc ★★★★

Still on sale, the partly barrel-fermented 2017 vintage (★★★★) has tropical-fruit aromas and flavours. Mouthfilling, with good richness, balanced acidity, and a subtle seasoning of oak, it's drinking well now.

DRY $18 V+

Crossings, The, Awatere Valley Marlborough Sauvignon Blanc ★★★★

Enjoyable young, the 2020 vintage (★★★☆) is a fresh and lively, clearly herbaceous style, with very good depth of melon and green-capsicum flavours, threaded with appetising acidity. (From Yealands.)

DRY $23 AV

Dashwood by Vavasour Marlborough Sauvignon Blanc ★★★★

This regional blend offers consistently good value. The 2019 vintage (★★★★) is punchy, with strong, fresh tropical-fruit and herbaceous flavours, and a basically dry (4.6 grams/litre of residual sugar), crisp finish. Marlborough in a glass.

DRY $16 V+

Decibel Crownthorpe Vineyard Hawke's Bay Sauvignon Blanc ★★★

Still fresh and lively in mid-2020, the 2018 vintage (★★★) is a bright, light lemon/green, medium-bodied wine, with good depth of ripely herbaceous flavours, fresh acidity, and a smooth finish. It's probably at its peak now.

DRY $19 AV

Deep Down Marlborough Sauvignon Blanc   ★★★★☆

Certified organic, the 2020 vintage (★★★★☆) is a single-vineyard wine, partly (35 per cent) fermented in seasoned French oak puncheons. Bright, light yellow/green, it is medium to full-bodied, with strong, ripe tropical-fruit flavours, showing a distinct touch of complexity, and a dry finish. Drink now or cellar. The 2019 vintage (★★★★☆), harvested from 20-year-old vines, was also partly (35 per cent) barrel-fermented. Ripely scented, it is a fresh and lively, medium to full-bodied wine, with ripe, non-herbaceous flavours, showing excellent vigour and intensity.

Vintage	20
WR	7
Drink	20-24

 DRY $27 AV

Delegat Awatere Valley Sauvignon Blanc   ★★★★

The 2019 vintage (★★★★☆) is a top buy. Bright, light lemon/green, it is fresh, mouthfilling and dry, with good vigour and intensity of ripe melon and green-capsicum flavours, lees-aging notes adding complexity, and a lingering finish.

 DRY $20 V+

Delta Estate Marlborough Sauvignon Blanc   ★★★★☆

The 2019 vintage (★★★★☆) is a single-vineyard wine, grown in the lower Wairau Valley. Aromatic and full-bodied, it has penetrating tropical-fruit and herbaceous flavours, dry (1.4 grams/litre of residual sugar) and lasting. Showing very good delicacy, drive and personality, it offers fine value.

 DRY $20 V+

Delta Hatters Hill Marlborough Sauvignon Blanc   ★★★★★

The highly aromatic 2019 vintage (★★★★☆) was grown in the Dillons Point district and handled in a mix of stainless steel tanks (60 per cent) and seasoned oak casks (40 per cent). Fresh and punchy, it is medium-bodied, with good intensity of tropical-fruit and herbaceous flavours, a gentle oak influence adding complexity, and a dry (1.9 grams/litre of residual sugar), crisp finish. Drink now to 2021.

DRY $28 V+

Doctors', The, Marlborough Sauvignon Blanc   ★★★

A good example of the low-alcohol style, the easy-drinking 2019 vintage (★★★) is light (9.5 per cent alcohol) and lively. Vibrantly fruity, it is clearly varietal, with fresh, citrusy, green-edged flavours, and an off-dry (5.4 grams/litre of residual sugar), smooth finish. (From Forrest Estate.)

 MED/DRY $22 –V

Dog Point Vineyard Marlborough Sauvignon Blanc ★★★★★

This classic wine offers a clear style contrast to Section 94, Dog Point's complex, barrel-aged Sauvignon Blanc (see the Branded and Other White Wines section). Hand-picked at several sites in the Wairau Valley, it is lees-aged in tanks but handled without oak. The classy 2019 vintage (★★★★★) is highly aromatic, weighty and sweet-fruited, with intense, ripely herbaceous flavours and a crisp, dry, very long finish. Best drinking 2021. Certified organic.

Vintage	19	18	17	16	15	14	13
WR	7	5	4	7	7	6	7
Drink	20-26	20-22	20-21	20-21	P	P	P

DRY $28 V+

Domain Road Vineyard Bannockburn Central Otago Sauvignon Blanc ★★★★

The 2018 vintage (★★★★☆) was mostly (58 per cent) barrel-fermented. Light lemon/green, it is a distinctive, mouthfilling wine, with a fresh, ripely herbaceous bouquet, strong, lively, tropical-fruit flavours, finely balanced acidity, and very good complexity and vigour.

DRY $23 AV

Durvillea Marlborough Sauvignon Blanc ★★★☆

Offering fine value, the 2020 vintage (★★★☆) is fresh, crisp and very lively, with tropical-fruit and herbaceous flavours, showing good delicacy and depth, and a fully dry finish.

DRY $17 V+

Eaton Marlborough Sauvignon Blanc (★★★★☆)

The distinctive 2018 vintage (★★★★☆) was grown in the Awatere Valley and at Flaxbourne, hand-picked, and fermented and matured for 11 months in oak casks (30 per cent new). Bright, light yellow/green, it is mouthfilling and dry, with generous tropical-fruit flavours, showing good complexity, and a finely textured finish.

Vintage	18
WR	7
Drink	20-22

DRY $39 –V

Eaton Thistle Hill Flaxbourne Marlborough Sauvignon Blanc ★★★★☆

The 2018 vintage (★★★★) is rare – only 378 bottles were produced. A single-vineyard wine, it was hand-picked in southern Marlborough, barrel-fermented with indigenous yeasts and oak-aged for 11 months. Pale gold, it is less vibrant than most of the region's Sauvignon Blancs, but weighty, with ripe tropical-fruit flavours, showing good concentration and complexity.

Vintage	18	17
WR	7	7
Drink	20-25	20-25

DRY $59 –V

Eradus Awatere Valley Marlborough Sauvignon Blanc   ★★★★

Offering excellent value, the 2020 vintage (★★★★) was harvested from 20-year-old vines. A full-bodied, freshly herbaceous wine, it is finely balanced, with very good delicacy and depth of passionfruit/lime flavours, lively acidity, and a fully dry finish.

 DRY $17 V+

Esk Valley Marlborough Sauvignon Blanc   ★★★★

The punchy 2019 vintage (★★★★) was grown in the Awatere and Wairau valleys. Mouthfilling and vibrantly fruity, it has strong tropical-fruit flavours, a herbaceous undercurrent, and a dry (2.8 grams/litre of residual sugar), long finish.

Vintage	19	18
WR	6	6
Drink	20-22	P

 DRY $20 V+

Fairbourne Marlborough Sauvignon Blanc   ★★★★★

From elevated, north-facing slopes in the Wairau Valley, the 2017 vintage (★★★★★) of this single-vineyard wine was hand-picked and fermented to full dryness. It was mostly handled in tanks, but a small portion of the blend (2 per cent) was French oak-fermented. Fragrant and full-bodied, it has concentrated, ripe tropical-fruit flavours to the fore, a herbaceous undercurrent, balanced acidity, and excellent complexity, drive and length.

Vintage	17	16	15	14	13
WR	6	7	6	7	7
Drink	20-21	20-22	20-21	P	P

 DRY $30 AV

Falconhead Marlborough Sauvignon Blanc   ★★★☆

The very good-value 2020 vintage (★★★☆) is a fresh and lively, medium-bodied wine, with ripe tropical-fruit flavours, including a distinct hint of passionfruit, and a crisp, smooth (4.3 grams/litre of residual sugar) finish.

Vintage	20
WR	7
Drink	20-22

 DRY $16 V+

Folium Reserve Marlborough Sauvignon Blanc   ★★★★★

The impressive 2018 vintage (★★★★★) was hand-picked in the Brancott Valley and handled entirely in tanks. A distinctive wine, it is fragrant, fresh and full-bodied, with concentrated tropical-fruit flavours, a herbaceous undercurrent, and a long finish. An age-worthy wine, it is full of personality.

Vintage	18	17	16
WR	4	5	6
Drink	20-25	20-25	20-30

 DRY $32 AV

Folium Vineyard Marlborough Sauvignon Blanc ★★★★★

The 2018 vintage (★★★★☆) was hand-harvested in the Brancott Valley and handled entirely in tanks. Bright, light lemon/green, it is fresh and lively, with very good weight and intensity of tropical-fruit and herbaceous flavours, crisp, dry and lingering.

Vintage	18	17
WR	4	5
Drink	20-21	P

 DRY $26 V+

Forrest Marlborough Sauvignon Blanc ★★★★

The 2019 vintage (★★★★) is enjoyable young. A medium to full-bodied, finely balanced wine, it has very good depth of lively tropical-fruit and herbaceous flavours, dry (3.3 grams/litre of residual sugar) and lingering.

 DRY $22 V+

Framingham Marlborough Sauvignon Blanc ★★★★☆

The 2019 vintage (★★★★☆) was grown in the Wairau Valley and given 'a quick tour inside oak and acacia barrels'. Bright, light lemon/green, it is mouthfilling, lively and dry (2 grams/litre of residual sugar), with generous, ripe tropical-fruit flavours, a subtle seasoning of oak, balanced acidity, and a lingering finish. Delicious now.

Vintage	17	16	15
WR	6	6	6
Drink	P	P	P

DRY $25 V+

Giesen 0% Marlborough Sauvignon Blanc (★)

'For health-conscious Kiwis', the non-vintage wine (★) released in early 2020 reminded me of biting into a Granny Smith apple. Harbouring no more than 0.5 per cent alcohol by volume, it was made by extracting alcohol, using spinning cone technology, so 'you can have a tipple or two of your favourite wine, without the pesky after-effects'. Sweetish (13 grams/litre of residual sugar), appley and crisp, it's bland, lacking the flavour delights of fine-quality Marlborough Sauvignon Blanc.

 MED/DRY $16 –V

Giesen Marlborough Sauvignon Blanc ★★★☆

This huge-volume wine from Giesen enjoys major export success. Grown in estate-owned and contract growers' vineyards, mostly in the Wairau Valley, with a smaller portion from the Awatere Valley, it is typically medium to full-bodied, with ripely herbaceous flavours, showing very good freshness, vigour and depth.

 DRY $17 V+

Gladstone Vineyard Sauvignon Blanc ★★★★

The 2018 vintage (★★★★) was grown in the northern Wairarapa and 50 per cent barrel-fermented; the rest was handled in tanks. It is mouthfilling, with ripe tropical-fruit flavours to the fore, hints of toasty oak adding complexity, and a dry (1.5 grams/litre of residual sugar), smooth finish.

Vintage	18
WR	6
Drink	20-22

 DRY $25 AV

Goldwater Wairau Valley Marlborough Sauvignon Blanc ★★★★☆

The 2019 vintage (★★★★☆) is delicious young. It has concentrated, ripe tropical-fruit flavours to the fore, mingled with fresh, herbaceous notes, excellent delicacy and vibrancy, and a smooth (4.7 grams/litre of residual sugar), persistent finish.

 DRY $25 V+

Graham Norton's Own Marlborough Sauvignon Blanc ★★★★

From 'chief winemaker Graham Norton', Invivo's instantly appealing 2020 vintage (★★★★☆) is a punchy, aromatic, strongly varietal wine. Medium to full-bodied, it is crisp and zingy, with penetrating passionfruit/lime flavours, tightly structured, dry (4.3 grams/litre of residual sugar) and lingering.

 DRY $19 V+

Greenhough Hope Vineyard Nelson Sauvignon Blanc ★★★★☆

Certified organic, the 2017 vintage (★★★★★) was estate-grown, hand-picked and fermented with indigenous yeasts in French oak barrels (17 per cent new). Wood-aged for eight months, it is a notably complex, very harmonious wine, with a fragrant, inviting bouquet. Mouthfilling, it is vibrant and concentrated, with deliciously ripe flavours, fresh but not high acidity, and a sustained finish. Ready.

 DRY $32 –V

Greenhough River Garden Nelson Sauvignon Blanc ★★★★☆

Certified organic, this consistently rewarding wine is mostly handled in tanks, but a small portion is fermented with indigenous yeasts and lees-aged in French oak casks. The 2019 vintage (★★★★★) is the first to be labelled 'River Garden'. Fresh and mouthfilling, it is sweet-fruited, with generous, ripe tropical-fruit flavours, a subtle seasoning of oak, good drive through the palate, finely balanced acidity, and a rounded finish. Delicious drinking now to 2021.

 DRY $22 V+

Greyrock Te Koru Marlborough Sauvignon Blanc (★★★★)

Priced right, the 2019 vintage (★★★★) is medium-bodied and finely balanced, with very good depth of tropical-fruit and herbaceous flavours, and a crisp, dry (3.1 grams/litre of residual sugar), lingering finish.

DRY $20 V+

Greystone Sauvignon Blanc Barrel Fermented ★★★★☆

Drinking well now, the 2019 vintage (★★★★☆) is a ripely scented, mouthfilling wine from North Canterbury. Fermented and matured for six months in old oak barriques, it is fleshy and sweet-fruited, with concentrated tropical-fruit flavours, slightly toasty notes adding complexity, and a dry, smooth finish.

Vintage	19
WR	6
Drink	20-26

DRY $26 AV

Greywacke Marlborough Sauvignon Blanc ★★★★★

Grown in the central Wairau Valley and the Southern Valleys, the 2019 vintage (★★★★★) was handled principally in tanks (a small percentage was fermented with indigenous yeasts in old oak casks). Fleshy, sweet-fruited and rounded, with generous, ripe tropical-fruit flavours, showing a distinct touch of complexity, and a dry, long finish, it's already very open and expressive. Bright, light lemon/green, the youthful 2020 vintage (★★★★★) is a very elegant, mouthfilling wine, with vigorous, tropical-fruit flavours, a herbaceous undercurrent, a distinct touch of complexity, and a crisp, long finish. Best drinking mid-2021+.

Vintage	20	19	18	17	16	15	14	13
WR	6	6	6	5	6	6	6	6
Drink	21-26	20-25	20-24	20-22	20-22	20-21	P	P

DRY $28 V+

Greywacke Marlborough Wild Sauvignon ★★★★★

This is a leading example of Marlborough Sauvignon Blanc from well outside the mainstream. Fermented with indigenous yeasts in old French oak barriques, the 2018 vintage (★★★★☆) is still unfolding. Bright, light yellow/green, it is mouthfilling, sweet-fruited and tightly structured, with concentrated, vigorous tropical-fruit flavours, oak complexity, and a crisp, dry, long finish. Best drinking 2022+.

Vintage	18	17	16	15	14	13
WR	6	6	6	6	6	6
Drink	20-28	20-27	20-26	20-25	20-24	20-23

DRY $37 AV

Grove Mill Wairau Valley Marlborough Sauvignon Blanc ★★★★

Offering good value, the 2019 vintage (★★★★) was mostly handled in tanks; 5 per cent of the blend was fermented in old French oak casks. Richly fragrant, with tropical-fruit aromas, it is vibrantly fruity, with strong, ripely herbaceous flavours, a touch of complexity, and a dry, lingering finish.

DRY $19 V+

Haha Marlborough Sauvignon Blanc ★★★☆

This is a good buy. Very fresh and lively, the 2019 vintage (★★★★) is medium-bodied, with a punchy, aromatic bouquet. Strongly varietal, it is sweet-fruited and tangy, with very good vigour and depth of passionfruit, lime and green-capsicum flavours, finely balanced, dry (1.4 grams/litre of residual sugar) and crisp.

DRY $18 V+

Hans Herzog Marlborough Sauvignon Blanc Barrel Fermented Sur Lie   ★★★★★

Outside the regional mainstream, the 2016 vintage (★★★★★) was estate-grown and hand-picked on the north side of the Wairau Valley, fermented with indigenous yeasts in French oak puncheons, and wood-aged for 15 months. It has good weight and mouthfeel, with concentrated, ripe tropical-fruit flavours, impressive complexity, and a dry, finely textured finish. Delicious now, it's certified organic.

Hunter's Home Block Marlborough Sauvignon Blanc   (★★★★★)

The 2019 vintage (★★★★★) of Hunter's new 'icon' Sauvignon Blanc was hand-picked from mature (25-year-old), low-cropped vines and partly (10 per cent) fermented in seasoned French oak puncheons. Medium to full-bodied, it is intense, crisp and dry, with punchy, ripe passionfruit/lime flavours, vague toasty notes, firm acid spine, and a long finish. Full of youthful vigour, it's well worth cellaring to mid-2021+.

Hunter's Kaho Roa Marlborough Sauvignon Blanc   ★★★★

The 2017 vintage (★★★☆), grown in the Omaka Valley, was fermented and aged for six months in seasoned French oak puncheons. Fragrant, it is medium-bodied, with ripe fruit flavours, a slightly minerally streak, and an appetisingly crisp, dry (1.8 grams/litre of residual sugar) finish.

Vintage	17
WR	4
Drink	20-25

Hunter's Marlborough Sauvignon Blanc   ★★★★

Hunter's fame rests on this wine. The goal is 'a strong expression of Marlborough fruit – a bell-clear wine with a mix of tropical and searing gooseberry characters'. The grapes are sourced from numerous sites in the Wairau Valley, all company-owned, and to retain their fresh, vibrant characters they are processed quickly, with some use of indigenous yeasts and lees-aging. The wine is usually at its best between one and two years old. The 2020 vintage (★★★★) was mostly handled in tanks, but 10 per cent of the blend was fermented in large French oak casks. Very fresh and youthful, it has vigorous melon, passionfruit and green-capsicum flavours, crisp and dry (3 grams/litre of residual sugar). It needs time; open mid-2021+.

Vintage	20
WR	7
Drink	20-23

DRY $19 V+

Hunting Lodge, The, Expressions Marlborough Sauvignon Blanc   ★★★★

Full of youthful vigour, the 2019 vintage (★★★★) was tank-fermented and matured on its yeast lees. Light lemon/green, it is vividly varietal, with strong, vibrant green-capsicum and passionfruit-like flavours, showing very good freshness, delicacy and length.

Hunting Lodge, The, Home Block Waimauku Sauvignon Blanc   ★★★★☆

Estate-grown in West Auckland, the classy, distinctive 2019 vintage (★★★★★) was hand-harvested (from vines principally planted in 2008, but dating back to 1979), and fermented and matured for eight months in French oak barriques (25 per cent new). Bright, light lemon/green, it is highly fragrant, weighty and dry, with rich, ripe tropical-fruit flavours, showing excellent complexity, fresh acidity, and a lasting finish. Already delicious, it's likely to be long-lived; best drinking 2022+.

 DRY $33 –V

Hunting Lodge, The, Waimauku Home Block Liberated Sauvignon Blanc   (★★★★☆)

Still unfolding, the distinctive 2018 vintage (★★★★☆) was estate-grown in West Auckland, hand-picked, barrel-fermented with indigenous yeasts and lees-aged in oak for nine months. Bright yellow/green, with a complex bouquet, it is fleshy, with deep, ripe tropical-fruit flavours to the fore, and good vigour and cellaring potential. Best drinking 2022+.

 DRY $45 –V

Invivo Marlborough Sauvignon Blanc   ★★★★

The 2020 vintage (★★★★) is pale lemon/green, with good intensity of ripe tropical-fruit flavours, a hint of passionfruit, and a fresh, dry (4 grams/litre of residual sugar), crisp finish.

DRY $19 V+

Invivo SJP Sarah Jessica Parker Marlborough Sauvignon Blanc   ★★★★☆

Aimed principally at the US market, the instantly likeable 2020 vintage (★★★★☆) is a good buy. Bright, light lemon/green, it is ripely scented and well-rounded, with excellent weight and depth of passionfruit/lime flavours, harmonious, dry (3 grams/litre of residual sugar) and lingering.

 DRY $22 V+

Jackson Estate Grey Ghost Barrique Wairau Valley
Marlborough Sauvignon Blanc   ★★★★★

Currently on sale, the 2016 vintage (★★★★★) is maturing very gracefully. Hand-picked from vines planted in 1988 and fermented in old oak barriques, it is a bright, light lemon/green wine, refined, complex and still youthful. Medium-bodied, it is ripely herbaceous, with tropical-fruit flavours, finely integrated oak, and a fully dry, long finish.

 DRY $30 AV

Vintage	16	15
WR	5	5
Drink	20-25	20-25

Jackson Estate Somerset Block 2 Single Vineyard
Waihopai Valley Marlborough Sauvignon Blanc   (★★★★★)

Still on sale, the concentrated 2017 vintage (★★★★★) was grown in the Waihopai Valley and handled entirely in tanks. An aromatic, intensely varietal wine, it is full-bodied and ripe, with strong tropical-fruit flavours, bottle-aged notes adding a toasty complexity, and a crisp, dry (3 grams/litre of residual sugar), lasting finish.

Vintage	17
WR	6
Drink	20-22

 DRY $29 V+

Jackson Estate Stich Marlborough Sauvignon Blanc   ★★★★

Unfolding well, the top-value 2019 vintage (★★★★☆) was estate-grown at three sites in the Wairau and Waihopai valleys. Bright, light lemon/green, it is ripely scented and mouthfilling, with very good vigour and depth of passionfruit/lime flavours, and a finely balanced, tightly structured, dry (3.2 grams/litre of residual sugar) finish. Best drinking 2021+.

Vintage	19	18
WR	6	5
Drink	20-24	20-23

 DRY $21 V+

Johanneshof Cellars Marlborough Sauvignon Blanc   ★★★☆

The bright, light lemon/green 2019 vintage (★★★☆) is an easy-drinking style, crisp and medium-bodied, with very good depth of tropical-fruit flavours, a herbaceous undercurrent, and lots of drink-young appeal.

 MED/DRY $25 –V

Joiy Marlborough Sauvignon Blanc   (★★★★)

The 2019 vintage (★★★★) is packaged in a 250-ml can, designed to be 'enjoiyed' at picnics or at the beach. Crisp and lively, with strong, ripely herbaceous flavours of melons and green capsicums, it's as good as most bottled wines, and priced sharply. (Note: the vintage date is stamped on the base of the can.)

DRY $6 (250ML) V+

Jules Taylor Marlborough Sauvignon Blanc   ★★★★☆

The punchy, lively 2020 vintage (★★★★☆) was grown in the lower Wairau, Awatere and Southern valleys. A pale, aromatic wine, it is mouthfilling, with fresh, ripe flavours, showing good intensity, and a fully dry (1.4 grams/litre of residual sugar), tangy finish.

Vintage	20
WR	5
Drink	20-22

 DRY $25 V+

Jules Taylor OTQ Limited Release Single Vineyard
Marlborough Sauvignon Blanc   ★★★★★

Made 'On The Quiet', the 2018 vintage (★★★★★) is a single-vineyard wine, fermented and matured for nine months in old French oak barriques. Delicious now, it has a fragrant, complex bouquet. Fleshy, rich and rounded, it has well-ripened tropical-fruit flavours, finely integrated oak, and a long, fully dry (1.3 grams/litre of residual sugar) finish.

Vintage	18
WR	6
Drink	20-23

 DRY $35 AV

Julicher Martinborough Sauvignon Blanc   (★★★★☆)

Probably at or near its peak, the distinctive 2018 vintage (★★★★☆) was estate-grown at Te Muna, hand-picked and mostly handled in tanks; 25 per cent of the blend was matured in seasoned oak casks. Bright, light lemon/green, it is ripely scented, mouthfilling, fleshy and sweet-fruited, with vibrant peach and passionfruit flavours, showing good concentration, and a subtle oak influence adding complexity. Worth discovering.

 DRY $21 V+

Junction Red Card Central Hawke's Bay Sauvignon Blanc   (★★★☆)

Priced right, the 2019 vintage (★★★☆) was hand-picked on the Takapau Plains. Freshly aromatic, with tropical-fruit and herbaceous flavours, crisp and zingy, and a smooth finish, it has lots of youthful impact.

 DRY $16 V+

Kahurangi Estate Mt Arthur Reserve Nelson Fumé Blanc   ★★★★☆

The 2019 vintage (★★★★☆) was fermented and matured in seasoned French oak puncheons and barriques. Bright, light yellow/green, it is mouthfilling, with concentrated, ripe tropical-fruit flavours, a gentle oak influence, very good complexity, and a dry finish. Best drinking 2021+.

 DRY $21 V+

Kahurangi Estate Nelson Sauvignon Blanc   (★★★☆)

Offering good value, the 2020 vintage (★★★☆) is fresh and lively, in a medium to full-bodied style with ripely herbaceous flavours, fresh acidity, and a dry finish.

DRY $17 V+

Kelly Washington Southern Valleys Marlborough Sauvignon Blanc   (★★★★☆)

Certified organic, the 2017 vintage (★★★★☆) was hand-picked, fermented with indigenous yeasts and lees-aged for 10 months, with 'a portion rested in old French oak'. A distinctive wine, still youthful, it has good intensity of crisp, ripely herbaceous flavours, a very subtle seasoning of oak, and a tightly structured finish.

 DRY $28 AV

Kina Beach Vineyard Nelson Sauvignon Blanc ★★★★

Currently on sale, the 2016 vintage (★★★★) was estate-grown. Bright, light yellow/green, with a fragrant, mature but still lively bouquet, it is vigorous, with strong, citrusy, limey flavours, showing bottle-aged complexity. It's drinking well now.

Vintage	16
WR	7
Drink	20-21

DRY $20 V+

Kina Cliffs By The Sea Nelson Sauvignon Blanc (★★★☆)

Enjoyable young, the 2019 vintage (★★★☆) is a single-vineyard wine, briefly lees-aged. Freshly aromatic, it is medium-bodied, with strong, ripely herbaceous flavours, and a crisp, off-dry (8 grams/litre of residual sugar) finish.

MED/DRY $25 –V

Koha Marlborough Sauvignon Blanc (★★★)

Light and lively, the 2019 vintage (★★★) is a strongly varietal wine, with fresh, herbaceous aromas and flavours, dry (3.5 grams/litre of residual sugar) and crisp. (From te Pā.)

DRY $19 AV

Kono Marlborough Sauvignon Blanc ★★★

The 2019 vintage (★★★) is a direct, uncomplicated wine, with fresh, herbaceous aromas and lively melon and green-capsicum flavours, showing good depth.

DRY $18 AV

Kumeu River Rays Road Sauvignon Blanc ★★★★☆

The refined 2019 vintage (★★★★☆) is from the company's vineyard on an elevated, north-facing site in Hawke's Bay. Hand-harvested, fermented with indigenous yeasts and handled without oak, it is a distinctive, subtle wine, bright, light lemon/green, with incisive, citrusy flavours, a hint of green capsicums, very good intensity, and a dry finish.

DRY $25 V+

Lake Chalice The Falcon Marlborough Sauvignon Blanc ★★★★

The 2019 vintage (★★★★) was grown in the lower Wairau Valley. Fresh and lively, it is medium-bodied, with good intensity of clearly herbaceous flavours, some tropical-fruit notes, a hint of saltiness, and appetising acidity.

DRY $19 V+

Lake Chalice The Raptor Marlborough Sauvignon Blanc ★★★★

Drinking well now, the 2018 vintage (★★★★☆) is a fleshy, concentrated wine, grown mostly at Dillons Point, in the lower Wairau Valley. Fresh and lively, it has strong, ripe tropical-fruit flavours to the fore, a herbal undercurrent, and a dry, lingering finish.

DRY $23 AV

Lawson's Dry Hills Marlborough Sauvignon Blanc ★★★★★

One of the region's best, widely available Sauvignon Blancs, this stylish wine is vibrant, intense and finely structured. The grapes are grown at several sites, mostly in the Southern Valleys, and to add a subtle extra dimension, part of the blend (5 per cent in 2020) is fermented with indigenous yeasts in old French oak barrels. The wine typically has strong impact in its youth, but also has a proven ability to age, acquiring toasty, minerally complexities. The 2020 vintage (★★★★☆) is still extremely youthful. Light lemon/green, it is mouthfilling, with punchy, yet delicate, passionfruit, lime and green-capsicum flavours that build to a long, very harmonious finish.

Vintage	20	19
WR	7	7
Drink	20-25	20-23

DRY $20 V+

Lawson's Dry Hills Reserve Marlborough Sauvignon Blanc ★★★★★

Retasted in mid-2020, the 2019 vintage (★★★★★) was grown in the Waihopai, Awatere and Wairau valleys, and made with some use of indigenous yeasts and barrel fermentation. Bright, light lemon/green, it is very lively, with intense tropical-fruit and herbaceous flavours, punchy and youthful, a distinct touch of complexity, and a long, crisp, dry (1.8 grams/litre of residual sugar) finish. Drink now or cellar. Good value. The 2020 vintage (★★★★☆) was partly (10 per cent) fermented in old oak barrels. Medium to full-bodied, it is very fresh and lively, with good intensity of ripely herbaceous flavours, showing considerable complexity, and finely balanced acidity. Best drinking mid-2021+.

Vintage	20	19
WR	6	7
Drink	21-26	20-23

DRY $25 V+

Left Field New Zealand Sauvignon Blanc ★★★★

The lively 2020 vintage (★★★★) is a blend of various regions. Pale lemon/green, it is medium-bodied, with lively tropical-fruit and herbaceous flavours, basically dry (4.5 grams/litre of residual sugar) and lingering. (From Te Awa.)

DRY $18 V+

Leveret Estate Marlborough Sauvignon Blanc ★★★☆

Still on sale, the 2018 vintage (★★★☆) is full-bodied, with tropical-fruit and herbaceous flavours, lively, crisp and strong, and a basically dry (4.2 grams/litre of residual sugar), finely balanced finish.

DRY $22 AV

Loveblock Marlborough Sauvignon Blanc ★★★★

Estate-grown in the lower Awatere Valley, the 2019 vintage (★★★★) is a punchy wine, fermented in tanks (75 per cent) and old French oak barrels (25 per cent). Fresh and weighty, it has good intensity of ripe tropical-fruit flavours, a touch of complexity, and a dry, appetisingly crisp finish.

DRY $22 V+

Loveblock Orange Marlborough Sauvignon Blanc ★★★☆

Certified organic, the 2019 vintage (★★★☆) of this estate-grown, lower Awatere Valley wine was made with 'absolutely zero added sulphur', using 'green tea powder as a natural antioxidant'. Mouthfilling and crisp, it is youthful, with restrained aromatics, but very good weight and depth of tropical-fruit and herbaceous flavours.

DRY $22 AV

Loveblock Tee Marlborough Sauvignon Blanc (★★★☆)

The pale gold 2019 vintage (★★★☆) was estate-grown in the lower Awatere Valley and handled without sulphur, using green tea as a natural antioxidant. It lacks the fresh, aromatic intensity of most Marlborough Sauvignon Blancs, but it is mouthfilling, with strong, ripe fruit flavours, and a smooth (4.9 grams/litre of residual sugar) finish. A distinctive wine, it's drinking well now. Certified organic.

DRY $27 –V

Mahi Marlborough Sauvignon Blanc ★★★★★

Offering good value, the 2019 vintage (★★★★☆) was mostly handled in tanks; the ripest, hand-picked fruit (12 per cent of the blend) was barrel-fermented with indigenous yeasts. Matured on its yeast lees for nine months, with some inclusion of Sémillon, it is a bright, light lemon/green, weighty wine, with deep, vibrant tropical-fruit flavours, showing very good complexity, and a finely textured, dry (below 2 grams/litre of residual sugar), lingering finish. It's drinking well now.

Vintage	19	18	17	16	15
WR	7	6	6	7	6
Drink	20-25	20-23	20-22	P	P

DRY $22 V+

Mahi Single Vineyard Boundary Farm Marlborough Sauvignon Blanc ★★★★★

Retasted in August 2020, the classy 2017 vintage (★★★★★) is maturing very gracefully. Grown on the lower slopes of the Wither Hills, on the south side of the Wairau Valley, it was hand-picked, and fermented and matured for 11 months in French oak barriques. Bright, light yellow/green, it is weighty, with concentrated tropical-fruit flavours, showing excellent complexity, that build to a fully dry (below 2 grams/litre of residual sugar), lasting finish. Drink now to 2021.

Vintage	17
WR	5
Drink	20-24

DRY $34 AV

Main Divide North Canterbury Sauvignon Blanc ★★★★

Very lively and youthful, the 2020 vintage (★★★★) is a bright, light lemon/green, medium to full-bodied wine, with fresh, punchy passionfruit/lime flavours, dry and crisp. Best drinking mid-2021+. (From Pegasus Bay.)

Vintage	20	19
WR	7	5
Drink	20-23	20-21

DRY $21 V+

Man O' War Gravestone Sauvignon Blanc/Sémillon   ★★★★★

The impressive 2018 vintage (★★★★★) is a 3:1 blend of Sauvignon Blanc and Sémillon, estate-grown on Waiheke Island and fully barrel-fermented. Bright, light lemon/green, it has a complex, ripely herbaceous bouquet. Mouthfilling, it is vibrantly fruity, with tropical-fruit flavours, finely integrated oak, and a long finish. A 'serious', very age-worthy wine, it's well worth cellaring to 2022+.

 DRY $30 AV

Man O' War Waiheke Island Sauvignon Blanc   ★★★☆

'Fresh and feisty', the youthful 2019 vintage (★★★☆) was estate-grown and hand-harvested at the eastern end of the island. Pale lemon/green, it is a fresh and lively, medium-bodied wine, with good depth of tropical-fruit and herbaceous flavours, crisp and dry.

Vintage	16	15	14
WR	6	6	5
Drink	20-21	P	P

 DRY $20 AV

Map Maker Marlborough Sauvignon Blanc   ★★★★

Priced sharply, the 2019 vintage (★★★★) was estate-grown at Rapaura, in the Wairau Valley. It has a punchy, aromatic bouquet, leading into a lively, intensely varietal wine, with strong tropical-fruit and herbaceous flavours, crisp, bone-dry and lingering. (From Staete Landt.)

 DRY $18 V+

Martinborough Vineyard Martinborough Sauvignon Blanc   ★★★★

Still on sale, the 2018 vintage (★★★★) was mostly handled in tanks; 10 per cent of the blend was fermented and matured in old oak barrels. Ripely scented, it has tropical-fruit flavours, showing a distinct touch of complexity, and a dry, crisp finish. Ready.

 DRY $24 AV

Martinborough Vineyard Te Tera Sauvignon Blanc   ★★★★

The 2019 vintage (★★★★) is a ripely scented, lively, medium-bodied wine, with good intensity of tropical-fruit flavours, a herbaceous undercurrent, and a basically dry (4 grams/litre of residual sugar), crisp finish. Good value.

Vintage	19	18	17
WR	7	7	7
Drink	20-23	20-23	20-22

 DRY $20 V+

Matahiwi Estate Wairarapa Sauvignon Blanc   ★★★★

The 2020 vintage (★★★★) is a freshly scented, lively, medium to full-bodied wine, with very good vigour and depth of passionfruit, lime and green-capsicum flavours, dry (2 grams/litre of residual sugar) and crisp.

Vintage	20	19
WR	6	5
Drink	20-23	P

DRY $23 AV

Maui Waipara Sauvignon Blanc   (★★★☆)

Bargain-priced, the 2019 vintage (★★★☆) is a lively, herbaceous style, with some riper tropical-fruit notes. Medium-bodied, it is fresh and finely balanced, with a basically dry (4 grams/litre of residual sugar), crisp finish. (From Tiki.)

`DRY $14 V+`

ME by Matahiwi Wairarapa Sauvignon Blanc   (★★★)

Enjoyable young, the 2020 vintage (★★★) is a fresh and lively, medium-bodied wine, with crisp tropical-fruit and herbaceous flavours, showing good depth, and a dry (2 grams/litre of residual sugar) finish.

Vintage	20
WR	6
Drink	20-23

`DRY $20 –V`

Mills Reef Estate Marlborough Sauvignon Blanc   ★★★

The 2020 vintage (★★☆) is bright, light lemon/green, with grassy aromas. It has fresh, appley, green-edged flavours, and a basically dry (4.2 grams/litre of residual sugar), crisp finish.

Vintage	20
WR	6
Drink	21-23

`DRY $19 AV`

Mills Reef Reserve Hawke's Bay Sauvignon Blanc   ★★★☆

The 2019 vintage (★★★☆) is a medium-bodied, vibrantly fruity wine, with very good depth of melon, passionfruit and lime flavours, fresh, dry (2 grams/litre of residual sugar) and smooth.

Vintage	19	18	17	16
WR	7	7	5	7
Drink	20-21	P	P	P

`DRY $23 –V`

Misha's Vineyard The Starlet Central Otago Sauvignon Blanc   ★★★★

The 2019 vintage (★★★☆) was estate-grown at Bendigo, in the Cromwell Basin. Hand-harvested, it was mostly handled in tanks, but 34 per cent of the blend was fermented with indigenous yeasts in seasoned French oak casks. Pale lemon/green, it is full-bodied and youthful, with restrained, appley, citrusy flavours, showing a distinct touch of complexity, fresh, mouth-watering acidity, and a dry (4 grams/litre of residual sugar) finish. Best drinking 2021+.

Vintage	19	18	17	16	15	14	13
WR	7	7	6	7	7	6	7
Drink	20-28	20-27	20-25	20-24	20-23	20-22	20-23

`DRY $28 –V`

Mission Barrique Reserve Marlborough Sauvignon Blanc   (★★★★☆)

Youthful, with obvious potential, the 2019 vintage (★★★★☆) was estate-grown in the Awatere Valley and fermented and lees-aged for nine months in French oak barrels. Bright, light lemon/green, with a fragrant, ripely herbaceous, complex bouquet, it is full-bodied, with concentrated tropical-fruit flavours, a subtle seasoning of oak, good acid spine, and a long, dry (3 grams/litre of residual sugar) finish.

 DRY $23 V+

Mission Marlborough Sauvignon Blanc   ★★★☆

Priced sharply, the punchy 2020 vintage (★★★☆) was estate-grown in the Awatere Valley. Pale lemon/green, it is fresh and lively, with good depth of tropical-fruit and herbaceous flavours, and a dryish (6 grams/litre of residual sugar), appetisingly crisp finish.

 MED/DRY $16 V+

Momo Organic Marlborough Sauvignon Blanc   ★★★★

From Seresin, the very youthful 2020 vintage (★★★★) is full-bodied and dry, with very good depth of ripe tropical-fruit flavours, crisp and lively. Certified organic, it should be at its best mid-2021+.

 DRY $22 V+

Montana New Zealand Collection Crisp & Zingy Marlborough Sauvignon Blanc   (★★★☆)

The 2019 vintage (★★★☆) is pale lemon/green, with a strong, nettley bouquet. Medium-bodied, it is fresh, with good depth of clearly herbaceous, green-apple flavours, and lots of youthful impact.

 DRY $20 AV

Montford Estate Marlborough Sauvignon Blanc   (★★★☆)

The attractive 2019 vintage (★★★☆) was grown in the Wairau and Awatere valleys. Full-bodied, it is fresh and lively, with ripe tropical-fruit and herbaceous flavours, showing good vigour and depth, and a finely balanced, dry (3.5 grams/litre of residual sugar) finish. (From te Pā.)

 DRY $20 AV

Mount Brown Estates North Canterbury Sauvignon Blanc   ★★★☆

Offering good value, the 2019 vintage (★★★☆) is a fresh, lively, medium-bodied wine with good depth of ripely herbaceous flavours, appetising acidity, and a tangy, dryish (5 grams/litre of residual sugar) finish. The 2002 vintage (★★★☆) is a single-vineyard wine, mouthfilling, with good depth of ripe tropical-fruit flavours, and a smooth (5 grams/litre of residual sugar) finish.

Vintage	20	19	18
WR	7	5	6
Drink	20-22	20-21	P

MED/DRY $16 V+

Mount Riley 17 Valley Marlborough Sauvignon Blanc ★★★★☆

Offering fine value, the 2019 vintage (★★★★☆) is a ripely scented wine, hand-picked and lees-aged for eight months in seasoned French oak casks. Still youthful, it is fleshy, with generous tropical-fruit flavours, showing excellent delicacy, slightly creamy and biscuity notes, and a crisp, dry, lengthy finish. Best drinking 2021+.

DRY $22 V+

Mount Riley Limited Release Marlborough Sauvignon Blanc ★★★★

Offering great value, the 2020 vintage (★★★★) was made from the company's 'most expressive fruit from the 2020 vintage'. Bright, light lemon/green, it has a fresh, aromatic, ripely herbal bouquet, leading into a mouthfilling wine with lively melon and lime flavours, showing very good delicacy and length.

DRY $17 V+

Mount Riley Marlborough Sauvignon Blanc ★★★☆

Priced sharply, the 2020 vintage (★★★☆) is a lively wine, with good depth of melon, passionfruit and capsicum flavours, crisp, and finely balanced for early enjoyment.

DRY $15 V+

Mount Vernon Marlborough Sauvignon Blanc ★★★☆

From Lawson's Dry Hills, the 2019 vintage (★★★☆) is a lively, medium-bodied wine, with herbaceous flavours, fresh and direct, a crisp, dry (2.7 grams/litre of residual sugar) finish, and lots of youthful impact.

Vintage	19	18
WR	5	5
Drink	20-21	P

DRY $18 V+

Moutere Hills Nelson Sauvignon Blanc ★★★★

The 2019 vintage (★★★★) is a single-vineyard wine, grown at Hope, on the Waimea Plains. Crisp and lively, it has ripely herbaceous flavours, showing good vigour and intensity, and a dry, lingering finish.

DRY $21 V+

Mt Beautiful North Canterbury Sauvignon Blanc ★★★★☆

Estate-grown at Cheviot, north of Waipara, the 2019 vintage (★★★★☆) is a distinctive wine – ripely scented and weighty. Sweet-fruited, it has vibrant, concentrated passionfruit/lime flavours, crisp, dry and sustained. Best drinking 2021+.

DRY $21 V+

Nautilus Marlborough Sauvignon Blanc ★★★★

This is typically a fragrant, sweet-fruited wine, with crisp, concentrated flavours. The punchy 2020 vintage (★★★★) is bright, light lemon/green, with a slightly nettley bouquet. Full-bodied, it is strongly varietal, with fresh green-apple and lime flavours, showing very good vigour and intensity, and a crisp, dry (2 grams/litre of residual sugar), lingering finish.

Vintage	20	19	18	17
WR	7	7	7	7
Drink	20-23	20-22	20-21	P

 DRY $25 AV

Nautilus The Paper Nautilus Marlborough Sauvignon Blanc ★★★★★

Named after a paper-thin shell, the estate-grown 2019 vintage (★★★★★) was hand-harvested from mature vines at Renwick, in the Wairau Valley, and fermented and matured for eight months in an 1800-litre oak foudre and a 3000-litre oak cuve. Bright, light lemon/green, it is ripely scented, youthful and tightly structured, with passionfruit-like flavours, a very subtle oak influence, lively acidity, excellent delicacy and vigour, and a lasting finish. A stylish, distinctive wine with obvious potential, it should be at its best 2022+.

Vintage	19
WR	7
Drink	20-26

 DRY $35 AV

Nga Waka Martinborough Sauvignon Blanc ★★★★

A great buy, the 2020 vintage (★★★★☆) is a highly aromatic, sweet-fruited and punchy wine, with good weight, vigorous, ripely herbaceous flavours, fresh acidity, and a dry, lingering finish. Best drinking mid-2021+.

 DRY $19 V+

Nikau Point Reserve Marlborough Sauvignon Blanc ★★★☆

Priced sharply, the 2020 vintage (★★★☆) is a fresh, medium-bodied wine, with tropical-fruit flavours, a herbal undercurrent, very good vigour and depth, and a dry (4 grams/litre of residual sugar) finish.

Vintage	20
WR	6
Drink	20-22

DRY $16 V+

Nikau Point Select Marlborough Sauvignon Blanc ★★☆

Low-priced, the 2020 vintage (★★☆) is lively, with strongly herbaceous, slightly appley flavours, and a crisp, dry (4 grams/litre of residual sugar) finish.

Vintage	20
WR	5
Drink	20-22

 DRY $14 AV

Nobody's Hero Sauvignon Blanc (★★★☆)

From Framingham, the 2020 vintage (★★★☆) 'turns the flavour dial up to 11'. Grown in the Wairau Valley, it is aromatic and lively, with fresh, direct tropical-fruit and herbaceous flavours, crisp and dry (4.3 grams/litre of residual sugar), and lots of youthful impact.

DRY $20 AV

O:TU Marlborough Sauvignon Blanc ★★★☆

Estate-grown in the Awatere Valley, the zesty 2020 vintage (★★★☆) is medium-bodied, fresh and lively, with good depth of herbaceous, slightly appley flavours, dry (4.2 grams/litre of residual sugar) and crisp.

DRY $20 AV

Odyssey Marlborough Sauvignon Blanc (★★★★)

Still on sale, the 2018 vintage (★★★★) was estate-grown in the Brancott Valley. Certified organic, it is a medium to full-bodied, fresh and lively wine, sweet-fruited, with tropical-fruit flavours, good acid spine, and a dry (2.5 grams/litre of residual sugar), lasting finish.

DRY $20 V+

Old Coach Road Nelson Sauvignon Blanc ★★★

This is Seifried Estate's lowest-tier Sauvignon, priced sharply and enjoyable young. The 2020 vintage (★★★☆) offers great value. Bright, light lemon/green, it is aromatic, very fresh and direct, with good depth of ripe passionfruit/lime flavours, and a dry (3.9 grams/litre of residual sugar), crisp finish. Good drinking for the summer of 2020–21.

Vintage	20
WR	6
Drink	20-22

DRY $14 V+

Old House Vineyards Kaho Nelson Sauvignon Blanc ★★★★☆

Estate-grown at Upper Moutere, the 2018 vintage (★★★★☆) is a weighty, slightly creamy wine, fermented and matured for eight months in French oak barrels (12 per cent new). Bright, light yellow/green, it is still unfolding, with strong, ripe tropical-fruit flavours, showing good complexity, fresh acidity, and a lingering finish. Best drinking 2021+.

Vintage	18	17
WR	7	6
Drink	20-26	20-25

DRY $30 –V

Old House Vineyards Nelson Sauvignon Blanc ★★★★

Estate-grown at Upper Moutere, the 2018 vintage (★★★★) is a tank-fermented wine. Mouthfilling and sweet-fruited, it is fresh and vigorous, with good intensity of ripely herbaceous flavours, and a crisp, fully dry finish. Ready.

Vintage	18	17
WR	7	6
Drink	20-23	20-22

DRY $21 V+

Opawa Marlborough Sauvignon Blanc
★★★★

Enjoyable young, the 2020 vintage (★★★★☆) was mostly handled in tanks; 5 per cent of the blend was fermented with indigenous yeasts in large oak cuves. Bright, light lemon/green, it is vibrantly fruity, with good intensity of fresh tropical-fruit and herbaceous flavours, dry (3 grams/litre of residual sugar) and crisp. (From Nautilus.)

DRY $22 V+

Orchard Lane Marlborough Sauvignon Blanc
★★★☆

Bargain-priced, the 2020 vintage (★★★☆) is a pale lemon/green, mouthfilling wine, with fresh, ripe tropical-fruit flavours, showing good depth, and a dry finish. Enjoyable young. (From Sugar Loaf.)

DRY $15 V+

Oyster Bay Marlborough Sauvignon Blanc
★★★★

Oyster Bay is a Delegat brand, focused mostly on Marlborough wines and enjoying huge success in global markets. Two-thirds estate-grown, this wine is grown at a multitude of sites around the Wairau (mostly) and Awatere valleys, handled entirely in stainless steel tanks, and made in a dry style with tropical-fruit and herbaceous flavours, crisp and punchy. The 2019 vintage (★★★★) is mouthfilling and lively, with fresh, tangy tropical-fruit and herbaceous flavours, showing good intensity, and a dry, appetisingly crisp finish.

DRY $20 V+

Pā Road Marlborough Sauvignon Blanc
★★★☆

The 2019 vintage (★★★☆) is full of youthful vigour, with good depth of fresh, lively tropical-fruit and herbaceous flavours, dry (3 grams/litre of residual sugar) and crisp. (From te Pā.)

DRY $20 AV

Paddy Borthwick Wairarapa Sauvignon Blanc
★★★★

Full of personality, the explosively flavoured 2019 vintage (★★★★★) is a single-vineyard wine, with a pungently, ripely aromatic, very fresh and lively bouquet. Mouthfilling and racy, it is sweet-fruited, with penetrating, ripely herbaceous flavours, threaded with crisp acidity, and a dry, persistent finish. A top buy.

DRY $22 V+

Palliser Estate Martinborough Sauvignon Blanc
★★★★☆

The delicious 2019 vintage (★★★★☆) is a strongly varietal wine, with generous passionfruit-like flavours, combining excellent ripeness and vibrancy, and a dry (3.2 grams/litre of residual sugar), mouth-wateringly crisp finish.

DRY $28 AV

Paritua Grace Hawke's Bay Sauvignon Blanc   (★★★★)

The youthful 2018 vintage (★★★★) was estate-grown in the Bridge Pa Triangle, barrel-fermented and oak-aged for 11 months. Pale lemon/green, it is a fragrant, medium to full-bodied wine, with gentle, ripely herbaceous flavours, showing good delicacy, a touch of complexity, fresh acidity, and a dry finish.

DRY $35 –V

Pask Instinct Bud Burst Marlborough Sauvignon Blanc   (★★★)

Enjoyable young, the 2019 vintage (★★★) is fresh and lively, with ripely herbaceous flavours, and a finely balanced finish, dry (3.2 grams/litre of residual sugar) and smooth.

DRY $17 AV

Passage Rock Waiheke Island Sauvignon Blanc   (★★★★★)

Delicious young, the 2019 vintage (★★★★★) was estate-grown and hand-picked at Te Matuku Bay. Weighty, fleshy and sweet-fruited, it is attractively aromatic, with balanced acidity and fresh, concentrated, distinctly tropical-fruit flavours. A top example of the North Island style of Sauvignon Blanc.

DRY $33 AV

Pegasus Bay Sauvignon/Sémillon   ★★★★★

This distinctive Waipara, North Canterbury wine is concentrated and complex, with loads of personality. It is typically a 70:30 blend of Sauvignon Blanc and Sémillon, partly (35 per cent) fermented and matured in French oak barrels. From vines over 30 years old, the 2017 vintage (★★★★★) is bright, light yellow/green, with a complex bouquet. Crisp, full-bodied and dry (0.9 grams/litre of residual sugar), it is a youthful, very vigorous wine, with ripe tropical-fruit flavours, a subtle seasoning of oak, fresh acidity, and a tightly structured, lasting finish. Full of personality, the 2018 vintage (★★★★★) is mouthfilling and very youthful. Mouthfilling, it has intense peachy, limey flavours, a gentle seasoning of oak adding complexity, and a fully dry (1.2 grams/litre of residual sugar), long finish. Best drinking 2023+.

Vintage	18	17	16	15	14
WR	7	7	6	6	6
Drink	20-29	20-27	20-26	20-27	20-25

DRY $34 AV

Pencarrow Martinborough Sauvignon Blanc   ★★★★

The 2019 vintage (★★★★) is 'crisp and delicious, like a dip in the ocean'. Lively and punchy, it is freshly aromatic, with strong tropical-fruit flavours, a herbaceous undercurrent, appetising acidity, and a lingering finish. (From Palliser Estate.)

DRY $22 V+

Peregrine Central Otago Sauvignon Blanc   ★★★☆

Certified organic, the bright, light lemon/green 2020 vintage (★★★★) was grown at Pisa and Bendigo. Full of youthful impact, it is fresh and crisp, with stone-fruit and herbaceous flavours, showing very good vigour and depth, and a dry (2 grams/litre of residual sugar) finish.

DRY $27 –V

Pyramid Valley Marlborough Sauvignon Blanc   (★★★★★)

The debut 2018 vintage (★★★★★) was hand-harvested in the Churton Vineyard, an elevated site between the Waihopai and Omaka valleys, and fermented and lees-aged for six months in seasoned French oak demi-muids. Scented and mouthfilling, it has penetrating, ripe tropical-fruit flavours, and a long, tightly structured finish. A distinctive, subtle, minerally wine, finely poised, it should be at its best 2021+.

DRY $35 AV

Pyramid Valley North Canterbury Sauvignon Blanc   (★★★★★)

Showing strong personality, the bright, light lemon/green 2019 vintage (★★★★★) is mouthfilling and sweet-fruited, with concentrated, ripe tropical-fruit flavours, and a finely balanced, lingering finish. An impressive debut.

DRY $28 V+

Quarter Acre Hawke's Bay Sauvignon Blanc   ★★★★☆

Still on sale, the stylish 2017 vintage (★★★★☆) was hand-picked at Maraekakaho and fermented and lees-aged for nine months in seasoned puncheons and barriques. It is medium to full-bodied, with vigorous, ripely herbaceous flavours, a subtle seasoning of oak, good complexity, and a long, dry finish. Drink now.

DRY $28 AV

Ra Nui Marlborough Sauvignon Blanc   ★★★★

Currently available, the 2018 vintage (★★★★) is a single-vineyard wine, grown in the lower Wairau Valley and mostly handled in tanks; 5 per cent was barrel-fermented. It is weighty, with ripe tropical-fruit flavours, a touch of complexity, fresh acidity, and very good vigour and depth.

DRY $25 AV

Rapaura Springs Bull Paddock Vineyard Dillons Point
Marlborough Sauvignon Blanc   ★★★★★

The very classy, youthful 2020 vintage (★★★★★) was grown in the lower Wairau Valley. Bright, light lemon/green, it is weighty and dry (3 grams/litre of residual sugar), with vibrant melon/lime flavours, showing lovely delicacy and depth. A very harmonious wine, with a long finish, it's well worth discovering.

DRY $28 V+

Rapaura Springs Classic Marlborough Sauvignon Blanc   ★★★☆

Priced sharply, the light lemon/green 2020 vintage (★★★) is very fresh and lively, with strong, herbaceous flavours, and a crisp, dryish (5 grams/litre of residual sugar) finish.

Vintage	20	19
WR	7	7
Drink	20-23	20-22

MED/DRY $14 V+

Rapaura Springs Reserve Marlborough Sauvignon Blanc ★★★★

Offering good value, the 2020 vintage (★★★★) 'practically defines Marlborough Sauvignon Blanc'. Light lemon/green, it is mouthfilling, with fresh, generous passionfruit/lime flavours to the fore, a herbal undercurrent, and a crisp, dry (4 grams/litre of residual sugar), very harmonious finish.

Vintage	20	19	18	17
WR	5	7	6	6
Drink	20-23	20-22	20-21	P

DRY $19 V+

Rapaura Springs Rohe Blind River Marlborough Sauvignon Blanc ★★★★☆

Grown in the Blind River district, south of the Awatere Valley, the 2020 vintage (★★★★★) is highly aromatic, mouthfilling and dry (2 grams/litre of residual sugar). Bright, light lemon/green, it has impressive freshness, intensity and delicacy, with deep, ripe tropical-fruit and herbaceous flavours, finely poised and persistent. A top buy.

Vintage	20
WR	6
Drink	20-24

DRY $25 V+

Rapaura Springs Rohe Dillons Point Marlborough Sauvignon Blanc ★★★★★

Grown in the lower Wairau Valley, the 2020 vintage (★★★★★) is mouthfilling and sweet-fruited, with fresh, lively tropical-fruit and herbaceous flavours, showing excellent depth, a slightly salty streak, and a dry (3.5 grams/litre of residual sugar), lingering finish.

Vintage	20
WR	7
Drink	20-24

DRY $25 V+

Renato Nelson Sauvignon Blanc ★★★★

Very fresh and lively, the 2019 vintage (★★★★) is a medium to full-bodied wine, with good intensity of ripe tropical-fruit flavours, a herbaceous undercurrent, and a crisp, dry (3 grams/litre of residual sugar) finish. Vibrant and punchy, it's drinking well now.

Vintage	19	18	17
WR	7	6	6
Drink	20-23	20-22	20-21

DRY $18 V+

Riverby Estate Marlborough Sauvignon Blanc ★★★☆

The 2019 vintage (★★★☆) is a single-vineyard wine, grown at Rapaura. Fresh and lively, it is medium-bodied, with good depth of tropical-fruit and herbaceous flavours, dry and crisp. It's drinking well now.

Vintage	20	19
WR	6	7
Drink	20-24	20-22

DRY $20 AV

Roaring Meg Central Otago Sauvignon Blanc   ★★★☆

The attractive 2019 vintage (★★★★) is mouthfilling, with a freshly herbaceous bouquet. Vibrantly fruity, it has very good depth of tropical-fruit and herbaceous flavours, crisp and dry (3 grams/litre of residual sugar), and lots of drink-young appeal. (From Mt Difficulty.)

Rock Ferry 3rd Rock Marlborough Sauvignon Blanc   ★★★★★

Certified organic, the 2019 vintage (★★★★☆) was partly (7 per cent) barrel-fermented. Bright, light lemon/green, it is medium-bodied, with concentrated, lively tropical-fruit and herbaceous flavours, a touch of complexity, and a dry (3 grams/litre of residual sugar), crisp finish. Best drinking 2021+.

Russian Jack Marlborough Sauvignon Blanc   ★★★

Priced right, the 2019 vintage (★★★☆) is a medium-bodied wine, aromatic, with ripely herbaceous flavours, showing good vigour and depth, and a finely balanced, crisp, dry finish.

DRY $19 AV

Rusty Bell Single Vineyard Marlborough Sauvignon Blanc   (★★★★)

From a Wairau Valley site, west of Blenheim, the 2019 vintage (★★★★) was hand-harvested and mostly handled in tanks; 20 per cent of the blend was fermented and matured for seven months in seasoned French oak barriques. Pale lemon/green, with a restrained bouquet, it is fresh, youthful and lively, with strong tropical-fruit flavours to the fore, some herbaceous notes, a distinct touch of complexity, and a crisp, dry, lengthy finish. Best drinking 2021.

Sacred Hill Reserve Marlborough Sauvignon Blanc   (★★★★)

Still on sale, the 2018 vintage (★★★★) was 60 per cent barrel-fermented (French oak, 15 per cent new). Medium-bodied, it has strong, vibrant tropical-fruit flavours, slightly toasty notes adding complexity, and a dry (4 grams/litre of residual sugar), crisp finish.

Saint Clair James Sinclair Marlborough Sauvignon Blanc   ★★★★

Still on sale, the 2018 vintage (★★★★☆) was grown at Dillons Point, in the lower Wairau Valley. It is mouthfilling and vigorous, with excellent intensity of ripely herbaceous flavours, a slightly salty streak, balanced acidity, and a finely poised, dry (2.7 grams/litre of residual sugar), lingering finish.

Saint Clair Origin Marlborough Sauvignon Blanc   ★★★★

The 2019 vintage (★★★★☆) is a vibrant, punchy wine, grown mostly in the lower Wairau Valley. It has concentrated, tropical-fruit and herbaceous flavours, a slightly salty streak, and a lengthy finish. Fine value.

DRY $20 V+

Saint Clair Pioneer Block 1 Foundation Marlborough Sauvignon Blanc ★★★★☆

The youthful 2019 vintage (★★★★★) is a full-on style, with mouthfilling body, penetrating, clearly herbaceous, slightly salty flavours, showing impressive delicacy, vigour and intensity, and a crisp, dry (2.4 grams/litre of residual sugar), lasting finish.

Saint Clair Pioneer Block 20 Cash Block Marlborough Sauvignon Blanc ★★★★☆

The very lively, finely balanced 2019 vintage (★★★★☆) was grown at Dillons Point, in the lower Wairau Valley. Mouthfilling, it has good intensity of ripe tropical-fruit flavours, a herbaceous undercurrent, balanced acidity, and a long, dry (2.6 grams/litre of residual sugar) finish.

Saint Clair Pioneer Block 21 Bell Block Marlborough Sauvignon Blanc ★★★★☆

Grown at Dillons Point, in the lower Wairau Valley, the 2019 vintage (★★★★) is a single-vineyard wine, full-bodied, with fresh, strong tropical-fruit flavours to the fore, a herbaceous undercurrent, and a crisp, lively finish.

Saint Clair Pioneer Block 3 43 Degrees Marlborough Sauvignon Blanc ★★★★☆

Full of youthful impact, the outstanding 2019 vintage (★★★★★) was grown at Dillons Point, in the lower Wairau Valley. Pale lemon/green, it is punchy and vibrantly fruity, with intense tropical-fruit and herbaceous flavours, a slightly salty streak, and a tight, dry (2 grams/litre of residual sugar), lasting finish. Benchmark stuff.

Saint Clair Wairau Reserve Marlborough Sauvignon Blanc ★★★★★

Marlborough's largest family-owned wine producer has an extensive array of Sauvignon Blancs. This is not the region's most complex Savvy, but in terms of sheer pungency, it's a star, having won countless gold medals and trophies since the first, 2001 vintage. Grown in the cooler, coastal end of the Wairau Valley and handled entirely in stainless steel tanks, it is typically super-charged, in an exuberantly fruity, very pure and zesty style. The 2019 vintage (★★★★★) was grown at Dillons Point. Fresh and vibrant, it has deep, delicate tropical-fruit and herbaceous flavours, pure and searching, and a dry (2.5 grams/litre of residual sugar), persistent finish.

Sanctuary Marlborough Sauvignon Blanc ★★★

Enjoyable young, the 2019 vintage (★★★) is fresh, lively and crisp, with tropical-fruit flavours to the fore, gentle herbaceous notes, and lots of youthful impact. (From Grove Mill.)

Satellite Marlborough Sauvignon Blanc ★★★☆

From Spy Valley, the 2019 vintage (★★★☆) is a lively, strongly varietal, medium-bodied wine. Bright, light lemon/green, it has good depth of tropical-fruit and herbaceous flavours, fresh and strong. Good value.

Saveé Sea Marlborough Sauvignon Blanc ★★★

Priced sharply, the 2019 vintage (★★★) is a very easy-drinking style, with faint sweetness (5.5 grams/litre of residual sugar) and good depth of ripe tropical-fruit and herbaceous flavours, fresh and crisp. (From Awatere River.)

MED/DRY $14 V+

Scott Base Central Otago Sauvignon Blanc (★★★★)

Despite its back label references to being 'estate-grown' and 'Our Place' (the Scott Base Vineyard in the Cromwell Basin), the highly attractive 2019 vintage (★★★★) was in fact grown in the Matapari Vineyard, at Gibbston. Fermented with indigenous yeasts and lees-aged, it is a very fresh and vibrant wine, with ripely herbaceous flavours, crisp, dry (1.9 grams/litre of residual sugar) and lingering.

DRY $31 –V

Seifried Nelson Sauvignon Blanc ★★★★

Priced right, the 2020 vintage (★★★★) is full of youthful impact. Highly aromatic, it is an intensely varietal, medium-bodied wine with fresh, penetrating tropical-fruit and herbaceous flavours, appetising acidity, and a dry (3.3 grams/litre of residual sugar), tangy finish. If you enjoy a punchy, 'leap out of the glass' style, try this.

Vintage	20	19	18
WR	7	7	6
Drink	20-22	20-21	P

DRY $19 V+

Seresin Marama Marlborough Sauvignon Blanc ★★★★★

Currently on sale, the distinctive, powerful 2016 vintage (★★★★★) was hand-picked from mature vines, and fermented and matured for 18 months in French oak barriques (11 per cent new). Bright, light yellow/green, it is weighty, with lively, very ripe tropical-fruit flavours, finely integrated oak, fresh acidity, and a dry (3 grams/litre of residual sugar), harmonious finish. Maturing very gracefully, it's certified organic.

DRY $40 AV

Seresin Marlborough Sauvignon Blanc ★★★★★

This is one of the region's most sophisticated, subtle and satisfying Sauvignons. It's also one of the most important, given its widespread international distribution and certified BioGro status. The wine (which includes 5 to 9 per cent Sémillon) is mostly fermented in tanks with indigenous yeasts, but 15 to 20 per cent of the blend is fermented and lees-aged in seasoned French oak casks. The impressive 2018 vintage (★★★★★) was hand-picked in the central Wairau Valley and Omaka Valley. Bright, light lemon/green, it is ripely scented, mouthfilling and lively, with tropical-fruit flavours, showing excellent intensity and vigour, and a dry, long finish. Drink now to 2022.

DRY $25 V+

Sherwood Estate Sherwood Waipara Valley Sauvignon Blanc   ★★★☆

The easy-drinking 2019 vintage (★★★☆) is fresh and full-bodied, with lively, ripe passionfruit/lime flavours, showing good depth, balanced acidity, and a smooth finish.

DRY $20 AV

Sherwood Estate Stoney Range Waipara Valley Sauvignon Blanc   ★★★

The 2019 vintage (★★★) is a fresh, medium-bodied wine, with tangy tropical-fruit and herbaceous flavours, crisp and lively.

DRY $17 V+

Sileni Cellar Selection Marlborough Sauvignon Blanc   ★★★☆

The 2020 vintage (★★★☆) is a strongly varietal, very fresh and lively wine, medium-bodied with crisp, youthful, herbaceous flavours, showing good depth.

DRY $20 AV

Sileni Grand Reserve Cape Hawke's Bay Sauvignon Blanc   (★★★★

The tightly structured 2018 vintage (★★★★) is a fresh, medium to full-bodied wine, with tropical-fruit flavours, showing excellent delicacy and vigour, a hint of toasty oak, and a dry (2.9 grams/litre of residual sugar) finish. Best drinking 2021+.

DRY $25 AV

Sileni Grand Reserve Straits Marlborough Sauvignon Blanc   (★★★★☆

The punchy, intensely varietal 2019 vintage (★★★★☆) was fermented and lees-aged in tanks. Bright, light lemon/green, it is highly aromatic, with good body and vibrant, concentrated herbaceous and tropical-fruit flavours, dry (2.9 grams/litre of residual sugar) and crisp.

DRY $25 V+

Smith & Sheth Cru Wairau Sauvignon Blanc   ★★★★★

The classy 2019 vintage (★★★★★) was harvested (partly by hand) from mature vines at Renwick and in the Churton Vineyard, in the Waihopai Valley. A richly fragrant, weighty wine, it is sweet-fruited and tightly structured. Bright, light lemon/green, it is highly concentrated, with lively tropical-fruit flavours, pure, focused and long. Benchmark stuff, it's already delicious but should be drinking well through 2021.

DRY $28 V+

Snapper Rock Marlborough Sauvignon Blanc   (★★★★

Offering very good drinking for the summer of 2020–21, the 2020 vintage (★★★★) is a medium to full-bodied wine with freshly herbaceous aromas. Strongly varietal, it is punchy and vigorous, with tropical-fruit and herbaceous flavours, and a finely balanced (4 grams/litre of residual sugar), lingering finish.

DRY $17 V+

Soljans Marlborough Sauvignon Blanc ★★★

The easy-drinking 2020 vintage (★★★) is a lively, medium-bodied wine, with ripely herbaceous flavours, fresh acidity, and a smooth finish.

 DRY $19 AV

Spinyback Nelson Sauvignon Blanc ★★★

Offering good value, the 2020 vintage (★★★) was grown at two sites on the Waimea Plains. Light lemon/green, with fresh, herbaceous aromas, it is very youthful, with slightly appley flavours, crisp and punchy. (From Waimea Estates.)

 DRY $15 V+

Spy Valley E Block Marlborough Sauvignon Blanc ★★★★☆

The punchy 2019 vintage (★★★★★) was harvested from estate-grown vines in the Waihopai Valley, planted in 1995, and matured for seven months on its yeast lees in tanks. Bright, light lemon/green, it is a youthful, intensely varietal wine, with excellent intensity of tropical-fruit and herbaceous flavours, pure and searching, and a tight, dry (4 grams/litre of residual sugar), long finish.

 DRY $25 V+

Spy Valley Marlborough Sauvignon Blanc ★★★★

Typically a good buy. The vigorous 2019 vintage (★★★★☆) was grown (partly in estate vineyards) in the Waihopai and Wairau valleys, and made in a dry style (2.9 grams/litre of residual sugar). Light lemon/green, it is a fresh and lively wine, full of youthful impact, with excellent depth of tropical-fruit and herbaceous flavours, and a crisp, tightly structured finish. Best drinking 2021+.

Vintage	19	18	17	16	15
WR	6	5	5	7	6
Drink	20-22	20-21	P	P	P

 DRY $20 V+

Staete Landt Annabel Marlborough Sauvignon Blanc ★★★★★

Estate-grown at Rapaura, on the relatively warm north side of the Wairau Valley, the 2018 vintage (★★★★☆) was partly hand-picked and 30 per cent barrel-fermented. Medium to full-bodied, it has good intensity of fresh, ripe tropical-fruit flavours, showing a distinct touch of complexity, and a fully dry, crisp finish. Best drinking 2021+.

 DRY $22 V+

Stanley Estates Wild Awatere Valley Marlborough Sauvignon Blanc (★★★★☆)

Drinking well now, but also worth cellaring, the 2018 vintage (★★★★☆) was estate-grown in the Awatere Valley, hand-picked, and fermented and lees-aged in barrels for 10 months. Bright, light yellow/green, it is mouthfilling and fleshy, with concentrated, lively tropical-fruit flavours, oak complexity, and a dry, very harmonious finish.

DRY $22 V+

Starborough Family Estate Marlborough Sauvignon Blanc   ★★★★

This label typically offers good value. Estate-grown in the Awatere (75 per cent) and Wairau (25 per cent) valleys, the 2020 vintage (★★★★) is aromatic and full-bodied, with punchy, vibrant tropical-fruit and herbaceous flavours, and a dry (3 grams/litre of residual sugar), crisp, lingering finish.

DRY $20 V+

State of Flux Yealands Estate Awatere Valley
Marlborough Sauvignon Blanc   (★★★★☆)

The distinctive 2018 vintage (★★★★☆) was estate-grown inland (over 10 km from the coast) and fermented and aged for 11 months in a concrete egg. Bright, light lemon/green, with a restrained bouquet, it has mouthfilling body, concentrated, ripe tropical-fruit flavours, showing good complexity, fresh acidity, and a long finish. Best drinking 2021+.

DRY $36 –V

Stoneburn Marlborough Sauvignon Blanc   ★★★

From Hunter's, the 2019 vintage (★★★) is a good value, strongly varietal wine, briefly lees-aged, with herbaceous and tropical-fruit flavours, fresh, crisp and lively.

DRY $12 V+

Stoneleigh Latitude Marlborough Sauvignon Blanc   ★★★★

Marlborough in a glass, the youthful 2020 vintage (★★★★★) is designed as a 'full-on style' with 'big aromatics'. Grown at Rapaura, on the north side of the Wairau Valley, it is mouthfilling and vibrantly fruity, with deep, ripe tropical-fruit flavours, balanced acidity, and a dry, very harmonious finish. Best drinking mid-2021+. Great value.

DRY $20 V+

Stoneleigh Lighter Marlborough Sauvignon Blanc   ★★

The 2020 vintage (★★) is '25 per cent lighter in alcohol' (9.5 per cent by volume) than the classic Stoneleigh Marlborough Sauvignon Blanc. Pale lemon/green, it has green-apple aromas and flavours, crisp and light. Basically bland.

MED/DRY $18 –V

Stoneleigh Marlborough Sauvignon Blanc   ★★★☆

From Pernod Ricard NZ, this very large-volume but typically satisfying wine flows from the stony, relatively warm Rapaura district of the Wairau Valley, which produces a ripe style of Sauvignon Blanc, yet retains good acidity and vigour. The 2020 vintage (★★★☆) is an aromatic, very fresh and lively wine, medium-bodied, with tropical-fruit and herbaceous flavours, crisp and dry. Offering good drinking for the summer of 2020–21, it's priced sharply.

DRY $16 V+

Stoneleigh Organic Marlborough Sauvignon Blanc   (★★★☆)

Certified organic, the 2020 vintage (★★★☆) has fresh, herbaceous aromas, leading into a lively, medium-bodied wine with citrusy, appley, limey flavours, a touch of complexity, and a crisp, lingering finish.

DRY $20 AV

Stoneleigh Rapaura Series Single Vineyard Marlborough Sauvignon Blanc   ★★★★☆

Labelled as 'the absolute best of Stoneleigh', this richly flavoured, single-vineyard wine is grown in the relatively warm, shingly soils of the Rapaura district and partly fermented in large oak cuves. Drinking well now, the 2019 vintage (★★★★☆) is a bright, light lemon/green, full-bodied wine, with strong, ripe tropical-fruit flavours, crisp and dry.

DRY $25 V+

Stoneleigh Wild Valley Marlborough Sauvignon Blanc   ★★★★

'Wild fermented by the micro-flora that occur naturally in the Rapaura environment', the 2020 vintage (★★★★☆) offers great value. Bright, light lemon/green, it is mouthfilling, fleshy and sweet-fruited, with vibrant tropical-fruit flavours, crisp, dry and strong.

DRY $18 V+

Sugar Loaf Leo Barrel Fermented Marlborough Sauvignon Blanc   ★★★★☆

The 2019 vintage (★★★★☆) was estate-grown at Rapaura, hand-harvested from mature vines and fermented in large, old oak barrels. Bright, light lemon/green, it is fresh and full-bodied, with concentrated, ripely herbaceous flavours, a subtle seasoning of oak adding complexity, and a finely balanced, dry, smooth finish. Drink now or cellar.

DRY $26 AV

Sugar Loaf Marlborough Sauvignon Blanc   ★★★★☆

Offering excellent value, the 2020 vintage (★★★★☆) from this Rapaura-based producer is a finely balanced regional blend. Skilfully crafted, it is aromatic and punchy, with melon and green-capsicum flavours, showing very good delicacy and depth, a touch of complexity, and a long finish.

DRY $20 V+

Summerhouse Marlborough Sauvignon Blanc   ★★★★

The 2020 vintage (★★★☆) was grown at Blind River, on the south side of the Awatere Valley. Pale lemon/green, it is a crisp, strongly varietal, clearly herbaceous wine, with a hint of passionfruit, and very good depth.

Vintage	20	19	18	17
WR	6	7	7	6
Drink	20-23	20-22	20-21	20-21

DRY $19 V+

Supernatural, The, Hawke's Bay Sauvignon Blanc ★★★★☆

Closed with a crown seal, the 2018 vintage (★★★★☆) is certified organic. Handled without oak, it was grown on a hill site in the Tuki Tuki Valley, held on its skins for six hours before pressing, fermented with indigenous yeasts, and matured on its yeast lees, with stirring, for a year before bottling. Light yellow/green, it is a powerful wine, ripely scented and fleshy, with strong tropical-fruit flavours, finely balanced acidity, and a dry finish. A wine of real individuality, it's not highly aromatic, but shows excellent body and texture.

DRY $32 –V

Te Awanga Estate Hawke's Bay Sauvignon Blanc ★★★★

The 2019 vintage (★★★★) is a vigorous, medium-bodied wine, fresh and sweet-fruited, with crisp passionfruit/lime flavours, and a dry, lingering finish.

DRY $20 V+

Te Kairanga Estate Martinborough Sauvignon Blanc ★★★★

The 2019 vintage (★★★★) is a partly (12 per cent) barrel-fermented wine. Medium to full-bodied, it is fresh and vigorous, with good intensity of ripely herbaceous flavours, dry (3.3 grams/litre of residual sugar) and lingering.

DRY $25 AV

Te Mata Cape Crest Sauvignon Blanc ★★★★★

This oak-aged Hawke's Bay label is impressive for its ripely herbal, complex, sustained flavours. Most of the grapes are hand-picked in the company's relatively warm Bullnose Vineyard, inland from Hastings (the rest is grown at Woodthorpe, in the Dartmoor Valley), and the blend includes small proportions of Sémillon (to add longevity) and Sauvignon Gris (which contributes weight and mouthfeel). The wine is fully fermented and lees-aged for about eight months in French oak barriques (partly new). The youthful 2019 vintage (★★★★★) is a fragrant, powerful wine, with concentrated, ripe, distinctly tropical-fruit flavours, gently enriched with oak, fresh acidity, and a dry, very harmonious finish. Best drinking 2022+.

Vintage	19
WR	7
Drink	20-23

DRY $30 AV

Te Mata Estate Vineyards Hawke's Bay Sauvignon Blanc ★★★★

The 2020 vintage (★★★★) was estate-grown in the Bridge Pa Triangle and at Havelock North. Made without oak, it is a bright, light lemon/green, very fresh and vibrant wine, with strong, ripely herbaceous aromas and flavours, crisp and dry.

Vintage	20
WR	7
Drink	20-22

DRY $22 V+

te Pā Marlborough Sauvignon Blanc   ★★★★

The 2019 vintage (★★★☆) is mouthfilling, with generous tropical-fruit and herbaceous flavours, slightly spicy notes, and a dry (3 grams/litre of residual sugar), finely balanced finish.

 DRY $20 V+

te Pā Oke Marlborough Sauvignon Blanc   ★★★★☆

Estate-grown in the lower Wairau Valley, the age-worthy 2018 vintage (★★★★) was hand-picked and fermented and lees-aged in French oak barrels (50 per cent new). It is mouthfilling, with strong, ripe tropical-fruit flavours, oak-derived complexity, fresh acidity, and a fully dry, long finish. Best drinking 2021+.

Vintage	18	17
WR	6	6
Drink	20-23	20-22

 DRY $25 V+

te Pā The Reserve Collection Hillside Marlborough Sauvignon Blanc   (★★★★)

The 2019 vintage (★★★★) is a single-vineyard wine, hand-picked in the Awatere Valley. Very fresh and delicate, it has subtle, green capsicum-like flavours, vigorous, dry (2 grams/litre of residual sugar) and crisp. Best drinking 2021+.

 DRY $25 AV

te Pā The Reserve Collection Seaside Marlborough Sauvignon Blanc   (★★★★☆)

The 2019 vintage (★★★★☆) was hand-picked in the lower Wairau Valley. Mouthfilling, it has good intensity of melon, passionfruit and capsicum flavours, vigorous, dry (2 grams/litre of residual sugar) and lingering.

 DRY $25 V+

Thornbury Marlborough Sauvignon Blanc   ★★★★

Offering top value, the 2020 vintage (★★★★) is already drinking well. Bright, light lemon/green, it is mouthfilling, with fresh, generous tropical-fruit and herbaceous flavours, and a dry (3.5 grams/litre of residual sugar) finish. (From Villa Maria.)

Vintage	20	19	18
WR	6	5	5
Drink	20-22	P	P

 DRY $16 V+

Tiki Estate Marlborough Sauvignon Blanc   ★★★☆

The 2019 vintage (★★★★) is mouthfilling and punchy, with vigorous passionfruit, lime and green-capsicum flavours, fresh, appetising acidity, and a basically dry (4.7 grams/litre of residual sugar), smooth finish.

Vintage	19	18	17
WR	6	6	7
Drink	20-21	P	P

DRY $20 AV

Tohu Awatere Valley Marlborough Sauvignon Blanc   ★★★★

Offering good value, the 2019 vintage (★★★★) is an aromatic, lively, medium-bodied wine, with passionfruit, capsicum and lime flavours, showing excellent delicacy and vibrancy, balanced acidity, and a dry (3.5 grams/litre of residual sugar) finish.

Vintage	19
WR	7
Drink	20-22

Tohu Single Vineyard Whenua Awa Awatere Valley
Marlborough Sauvignon Blanc   (★★★★☆)

The punchy, highly aromatic 2018 vintage (★★★★☆) was estate-grown in the upper Awatere Valley. It is crisp and mouthfilling, with excellent vigour and depth of tropical-fruit and herbaceous flavours, lively and long.

Toi Toi Marlborough Sauvignon Blanc   ★★★☆

The vigorous 2019 vintage (★★★☆) of this regional blend is a strongly varietal, medium-bodied style with youthful melon and green capsicum-like flavours, crisp and lively. Good value.

Toi Toi Reserve Marlborough Sauvignon Blanc   ★★★★☆

Grown in the Wairau Valley, the 2019 vintage (★★★★☆) is a weighty, fleshy wine with strong, ripe tropical-fruit flavours, and a finely balanced, smooth (3.9 grams/litre of residual sugar) finish. Ready to roll, it offers good value.

Toi Toi Winemakers Selection Marlborough Sauvignon Blanc   (★★★★)

The punchy 2019 vintage (★★★★) is full-bodied and vibrant, with fresh, strong passionfruit and green-capsicum flavours, lively acidity, and a finely balanced finish. Good value.

Twin Islands Marlborough Sauvignon Blanc   ★★★★

Already enjoyable, the 2020 vintage (★★★★) is a bright, light lemon/green, full-bodied wine, with fresh, ripe tropical-fruit flavours to the fore, gentle herbaceous notes, balanced acidity, and a dry (3 grams/litre of residual sugar), harmonious finish. A good buy. (From Nautilus.)

Two Rivers Marlborough Convergence Sauvignon Blanc   ★★★★★

The very lively, harmonious 2020 vintage (★★★★★) was grown in the Awatere and Wairau valleys, and matured for three months on its yeast lees in a mix of stainless steel tanks (principally), concrete, egg-shaped vessels and clay amphorae. Bright, light lemon/green, it is highly aromatic, mouthfilling and vibrantly fruity, with penetrating tropical-fruit flavours, ripe and fresh, a herbal undercurrent, and a long, dry (3 grams/litre of residual sugar) finish. Best drinking mid-2021+.

Vintage	20	19
WR	7	7
Drink	20-23	20-22

Unison Snazzy Hawke's Bay Sauvignon Blanc   (★★★★)

Well worth cellaring, the 2019 vintage (★★★★) was hand-picked and mostly handled in tanks; 25 per cent of the blend was fermented in a seasoned French oak barrel. Pale lemon/green, it is a freshly aromatic, vigorous, medium to full-bodied wine, with good intensity of ripely herbaceous flavours, crisp and fully dry. Best drinking mid 2021+.

Urlar Gladstone Sauvignon Blanc   ★★★★☆

Certified organic, the highly aromatic 2018 vintage (★★★★☆) was mostly handled in tanks; 10 per cent was fermented in old oak barrels. It is a fresh, medium to full-bodied wine, with vigorous peach, lime and herb flavours, barrel-ferment notes adding richness, crisp acidity, and excellent intensity and complexity. The 2019 vintage (★★★★) was handled without oak. Bright, light lemon/green, it is fresh and lively, mouthfilling and sweet-fruited, with good intensity of ripe, tropical-fruit flavours, and a basically dry (below 5 grams/litre of residual sugar) finish.

DRY $25 V+

Urlar Select Parcels Gladstone Sauvignon Blanc   ★★★★☆

Developing good complexity with age, the 2017 vintage (★★★★☆) was estate-grown in the northern Wairarapa and fermented and lees-aged for 10 months in seasoned French oak barrels. Retasted in 2019, it is a light yellow, medium to full-bodied wine, sweet-fruited, with generous, ripe tropical-fruit flavours to the fore, some herbal notes, a subtle seasoning of toasty oak, balanced acidity, and impressive harmony. Drink now or cellar. Certified organic.

Vintage	17
WR	6
Drink	20-25

DRY $29 AV

Vavasour Awatere Valley Marlborough Sauvignon Blanc   ★★★★☆

The tightly structured 2019 vintage (★★★★☆) is a medium to full-bodied wine, strongly varietal, with very good intensity of fresh melon and green-capsicum flavours, showing excellent delicacy, and a crisp, dry (3.5 grams/litre of residual sugar), lingering finish.

Vegan, The, Wine Project Marlborough Sauvignon Blanc   (★★★★)

From Nautilus, the debut 2020 vintage (★★★★) is the fruit of a project to remove animal-based fining agents from the company's winemaking. Bright, light yellow/green, it is a lively, medium-bodied wine with generous, ripely herbaceous flavours, fresh acidity, and a dry, harmonious finish.

DRY $18 V+

Vidal Marlborough Sauvignon Blanc   ★★★☆

The 2020 vintage (★★★☆) was grown principally in the Wairau Valley. Light lemon/green, with fresh, herbaceous aromas, it is a clearly varietal style with good depth of melon and green-capsicum flavours, dry (3.5 grams/litre of residual sugar) and crisp. Good value.

Vintage	20	19	18	17
WR	7	6	7	6
Drink	20-22	20-21	P	P

DRY $16 V+

Vidal Reserve Marlborough Sauvignon Blanc   ★★★★

Offering great value, the 2019 vintage (★★★★☆) was grown in the Wairau Valley (85 per cent) and the Awatere Valley (15 per cent), and matured for four months on its yeast lees. Mouthfilling and sweet-fruited, it has passionfruit-like flavours, showing a distinct touch of complexity, and a dry (2.4 grams/litre of residual sugar), lengthy finish.

Vintage	19	18
WR	6	7
Drink	20-21	P

DRY $20 V+

Villa Maria Cellar Selection Marlborough Sauvignon Blanc   ★★★★☆

Typically of a high standard, this great-value wine is blended from Wairau Valley and Awatere Valley grapes, and fermented and lees-aged in tanks. Still very youthful, the 2020 vintage (★★★★) is ripely scented, full-bodied and fleshy, with strong passionfruit/lime flavours, balanced acidity, and a dry (3.5 grams/litre of residual sugar) finish. Best drinking mid-2021+.

Vintage	20
WR	6
Drink	20-22

DRY $18 V+

Villa Maria Cellar Selection Organic Marlborough Sauvignon Blanc   ★★★★

Certified organic, the 2019 vintage (★★★★) is medium-bodied, fresh and vibrant, with strong, ripe tropical-fruit and herbaceous flavours, dry (3.1 grams/litre of residual sugar) and crisp.

DRY $18 V+

Villa Maria Platinum Selection Organic Marlborough Sauvignon Blanc   ★★★★☆

Certified organic, the 2019 vintage (★★★★★) is a lees-aged wine, freshly aromatic, weighty, crisp and dry, with ripe tropical-fruit flavours, showing excellent vigour and intensity, good complexity, and a finely balanced, long finish.

DRY $25 V+

Villa Maria Private Bin Marlborough Sauvignon Blanc ★★★★

This huge-volume label consistently offers very good quality and value. Already delicious, the 2020 vintage (★★★★) is bright, light lemon/green, with a fresh, aromatic bouquet. Mouthfilling, it has strong tropical-fruit and herbaceous flavours, hints of passionfruit and green capsicum, and a crisp, slightly off-dry (6 grams/litre of residual sugar) finish.

Vintage	20
WR	5
Drink	20-22

 MED/DRY $15 V+

Villa Maria Private Bin Organic Marlborough Sauvignon Blanc ★★★☆

Priced sharply, the 2019 vintage (★★★☆) is mouthfilling, fresh and ripe, with tropical-fruit flavours, crisp and dry (3.3 grams/litre of residual sugar), and very good depth. Certified organic.

 DRY $15 V+

Villa Maria Reserve Clifford Bay Awatere Valley
Marlborough Sauvignon Blanc ★★★★★

Named after Clifford Bay, into which the Awatere River empties, this is a very classy Marlborough wine. Seddon Vineyards and the Taylors Pass Vineyard – both managed but not owned by Villa Maria – are the key sources of fruit. Handled entirely in stainless steel tanks and aged on its light yeast lees for several months, the wine typically exhibits the leap-out-of-the-glass fragrance and zingy, explosive flavour of Marlborough Sauvignon Blanc at its best. The outstanding 2019 vintage (★★★★★) is a powerful, punchy wine, with lifted, freshly herbaceous aromas. Already delicious, it is weighty and vibrant, with pure, penetrating flavours of passionfruit, lime and green capsicums, that build across the palate to a dry (2.5 grams/litre of residual sugar), lasting finish. A great buy.

Vintage	19
WR	7
Drink	20-22

 DRY $25 V+

Villa Maria Reserve Wairau Valley Sauvignon Blanc ★★★★★

An authoritative wine, it is typically ripe and zingy, with impressive weight and length of flavour, and tends to be fuller in body, less herbaceous and rounder than its Clifford Bay stablemate (above). The contributing vineyards vary from vintage to vintage, but Peter and Deborah Jackson's warm, stony vineyard in the heart of the valley has long been a key source of grapes, and sometimes a small part of the blend is barrel-fermented, to enhance its complexity and texture. The youthful 2020 vintage (★★★★★) was handled entirely in tanks. Bright, light yellow/green, it is mouthfilling, with concentrated, ripe tropical-fruit flavours, fresh, dry (2.9 grams/litre of residual sugar), crisp and long.

Vintage	20	19
WR	6	7
Drink	20-22	20-21

 DRY $25 V+

Villa Maria Single Vineyard Southern Clays Marlborough Sauvignon Blanc ★★★★☆

From north-facing clay slopes on the south side of the Wairau Valley, the delicious 2018 vintage (★★★★★) has ripe tropical-fruit aromas and flavours. Weighty and sweet-fruited, it's a very non-herbaceous style, dry (3.8 grams/litre of residual sugar) and crisp, with a lasting finish.

DRY $30 –V

Villa Maria Single Vineyard Taylors Pass Marlborough Sauvignon Blanc ★★★★★

Taylors Pass Vineyard lies 100 metres above sea level in the Awatere Valley. This is typically a classic example of the sub-regional style – vibrant, punchy, minerally and herbal, with intense capsicum and 'tomato stalk' aromas and a long, dry, racy finish. The 2019 vintage (★★★★★) was handled entirely in tanks. It is mouthfilling, fresh and lively, with strong, herbaceous flavours, some riper, tropical-fruit notes, a minerally streak, and a tightly structured, dry (2.8 grams/litre of residual sugar), sustained finish.

Vintage	19
WR	7
Drink	20-22

DRY $30 AV

Volcanic Hills Marlborough Sauvignon Blanc (★★★★)

Punchy and finely balanced, the 2019 vintage (★★★★) of this Awatere Valley wine is freshly aromatic and intensely varietal, with very good flavour depth and a crisp, dry, lengthy finish.

DRY $23 AV

Waimea Nelson Sauvignon Blanc ★★★★

The punchy 2020 vintage (★★★★) was grown at two sites on the Waimea Plains and lees-aged in tanks. Mouthfilling, it has very good depth of fresh tropical-fruit flavours, a herbaceous undercurrent, and a crisp, dry finish. It's already drinking well.

DRY $18 V+

Wairau River Marlborough Sauvignon Blanc ★★★★

The 2019 vintage (★★★★) is a fresh, punchy, medium-bodied wine, with ripe passionfruit-like flavours to the fore, a herbaceous undercurrent, good intensity, and a crisp, dry finish.

DRY $20 V+

Walnut Block Nutcracker Marlborough Sauvignon Blanc ★★★★☆

Certified organic, the classy 2019 vintage (★★★★★) is a Wairau Valley wine, hand-picked and 30 per cent barrel-fermented. Bright, light lemon/green, it is fleshy and dry, with strong, ripe tropical-fruit flavours, slightly creamy notes, and excellent complexity and texture. Drink now or cellar.

DRY $25 V+

Ward Valley Triple Block Marlborough Sauvignon Blanc   (★★★☆)

Fresh and lively, with plenty of youthful impact, the 2019 vintage (★★★☆) is a strongly varietal wine, with crisp, direct melon and green-capsicum flavours, and a basically dry (4 grams/litre of residual sugar) finish. (From Snapper Rock.)

DRY $18 V+

Weaver Estate Alexandra Basin Central Otago Sauvignon Blanc   (★★★★)

The 2019 vintage (★★★★) was partly barrel-fermented. It is a medium-bodied, vibrantly fruity wine, with ripely herbaceous flavours, showing very good vigour and depth, and a dry (3.5 grams/litre of residual sugar), crisp finish.

DRY $27 –V

Whitehaven Greg Awatere Valley Single Vineyard
Marlborough Sauvignon Blanc   ★★★★★

The 2019 vintage (★★★★☆) is a mouthfilling, punchy, tangy wine, fresh and forthright, with good intensity of ripely herbaceous flavours, dry (4.2 grams/litre of residual sugar) and mouthwateringly crisp.

DRY $28 V+

Whitehaven Marlborough Sauvignon Blanc   ★★★★

The 2019 vintage (★★★★) is mouthfilling and dry (3.7 grams/litre of residual sugar), with strong, ripely herbaceous flavours, tightly structured and crisp.

DRY $22 V+

Wild River North Canterbury Sauvignon Blanc   (★★★☆)

From Mount Brown, the 2019 vintage (★★★☆) is bargain-priced. Light lemon/green, it is a highly aromatic, medium-bodied wine, with punchy, ripely herbaceous flavours, fresh, crisp and direct.

DRY $13 V+

Wither Hills Cellar Selection Barrel Fermented Sauvignon Blanc   (★★★★☆)

The 2018 vintage (★★★★☆) is rare: only 933 bottles were produced. Estate-grown at Rarangi, it is very pale straw, with a slightly biscuity, oaky bouquet. Full-bodied, it is still youthful, with generous, ripe tropical-fruit flavours, showing good complexity, and a rounded finish. Worth cellaring.

DRY $26 AV

Wither Hills Cellar Selection Organic Marlborough Sauvignon Blanc   (★★★★☆)

The 2018 vintage (★★★★☆) is a single-vineyard wine, drinking well now. Weighty and harmonious, it has strong, ripe tropical-fruit flavours, showing a distinct touch of complexity, and a dry, well-rounded finish.

DRY $26 AV

Wither Hills Marlborough Sauvignon Blanc ★★★☆

This popular wine is typically vibrantly fruity, with strong passionfruit/lime flavours, finely balanced and lingering. (From Lion.)

DRY $18 V+

Wither Hills Rarangi Marlborough Sauvignon Blanc ★★★★☆

Still on sale, the distinctive 2016 vintage (★★★★☆) is from a coastal site at the north-east edge of the Wairau Valley. Still drinking well, it is fragrant, mouthfilling, crisp and dry, with a slightly salty streak running through its melon/lime flavours, which show excellent vigour, intensity and length.

DRY $26 AV

Woven Stone Single Vineyard Ohau Sauvignon Blanc (★★★)

Grown in the Horowhenua, the strongly varietal 2019 vintage (★★★) is a fresh and lively, medium-bodied wine with a fairly restrained bouquet, but good depth of melon, lime and green-capsicum flavours. Bargain-priced. (From Ohau Wines.)

DRY $14 V+

Yealands Estate Single Block S1 Awatere Valley
Marlborough Sauvignon Blanc (★★★★★)

From an elevated site within Yealand's huge vineyard in the lower Awatere Valley, the 2019 vintage (★★★★★) is a very refined wine with obvious cellaring potential. Bright, light lemon/green, it has deep passionfruit and lime flavours, showing excellent delicacy and purity, gentle acidity, and a persistent finish.

DRY $28 V+

Yealands Lighter Marlborough Sauvignon Blanc ★★

Labelled as 'a great alternative to enjoy at lunch', the 2020 vintage (★★) is a low-alcohol style (9.5 per cent alcohol by volume). Pale, it is light-bodied, with green-edged, lemony, appley flavours, and a basically dry (4.6 grams/litre of residual sugar), crisp finish.

Vintage	20
WR	5
Drink	20-22

DRY $16 –V

Yealands Marlborough Sauvignon Blanc ★★★★

Offering good value, the punchy 2020 vintage (★★★★) is a Marlborough regional blend. Fresh and crisp, it has strong, herbaceous and tropical-fruit flavours, finely balanced, lively and dry (3.7 grams/litre of residual sugar).

DRY $16 V+

Yealands Reserve Awatere Valley Marlborough Sauvignon Blanc   ★★★★☆

Estate-grown in the Awatere Valley, the 2020 vintage (★★★★☆) is a great buy. Mouthfilling and dry (3.5 grams/litre of residual sugar), it has concentrated, ripe tropical-fruit flavours, a herbaceous undercurrent, fresh, balanced acidity, and a rich finish.

Vintage	20	
WR	7	
Drink	20-22	

`DRY $19 V+`

Zephyr MK III Marlborough Sauvignon Blanc   (★★★★☆)

Wood-aged, the bright, light yellow/green 2018 vintage (★★★★☆) is a refined wine, fragrant and weighty, with ripe tropical-fruit flavours, showing good complexity, and a long, dry, harmonious finish.

`DRY $33 –V`

Sémillon

You'd never guess it from the tiny selection of labels on the shelves, but Sémillon is New Zealand's eighth most widely planted white-wine variety. The few winemakers who once played around with Sémillon could hardly give it away, so aggressively stemmy and spiky was its flavour. Now, there is a new breed of riper, richer, rounder Sémillons on the market – and they are ten times more enjoyable to drink.

The Sémillon variety is beset by a similar problem to Chenin Blanc. Despite being the foundation of outstanding white wines in Bordeaux and Australia, Sémillon is out of fashion in the rest of the world, and in New Zealand its potential is still largely untapped. The area of bearing Sémillon vines contracted markedly between 2007 and 2020, from 230 to 46 hectares.

Sémillon is highly prized in Bordeaux, where as one of the two key varieties both in dry wines, most notably white Graves, and the inimitable sweet Sauternes, its high levels of alcohol and extract are perfect foils for Sauvignon Blanc's verdant aroma and tartness. With its propensity to rot 'nobly', Sémillon forms about 80 per cent of a classic Sauternes.

Cooler climates like those of New Zealand's South Island, however, bring out a grassy-green character in Sémillon which, coupled with its higher acidity in these regions, can give the variety strikingly Sauvignon-like characteristics.

Grown principally in Hawke's Bay (over half of the variety's plantings) and Marlborough (29 per cent), Sémillon is mostly used in New Zealand not as a varietal wine but as a minor (and anonymous) partner in wines labelled Sauvignon Blanc, contributing complexity and aging potential. By curbing the variety's natural tendency to grow vigorously and crop bountifully, winemakers are now overcoming the aggressive cut-grass characters that in the past plagued the majority of New Zealand's unblended Sémillons. The spread of clones capable of giving riper fruit characters has also contributed to quality advances. However, very few wineries in New Zealand are exploring Sémillon's potential to produce complex, long-lived dry whites.

Askerne Hawke's Bay Sémillon ★★★★

The 2017 vintage (★★★☆) was made with a 'dash of fine-grained oak'. Bright, light lemon/ green, it is a fresh and lively, medium-bodied wine, with stone-fruit and spice flavours, a hint of herbs, a touch of complexity, and a dry, crisp finish. Best drinking 2022+.

DRY $23 AV

Kaimira Estate Brightwater Sémillon (★★★★)

Currently on sale, the 2009 vintage (★★★★) offers a rare chance to buy a decade-old New Zealand white wine. Estate-grown and hand-harvested on the Waimea Plains, in Nelson, it is still lively, with bright, light, yellow/green colour. Highly fragrant, it is medium-bodied, with citrusy, limey, lingering flavours, toasty, bottle-aged notes adding complexity, and a fully dry finish. Ready; no rush.

DRY $25 AV

Kelly Washington Wairau Valley Marlborough Sémillon/Sauvignon Blanc (★★★★☆)

From Auckland-based Tamra Kelly (formerly chief winemaker at Yealands Estate), the 2017 vintage (★★★★☆) is built to last. Fermented and aged in a concrete, egg-shaped tank, it shows good complexity, with lively tropical-fruit and herbal flavours, dry, crisp and lengthy. Certified organic.

DRY $35 –V

Mission Reserve Old Vine Hawke's Bay Sémillon   (★★★★★)

From estate-grown vines planted at Greenmeadows, in Taradale, 40 years ago, the powerful, complex 2018 vintage (★★★★★) was fermented with indigenous yeasts and matured on its yeast lees for 15 months. Pale gold, it is sturdy and weighty, with concentrated, ripe stone-fruit and lime flavours, and a dry, highly sustained finish. Already drinking well, it should be long-lived.

DRY $29 V+

Sileni Grand Reserve Circle Hawke's Bay Sémillon   ★★★★

Still extremely youthful, the 2019 vintage (★★★★) is a pale, mouthfilling wine with restrained, ripe peach and lime flavours, showing a distinct touch of complexity, and a dry, tightly structured finish. Best drinking 2023+.

DRY $24 AV

Verdelho

A Portuguese variety traditionally grown on the island of Madeira, Verdelho preserves its acidity well in hot regions, yielding enjoyably full-bodied, lively, lemony table wines in Australia. However, it is still extremely rare in New Zealand, with only 7 hectares of bearing Verdelho vines in 2020, mostly in Hawke's Bay and Auckland.

Esk Valley Gimblett Gravels Verdelho ★★★★

The 2018 vintage (★★★★) was grown in the company's Omahu Gravels and Joseph Soler vineyards, and 30 per cent of the blend was barrel-fermented with indigenous yeasts; the rest was handled in tanks. Full-bodied and vigorous, it has strong, lively, citrusy flavours, a sliver of sweetness (5.1 grams/litre of residual sugar), appetising acidity, minerally notes, and lots of youthful impact.

Vintage	18	17	16	15
WR	6	5	7	7
Drink	20-22	P	P	P

MED/DRY $20 V+

Hans Herzog Marlborough Verdelho (★★★★★)

Certified organic, the 2018 vintage (★★★★★) has a powerful personality. Estate-grown, handled without oak, and bottled unfined and unfiltered, it is light gold, mouthfilling and fleshy, with rich, ripe tropical-fruit flavours, balanced acidity, and a dry, well-rounded finish.

DRY $39 AV

Rapaura Springs The Springs Vineyard Marlborough Verdelho (★★★★)

Still unfolding, the vigorous 2017 vintage (★★★★) was hand-picked at Rapaura and barrel-fermented. Bright, light yellow/green, it is a medium-bodied wine, with strong, lemony, appley, slightly spicy flavours, a touch of complexity, and a basically dry (4 grams/litre of residual sugar), crisp finish. Best drinking 2022+.

DRY $33 –V

Viognier

A classic grape of the Rhône Valley, in France, Viognier is renowned for its exotically perfumed, substantial, peach and apricot-flavoured dry whites. A delicious alternative to Chardonnay, Viognier (pronounced 'Vee-yon-yay') is an internationally modish variety, popping up with increasing frequency in shops and restaurants here.

Viognier accounts for only 0.2 per cent of the national vineyard, but the area of bearing vines expanded from 15 hectares in 2002 to 93 hectares in 2020. Over two-thirds of the vines are clustered in Hawke's Bay and Gisborne, with further significant plantings in Marlborough (15 per cent) and Auckland (6 per cent).

As in the Rhône, Viognier's flowering and fruit set have been highly variable here. The deeply coloured grapes go through bud-burst, flowering and 'veraison' (the start of the final stage of ripening) slightly behind Chardonnay and are harvested about the same time as Pinot Noir.

The wine is often fermented in seasoned oak barrels, yielding scented, substantial, richly alcoholic wines with gentle acidity and subtle flavours. If you enjoy mouthfilling, softly textured, dry or dryish white wines, but feel like a change from Chardonnay and Pinot Gris, try Viognier. You won't be disappointed.

Askerne Hawke's Bay Viognier ★★★★

The youthful 2019 vintage (★★★★) was hand-picked and fermented and matured for nine months in French oak barrels (20 per cent new). Pale lemon/green, it is mouthfilling, fresh and lively, with ripe stone-fruit and spice flavours, a subtle seasoning of oak, balanced acidity, and a dryish (5 grams/litre of residual sugar) finish. Best drinking mid-2021+.

MED/DRY $24 AV

Brookfields Barrique Fermented Hawke's Bay Viognier ★★★★

Still very youthful, the 2019 vintage (★★★★☆) was estate-grown, hand-picked and fermented in oak barriques. Pale lemon/green, it is sturdy and dry, with ripe stone-fruit flavours, a hint of spice, wood-aging complexity, and impressive weight and concentration. A slightly Chardonnay-like wine, it's well worth cellaring to 2022+.

DRY $25 AV

Church Road McDonald Series Hawke's Bay Viognier (★★★★☆)

The 2018 vintage (★★★★☆) is a pale gold, fleshy wine, estate-grown in the Redstone Vineyard, in the Bridge Pa Triangle, and matured for 10 months in French oak barrels (25 per cent new). Full-bodied and sweet-fruited, it has ripe, peachy, slightly spicy flavours, gently seasoned with oak, very good complexity and a dry, smooth finish. Drink now or cellar.

DRY $27 AV

Clos de Ste Anne Viognier Les Arbres ★★★★★

This biodynamically certified Gisborne wine from Millton shows impressive richness and complexity. Hill-grown, it is hand-harvested and fermented with indigenous yeasts in large, 600-litre oak barrels. The 2015 vintage (★★★★★) is instantly seductive. Weighty and fleshy, it is rich, sweet-fruited and soft, with generous, peachy flavours, a creamy texture, and a very harmonious, dry (4 grams/litre of residual sugar), lasting finish.

DRY $60 AV

Coopers Creek Select Vineyards Chalk Ridge Hawke's Bay Viognier   ★★★★

Fresh, mouthfilling and sweet-fruited, the 2018 vintage (★★★★) was hand-picked near Havelock North and barrel-fermented. It has very good vigour and depth of stone-fruit flavours, a subtle seasoning of biscuity oak adding complexity, balanced acidity, and some cellaring potential; best drinking 2021+.

DRY $25 AV

Dancing Petrel Paewhenua Island Mangonui Northland Viognier   ★★★★☆

From a coastal vineyard in the Far North, the generous 2019 vintage (★★★★☆) was hand-harvested and matured in French oak casks. A powerful, youthful wine, it is softly mouthfilling, with generous, ripe peach and pear flavours, biscuity notes adding complexity, balanced acidity, and a long finish. Best drinking 2022+.

DRY $30 –V

De la Terre Reserve Viognier   ★★★★☆

Estate-grown at Havelock North, the 2016 vintage (★★★★☆) was fermented in seasoned French oak casks. Bright yellow/green, it is fragrant and robust, with strong stone-fruit flavours, oak complexity, balanced acidity, and a dry finish. Tasted in September 2020, it's probably at its peak now.

Vintage	16
WR	6
Drink	20-28

DRY $40 –V

Decibel Bridge Pa Triangle Vineyard Hawke's Bay Viognier   ★★★★

Delicious in its youth, the 2019 vintage (★★★★☆) was grown in the Bridge Pa Triangle and handled without oak. Bright, light lemon/green, it is fresh, full-bodied and vibrantly fruity, with ripe, peachy, slightly spicy flavours, showing good concentration, and finely balanced acidity. Best drinking 2021+.

DRY $26 –V

Elephant Hill Hawke's Bay Sea Viognier   ★★★★☆

The skilfully crafted 2019 vintage (★★★★★) was estate-grown at Te Awanga and partly (55 per cent) barrel-fermented. Pale straw, with a fresh, slightly biscuity bouquet, it is mouthfilling, fleshy and sweet-fruited, with generous, vibrant peach, pear, lychee and spice flavours, a subtle seasoning of oak, a slightly oily richness, and a finely textured, smooth, very harmonious finish. Best drinking 2022+.

DRY $34 –V

Falconhead Hawke's Bay Viognier ★★★☆

Offering top value, the 2019 vintage (★★★☆) is already drinking well. Bright, light lemon/green, it is mouthfilling and fleshy, with ripe stone-fruit and spice flavours, a touch of complexity, and a well-rounded, dry (3 grams/litre of residual sugar) finish.

Vintage	19	
WR	7	
Drink	20-24	DRY $16 V+

Gladstone Vineyard Viognier ★★★★

A 'floral tease', the 2018 vintage (★★★★☆) was hand-harvested in the northern Wairarapa and fermented in oak barrels (50 per cent new). Fragrant and softly mouthfilling, it is fresh and vibrant, with peachy, citrusy flavours, a subtle seasoning of oak adding complexity, and a fully dry, slightly creamy finish.

DRY $27 –V

Hans Herzog Marlborough Viognier ★★★★★

Certified organic, the 2017 vintage (★★★★★) was hand-harvested from mature, estate-grown vines on the north side of the Wairau Valley, fermented and matured for 18 months in French oak puncheons, and bottled unfined and unfiltered. Bright, light yellow, it has a fragrant, slightly toasty bouquet. Sturdy, with fresh, ripe stone-fruit flavours, it shows excellent concentration, with oak complexity, and a long, dry, savoury finish.

DRY $44 AV

Hopesgrove Estate Single Vineyard Hawke's Bay Viognier ★★★★☆

Showing obvious cellaring potential, the 2019 vintage (★★★★☆) was hand-harvested. Bright, light lemon/green, it is fresh, full-bodied and sweet-fruited, with strong, ripe stone-fruit flavours, a subtle seasoning of oak adding complexity, and a lingering finish. Best drinking 2022+.

DRY $30 –V

Johner Estate Gladstone Viognier (★★★★☆)

Enjoyable young, the 2018 vintage (★★★★☆) was matured for nine months in seasoned oak casks. Fresh and mouthfilling, it is vibrantly fruity, with good intensity of stone-fruit flavours, a subtle twist of oak, and a fully dry, very harmonious finish. Best drinking 2021+.

Vintage	18	DRY $26 AV
WR	6	
Drink	20-22	

Marsden Bay of Islands Viognier ★★★☆

The 2019 vintage (★★★★) was hand-picked and aged in seasoned oak barrels. Pale lemon/green, it is mouthfilling and vibrantly fruity, with youthful, ripe peach, pear and spice flavours, a very subtle seasoning of oak, balanced acidity, and a basically dry, lingering finish. Best drinking mid-2021+.

DRY $30 –V

Millton Riverpoint Vineyard Gisborne Viognier   ★★★★☆

Certified organic, the 2018 vintage (★★★★☆) was hand-harvested and fermented with indigenous yeasts in tanks and French oak hogsheads. Light gold, it is fragrant and fleshy, with rich, peachy, slightly honeyed flavours, showing good complexity, a slightly oily texture, balanced acidity, and a dry finish (1.5 grams/litre of residual sugar). Best drinking 2021+.

DRY $28 AV

Moutere Hills Nelson Viognier   ★★★☆

Estate-grown at Upper Moutere, the 2019 vintage (★★☆) is rare – only 23 cases were produced. Hand-picked and matured for 11 months in old French oak barrels, it is a light yellow/green wine, medium-bodied, with crisp, ripe, peachy, tightly structured flavours, but lacks the beguiling texture and fragrance typical of Viognier.

DRY $44 –V

Pask Gimblett Gravels Small Batch Hawke's Bay Viognier   ★★★★

Already drinking well, the bright, light lemon/green 2019 vintage (★★★★☆) is a full-bodied, sweet-fruited wine with a slightly toasty, buttery bouquet. Strongly varietal, it has good intensity of ripe stone-fruit flavours, and a softly seductive finish.

DRY $25 AV

Passage Rock Reserve Waiheke Island Viognier   ★★★★☆

Full of personality, the 2019 vintage (★★★★★) was barrel-matured. Bright, light lemon/green, it has a complex, slightly creamy and nutty bouquet. Weighty and fleshy, it is still youthful, with concentrated, ripe stone-fruit flavours, oak complexity, and a rich, fully dry (2 grams/litre of residual sugar) finish. Best drinking mid-2021+.

Vintage	19
WR	7
Drink	20-25

DRY $50 –V

Petane Tracks Block Hawke's Bay Viognier   ★★★★

The impressive 2019 vintage (★★★★☆) was grown at Eskdale, hand-harvested and fermented in seasoned French oak barrels. Bright, light yellow/green, it is weighty and fleshy, with concentrated, ripe stone-fruit flavours, slightly mealy and toasty notes adding complexity, finely balanced acidity, and a dryish (7 grams/litre of residual sugar) finish. An age-worthy wine, it's well worth cellaring to mid-2021+.

MED/DRY $31 –V

Quarter Acre Hawke's Bay Viognier   ★★★★☆

The classy 2018 vintage (★★★★★) is a single-vineyard wine, grown in the Bridge Pa Triangle, hand-harvested and mostly barrel-fermented. Seductively weighty and rich, it has lush stone-fruit flavours, finely integrated oak, gentle acidity, and a long, well-rounded finish.

DRY $35 –V

Stonecroft Gimblett Gravels Hawke's Bay Viognier ★★★★☆

Certified organic, the fine-value 2019 vintage (★★★★★) was estate-grown in the Roys Hill Vineyard and fermented and matured for six months in seasoned French oak barrels. Bright, light yellow/green, it is a powerful, fleshy, sweet-fruited wine, with concentrated, ripe stone-fruit and spice flavours, a subtle seasoning of oak, good complexity, a slightly oily texture, and a dry, well-rounded finish. A very age-worthy wine, it should break into full stride from 2022 onwards.

Vintage	19	18	17	16
WR	6	6	5	5
Drink	20-24	20-23	20-22	20-21

 DRY $27 AV

Te Mata Estate Zara Hawke's Bay Viognier ★★★★★

This estate-grown wine is from Woodthorpe Terraces, on the south side of the Dartmoor Valley. Hand-picked, in 2018 it was fermented and lees-aged for seven months in French oak barrels (partly new). The 2018 vintage (★★★★★) is fragrant and fleshy, with good weight and intensity of fresh, ripe stone-fruit flavours, finely integrated biscuity oak, gentle acidity, and a long, savoury, dry finish. Seductively rich and soft, it's drinking well now.

Vintage	18
WR	7
Drink	20-21

 DRY $30 AV

Villa Maria Cellar Selection Hawke's Bay Viognier ★★★★

Weighty and sweet-fruited, the partly (20 per cent) barrel-fermented 2018 vintage (★★★★) offers good value. Fresh, full-bodied and vibrantly fruity, it has stone-fruit flavours, showing a distinct touch of complexity, and a dry, well-rounded finish. Best drinking 2021+.

 DRY $19 V+

Wairau River Reserve Marlborough Viognier ★★★★

The 2018 vintage (★★★★) was estate-grown in The Angler Vineyard, on the banks of the Wairau River, hand-picked and fermented in a seasoned French oak barrique. Vibrantly fruity, it is freshly scented and weighty, with strong pear and citrus-fruit flavours, lively acidity, and a dry (1.8 grams/litre of residual sugar) finish.

 DRY $30 –V

Walnut Block Nutcracker Marlborough Viognier (★★★★)

Still on sale and probably at its peak, the 2016 vintage (★★★★) was hand-harvested and barrel-fermented. Bright, light gold, with bottle-aged complexity, it has strong, peachy, slightly toasty flavours, fresh acidity and a dry finish. Certified organic.

DRY $32 –V

Würzer

A German crossing of Gewürztraminer and Müller-Thurgau, Würzer is extremely rare in New Zealand, with 0.4 hectares of bearing vines in 2020, all in Nelson, where Seifried has 'a few rows' at its Redwood Valley Vineyard.

Seifried Nelson Würzer   ★★★★

The 2019 vintage (★★★★) is very fresh, with vibrant, citrusy, appley, gently spicy flavours, showing excellent delicacy, and an off-dry (12 grams/litre of residual sugar), crisp finish. Tasting like a gentle Gewürztraminer, it shows obvious potential and should be at its best 2021+.

MED/DRY $25 AV

Sweet White Wines

New Zealand's sweet white wines (often called dessert wines) are hardly taking the world by storm, with only a few thousand cases exported each year (about 64,000 half bottles in 2019). Yet around the country, winemakers work hard to produce some ravishingly beautiful, honey-sweet white wines that are worth discovering and can certainly hold their own internationally.

New Zealand's most luscious, concentrated and honeyish sweet whites are made from grapes which have been shrivelled and dehydrated on the vines by 'noble rot', the dry form of the *Botrytis cinerea* mould. Misty mornings, followed by clear, fine days with light winds and low humidity, are ideal conditions for the spread of noble rot, but in New Zealand this favourable interplay of weather factors occurs irregularly.

Some enjoyable but rarely exciting dessert wines are made by the 'freeze-concentration' method, whereby a proportion of the natural water content in the grape juice is frozen out, leaving a sweet, concentrated juice to be fermented.

Marlborough has so far yielded a majority of the finest sweet whites. Most of the other wine regions, however, can also point to the successful production of botrytised sweet whites in favourable vintages.

Riesling has been the foundation of the majority of New Zealand's most opulent sweet whites, but Sauvignon Blanc, Sémillon, Gewürztraminer, Muscat, Pinot Gris, Petit Manseng, Chenin Blanc, Viognier, Chardonnay — even Pinot Noir — have all yielded fine dessert styles. With their high levels of extract and firm acidity, most of these wines mature well for two to three years, although few are very long-lived.

Askerne Hawke's Bay Noble Sémillon ★★★★☆

The powerful 2017 vintage (★★★★★) was estate-grown, hand-picked and matured for 20 months in oak barrels (25 per cent new). Gold/amber, with a slightly oily texture, it is mouthfilling and complex, with concentrated peach, apricot and honey flavours, woven with fresh acidity, and abundant sweetness (126 grams/litre of residual sugar). It's delicious now.

SW $33 (375ML) AV

Askerne Late Harvest Hawke's Bay Gewürztraminer ★★★★☆

Already delicious, the 2019 vintage (★★★★★) is gold/amber, with an inviting, honeyed fragrance. Weighty and rich, it has highly concentrated, peachy, spicy flavours, enriched but not swamped by botrytis, finely balanced acidity, an oily texture, and a sweet (108 grams/litre of residual sugar), seductively smooth finish.

SW $24 (375ML) V+

Astrolabe Wrekin Vineyard Late Harvest Marlborough Chenin Blanc ★★★★☆

The 2018 vintage (★★★★) was grown in the Wrekin Vineyard, in the Southern Valleys, hand-picked and 50 per cent barrel-fermented. Made from 'lightly botrytised' grapes, it is a fresh, medium-bodied wine, attractively scented, with rich, ripe, peachy, slightly honeyed flavours, abundant sweetness (108 grams/litre of residual sugar), balanced acidity, and a smooth finish. A gentle, very harmonious wine, it's a drink-now or cellaring proposition.

Vintage	18
WR	7
Drink	20-30

SW $30 (375ML) AV

Ata Rangi Kahu Martinborough Botrytis Riesling ★★★★★

Hard to resist, the 2018 vintage (★★★★★) is golden, with a rich, honeyed fragrance. Strongly botrytis-affected, it has highly concentrated peach, apricot and honey flavours, lush, sweet (120 grams/litre of residual sugar) and crisp, with lovely depth and harmony.

Vintage	18	SW $34 (375ML) V+
WR	7	
Drink	20-27	

Blank Canvas Marlborough Meta Riesling (★★★★★)

For sheer hedonistic pleasure, the botrytised 2018 vintage (★★★★★) is hard to beat. Hand-picked in the Wairau Valley and fermented and aged in seasoned French oak puncheons, it is pale gold, with a highly fragrant, honeyed bouquet. Showing lovely concentration and harmony, it has rich, sweet apricot and honey flavours, good acid spine, an oily texture, and delicious vibrancy, poise and depth.

SW $40 (375ML) AV

Church Road Grand Reserve Hawke's Bay Noble Pinot Gris (★★★★★)

The delicious, distinctive 2018 vintage (★★★★★) was hand-picked at Matapiro, and fermented and lees-matured for nine months in French and Hungarian oak barrels (50 per cent new). Golden and robust (15 per cent alcohol), it has beautifully ripe, peachy, spicy, gently honeyed flavours, balanced acidity, a slightly oily richness, and notable complexity and harmony.

SW $30 (375ML) V+

Churton Marlborough Petit Manseng ★★★★★

The 2017 vintage (★★★★★) of this traditional variety of Jurancon, in south-west France, was estate-grown in the Waihopai Valley and fermented in seasoned oak casks of various sizes. Highly seductive, it is the first to be made from raisined, botrytis-affected grapes. Green/gold, it is full-bodied, rich, peachy and honeyed, in an instantly appealing style, threaded with mouth-watering acidity. Certified organic.

Vintage	17	16	15	14	13	12	SW $49 (500ML) AV
WR	7	7	7	NM	6	7	
Drink	20-30	20-35	20-30	NM	20-28	20-30	

Domain Road Central Otago Bannockburn Symposium (★★★★)

The estate-grown, hand-picked 2018 vintage (★★★★) is a late-harvested Sauvignon Blanc, partly (40 per cent) barrel-fermented. Light lemon/green, it has vibrant, ripe, peachy, citrusy, limey flavours, showing good delicacy, a touch of complexity, moderate acidity, and a sweet (121 grams/litre of residual sugar), very harmonious finish. Delicious young.

SW $32 (375ML) –V

Dry River Martinborough Gewürztraminer Botrytis Bunch Selection Lovat Vineyard (★★★★★)

Sweet but not super-sweet, the 2018 vintage (★★★★★) is a very 'complete' wine, already delicious but also well worth cellaring. Made from 100 per cent botrytis-infected grapes and handled without oak, it is light gold, with a spicy, honeyed fragrance. It has rich stone-fruit, spice and honey flavours, a hint of ginger, and a sweet (160 grams/litre of residual sugar), very harmonious finish. Hard to resist.

 SW $59 (750ML) V+

Eradus Awatere Valley Sticky Mickey (★★★★★)

Bargain-priced, the 2017 vintage (★★★★★) was made from Sauvignon Blanc. Bright green/gold, with a richly honeyed bouquet, it is a strongly botrytised style, concentrated, crisp and sweet (204 grams/litre of residual sugar), with passionfruit and honey flavours, a slightly oily richness, and loads of current-drinking charm.

 SW $15 (375ML) V+

Esk Valley Late Harvest Hawke's Bay Chenin Blanc ★★★★★

Hard to resist, the 2018 vintage (★★★★★) is a pale gold wine with an intense, honeyed fragrance. Showing lovely depth and harmony, it has concentrated, vibrant, peachy, botrytis-enriched flavours, abundant sweetness, finely poised acidity, and excellent vigour and richness.

Vintage	18
WR	6
Drink	20-29

 SW $30 (375ML) V+

Felton Road Block 1 Central Otago Riesling ★★★★★

Estate-grown in The Elms Vineyard, from mature vines on a 'steeper slope' which yields 'riper fruit' without noble rot, this Bannockburn wine is made in a style 'similar to a late-harvest, Mosel spätlese'. The 2020 vintage (★★★★★) is a very Mosel-like wine. Bright, light lemon/green, it is lemon-scented, with vibrant, citrusy, appley flavours, gentle sweetness (69 grams/litre of residual sugar), appetising acidity, and lovely poise, delicacy and depth. Already seductive, it's well worth cellaring.

Vintage	20	19	18
WR	7	7	7
Drink	20-44	20-44	20-43

 SW $51 (750ML) AV

Folium Late Harvest Marlborough Sauvignon Blanc   (★★★★★)

The distinctly Sauternes-style 2018 vintage (★★★★★) is a lovely young wine, handled in French oak casks (10 per cent new). Bright, light yellow/green, it is mouthfilling and sweet (140 grams/litre of residual sugar), with ripe, vibrant tropical-fruit flavours, gentle honeyed notes, a hint of apricot, and a subtle seasoning of oak adding complexity. The producer suggests cellaring up to 2050, but it's already delicious.

Vintage	18
WR	7
Drink	20-50

 SW $52 (750ML) V+

Forrest Botrytised Marlborough Riesling   ★★★★★

The 2018 vintage (★★★★★) is a richly botrytised style with a fragrant, honeyed bouquet. Bright, light gold/green, it has concentrated, peachy, honeyed flavours, abundant sweetness (213 grams/litre of residual sugar), balanced acidity, and a slightly oily richness. Drink now or cellar.

 SW $30 (375ML) V+

Forrest Marlborough Petit Manseng   ★★★★

Forrest Estate says this is their most popular wine at the cellar door over summer. The tangy 2018 vintage (★★★★) is delicious young. Light-bodied, it is gently sweet (80 grams/litre of residual sugar), with peachy flavours, a hint of apricot, and lots of youthful impact.

 SW $20 (750Ml) V+

Framingham Noble Riesling   ★★★★★

The 2017 vintage (★★★★★) is an oily-rich, sweet (176 grams/litre of residual sugar), vibrantly fruity wine, handled in a mix of tanks (55 per cent) and barrels (45 per cent). Pale gold, with a green tinge, it has fresh, concentrated lemon, apple, apricot and honey flavours, enriched but not swamped by botrytis, good acid spine, and a very harmonious, lasting finish. Delicious young, it's a drink-now or cellaring proposition.

 SW $40 (375ML) AV

Framingham Select Marlborough Riesling   ★★★★★

An 'aperitif' style, the beautifully poised 2019 vintage (★★★★★) was grown in the Wairau Valley. Bright, light lemon/green, it is highly scented, vivacious and intense, in a light, lively style with searching, lemony, appley flavours, a distinct splash of sweetness (66 grams/litre of residual sugar), and a very harmonious, lasting finish. Drink now or cellar.

SW $40 (750ML) V+

Fromm Riesling Spätlese (★★★★★)

An outstanding young wine, the 2019 vintage (★★★★★) was hand-picked in Marlborough and made in a low-alcohol (7.5 per cent), sweet (81 grams/litre of residual sugar) style. Light lemon/green, it is beautifully scented, light and racy, with intense, lemony, appley flavours, lovely sugar/acid balance, and a lasting finish. Certified organic.

Vintage	14	13	12
WR	7	7	7
Drink	17-24	17-23	17-22

SW $30 (750ML) V+

Greywacke Botrytis Marlborough Pinot Gris ★★★★★

Lovely now, the 2015 vintage (★★★★★) is a single-vineyard wine, grown in the Wairau Valley, and fermented and matured for a year in old barrels. Pale gold, it is mouthfilling, rich and complex, with concentrated stone-fruit and spice flavours, sweet (105 grams/litre of residual sugar), rounded and lasting. Drink now or cellar.

Vintage	15
WR	6
Drink	20-25

SW $37 (375ML) AV

Grove Mill Wairau Valley Marlborough Botrytis Riesling (★★★★★)

Delicious now, the 2017 vintage (★★★★★) is a strongly botrytised style, with a richly honeyed fragrance and flavours. Light gold, it has concentrated peach and apricot flavours, showing a slightly oily richness, abundant sweetness (215 grams/litre of residual sugar), finely balanced acidity, and a long finish.

Vintage	17
WR	7
Drink	20-29

SW $50 (375ML) AV

Jackson Estate Botrytis Marlborough Riesling ★★★★★

The lovely 2018 vintage (★★★★★) was estate-grown in the heart of the Wairau Valley. Light gold, it is fresh and lively, with concentrated peach and apricot flavours, enriched by botrytis-derived honey notes, abundant sweetness (216 grams/litre of residual sugar), balanced acidity, and a slightly oily texture. Drink now or cellar.

SW $45 (375ML) AV

Johanneshof Noble Late Harvest Marlborough Riesling ★★★★★

The striking 2018 vintage (★★★★★) has a 'Wow!' factor. Amber-hued, it was produced from 100 per cent botrytis-affected fruit, harvested at a soaring 45 brix (natural sugar level in the grapes). Already delicious, it has intense apricot and honey aromas and flavours, enlivened by fresh acidity, abundant sweetness (176 grams/litre of residual sugar), and a rich, oily texture. Hugely concentrated, it's a drink-now or cellaring proposition.

SW $42 (375ML) AV

Jules Taylor Late Harvest Marlborough Sauvignon Blanc   ★★★★☆

Maturing well, the powerful 2018 vintage (★★★★☆) is rich and full-bodied. Gold/amber, it has ripe peach and apricot flavours, a hint of honey, gentle sweetness, good acid spine, a slightly oily texture, and excellent harmony. Drink now to 2023.

Vintage	18	SW $30 (375ML) AV
WR	5	
Drink	20-23	

Misha's Vineyard The Cadenza Late Harvest Gewürztraminer   ★★★★☆

The 2019 vintage (★★★★☆) was estate-grown and hand-picked on 6 June at Bendigo, in Central Otago, at 30.2 brix, with 15 per cent of the fruit botrytis-affected, and handled without oak. Pale lemon/green, with an invitingly perfumed, gently spicy bouquet, it is an elegant, light-bodied style (9.5 per cent alcohol), with very youthful, vibrant, citrusy, spicy flavours, showing excellent delicacy and depth, and a sweet (120 grams/litre of residual sugar), smooth finish. A very harmonious wine, it is well worth cellaring; best drinking 2021+.

Vintage	19	18	17	16	15	14	SW $32 (375ML) AV
WR	6	7	6	7	7	6	
Drink	20-29	20-28	20-26	20-26	20-25	20-24	

Mission Late Harvest   (★★★☆)

The youthful 2018 vintage (★★★☆) was made from botrytis-affected Riesling, grown in Hawke's Bay. Fresh, lively and crisp, it has citrusy, slightly spicy flavours, a hint of apricot and good sugar/acid balance (90 grams/litre of residual sugar). Best drinking 2021+.

SW $16 (375ML) V+

Mondillo Central Otago Nina   ★★★★★

A lovely late-harvest style, the 2019 vintage (★★★★★) was made from Riesling, hand-picked at Bendigo. Bright, light lemon/green, it is invitingly scented and light-bodied, with pure, vibrant, peachy, slightly citrusy and appley flavours, abundant sweetness (147 grams/litre of residual sugar), and excellent delicacy, depth and harmony. Already delicious, it should be at its best 2022+.

SW $38 (375ML) AV

Mt Difficulty Single Vineyard Long Gully Bannockburn Late Harvest Riesling   ★★★★☆

The vigorous 2016 vintage (★★★★☆) has strong, peachy, citrusy flavours, a hint of honey, gentle sweetness (72 grams/litre of residual sugar), lively acidity, and complex, bottle-aged notes emerging. Best drinking 2021+.

Vintage	16	SW $70 (750ML) –V
WR	5	
Drink	20-28	

Pegasus Bay Aria Late Picked Riesling   ★★★★★

Estate-grown at Waipara, the delicious 2018 vintage (★★★★★) is packaged in a full-sized (750-ml) bottle. Bright, light yellow/green, it has rich, ripe, peachy flavours, sweet but not super-sweet, a hint of honey, and notable depth and harmony. It should be long-lived, but is already a lovely mouthful.

SW $40 (750ML) V+

Pegasus Bay Encore Noble Riesling   ★★★★★

Grown at Waipara, in North Canterbury, this beauty is from hand-selected, botrytised bunches and berries, harvested late in the season in multiple passes through the vineyard. The 2016 vintage (★★★★★) has a scented, honeyed bouquet. A very elegant wine, it has concentrated, citrusy, peachy, honeyed flavours, sweet (177 grams/litre of residual sugar), crisp, finely balanced and lasting. Drink now or cellar.

Vintage	16
WR	6
Drink	20-42

SW $40 (375ML) AV

Pegasus Bay Finale Noble Barrique Matured Sauvignon Blanc/Sémillon   ★★★★★

A wine with a real 'Wow!' factor, the 2019 vintage (★★★★★) is a light gold, honey-sweet North Canterbury wine, made in the classic Sauternes style. French oak-aged, with an invitingly honeyed bouquet, it is mouthfilling, with concentrated stone-fruit and honey flavours, a slightly oily texture, and great richness and harmony. Drink now or cellar.

SW $42 (375ML) AV

Pegasus Bay Fortissimo Waipara Muscat   (★★★★★)

The very rare 2016 vintage (★★★★★) was estate-grown in North Canterbury. Modelled on Muscat de Beaumes de Venise, a traditional fortified Muscat from the Rhône Valley, it is richly perfumed and full-bodied (17 per cent alcohol), with lovely, vibrant, pure lemon and orange flavours, sweet (142 grams/litre of residual sugar) and strong. Finely balanced, with gentle acidity, it's delicious now.

Vintage	16
WR	7
Drink	20-32

SW $40 (375ML) AV

Queensberry The Lazy Dog Sweet on Chenin
Central Otago Chenin Blanc/Gewürztraminer   (★★★★)

From 'later harvest' grapes, the 2018 vintage (★★★★) was estate-grown at Queensberry – midway between Cromwell and Wanaka – and fermented in 'pre-loved' barrels. It is fresh and vibrant, with gentle sweetness (70 grams/litre of residual sugar), strong, citrusy, spicy flavours, a hint of apricot, and a finely balanced, crisp finish. Already delicious, it should be at its best 2021+.

SW $29 (750 ML) V+

Rapaura Springs Gravel Lane Vineyard Marlborough
Botrytised Riesling   (★★★★★)

Already delicious, the 2018 vintage (★★★★★) was grown at Omaka and handled in old French oak barriques. Golden, with a richly honeyed bouquet, it has lovely vigour, richness and poise, with intense lemon and apricot flavours, a slightly oily texture, abundant sweetness (233 grams/litre of residual sugar), and good acid spine. Drink now or cellar.

SW $35 (375ML) AV

Riverby Estate Marlborough Cyrene   (★★★★★)

'Made exactly like Sauternes', the 2016 vintage (★★★★★) is a 3:1 blend of Sémillon and Sauvignon Blanc, matured for a year in oak barrels (50 per cent new). Amber-hued, with a strong botrytis influence, it has concentrated, ripe, peachy, honeyed flavours, abundant sweetness (145 grams/litre of residual sugar), finely balanced acidity, and a slightly oily richness. Lovely drinking now onwards.

SW $39 (375ML) AV

Riverby Estate Marlborough Noble Riesling   ★★★★★

Tasted together in mid-2019, the 2016 to 2018 vintages were an impressive trio. Estate-grown at Rapaura, the 2018 (★★★★★) is golden, with rich, peachy, honeyed aromas and flavours, a strong botrytis influence, and a sweet (187 grams/litre of residual sugar), finely poised finish; best drinking mid-2020+. The 2017 vintage (★★★★) shows some development, with very good flavour depth, gentle honeyed notes, and a sweet (157 grams/litre of residual sugar) finish. Delicious now, the 2016 vintage (★★★★★) is amber-hued, with apricot and honey flavours, sweet (200 grams/litre of residual sugar), and highly concentrated. The 2019 vintage (★★★★☆), tasted in mid to late 2020, is golden, with a honeyed bouquet. Already drinking well, it is rich, sweet (180 grams/litre of residual sugar) and smooth, with strong, ripe, peachy flavours, balanced acidity, and a very harmonious finish.

Vintage	19
WR	7
Drink	21-32

SW $35 (375ML) AV

Rock Ferry Botrytised Riesling   ★★★★☆

Certified organic, the delicious 2017 vintage (★★★★★) was hand-harvested in Marlborough and 50 per cent of the blend was fermented and matured for six months in barrels. Golden, with an inviting, richly honeyed bouquet, it has concentrated, apricot-like flavours, abundant sweetness (129 grams/litre of residual sugar), finely balanced acidity, good complexity, and a very harmonious, lasting finish. Drink now or cellar.

 SW $30 (375ML) AV

Seifried Winemaker's Collection Sweet Agnes Nelson Riesling   ★★★★★

Seifried's most celebrated wine. The 2019 vintage (★★★★★) is delicious young. Light yellow/green, it is lively and intense, with rich, peachy, citrusy, gently honeyed flavours, sweet (198 grams/litre of residual sugar), crisp and harmonious. Drink now or cellar. (In a tasting of the 2011, 2010 and 2008 vintages, held in September 2019, the star was the golden 2011 (★★★★★), which shows lovely richness, vigour and harmony.)

Vintage	19	18	17	16	15
WR	7	7	5	7	5
Drink	20-29	20-28	20-25	20-27	20-23

 SW $29 (375ML) V+

Seresin Late Harvest Marlborough Riesling   (★★★★★)

Certified organic, the 2018 vintage (★★★★★) was hand-harvested and fermented with indigenous yeasts in old French oak barrels. Gold/amber, it has a fragrant, complex, honeyed bouquet. Already delicious, it has concentrated stone-fruit and honey flavours, with a clear but not overwhelming botrytis influence, and a crisp, finely poised finish. Drink now or cellar.

 SW $25 (375ML) V+

Sileni Estate Selection Late Harvest Hawke's Bay Sémillon   ★★★☆

The 2018 vintage (★★★☆) was handled without oak. Light-bodied, it has fresh, delicate pear, lemon and apple flavours, a vague hint of honey, gentle sweetness (91 grams/litre of residual sugar), and moderate acidity. Drink now or cellar.

Vintage	18
WR	6
Drink	20-23

SW $20 (375ML) AV

Sileni Exceptional Vintage Marlborough Pourriture Noble   ★★★★☆

The lovely 2014 vintage (★★★★★) is light gold, very honeyed and rich, with lush stone-fruit flavours, advanced sweetness (245 grams/litre of residual sugar), an oily texture, and good acid spine. (Although not labelled by variety, it was made from botrytised Sauvignon Blanc grapes, picked in Marlborough at a super-ripe 46 brix.)

Vintage	14
WR	7
Drink	20-22

 SW $32 (375ML) AV

te Pā Marlborough Noble Sauvignon Blanc   (★★★☆)

The 2017 vintage (★★★☆) is a single-vineyard, botrytised wine, late-picked in the Awatere Valley and partly (30 per cent) barrel-fermented. Light gold/green, with a slightly herbal fragrance, it is medium-bodied, with very good depth of apricot, honey and herb flavours, and plentiful sweetness (150 grams/litre of residual sugar).

SW $30 (375ML) –V

Tohu Raiha Reserve Limited Release Marlborough Noble Riesling   ★★★★☆

The classy 2016 vintage (★★★★★) is an estate-grown, Awatere Valley wine. Delicious now, it has a scented, gently honeyed bouquet, with intense, peachy, honeyed flavours, a slightly oily richness, and lovely balance of sweetness and acidity.

SW $28 (375ML) V+

Urlar Late Harvest Gladstone Riesling   (★★★★★)

Estate-grown in the northern Wairarapa and hand-picked, the youthful 2019 vintage (★★★★★) is already delicious. Bright, light gold/green, it is finely scented and light-bodied, with rich, delicate, peachy, slightly honeyed flavours, abundant sweetness (105 grams/litre of residual sugar), lively acidity, and a finely poised finish. Certified organic.

SW $25 (375ML) AV

Villa Maria Reserve Marlborough Noble Riesling Botrytis Selection   ★★★★★

One of New Zealand's top sweet wines on the show circuit. It is typically stunningly perfumed, weighty and oily, with intense, very sweet honey/citrus flavours, and a lush, long finish. The grapes are grown mainly in the Fletcher Vineyard, in the centre of Marlborough's Wairau Plains, where trees create a 'humidity crib' around the vines and sprinklers along the vines' fruit zone create ideal conditions for the spread of noble rot. The luscious 2015 vintage (★★★★★), hand-harvested in mid-May, is a pale gold wine, light (10 per cent alcohol), peachy, sweet (240 grams/litre of residual sugar), oily-textured and long, with instant appeal.

Vintage	15
WR	7
Drink	20-25

SW $37 (375ML) AV

🍇🍇🍇

Wairau River Botrytised Reserve Riesling   ★★★★☆

The 2017 vintage (★★★★☆) is golden, with apricot and honey aromas and flavours, rich and sweet. A lush wine with a powerful botrytis ('noble rot') influence, it's ready to roll.

Vintage	17	16	15
WR	7	6	6
Drink	20-21	P	P

SW $30 (375ML) AV

Whitehaven Marlborough Noble Riesling   (★★★★★)

Delicious young, the 2018 vintage (★★★★★) is light green/gold, with a scented, honeyed bouquet. Light (9.5 per cent alcohol) and lovely, it has concentrated peach and apricot flavours, sweet (192 grams/litre of residual sugar) and crisp, and a slightly oily richness.

SW $30 (375ML) V+

Yealands Estate Single Vineyard Late Pick Awatere Valley
Marlborough Riesling   (★★★★☆)

The 2019 vintage (★★★★☆) is a highly approachable wine with a scented, gently honeyed bouquet and peachy, slightly spicy and honeyed flavours, fresh, deep and well-rounded. A youthful, very harmonious style, it's a drink-now or cellaring proposition.

SW $30 (375ML) AV

Yealands Estate Winemaker's Reserve Awatere Valley
Marlborough Noble Riesling   (★★★★★)

The 2019 vintage (★★★★★) has a richly fragrant, honeyed bouquet. Already a lovely mouthful, it has lush, sweet stone-fruit flavours, enriched but not dominated by botrytis, an oily texture, and excellent depth and harmony.

SW $40 (375ML) AV

Sparkling Wines

Fizz, bubbly, *méthode traditionnelle*, sparkling – whatever name you call it by (the word Champagne is reserved for the wines of that most famous of all wine regions), wine with bubbles in it is universally adored. How good are Kiwi bubblies? Good enough for the industry to export around 132,000 cases in 2019, although that accounts for less than 0.5 per cent of New Zealand's overseas wine shipments. The selection of New Zealand bubblies is not wide, but has been boosted in recent years by an influx of low-priced sparkling Sauvignon Blancs, sparkling Pinot Gris and the like. Most small wineries find the production of bottle-fermented sparkling wine too time-consuming and costly, and the domestic demand for premium bubbly is limited. The vast majority of purchases are under $15.

New Zealand's sparkling wines can be divided into two key classes. The bottom end of the market is dominated by sweet, simple wines which acquire their bubbles by simply having carbon dioxide pumped into them. Upon pouring, the bubbles race out of the glass. A few other sparklings are made by the 'Charmat' method, which involves a secondary fermentation in a sealed tank. At the middle and top end of the market are the much drier, bottle-fermented *méthode traditionnelle* (formerly *méthode Champenoise*, until the French got upset) labels, in which the wine undergoes its secondary, bubble-creating fermentation not in a tank but in the bottle, as in Champagne itself. Ultimately, the quality of any fine sparkling wine is a reflection both of the standard of its base wine and of its later period of maturation in the bottle in contact with its yeast lees. Only bottle-fermented sparkling wines possess the additional flavour richness and complexity derived from extended lees-aging. Pinot Noir and Chardonnay, both varieties of key importance in Champagne, are also the foundation of New Zealand's top sparkling wines.

Pinot Meunier, also extensively planted in Champagne, is still rare here, with 23 hectares of bearing vines in 2020. Marlborough, with its cool nights preserving the grapes' fresh natural acidity, has emerged as the country's premier region for bottle-fermented sparkling wines (10 producers launched a promotional group, Méthode Marlborough, in 2013), but there are also some very stylish examples flowing from Central Otago. The vast majority of sparkling wines are ready to drink when marketed, and need no extra maturation. A short spell in the cellar, however, can benefit the very best bottle-fermented sparklings.

Allan Scott Cecilia Brut Méthode Traditionnelle Brut NV ★★★☆

The non-vintage wine I tasted in late 2019 (★★★☆) was made from Chardonnay (principally) and Pinot Noir, and disgorged after at least 18 months on its yeast lees. Pale, fresh and lively, it's an easy-drinking style with good depth of crisp, citrusy flavours, gentle yeasty notes adding a touch of complexity, and a smooth finish.

MED/DRY $23 AV

Alpha Domus Cumulus Méthode Traditionnelle ★★★★☆

The vivacious 2017 vintage (★★★★★) is a 'blanc de blancs' style, estate-grown and hand-harvested in the Bridge Pa Triangle, Hawke's Bay. It has a fresh, lifted, very yeasty bouquet, with intense, citrusy, biscuity, nutty flavours, showing excellent vigour and complexity, and a crisp, dry, sustained finish.

DRY $30 AV

Amisfield Central Otago Méthode Traditionnelle Brut (★★★★★)

Still on sale, the classy 2015 vintage (★★★★★) was disgorged from its yeast lees in 2018. Pale straw, with a complex, yeasty fragrance, it is crisp and lively, with excellent vigour and intensity of citrusy, yeasty, biscuity flavours, and a dry (2 grams/litre of residual sugar), lasting finish.

DRY $45 AV

Aotea Nelson Méthode Traditionnelle ★★★★☆

The classy, distinctive, non-vintage wine (★★★★☆) I tasted in September 2020 is a blend of hand-picked Chardonnay and Pinot Noir, disgorged after four years on its yeast lees. Bright, light yellow-green, with a fragrant, yeasty bouquet, it is lively and intense, with citrusy, yeasty flavours, showing excellent complexity, and a crisp, dry, lasting finish. (From Seifried.)

DRY $39 –V

Aurum Rosé Vintage (★★★★)

Still on sale, the pale pink 2011 vintage (★★★★) was blended from estate-grown, Central Otago Pinot Gris and Pinot Noir, and disgorged after three years on its yeast lees. Mouthfilling and dryish (5 grams/litre of residual sugar), it has good complexity, vigour and intensity of berryish, gently spicy and yeasty flavours.

MED/DRY $34 –V

Brancott Estate New Zealand Brut Cuvée ★★★☆

There's a lot to like about this bottle-fermented blend of Pinot Noir and Chardonnay, including its sharp price. A non-vintage wine from unidentified regions, it is typically pale pink and lively, with fresh peach and strawberry flavours, biscuity, yeasty notes adding complexity, and a smooth, dryish finish.

MED/DRY $14 V+

Church Road Hawke's Bay Blanc de Blancs Méthode Traditionnelle (★★★★☆)

The vivacious 2016 vintage (★★★★☆) was made from Chardonnay, hand-picked at Haumoana, bottle-fermented and lees-aged for four years. Bright, light yellow/green, with a nutty, yeasty fragrance, it has strong, vibrant, citrusy, biscuity flavours, showing excellent complexity, and an appetisingly fresh, crisp, dry finish.

DRY $40 –V

Cloudy Bay Pelorus NV ★★★★★

'Designed as an aperitif', Cloudy Bay's non-vintage Marlborough bubbly is a Chardonnay-dominant style, with 30 per cent Pinot Noir, grown in the Wairau Valley and hand-picked. The base wines are fermented and aged in tanks, large oak vats and small French oak barrels, and the bottle-fermented blend is matured for at least two years on its yeast lees, before it is disgorged. It is typically refined, tightly structured and elegant. The sample I tasted in mid-2020 (★★★★☆) is pale straw, fragrant and vivacious, with strong, citrusy, yeasty, slightly biscuity flavours, crisp acidity, and very good complexity and harmony.

MED/DRY $35 AV

Cloudy Bay Pelorus Rosé ★★★★★

This classy, non-vintage wine is a blend of Pinot Noir (mostly) and Chardonnay, hand-picked in the Wairau Valley, partly fermented in old oak vats and French oak barrels, and disgorged after at least two years maturing on its yeast lees. The wine I tasted in mid-2020 (★★★★★) is salmon pink, with a fragrant, complex bouquet. It floats effortlessly across the palate, with lively strawberryish, spicy, yeasty flavours, showing excellent intensity, delicacy, complexity and length. A very 'complete' wine.

MED/DRY $45 AV

Daniel Le Brun Blanc de Blancs Méthode Traditionnelle ★★★★★

Disgorged after at least five years' maturation on its yeast lees, the fresh, elegant 2012 vintage (★★★★★), still on sale, was made entirely from Marlborough Chardonnay. Light lemon/green, it is highly scented, citrusy, yeasty, crisp and lively, with a hint of cashew nuts, excellent complexity, and a racy, dryish, lingering finish.

MED/DRY $40 AV

Daniel Le Brun Méthode Traditionnelle Brut NV ★★★★☆

This non-vintage blend of Chardonnay and Pinot Noir is grown in Marlborough and disgorged after at least two years on its yeast lees. The batch I tasted in 2019 (★★★★☆) was vivacious, with very good intensity of citrusy, peachy, appley, slightly nutty flavours. A very attractive and harmonious wine, it's produced by Lion, owner of Wither Hills.

MED/DRY $30 AV

Daniel Le Brun Méthode Traditionnelle Rosé NV ★★★★☆

The pale pink, non-vintage wine I tasted in 2019 (★★★★☆) was made from Pinot Noir grapes, hand-picked in Marlborough. Lively, with gentle strawberry, watermelon and peach flavours, it has yeasty notes adding complexity, and a finely balanced, very harmonious finish.

MED/DRY $30 AV

Daniel Le Brun Vintage Méthode Traditionnelle ★★★★★

The 2010 vintage (★★★★★), currently on sale, is a blend of Marlborough Pinot Noir and Chardonnay, disgorged after six years on its yeast lees. Bright, light lemon/green, it is very refined and vigorous, with a fresh, complex bouquet, yeasty and slightly nutty. A very 'complete' wine, it has generous, peachy, yeasty flavours, with a distinct hint of cashew nuts, and a long, rich finish.

MED/DRY $40 AV

De La Terre Blanc de Blancs Hawke's Bay Méthode Traditionnelle ★★★★★

The distinctive, refined 2015 vintage (★★★★★) was estate-grown at Havelock North and matured on its yeast lees for three years. Bright, light yellow/green, with a scented, citrusy bouquet, it has a real sense of immediacy, with intense, yeasty, complex flavours, delicate, crisp, dry and persistent.

De La Terre Blanc de Noirs Hawke's Bay Méthode Traditionnelle (★★★★☆)

The 2017 vintage (★★★★☆) was estate-grown at Havelock North. Pale gold, it is crisp, with peachy, yeasty flavours, showing very good vigour, intensity and complexity, and a dry finish.

De La Terre Cuvée 11 Hawke's Bay Méthode Traditionnelle ★★★★☆

The 2017 vintage (★★★★☆), designed as a 'more fruit-driven' style, was estate-grown at Havelock North and matured for two years on its yeast lees. Light gold, it is characterful, with strong, peachy, yeasty, slightly toasty flavours, showing good vibrancy and complexity, and a crisp, dry finish.

Deutz Marlborough Cuvée Blanc de Blancs ★★★★★

New Zealand's most awarded bubbly on the show circuit. This Chardonnay-predominant blend is hand-harvested on the south side of the Wairau Valley, at Renwick Estate and in the Brancott Vineyard, and matured for up to three years on its yeast lees. It is typically a very classy wine with delicate, piercing, lemony, appley flavours, well-integrated yeastiness, and a slightly creamy finish. The 2015 vintage (★★★★★) is a light lemon/green, vivacious wine with a scented, lemony, yeasty bouquet. It has fresh, citrusy, yeasty flavours, showing excellent intensity, delicacy and complexity, that build across the palate to a dryish, lasting finish.

Deutz Marlborough Cuvée Brut NV ★★★★☆

The marriage of Pernod Ricard NZ's fruit at Marlborough with the Champagne house of Deutz's 150 years of experience created an instant winner. Bottled-fermented and matured on its yeast lees for two to three years, this non-vintage wine has evolved over the past decade into a less overtly fruity, more delicate and flinty style. The Pinot Noir grapes are drawn principally from Kaituna Estate, on the north side of the Wairau Valley; the Chardonnay comes mostly from Renwick Estate, in the middle of the valley. Before being bottled, the base wine is lees-aged for up to three months and given a full malolactic fermentation. Reserve wines, a year or two older than the rest, are added to each batch, contributing consistency and complexity to the final blend. The bottlings I have tasted are typically vivacious and smooth, with vibrant, citrusy, biscuity, yeasty flavours, showing excellent complexity and harmony.

Deutz Marlborough Cuvée Rosé   ★★★★

Offering easy drinking, this non-vintage wine (★★★★) is a pale pink sparkling, made principally from Pinot Noir. Lively and finely balanced, it typically has peachy, strawberryish, yeasty flavours, showing good freshness and complexity, and an off-dry, crisp finish.

 MED/DRY $27 AV

Deutz Marlborough Prestige Cuvée   ★★★★★

Well worth discovering, this is typically a very classy wine, disgorged after three years on its yeast lees. A vigorous blend of Chardonnay (mostly) and Pinot Noir, the 2016 vintage (★★★★★) is invitingly scented, with intense, citrusy, yeasty aromas and flavours, tight-knit, long and harmonious.

 MED/DRY $33 V+

Dulcét Brut   (★★★☆)

This easy-drinking, non-vintage wine is a blend of Gisborne Chardonnay and Pinot Noir, given its secondary, bubble-inducing fermentation in tanks. Fresh, crisp, peachy and citrusy, with a touch of complexity, it is vibrantly fruity, with good depth, and a slightly sweet finish. (From Villa Maria.)

MED/DRY $20 AV

Gibbston Valley Blanc de Blancs Méthode Traditionnelle   (★★★★★)

The classy 2013 vintage (★★★★★), made entirely from Chardonnay, was estate-grown at Bendigo, in Central Otago, and disgorged after nearly five years of maturation on its yeast lees. Bright, light yellow/green, it has a highly fragrant, yeasty bouquet. Lively and intense, it has rich, citrusy, yeasty flavours, showing notable complexity and harmony, and a smooth, lasting finish. A very 'complete' wine.

 MED/DRY $110 –V

Gibbston Valley NV Méthode Traditionnelle   ★★★★★

This classy wine, from grapes hand-picked in Central Otago, is disgorged after more than two years on its yeast lees. The sample I tasted in September 2020 (★★★★☆) was disgorged in late 2019. It is very pale straw, with lively, lemony, appley flavours, yeasty and biscuity notes adding complexity, fresh acidity, and a dryish (6 grams/litre of residual sugar) finish.

 MED/DRY $50 AV

Gibbston Valley Rosé Méthode Traditionnelle   ★★★★★

Disgorged in late 2018, the delicious 2013 vintage (★★★★★) was made from Pinot Noir, grown at Gibbston, bottle-fermented and matured on its yeast lees for nearly five years. Straw-hued, with a hint of orange, it has a highly fragrant, complex bouquet. Vivacious, it's a distinctive wine with intense, peachy, strawberryish, spicy, yeasty flavours, showing lovely vigour and depth, and a smooth, resounding finish. Pricey, but memorable.

 DRY $120 AV

Gold Digger Frizzante Naturally Sparkling Rosé   (★★★★)

From Maori Point, in Central Otago, this non-vintage wine is instantly appealing. Bright, light pink, it is light and lively, with vibrant strawberry and watermelon flavours, yeasty notes, and a crisp, off-dry (8 grams/litre of residual sugar), lingering finish.

MED/DRY $12 (330ML) AV

Greystone Organic Pétillant Naturel   (★★★★)

Closed with a crown seal, the 2019 vintage (★★★★) is the first bubbly from this North Canterbury producer. Made from Riesling, it was 'bottled prior to fully completing its first fermentation, allowing carbon dioxide to be produced by the natural sugars found in the grapes'. Certified organic, it was made with 'no added sulphur'. Light straw, it's a distinctive wine, crisp and lively, with plenty of peachy, citrusy flavour, yeasty notes and a dry feel.

DRY $43 –V

Haha Brut Cuvée NV   ★★★★

The impressive non-vintage wine (★★★★☆) I tasted in June 2020 offers great value. Blended from grapes grown in Hawke's Bay and Marlborough, it is a pale straw, vivacious, harmonious wine, with strong, peachy, biscuity, yeasty flavours, showing good complexity, and a tightly structured, crisp, dryish (6 grams/litre of residual sugar), lingering finish.

MED/DRY $22 V+

Haha Brut Rosé NV   ★★★★

Past releases have been blended from Chardonnay and Pinot Noir, grown in Marlborough and Hawke's Bay. The non-vintage wine I tasted in August 2020 (★★★☆) is pale pink, very crisp and lively, with strawberryish, spicy flavours, gently yeasty notes adding a touch of complexity, and a dry finish.

DRY $22 V+

Hans Herzog Cuvée Therese Rosé Méthode Traditionnelle Brut   ★★★★★

The 2014 vintage (★★★★★) was barrel-aged for 18 months, bottle-fermented and made in a bone-dry style. Light red, with a fragrant, complex bouquet, it is crisp and very lively, with strawberryish, slightly spicy flavours, showing excellent intensity. A highly distinctive wine, it's well worth discovering. The 2015 vintage (★★★★☆) was also barrel-aged for 18 months and bottle-fermented. Light red, it has strong strawberry and spice flavours, showing good complexity, and a dry (4 grams/litre of residual sugar), smooth finish.

DRY $64 AV

Hunter's Miru Miru NV   ★★★★☆

'Miru Miru' means 'Bubbles'. This Marlborough wine is disgorged after a minimum of 18 months on its yeast lees (earlier than its Reserve stablemate, below), has a lower Pinot Noir content and a crisper finish. The non-vintage wine (★★★★☆) I tasted in late 2019 is a blend of Chardonnay, Pinot Noir and Pinot Meunier. Bright, light lemon/green, it is fresh and vivacious, with citrusy, peachy, slightly nutty flavours, showing good complexity, and a crisp, dryish (8 grams/litre of residual sugar) finish. Good value.

MED/DRY $29 V+

Hunter's Miru Miru Reserve ★★★★★

This has long been one of Marlborough's best sparklings, full and lively, with loads of peachy, yeasty, nutty flavour, and a creamy, long finish. It is matured on its yeast lees for an average of three and a half years. The 2015 vintage (★★★★★) is a blend of Pinot Noir, Chardonnay and Pinot Meunier, principally (60 per cent) barrel-fermented. Full of personality, it is bright, light yellow/green, with an inviting, scented, complex bouquet. Crisp and dryish (6 grams/litre of residual sugar), it has excellent vigour and richness, with a lasting finish.

MED/DRY $40 AV

Hunter's Miru Miru Rosé NV ★★★★☆

The non-vintage wine (★★★★☆) I tasted in late 2019 is a blend of Marlborough Pinot Noir, Chardonnay and Pinot Meunier. Pale pink, it is very fresh, light and lively, with gentle strawberryish, peachy, spicy flavours, yeasty notes adding complexity, and a slightly off-dry (7 grams/litre of residual sugar), smooth finish.

MED/DRY $35 –V

Hunter's Offshoot Marlborough Sauvignon Blanc ★★★

Closed with a crown seal, the highly distinctive 2019 vintage (★★★) is a 'pétillant naturel style', grown at Rapaura and bottled while still fermenting in tanks, 'to create a naturally carbonated sparkling wine'. Light and vivacious, it is hazy, with plenty of crisp, uncomplicated, appley, slightly sweet (15 grams/litre of residual sugar) flavour.

MED $25 –V

Johanneshof Cellars Blanc de Blancs NV ★★★★☆

Released after a minimum of five years' maturation on its yeast lees, this Chardonnay-based Marlborough wine is hand-picked and barrel-fermented. The very refreshing, non-vintage batch (★★★★☆) I tasted in 2018 has a lemony, gently yeasty fragrance. Crisp, lively and tightly structured, it is vivacious, with strong, citrusy, moderately yeasty flavours, and a very persistent finish.

MED/DRY $38 –V

Johanneshof Cellars Emmi ★★★★☆

Still on sale, the 2009 vintage (★★★★★) is a blend of Pinot Noir and Chardonnay, hand-picked in Marlborough and disgorged after at least five years on its yeast lees. Very pale straw, it shows excellent complexity, with rich, peachy, citrusy, yeasty, gently toasty flavours, and a smooth, very harmonious finish. It's delicious now.

MED/DRY $40 –V

Johanneshof Cellars New Dawn Marlborough Brut   (★★★★★)

Still on sale, the classy, deliciously smooth 2010 vintage (★★★★★) was made from Pinot Noir, hand-harvested in Marlborough and disgorged after a minimum of five years on its yeast lees. Very pale pink, it is highly scented, with gentle strawberry, peach and spice flavours, showing lovely delicacy and complexity. Yeasty and dryish, with excellent harmony, it's well worth discovering.

MED/DRY $38 AV

Johner Estate Wairarapa Méthode Traditionnelle Brut   (★★★★☆)

The characterful 2016 vintage (★★★★☆) is a blend of Pinot Noir (55 per cent) and Chardonnay (45 per cent), oak-aged for six months, then bottle-fermented and lees-aged. Bright, light yellow, it is crisp and lively, with peachy, citrusy, yeasty flavours, showing excellent vigour, complexity and intensity, and a finely balanced, dryish finish.

MED/DRY $36 –V

Kahurangi Estate Vintage Reserve Blanc de Blancs   (★★★★☆)

The elegant 2016 vintage (★★★★☆) is a single-vineyard Nelson wine, made from Chardonnay and disgorged after 18 months on its yeast lees. Bright, light lemon/green, with fragrant, citrusy, yeasty aromas, it is very lively, with strong, citrusy, gently yeasty flavours, showing excellent intensity and vigour, and a crisp, dry (1.5 grams/litre of residual sugar) finish.

DRY $38 –V

Karikari Estate Sparkling Rosé   (★★☆)

Closed with a crown seal, the 2018 vintage (★★☆) is a deep orange wine, grown on the Karikari Peninsula, in the Far North. It has plenty of peachy, strawberryish, slightly sweet, crisp flavour, but also shows a slight lack of freshness and vivacity. Ready.

MED/DRY $30 –V

Kumeu River Kumeu Crémant   (★★★★★)

Bottled in early 2015 and disgorged in late 2018, the non-vintage wine (★★★★★) I tasted in August 2019 is impressive. Light lemon/green, it is crisp and fully dry, with strong, citrusy, slightly nutty flavours, showing excellent vigour, intensity and complexity. Fragrant, it's a highly distinctive wine, well worth trying.

DRY $50 AV

Leveret IQ Premium Brut NV   ★★★★

This fragrant, fresh and lively Hawke's Bay sparkling is a blend of Pinot Noir, Chardonnay and Pinot Meunier, disgorged after a minimum of 18 months on its yeast lees. The non-vintage wine I tasted in mid-2020 (★★★★) is bright, light yellow, with citrusy, biscuity, gently yeasty flavours, showing good complexity, and a crisp, finely balanced finish. Good value.

MED/DRY $22 V+

Leveret IQ Rosé Méthode Traditionnelle   ★★★

The non-vintage wine (★★★) I tasted in mid to late 2019 is a Hawke's Bay blend of Pinot Noir, Chardonnay and Pinot Meunier. Orange/slight amber, it is gently yeasty, with plenty of mature, peachy, spicy flavour, and an off-dry (9.5 grams/litre of residual sugar), crisp finish.

MED/DRY $22 –V

Lindaeur Special Reserve Cuvée Riche   ★★★☆

The non-vintage wine (★★★☆) I tasted in late 2018 was grown in Hawke's Bay and Gisborne. Straw-coloured, with a hint of orange, it was a sweetish style, with good depth of strawberryish, peachy flavours, showing some yeasty complexity, and a crisp, smooth finish.

MED $16 V+

Lindauer Brut Cuvée NV   ★★★

Given its track record of good quality, low price and huge volumes (batch variation is inevitable), this non-vintage bubbly has been a miracle of modern winemaking for several decades. Made from Pinot Noir and Chardonnay, grown in Gisborne and Hawke's Bay, it is matured for a year on its yeast lees, and blended with some reserve wine from past vintages. Fractionally sweet (12 grams/litre of residual sugar), it typically has good vigour and depth, with moderate complexity and lively, lemony, slightly nutty and yeasty flavours.

MED/DRY $10 V+

Lindauer Enlighten Moscato Rosé   ★★★

'Enlighten' is – you guessed it – a range of light wines, and this charmer is just 8.5 per cent alcohol. Based on Muscat grapes, grown in Gisborne, it was blended with a splash of Pinotage (hence its enticing, pale pink hue). Deliciously light and lively, it is unabashedly sweet (60 grams/litre of residual sugar), but very crisp, fruity and well-balanced, in a simple but vivacious style that offers plenty of pleasure.

SW $13 V+

Lindauer Enlighten Pinot Gris   (★★☆)

Offering easy drinking, the lively non-vintage wine (★★☆) I tasted in 2018 was low in alcohol (8.5 per cent), with a gentle stream of bubbles and fresh, peachy, citrusy flavours, fruity and smooth.

MED $13 AV

Lindauer Enlighten Sauvignon Blanc   ★★

The non-vintage wine (★★) I tasted in 2018 was light-bodied (8.5 per cent alcohol), with slightly appley aromas and lively, green-edged flavours, fresh and smooth.

MED/DRY $13 –V

Lindauer Fraise   (★★)

The non-vintage wine (★★) I tasted in 2018 was labelled 'Lindauer and Strawberry', meaning it has been 'infused with natural strawberry essence'. It offers crisp, easy drinking, with – you guessed it – fresh, strawberryish aromas and flavours.

MED $13 –V

Lindauer Pinot Gris ★★★

The non-vintage wine (★★★) I tasted in 2018 was fresh and lively, with good depth of peach and pear-like flavours, gentle sweetness, balanced acidity, and lots of easy-drinking charm.

MED/DRY $13 V+

Lindauer Rosé ★★★

The non-vintage wine (★★☆) I tasted in 2018 is a blend of Chardonnay and Pinot Noir, grown in Gisborne and Hawke's Bay. Pink/orange, with a hint of development, it is dryish, with peachy, strawberryish flavours.

MED/DRY $13 V+

Lindauer Sauvignon Blanc (★★☆)

The non-vintage wine (★★☆) I tasted in 2018 is aromatic, with herbaceous, uncomplicated flavours, fresh and lively.

MED/DRY $13 AV

Lindauer Special Reserve Blanc de Blancs ★★★★

The non-vintage wine (★★★★) I tasted in 2019 was made from Gisborne Chardonnay and bottle-fermented. Very pale straw, with a yeasty fragrance, it is lively and lemony, with very good intensity, and a finely balanced, dryish finish. Great value.

MED/DRY $15 V+

Lindauer Special Reserve Brut Cuveé ★★★★

The non-vintage wine (★★★★) I tasted in late 2018 was a bottle-fermented blend of Pinot Noir and Chardonnay, grown in Hawke's Bay and Gisborne. Pale pink, it looks like a sparkling rosé, with fresh, strawberryish, yeasty aromas and flavours, a hint of apricot, and impressive intensity and length. A great buy.

MED/DRY $16 V+

Lindauer Special Reserve Rosé ★★★★

The non-vintage wine (★★★★) I tasted in 2018 offered fine value. Bottle-fermented, it is pink/pale red, with a fresh, yeasty bouquet, lively, strawberryish flavours, yeasty notes adding complexity, and a finely balanced, dryish finish.

MED/DRY $15 V+

Lindauer Summer Blush (★★★)

The non-vintage wine (★★★) I tasted in 2018 was a 'sparkling rosé', made from Pinot Noir and other varieties. Pale pink, it is fresh and crisp, with gentle peach, strawberry and spice flavours, a touch of complexity, and a dryish finish.

MED/DRY $13 V+

Lindauer White Moscato   (★★★☆)

'Perfect for lunching with the girls', this fairly recent addition to the Lindauer range (★★★☆) is from Muscat grapes grown in Gisborne. Light lemon/green, it is perfumed, frothy, very lively and light (9 per cent alcohol), with fresh, ripe, peachy, slightly appley flavours, and a sweetish finish. Asti Spumante-like, it's priced sharply.

SW $14 V+

LV Marlborough Méthode Traditionnelle NV   ★★★★★

The refined, non-vintage wine (★★★★☆) I tasted in late 2019 is a blend of Pinot Noir (principally) and Chardonnay, disgorged after more than two years on its yeast lees. Light lemon/green, it is invitingly scented, with very good intensity of peachy, citrusy, yeasty, biscuity flavours, showing excellent vigour and complexity. (From Awatere River Wine Co.)

MED/DRY $49 AV

Matahiwi Estate Brut Rosé   (★★★☆)

Grown in the Wairarapa, the non-vintage wine (★★★☆) I tasted in late 2020 is pink-hued, with good depth of strawberryish, slightly spicy flavours, crisp and lively, and a dryish (9 grams/ litre of residual sugar) finish.

MED/DRY $27 –V

Matahiwi Estate Hawke's Bay Blanc de Blancs NV   (★★★★)

The fresh, finely poised wine (★★★★) I tasted in late 2020 was made from Chardonnay. Bright, light lemon/green, it has strong, vibrant, peachy, citrusy, yeasty flavours, showing good vigour, and a crisp, dryish (9 grams/litre of residual sugar) finish.

MED/DRY $22 V+

Mission Fete   (★★★★)

Offering fine value, the non-vintage wine (★★★★) I tasted in late 2019 was made from Pinot Gris, estate-grown and hand-picked at Taradale, in Hawke's Bay. Bright, light lemon/green, it is a distinctive, vivacious wine, crisp and lively, with peachy, gently yeasty flavours, showing good intensity, and an off-dry (9 grams/litre of residual sugar) finish.

MED/DRY $20 V+

Nautilus Cuvée Marlborough   ★★★★★

Recent releases of this non-vintage, bottle-fermented sparkling have revealed an intensity and refinement that positions the label among the finest in the country. Made with Pinot Noir (mostly) and Chardonnay, it is blended with older reserve stocks held in old oak barriques and disgorged after a minimum of three years aging on its yeast lees. Rich, piercing, crisp and long, it's a beautifully tight, vivacious and refined wine, its vibrant Marlborough fruit characters enriched with intense, bready aromas and flavours. The sample I tasted in September 2020 (★★★★☆) was – as the back label indicates helpfully – disgorged in December 2019. A blend of Pinot Noir (75 per cent) and Chardonnay (25 per cent), it was blended with 12 per cent reserve stocks. Light lemon/green, it is very lively, with citrusy, peachy, yeasty flavours, showing very good complexity, slightly toasty notes, and a long, dryish (6 grams/litre of residual sugar) finish.

MED/DRY $39 AV

Nautilus Cuvée Marlborough Vintage Rosé ★★★★★

The vivacious 2017 vintage (★★★★★), made from Pinot Noir, was bottle-fermented and disgorged after lengthy maturation (typically well over two years) on its yeast lees. Pale pink, with strawberryish, spicy, yeasty flavours, it shows excellent delicacy and complexity, with a long, basically dry (7 grams/litre of residual sugar), smooth finish.

MED/DRY $49 AV

Nikau Point Gold Méthode Traditionnelle ★★★

The non-vintage wine (★★★) I tasted in late 2019 is a blend of Chardonnay, Pinot Noir and Pinot Meunier. Pale straw, it's a crisp, gently sweet style (12 grams/litre of residual sugar), with a touch of complexity and plenty of citrusy, peachy, gently yeasty flavour.

MED/DRY $16 AV

No. 1 Family Estate Cuvée No. 1 NV ★★★★☆

The non-vintage wine (★★★★☆) I tasted in late 2019 was made from Marlborough Chardonnay and disgorged after two years on its yeast lees. Bright, light lemon/green, it has generous, citrusy, yeasty flavours, hints of oranges and toast, and a dryish (6 grams/litre of residual sugar), crisp finish.

MED/DRY $36 –V

Oyster Bay Sparkling Cuvée Brut ★★★☆

Chardonnay-based, this Hawke's Bay wine is a blanc de blancs style, with fresh, citrusy fruit flavours to the fore. Made by the Charmat method (where the secondary, bubble-inducing fermentation occurs in tanks, rather than in the individual bottles), the wine I tasted in mid to late 2019 (★★★★) is instantly likeable. Bright, light lemon/green, it has a fragrant, fresh, citrusy, gently yeasty bouquet. Vivacious, it has good vigour and intensity, with a distinct touch of complexity, and a dryish finish.

MED/DRY $22 AV

Oyster Bay Sparkling Cuvée Rosé ★★★☆

The non-vintage wine (★★★★) I tasted in mid to late 2019 was blended from Hawke's Bay Chardonnay (mostly) and Marlborough Pinot Noir. Pale pink, it is lively, with strong, strawberryish, peachy, spicy flavours, gentle yeasty notes adding complexity, and a dryish, finely balanced finish.

MED/DRY $22 AV

Palliser Estate The Griffin Martinborough Méthode Traditionnelle   ★★★★★

The 2017 vintage (★★★★★) is an elegant, bottle-fermented blend of Pinot Noir and Chardonnay, matured for over three years on its yeast lees. Pale straw, with an invitingly fragrant, yeasty bouquet, it is vivacious, with crisp, intense, citrusy, yeasty flavours, tightly structured and complex, and a dryish, racy finish.

MED/DRY $53 AV

Palliser Estate The Rose Méthode Traditionnelle   (★★★★★)

Labelled 'The Rose', rather than 'The Rosé', the vivacious 2017 vintage (★★★★★) is a delicious, pale orange Martinborough wine, based entirely on Pinot Noir. A 'serious' style, it is crisp and dryish, with incisive, peachy, strawberryish, spicy, yeasty flavours, showing excellent complexity, and a very harmonious, lasting finish.

MED/DRY $56 AV

Pask Declaration Gimblett Gravels Méthode Traditionnelle   ★★★★☆

Currently on sale, the elegant 2011 vintage (★★★★★) is still extremely lively. Closed with a crown seal, it is a blend of Chardonnay (80 per cent) and Pinot Noir (20 per cent), bottle-fermented and disgorged in July 2020 after nine years on its yeast lees. Bright yellow/green, it is crisp and intense, with vigorous, citrusy, yeasty flavours, and a long, fully dry (2 grams/litre of residual sugar) finish.

DRY $30 AV

Porters Reserve Martinborough Cuvée Zoe   (★★★★☆)

Still on sale, the 2012 vintage (★★★★☆) was handled in old oak casks. Pale straw, with a biscuity, yeasty fragrance, it's a distinctive wine, with strong, citrusy, peachy flavours, showing excellent vigour and complexity, and a basically dry (5 grams/litre of residual sugar) finish.

MED/DRY $60 –V

Quartz Reef Méthode Traditionnelle Brut NV   ★★★★☆

This increasingly Champagne-like, non-vintage bubbly is estate-grown at Bendigo, in Central Otago, and lees-aged for at least two years. The batches vary in their varietal composition, but the release I tasted in 2018 (★★★★☆) is a blend of Pinot Noir (62 per cent) and Chardonnay (38 per cent), disgorged from autumn 2018 onwards. Very pale straw, with a refined, yeasty bouquet, it has very harmonious, citrusy, biscuity, yeasty flavours, and a smooth, dry (4 grams/litre of residual sugar), lingering finish. Certified biodynamic.

DRY $35 –V

Quartz Reef Méthode Traditionnelle Late Disgorged Vintage   (★★★★★)

Chosen to help celebrate Quartz Reef's 21 years at Bendigo, in Central Otago, the 2010 vintage (★★★★★) is a real conversation piece. An estate-grown blend of Chardonnay (93 per cent) and Pinot Noir (7 per cent), it was disgorged in May 2019, after maturing for eight and a half years on its yeast lees. A unique wine, it is rare (only 500 bottles were produced), with mature colour and a fragrant, very yeasty bouquet. Still vigorous, it has intense, yeasty, toasty, nutty flavours, showing real complexity, and an unusually dry (4 grams/litre of residual sugar) finish. Ready.

DRY $125 AV

Quartz Reef Méthode Traditionnelle Rosé   ★★★★☆

Instantly appealing, the vivacious, non-vintage wine (★★★★★) I tasted in 2018 was estate-grown at Bendigo, in Central Otago. Made entirely from Pinot Noir and disgorged in autumn 2018, it is bright pink, with a fragrant, berryish, gently yeasty bouquet. Crisp and tightly structured, it has lively peach, strawberry and apricot flavours, showing impressive depth and complexity, and a finely textured, smooth, dry (4 grams/litre of residual sugar) finish.

DRY $45 –V

Quartz Reef Méthode Traditionnelle Vintage Blanc de Blancs   ★★★★★

Top vintages are outstanding, showing great vigour and complexity in a Champagne-like style, intense and highly refined. A wine of great presence, the vivacious 2013 vintage (★★★★★) is promoted as the 'crown jewel' of Quartz Reef's Central Otago sparklings. A blend of Chardonnay (91 per cent) and Pinot Noir (9 per cent), estate-grown at Bendigo, it is pale straw, with very intense, citrusy, yeasty, biscuity flavours, crisp acidity, and a lasting, dry (4 grams/litre of residual sugar) finish.

DRY $75 AV

Rock Ferry Central Otago Brut Rosé   (★★★★★)

Certified organic, the 2014 vintage (★★★★★) is a classy, distinctive wine. Estate-grown in the Trig Hill Vineyard, at Bendigo, it was fermented in a 50:50 split of seasoned oak barrels and stainless steel barrels, and disgorged after maturing for three and a half years on its yeast lees. Pale pink, it is vivacious, with intense, strawberryish, spicy, yeasty flavours, showing good complexity, and a very finely balanced, dry (5 grams/litre of residual sugar), lingering finish.

MED/DRY $55 AV

Rock Ferry Marlborough Blanc de Blancs   ★★★★☆

The very lively 2015 vintage (★★★★☆) was made from Chardonnay, estate-grown in The Corners Vineyard at Rapaura, in Marlborough. Hand-picked and fermented in a mix of old oak (30 per cent) and stainless steel (70 per cent) barrels, it was disgorged after two years on its yeast lees. Bright, light lemon/green, with a fragrant, citrusy bouquet, it is vigorous, with strong, grapefruit-like flavours, gentle yeasty notes adding complexity, and a crisp, unusually dry (4 grams/litre of residual sugar) finish. Certified organic.

DRY $50 –V

Saint Clair Dawn Méthode Traditionnelle   ★★★★☆

A blend of Marlborough Pinot Noir, Chardonnay and Pinot Meunier, the 2015 vintage (★★★★) was hand-picked and disgorged after more than three years on its yeast lees. Light lemon/green, it is youthful, with citrusy, gently yeasty flavours, showing excellent delicacy and vigour, and a dryish (6 grams/litre of residual sugar), crisp, finely balanced finish.

MED/DRY $50 –V

Sileni Sparkling Cuvée Brut (★★★)

The non-vintage wine (★★★) I tasted in late 2019 was made from Hawke's Bay Chardonnay. Bright, light yellow/green, it is fresh and lively, in a simple but attractive style with good depth of citrusy, slightly peachy flavours, finely balanced, dry (2.6 grams/litre of residual sugar) and crisp.

DRY $20 –V

Sileni Sparkling Cuvée Pinot Gris (★★★)

Offering very easy drinking, the non-vintage wine (★★★) I tasted in late 2019 is pale straw, lively and smooth, with peach, pear and spice flavours, showing good varietal character, balanced acidity, and a dryish (6 grams/litre of residual sugar) finish.

MED/DRY $20 –V

Sileni Sparkling Cuvée Rosé (★★☆)

The non-vintage wine (★★☆) I tasted in late 2019 is pink/orange, with strawberryish, slightly spicy flavours, and an off-dry (5.6 grams/litre of residual sugar) finish. Solid, easy drinking.

MED/DRY $20 –V

Sileni Sparkling Cuvée Sauvignon Blanc (★★☆)

The non-vintage wine (★★☆) I tasted in late 2019 is an uncomplicated style with ripely herbaceous flavours, fresh and crisp, a sliver of sweetness (7.7 grams/litre of residual sugar), and an easy-drinking appeal.

MED/DRY $20 –V

Soljans Fusion Sparkling Moscato ★★★★

This 'Asti-style' bubbly has a long, proud history. The wine I tasted in 2019 (★★★★) is perfumed and light (8.5 per cent alcohol), with vivacious, crisp, sweetly seductive flavours, simple but full of charm.

SW $15 V+

Soljans Legacy Méthode Traditionnelle ★★★★☆

Still on sale, the 2013 vintage (★★★★☆) is a blend of Hawke's Bay Chardonnay (60 per cent) and Marlborough Pinot Noir (40 per cent), disgorged after three years on its yeast lees. Light yellow/green, it is rich and lively, with peachy, yeasty, toasty flavours, showing very good complexity, and a finely balanced, smooth (9.5 grams/litre of residual sugar) finish.

MED/DRY $33 AV

Spy Valley Echelon Marlborough Méthode Traditionnelle ★★★★☆

Currently on sale, the 2012 vintage (★★★★☆) is a blend of Chardonnay (52 per cent) and Pinot Noir (48 per cent), estate-grown and hand-harvested at Johnson Estate, in the Waihopai Valley. Matured for a year in old oak casks, then bottled and matured on its yeast lees for three and a half years, it is a bright, light lemon/green, vigorous, citrusy wine, with very good intensity, and a long, dry (4 grams/litre of residual sugar) finish.

DRY $37 –V

Thomas Waiheke Island Blanc De Gris   ★★★★

The vivacious 2018 vintage (★★★★☆) of this Waiheke Island sparkling is a distinctive blend of Pinot Gris (56 per cent) and Flora (44 per cent). Bright, light lemon/green, it is a slightly Muscat-like wine, with pear, lemon and apple flavours, showing very good delicacy and depth, a gentle splash of sweetness (13.4 grams/litre of residual sugar), fresh acidity, and a lingering finish. Excellent summer drinking.

MED/DRY $46 –V

Tohu Rewa Marlborough Blanc de Blancs Méthode Traditionnelle   ★★★★☆

The attractive 2015 vintage (★★★★☆) is a very fresh, elegant sparkling, from hand-picked Chardonnay grapes. Disgorged after 27 months on its yeast lees, it is bright, light lemon/green, with a fragrant, citrusy, yeasty bouquet. Crisp and lively, it is a tight-knit, complex wine with lemony, slightly appley flavours, showing good intensity and harmony, and a lingering finish.

DRY $34 AV

Tohu Rewa Marlborough Rosé Méthode Traditionnelle   (★★★★☆)

The 2015 vintage (★★★★☆) was made from Pinot Noir, disgorged after two years on its yeast lees. Bright, light pink, it is fragrant, fresh and vivacious, with crisp, strawberryish, yeasty flavours, showing excellent delicacy, harmony and length.

MED/DRY $34 AV

Toi Toi Sparkling Rosé   (★★★)

The non-vintage wine (★★★) I tasted in late 2019 is an unusual blend of Riesling and barrel-aged Merlot. Made in a very easy-drinking style, it is pink/slight orange, with strawberryish, peachy flavours, strong and lively, although not complex, and a crisp, slightly sweet (26 grams/litre of residual sugar) finish.

MED $17 AV

Twin Islands Pinot Noir/Chardonnay Brut NV   ★★★★

Nautilus's sparkling is a bottle-fermented, non-vintage style. It is typically dryish, crisp and vivacious, with strong, citrusy, slightly appley, gently yeasty flavours, showing considerable complexity.

MED/DRY $25 AV

Wildsong Sauvignon Blanc Sparkling Cuvée   (★★★☆)

From Te Awanga Estate, the distinctive 2018 vintage (★★★☆) was grown in Hawke's Bay. It has ripe tropical-fruit aromas and flavours, fresh, lively and strong, in an uncomplicated but highly attractive style, dry and crisp.

DRY $25 –V

Rosé Wines

The number of rosé labels on the market has exploded recently, as drinkers discover that rosé is not an inherently inferior lolly water, but a worthwhile and delicious wine style in its own right. New Zealand rosé is even finding offshore markets (over 577,000 cases in 2019, a steep rise from 104,666 cases in 2016) and collecting overseas awards.

In Europe many pink or copper-coloured wines, such as the rosés of Provence, Anjou and Tavel, are produced from red-wine varieties. (Dark-skinned grapes are even used to make white wines: Champagne, heavily based on Pinot Meunier and Pinot Noir, is a classic case.) To make a rosé, after the grapes are crushed, the time the juice spends in contact with its skins is crucial; the longer the contact, the greater the diffusion of colour, tannin and flavour from the skins into the juice.

'Saignée' (bled) is a French term that is seen occasionally on rosé labels. A technique designed to produce a pink wine or a more concentrated red wine – or both – it involves running off or 'bleeding' free-run juice from crushed, dark-skinned grapes after a brief, pre-ferment maceration on skins. An alternative is to commence the fermentation as for a red wine, then after 12 or 24 hours, when its colour starts to deepen, drain part of the juice for rosé production and vinify the rest as a red wine.

Pinot Noir and Merlot are the grape varieties most commonly used in New Zealand to produce rosé wines. Regional differences are emerging. South Island and Wairarapa rosés, usually made from Pinot Noir, are typically fresh, crisp and often slightly sweet, while those from the middle and upper North Island – Hawke's Bay, Gisborne and Auckland – tend to be Merlot-based, fuller-bodied and drier.

These are typically charming, 'now-or-never' wines, peaking in their first 12 to 18 months with seductive strawberry/raspberry-like fruit flavours. Freshness is the essence of the wines' appeal.

Alexander Raumati Martinborough Pinot Noir Rosé ★★★★☆

The 2020 vintage (★★★★★) was estate-grown, hand-picked and made in a fully dry (1.3 grams/litre of residual sugar) style. Bright, light pink, it is mouthfilling, with ripe strawberry, peach and spice flavours, showing good concentration. Best drinking 2021+.

DRY $24 V+

Allan Scott Marlborough Rosé ★★★☆

Opening out well, the 2019 vintage (★★★☆) is a bright, light pink wine, offering very easy drinking. Fresh and lively, it has good depth of peach, strawberry and spice flavours, balanced acidity, and a gently sweet (11 grams/litre of residual sugar), smooth finish.

MED/DRY $18 V+

Ash Ridge Estate Hawke's Bay Rosé (★★★★☆)

Invitingly scented, the 2019 vintage (★★★★☆) was made from Merlot, estate-grown in the Bridge Pa Triangle. Bright pink, it is fresh, with vibrant watermelon, cherry and spice flavours, showing very good vigour and intensity, and a bone-dry finish.

DRY $22 V+

Astrolabe Comelybank Vineyard Marlborough Pinot Rosé ★★★★★

The classy 2019 vintage (★★★★★) was grown in the lower Waihopai Valley. A blend of Pinot Noir (85 per cent) and Pinot Gris (15 per cent), it is a bright, light pink, very fragrant and fleshy wine, with strong peach, strawberry and spice flavours, and a smooth, fully dry finish. Delicious young.

Vintage	19	
WR	7	
Drink	P	

 DRY $25 V+

Aurum Organic Central Otago Pinot Gris Rosé ★★★★☆

The distinctive 2019 vintage (★★★★☆) was made from estate-grown, hand-harvested Pinot Gris. Straw/orange in colour, it is full-bodied, with concentrated, peachy, slightly spicy flavours, a hint of apricot, a touch of complexity, and a fresh, dry (3 grams/litre of residual sugar) finish. Full of personality, it's delicious young. Certified organic.

 DRY $28 AV

Bald Hills Friends & Lovers Single Vineyard Bannockburn Central Otago Rosé (★★★★☆)

Made from hand-picked Pinot Noir, the pale pink, floral 2019 vintage (★★★★☆) has strong strawberry, watermelon and spice flavours. Vivacious, with good delicacy, it's a dryish style (5 grams/litre of residual sugar), with fresh acidity, and excellent harmony.

MED/DRY $30 –V

Black Barn Hawke's Bay Rosé ★★★★

The impressive 2019 vintage (★★★★☆) was made from Merlot grapes, hand-picked in the Havelock North hills. Pink/slight orange, it has strong, peachy, slightly strawberryish and spicy flavours, showing good complexity, balanced acidity, and a dry, lengthy finish.

 DRY $23 AV

Black Cottage Marlborough Rosé ★★★☆

Priced right, the bright, light pink 2020 vintage (★★★☆) was made mostly from Pinot Noir grapes, grown in the Wairau Valley. Fermented and briefly lees-aged in tanks, it is freshly scented, with very lively, strawberryish flavours, hints of watermelon and spices, and a crisp, dry (2 grams/litre of residual sugar) finish. (From Two Rivers.)

 DRY $18 V+

Black Estate North Canterbury Treble Rosé (★★★★)

'Treble' refers to Black Estate's three vineyard sites. Pink/red, with a hint of development, the 2020 vintage (★★★★) is a blend of co-fermented Pinot Noir, Riesling, Cabernet Franc, Chenin Blanc and Chardonnay. Fresh and lively, it is sweet-fruited, with good concentration of cherry, plum and spice flavours, crisp and dry. Certified organic.

 DRY $29 –V

Blackenbrook Nelson Pinot Rosé   ★★★★☆

The attractive 2020 vintage (★★★★☆) was made from hand-picked Nelson Pinot Noir, partly (9 per cent) aged in old oak barrels. Made in a dryish style (5 grams/litre of residual sugar), it is a light pink/red, full-bodied wine with ripe, berryish, plummy, slightly spicy flavours, showing excellent depth, balanced acidity and a rounded finish. Good drinking for the summer of 2020–21.

Vintage	20	19	18
WR	7	6	7
Drink	20-21	20-21	P

 MED/DRY $25 V+

Bladen Marlborough Pinot Rosé   (★★★★)

The 2019 vintage (★★★★) is a single-vineyard wine, made from Pinot Noir grapes hand-picked in the Wairau Valley. Bright, light pink, it is fresh, full-bodied and fleshy, with stone-fruit, watermelon and spice flavours, a touch of tannin, and a soft, dry (3.5 grams/litre of residual sugar), rounded finish.

DRY $25 AV

Blushing Rogue Bay of Islands Tempranillo Rosé   (★★★★)

Delicious young, the 2019 vintage (★★★★) was made from Tempranillo, estate-grown at Kerikeri, in Northland. Pink-hued, it is full-bodied, fresh and smooth, with plenty of peachy, strawberryish, spicy flavour, finely balanced for easy drinking. (From Rogue Vine Vineyard.)

 MED/DRY $24 AV

Boneline, The, Pink Noise Rosé   (★★★★☆)

The delicious 2019 vintage (★★★★☆) is from mature Merlot vines, estate-grown at Waipara and fermented in old oak barrels. Bright pink/pale red, it has fresh, berryish scents, leading into a lively, medium-bodied wine with strong, berryish, plummy, spicy flavours, hints of watermelon and strawberry, and a finely balanced, dry, smooth finish.

 DRY $32 –V

Brick Bay Matakana Rosé   ★★★★

Estate-grown, this is a blend of traditional Bordeaux red-wine varieties. Delicious young, the 2020 vintage (★★★★☆) is a bright, light pink wine, full-bodied, fresh and lively, with generous, ripe peach, strawberry and spice flavours, and an off-dry, very smooth and harmonious finish.

 MED/DRY $50 –V

Brightwater Gravels Nelson Rosé   (★★★☆)

Fresh, medium-bodied and lively, the 2020 vintage (★★★☆) is bright pink, with watermelon and spice flavours, a sliver of sweetness, balanced acidity, and a smooth finish. Offering good drinking for the summer of 2020–21, it's priced sharply.

 MED/DRY $16 V+

Brightwater Vineyards Sophie's Kiss Nelson Rosé   ★★★★☆

The delicious 2019 vintage (★★★★☆) is Pinot Noir-based. Bright pink, it is full-bodied, with fresh watermelon and spice flavours, showing excellent vibrancy and depth, and a finely balanced, off-dry (9 grams/litre of residual sugar) finish.

Vintage	19	18
WR	6	6
Drink	20-21	P

MED/DRY $22 V+

Bronte Nelson Pinot Rosé   (★★★★)

From Rimu Grove, the 2019 vintage (★★★★) is a deep pink, fleshy wine with strong, berryish, slightly spicy flavours, fresh and lively, and a dryish (5 grams/litre of residual sugar), crisp finish. Drink now and over the summer of 2020–21.

Vintage	19
WR	7
Drink	20-25

MED/DRY $25 AV

Coal Pit Central Otago Pinot Noir Rosé   ★★★★☆

The lovely 2019 vintage (★★★★★) was hand-picked at Gibbston. Bright pink, with a highly attractive, floral bouquet, it is fresh and dry, with mouthfilling body and strong peach, watermelon, strawberry and spice flavours, showing excellent delicacy and length. Retasted in mid-2020, it was developing very gracefully.

DRY $31 –V

Coopers Creek Kumeu Rosé   ★★★★

Full of drink-young charm, the 2019 vintage (★★★★) of this West Auckland rosé is a 2:1 blend of Malbec and Merlot. Bright pink, with fresh, floral aromas, it is lively and medium-bodied, with strawberry and spice flavours, a hint of peaches, balanced acidity, and a dry finish.

DRY $18 V+

Craggy Range Gimblett Gravels Vineyard Hawke's Bay Rosé   ★★★★

The pale pink 2019 vintage (★★★★☆) is a blend of red-wine varieties, estate-grown, hand-picked and oak-aged for three months. Full-bodied, it has excellent depth of watermelon, peach and spice flavours, a hint of oranges, a distinct touch of complexity, and a dry (1.5 grams/litre of residual sugar) finish.

DRY $32 –V

Dancing Petrel Mangonui Northland Rosé   (★★★★)

Grown in the Far North, the 2019 vintage (★★★★) was blended from Syrah and Cabernet Franc. Bright, light pink, it is lively and full-bodied, with strong, fresh berry and spice flavours, a touch of tannin, and a smooth, dryish finish.

MED/DRY $22 V+

Dashwood by Vavasour New Zealand Rosé ★★★☆

The 2019 vintage (★★★☆) makes no claims about regional origin or varieties, but it was grown in Marlborough and offers great value. Bright pink, it is a charming, vibrantly fruity wine with watermelon and peach flavours, hints of strawberry and spices, and an ultra-smooth finish.

MED/DRY $16 V+

Decibel Crownthorpe Vineyard Hawke's Bay Rosé ★★★

The 2019 vintage (★★★☆) is a single-vineyard wine, grown inland at Crownthorpe. Pale pink, with fresh strawberry and spice aromas, it is crisp and lively, with a sliver of sweetness, and plenty of peachy, slightly spicy flavour.

MED/DRY $24 –V

Delta Estate Marlborough Rosé ★★★☆

The very pale pink 2019 vintage (★★★☆) was made from Pinot Gris and Malbec grapes, grown in the Wairau Valley. A fresh, medium-bodied wine, it has strong, peachy, strawberryish flavours, hints of spices and apricots, and a smooth, dry (2.8 grams/litre of residual sugar) finish.

DRY $20 AV

Doctors', The, Marlborough Rosé ★★★

The 2019 vintage (★★★) was crafted as 'a lower alcohol rosé' (9.5 per cent). Pale pink, it is fresh and lively, with gentle watermelon and strawberry flavours, and a slightly sweet (6 grams/litre of residual sugar), crisp finish.

MED/DRY $22 –V

Dunleavy The Shed Waiheke Island Rosé (★★★★☆)

The pale pink 2019 vintage (★★★★☆) was made from Merlot, grown at the eastern end of the island. A distinctive, lively, medium-bodied wine, it is attractively scented, with strong, peachy, spicy flavours, a hint of apricots, fresh acidity, and a dry finish.

DRY $35 –V

Durvillea Marlborough Rosé ★★★★

Offering good value, the 2020 vintage (★★★★) is a 50:50 blend of Pinot Noir and Pinot Gris, grown at a single site in the Awatere Valley. Bright, light pink, it is very fresh and lively, with strong, strawberryish, slightly peachy and spicy flavours, and a dry (1.2 grams/litre of residual sugar) finish. Enjoyable from the start.

Vintage	20
WR	7
Drink	20-22

DRY $20 V+

Eradus Sadie Awatere Valley Marlborough Rosé ★★★☆

Priced sharply, the 2019 vintage (★★★★) is a pale pink, fresh and lively wine, with watermelon and peach flavours, showing excellent delicacy, and a lingering, finely balanced, off-dry finish.

MED/DRY $17 V+

Esk Valley Hawke's Bay Rosé ★★★★☆

For many years, this was New Zealand's most successful rosé on the show circuit. Retasted in mid-2020, the 2019 vintage (★★★★★) is a Merlot-based wine with a highly inviting, light pink hue. Fragrant and lively, it is medium-bodied, with excellent depth of vibrant peach, strawberry and spice flavours, and a beautifully poised, dry (2.6 grams/litre of residual sugar), smooth finish. Drink now to 2021.

Vintage	19	18
WR	7	6
Drink	20-21	P

Falconhead Hawke's Bay Rosé ★★★

The 2019 vintage (★★★☆) was mostly handled in tanks, but 25 per cent of the blend was barrel-fermented. Pale pink, it is mouthfilling, with generous, fresh peach, watermelon and spice flavours, and a dryish (5 grams/litre of residual sugar) finish. Good value.

Flaxmore Moutere Rosé ★★★★

Bargain-priced, the 2019 vintage (★★★★☆) is a 'serious' style of rosé, from hand-picked Pinot Noir, estate-grown in the Moutere hills. Pale pink, it is mouthfilling, with strong peach, apricot and spice flavours, a touch of tannin, and a dry finish. Delicious drinking now onwards.

Forrest Marlborough Rosé ★★★★

The delicious 2019 vintage (★★★★☆) is a bright pink, vibrant wine, with strong watermelon and strawberry flavours, a hint of spice, fresh acidity, a sliver of sweetness (5.4 grams/litre of residual sugar), and a lively, long finish.

Georges Road Les Terrasses Waipara Rosé ★★★★☆

The very lively 2020 vintage (★★★★) is a single-vineyard wine, made from Syrah, hand-picked in North Canterbury, fermented with indigenous yeasts and lees-aged. Bright pink, it is light-bodied, with vibrant red-berry and watermelon flavours, crisp and dry. Good drinking for the summer of 2020–21.

Gibbston Valley GV Collection Central Otago Rosé ★★★★

The fragrant, very lively 2019 vintage (★★★★) was hand-harvested and cool-fermented in tanks. Bright pink, it has good intensity of ripe cherry, plum and spice flavours, fresh acidity, and a finely poised, basically dry (4 grams/litre of residual sugar) finish.

DRY $28 –V

Giesen Blush Sauvignon   (★★★★)

Simple but delightful, the 2019 vintage (★★★★) is designed as 'an alluring, playful wine'. A blend of Marlborough Sauvignon Blanc (mostly) and Hawke's Bay Merlot, it is light pink, fresh and vivacious, with watermelon, strawberry and spice flavours, and a crisp, finely balanced, basically dry (4 grams/litre of residual sugar), lingering finish. Fine value.

DRY $16 V+

Giesen Riesling Blush   (★★★☆)

'Share this wine while getting ready for a night out', suggests Giesen. The 2019 vintage (★★★☆) is a blend of Riesling, grown in Marlborough and Waipara, with 'a dash of Marlborough-grown Syrah'. Pale pink, it is light-bodied, with fresh watermelon-like flavours, hints of peaches and spices, balanced acidity, and a gently sweet (20 grams/litre of residual sugar) finish.

MED $16 V+

Gillman Clairet   ★★★★

Labelled as 'slightly darker than a modern rosé, with more fruit richness and structure', the distinctive 2017 vintage (★★★★) was made from Cabernet Franc and Merlot, grown at Matakana, and barrel-aged for a year. A rare wine, it has light red colour and a fragrant, spicy bouquet. A complex, dry style, it has a gentle touch of tannin and strong, berryish, nutty, slightly earthy flavours.

DRY $46 –V

Graham Norton's Own Pink by Design Rosé   ★★★★

The 2020 vintage (★★★★) was blended from grapes grown in Marlborough and Gisborne. Pale pink, it is fresh and lively, with very good depth of peach, apricot, strawberry and spice flavours, and a dry (3 grams/litre of residual sugar), finely balanced finish.

DRY $19 V+

Greystone Organic Waipara Valley North Canterbury Rosé   (★★★★★)

Certified organic, the impressive 2020 vintage (★★★★★) was made from estate-grown Pinot Noir, briefly lees-aged. Bright pink, it is finely scented, sweet-fruited and vivacious, with peach, strawberry and spice flavours, showing excellent delicacy, and a harmonious, dryish (5 grams/litre of residual sugar), lingering finish.

Vintage	20
WR	6
Drink	20-23

MED/DRY $25 V+

Haha Hawke's Bay Rosé   ★★★☆

The bright pink 2020 vintage (★★★☆) is a blend of varieties, including Merlot and Malbec. Fresh, crisp and lively, it is medium-bodied, with youthful watermelon and spice flavours, and a dry (3 grams/litre of residual sugar), smooth finish. Enjoyable from the start, it offers good value.

DRY $18 V+

Hawkshead Central Otago Rosé ★★★★

The 2019 vintage (★★★★☆) is 'a sexy little number', according to the back label. Based entirely on Pinot Noir, it is pink, with a hint of orange. Fresh and vivacious, it is full-bodied, with strong strawberry, apricot and spice flavours, and a very harmonious, dry (3 grams/litre of residual sugar), appetisingly crisp finish.

DRY $29 –V

Hunter's Pinot Noir Marlborough Rosé ★★★☆

The pale pink 2019 vintage (★★★☆) was grown in the Wairau Valley. It has good depth of fresh, lively, peachy, slightly spicy flavours, finely balanced acidity, and a smooth, dry finish.

DRY $20 AV

Hunting Lodge, The, Central Otago Pinot Noir Rosé (★★★★)

The pale pink 2019 vintage (★★★★) is light and lively, in a vivacious, off-dry style with fresh, gentle strawberry, watermelon and spice flavours, showing very good delicacy and length.

MED/DRY $26 –V

Johanneshof Marlborough Pinot Noir Rosé Maybern Single Vineyard ★★★★

Released in 2020, the 2018 vintage (★★★★) was estate-grown in a hillside vineyard at Koromiko. Made from hand-picked Pinot Noir, it is orange-hued, with mouthfilling body, good depth of strawberry, peach and spice flavours, a hint of apricot, fresh acidity, and a rounded, dry (1 gram/litre of residual sugar) finish.

DRY $25 AV

Johner Estate Pinot Noir Rosé ★★★★

The 2019 vintage (★★★★) was grown at Gladstone, in the Wairarapa. Pink/pale red, with floral, berryish scents, it is fresh and full-bodied, with vibrant berry and plum flavours, vague sweetness (5 grams/litre of residual sugar), and lively acidity.

MED/DRY $20 V+

Jules Taylor OTQ Single Vineyard Marlborough Pinot Noir Rosé ★★★★☆

Strikingly packaged, the 2020 vintage (★★★★☆) was produced 'OTQ' (On The Quiet) and handled without oak. Light pink, it is full of youthful vigour, with strong, yet delicate, watermelon and spice flavours, fresh acidity, and a dry (2 grams/litre of residual sugar), lingering finish. Best drinking 2021+.

DRY $35 –V

Jules Taylor The Jules Rosé   (★★★★☆)

The delicious 2020 vintage (★★★★☆) is perfect 'with cucumber sandwiches'. Made from Merlot grown in Gisborne, it is bright pink, mouthfilling and lively, with fresh, strong berry, plum, watermelon and spice flavours, and a finely poised, dry (3.6 grams/litre of residual sugar) finish.

Vintage	20	DRY $25 V+
WR	5	
Drink	20-22	

Kahurangi Estate Nelson Rosé   ★★★☆

Already drinking well, the 2020 vintage (★★★☆) is a bright pink, fruity wine with very good depth of fresh, lively, berryish, plummy flavours, balanced acidity, and an off-dry finish.

MED/DRY $17 V+

Karikari Estate Calypso Rosé   (★★★)

Still on sale, the 2018 vintage (★★★) was grown on the Karikari Peninsula, in Northland. A blend of Merlot and Syrah, it has deep orange colour, in a mouthfilling, dry style with peachy, spicy flavours. Don't expect 'fresh and fruity', but this is a distinctive wine, ready to roll.

DRY $27 –V

Kina Beach Vineyard Nelson Pinot Noir Rosé   (★★★☆)

Estate-grown at a coastal site, the 2019 vintage (★★★☆) is bright pink, crisp and lively. Medium-bodied, it has fresh berry and plum flavours, balanced for good, easy drinking over the summer of 2020–21.

MED/DRY $20 AV

Kina Cliffs Three Girls Blush Nelson Pinot Rosé   (★★★★)

Made from Pinot Noir, the charming 2019 vintage (★★★★) is bright pink, with a floral bouquet. A vivacious, harmonious wine, it is vibrantly fruity, with cherryish, plummy flavours, a sliver of sweetness (7 grams/litre of residual sugar), and a smooth finish.

MED/DRY $25 AV

Lake Chalice The Falcon Marlborough Rosé   ★★★

The 2019 vintage (★★★☆) was 'made seriously for serious fun'. Very pale pink, it is a blend of Pinot Gris and Malbec, grown in the central Wairau Valley. Vibrantly fruity, it is medium-bodied, with fresh, peachy, slightly spicy flavours, lively acidity, and a dry finish.

DRY $19 AV

Landing, The, Bay of Islands Rosé   ★★★☆

Pale pink, the 2019 vintage (★★★☆) of this Northland rosé is a blend of Merlot and Syrah. Medium to full-bodied, it has peach, spice and strawberry flavours, a hint of apricot, and a dry (4 grams/litre of residual sugar), very smooth finish.

DRY $27 –V

Lawson's Dry Hills Pink Pinot   (★★★★☆)

The 2019 vintage (★★★★☆) is a characterful Marlborough rosé, brimful of flavour. Bright pink, it has generous strawberry and watermelon flavours, slightly spicy notes, and excellent vigour and length, with a dry (2.9 grams/litre of residual sugar) finish.

Vintage	19
WR	6
Drink	P

DRY $25 V+

Left Field Hawke's Bay Rosé   ★★★★

Bright pink, the 2020 vintage (★★★★) is a top buy. Delicious young, it is very fresh, with vibrant, delicate watermelon and spice flavours and a very harmonious, almost dry (4.5 grams/litre of residual sugar) finish. (From Te Awa.)

Vintage	20
WR	7
Drink	20-22

DRY $18 V+

Leveret Estate Hawke's Bay Rosé   (★★★☆)

Bright, light pink, the 2019 vintage (★★★☆) was 30 per cent barrel-fermented and made in a basically dry (4.5 grams/litre of residual sugar) style. Fresh and lively, it has finely balanced acidity, and very good depth of watermelon and peach flavours.

DRY $22 AV

Luna Martinborough Rosé   ★★★★☆

From Pinot Meunier and Pinot Noir vines in the Blue Rock Vineyard, the lovely 2019 vintage (★★★★★) was made with some use of barrel fermentation. Bright pink, it is floral, sweet-fruited and full-bodied, with strong, yet delicate, cherry, strawberry and watermelon flavours, rich, dry (3 grams/litre of residual sugar) and smooth.

DRY $26 AV

Madam Sass Central Otago Pinot Noir Rosé   ★★★★

Scented, pink and lively, the 2019 vintage (★★★★) is a single-vineyard wine, made from Pinot Noir grown at Bendigo. Crisp and vivacious, it has strong strawberry, watermelon and spice flavours, with a sliver of sweetness balanced by refreshing acidity.

MED/DRY $25 AV

Main Divide North Canterbury Rosé   ★★★★

The fresh, vivacious 2019 vintage (★★★★) is a blend of Pinot Noir, Cabernet Sauvignon and Cabernet Franc. Bright, light pink, it has strong, yet delicate, flavours of peaches, srawberries and watermelon, and a slightly sweet (6 grams/litre of residual sugar), crisp finish.

Vintage	19	18
WR	5	6
Drink	P	P

MED/DRY $21 V+

Maison Noire Hawke's Bay Rosé ★★★☆

From hand-harvested grapes, the bright, light pink 2020 vintage (★★★☆) is light and lively, with good depth of youthful watermelon and spice flavours, peachy notes, and a dry (3 grams/litre of residual sugar) finish. Best drinking 2021+.

Vintage	17
WR	6
Drink	P

DRY $20 AV

Man O' War Waiheke and Ponui Islands Pinque Rosé ★★★★

Estate-grown at the eastern end of Waiheke Island and on the adjacent Ponui Island, the 2020 vintage (★★★★) is bright pink, fresh, light-bodied and lively, with gentle strawberry and spice flavours, and a crisp, bone-dry (0.7 grams/litre of residual sugar), lingering finish.

DRY $28 –V

Maori Point Single Vineyard Central Otago Pinot Noir Rosé ★★★★

Estate-grown and hand-picked at Tarras, in the Cromwell Basin, the 2020 vintage (★★★★) is a bright pink wine with vibrant watermelon, strawberry and spice flavours, a sliver of sweetness and a seductively smooth finish. Full-bodied, yet with a sense of lightness, it's delicious young.

MED/DRY $25 AV

Marsden Bay of Islands Rosé ★★★☆

The 2020 vintage (★★★☆) of this Northland rosé was made principally from Merlot. A medium-bodied wine, it is lively, with good depth of strawberry and peach flavours, a hint of apricot, and an off-dry, smooth finish. Fresh, attractive drinking.

MED/DRY $20 AV

Matawhero Single Vineyard Gisborne Pinot Rosé ★★★★

The attractive, pale pink 2019 vintage (★★★★) was made from Pinot Noir. Very fresh and lively, it is medium-bodied, with delicate watermelon and spice flavours, a hint of apricot, appetising acidity, and a smooth (4.5 grams/litre of residual sugar) finish.

DRY $23 AV

Maui Waipara Rosé (★★☆)

The 2019 vintage (★★☆) was blended from Pinot Noir (70 per cent) and Pinot Gris (30 per cent). Pink/pale red, it has fresh, berryish flavours, which show a slight lack of delicacy, some earthy notes, and an off-dry (6 grams/litre of residual sugar) finish. Solid but plain.

MED/DRY $20 –V

ME by Matahiwi Estate New Zealand Rosé (★★★☆)

The 2020 vintage (★★★☆) was grown in the Wairarapa. Bright pink/pale red, it is vibrantly fruity, with fresh, berryish aromas and flavours, finely balanced, dryish (5 grams/litre of residual sugar) and smooth. Good drinking for the summer of 2020–21.

MED/DRY $20 AV

Middle-Earth Nelson Pinot Meunier Rosé (★★★☆)

Bright, light pink, the easy-drinking 2020 vintage (★★★☆) was made solely from Pinot Meunier, a variety planted widely in Champagne. Freshly scented, it is medium-bodied, with good depth of peach, watermelon and spice flavours, and fresh acidity keeping things lively.

 MED/DRY $21 AV

Mills Reef Reserve Hawke's Bay Rosé ★★★★

The generous 2020 vintage (★★★★) is already delicious. Bright pink, it has very good body and depth of berryish, slightly spicy flavours, and a smooth, basically dry (4.7 grams/litre of residual sugar) finish.

Vintage	20
WR	7
Drink	21-23

 DRY $25 AV

Misha's Vineyard The Soloist Central Otago Pinot Rosé ★★★★☆

The 2019 vintage (★★★★☆) was made from Pinot Noir, estate-grown at Bendigo. Bright pink, it has vibrant strawberry, watermelon, peach and spice flavours, showing excellent freshness, delicacy and depth, balanced acidity, and a finely poised, dry (4 grams/litre of residual sugar) finish.

Vintage	19	18	17	16
WR	6	7	6	7
Drink	20-23	20-22	20-21	P

 DRY $27 AV

Mission Hawke's Bay Rosé ★★★☆

The bright pink, very pale red 2019 vintage (★★★☆) was blended from red-wine varieties. Very fresh and lively, it has good depth of vibrant strawberry, watermelon and spice flavours, slightly peachy notes, and a finely balanced, dryish finish. Good value.

MED/DRY $16 V+

Mission Vineyard Selection Hawke's Bay Rosé ★★★☆

The highly attractive 2019 vintage (★★★★) is fragrant and full-bodied. Made mostly from Merlot and Cabernet Sauvignon, with a splash of Syrah, it is pink/very pale red, with generous strawberry and spice flavours, a hint of apricot, and a finely poised, dry (4 grams/litre of residual sugar) finish.

 DRY $20 AV

Momo Organic Marlborough Rosé (★★★★☆)

Already delicious, the 2020 vintage (★★★★☆) from Seresin is a bright pink, finely poised wine with peach, strawberry and watermelon flavours, showing excellent delicacy and depth, and a dry finish. Certified organic.

 DRY $18 V+

Mondillo Central Otago Rosé ★★★★

The 2020 vintage (★★★★) was made from Pinot Noir, estate-grown at Bendigo. Bright pink, it is fragrant and very lively, with vibrant, plummy flavours, fresh acidity, and a dryish (5.7 grams/litre of residual sugar), smooth finish. Best drinking mid-2021+.

MED/DRY $28 –V

Montana New Zealand Collection Delicate & Fruity Marlborough Rosé (★★★☆)

Made from Pinot Noir, the very easy-drinking 2019 vintage (★★★☆) is pale pink and freshly scented, with good depth of lively strawberry, peach and spice flavours, and an off-dry finish.

MED/DRY $20 AV

Mount Brown Estates North Canterbury Rosé ★★★☆

Offering good drinking for the summer of 2020–21, the 2020 vintage (★★★☆) is not labelled by variety. Bright pink, it is a freshly scented, lively, medium-bodied wine, with gentle watermelon and berry flavours, showing good delicacy and depth, and an off-dry (7 grams/litre of residual sugar) finish. Priced sharply.

Vintage	20
WR	6
Drink	20-22

MED/DRY $16 V+

Mount Edward Central Otago Rosé (★★★★☆)

The salmon pink 2019 vintage (★★★★☆) was grown in the Muirkirk Vineyard at Bannockburn, fermented with indigenous yeasts and handled entirely in tanks. Fragrant and full-bodied, it has strong, peachy, spicy, strawberryish flavours, a hint of apricot, fresh acidity, and a dry finish. Delicious young, it's ready to roll.

DRY $29 AV

Mount Riley The Bonnie Marlborough Pinot Rosé ★★★☆

The 2020 vintage (★★★☆) is a bright, light pink wine, blended from Pinot Noir and Pinot Gris. A drink-young charmer, it is very lively, with good depth of watermelon and strawberry flavours, hints of peaches and spices, and a dryish finish.

DRY $17 V+

Moutere Hills Nelson Pinot Rosé ★★★☆

The 2019 vintage (★★★★) is a light pink, single-vineyard wine, grown near Brightwater, on the Waimea Plains. Fresh and lively, it is medium-bodied, with vivacious strawberry, watermelon and spice flavours, dry and lingering.

DRY $25 –V

Mt Beautiful North Canterbury Rosé ★★★★

Full of personality, the 2019 vintage (★★★★☆) is a blend of co-fermented Pinot Noir (65 per cent) and Pinot Gris (35 per cent). Pink/orange, it is fragrant and mouthfilling, with concentrated peach, strawberry and spice flavours, hints of watermelon and apricot, balanced acidity, and a dry (2 grams/litre of residual sugar), lingering finish.

DRY $22 V+

Mt Rosa Central Otago Rosé (★★★★☆)

Delicious from the start, the 2019 vintage (★★★★☆) from this Gibbston-based producer was made solely from Gamay. Pink/pale red, it is floral and vibrantly fruity, with generous, berryish, plummy flavours, fresh acidity, and a dry (2 grams/litre of residual sugar), smooth finish.

DRY $28 AV

Nga Waka Martinborough Rosé ★★★★

Priced right, the 2019 vintage (★★★☆) is 'essentially our Nga Waka Pinot Noir, without the colour, tannin and oak'. Pink-hued, with a hint of development, it is fresh, crisp and lively, with peach, watermelon and spice flavours, and a dry finish. Ready.

DRY $18 V+

O:TU Hawke's Bay Rosé ★★★☆

The refreshing 2020 vintage (★★★☆) is a bright pink wine, made from Merlot. Fresh and lively, it is medium-bodied, with good depth of strawberry, watermelon and spice flavours, and a dry (3.8 grams/litre of residual sugar) finish.

DRY $20 AV

Obsidian Estate Waiheke Island Rosé ★★★★☆

Estate-grown and hand-harvested, the 2019 vintage (★★★★☆) is a blend of Tempranillo and Merlot. Pink/pale red, it is mouthfilling, smooth and dry, with good concentration of strawberryish, spicy flavours, a touch of tannin, and a lengthy finish.

DRY $29 AV

Ohau Not the Norm Pinot Rosé (★★★★)

Grown in the Horowhenua, on the west coast of the North Island (itself 'Not the Norm', in terms of wine regions), the attractive 2019 vintage (★★★★) is also a bit different in terms of its sweetness (9.8 grams/litre of residual sugar). Blended from Pinot Gris and Pinot Noir, it is bright pink, fresh and lively, with strong peach, strawberry and spice flavours, a hint of apricots, and lots of drink-young charm.

MED/DRY $24 AV

Opawa Marlborough Pinot Noir Rosé ★★★★

The 2020 vintage (★★★★☆) is impressive. Showing strong personality, it is pink/pale orange, with very satisfying depth of strawberry, peach and spice flavours, a distinct touch of complexity, and a finely balanced (5 grams/litre of residual sugar), lingering finish. Excellent drinking for the summer of 2020–21.

MED/DRY $22 V+

Oyster Bay Marlborough Rosé ★★★★

The fresh, medium-bodied 2019 vintage (★★★★) was made from Pinot Noir. Bright, pale pink, it is vibrantly fruity, with watermelon and spice flavours, slightly peachy notes, good intensity and a dry finish.

Pā Road Marlborough Rosé ★★★

Balanced for easy drinking, the pale pink 2019 vintage (★★★) is fresh and light, with gentle strawberry and spice flavours, hints of peaches and watermelon, and a crisp, smooth finish. (From te Pā.)

Paddy Borthwick Wairarapa Pinot Rosé ★★★★☆

Full of drink-young charm, the vivacious 2020 vintage (★★★★★) was estate-grown at Gladstone, in the northern Wairarapa. Bright pink, it is full-bodied, vibrantly fruity and dry, with strong watermelon and spice flavours, showing excellent delicacy and depth.

Pask Instinct Berry Blush Rosé ★★★☆

The easy-drinking 2020 vintage (★★★☆) was grown in Hawke's Bay. Bright, light pink, it is fresh and lively, with good depth of peach, strawberry and spice flavours, and a dryish (4.6 grams/litre of residual sugar), smooth finish. Good value.

Pinot 3 – The Pink Edition ★★★★

The 2019 and 2020 vintages offer good value. The 2019 vintage (★★★★) is a blend of Pinot Noir, Pinot Gris and Pinot Blanc, grown in Marlborough and Gisborne, and handled in old oak barriques. Bright, light pink, it is highly fragrant, with generous peach, watermelon and spice flavours, showing a distinct touch of complexity, and a smooth finish. The 2020 vintage (★★★★) is bright pink, very fresh and lively, with good intensity of strawberry and watermelon flavours, and a dry, lingering finish. (From Untitled Wines, based in West Auckland.)

DRY $20 V+

Q Waitaki Valley Rosé (★★★★★)

The delicious 2019 vintage (★★★★★) is a single-vineyard, Waitaki Valley wine. Made from Pinot Noir and partly barrel-fermented, it is weighty, dry (2 grams/litre of residual sugar) and smooth, with mouthfilling body, fresh acidity, and rich strawberry, watermelon and spice flavours. Pink/faint orange, it's a very finely balanced, complex wine, full of personality.

Rapaura Springs Reserve Marlborough Pinot Rosé   ★★★★

Enjoyable from the start, the 2019 vintage (★★★★) is pale pink, fresh and mouthfilling, with very good depth of peachy, spicy flavours, a hint of apricot, and an off-dry (6.8 grams/litre of residual sugar) finish. A 50:50 blend of Pinot Noir and Pinot Gris, it offers fine value.

Vintage	20	19
WR	6	6
Drink	20-24	20-21

MED/DRY $19 V+

Redmetal Vineyards Bridge Pa Triangle Hawke's Bay Cabernet Franc Rosé   ★★★★

The 2020 vintage (★★★★) is a bright pink blend of Cabernet Franc (86 per cent), Albariño (13 per cent) and Syrah (1 per cent), lees-aged for three months. Full-bodied, it has strong, youthful berry, plum and spice flavours, with a dry (2.8 grams/litre of residual sugar) finish.

Vintage	20
WR	5
Drink	20-22

DRY $22 V+

Rogue Vine Bay of Islands Rosé   (★★★☆)

Grown in Northland, the very easy-drinking 2020 vintage (★★★☆) is pink and full-bodied, with generous stone-fruit flavours, a hint of spice, gentle acidity and a smooth, slightly off-dry (5 grams/litre of residual sugar) finish.

MED/DRY $21 AV

Ruru Central Otago Rosé   ★★★★

From Immigrant's Vineyard, at Alexandra, the bright pink 2019 vintage (★★★★) was made from hand-picked Pinot Noir. Freshly scented, it is vivacious, with very good depth of strawberry, watermelon and spice flavours, and a finely balanced, off-dry (5 grams/litre of residual sugar) finish. Drink now to 2021. Good value.

MED/DRY $20 V+

Sacred Hill Reserve Marlborough Pinot Noir Rosé   (★★★☆)

The 2019 vintage (★★★☆) is a bright pink, attractively scented wine with good depth of lively red-berry and plum flavours, fresh acidity, and an off-dry, smooth finish.

MED/DRY $22 AV

Saddleback Central Otago Pinot Noir Rosé   (★★★★)

From Peregrine, the 2019 vintage (★★★★) is a very easy-drinking wine, hand-picked at Pisa and Gibbston. Pink-hued, it is invitingly aromatic, with strong, lively strawberry and spice flavours, and a crisp, off-dry finish. Delicious young.

MED/DRY $20 V+

Saint Clair Origin Marlborough Pinot Gris Rosé ★★★☆

The 2019 vintage (★★★☆) is a bright, light pink wine, made principally from Pinot Gris, blended with Pinot Noir. Drinking well from the start, it is fresh and vibrantly fruity, with peachy, strawberryish, slightly spicy flavours, a touch of tannin, and very good depth.

DRY $20 AV

Seifried Nelson Pinot Noir Rosé (★★★★)

The very charming 2019 vintage (★★★★) is pale pink, with a floral, scented bouquet. A vivacious wine, it has vibrant plum, red-berry, strawberry and spice flavours, with an off-dry (5.6 grams/litre of residual sugar) finish. Fine value.

MED/DRY $18 V+

Sherwood Estate Stoney Range Waipara Valley Rosé ★★★★

Showing good personality and priced sharply, the 2019 vintage (★★★★) was blended from Pinot Noir, Pinot Gris and Syrah. Very pale pink, it has strong peach, strawberry, watermelon and spice flavours, a hint of apricot, and a crisp, dry finish.

DRY $18 V+

Sileni Cellar Selection Hawke's Bay Cabernet Franc Rosé ★★★☆

The 2019 vintage (★★★★) is a pale pink, fresh and lively wine, with generous peach, spice and watermelon flavours, a hint of apricot, and a finely balanced, basically dry (4.2 grams/litre of residual sugar) finish.

DRY $20 AV

Snapper Rock Marlborough Sauvignon Rosé (★★★☆)

The 2020 vintage (★★★☆) is a blend of Sauvignon Blanc and Pinot Noir. Bright pink, with freshly herbaceous aromas, it is crisp and lively, with punchy strawberry, watermelon and spice flavours, and a basically dry (4 grams/litre of residual sugar) finish. Priced right.

DRY $17 V+

Spy Valley Pinot Noir Marlborough Rosé ★★★★☆

The bright pink 2019 vintage (★★★★☆) was grown in the Waihopai and Wairau valleys. A vivacious dry wine (4 grams/litre of residual sugar), it has strong strawberry and spice flavours, a hint of apricot, fresh acidity, and a finely poised, long finish. Drink now to 2021.

DRY $25 V+

Stables Ngatarawa Rosé ★★☆

Bright pink, the 2020 vintage (★★☆) is a blend of varieties grown in Hawke's Bay. A pleasant but simple wine, it has lively, herbaceous, berryish flavours, slightly sweet and crisp. Drink young. (From Mission.)

MED/DRY $16 AV

Stoneleigh Lighter Marlborough Rosé   (★★☆)

Very pale pink, the easy-drinking 2020 vintage (★★☆) is a low-alcohol (9 per cent) style. Crisp and light-bodied, it is fresh, with watermelon-like flavours, hints of peaches and spices, and an off-dry, crisp finish. Priced right.

MED/DRY $14 AV

Stoneleigh Marlborough Pinot Noir Rosé   ★★★☆

Full of drink-young charm, the lively 2020 vintage (★★★★) is pale pink, with fresh, strong, peachy, strawberryish flavours and a finely balanced, off-dry finish. Showing very good vigour and depth, it offers fine value.

MED/DRY $17 V+

Stoneleigh Organic Marlborough Rosé   (★★★★)

Certified organic, the 2020 vintage (★★★★) is a bright, light pink, full-bodied wine with generous, fresh strawberry and spice flavours, a hint of apricot, and a well-rounded finish. Delicious young.

MED/DRY $18 V+

Stoneleigh Wild Valley Marlborough Rosé   ★★★☆

Tasted in September 2020, the 2019 vintage (★★★) is soft and ready. It was produced from Pinot Noir, fermented with indigenous ('wild') yeasts – hence the Wild Valley brand. Pink/orange, it is full-bodied, with good depth of peachy, slightly spicy flavours and an off-dry finish.

MED/DRY $18 V+

Summerhouse Marlborough Pinot Rosé   ★★★★

The 2020 vintage (★★★☆) is labelled 'Pinot', rather than Pinot Noir, suggesting the inclusion of Pinot Gris. Bright, light pink, it is very lively, with fresh, gentle watermelon and spice flavours, a hint of apricot, and a finely poised, dryish (4.8 grams/litre of residual sugar) finish.

Vintage	20	19
WR	7	6
Drink	20-24	P

DRY $19 V+

Te Awa Single Estate Hawke's Bay Cabernet Franc Rosé   (★★★★★)

The classy, distinctive 2020 vintage (★★★★★) was handled without oak. Light pink, it is full-bodied, with an array of peach, strawberry, watermelon and spice flavours, showing excellent vigour, delicacy and length, and a fresh, dry (2 grams/litre of residual sugar) finish. Well worth trying.

Vintage	20
WR	7
Drink	20-22

DRY $25 V+

Te Kairanga Martinborough Pinot Rosé ★★★★☆

Full of drink-young charm, the 2019 vintage (★★★★☆) is a bright pink, full-bodied wine. It has watermelon and spice flavours, showing excellent vibrancy, delicacy and depth, and an off-dry (9.9 grams/litre of residual sugar) finish.

 MED/DRY $25 V+

te Pā Marlborough Pinot Noir Rosé ★★★★

The 2020 vintage (★★★★) offers delicious drinking for this summer. Pale pink, it is very fresh and lively, with strawberry, watermelon and spice flavours, a hint of apricot, and a dry finish (3 grams/litre of residual sugar).

 DRY $19 V+

Terra Sancta Bannockburn Central Otago Pinot Noir Rosé ★★★★★

From one vintage to the next, this is one of the country's leading rosés. The 2019 vintage (★★★★★) was mostly handled in tanks, but a significant 40 per cent of the blend was fermented and aged in old French oak barriques. Bright, pale pink, it is vibrantly fruity, with strong peach, strawberry and spice flavours, showing excellent delicacy and freshness, and a dryish (5.4 grams/litre of residual sugar), lingering finish.

Vintage	19	18	17
WR	7	7	7
Drink	20-22	20-21	P

 MED/DRY $28 V+

Terra Sancta Special Release First Vines Pinot Noir Rosé ★★★★★

This unusually complex wine is New Zealand's highest-priced rosé to date. The 2019 vintage (★★★★★), estate-grown in Central Otago, was hand-picked from vines planted at Bannockburn in 1991 and 1995, and fermented with indigenous yeasts in large old French oak barrels. Pale pink, it is full-bodied, with notable depth of peach, strawberry and spice flavours, showing considerable complexity, fresh acidity, and a dry (2 grams/litre of residual sugar), lasting finish. Well worth discovering.

Vintage	19	18
WR	7	7
Drink	20-27	20-26

DRY $55 AV

Terrace Edge North Canterbury Rosé ★★★★★

Certified organic, the 2020 vintage (★★★★☆) was made principally from Syrah grapes, grown at Waipara. Bright pink, it is still unfolding, with good intensity of vibrant peach, strawberry and spice flavours, a touch of tannin, and an off-dry (6 grams/litre of residual sugar), lingering finish.

 MED/DRY $24 V+

Tiki Estate Waipara Pinot Noir Rosé   ★★★☆

The 2019 vintage (★★★★) is a real charmer. Bright pink/very pale red, it is finely balanced, with strong, vibrant plum, red-berry and watermelon flavours, and an off-dry (6 grams/litre of residual sugar), smooth finish.

Vintage	19
WR	6
Drink	20-21

MED/DRY $24 –V

Tohu Nelson Pinot Rosé   ★★★★

Estate-grown at Upper Moutere, the 2019 vintage (★★★★) was made from Pinot Noir. Bright pink/pale red, it has fresh, berryish scents and flavours, in a very lively, buoyantly fruity style, with a dry (4.4 grams/litre of residual sugar) finish. Fine value.

Vintage	19
WR	6
Drink	20-22

DRY $18 V+

Two Paddocks Rosé   (★★★★★)

The 2019 vintage (★★★★★) is an auspicious debut. Made from Pinot Noir, estate-grown in the Last Chance Vineyard at Earnscleugh, near Alexandra, it is bright pink/pale red, with very fresh, berryish aromas. Mouthfilling, it is rich and lively, with vibrant strawberry, watermelon and spice flavours, and a crisp, basically dry (4 grams/litre of residual sugar) finish. Delicious from the start, it's certified organic.

DRY $33 AV

Two Rivers New Zealand Isle of Beauty Rosé   ★★★★☆

Grown at four sites in the Southern Valleys of Marlborough, the 2020 vintage (★★★★☆) is a 'field blend of multiple red and white varieties'. It was handled mostly in stainless steel tanks, but a small portion of the blend was fermented and aged for 10 weeks in concrete, egg-shaped tanks. Pale pink, it is a vivacious, medium-bodied wine with fresh, youthful, strawberryish flavours, hints of spices and apricots, good intensity, and a dry (1.3 grams/litre of residual sugar), lingering finish. Well worth trying.

Vintage	20
WR	7
Drink	20-22

 DRY $24 V+

Two Sisters Central Otago Pinot Rosé   (★★★★)

The vivacious 2019 vintage (★★★★) is a single-vineyard wine, hand-picked at Lowburn, in the Cromwell Basin. Bright pink, it is medium-bodied, with fresh, strong watermelon and spice flavours, crisp, dry and finely balanced.

Vintage	19
WR	7
Drink	20-21

DRY $30 –V

Untitled Pink Blend ★★★★

The first release, from the 2018 vintage (★★★★), was grown mostly in Auckland and Marlborough, and handled in old oak barriques. Bright, light pink, it is lively, with strong, peachy, spicy flavours, showing a touch of complexity, gentle tannins and a dry finish. The non-vintage wine (★★★★) I tasted in August 2020 is pale pink, mouthfilling and lively, with fresh, ripe flavours of watermelon, peaches and spices, and a dry, crisp finish. (From Untitled Wines, based in West Auckland.)

DRY $20 V+

Urlar Gladstone Pinot Rosé (★★★★☆)

Already drinking well, the very fresh and lively 2020 vintage (★★★★☆) was grown in the northern Wairarapa and fermented in seasoned oak barrels. Pink/very pale red, it is mouthfilling, with concentrated berry, plum and spice flavours, a touch of tannin, and a basically dry (less than 5 grams/litre of residual sugar) finish.

DRY $25 V+

Vavasour Awatere Valley Marlborough Rosé ★★★★★

The classy 2019 vintage (★★★★★) is pink/pale red, with loads of youthful vigour and charm. It has fresh, strong strawberry, watermelon and spice flavours, with a dry (3.6 grams/litre of residual sugar), lasting finish. Top drinking.

DRY $23 V+

Villa Maria Cellar Selection Marlborough Pinot Rosé ★★★★

Made from Pinot Noir, the 2020 vintage (★★★☆) is a pink, floral, vibrant wine, medium-bodied, with fresh, youthful, straightforward strawberry/spice flavours, and a dry (3 grams/litre of residual sugar) finish.

Vintage	20
WR	7
Drink	20-22

DRY $15 V+

Villa Maria Private Bin Hawke's Bay Rosé ★★★★

The 2020 vintage (★★★★) is a pink-hued, mouthfilling wine with ripe watermelon, strawberry and spice flavours, a hint of apricot, and a fresh, smooth, finely balanced (4.5 grams/litre of residual sugar) finish. Great value.

Vintage	20
WR	7
Drink	20-22

DRY $15 V+

Villa Maria Single Vineyard The Attorney Marlborough Pinot Noir Rosé (★★★★☆)

Certified organic, the delicious 2019 vintage (★★★★☆) is a bright pink wine, grown in the Southern Valleys. Invitingly floral, it is medium-bodied and sweet-fruited, with cherryish, slightly spicy flavours, balanced acidity, and excellent depth.

DRY $30 –V

Waimea Nelson Pinot Noir Rosé   (★★★★☆)

Instantly appealing, the 2020 vintage (★★★★☆) is an attractively scented, pale pink wine. It is very lively, with fresh, strong, strawberryish, slightly peachy and spicy flavours, finely balanced for the summer of 2020–21.

MED/DRY $20 V+

Waipara Hills Waipara Valley Pinot Noir Rosé   ★★★★

The 2019 vintage (★★★★) is a bright pink, vivacious wine, grown in the Home Block (mostly) and briefly lees-aged. Medium-bodied, it is fresh and vibrant, with lively strawberry and spice flavours, a touch of tannin, and a basically dry (4.2 grams/litre of residual sugar), appetisingly crisp finish. Fine value.

DRY $18 V+

Westbrook Single Vineyard Waimauku Crackling Rosé   ★★★☆

The bright pink 2020 vintage (★★★☆) is a spritzing (gently bubbly) style, with fresh, lively berry and plum flavours, a hint of watermelon, good delicacy and vibrancy, and a slightly sweet, crisp finish.

MED/DRY $25 –V

Whitehaven Marlborough Pinot Noir Rosé   ★★★★

Showing plenty of personality, the attractively scented 2019 vintage (★★★★☆) is a light pink, mouthfilling wine, with strawberryish, spicy flavours, peachy notes, a touch of tannin, and a dry, lasting finish. A 'serious' but vivacious wine, it's delicious now.

DRY $23 AV

Wild Earth Central Otago Pinot Noir Rosé   (★★★★☆)

Full of drink-young charm, the 2019 vintage (★★★★☆) is a single-vineyard wine, hand-picked at Gibbston. Freshly scented, it is very lively, with strong, strawberryish, spicy flavours, and a crisp, finely balanced finish.

DRY $29 AV

Yealands Estate Single Vineyard Awatere Valley Marlborough Pinot Noir Rosé   (★★★★)

Estate-grown, the 2019 vintage (★★★★) is pink/pale red, dryish and smooth, with strong, strawberryish, slightly spicy flavours, a touch of tannin, fresh acidity and a slightly creamy finish.

DRY $25 AV

Yealands Marlborough Rosé   (★★★★)

The bargain-priced 2020 vintage (★★★★) is already delicious. A blend of Pinot Gris and Pinot Noir, it is pale pink, fresh and vibrant, with good intensity of strawberry, spice and peach flavours, and a basically dry (4 grams/litre of residual sugar) finish.

Vintage	20
WR	6
Drink	20-22

DRY $15 V+

Zephyr MK I Rosé   (★★★★☆)

A single-vineyard Marlborough wine, the 2019 vintage (★★★★☆) is bright pink, crisp and vivacious, with watermelon, strawberry and spice flavours, showing excellent intensity, and a long, dry finish. (From Glover Family Wines.)

DRY $28 AV

Red Wines

Branded and Other Red Wines

Most New Zealand red wines carry a varietal label, such as Pinot Noir, Syrah, Merlot or Cabernet Sauvignon (or blends of the last two). Those not labelled prominently by their principal grape varieties – often prestigious wines such as Te Mata Coleraine or Esk Valley Heipipi The Terraces – can be found here. Although not varietally labelled, these wines are mostly of high quality and sometimes outstanding.

Alpha Domus AD The Aviator   ★★★★★

Estate-grown in the Bridge Pa Triangle, this is a blend of classic Bordeaux varieties. The outstanding 2015 vintage (★★★★★) is a marriage of Cabernet Sauvignon (50 per cent), Cabernet Franc (22 per cent), Merlot (21 per cent) and Malbec (7 per cent). Matured in French oak barriques (46 per cent new), it is deeply coloured, with a fragrant, very refined bouquet. Full-bodied, it is youthful, with concentrated, deliciously ripe blackcurrant, plum and spice flavours, excellent complexity, and a long finish. A very elegant, rich wine, showing lovely delicacy and depth, it's already very approachable, but likely to be at its best 2021+.

Vintage	15	DRY $98 AV
WR	7	
Drink	20-25	🍇🍇

Awaroa Waiheke Island The Dan   (★★★★☆)

The distinctive 2017 vintage (★★★★☆) is a youthful blend of Syrah (50 per cent) and Cabernet Sauvignon (40 per cent), with small amounts of Merlot and Malbec. Matured for a year in French oak barriques (100 per cent new), it is deeply coloured, fragrant and full-bodied, with good density of blackcurrant, plum and spice flavours, hints of olives and herbs, savoury, nutty notes adding complexity, and good tannin backbone.

DRY $75 –V

Babich Heritage Anniversary Label Hawke's Bay Premium Red Blend   (★★★★★)

Clad in the company's Cabernet Sauvignon label from the 1970s, the classy 2016 vintage (★★★★★) is a celebration of Babich's 100-year history, produced in quite large volumes (about 1000 cases). French oak-matured for 15 months, it is a blend of Cabernet Sauvignon, Merlot and Cabernet Franc, grown in the Gimblett Gravels and French oak-aged for 16 months. A very elegant, 'complete' wine, it is deeply coloured, with concentrated blackcurrant, plum and spice flavours, showing excellent complexity, fine-grained tannins, and impressive vigour and harmony.

DRY $80 AV

Babich The Patriarch ★★★★★

This is promoted as Babich's greatest red, regardless of the variety or region of origin, but all vintages have been grown in the company's shingly Irongate Vineyard in Gimblett Road, Hawke's Bay (in other words, they have been Cabernet Sauvignon or Merlot-based blends, rather than Pinot Noirs from further south). It is typically a dark, ripe and complex, deliciously rich red. The 2016 vintage (★★★★★) is a boldly coloured blend of Merlot (40 per cent), Malbec (33 per cent) and Cabernet Sauvignon (27 per cent), matured for 16 months in French oak barriques. A powerful young wine, it is sturdy, with concentrated, ripe berry, plum and spice flavours, finely integrated oak, good tannin backbone, and obvious potential. Well worth cellaring to 2022+.

Vintage	16	15	14	13	12	11	10
WR	6	7	7	7	5	5	7
Drink	20-26	20-25	20-25	20-25	20-21	P	20-22

DRY $90 AV

Boneline, The, Waipara Iridium (★★★★★)

Deeply coloured, the 2016 vintage (★★★★★) is a commanding North Canterbury red, blended from Cabernet Franc, Merlot and Cabernet Sauvignon. Matured in French oak casks (35 per cent new), it has a fragrant, slightly herbal bouquet, leading into a sturdy wine (15 per cent alcohol), with notable density. Youthful, it has highly concentrated blackcurrant, plum, herb and spice flavours, with a firmly structured, lasting finish. A very distinctive red, it's well worth cellaring to 2022+.

DRY $50 AV

Brick Bay Martello Rock ★★★★

The 2019 vintage (★★★★) is a blend of Malbec, Merlot and Petit Verdot, estate-grown at Matakana and matured for nine months in French oak casks (partly new). Still very youthful, it has deep, purple-flushed colour and a fresh, spicy bouquet. Mouthfilling and fruit-packed, it has strong, plummy, berryish, spicy flavours, fresh acidity and obvious potential; best drinking 2022+.

DRY $52 –V

Brick Bay Pharos ★★★★☆

Still unfolding, the 2015 vintage (★★★★★) is a blend of Merlot and Petit Verdot, with minor portions of Cabernet Franc and Malbec, estate-grown at Matakana and matured in French oak barriques (mostly new). Full-coloured, with good personality, it is mouthfilling, savoury and complex, with obvious cellaring potential. Plummy and spicy, with a slightly earthy streak, it is strongly flavoured, ripe and finely textured, with a long finish.

DRY $68 –V

Clearview Hawke's Bay Enigma ★★★★★

Entirely estate-grown at Te Awanga, the lovely 2016 vintage (★★★★★) is a deeply coloured blend of Merlot (70 per cent), Malbec (20 per cent) and Cabernet Franc (10 per cent), matured for 16 months in French oak casks (40 per cent new). Sturdy, rich and youthful, it has concentrated blackcurrant, plum and spice flavours, savoury and complex, a hint of dark chocolate, fine-grained tannins and obvious cellaring potential. Already drinking well, it's a very 'complete' wine, likely to be at its best 2021+.

DRY $55 AV

Clearview Old Olive Block ★★★★★

This Hawke's Bay red is named after the estate vineyard at Te Awanga, which has an old olive tree in the centre. It is grown there and in the Gimblett Gravels. Still youthful, the 2016 vintage (★★★★★) is a deeply coloured blend of Cabernet Sauvignon (63 per cent), Malbec (20 per cent) and Cabernet Franc (17 per cent), matured for 16 months in French oak casks (25 per cent new). Grown principally (70 per cent) in the Gimblett Gravels, it is well worth cellaring, with a fragrant, slightly herbal bouquet and concentrated blackcurrant, herb and spice flavours. Complex, savoury and nutty, it is an elegant, very finely structured red, likely to break into full stride from 2021 onwards.

Vintage	16	15
WR	6	6
Drink	21-26	20-25

DRY $45 AV

Clearview The Basket Press ★★★★★

The distinguished 2016 vintage (★★★★★) is a blend of Cabernet Sauvignon (41 per cent), Merlot (39 per cent) and Malbec (20 per cent), grown at Te Awanga (59 per cent) and in the Gimblett Gravels (41 per cent). Hand-picked and matured for nearly two years in new French oak barrels, it is a powerful, deeply coloured red, with mouthfilling body and dense, ripe blackcurrant, plum and spice flavours. Still youthful, with impressive complexity and the structure to mature gracefully for many years, it should break into full stride 2023+.

DRY $175 –V

Craggy Range Aroha ★★★★★

The delicious 2017 vintage (★★★★★) is a single-vineyard Pinot Noir, estate-grown at Te Muna, on the edge of Martinborough. Hand-picked, it was fermented with indigenous yeasts and matured for 11 months in French oak barriques (28 per cent new). Deep, bright ruby, it is mouthfilling and savoury, with generous cherry, plum and spice flavours, oak complexity, and ripe, supple tannins. A very refined, youthful, harmonious red, it's well worth cellaring to 2022+.

Vintage	17	16	15	14	13	12	11
WR	6	7	7	7	7	7	7
Drink	20-27	20-27	20-26	20-25	20-25	20-24	20-23

DRY $150 –V

Craggy Range Le Sol

This famous Syrah impresses with its lovely fragrance and finesse. Estate-grown in the Gimblett
Gravels of Hawke's Bay, the densely packed 2016 vintage (★★★★★) was hand-picked and
matured for 17 months in French oak barriques (35 per cent new). Still youthful, it is dark
and purple-flushed, mouthfilling and supple, with highly concentrated plum and black-pepper
flavours, refined tannins, and a lasting finish. It needs time; open 2021+. (There is no 2017.)

Vintage	17	16	15	14	13	12	11	10
WR	NM	7	7	7	7	NM	7	7
Drink	NM	20-31	20-30	20-30	20-30	NM	20-25	20-27

DRY $150 AV

Craggy Range Sophia

This is Craggy Range's premier Merlot-based red. The 2016 vintage (★★★★★) is a Gimblett
Gravels, Hawke's Bay blend of Merlot, Cabernet Sauvignon, Cabernet Franc and Petit Verdot,
hand-picked and matured for 18 months in French oak barriques (45 per cent new). Dark
and purple-flushed, it is weighty and highly concentrated, with very vibrant plum, spice and
blackcurrant flavours, oak complexity, and a finely textured finish. It's still youthful; open
2021+. (There is no 2017.)

Vintage	17	16	15	14	13	12	11	10
WR	NM	7	7	7	7	NM	7	7
Drink	NM	20-31	20-30	20-30	20-30	NM	20-25	20-27

DRY $140 AV

Craggy Range Te Kahu   ★★★★☆

Estate-grown in the Gimblett Gravels, the youthful 2017 vintage (★★★★☆) of this Hawke's
Bay red is Merlot-based (66 per cent), with smaller portions of Cabernet Franc and Cabernet
Sauvignon and splashes of Petit Verdot and Malbec. Matured for 17 months in oak barriques
(20 per cent new), it is full-coloured, fresh and mouthfilling, with generous, ripe blackcurrant,
plum and spice flavours, firm tannins, and the depth and structure to mature well. Best drinking
2022+.

DRY $30 AV

Craggy Range The Quarry   ★★★★★

The impressive 2016 vintage (★★★★★) is the first since 2011. From hand-harvested Cabernet
Sauvignon grapes, estate-grown in the Gimblett Gravels, it was matured for 18 months in
French oak barriques (50 per cent new). Densely coloured, it is a sturdy, youthful red, sweet-
fruited, with highly concentrated, pure blackcurrant-like flavours, very finely structured and set
for the long haul. Open 2023+.

DRY $150 AV

Dry River The Twelve Spies   ★★★★☆

The 2018 vintage (★★★★☆) is an estate-grown Martinborough blend of Pinot Noir (50 per
cent), Tempranillo (25 per cent) and Syrah/Viognier (25 per cent), oak-matured for 12 to 18
months. Deeply coloured, with a fragrant, spicy bouquet, it is a fresh, medium to full-bodied
red, with vibrant, ripe blackcurrant, plum, spice and nutty oak flavours, showing excellent
complexity and harmony, and lots of youthful impact.

DRY $75 –V

Elephant Hill Hawke's Bay Hieronymus   ★★★★★

The powerful, very age-worthy 2017 vintage (★★★★★) is a blend of Cabernet Sauvignon, Cabernet Franc, Merlot and Malbec, estate-grown in the Gimblett Gravels and the Bridge Pa Triangle. Matured in French oak casks (65 per cent new), it is dark, with dense, youthful blackcurrant, plum and spice flavours, good tannin backbone, and impressive richness, structure and complexity. Best drinking 2025+.

DRY $120 AV

Elephant Hill Hawke's Bay Le Phant Rouge   ★★★★

The 2017 vintage (★★★★) is a full-coloured blend of Merlot, Syrah and Cabernet Sauvignon. Already drinking well, it is mouthfilling, with strong blackcurrant, plum and spice flavours, hints of herbs and nuts, good complexity and a smooth, lengthy finish. Good value.

DRY $24 V+

Esk Valley Heipipi The Terraces   ★★★★★

Grown on a steep, terraced, north-facing hillside at Bay View, in Hawke's Bay, this is typically a strikingly bold, dark wine with bottomless depth of blackcurrant, plum and strongly spicy flavour. Malbec (43 per cent of the vines) and Merlot (35 per cent) are the major ingredients, supplemented by Cabernet Franc; the Malbec gives 'perfume, spice, tannin and brilliant colour'. Yields in the 1-hectare vineyard are very low, and the wine is matured for 17 to 22 months in French oak barriques (55 per cent new in 2018). 'En primeur' (payment at a reduced price, in advance of delivery) has been the best way to buy. It typically matures well, developing a beautiful fragrance and spicy, Rhône-like complexity. The 2018 vintage (★★★★★) is a deeply coloured blend of Malbec (43 per cent), Merlot (38 per cent) and Cabernet Franc (19 per cent). Fragrant, with a spicy bouquet, it is powerful but refined, with concentrated, ripe blackcurrant, plum and spice flavours, that build to a supple, very harmonious, lasting finish.

Vintage	18	16	15	14	13	12	11	10
WR	7	7	7	7	7	NM	NM	NM
Drink	20-40	20-30	20-30	20-30	20-35	NM	NM	NM

DRY $160 AV

Frenchmans Hill Estate Waiheke Island Blood Creek 8   ★★★★★

Still on sale, the fragrant, highly concentrated 2014 vintage (★★★★★) is a blend of eight varieties – principally Cabernet Sauvignon (36 per cent), Merlot (17 per cent) and Petit Verdot (15 per cent), plus smaller portions of Cabernet Franc, Tannat, Syrah, Viognier and Koler. Matured for 16 months in all-new French oak barriques, it is dark, fresh and full-bodied, with dense, ripe blackcurrant, plum and spice flavours, good tannin backbone, and impressive power through the palate. Best drinking 2021+.

DRY $125 –V

Gillman ★★★★★

This rare, estate-grown Matakana red is a blend of Cabernet Franc, Merlot and Malbec, matured in French oak barrels. In late 2018, I tasted the 2016, 2015, 2014 and 2012 vintages. Fleshy, savoury and full-coloured, the 2016 (★★★★★) is a classy red, likely to be long-lived, with deep blackcurrant/spice flavours, leathery notes adding complexity, good tannin support, and a very harmonious finish. Drinking well now, the 2015 vintage (★★★★☆) is elegant, with good but not great intensity of plum, spice, herb and nut flavours, a hint of coffee, and supple tannins. The 2014 (★★★★★), oak-aged for two years (50 per cent new), is a powerful, almost robust red, very fragrant, savoury and concentrated, with a long future ahead; open 2021+. The 2012 vintage (★★★★★), still fairly youthful in colour, has an earthy streak running through its savoury, complex flavours, which are fresh, smooth and strong. Drink now or cellar.

DRY $85 AV

Linden Estate Hawke's Bay Dam Block ★★★★☆

Already drinking well, the 2017 vintage (★★★★☆) is a blend of Cabernet Sauvignon (47 per cent), Merlot (47 per cent) and Cabernet Franc (6 per cent), matured in French oak casks (20 per cent new). Full-coloured, it is savoury and complex, with mouthfilling body, deep, berryish, spicy, nutty flavours, and the structure to age well.

DRY $55 –V

Man O' War Ironclad ★★★★☆

This powerful red is estate-grown at the eastern end of Waiheke Island. The 2017 vintage (★★★★★) is a blend of Cabernet Franc, Merlot, Petit Verdot, Cabernet Sauvignon and Malbec, matured in French oak barriques (32 per cent new). Deeply coloured, with a fragrant, slightly earthy bouquet, it is sturdy and complex, with deep blackcurrant, red-berry, plum and spice flavours, seasoned with nutty oak, and ripe, supple tannins. A very harmonious red, it's a drink-now or cellaring proposition.

Vintage	17
WR	3
Drink	20-27

DRY $52 –V

Mission Jewelstone Gimblett Gravels Hawke's Bay Antoine ★★★★★

Named after pioneer winemaker Father Antoine Gavin, the 2016 vintage (★★★★★) is a classy blend of Cabernet Sauvignon (41 per cent), Cabernet Franc (33 per cent) and Merlot (26 per cent), matured for 18 months in French oak barriques. Deeply coloured, it is fragrant and youthful, with deep blackcurrant, red-berry and spice flavours, and fine-grained tannins. Showing excellent delicacy and finesse, it's a very age-worthy wine, likely to be at its best 2023+.

DRY $50 AV

Mokoroa   ★★★☆

From Puriri Hills, the 2017 vintage (★★★☆) was estate-grown at Clevedon, in South Auckland. Promoted as 'a good lunchtime wine', it is a blend of Merlot (84 per cent), Cabernet Franc (13 per cent), Malbec (2 per cent) and Carménère (1 per cent). It has fullish, fairly youthful colour and a fresh, slightly herbal bouquet. Medium-bodied, with good depth of plum, berry and spice flavours, savoury notes adding complexity, and a smooth finish, it's already drinking well.

 DRY $30 –V

Moutere Hills Nelson Rumer   ★★★

The 2018 vintage (★★☆) is a blend of Syrah, Merlot and Cabernet Sauvignon, hand-harvested at Upper Moutere and matured for 10 months in French and American oak casks. Mouthfilling, with fullish, fairly youthful colour, it has moderately rich, berryish, slightly herbal flavours, showing some leathery, savoury complexity, but lacks real fragrance and finesse.

Vintage	18
WR	7
Drink	20-33

 DRY $55 –V

Newton Forrest Estate Cornerstone   ★★★★★

Grown in the Cornerstone Vineyard, on the corner of Gimblett Road and State Highway 50 – where the first vines were planted in 1989 – this is a distinguished Hawke's Bay blend of Cabernet Sauvignon, Merlot and Malbec, matured in French (principally) and American oak barriques. Still on sale, the highly refined 2015 vintage (★★★★★) is dark, full-bodied and tightly structured, with concentrated, ripe blackcurrant, plum and spice flavours, complex and savoury, fine-grained tannins, and a very harmonious finish. Already delicious, it's well worth cellaring.

 DRY $60 AV

Obsidian Reserve The Obsidian   ★★★★

The Obsidian Vineyard at Onetangi produces one of the most stylish Waiheke Island reds. Blended from classic Bordeaux red varieties – Cabernet Franc, Merlot, Cabernet Sauvignon, Petit Verdot and Malbec – it is matured in French oak barriques. The 2014 vintage (★★★★★) has deep, youthful colour. Fragrant and supple, it has deep blackcurrant, plum, herb and spice flavours, showing excellent complexity, fine-grained tannins, and a rich, harmonious finish. A graceful wine, it's delicious now, but well worth cellaring.

Vintage	15	14	13	12	11	10
WR	6	7	7	6	6	7
Drink	20-24	20-24	20-23	P	P	P

 DRY $68 AV

Obsidian Reserve Waiheke Island The Mayor   ★★★★☆

Still youthful, the 2018 vintage (★★★★☆) is a bold, vibrantly fruity blend of Cabernet Franc (50 per cent), Petit Verdot (25 per cent) and Malbec (25 per cent), matured in new French and seasoned American oak barrels. Full-coloured, it has fresh, berryish, spicy aromas and flavours, showing excellent depth and complexity, fine-grained tannins and good aging potential.

 DRY $58 –V

Paritua 21:12   ★★★★★

The powerful, still youthful 2015 vintage (★★★★★) is a blend of Cabernet Sauvignon (52 per cent), Merlot (31 per cent) and Cabernet Franc (17 per cent), estate-grown in the Bridge Pa Triangle, Hawke's Bay, and matured for 22 months in French oak barriques (50 per cent new). Retasted in mid-2020, it is a classic, claret-style red, dark, rich and robust, with highly concentrated blackcurrant, plum, spice and nut flavours. A dense, firmly structured wine, it should flourish for at least 15 years.

Vintage	15
WR	6
Drink	20-30

 DRY $130 –V

Paritua Hawke's Bay Red   ★★★★★

Already highly approachable, the 2018 vintage (★★★★★) is a blend of Merlot (58 per cent), Cabernet Sauvignon (26 per cent) and Cabernet Franc (16 per cent), matured for 18 months in French oak casks (40 per cent new). Dark, fragrant, sturdy and supple, it has deep, ripe blackcurrant and plum flavours, seasoned with nutty oak, impressive complexity and a finely textured, long finish. A subtle, satisfying red, it's well worth cellaring to 2023+.

Vintage	18
WR	6
Drink	20-30

 DRY $49 AV

Paritua Stone Paddock Hawke's Bay Scarlet   ★★★★

Enjoyable now, the 2016 vintage (★★★★) is a blend of Merlot (42 per cent), Cabernet Franc (30 per cent), Cabernet Sauvignon (20 per cent) and Malbec (8 per cent), matured for a year in old French oak casks. Full-coloured, it is sturdy, with strong, ripe, plummy, spicy flavours, and nutty, savoury notes adding complexity. Best drinking 2021+.

Vintage	16
WR	4
Drink	20-24

DRY $25 AV

Pask Small Batch Trilliant   (★★★★)

Retasted in early 2020, the 2016 vintage (★★★★) is a full-coloured Hawke's Bay red, blended from Merlot (52 per cent), Malbec (28 per cent) and Cabernet Sauvignon (20 per cent), grown in the Gimblett Gravels. Matured for 14 months in American oak casks (50 per cent new), it has a fresh, spicy, slightly herbal bouquet. Still youthful, with blackcurrant, plum, spice and herb flavours, seasoned with nutty oak, and good complexity, it's well worth cellaring to 2021+.

Vintage	16
WR	6
Drink	20-28

 DRY $35 –V

Passage Rock Waiheke Island Magnus   ★★★★★

The impressive 2017 vintage (★★★★★) is a rare blend of Syrah, Cabernet Sauvignon, Montepulciano, Merlot and Malbec, grown on Waiheke Island and matured for a year in French oak casks (30 per cent new). A rich, very 'complete' wine, it's already delicious. Deeply coloured and sturdy, with concentrated blackcurrant, plum, berry and spice flavours, hints of liquorice and nuts, and good tannin backbone, it should be at its best 2022+.

Vintage	17
WR	6
Drink	20-25

 DRY $98 AV

Pegasus Bay Maestro   ★★★★★

The 2016 vintage (★★★★★) is a Waipara, North Canterbury blend of Merlot, Cabernet Sauvignon and Malbec, from vines over 30 years old. Barrel-aged for two years (60 per cent new), it is a powerful, dense, youthful red, set for a very long life. Dark and still purple-flushed, it has rich, harmonious plum, blackcurrant, herb and spice flavours, fine-grained tannins and an enticingly fragrant bouquet. One of the South Island's greatest 'Bordeaux-style' reds, it should flourish for a decade.

Vintage	16	15
WR	7	6
Drink	20-34	20-28

 DRY $50 AV

Pinot 3 – The Red Edition   (★★★☆)

Floral and fresh, the 2019 vintage (★★★☆) is an unusual blend of Pinot Noir, Pinot Gris and Pinot Blanc, grown in Marlborough and Gisborne, and handled without oak. Bright pink/pale red, it is light and lively, with fruity, berryish flavours, in a highly enjoyable, smooth, drink-young style with a Beaujolais-like charm. (From Untitled Wines, based in West Auckland.)

DRY $20 AV

Prophet's Rock Central Otago Cuvée Aux Antipodes ★★★★★

The 2017 vintage (★★★★★) is a Pinot Noir, estate-grown at an elevated site (320 to 400 metres above sea level) at Bendigo, in Central Otago, and matured in French oak casks. Deeply coloured, it is a powerful red, with substantial body and concentrated, vibrant, plummy, spicy flavours, showing real depth through the palate. Still youthful, it should break into full stride 2023+.

DRY $118 –V

Puriri Hills Clevedon Estate ★★★★★

Estate-grown at Clevedon, in South Auckland, this is a classy, Merlot-based red. Still youthful, the very refined and harmonious 2014 vintage (★★★★★) is a blend of Merlot (77 per cent), Cabernet Sauvignon (13 per cent), Cabernet Franc (7 per cent) and Malbec (3 per cent). Deeply coloured, it is a sweet-fruited, medium to full-bodied red, with concentrated, ripe blackcurrant, plum, herb and spice flavours, finely integrated oak, supple tannins and obvious cellaring potential. Best drinking 2022+.

Vintage	14	13	12	11	10
WR	7	7	6	6	7
Drink	20-31	20-30	20-28	P	20-27

DRY $45 AV

Puriri Hills Clevedon Pope ★★★★★

Named after Ivan Pope, who planted and tended the vines at this Clevedon, South Auckland vineyard. Still on sale, the 2013 vintage (★★★★★) is a classy blend of Merlot (70 per cent), Cabernet Franc (10 per cent), Carménère (10 per cent), Cabernet Sauvignon (5 per cent) and Malbec (5 per cent), matured in French oak casks (100 per cent new). Deeply coloured, it has a fragrant, berryish, spicy bouquet, leading into a full-bodied, very approachable wine, with densely packed, complex plum, blackcurrant and spice flavours, savoury and persistent. The very elegant 2014 vintage (★★★★★) is a blend of Merlot (41 per cent), Cabernet Franc (31 per cent), Carménère (18 per cent) and Malbec (10 per cent). Fragrant, rich and still youthful, with deep, bright colour, it is concentrated and finely structured, with concentrated, plummy, spicy flavours, a hint of dark chocolate, and a savoury, silky, long finish. Best drinking 2023+.

DRY $160 –V

Puriri Hills Harmonie Du Soir ★★★★★

Formerly called 'Puriri Hills Reserve', this regional classic has been labelled as 'Harmonie Du Soir' since the 2012 vintage. Estate-grown at Clevedon, in South Auckland, it is blended from varying proportions of Merlot (principally), Cabernet Franc, Carménère, Cabernet Sauvignon and Malbec, and typically matured for two years in French oak barriques (a high percentage new). The benchmark 2013 vintage (★★★★★) is notably refined, beautifully rich and silky-textured. The lovely 2014 vintage (★★★★★) is a blend of Merlot (42 per cent), Cabernet Franc (25 per cent), Carménère (17 per cent), Cabernet Sauvignon (8 per cent) and Malbec (8 per cent). A classic claret-style red, still unfolding, it has ripe blackcurrant, plum and spice flavours, seasoned with nutty oak, good tannin backbone, and impressive density and complexity. Already delicious, it's well worth cellaring to 2023+.

DRY $85 AV

Sacred Hill Brokenstone ★★★★★

Merlot-based, this is a typically outstanding Hawke's Bay red from the Gimblett Gravels (principally the company's Deerstalkers Vineyard). The highly attractive 2015 vintage (★★★★★), matured for 19 months in French oak casks (22 per cent new), is Merlot-dominant (87 per cent), with minor portions of Malbec (4 per cent), Syrah (4 per cent), Cabernet Sauvignon (3 per cent) and Cabernet Franc (2 per cent). Full-coloured, it is vibrantly fruity, with concentrated, ripe, plummy, spicy flavours, well-integrated oak, savoury notes adding complexity, and supple tannins. Already delicious, it should be at its best 2021+.

Vintage	15	14	13	12	11	10
WR	7	7	7	NM	6	7
Drink	20-30	20-26	20-23	NM	P	P

DRY $50 AV

Sacred Hill Helmsman ★★★★★

This is a classy, single-vineyard Gimblett Gravels red from Hawke's Bay. The highly refined 2017 vintage (★★★★★), blended from Cabernet Sauvignon (55 per cent), Merlot (34 per cent) and Cabernet Franc (11 per cent), was hand-picked and matured for 16 months in French oak barriques (55 per cent new). Full-coloured, it is fragrant, with strong, youthful blackcurrant, plum and spice flavours, revealing excellent complexity, and ripe, supple tannins. Best drinking 2022+.

DRY $85 AV

Sileni Ruber Grand Reserve Hawke's Bay Red Blend ★★★★☆

The attractive 2018 vintage (★★★★☆) is a distinctive blend of Merlot, Syrah and Cabernet Franc, grown in the Bridge Pa Triangle. Full-coloured, it is mouthfilling and sweet-fruited, with concentrated, plummy, spicy flavours, showing good backbone and complexity, and a fragrant bouquet. Best drinking 2021+.

DRY $37 AV

Smith & Sheth Cru Omahu Cantera ★★★★★

The very age-worthy 2018 vintage (★★★★★) is a Hawke's Bay blend of Cabernet Sauvignon (48 per cent), Tempranillo (32 per cent) and Cabernet Franc (20 per cent), hand-picked in the Gimblett Gravels and matured for 20 months in American and French oak barriques (30 per cent new). Named after the Spanish word for quarry (cantera), it is full-bodied, with deep, purple-flushed colour. Fragrant, with concentrated, ripe blackcurrant, plum and spice flavours, complex and savoury, and good tannin backbone, it's well worth cellaring to 2022+.

DRY $60 AV

Soho Blue Blood Zabeel Reserve ★★★★★

The powerful 2015 vintage (★★★★★) is a distinctive Waiheke Island blend of Syrah (51 per cent), Petit Verdot (35 per cent) and Malbec (14 per cent), estate-grown at Onetangi and matured for nine months in French oak casks (75 per cent new). Deeply coloured, with a fragrant, spicy bouquet, it's a full-on, bold style, weighty and fruit-packed, with fresh, highly concentrated, still youthful plum, spice and blackcurrant flavours, rich, savoury and long. Best drinking 2021+.

DRY $99 AV

Stonyridge Larose ★★★★★

Typically a stunning Waiheke Island wine. Dark and seductively perfumed, with smashing fruit flavours, at its best it is a magnificently concentrated red that matures superbly for a decade or longer, acquiring great complexity. The vines – Cabernet Sauvignon, Merlot, Cabernet Franc, Malbec and Petit Verdot – are grown in free-draining clay soils on a north-facing slope, a kilometre from the sea at Onetangi, and are very low-yielding (4 tonnes/hectare). The wine is matured for a year in French (80 to 90 per cent) and American oak barriques (half new, half one year old), and is sold largely on an 'en primeur' basis, whereby the customers, in return for paying for their wine about nine months in advance of its delivery, secure a substantial price reduction. The most recent vintage I have tasted is the 2015 (★★★★★). A classic claret-style red, it is dense but not tough, with power through the palate and obvious potential. Dark, sturdy, rich and supple, it has very ripe blackcurrant, plum and spice flavours, showing lovely freshness, harmony and length. It should mature gracefully for decades.

Vintage	15	14	13	12	11	10
WR	5	6	7	6	5	7
Drink	23-33	23-33	23-33	20-25	20-23	20-30

DRY $280 –V

Tantalus Waiheke Island Écluse Reserve ★★★★

The powerful, concentrated and classy 2015 vintage (★★★★★) is a blend of Cabernet Sauvignon, Cabernet Franc, Merlot and Malbec. Estate-grown at Onetangi, it was matured for a year in French oak barriques. Deeply coloured, it is youthful, with dense, firm blackcurrant, plum and spice flavours, complex, well-structured and likely to be long-lived. Well worth discovering, it should be at its best 2022+.

DRY $95 –V

Tantalus Waiheke Island Évoque Reserve ★★★★★

The impressive 2015 vintage (★★★★★), estate-grown at Onetangi, is a blend of Merlot, Malbec, Cabernet Sauvignon and Cabernet Franc, matured for a year in French oak barriques. A powerful but approachable red, it is dark, fragrant and full-bodied, with highly concentrated, plummy, spicy flavours, showing excellent ripeness and complexity, good tannin backbone, and a rich, harmonious finish. Already delicious, it's well worth cellaring to 2022+.

DRY $90 AV

Tantalus Waiheke Island Voilé Reserve (★★★★☆)

The deeply coloured, powerful 2015 vintage (★★★★☆) is a very age-worthy Syrah. Estate-grown at Onetangi and matured for a year in French oak barriques, it is fragrant, with concentrated, ripe blackcurrant, plum, spice and nut flavours – less overtly peppery than southern styles – and a well-structured, harmonious finish. Best drinking 2021+.

DRY $80 –V

Te Mata Coleraine ★★★★★

Breed, rather than brute power, is the hallmark of Coleraine (correctly pronounced Cole-raine rather than Coler-aine), which since its first vintage in 1982 has carved out an illustrious reputation among New Zealand's claret-style reds. In all vintages since 2007, Cabernet Sauvignon has been the predominant variety. At its best, it is a magical Hawke's Bay wine, with a depth, complexity and subtlety on the level of a top-class Bordeaux. The grapes are grown and hand-picked in the Havelock North hills, in the company's warm, north-facing Buck and 1892 vineyards, and the wine is matured for 17 to 20 months in French oak barriques, predominantly new. The 2018 vintage (★★★★★) is described by Toby Buck, Te Mata's marketing and communications manager, as '60 per cent 2014, 40 per cent 2013', meaning it veers towards the robust, ripe, richly flavoured style of the 2014 reds from Hawke's Bay, while retaining some of the sheer elegance and obvious longevity of the 2013. A very elegant blend of Cabernet Sauvignon (52 per cent), Merlot (33 per cent) and Cabernet Franc (15 per cent), it is deeply coloured, with concentrated, well-ripened blackcurrant, plum and spice flavours, and good tannin backbone. A finely poised, very 'complete' red, it has obvious potential for long-term cellaring.

Vintage	18	17	16	15	14	13	12	11	10
WR	7	6	7	7	7	7	NM	7	7
Drink	20-38	20-32	20-30	20-30	20-28	20-33	NM	20-23	20-22

DRY $129 AV

Te Motu ★★★★★

This Waiheke Island red is grown at Onetangi, over the fence from Stonyridge. Compared to its neighbour, it has typically been less opulent than Larose, in a more earthy, slightly leafy style, but the latest releases are the finest yet. Cabernet Sauvignon-predominant, with Merlot and Cabernet Franc, the 2014 vintage (★★★★★) was matured in French oak casks and bottle-aged for several years prior to its release. Full-coloured, it is fragrant and mouthfilling, with deep, still youthful blackcurrant, plum and spice flavours and refined tannins. A very savoury, distinctly Bordeaux-like style, complex and well-structured, it should be at its best 2022+.

DRY $140 –V

Te Motu Kokoro ★★★★★

Estate-grown at Onetangi, on Waikehe Island, the 2014 vintage (★★★★★) was blended from Merlot (principally), with smaller amounts of Cabernet Sauvignon, Cabernet Franc, Malbec and Syrah. Made 'in a more forward style' (meaning not requiring lengthy cellaring), it is deeply coloured, fragrant and softly mouthfilling. Rich, savoury and complex, with ripe, berryish, spicy, nutty flavours, showing excellent depth and harmony, it's drinking well now.

DRY $85 –V

Terra Sancta Special Release The Italian   (★★★★☆)

The non-vintage wine (★★★★☆) released in late 2019 is a blend of Dolcetto, Lagrein and Barbera, estate-grown at Bannockburn, in Central Otago, and harvested from the 2016, 2017, 2018 and 2019 vintages. Matured mostly in seasoned French oak casks, with some use of new French and American oak, it is a fresh, fragrant, medium-bodied red, full-coloured, savoury and supple, with strong, youthful, plummy, spicy flavours, well-integrated oak, lively acidity, and good immediacy.

DRY $55 –V

Trinity Hill Gimblett Gravels The Gimblett   ★★★★★

The sturdy, dark 2018 vintage (★★★★★) is a Hawke's Bay blend of Cabernet Sauvignon and Cabernet Franc. Set for a long life, it is fragrant and full-bodied, with concentrated, ripe blackcurrant, plum and spice flavours, well-integrated oak and a fresh, finely structured finish. Best drinking 2024+.

DRY $40 AV

Unison Rocky Red   (★★★★)

Drinking well now, the 2017 vintage (★★★★) is a blend of Merlot (89 per cent) and Cabernet Sauvignon (11 per cent), grown in the Gimblett Gravels and barrel-aged. Full-coloured, it is mouthfilling, with fresh, generous, plummy, spicy flavours, showing considerable complexity, and a very harmonious, smooth finish.

DRY $24 V+

Vergence Red by Pegasus Bay Mk 1   ★★★★★

The Vergence label is used by Pegasus Bay for 'experimental, non-traditional wines'. The 2018 vintage (★★★★★) is a Central Otago Pinot Noir, fully whole-bunch fermented. A distinctive, generous red, it is full-coloured and fragrant, with concentrated plum and spice flavours, showing impressive complexity, and a firmly structured, long, spicy finish.

DRY $40 V+

Villa Maria Ngakirikiri The Gravels   ★★★★★

The debut 2013 vintage (★★★★★) was promoted as the company's 'icon' Bordeaux-style red. From vines planted in the Gimblett Gravels between 1998 and 2000, it is Cabernet Sauvignon-based (97 per cent), with a splash of Merlot (3 per cent). Matured for 18 months in French oak barrels (52 per cent new), it is densely coloured, with substantial body (14 per cent alcohol) and bold, still youthful, blackcurrant and plum-evoking flavours, showing lovely richness, purity and complexity. It should flourish for decades; open 2021 onwards. The 2014 vintage (★★★★★), made entirely from Cabernet Sauvignon, was matured for 18 months in French oak barriques (40 per cent new). A powerful, lush red, it is sturdy, boldly coloured and fleshy, with dense, very ripe blackcurrant and plum flavours, hints of nuts, spices and liquorice, and a rich, harmonious finish. Combining power and grace, it will be very long-lived; best drinking 2022+.

Vintage	14	13
WR	7	7
Drink	20-30	20-30

DRY $150 AV

Cabernet Franc

New Zealand's sixth most widely planted red-wine variety, Cabernet Franc is probably a mutation of Cabernet Sauvignon, the much higher-profile variety with which it is so often blended. Jancis Robinson's phrase, 'a sort of claret Beaujolais', aptly sums up the nature of this versatile and underrated red-wine grape.

As a minority ingredient in the recipe of many of New Zealand's top reds, Cabernet Franc lends a delicious softness and concentrated fruitiness to its blends with Cabernet Sauvignon and Merlot. However, admirers of Château Cheval Blanc, the illustrious St Émilion (which is two-thirds planted in Cabernet Franc), have long appreciated that Cabernet Franc need not always be Cabernet Sauvignon's bridesmaid, but can yield fine red wines in its own right. The supple, fruity wines of Chinon and Bourgueil, in the Loire Valley, have also proved Cabernet Franc's ability to produce highly attractive, soft light reds.

According to the latest national vineyard survey, the bearing area of Cabernet Franc was 96 hectares in 2020 – well below the 213 hectares in 2004. Over two-thirds of the vines are clustered in Hawke's Bay and most of the rest are in Auckland. As a varietal red, Cabernet Franc is lower in tannin and acid than Cabernet Sauvignon; or as Michael Brajkovich, of Kumeu River, has put it: 'more approachable and easy'.

Aotea by the Seifried Family Nelson Cabernet Franc (★★★★☆)

From 'great fruit in perfect condition', the 2019 vintage (★★★★☆) was estate-grown at Brightwater and matured in French oak barriques (one and two years old). A powerful, youthful red, it has deep, purple-flushed colour. Full-bodied, it has fresh blackcurrant, plum and spice flavours, showing excellent ripeness and depth, a gentle seasoning of oak, lively acidity, and supple tannins. Worth discovering.

DRY $39 AV

Askerne Hawke's Bay Cabernet Franc ★★★★☆

Priced well, the 2018 vintage (★★★★) was estate-grown and matured for a year in French oak casks (30 per cent new). Full-coloured, it is fragrant, with a fresh bouquet of berries, herbs and spices. Mouthfilling, with good concentration, complexity and structure, it's a youthful wine, likely to be at its best 2022+.

DRY $24 V+

Black Estate Home North Canterbury Cabernet Franc ★★★★

Certified organic, the 2018 vintage (★★★★☆) was estate-grown, hand-harvested, fermented with indigenous yeasts, and matured in a mix of aged oak barrels (18 per cent) and egg-shaped, Spanish clay vessels called tinaja (82 per cent). Fresh and full-bodied, it has very good density and vigour, with strong, youthful, berryish, spicy flavours, a hint of herbs, and refined tannins. Well worth cellaring, it should be at its best 2022+.

DRY $45 –V

Boneline, The, Amphitheatre Waipara Cabernet Franc ★★★★☆

The striking 2018 vintage (★★★★★) was harvested from mature, estate-grown vines. Deeply coloured, it is very fragrant and full-bodied, with highly concentrated blackcurrant, plum and spice flavours, a hint of herbs, finely integrated oak, fresh acidity and a finely textured, long finish. One of the finest Cabernet Francs ever produced in the South Island, it's already delicious, but likely to be at its best 2021+.

DRY $50 –V

Dancing Petrel Paewhenua Island Mangonui Northland Cabernet Franc   (★★★★☆)

Likely to be long-lived, the 2019 vintage (★★★★☆) was hand-harvested and matured in French oak casks (30 per cent new). Deeply coloured, with a fragrant, slightly herbal and spicy bouquet, it is mouthfilling, with concentrated, ripe, plummy, spicy flavours, a hint of herbs, good complexity, and firm tannin backbone. Best drinking 2023+.

DRY $30 AV

Elephant Hill Reserve Cabernet Franc/Cabernet/Merlot   (★★★★★)

The powerful, weighty, youthful 2016 vintage (★★★★★) is a blend of Cabernet Franc (34 per cent), Cabernet Sauvignon (32 per cent) and Merlot (26 per cent), with a splash of Malbec. Hand-harvested in the Gimblett Gravels (75 per cent) and the Bridge Pa Triangle (25 per cent), it was matured for 21 months in French oak casks (48 per cent new). Dark and purple-flushed, it is fragrant, with substantial body, concentrated blackcurrant, plum and spice flavours, and firm tannin backbone. Set for a long life, it should be at its best 2023+.

DRY $54 AV

Kelly Washington Bridge Pa Hawke's Bay Cabernet Franc   (★★★★☆)

From Auckland-based Tamra Kelly (formerly chief winemaker at Yealands Estate), the 2018 vintage (★★★★☆) was barrel-aged for 10 months. A medium to full-bodied red, it is deeply coloured, with concentrated, vibrant flavours of berries, plums and spices, showing good complexity and obvious cellaring potential.

DRY $50 –V

Lime Rock Central Hawke's Bay Cabernet Franc   ★★★★

The highly attractive 2015 vintage (★★★★☆) was estate-grown, hand-harvested and matured in seasoned French oak barriques. Full and bright in colour, it is fragrant and full-bodied, with strong, ripe berry, plum and spice flavours, showing excellent complexity. The 2016 vintage (★★★★) is medium to full-bodied, with vibrant plum, spice and herb flavours, oak complexity, gentle tannins, and a lingering finish.

Vintage	16	15
WR	7	7
Drink	20-23	20-22

DRY $28 AV

Maison Noire Hawke's Bay Cabernet Franc   ★★★☆

Still on sale, the 2015 vintage (★★★☆) was matured in French oak barrels (25 per cent new). A medium-bodied style with fullish colour, it has moderately concentrated, plummy, spicy, slightly herbal flavours, showing some savoury complexity, fresh acidity, and a fairly firm finish.

Vintage	15
WR	6
Drink	20-22

DRY $25 –V

Maison Noire Hawke's Bay Cabernet/Merlot   (★★★★)

The 2016 vintage (★★★★) is maturing gracefully. A medium-bodied style, it is a blend of Cabernet Franc (48 per cent), Merlot (45 per cent) and Cabernet Sauvignon (7 per cent), matured for a year in French oak barrels (25 per cent new). It has very satisfying depth of ripe, berryish, plummy, slightly spicy flavours, showing good complexity, and a smooth, finely textured finish.

Vintage	16
WR	5
Drink	P

 DRY $25 AV

Mills Reef Elspeth Gimblett Gravels Hawke's Bay Cabernet Franc   ★★★★

Revealing good personality, the elegant 2016 vintage (★★★★☆) is a full-coloured, sweet-fruited red, matured for 17 months in French oak barrels (24 per cent new). Rich and supple, with red-berry, plum and spice flavours, good complexity and fine-grained tannins, it shows obvious potential; best drinking 2022+.

Vintage	16
WR	7
Drink	20-24

 DRY $50 –V

Sileni Grand Reserve Pacemaker Hawke's Bay Cabernet Franc   ★★★★

Grown in the Bridge Pa Triangle, the 2018 vintage (★★★★☆) is full-coloured and fleshy, with mouthfilling body and deep, berryish, plummy, spicy, slightly nutty flavours, showing good complexity. A youthful, very age-worthy red, it's well worth cellaring to 2021+.

 DRY $40 –V

Sileni Reserve Hawke's Bay Cabernet Franc/Merlot   (★★★☆)

Grown mostly in the Bridge Pa Triangle and briefly oak-aged, the easy-drinking 2018 vintage (★★★☆) has fullish colour and fresh berry and spice aromas. Mouthfilling, it is vibrantly fruity, with very good depth of berryish, slightly spicy flavours, and a smooth finish. Best drinking 2020–21.

 DRY $22 AV

Smith & Sheth Cru Heretaunga Cabernet Franc   (★★★★☆)

The age-worthy 2018 vintage (★★★★☆) was hand-picked in the Bridge Pa Triangle and matured for a year in French oak barrels (50 per cent new). Full-coloured, it is mouthfilling, with concentrated, ripe blackcurrant, red-berry and spice flavours, gentle acidity, and a fairly firm finish. Best drinking 2022+.

DRY $35 AV

Thomas Cabernet Franc/Merlot   ★★★★☆

The 2014 vintage (★★★★☆) is a blend of Cabernet Franc (48 per cent) and Merlot (45 per cent), with splashes of Syrah (4 per cent) and Cabernet Sauvignon (3 per cent). Hand-harvested at Onetangi, on Waiheke Island, it was matured for 15 months in French oak barriques (26 per cent new). Full-coloured, it is mouthfilling and smooth, with strong, ripe plum, red-berry and spice flavours, seasoned with nutty oak. An elegant, supple red, it should be at its best 2021+. (From Batch Winery.)

DRY $46 –V

Waimea Estates Nelson Cabernet Franc/Syrah   (★★★)

A drink-young charmer, the 2017 vintage (★★★) is a medium-bodied blend with fullish colour and fresh, berryish flavours. Fruity and smooth, it's a very easy-drinking style.

DRY $18 AV

Cabernet Sauvignon and Cabernet-predominant blends

Cabernet Sauvignon has proved a tough nut to crack in New Zealand. Mid-priced models were – until recently – usually of lower quality than a comparable offering from Australia, where the relative warmth suits the late-ripening Cabernet Sauvignon variety. Yet a top New Zealand Cabernet-based red from a favourable vintage can hold its own in illustrious company and the overall standard of today's middle-tier, $20 bottlings is far higher than many wine lovers realise – which makes for some great bargains.

Cabernet Sauvignon was widely planted here in the nineteenth century. The modern resurgence of interest in the great Bordeaux variety was led by Tom McDonald, the legendary Hawke's Bay winemaker, whose string of elegant (though, by today's standards, light) Cabernet Sauvignons under the McWilliam's label, from the much-acclaimed 1965 vintage to the gold medal-winning 1975, proved beyond all doubt that fine-quality red wines could be produced in New Zealand.

During the 1970s and 1980s, Cabernet Sauvignon ruled the red-wine roost in New Zealand. Since then, as winemakers – especially in the South Island, but also Hawke's Bay – searched for red-wine varieties that would ripen more fully and consistently in our relatively cool grape-growing climate than Cabernet Sauvignon, it has been pushed out of the limelight by Merlot, Pinot Noir and Syrah. Between 2003 and 2020, the country's total area of bearing Cabernet Sauvignon vines contracted from 741 to 255 hectares. Growers with suitably warm sites have often retained faith in Cabernet Sauvignon, but others have moved on to less challenging varieties.

Over 87 per cent of the country's Cabernet Sauvignon vines are clustered in Hawke's Bay, and Auckland also has significant plantings. In the South Island, Cabernet-based reds have typically lacked warmth and richness. This magnificent but late-ripening variety's future in New Zealand clearly lies in the warmer vineyard sites of the north.

What is the flavour of Cabernet Sauvignon? When newly fermented a herbal character is common, intertwined with blackcurrant-like fruit aromas. New oak flavours, firm acidity and taut tannins are other hallmarks of young, fine Cabernet Sauvignon. With maturity the flavour loses its aggression and the wine develops roundness and complexity, with assorted cigar-box, minty and floral scents emerging. It is unwise to broach a Cabernet Sauvignon-based red with any pretensions to quality at less than three years old; at about five years old the rewards of cellaring really start to flow.

Ashwell Martinborough Cabernet Sauvignon ★★★☆

French oak-aged for a year, the 2019 vintage (★★★★) was grown on the Martinborough Terraces. Full-coloured, it is fragrant and full-bodied, with youthful, ripe berry, plum and spice flavours, showing good concentration, balanced tannins, and obvious potential; best drinking 2023+.

Vintage	19
WR	5
Drink	20-29

DRY $28 –V

Awaroa Requiem Waiheke Island Cabernet/Merlot/Malbec ★★★★★

The 2016 vintage (★★★★★) is a powerful blend of Cabernet Sauvignon (50 per cent), Merlot (30 per cent) and Cabernet Franc (20 per cent), matured in French oak barriques (70 per cent new). Dark and fragrant, it is mouthfilling, with deep blackcurrant, plum and spice flavours, savoury, nutty notes adding complexity, and supple tannins. It's already quite expressive; drink now or cellar.

Vintage	16	15	14
WR	6	7	7
Drink	20-25	20-25	20-25

DRY $75 AV

Awaroa Waiheke Island Cabernet/Merlot/Malbec   ★★★★

The fragrant, fleshy 2016 vintage (★★★★☆) is a blend of Cabernet Sauvignon (50 per cent), Merlot (30 per cent) and Cabernet Franc (20 per cent), matured in French oak barriques. Deep and youthful in colour, it is full-bodied, with strong blackcurrant, plum and spice flavours, showing excellent ripeness and complexity, and a firm tannin grip. Best drinking 2022+.

DRY $45 –V

Babich Irongate Gimblett Gravels Hawke's Bay Cabernet/Merlot/Franc   ★★★★★

Estate-grown in the Irongate Vineyard and matured in French oak barriques (40 per cent new in 2016), this elegant, complex, firmly structured red is made for cellaring. Still on sale, the 2016 vintage (★★★★★) has deep, youthful colour. Fragrant and mouthfilling, it is well-structured, with strong blackcurrant, plum and spice flavours, oak complexity, good tannin backbone, and excellent cellaring potential; open 2022+.

Vintage	16	15	14	13	12	11	10
WR	6	7	7	7	5	4	7
Drink	20-26	20-27	20-25	20-25	20-22	P	20-22

DRY $40 AV

Babich Limited Edition 100 Years Cabernet Sauvignon   (★★★★★)

Launched in 2016 – a century after Babich's first vintage in 1916 – the rare 2013 vintage (★★★★★) was not shown to critics. Still on sale, it was estate-grown in the Gimblett Gravels, Hawke's Bay, and French oak-aged. Deeply coloured and weighty, it is sweet-fruited and savoury, with complex flavours of blackcurrant, plums and spices, and a tight, exceptionally long finish.

DRY $399 –V

Brookfields Ohiti Estate Cabernet Sauvignon   ★★★★

Veteran Hawke's Bay winemaker Peter Robertson says the shingly Ohiti Estate, inland from Fernhill, yields 'sound Cabernet Sauvignon year after year – which is a major challenge to any vineyard'. The 2018 vintage (★★★★☆) was matured for a year in French and American oak barrels (10 per cent new). Deeply coloured, it is sturdy, sweet-fruited and firm, with strong, vibrant blackcurrant, plum and spice flavours, seasoned with nutty oak, and good freshness and complexity. Still very youthful, it should be long-lived; open 2022+. A great buy.

Vintage	18	17
WR	7	7
Drink	20-28	20-28

DRY $21 V+

Brookfields Reserve Vintage Hawke's Bay Cabernet/Merlot   ★★★★★

Brookfields' top red is one of the most powerful, long-lived reds in Hawke's Bay. At its best, it is a thrilling wine – robust, tannin-laden and overflowing with very rich cassis, plum and mint flavours. The grapes are sourced from the Lyons family's sloping, north-facing vineyard at Bridge Pa, and the wine is matured for a year in predominantly new French oak barriques. The youthful 2018 vintage (★★★★★) is a blend of Cabernet Sauvignon (80 per cent), Merlot

(15 per cent) and Cabernet Franc (5 per cent.) Deeply coloured, with a fragrant, slightly herbal bouquet, it is mouthfilling and highly concentrated, with densely packed blackcurrant, red-berry, herb and spice flavours, and a firmly structured, lasting finish. Best drinking 2023+.

Church Road 1 Single Vineyard Redstone Cabernet Sauvignon   NA

The 2018 vintage was tasted in July 2020, before it was bottled, so is not rated. Estate-grown in the Redstone Vineyard, in the Bridge Pa Triangle, Hawke's Bay, it was matured for 18 months in French oak barriques (34 per cent new). Dark and full-bodied, with pure, ripe blackcurrant-like flavours and supple tannins, it looked brimful of promise.

DRY $90 NA

Church Road McDonald Series Hawke's Bay Cabernet Sauvignon   ★★★★★

This consistently impressive wine is grown principally in the company's Redstone Vineyard, in the Bridge Pa Triangle. The 2017 vintage (★★★★☆), which includes 12 per cent Merlot, is a very age-worthy, harmonious red, matured for 18 months in French (mostly) and Hungarian oak barrels (30 per cent new). Dark and youthful, it is mouthfilling, with concentrated blackcurrant, plum and spice flavours, nutty and savoury, excellent complexity and supple tannins. Best drinking 2022+.

DRY $28 V+

Church Road Tom Cabernet Sauvignon/Merlot – see Church Road Tom Merlot/Cabernet.

Coopers Creek Reserve Gimblett Gravels Hawke's Bay Cabernet Sauvignon   ★★★★★

Still youthful, the 2016 vintage (★★★★★) is a dark, purple-flushed red, maturing very gracefully. A single-vineyard wine, it has a dense, structured palate. Full-bodied and highly concentrated, with cassis, plum and spice flavours, oak complexity and a well-structured finish, it should be at its best 2022+.

DRY $60 AV

Coopers Creek Select Vineyards Gimblett Gravels
Hawke's Bay Cabernet/Merlot   ★★★★☆

The 2016 vintage (★★★★☆) was blended from almost equal portions of Cabernet Sauvignon and Merlot. A full-coloured, youthful red with good substance, it is mouthfilling, vibrantly fruity and firmly structured, with strong, ripe blackcurrant, berry, plum and spice flavours. Open 2021+.

DRY $28 V+

Cornerstone Cabernet/Merlot/Malbec – see Newton Forrest Estate
Cornerstone in the Branded and Other Red Wines section

Esk Valley Winemakers Reserve Gimblett Gravels
Cabernet Sauvignon/Merlot/Malbec/Cabernet Franc   ★★★★★

The bold 2018 vintage (★★★★★) is a blend of Cabernet Sauvignon (38 per cent), Merlot (28 per cent), Malbec (19 per cent) and Cabernet Franc (15 per cent). Hand-harvested and matured for 16 months in French oak barriques (45 per cent new), it is deeply coloured, with a fragrant, slightly spicy bouquet. Weighty, it has concentrated, vibrant blackcurrant, plum, red-berry, spice and nutty oak flavours, with good tannin backbone. Still very youthful, but highly expressive in its youth, it's well worth cellaring to 2023+.

DRY $70 AV

Fino Valley Proprietors Cellar Hawke's Bay Cabernet Sauvignon   (★★★)

From a long-established producer at Henderson, in West Auckland, the 2018 vintage (★★★) was French oak-aged for a year. An easy-drinking style, it has fullish colour, with decent depth of ripe blackcurrant, plum and spice flavours, a touch of complexity, and a smooth finish. Drink now or cellar.

DRY $15 V+

Linden Estate Reserve Hawke's Bay Cabernet Sauvignon   (★★★★)

The full-coloured 2017 vintage (★★★★) was matured in French oak barriques (14 per cent new). It has a fragrant, savoury bouquet, leading into a mouthfilling wine with strong, berryish, spicy flavours, showing considerable complexity, and good tannin backbone. Best drinking 2021+.

DRY $65 –V

Maison Noire Single Vineyard Hawke's Bay Cabernet Sauvignon   (★★★☆)

The youthful 2018 vintage (★★★☆) was barrel-matured for 16 months. Bright ruby, it is medium-bodied and lively, with fresh acidity and moderately concentrated, ripe blackcurrant/plum flavours. Best drinking 2022+.

Vintage	18
WR	5
Drink	20-23

DRY $25 –V

Mills Reef Arthur Edward Gimblett Gravels Cabernet/Merlot   (★★★★★)

After tasting the debut 2013 vintage (★★★★★) 'blind' (identity hidden) against acclaimed French reds, Mills Reef decided they were of similar quality. Released in late 2018 at an eye-catching $350, it was hand-picked from the oldest vines, pruned to extremely low yields, and matured for 20 months in 100 per cent new French oak hogsheads. A 50:50 blend of Cabernet Sauvignon and Merlot, it is deeply coloured, fragrant, mouthfilling, elegant and supple, with rich blackcurrant, plum and spice flavours, in a classic Bordeaux style. Best drinking 2023+.

DRY $350 –V

Mills Reef Elspeth Gimblett Gravels Hawke's Bay Cabernet Sauvignon ★★★★★

Fragrant, fresh and full-bodied, the 2016 vintage (★★★★☆) was hand-picked from mature, 21-year-old vines in the company's Mere Road Vineyard, and matured for 17 months in French (90 per cent) and American oak hogsheads (48 per cent new). Likely to be at its best from 2022 onwards, it has strong, vibrant, well-ripened blackcurrant and plum flavours, spicy and nutty characters adding complexity, and obvious potential for cellaring.

Vintage	16	15	14	13	12	11	10
WR	7	7	7	7	NM	7	7
Drink	20-25	20-25	20-24	20-25	NM	P	P

DRY $50 AV

Mills Reef Elspeth Gimblett Gravels Hawke's Bay Cabernet/Merlot ★★★★★

Grown and hand-picked at the company's close-planted Mere Road site, this is a consistently impressive wine. The 2016 vintage (★★★★☆) was matured for 17 months in French oak hogsheads (37 per cent new). It is a youthful, full-coloured, medium to full-bodied red. Fresh and vibrant, it is sweet-fruited, with concentrated blackcurrant, plum and slight nut flavours, oak complexity, and refined tannins. Best drinking 2022+.

Vintage	16
WR	7
Drink	20-26

DRY $50 AV

Mills Reef Reserve Gimblett Gravels Hawke's Bay Cabernet/Merlot ★★★★

The 2018 vintage (★★★★) is a blend of Cabernet Sauvignon (68 per cent) and Merlot (32 per cent), matured for 15 months in French oak hogsheads (36 per cent new). Full-coloured, it is mouthfilling and supple, with ripe blackcurrant, plum and spice flavours. A generous wine, finely balanced for early enjoyment, it should be at its best 2021+.

Vintage	18
WR	7
Drink	20-25

DRY $25 AV

Mission Barrique Reserve Hawke's Bay Cabernet Sauvignon ★★★★☆

The 2018 vintage (★★★★★) is a great buy. The label makes no mention of the Gimblett Gravels, but the wine was grown at two sites (in Mere Road and Gimblett Road, both in the Gimblett Gravels), and matured for a year in French oak barrels (25 per cent new). Deeply coloured, with a fragrant bouquet, it is full-bodied and savoury, with generous blackcurrant, red-berry and spice flavours, revealing excellent ripeness and density, oak complexity, good tannin backbone, and a rich, harmonious finish. Already approachable, it's well worth cellaring to 2023+.

DRY $30 AV

Mission Barrique Reserve Hawke's Bay Cabernet/Merlot ★★★★☆

The powerful, very age-worthy 2018 vintage (★★★★☆) is a blend of Cabernet Sauvignon (62 per cent), Merlot (24 per cent) and Cabernet Franc (14 per cent), matured for a year in French oak barriques. Deeply coloured, it is fragrant, with strong, ripe blackcurrant, plum and spice flavours, and a fairly firm finish. Best drinking 2023+.

DRY $29 V+

Mission Hawke's Bay Cabernet Sauvignon ★★★

Priced right, the 2018 vintage (★★★) is a blend of Cabernet Sauvignon (86 per cent) and Merlot (14 per cent), partly barrel-aged. Full-coloured, it is mouthfilling and vibrantly fruity, with good depth of blackcurrant, herb and spice flavours, and a well-rounded finish.

DRY $16 V+

Pask Declaration Gimblett Gravels Hawke's Bay Cabernet/Merlot/Malbec ★★★★☆

The 2014 vintage (★★★★☆) was matured for two years in French and American oak puncheons (100 per cent new). Full-coloured, it shows good concentration, with ripe blackcurrant, plum and spice flavours, complex and savoury, and fine-grained tannins.

Vintage	14	13	12	11	10
WR	7	7	NM	NM	6
Drink	20-25	20-25	NM	NM	P

DRY $50 –V

Pask Gimblett Gravels Cabernet/Merlot ★★★★

The fresh, supple, medium to full-bodied 2016 vintage (★★★☆) is a blend of Cabernet Sauvignon (71 per cent) and Merlot (29 per cent), matured for 14 months in seasoned French oak barrels. Retasted in mid-2020, it is full-coloured, with a slightly leafy bouquet, very good depth of blackcurrant, plum and herb flavours, and nutty, savoury notes adding complexity. It's drinking well now.

DRY $22 V+

Passage Rock Reserve Waiheke Island Cabernet Sauvignon/Merlot ★★★★☆

The sturdy 2015 vintage (★★★★★) was matured for a year in French oak barrels (30 per cent new). Highly fragrant and deeply coloured, it is built to last, with deep, fairly youthful blackcurrant, plum, spice and nut flavours, showing excellent structure and complexity. Best drinking 2022+.

Vintage	15
WR	6
Drink	20-25

DRY $55 –V

Saint Clair James Sinclair Gimblett Gravels Hawke's Bay Cabernet/Merlot ★★★☆

Enjoyable young, the 2018 vintage (★★★☆) is a deeply coloured blend of Cabernet Sauvignon (59 per cent) and Merlot (41 per cent), matured in tanks and French oak barrels (partly new). It has a fresh, vibrantly fruity bouquet, leading into a full-bodied wine with very good depth of blackcurrant and red-berry flavours, ripe and smooth.

DRY $28 –V

Saint Clair Pioneer Block 17 Plateau Gimblett Gravels Cabernet/Merlot   ★★★★☆

Still unfolding, the 2018 vintage (★★★★☆) is a single-vineyard, Gimblett Gravels blend of Cabernet Sauvignon (55 per cent), Merlot (41 per cent) and Malbec (4 per cent), matured for 10 months in French oak casks (35 per cent new). Deeply coloured, with a fragrant, fresh, slightly herbal bouquet, it is mouthfilling, with vibrant, ripe blackcurrant, red-berry and spice flavours, showing good density, and finely balanced tannins. Best drinking 2023+.

 DRY $38 AV

Settler Crownthorpe Hawke's Bay Cabernet/Merlot   (★★★★)

Enjoyable now, the 2015 vintage (★★★★) is an estate-grown blend of Cabernet Sauvignon (50 per cent), Merlot (45 per cent) and Cabernet Franc (5 per cent), barrel-aged for five months. Deep and youthful in colour, with a fresh, slightly herbal bouquet, it's a distinctive wine, with generous blackcurrant, plum and spice flavours, savoury notes adding complexity, and a smooth finish. Drink now to 2022.

 DRY $25 AV

Squawking Magpie SQM Gimblett Gravels Cabernets/Merlot   ★★★★★

The very age-worthy 2017 vintage (★★★★★) is a classy Hawke's Bay blend of Cabernet Sauvignon (66 per cent), Merlot (23 per cent) and Cabernet Franc (11 per cent), matured for 15 months in French oak casks (22 per cent new). Mouthfilling, with deep, purple-flushed colour, it has rich, ripe blackcurrant, plum and spice flavours, good tannin backbone, and excellent complexity and cellaring potential. Best drinking 2022+.

 DRY $79 AV

Stonecroft Gimblett Gravels Hawke's Bay Cabernet Sauvignon   ★★★★★

The youthful 2018 vintage (★★★★☆) is a single-vineyard, organically certified red, matured for 18 months in French oak barrels. Deeply coloured, it is medium to full-bodied, with good concentration of blackcurrant, plum and spice flavours, finely integrated oak and obvious potential; open 2023+.

Vintage	18
WR	6
Drink	22-32

DRY $45 AV

Stonecroft Ruhanui Gimblett Gravels Hawke's Bay
Cabernet Sauvignon/Merlot   ★★★★☆

The youthful 2017 vintage (★★★★☆) is a blend of Cabernet Sauvignon (90 per cent) and Merlot (10 per cent), matured for 20 months in seasoned French oak barrels. Deeply coloured, it is medium-bodied, with good density of blackcurrant, plum and spice flavours, savoury notes adding complexity, and fine-grained tannins. A very harmonious young red, well worth cellaring, it should be at its best 2022+.

Vintage	17
WR	4
Drink	20-25

 DRY $31 AV

Te Mata Awatea Cabernets/Merlot   ★★★★★

Positioned below its Coleraine stablemate in Te Mata's hierarchy of Hawke's Bay, claret-style reds, since 1995 Awatea has been grown at Havelock North and in the Bullnose Vineyard, inland from Hastings. A blend of Cabernet Sauvignon, Merlot and Cabernet Franc – with a splash of Petit Verdot in most years since 2001 – it is hand-harvested and matured for 15 to 18 months in French oak barriques (partly new). Compared to Coleraine, in its youth Awatea is more seductive, more perfumed, and tastes more of sweet, ripe fruit, but it is more forward and slightly less concentrated. The wine can mature gracefully for many years, but is also typically delicious in its youth. The stylish 2018 vintage (★★★★★) is a blend of Cabernet Sauvignon (48 per cent), Merlot (37 per cent) and Cabernet Franc (15 per cent). Deeply coloured, it is mouthfilling, with concentrated blackcurrant and spice flavours, finely integrated oak and ripe, supple tannins. A very harmonious, age-worthy red, it should break into full stride 2023+.

Vintage	18	17	16	15	14	13	12	11	10	DRY $40 AV
WR	7	6	7	7	6	7	6	7	7	
Drink	20-28	20-27	20-26	20-25	20-25	20-23	P	P	P	

Te Mata Estate Vineyards Hawke's Bay Cabernets/Merlot   (★★★☆)

The 2017 vintage (★★★☆) is a blend of Cabernet Sauvignon, Merlot and Cabernet Franc, matured for 11 months in French oak barrels (partly new). Full-coloured, with a fresh, berryish bouquet, it is medium-bodied, with vibrant, ripe red-berry and plum flavours, showing moderate complexity, fresh acidity and gentle tannins. Enjoyable young, it offers good drinking now to 2021. (The 2019 vintage is a Merlot/Cabernets blend – see the Merlot section).

Vintage	18	DRY $20 AV
WR	6	
Drink	20-23	

Thomas Legacy Waiheke Island Cabernet Sauvignon   (★★★★★)

Still on sale, the promisingly dark 2013 vintage (★★★★★) was made solely from Cabernet Sauvignon, hand-harvested at Onetangi and matured for 18 months in French oak barriques (33 per cent new). Fragrant, with blackcurrant and herb aromas and flavours, it is sturdy, with excellent structure, density and complexity. Approachable now, it should be long-lived. (From Batch Winery.)

DRY $90 –V

Thomas Legacy Waiheke Island Cabernet/Merlot/Franc   (★★★★★)

Still on sale and set for the long haul, the fragrant, youthful 2013 vintage (★★★★★) is a blend of Cabernet Sauvignon (72 per cent), Merlot (23 per cent) and Cabernet Franc (5 per cent), matured for 18 months in French oak barriques (62 per cent new). Deeply coloured, it is full-bodied and fresh, with generous blackcurrant, plum, spice and herb flavours, seasoned with nutty oak, excellent complexity, good tannin backbone, and a lasting finish.

DRY $120 –V

Trinity Hill Prison Block Single Vineyard Gimblett Gravels Cabernet Sauvignon (★★★★★)

From a site earmarked originally for a prison, but 'better suited to vines than villains', the very classy 2018 vintage (★★★★★) is dark and full-bodied, with blackcurrant and spice flavours, showing lovely ripeness and density, and fine, supple tannins. Still a baby, it's a well-structured red with obvious potential; open 2023+.

DRY $120 AV

Unison Selection Gimblett Gravels Cabernet Sauvignon/Merlot ★★★★☆

Still youthful, the 2015 vintage (★★★★☆) is a blend of chiefly Cabernet Sauvignon (64 per cent) and Merlot (34 per cent), estate-grown, hand-picked and matured for nearly two years in French oak casks (50 per cent new). Full-coloured, with a fragrant, spicy, slightly herbal bouquet, it is mouthfilling, with fresh acidity, and concentrated berry, spice and herb flavours, seasoned with nutty oak. Best drinking 2022+.

DRY $60 –V

Vidal Legacy Gimblett Gravels Hawke's Bay Cabernet Sauvignon/Merlot ★★★★★

The refined 2018 vintage (★★★★★) is a blend of Cabernet Sauvignon (64 per cent) and Merlot (36 per cent), hand-picked and matured for 20 months in French oak barriques (54 per cent new). Deeply coloured, it is fragrant and full-bodied, with concentrated blackcurrant, herb and spice flavours, good complexity, and ripe, supple tannins. An elegant, supple red, it's well worth cellaring to 2023+.

Vintage	18
WR	7
Drink	20-30

DRY $70 AV

Vidal Soler Gimblett Gravels Hawke's Bay Cabernet Sauvignon ★★★★☆

Still very youthful, the 2018 vintage (★★★★☆) contains 10 per cent Merlot. Grown at two sites in the Gimblett Gravels, it was matured for 20 months in French oak barriques (49 per cent new). Full-coloured, it is mouthfilling and vibrant, with concentrated plum, spice and herb flavours, well-integrated oak adding complexity, and obvious cellaring potential; open 2022+.

Vintage	18	17
WR	7	6
Drink	20-27	20-27

DRY $35 AV

Villa Maria Platinum Selection Organic Hawke's Bay Cabernet Sauvignon (★★★★☆)

Certified organic, the impressive 2018 vintage (★★★★☆) was estate-grown in the Soler Vineyard and matured for 14 months in oak barriques (15 per cent new). Deeply coloured, with a fragrant, fresh, slightly herbal bouquet, it is mouthfilling, with concentrated, youthful berry, spice and herb flavours, nutty oak adding complexity, and obvious cellaring potential. Best drinking 2022+.

DRY $30 AV

Villa Maria Reserve Gimblett Gravels Hawke's Bay Cabernet Sauvignon/Merlot ★★★★★

Deeply coloured, the lovely 2018 vintage (★★★★★) is a blend of Cabernet Sauvignon (78 per cent), Merlot (14 per cent) and Malbec (8 per cent), matured for 16 months in French oak barriques (35 per cent new). A refined, very youthful red, it is fragrant and full-bodied, with dense, well-ripened blackcurrant, plum and spice flavours, finely integrated oak, excellent complexity, and a long life ahead. Best drinking 2023+.

Vintage	18	17	16	15	14	13	12	10
WR	7	NM	7	7	7	7	6	7
Drink	20-30	NM	20-28	20-25	20-25	20-25	20-22	20-25

DRY $70 AV

Waiheke Road Waiheke Island Cabernet/Merlot (★★★★)

From Awaroa Winery, the 2017 vintage (★★★★) was grown in the Te Whau Vineyard. Based mostly on Cabernet Sauvignon (49 per cent) and Merlot (36 per cent), with smaller amounts of Cabernet Franc, Malbec and Petit Verdot, it is a youthful, age-worthy wine. Full-coloured, it is generous, with very good depth of fresh blackcurrant, herb and spice flavours, firm and youthful, and considerable complexity.

DRY $45 –V

Chambourcin

Chambourcin is one of the more highly rated French hybrids, well known in Muscadet for its good disease-resistance and bold, crimson hue. Rare in New Zealand (with 4 hectares of bearing vines in 2020), it is most often found as a varietal red in Northland.

Byrne Northland Chambourcin ★★★★☆

Byrne rates among the region's top producers of Chambourcin. The 2016 vintage (★★★★), matured in old oak barriques, is full-coloured, with fresh, berryish, spicy aromas and flavours. Vibrantly fruity, with the slightly rustic note typical of the variety, gentle tannins, and a lingering finish, it's a highly attractive, drink-young style.

DRY $21 V+

Marsden Bay of Islands Chambourcin ★★★★☆

Top vintages of this Northland red are generous, dark and flavour-packed. The youthful, finely balanced 2019 vintage (★★★★☆) was matured for 16 months in French and American oak casks (30 per cent new). Deeply coloured, it is fresh, sturdy and sweet-fruited, with strong, vibrant plummy, spicy flavours, a hint of liquorice, ripe, supple tannins and a deliciously smooth finish. Best drinking mid-2021+.

DRY $26 AV

Gamay Noir

Gamay Noir is single-handedly responsible for the seductively scented and soft red wines of Beaujolais. The grape is still very rare in New Zealand, with 10 hectares of bearing vines in 2020, mostly in Hawke's Bay. In the Omaka Springs Vineyard in Marlborough, Gamay ripened later than Cabernet Sauvignon (itself an end-of-season ripener), with higher levels of acidity than in Beaujolais, but at Te Mata's Woodthorpe Terraces Vineyard in Hawke's Bay, the crop is harvested as early as mid-March.

Easthope Two Terraces Vineyard Hawke's Bay Gamay (★★★★)

Still unfolding, the 2019 vintage (★★★★) was hand-picked at Maraekakaho and matured for 10 months in French oak puncheons and 'cast-stone, egg shaped tanks'. Deep, bright ruby, it has a fragrant, spicy, slightly herbal bouquet. Fresh, lively and smooth, with generous berry, plum and spice flavours, vibrant acidity, and some savoury complexity, it should be at its best for drinking mid-2021+.

DRY $40 –V

Mount Edward Central Otago Gamay (★★★★★)

The 2019 vintage (★★★★★) is one of New Zealand's finest Gamays to date. Certified organic, it was grown in the Muirkirk Vineyard at Bannockburn, matured in tanks (60 per cent) and old oak barrels (40 per cent), and bottled unfined and unfiltered. Deeply coloured, it is deliciously floral, rich and supple, with vibrant, sweet-fruit flavours of plums and red berries, showing surprising depth, and loads of drink-young charm.

DRY $35 AV

Rippon Lake Wanaka Central Otago Gamay (★★★★★)

If there is a more striking New Zealand Gamay around, I certainly haven't tasted it. Ruby-hued, the 2019 vintage (★★★★★) was hand-picked from vines over 25 years old, matured for 10 months in old oak barrels, and bottled unfined and unfiltered. Still unfolding, with a strong sense of youthful drive, it is medium-bodied, fresh and concentrated, with deep, berryish, plummy, slightly spicy flavours, fresh acidity and a lasting finish. Benchmark stuff, it should be at its best for drinking mid-2021+.

DRY $57 AV

Te Mata Estate Vineyards Hawke's Bay Gamay Noir ★★★★

The very youthful 2020 vintage (★★★★☆) was estate-grown inland, at the Woodthorpe Terraces Vineyard, and matured for seven weeks in seasoned French oak barrels. It could easily be mistaken for a Pinot Noir. Purple-flushed, it is sweet-fruited, very lively and fruit-packed, with good density of fresh, plummy, berryish, slightly spicy flavours, a touch of tannin, and some aging potential. Best drinking mid-2021+.

Vintage	20
WR	7
Drink	20-22

DRY $22 V+

Grenache

Grenache, one of the world's most extensively planted grape varieties, thrives in the hot, dry vineyards of Spain and southern France. It is also yielding exciting wines in Australia, especially from old, unirrigated, bush-pruned vines, but is exceedingly rare in New Zealand, with a total producing area in 2020 of 1 hectare, all in Hawke's Bay.

Villa Maria Cellar Selection Hawke's Bay Grenache ★★★★☆

The 2018 vintage (★★★★☆) of this very late-ripening variety was blended with Syrah (7 per cent) and matured in small and large French oak vessels. Deep ruby, with a fragrant, berryish, spicy bouquet, it is sturdy and supple, with strong, ripe berry and spice flavours, oak complexity, and gentle tannins. A powerful young red, it's well worth cellaring to 2021+.

 DRY $25 V+

Lagrein

Cultivated traditionally in the vineyards of Trentino-Alto Adige, in north-east Italy, Lagrein yields deeply coloured, slightly astringent reds with fresh acidity and plum/cherry flavours, firm and strong. The area of bearing vines in New Zealand will leap from 2 hectares in 2015 to 10 hectares in 2020, mostly in Hawke's Bay (8 hectares), but also in Marlborough and Nelson.

Hans Herzog Marlborough Lagrein (★★★★☆)

Still a baby, the 2018 vintage (★★★★☆) was estate-grown, hand-picked, matured in a single French oak puncheon, and bottled unfined and unfiltered. Deeply coloured, it is fragrant and full-bodied, with concentrated plum, blackcurrant and spice flavours, oak complexity, lively acidity, and obvious potential; open 2022+. Certified organic.

DRY $60 –V

Hunting Lodge, The, Marlborough Lagrein ★★★★★

Full of personality, the 2019 vintage (★★★★★) is described on the back label as 'an Italian hillbilly on OE in Marlborough'. From a variety related to Syrah and Pinot Noir, it is a deeply coloured, single-vineyard red, grown in the Awatere Valley and matured for 14 months in French oak barriques (35 per cent new). It has dark, youthful colour and a highly fragrant, spicy bouquet. Fresh and vibrant, it is supple, with strong, vigorous, plummy, spicy flavours, and a long, harmonious, spicy finish. Well worth discovering.

DRY $36 AV

Malbec

With a rise from 25 hectares of bearing vines in 1998 to 120 hectares in 2020, this old Bordeaux variety is starting to make its presence felt in New Zealand, where nearly 75 per cent of all plantings are clustered in Hawke's Bay (most of the rest are in Auckland). It is often used as a blending variety, adding brilliant colour and rich, sweet-fruit flavours to its blends with Merlot, Cabernet Sauvignon and Cabernet Franc. Numerous unblended Malbecs have also been released recently, possessing loads of flavour and often the slight rusticity typical of the variety (or at least some of the clones established here).

Ash Ridge Premium Estate Hawke's Bay Malbec ★★★★☆

The charming 2018 vintage (★★★★☆) was estate-grown in the Bridge Pa Triangle and matured for 10 months in French and American oak barrels (15 per cent new). Full-coloured, mouthfilling and supple, it has good intensity of vibrant, plummy, gently spicy flavours, a hint of dark chocolate, and a long, spicy finish. Drink now or cellar.

DRY $32 AV

Brookfields Hawke's Bay Sun Dried Malbec ★★★★☆

Promoted as 'Malbec on steroids', the 2019 vintage (★★★★★) was made from grapes sun-dried to concentrate their sugars and flavours, then matured for a year in French and American oak casks. If you like your reds sturdy, sweet-fruited and smooth, this is for you. Deeply coloured, it is mouthfilling and fragrant, with rich, plummy, spicy flavours and supple tannins. A top vintage of this label, powerful and lacking the rusticity often seen in Malbec, it's already delicious.

Vintage	19	18
WR	7	7
Drink	20-29	20-29

DRY $27 V+

Church Road 1 Single Vineyard Gimblett Gravels Hawke's Bay Malbec (★★★★★)

More elegant, less gutsy than many Malbecs, the 2017 vintage (★★★★★) is a powerful red, matured in French (80 per cent) and Hungarian (20 per cent) oak casks (38 per cent new). Deeply coloured, it is mouthfilling and youthful, with fresh, dense, plummy, spicy flavours, and firm, but not grippy, tannins. Well worth cellaring to 2023 onwards, it should be long-lived.

DRY $90 AV

Coopers Creek Gisborne Malbec ★★★☆

The 2016 vintage (★★★☆) was barrel-aged for a year. An easy-drinking red, offering good value, it is full-coloured and mouthfilling, with satisfying depth of fresh, vibrant, berryish, slightly spicy flavours, a subtle seasoning of oak, and a smooth finish.

DRY $18 V+

Decibel Gimblett Gravels Malbec ★★★★

The 2018 vintage (★★★★) is a highly approachable, but age-worthy, Hawke's Bay red, grown in the Gimblett Gravels. It has deep, purple-flushed colour. Fresh and vibrantly fruity, it is full-bodied, with plummy, spicy aromas and flavours, showing very good ripeness and depth, and supple tannins. Best drinking 2022+.

DRY $28 AV

Esk Valley The Hillside Malbec/Cabernet Franc/Merlot   (★★★★★)

Showing strong personality, the 2017 vintage (★★★★★) is a declassified year of Esk Valley Heipipi The Terraces (see the Branded Reds section), 'to enjoy while you wait for the greatest vintages . . . to mature'. Matured for 18 months in French oak barriques (50 per cent new), and bottled unfined and unfiltered, it is dark and purple-flushed, with a very fragrant, spicy bouquet. Already approachable, it's a powerful, mouthfilling red, with fresh, dense plum, blackcurrant and spice flavours, complex and savoury, and good tannin backbone.

Vintage	17	DRY $90 AV
WR	7	
Drink	20-35	

Fromm Malbec Fromm Vineyard   ★★★★☆

Estate-grown in Marlborough and hand-picked from mature vines, this red is recommended by winemaker Hätsch Kalberer for drinking with 'a large piece of wild venison'. The 2017 vintage (★★★★☆) is rare – only four barrels were made. Oak-aged for 19 months, it has deep, purple-flushed colour. Fresh, spicy aromas lead into a full-bodied, very youthful wine, with strong plum, spice and blackcurrant flavours, good tannin backbone and a long finish. Unusually refined for Malbec, it should break into full stride 2021+. Certified organic.

 DRY $65 –V

Hunting Lodge, The, Hawke's Bay Malbec/Merlot   (★★★★☆)

The deeply coloured 2019 vintage (★★★★☆) was grown in 'the Gravels' and matured for 14 months in French oak casks (30 per cent new). Bold and smooth-flowing, it has rich, vibrant, plummy, spicy flavours, a hint of liquorice, fresh acidity and ripe, supple tannins giving it plenty of drink-young appeal.

 DRY $32 AV

Left Field Hawke's Bay Malbec   (★★★★)

The 2019 vintage (★★★★) was French and American oak-aged. Deeply coloured, with a fresh, spicy bouquet, it is mouthfilling and vibrantly fruity, with strong, plummy, spicy flavours. A 'fruit-driven' style, it is supple, with loads of drink-young charm. (From Te Awa.)

Vintage	19	DRY $25 AV
WR	6	
Drink	23-28	

Matawhero Church House Single Vineyard Gisborne Malbec   ★★★☆

The easy-drinking 2018 vintage (★★☆) is bright ruby (light for Malbec), with fresh, berryish aromas. Fruity and smooth, with berryish, slightly spicy flavours, it's an uncomplicated red, with an off-dry (5 grams/litre of residual sugar) finish.

MED/DRY $26 –V

Saint Clair James Sinclair Hawke's Bay Malbec   ★★★☆

The easy-drinking 2017 vintage (★★★☆) is a medium-bodied, supple red with strong, fresh, berryish, plummy, slightly earthy flavours, and oak-derived complexity. Drink now or cellar.

DRY $28 –V

Stonyridge Luna Negra Waiheke Island Hillside Malbec   ★★★★★

Promoted as 'like going on an energetic dance with a Cuban beauty queen', this bold, classy red is estate-grown in the Vina del Mar Vineyard at Onetangi and matured in American oak barriques. The most recent vintage I have tasted is the 2015 (★★★★★), which had dense, inky, purple-flushed colour. A powerful, sturdy wine, with concentrated, well-ripened blackcurrant and plum flavours, it's a structured, age-worthy style, delicious young, but likely to be at its best 2021+.

DRY $95 –V

Testify by Decibel Hawke's Bay Malbec   (★★★★)

Drinking well now, the 2016 vintage (★★★★) was grown in the Gimblett Gravels and matured in French oak barrels (partly new). Deeply coloured, it is fresh, fragrant and vibrantly fruity, with a seasoning of nutty oak adding complexity. It's not a blockbuster (unlike many Malbecs), but skilfully crafted.

DRY $56 –V

Tironui Hawke's Bay Malbec/Merlot/Cabernet   ★★★★☆

From an elevated site at Taradale, the single-vineyard, youthful 2018 vintage (★★★★☆) is a blend of Malbec (70 per cent), Merlot (22 per cent) and Cabernet Sauvignon (8 per cent). Matured for 20 months in seasoned French oak barrels, it is a full-coloured, elegant, supple red, with vibrant, ripe blackcurrant and spice flavours, gently seasoned with oak, and good tannin support. Best drinking 2022+.

DRY $35 AV

Villa Maria Reserve Gimblett Gravels Hawke's Bay Malbec   ★★★★★

Still on sale, the dark, rich 2015 vintage (★★★★☆) was estate-grown in the Omahu Gravels Vineyard and matured for 18 months in French oak barriques (25 per cent new). It is vibrantly fruity, with deep, plummy, berryish flavours, woven with fresh acidity, and fine-grained tannins.

DRY $50 AV

Marzemino

Once famous, but today rare, Marzemino is cultivated in northern Italy, where it typically yields light, plummy reds. Established in New Zealand in 1995, Marzemino has been made commercially by Pernod Ricard NZ under the Church Road brand since 2005, but was not listed separately in New Zealand Winegrowers' *Vineyard Register Report 2017–2020*.

Church Road McDonald Series Hawke's Bay Marzemino ★★★★

The deeply coloured, easy-drinking 2018 vintage (★★★★) was estate-grown in the Redstone Vineyard, in the Bridge Pa Triangle, and matured for 14 months in French oak casks (21 per cent new). Fresh and full-bodied, it has strong, plummy, spicy flavours, a slightly earthy streak, considerable complexity, and a well-rounded finish.

DRY $42 –V

Merlot

Pinot Noir is New Zealand's red-wine calling card on the world stage, but our Merlots are also proving competitive. Interest in this most extensively cultivated red-wine grape in Bordeaux is especially strong in Hawke's Bay. Everywhere in Bordeaux – the world's greatest red-wine region – except in the Médoc and Graves districts, the internationally higher-profile Cabernet Sauvignon variety plays second fiddle to Merlot. The elegant, fleshy wines of Pomerol and St Émilion bear delicious testimony to Merlot's capacity to produce great, yet relatively early-maturing, reds.

In New Zealand, after initial preoccupation with the more austere and slowly evolving Cabernet Sauvignon, the rich, rounded flavours and (more practically) earlier-ripening ability of Merlot are now fully appreciated. Poor set can be a major drawback with the older clones, reducing yields, but Merlot ripens ahead of Cabernet Sauvignon, a major asset in cooler wine regions, especially in vineyards with colder clay soils. Merlot grapes are typically lower in tannin and higher in sugar than Cabernet Sauvignon's; its wines are thus silkier and a shade stronger in alcohol.

Hawke's Bay had 87.5 per cent of New Zealand's bearing Merlot vines in 2020; the rest were clustered in Gisborne, Auckland and Marlborough. The country's fifth most widely planted variety, Merlot covers well over four times the area of Cabernet Sauvignon. Between 2003 and 2020, the total area of bearing Merlot vines barely changed, from 1249 to 1197 hectares, but in most vintages the wines offer terrific value.

Merlot's key role in New Zealand was traditionally that of a minority blending variety, bringing a soft, mouthfilling richness and floral, plummy fruitiness to its marriages with the predominant Cabernet Sauvignon. Now, with a host of straight Merlots and Merlot-predominant blends on the market, this aristocratic grape is fully recognised as a top-flight wine in its own right.

Alexander Martinborough Merlot ★★★★☆

Still extremely youthful, the outstanding 2019 vintage (★★★★★) was estate-grown, hand-picked and matured for 11 months in French oak barriques (33 per cent new). Dark and purple-flushed, it is a powerful, vibrant, sweet-fruited wine with dense, ripe blackcurrant, plum and spice flavours, showing good complexity, and firm but not grippy tannins. It should mature well for a decade.

Vintage	19
WR	6
Drink	22-26

DRY $32 AV

Ash Ridge Estate Hawke's Bay Merlot ★★★★

Already drinking well, the 2018 vintage (★★★★) was estate-grown in the Bridge Pa Triangle. A fragrant, generous red, it has vibrant red-berry, plum and spice flavours, showing considerable complexity. Good value.

DRY $22 V+

Askerne Hawke's Bay Merlot/Cabernet Franc/Malbec ★★★☆

Drinking well in its youth, the 2018 vintage (★★★★) is a blend of principally Merlot (34 per cent), Cabernet Franc (28 per cent) and Malbec (28 per cent), with minor amounts of Cabernet Sauvignon and Petit Verdot. Matured for over a year in oak barrels (43 per cent new), it is full-coloured, fleshy and sweet-fruited, with generous red-berry, plum and spice flavours, oak complexity, and a smooth, harmonious finish.

DRY $24 AV

Askerne Reserve Hawke's Bay Merlot/Cabernet Sauvignon/Cabernet Franc   ★★★★☆

Still extremely youthful, the 2019 vintage (★★★★☆) is a blend of principally Merlot (43 per cent) and Cabernet Sauvignon (31 per cent), with smaller amounts of Cabernet Franc and Malbec. Matured for 10 months in oak barrels (47 per cent new), it is deeply coloured, full-bodied and savoury, with strong, ripe, plummy, spicy, slightly nutty flavours, showing good complexity, fresh acidity, and a rich, smooth finish. Best drinking 2023+.

 DRY $33 AV

Ataahua Waipara Merlot   ★★★★

Showing good density, the 2017 vintage (★★★★) of this North Canterbury red was hand-picked from mature vines and barrel-aged for over a year. Full-coloured, it is fresh and full-bodied, with generous, plummy, spicy, slightly nutty flavours, savoury notes adding complexity, and a finely structured, smooth finish. Well worth cellaring, it should be at its best 2022+.

 DRY $30 –V

Babich Hawke's Bay Merlot/Cabernet   ★★★☆

Priced right, the 2017 vintage (★★★☆) is full-coloured, mouthfilling and smooth. Wood-aged for a year, it has good depth of fresh, berryish, slightly spicy flavours, finely balanced tannins, and some savoury complexity. Best drinking 2021+.

Vintage	17
WR	5
Drink	20-23

 DRY $20 AV

Babich Winemakers' Reserve Hawke's Bay Merlot   ★★★★☆

Grown in the Irongate Vineyard, in the Gimblett Gravels, the 2016 vintage (★★★★☆) was French oak-aged for a year. Full-coloured and fragrant, it is fresh and full-bodied, with strong berry, plum and spice flavours, savoury and complex, supple tannins, and obvious potential. A refined, silky-textured red, it should be at its best 2022+.

Vintage	16	15
WR	6	7
Drink	20-22	20-22

 DRY $35 AV

Brookfields Burnfoot Hawke's Bay Merlot   ★★★★

Typically great value. The 2015 vintage (★★★☆), grown in the Tuki Tuki Valley, was matured for a year in seasoned French and American oak casks. A mouthfilling red with fullish, bright colour, it is vibrantly fruity, with fresh acidity and strong, plummy, slightly herbal flavours, gently seasoned with oak.

Vintage	15
WR	7
Drink	20-21

DRY $20 V+

Brookfields Highland Hawke's Bay Merlot/Cabernet ★★★★☆

The 2015 vintage (★★★★☆) is a blend of Merlot and Cabernet Sauvignon, matured for a year in new and one-year-old French and American oak casks. Deeply coloured, with plenty of personality, it has mouthfilling body and rich, vibrant plum, cassis and spice flavours, with a hint of coffee. Complex and savoury, it should be at its best 2021+.

Vintage	15	14
WR	7	7
Drink	20-26	20-25

DRY $45 –V

Church Road 1 Single Vineyard Gimblett Gravels Merlot (★★★★★)

The very classy 2016 vintage (★★★★★) is a still youthful Hawke's Bay red, matured for 18 months in French oak barriques (54 per cent new). Deeply coloured, with a fragrant, inviting bouquet, it is mouthfilling and sweet-fruited, but not heavy, with highly concentrated red-berry and plum flavours, a hint of liquorice, well-integrated oak, and a very harmonious, seductively smooth finish. Best drinking 2023+.

DRY $90 AV

Church Road Grand Reserve Hawke's Bay Merlot/Cabernet Sauvignon ★★★★★

The powerful, yet very approachable, 2016 vintage (★★★★★) is a blend of Merlot (74 per cent) and Cabernet Sauvignon (26 per cent), grown in the Gimblett Gravels (mostly) and the Bridge Pa Triangle, and matured for 18 months in French oak barrels (41 per cent new). It has bold, youthful colour, lush, concentrated plum, blackcurrant and spice flavours, impressive complexity, and supple tannins. Best drinking 2023+.

DRY $45 AV

Church Road Hawke's Bay Merlot/Cabernet Sauvignon ★★★★

This full-flavoured, claret-style red from Pernod Ricard NZ can offer wonderful value. Merlot-based, it is typically estate-grown, principally in the Redstone Vineyard, in the Bridge Pa Triangle, and fully barrel-aged. Surprisingly complex for its price, the 2018 vintage (★★★★☆) is a blend of Merlot (92 per cent) and Cabernet Sauvignon (8 per cent), matured for a year in Hungarian and French oak casks (35 per cent new). Deeply coloured, it is full-bodied and sweet-fruited, with very good density of plum, blackcurrant and spice flavours, nutty, well-structured, and very age-worthy.

DRY $20 V+

Church Road McDonald Series Hawke's Bay Merlot ★★★★★

The 2016 vintage (★★★★★) is a rich, savoury, smooth red, still unfolding. Merlot-based (92 per cent), with a splash of Cabernet Sauvignon (8 per cent), it was grown in the Bridge Pa Triangle (mostly) and the Gimblett Gravels, and matured for 18 months in Hungarian and French oak barrels (28 per cent new). Deep and youthful in colour, it is fragrant and full-bodied, with dense, ripe plum, blackcurrant and spice flavours, finely integrated oak, and a very harmonious, lingering finish. Best drinking 2022+.

DRY $28 V+

Church Road Tom Merlot/Cabernet   ★★★★★

Pernod Ricard NZ's top Hawke's Bay red honours pioneer winemaker Tom McDonald, a driving force behind New Zealand's first prestige red, McWilliam's Cabernet Sauvignon (first vintage 1965). The early releases of Tom in the mid-1990s were Cabernet Sauvignon-predominant, but from 1998 onwards, Merlot emerged as an equally crucial part of the recipe. Typically a wine of great finesse, it is savoury, complex and more akin to a quality Bordeaux than other New World reds. The 2016 vintage (★★★★★) is a blend of Merlot (81 per cent), estate-grown in the Gimblett Gravels, and Cabernet Sauvignon (19 per cent), estate-grown in the Redstone Vineyard, in the Bridge Pa Triangle. It was matured for 18 months in French oak barrels (62 per cent new). Already delicious, it is a powerful, fleshy, rich red, with impressive concentration and fine, supple tannins. Highly fragrant, it is sweet-fruited, with dense, plummy, spicy flavours, still unfolding. Is it as profound as the commanding, more Cabernet Sauvignon-based 2015 vintage? I don't think so, but it's still a very classy red. Open 2023+.

DRY $220 AV

Collaboration Impression Merlot/Cabernet/Cabernet Franc   ★★★★☆

The distinctive, attractive 2016 vintage (★★★★☆) is a blend of Merlot, Cabernet Sauvignon and Cabernet Franc. Matured for 18 months in seasoned French oak barrels, and bottled unfined and unfiltered, it is full-coloured, with a fragrant, berryish, slightly herbal bouquet. Medium to full-bodied, it is vibrantly fruity, with strong plum, red-berry and spice flavours, showing good complexity, and fine-grained tannins. Already highly enjoyable, it should also reward cellaring; best drinking 2021+.

DRY $30 AV

Coopers Creek Select Vineyards Gimblett Gravels
Hawke's Bay Merlot/Malbec   ★★★★

Well worth cellaring, the 2016 vintage (★★★★) is a blend of Merlot (54 per cent) and Malbec (46 per cent), matured in French oak casks. Full-coloured, it is fresh and vibrant, with strong, ripe plum and spice flavours, finely balanced tannins, and savoury notes adding complexity. Best drinking 2021+.

DRY $25 AV

Craggy Range Gimblett Gravels Vineyard Hawke's Bay Merlot   ★★★★☆

The 2016 vintage (★★★★☆) was matured for 17 months in French oak barriques (30 per cent new). Dark and purple-flushed, it is mouthfilling and vibrantly fruity, with fresh, ripe, concentrated, plummy, spicy flavours that build across the palate to a long finish. A stylish, youthful red, it's well worth cellaring to 2021+.

DRY $40 –V

Delegat Gimblett Road Merlot

Offering outstanding value, the debut 2018 vintage (★★★★☆) was grown in the Gimblett Gravels, Hawke's Bay, and matured for 14 months in oak barriques (new and one year old). Richly coloured, with fresh, spicy aromas, it is mouthfilling and vibrantly fruity, with concentrated, plummy, spicy flavours, finely integrated oak, good tannin support, and obvious cellaring potential. A distinctive, youthful wine, it should be at its best 2021+.

DRY $20 V+

Delta Hawke's Bay Merlot   ★★★★

Offering good value, the 2019 vintage (★★★★) was matured for nine months in tanks and seasoned French oak casks. Deeply coloured, it is mouthfilling and vibrantly fruity, with very good density of ripe, plummy, spicy flavour. Full of youthful impact, it's an age-worthy red, likely to be at its best 2022+.

DRY $20 V+

Elephant Hill Reserve Hawke's Bay Merlot/Cabernet Franc/Cabernet   ★★★★★

The classy 2017 vintage (★★★★★) was estate-grown and hand-harvested in the Gimblett Gravels and the Bridge Pa Triangle, and matured in French oak casks (35 per cent new). Fragrant and full-bodied, it is deeply coloured, with concentrated blackcurrant, plum and spice flavours, seasoned with nutty oak, excellent complexity, and a finely structured, very harmonious finish. Best drinking 2023+.

DRY $54 AV

Esk Valley Gimblett Gravels Merlot/Cabernet Sauvignon/Malbec   ★★★★☆

Offering outstanding value, the 2018 vintage (★★★★☆) is a blend of Merlot (49 per cent), Cabernet Sauvignon (33 per cent), Malbec (16 per cent) and Cabernet Franc (2 per cent), grown in the Gimblett Gravels, Hawke's Bay, and matured for a year in French oak barriques. Full-coloured, it is weighty and generous, with ripe, berryish, spicy flavours, showing very good complexity. Already approachable, it's well worth cellaring to at least 2022.

Vintage	18	17	16	15	14	13	12	11
WR	6	5	6	6	7	7	6	5
Drink	20-27	20-23	20-22	20-21	20-21	P	P	P

DRY $20 V+

Falconhead Hawke's Bay Merlot/Cabernet   ★★★☆

Priced sharply, the 2016 vintage (★★★) was barrel-aged for two years. It has full, moderately youthful colour, mouthfilling body, plenty of fresh, berryish, spicy, slightly earthy flavour, and a fairly firm finish.

Vintage	16
WR	5
Drink	20-22

DRY $17 V+

Greyrock Te Koru Hawke's Bay Merlot   (★★★☆)

The 2018 vintage (★★★☆) is full-coloured, fresh and fragrant, with very good depth of berry, plum and spice flavours. A firmly structured red with considerable complexity, it should be at its best 2021+. (From Sileni.)

DRY $20 AV

Haha Hawke's Bay Merlot   ★★★

The easy-drinking 2019 vintage (★★★) is a deeply coloured, fragrant, very fresh and fruity red, with mouthfilling body, generous, plummy, spicy flavours and a smooth finish.

DRY $18 AV

Hans Herzog Spirit of Marlborough Merlot/Cabernet   ★★★★★

Who says you can't make outstanding claret-style reds in the South Island? Estate-grown on the banks of the Wairau River, matured for at least two years in new and one-year-old French oak barriques, and then bottle-aged for several years, this is typically a densely coloured wine with a classy fragrance, substantial body and notably concentrated blackcurrant, plum, herb and spice flavours. The 2014 vintage (★★★★★) is a blend of equal portions of Merlot, Cabernet Franc and Cabernet Sauvignon. Fragrant, with deep, fairly youthful colour, it is sturdy, with concentrated blackcurrant, plum and spice flavours, showing excellent ripeness and depth, good complexity, and a well-structured, long finish. Best drinking 2022+. Certified organic.

Vintage	14	13
WR	7	7
Drink	20-28	20-28

DRY $69 AV

Hunter's Marlborough Merlot   ★★★

Estate-grown at Rapaura, in the Wairau Valley, the 2016 vintage (★★★☆)· is a single-vineyard red, hand-picked from mature vines, matured for a year in French oak barrels (50 per cent new), and bottled unfined and unfiltered. Fullish in colour, it is mouthfilling and youthful, with good depth of vibrant red-berry, plum, spice and herb flavours, showing considerable complexity, an earthy streak, and a fairly firm finish.

Vintage	16
WR	5
Drink	20-25

DRY $35 –V

Karikari Estate Hell Hole Merlot/Cabernet Franc   (★★☆)

The 2016 vintage (★★☆) is an estate-grown, Far North blend of Merlot (75 per cent) and Cabernet Franc (25 per cent), hand-harvested and matured for two years in old oak barrels, mostly American. 'Honest, raucous and a little rough' (according to the back label), it has mature colour. Full-bodied, it's a slightly gutsy, easy-drinking red, with red-berry, herb and spice flavours, and a smooth finish. Ready.

DRY $27 –V

Karikari Estate Toa Iti Merlot/Cabernet Franc/Tannat   (★★★)

Retasted in 2020, this distinctive, non-vintage wine (★★★) is a blend of 2016 and 2017 vintages. Merlot-based (50 per cent), with Cabernet Franc (40 per cent) and Tannat (10 per cent), it was hand-picked in the Far North and matured for two years in French (mostly) and American oak casks (25 per cent new). Very developed in colour, it is a distinctive, gutsy, full-flavoured wine, with hints of liquorice and spices, and moderately firm tannins. Savoury and mellow, it tastes ready.

DRY $27 –V

Kumeu River Melba's Vineyard Merlot   ★★★★

Still available, the 2013 vintage (★★★★) was estate-grown at Kumeu, in West Auckland, and barrel-aged for a year. Deeply coloured, it is an elegant rather than powerful red, sweet-fruited, with vibrant, plummy flavours, showing some savoury complexity, and a finely poised finish.

DRY $25 AV

Lake Chalice The Falcon Gimblett Gravels Hawke's Bay Merlot   ★★★☆

Priced right, the 2019 vintage (★★★☆) is a full-coloured, mouthfilling, youthful red with ripe, plummy, spicy, slightly nutty flavours, fresh acidity and very good depth. Best drinking 2021+. Enjoyable young, but also worth cellaring, the easy-drinking 2018 vintage (★★★☆) was matured for 10 months in French oak barriques. Full-coloured, it is vibrantly fruity, with good depth of youthful, ripe, plummy, spicy flavour, fresh and smooth.

DRY $19 V+

Left Field Hawke's Bay Merlot   ★★★★

If you haven't discovered the delights of Hawke's Bay Merlot, try the 2018 vintage (★★★★) of this easy-drinking, French and American oak-aged red. Full-coloured and fragrant, it's a mouthfilling, generous red with a sense of youthful drive and ripe berry, plum and spice flavours, strong and smooth. (From Te Awa.)

Vintage	18	17	16	15	14
WR	5	5	6	6	5
Drink	21-25	20-23	20-23	P	P

DRY $18 V+

Leveret Estate Hawke's Bay Merlot/Cabernet   ★★★★

Offering good value, the 2018 vintage (★★★★) was matured for 18 months in French oak (20 per cent new). A sturdy, full-coloured red, it has strong, ripe berry, plum and spice flavours, savoury notes adding complexity, and finely balanced tannins. Already drinking well, it's also well worth cellaring.

Vintage	18
WR	7
Drink	22-30

DRY $22 V+

Leveret Estate Reserve Hawke's Bay Merlot Cabernet ★★★★

Still youthful, the 2016 vintage (★★★★☆) was matured for two years in French oak casks (20 per cent new). A deeply coloured, mouthfilling red, it has fresh, concentrated blackcurrant, plum and spice flavours, finely structured and sustained. Best drinking 2022+.

Vintage	16	15	14	13
WR	7	7	6	7
Drink	22-30	20-25	20-24	20-25

DRY $29 AV

Main Divide North Canterbury Merlot/Cabernet ★★★★

Offering good value, the 2018 vintage (★★★★) from Pegasus Bay was grown at Waipara and matured for 18 months in French oak barriques (10 per cent new). It is a blend of Merlot (50 per cent), Cabernet Sauvignon (40 per cent) and Malbec (10 per cent). Full-coloured, it is mouthfilling, vibrant and supple, with strong, well-ripened plum, blackcurrant and spice flavours, showing considerable complexity, and a very harmonious finish. Best drinking mid-2021+.

DRY $21 V+

Marsden Bay of Islands The Winemaker's Daughter Merlot ★★★★

The attractive 2019 vintage (★★★★) of this Northland red was matured for a year in French oak casks (30 per cent new), and bottled unfined and unfiltered. Full-coloured, it is fragrant, sweet-fruited and supple, with rich plum and spice flavours, a hint of liquorice, good complexity, and a well-rounded finish. Drink now or cellar.

Vintage	14	13
WR	6	5
Drink	P	P

DRY $35 –V

Matawhero Single Vineyard Gisborne Merlot ★★★☆

The 2019 vintage (★★★☆) is a vibrantly fruity red, grown at Patutahi. Full-coloured, with plummy, slightly earthy aromas, it is full-bodied, with ripe blackcurrant, plum and spice flavours, fresh acidity, and a smooth finish.

DRY $23 AV

Mills Reef Bespoke Gimblett Gravels Merlot/Cabernet Franc (★★★★)

The very approachable 2016 vintage (★★★★) is a blend of Merlot (66 per cent) and Cabernet Franc (34 per cent), matured for 17 months in French (mostly) hogsheads (44 per cent new). Full-coloured, it is mouthfilling, with generous, well-ripened plum, spice and blackcurrant flavours, and hints of liquorice and nuts, in a smooth, moderately complex style, with lots of upfront appeal.

DRY $40 –V

Mills Reef Elspeth Gimblett Gravels Hawke's Bay Merlot ★★★★☆

Retasted in 2020, the 2016 vintage (★★★★☆) is a medium to full-bodied red, hand-harvested in the Mere Road Vineyard and matured for 17 months in French oak casks (34 per cent new). Sweet-fruited, it has strong blackcurrant, plum and spice flavours, with savoury oak adding complexity, and a smooth finish. Still developing, it's a good but not great vintage of this label.

Vintage	16
WR	7
Drink	20-26

 DRY $50 –V

Mills Reef Estate Hawke's Bay Merlot/Cabernet ★★★☆

Deeply coloured, with a fresh, slightly spicy, herbal bouquet, the 2018 vintage (★★★☆) is a blend of Merlot (54 per cent), Cabernet Sauvignon (33 per cent) and Cabernet Franc (13 per cent), French oak-matured for a year. Mouthfilling, it is vibrantly fruity and supple, with generous blackcurrant, plum, herb and spice flavours, showing a distinct touch of complexity. Retasted in mid-2020, it's drinking well now and offers good value.

 DRY $19 V+

Mills Reef Reserve Gimblett Gravels Hawke's Bay Merlot ★★★★

The 2018 vintage (★★★★) was hand-harvested and matured for a year in French oak barrels (25 per cent new). Retasted in mid-2020, it is deeply coloured, fragrant and full-bodied, with strong, vibrant plum, berry and spice flavours, a hint of herbs, a gentle seasoning of oak, and finely balanced tannins. Best drinking 2022+.

Vintage	18	17	16	15	14	13	12
WR	7	5	7	7	6	7	6
Drink	20-24	20-23	20-22	20-21	P	P	P

 DRY $25 AV

Mills Reef Reserve Gimblett Gravels Hawke's Bay Merlot/Malbec ★★★☆

The 2018 vintage (★★★☆) was barrel-matured for 14 months (80 per cent French; 35 per cent new). Retasted in mid-2020, it is unfolding well. Full-coloured, it is mouthfilling and smooth, with generous, youthful blackcurrant, plum and spice flavours, finely balanced tannins, and good complexity. Best drinking 2022+.

Vintage	18	17	16	15	14	13	12	11	10
WR	7	7	7	7	7	7	6	7	7
Drink	20-25	20-22	20-22	20-21	P	P	P	P	P

 DRY $25 –V

Mission Hawke's Bay Merlot ★★★☆

The deeply coloured 2019 vintage (★★★☆) is bargain-priced. A sturdy, generous red, matured in tanks to highlight its vibrant ripe-fruit flavours of blackcurrants, plums and spices, it has very good depth.

DRY $16 V+

Mission Hawke's Bay Merlot/Cabernet Sauvignon   ★★★

The 2018 vintage (★★★☆) of this sharply priced red is based on Merlot (77 per cent) and Cabernet Sauvignon (19 per cent), with splashes of Malbec and Cabernet Franc. Full-coloured, with a fragrant, slightly herbal bouquet, it is mouthfilling and supple, with generous, berryish, slightly spicy and herbal flavours, underlying tannins, and some aging potential.

 DRY $16 V+

Montford Estate Hawke's Bay Merlot/ Cabernet   (★★☆)

The debut 2017 vintage (★★☆) is a blend of Merlot (79 per cent) and Cabernet Sauvignon (21 per cent). Fullish in colour, it has a slightly rustic bouquet, leading into a fresh, firm palate with plenty of berryish, spicy, slightly earthy flavour. (From te Pā.)

DRY $25 –V

Mount Riley Marlborough Merlot/Malbec   ★★★☆

Offering fine value, the smooth 2019 vintage (★★★☆) was matured for 10 months in French and American oak barrels. Full-coloured, it has fresh, plummy, spicy, slightly earthy flavours, showing good depth, a touch of complexity, and plenty of drink-young appeal.

 DRY $18 V+

Moutere Hills Nelson Merlot   ★★★☆

Estate-grown at Upper Moutere, the 2019 vintage (★★★★) is a single-vineyard red, hand-picked from mature vines and matured for 10 months in French oak casks. Full-coloured, it is mouthfilling, fresh and youthful, with ripe, plummy, berryish flavours, seasoned with nutty oak, and finely balanced tannins. It needs time; open 2022+.

Vintage	19
WR	7
Drink	20-33

DRY $35 –V

Moutere Hills Sarau Reserve Nelson Merlot   ★★★☆

The 2018 vintage (★★★☆) is a single-vineyard red, estate-grown at Upper Moutere, hand-picked and matured for 11 months in French oak barriques. A rare wine, it has lightish, moderately youthful colour. Mouthfilling, with plenty of berryish, slightly herbal and spicy flavour, fresh acidity and some savoury complexity, it should be at its best 2021+.

Vintage	18
WR	6
Drink	20-28

DRY $55 –V

Oyster Bay Hawke's Bay Merlot   ★★★☆

From Delegat, this red accounts for a huge slice of New Zealand's exports of 'Bordeaux-style' wines (Merlot and/or Cabernet Sauvignon). Winemaker Michael Ivicevich aims for a wine with 'sweet fruit and silky tannins. The trick is – not too much oak.' Grown in the Gimblett Gravels and at Crownthorpe, it is typically fragrant and mouthfilling, with strong blackcurrant, herb and dark chocolate flavours, supple tannins, and plenty of drink-young appeal. The 2018 vintage (★★★☆) is deeply coloured, mouthfilling and smooth, with generous, berryish, plummy flavours, ripe and rounded.

DRY $20 AV

Paritua Red Hawke's Bay Merlot/Cabernets   ★★★★☆

The 2015 vintage (★★★★★) is a blend of Merlot (74 per cent), Cabernet Sauvignon (19 per cent) and Cabernet Franc (7 per cent), matured for 18 months in French oak barriques (40 per cent new). Deeply coloured, it has a fragrant, complex, nutty bouquet. A powerful, well-structured red, it has concentrated, berryish, spicy flavours, showing excellent complexity, and good tannin backbone. Still youthful, it should mature well for a decade.

DRY $49 –V

Paritua Stone Paddock Scarlet Merlot/Cabernet
Franc/Cabernet Sauvignon/Malbec   (★★★★☆)

Offering excellent value, the deeply coloured 2016 vintage (★★★★☆) is a Hawke's Bay blend of Merlot (42 per cent), Cabernet Franc (30 per cent), Cabernet Sauvignon (20 per cent) and Malbec (8 per cent), matured for a year in seasoned oak barrels. Fragrant, with a gently spicy bouquet, it is mouthfilling, with generous plum, berry and spice flavours, oak complexity, and good freshness and vigour. Drinking well now, it should be at its best 2021+.

DRY $26 V+

Pask Declaration Gimblett Gravels Hawke's Bay Merlot   ★★★★☆

Retasted in 2019, the 2013 vintage (★★★★☆) was estate-grown and matured for 18 months in French oak casks (80 per cent new). It has deep, still fairly youthful colour. Mouthfilling and savoury, with deep plum and red-berry flavours, strongly seasoned with oak, and a smooth finish, it's drinking well now but still youthful; best drinking 2021+.

Vintage	13
WR	7
Drink	20-25

DRY $50 –V

Pask Gimblett Gravels Merlot   ★★★☆

The 2018 vintage (★★★☆) was French oak-aged. Bright ruby, it is fresh and lively, in a medium to full-bodied style, with ripe plum and spice flavours, nutty, savoury notes adding complexity, balanced acidity, and good harmony. Best drinking 2022+.

DRY $22 AV

Pask Instinct Rich Royal Hawke's Bay Merlot   (★★★)

The 2018 vintage (★★★) is a bright ruby, medium-bodied red, matured for 10 months in seasoned French oak casks. Already drinking well, it has ripe, berryish, slightly spicy and nutty flavours, with a touch of complexity. Priced right.

DRY $17 AV

Pegasus Bay Merlot/Cabernet ★★★★☆

Still very youthful, the 2018 vintage (★★★★☆) of this Waipara Valley, North Canterbury red is a blend of Merlot (60 per cent), Cabernet Sauvignon (20 per cent), Cabernet Franc (10 per cent) and Malbec (10 per cent), matured for 18 months in French oak barriques (25 per cent new). Full-coloured, it is mouthfilling, with concentrated, vibrant blackcurrant, plum, herb and spice flavours, showing good complexity, finely balanced tannins, and obvious cellaring potential. Open 2022+.

DRY $33 AV

Quarter Acre Hawke's Bay Merlot/Malbec ★★★★☆

The youthful, fruit-packed 2016 vintage (★★★★☆) was matured for nine months in French oak barriques. Full-coloured, it is fragrant and mouthfilling, with strong, vibrant, plummy, spicy flavours, showing good complexity, and a firm, long finish. Well worth cellaring, it should be at its best 2021+.

DRY $35 AV

Radburnd Hawke's Bay Merlot/Cabernet (★★★★☆)

The debut 2018 vintage (★★★★☆) is from mature vines grown in the Bridge Pa Triangle and 'on the gravels'. Hand-picked, it is a blend of Merlot (70 per cent) and Cabernet Sauvignon (30 per cent), matured for 21 months in French oak barriques (partly new). Full-coloured, with a fragrant, savoury bouquet, it is an elegant, youthful red, with ripe plum/spice flavours, seasoned with nutty oak, and a fairly firm finish. Restrained in its youth, but showing excellent concentration and complexity, it's well worth cellaring to 2023+.

DRY $85 –V

Redmetal Vineyards Basket Press Bridge Pa Triangle Merlot/Cabernet Franc ★★★★☆

Retasted in 2019, the 2016 vintage (★★★★☆) was made almost entirely from Merlot and matured for 14 months in oak barrels (25 per cent new). Deeply coloured, it is mouthfilling, sweet-fruited and supple, with generous, vibrant, plummy, nutty flavours, a hint of liquorice, and a smooth finish.

Vintage	16
WR	5
Drink	20-26

DRY $36 AV

Redmetal Vineyards Bridge Pa Triangle Hawke's Bay Merlot/Cabernet Franc ★★★☆

Retasted in 2019, the 2016 vintage (★★★☆) was matured in tanks and barrels. Full and still fairly youthful in colour, it is fresh and vibrantly fruity, with smooth, ripe blackcurrant, plum and spice flavours, in an uncomplicated but generous style.

Vintage	18
WR	6
Drink	20-25

DRY $22 AV

Regent of Tantallon, The, Hawke's Bay Limited Edition Merlot/Cabernet ★★★★☆

Set for a long life, the 2015 vintage (★★★★☆) was matured for 30 months in oak barrels (36 per cent new). A sturdy, fleshy, youthful red, it is deeply coloured, with concentrated blackcurrant, plum and spice flavours, nutty, savoury notes adding complexity, and a firm foundation of tannin. Best drinking 2022+.

Renato Estate Nelson Merlot ★★★★

From mature, very low-cropped vines at Kina, the 2015 vintage (★★★★) was hand-harvested and matured for 11 months in French oak casks (15 per cent new). Full-coloured, it is full-bodied, with generous, ripe, plummy, spicy flavours, a hint of liquorice, considerable complexity, and good cellaring potential.

Vintage	15	14	13	12
WR	6	6	5	6
Drink	20-21	20-21	P	P

Roys Hill Hawke's Bay Merlot/Cabernet (★★★)

From Pask, the 2017 vintage (★★★) was grown in the Gimblett Gravels and partly barrel-aged. Enjoyable young, it has fullish colour, with ripe plum, berry and spice flavours, a touch of savoury complexity, and a smooth finish.

Saint Clair Origin Hawke's Bay Merlot ★★★★

Grown in the Gimblett Gravels, the 2018 vintage (★★★★) is a youthful, full-coloured red, with mouthfilling body and good concentration of ripe, berryish, spicy flavours. A well-structured, age-worthy wine, it should break into full stride 2022+.

Saint Clair Pioneer Block 17 Plateau Block Gimblett Gravels Merlot ★★★★☆

The 2018 vintage (★★★★☆) is a deeply coloured, vibrant, single-vineyard red, matured for 10 months in French oak casks (33 per cent new). Fleshy and full-bodied, it has concentrated, ripe, plummy, spicy, nutty flavours, showing good freshness and complexity, and a smooth finish. Well worth cellaring.

Saint Clair Rapaura Reserve Merlot ★★★★

From a single vineyard at Rapaura, on the northern side of the Wairau Valley, the 2019 vintage (★★★★) has deep, purple-flushed colour. Well worth cellaring, it is full-bodied, with strong, fresh, plummy, gently spicy and nutty flavours, a hint of liquorice, supple tannins, and a smooth finish. Best drinking 2022+.

DRY $35 –V

Selaks The Taste Collection Silky Smooth Hawke's Bay Merlot   (★★★)

The 2016 vintage (★★★) is a gutsy red, full-coloured and mouthfilling. It has plenty of ripe, plummy, spicy, slightly nutty flavour, with some rustic, earthy notes, and a fairly firm (rather than 'silky smooth') finish.

DRY $22 –V

Sileni Estates Cellar Selection Hawke's Bay Merlot   ★★★☆

The 2019 vintage (★★★★) is highly attractive. Full-coloured, it is mouthfilling and sweet-fruited, with generous blackcurrant, plum and spice flavours, and slightly nutty notes adding complexity. Already enjoyable, it should be at its best 2022+.

DRY $19 V+

Sileni Exceptional Vintage Hawke's Bay Merlot   ★★★★☆

The 2014 vintage (★★★★☆), estate-grown in the Bridge Pa Triangle, was matured for 14 months in French oak barriques (50 per cent new). A powerful, strapping red (15 per cent alcohol), it is deeply coloured and jam-packed with very ripe plum, spice and liquorice flavours. A super-charged style, it will appeal strongly to fans of 'big reds'. Best drinking 2021+.

Vintage	14	13
WR	7	7
Drink	20-25	20-25

DRY $70 –V

Sileni Grand Reserve Cut Cane Hawke's Bay Merlot   ★★★★☆

The 2018 vintage (★★★★☆) is a powerful red (15.5 per cent alcohol), made by 'cutting the bunch canes and allowing the fruit to shrivel prior to harvest [which] concentrated the juice within'. Deeply coloured, it is robust, with fresh, very ripe-tasting, berryish, plummy flavours and a hint of liquorice. If you like 'big' reds, try this.

DRY $50 –V

Sileni Grand Reserve Triangle Hawke's Bay Merlot   ★★★★☆

The very youthful 2018 vintage (★★★★★) was grown in the Bridge Pa Triangle and matured in French oak barriques. Deeply coloured, it is fresh and rich, with mouthfilling body, concentrated plum and spice flavours, seasoned with nutty oak, fine-grained tannins, impressive complexity, and the structure to age well. Best drinking 2022+.

DRY $35 AV

Snapper Rock Hawke's Bay Merlot/Cabernet   ★★★☆

The attractive 2018 vintage (★★★★) is unexpectedly satisfying for a sub-$20 red. A blend of Merlot (90 per cent) and Cabernet Sauvignon (10 per cent), it was hand-picked in the Bridge Pa Triangle and matured for 18 months in seasoned oak barrels. Deeply coloured, it is a fragrant, fresh, 'fruit-driven' style, with strong, ripe berry, plum and spice flavours to the fore, a subtle seasoning of oak, and a finely structured finish. Drink now or cellar.

DRY $19 V+

Soljans Tribute Hawke's Bay Merlot/Malbec   ★★★★

The 2016 vintage (★★★★) is a blend of Merlot (70 per cent) and Malbec (30 per cent), matured for 18 months in French oak barriques (partly new). Fresh and mouthfilling, with full, moderately youthful colour, it has generous, berryish, spicy flavours, with earthy, savoury notes adding complexity. Drink now onwards.

Vintage	16	15
WR	6	7
Drink	20-23	20-22

DRY $40 –V

Squawking Magpie the Nest Gimblett Gravels Hawke's Bay Merlot   (★★★★☆)

The sturdy, surprisingly youthful 2014 vintage (★★★★☆) is a single-vineyard blend of Merlot (86 per cent), Malbec (10 per cent) and Cabernet Franc (4 per cent), matured for 20 months in French oak casks (33 per cent new). It has bold, bright colour and a fragrant, fresh bouquet, with a hint of herbs. Mouthfilling, with vibrant plum and blackcurrant flavours, showing considerable complexity, it's well worth cellaring to 2022+.

DRY $50 –V

Stables Reserve Ngatarawa Hawke's Bay Merlot   ★★★☆

Retasted in 2020, the lightly oaked 2018 vintage (★★★☆) is maturing well. Full-coloured, fresh and vibrantly fruity, it has good depth of ripe berry, plum and spice flavours, showing some complexity, and a smooth finish. (From Mission.)

DRY $20 AV

Stonecroft Gimblett Gravels Hawke's Bay Undressed Merlot   (★★★★☆)

Certified organic, the debut 2019 vintage (★★★★☆) was estate-grown at Roys Hill and matured for five months in seasoned French oak barrels. Preservative-free (with no added sulphur), it was designed as a 'great wine to drink while it is young and vibrant'. Dark and purple-flushed, it is a distinctive red, fragrant, rich, buoyantly fruity and supple, with strong, ripe blackcurrant-evoking flavours, and gentle tannins. Delicious young.

DRY $31 AV

Stonecroft Ruhanui Gimblett Gravels Hawke's Bay
Merlot/Cabernet Sauvignon   ★★★★☆

Still very youthful, the 2016 vintage (★★★★) is a blend of Merlot (55 per cent) and Cabernet Sauvignon (45 per cent), estate-grown at Roys Hill and matured for 20 months in seasoned French oak barrels. Full-coloured, it is mouthfilling, with fresh, ripe plum and blackcurrant flavours, showing very good depth and considerable complexity, and a smooth, tightly structured finish. Best drinking 2020+.

Vintage	16	15	14	13
WR	5	6	7	7
Drink	20-27	19-26	19-26	19-25

DRY $31 AV

Te Awa Single Estate Gimblett Gravels Hawke's Bay
Merlot/Cabernet Sauvignon   ★★★★☆

The 2018 vintage (★★★★☆) is a blend of Merlot (80 per cent) and Cabernet Sauvignon (20 per cent), matured in French oak barriques (35 per cent new). Full-coloured, it is mouthfilling, with strong blackcurrant, plum and spice flavours, showing very good complexity, and a smooth, finely textured finish. An elegant, generous, supple red, it's already enjoyable, but well worth cellaring to 2023+.

Vintage	18
WR	6
Drink	23-28

 DRY $30 AV

Te Awanga Estate Hawke's Bay Merlot/Cabernet Franc   (★★★★☆)

The stylish 2015 vintage (★★★★☆) was estate-grown near the coast and oak-aged for nine months. Full-coloured, it is mouthfilling, with strong, ripe berry, plum and spice flavours, a hint of herbs, fresh acidity, and very good complexity. Best drinking 2021+.

 DRY $28 V+

Te Mata Estate Vineyards Merlot/Cabernets   ★★★★

The very age-worthy 2019 vintage (★★★★☆) is a great buy. A blend of Merlot, Cabernet Sauvignon and Cabernet Franc, it was matured for nine months in French oak barrels (partly new). Deeply coloured, it is fragrant, mouthfilling and fruit-packed, with strong, vibrant blackcurrant, plum and spice flavours, savoury notes adding complexity, fresh acidity, and obvious potential. Best drinking 2023+.

Vintage	19
WR	7
Drink	20-23

 DRY $22 V+

Thornbury Hawke's Bay Merlot   ★★★☆

Priced sharply, the 2019 vintage (★★★☆) was grown in the Gimblett Gravels and matured for over a year with French and American oak staves. Deeply coloured, it is mouthfilling, with fresh, ripe blackcurrant, plum and spice flavours, showing very good depth, and a smooth finish. Best drinking 2022+. (From Villa Maria.)

Vintage	19	18	17	16	15
WR	6	5	3	5	5
Drink	20-24	20-21	20-21	20-21	P

DRY $16 V+

Tiki Koro Hawke's Bay Merlot/Cabernet Sauvignon   (★★★★☆)

The age-worthy 2015 vintage (★★★★☆) was hand-picked and matured for 10 months in French oak barriques. Full-coloured, it is mouthfilling and youthful, with concentrated, ripe plum, spice, blackcurrant and nut flavours, oak complexity, and a fairly firm finish. Best drinking 2022+.

Vintage	15
WR	6
Drink	20-21

DRY $35 AV

Tironui Above & Beyond Single Vineyard Hawke's Bay Merlot   (★★★☆)

The 2015 vintage (★★★☆) was estate-grown at Taradale, hand-picked and matured for 20 months in French oak barrels. Fullish in colour, it is mouthfilling and smooth, with good depth of plummy, spicy flavours, and a subtle seasoning of oak adding complexity. Ready.

DRY $25 –V

Tohu Hawke's Bay Merlot   ★★★☆

An excellent drink-young style, the 2018 vintage (★★★★) was matured for eight months in French oak barriques (15 per cent new). Full-coloured, with a fragrant, gently spicy bouquet, it is mouthfilling and supple, with very good depth of berryish, plummy flavours, and a smooth finish. Fine value.

Vintage	18
WR	5
Drink	20-24

DRY $18 V+

Toi Toi Hawke's Bay Merlot   ★★★

The 2017 vintage (★★★) is a very easy-drinking red, ruby-hued and vibrantly fruity, with decent depth of berry, plum and spice flavours, some savoury notes adding complexity, and a dry, well-rounded finish.

DRY $17 AV

Unison Excalibur Gimblett Gravels Merlot/Cabernet Sauvignon/Syrah   (★★★★★)

Fragrant, with a slightly spicy, nutty bouquet, the 2014 vintage (★★★★★) is an estate-grown, hand-picked blend of Merlot (75 per cent), Cabernet Sauvignon (19 per cent) and Syrah (6 per cent), matured for nearly two years in French oak casks (20 per cent new). Deep and still fairly youthful in colour, it has impressive density, with rich, ripe blackcurrant, spice and nut flavours, and good tannin backbone. A distinctive red with strong personality, it's still maturing and should flourish for a decade. Fine value.

DRY $38 V+

Unison Merlin's Reserve Gimblett Gravels Merlot   (★★★★☆)

Barrel-aged for nearly two years, the 2015 vintage (★★★★☆) has fullish, moderately youthful colour. Full-bodied and savoury, it has fresh, ripe blackcurrant, red-berry, spice and nutty oak flavours, showing excellent complexity, and a finely balanced, lengthy finish. Drink now or cellar.

`DRY $32 AV`

Vidal Hawke's Bay Merlot/Cabernet Sauvignon   ★★★☆

Skilfully crafted for early enjoyment, the good-value 2018 vintage (★★★★) is a blend of Merlot (70 per cent) and Cabernet Sauvignon (28 per cent), with splashes of Malbec and Cabernet Franc. Partly barrel-aged (in seasoned French oak), it is full-coloured, mouthfilling, sweet-fruited and smooth, with gentle tannins, and very satisfying depth of plum, berry and spice flavours. Drink now to 2022.

Vintage	18	17	16	15
WR	6	5	6	6
Drink	20-22	20-21	20-21	P

 `DRY $16 V+`

Vidal Reserve Gimblett Gravels Merlot/Cabernet Sauvignon   ★★★★

A consistently good buy. Matured for 18 months in French oak barriques (15 per cent new), the 2018 vintage (★★★★) is a blend principally of Merlot (65 per cent), Cabernet Sauvignon (23 per cent) and Malbec (11 per cent). Full-coloured, it is mouthfilling, with strong, vibrant red-berry and spice flavours, nutty, savoury notes adding complexity, and ripe, supple tannins. A refined red, it should be at its best 2022+.

Vintage	18	17	16	15	14	13
WR	6	5	7	7	7	7
Drink	20-26	20-23	20-23	20-23	20-23	20-22

`DRY $20 V+`

Villa Maria Cellar Selection Hawke's Bay Merlot   ★★★★

Offering outstanding value, the 2019 vintage (★★★★☆) was matured for a year in French oak barriques (15 per cent new). Deeply coloured, with a fragrant, berryish, spicy bouquet, it is mouthfilling and supple, with concentrated, ripe blackcurrant, plum and spice flavours, oak complexity, and a long, very harmonious finish. Well worth cellaring.

Vintage	19	18	17
WR	7	7	6
Drink	20-25	20-24	20-23

`DRY $18 V+`

Villa Maria Cellar Selection Hawke's Bay Merlot/Cabernet Sauvignon   ★★★★

Sharply priced, the 2018 vintage (★★★★) is a blend of Merlot (63 per cent) and Cabernet Sauvignon (25 per cent), with minor portions of Malbec and Cabernet Franc, matured for a year in French, American and Hungarian oak barriques (10 per cent new). Retasted in mid-

2020, it is deeply coloured and youthful, with mouthfilling body, good concentration of vibrant blackcurrant, plum and spice flavours, a hint of herbs, and fine, supple tannins. Well worth cellaring, it should be at its best 2022+.

Vintage	19	18
WR	7	6
Drink	20-25	20-24

DRY $18 V+

Villa Maria Library Release Gimblett Gravels Merlot/Cabernet Sauvignon   (★★★★★)

The 2010 vintage (★★★★★), released in 2017, is a classy, very refined blend of Merlot (62 per cent) and Cabernet Sauvignon (38 per cent), matured in French oak barriques (60 per cent new) for 18 months. Currently delicious, it is deeply coloured, with concentrated, beautifully ripe blackcurrant and spice flavours, showing good, savoury complexity, and fine-grained tannins. Built to last, it should be at its best 2021+.

Vintage	10
WR	7
Drink	20-22

DRY $70 AV

Villa Maria Private Bin Hawke's Bay Merlot   ★★★

Enjoyable young, the full-coloured 2019 vintage (★★★) is a partly barrel-aged red, vibrantly fruity and supple, with generous, ripe, berryish, plummy flavours, a hint of herbs, and a smooth finish.

Vintage	19	18	17	16	15	14	13
WR	7	6	6	7	7	7	6
Drink	20-24	20-22	20-21	20-21	P	P	P

DRY $15 V+

Villa Maria Private Bin Hawke's Bay Merlot/Malbec/Cabernet Sauvignon   ★★★☆

The 2019 vintage (★★★☆) was matured in tanks and seasoned oak barrels. Deeply coloured, it is full-bodied, with strong, vibrant blackcurrant, plum and red-berry flavours, and a well-rounded finish. Drink now or cellar. Fine value.

Vintage	19
WR	7
Drink	20-24

DRY $15 V+

Villa Maria Private Bin Organic Hawke's Bay Merlot   ★★★☆

Certified organic, the 2019 vintage (★★★) is a great buy. Matured for nine months in tanks and seasoned oak barrels, it is full-coloured, mouthfilling and vibrantly fruity, with generous, ripe blackcurrant and plum flavours, rich and smooth. Already delicious, it's a drink-now or cellaring proposition.

Vintage	19
WR	7
Drink .	20-24

DRY $15 V+

Villa Maria Reserve Gimblett Gravels Hawke's Bay Merlot   ★★★★★

This is a consistently outstanding wine. Estate-grown, the 2018 vintage (★★★★★) was matured for 18 months in French oak barriques (50 per cent new). Deeply coloured, it is mouthfilling and savoury, with dense blackcurrant, plum and spice flavours, showing excellent complexity, and ripe, supple tannins. A refined, youthful, very harmonious red, it's well worth cellaring to 2023+.

Vintage	16	15	14	13
WR	7	7	7	7
Drink	20-26	20-25	20-26	20-23

DRY $50 AV

Wairau River Marlborough Merlot   ★★★

The easy-drinking 2017 vintage (★★★) is full-coloured and mouthfilling, with vibrant, plummy, spicy flavours, fresh and smooth.

Vintage	14
WR	6
Drink	P

DRY $20 –V

Wither Hills Hawke's Bay Merlot   (★★★☆)

Already drinking well, the 2018 vintage (★★★☆) was handled under 'different oak regimes'. Full-coloured, it is fresh and smooth, with very good depth of plummy, berryish flavours, and a well-rounded finish.

DRY $22 AV

Woodside Hill Emile Merlot/Cabernet Franc   ★★★★☆

Currently on sale, the fleshy, very generous 2015 vintage (★★★★☆) was matured for 11 months in French oak barriques (partly new). Full-coloured, with a fragrant, ripely scented bouquet, it is a sturdy red, with very ripe, plummy, spicy, nutty flavours, showing good complexity. Delicious now.

DRY $32 AV

Woodside Hill Reserve Merlot/Cabernet Franc   ★★★★★

Grown on Waiheke Island, the 2015 vintage (★★★★★) was matured for 16 months in French oak casks (partly new). Deeply coloured, it is a powerful, fleshy, rich red, with deep, ripe blackcurrant, plum and spice flavours, complex, savoury and supple. Drinking well now, it should mature gracefully for a decade.

Vintage	15	14	13
WR	6	6	7
Drink	20-24	20-23	20-23

DRY $45 AV

Montepulciano

Montepulciano is widely planted across central Italy, yielding deeply coloured, ripe wines with good levels of alcohol, extract and flavour. In the Abruzzi, it is the foundation of the often superb-value Montepulciano d'Abruzzo, and in the Marches it is the key ingredient in the noble Rosso Conero. In New Zealand, Montepulciano is a rarity and there has been confusion between the Montepulciano and Sangiovese varieties. Some wines may have been incorrectly labelled. According to the latest national vineyard survey, between 2005 and 2020, New Zealand's area of bearing Montepulciano vines expanded slightly from 6 to 8 hectares (mostly in Auckland, Hawke's Bay, Nelson and Marlborough).

Blackenbrook Family Reserve Nelson Montepulciano ★★★★☆

The youthful 2019 vintage (★★★★☆) was matured for a year in seasoned French oak barriques. Dark and purple-flushed, it is robust and sweet-fruited, with concentrated plum and spice flavours, woven with fresh acidity, supple tannins, and good cellaring potential; open 2022+.

Vintage	19
WR	7
Drink	20-25

DRY $43 –V

Coopers Creek SV Guido In Velvet Pants Huapai Montepulciano ★★★★

Estate-grown at Huapai, in West Auckland, the 2017 vintage (★★★★) is a characterful, savoury red, full-coloured and mouthfilling, with vibrant blackcurrant, plum, red-berry and spice flavours, oak complexity, and good tannin backbone. Best drinking 2021+.

Vintage	17	16	15	14	13
WR	5	6	6	6	6
Drink	20-22	20-21	P	P	P

DRY $28 AV

De La Terre Hawke's Bay Montepulciano ★★★★★

The classy 2018 vintage (★★★★★) is rare, but well worth tracking down. Hand-harvested at Havelock North and matured for 18 months in French oak barriques (40 per cent new), it's a full-coloured, ripely fragrant, sturdy red, fleshy, sweet-fruited and savoury, with generous, plummy, spicy, nutty flavours, showing good complexity. Best drinking 2022+. The 2017 vintage (★★★★☆) was also matured for 18 months in French oak barriques (40 per cent new). Deeply coloured, it is very fresh and vibrant, with good intensity of youthful, strongly spicy flavours, and a fairly firm finish. It should be long-lived; open 2022+.

Vintage	18	17	15	14	13
WR	6	6	6	7	6
Drink	21-31	20-30	20-27	20-25	20-28

DRY $45 AV

Hans Herzog Marlborough Montepulciano ★★★★★

This classy, estate-grown red is typically overflowing with sweet-fruit flavours. The 2015 vintage (★★★★☆) was hand-picked on the north side of the Wairau Valley, fermented with indigenous yeasts, matured for two and a half years in French oak barriques (partly new), and bottled unfined and unfiltered. Fragrant, with deep, youthful colour, it is mouthfilling, with fresh, youthful plum and spice flavours, showing excellent depth, refined tannins, and obvious potential; best drinking 2022+.

Kahurangi Estate Monte Nelson Montepulciano ★★★★

Worth cellaring, the 2019 vintage (★★★☆) was matured in seasoned French oak barrels. Deeply coloured, with a slightly earthy bouquet, it is a robust, fruit-packed red, with strong, fresh, plummy, spicy flavours, and a fairly firm finish. Best drinking 2022+.

Obsidian Estate Waiheke Island Montepulciano ★★★★☆

Clearly a top vintage, the 2019 (★★★★★) is a bold, well-structured, youthful red with full, bright colour. Sturdy, it is vibrantly fruity, with concentrated plum, blackcurrant and spice flavours, complex and savoury, good tannin support, and obvious potential. Best drinking 2023+.

DRY $43 –V

Nebbiolo

Nebbiolo is the foundation of Piedmont's most majestic red wines – Barolo, Barbaresco and Gattinara – renowned for their complex leather and tar flavours, powerful tannins and great longevity. In New Zealand, only 1 hectare of vines were bearing in 2020, mostly in Marlborough.

Hans Herzog Marlborough Nebbiolo
★★★★☆

Currently on sale, the rare 2013 vintage (★★★★) was estate-grown on the north side of the Wairau Valley and matured for 30 months in French oak puncheons (100 per cent new). Fullish and moderately developed in colour, it is savoury, with fresh, berryish, slightly nutty flavours, woven with fresh acidity, and good depth. Certified organic.

DRY $125 –V

Rock Ferry The Corners Vineyard Marlborough Nebbiolo
(★★★★☆)

Set for a long life, the 2016 vintage (★★★★☆) is certified organic. Barrel-aged for 17 months, it is full-coloured, with an earthy bouquet. Mouthfilling, it has concentrated, vigorous berry, plum, spice and nut flavours, fresh and firmly structured. Very much a 'food' wine, it has obvious cellaring potential; best drinking 2021+.

DRY $65 –V

Pinot Noir

New Zealand Pinot Noir enjoys strong overseas demand and there are now countless Pinot Noir labels, as producers launch second and even third-tier labels, as well as single-vineyard bottlings (and others under 'buyer's own' and export-only brands you and I have never heard of). The wines are enjoying notable success in international competitions, but you need to be aware that most of the world's elite Pinot Noir producers, especially in Burgundy, do not enter. Between 2000 and 2020, New Zealand's area of bearing Pinot Noir vines expanded from 1126 hectares to 5719 hectares, making it the country's most widely planted red-wine variety (far ahead of Merlot, with 1197 hectares).

Pinot Noir is the princely grape variety of red Burgundy. Cheaper wines typically display light, raspberry-evoking flavours, but great Pinot Noir has substance, suppleness and a gorgeous spread of flavours: cherries, fruit cake, spice and plums.

Pinot Noir is now New Zealand's most internationally acclaimed red-wine style. Nearly half of the country's total Pinot Noir plantings are in Marlborough, and the variety is also well established in Otago (27 per cent), Wairarapa (9 per cent), Canterbury (7.5 per cent), Hawke's Bay and Nelson.

Yet Pinot Noir is a frustrating variety to grow. Because it buds early, it is vulnerable to spring frosts; its compact bunches are also very prone to rot. One crucial advantage is that it ripens early, well ahead of Cabernet Sauvignon. Low cropping and the selection of superior clones are essential aspects of the production of fine wine.

Martinborough (initially) and Central Otago have enjoyed the highest profile for Pinot Noir over the past 30 years. As their output of Pinot Noir has expanded, average prices have fallen, reflecting the arrival of a tidal wave of 'entry-level' (drink-young) wines.

Of the other small regions, Nelson and Canterbury (especially Waipara) are also enjoying success. Marlborough's potential for the production of outstanding – but still widely underrated – Pinot Noir, in sufficient volumes to supply the burgeoning international demand, has also been tapped.

---

99 Rows Martinborough Pinot Noir ★★★★

From Julicher Estate, the attractive 2016 vintage (★★★★☆) is a single-vineyard red, estate-grown at Te Muna. Invitingly fragrant, with full, bright colour, it has vibrant cherry, plum and spice flavours, nutty, savoury notes adding good complexity, and plenty of youthful vigour. Best drinking 2021+.

> DRY $35 AV

Aitkins Folly Riverbank Road Wanaka Central Otago Pinot Noir ★★★★☆

Estate-grown at Wanaka, the 2017 vintage (★★★★☆) offers fine value. Deeply coloured, it is fresh, concentrated and youthful, with deep, ripe plum and spice flavours to the fore, a gentle oak influence, and obvious potential; best drinking 2023+. Still available (at a higher price of $45), the 2014 vintage (★★★★☆) is maturing very gracefully. Fragrant and full-coloured, it has strong, spicy, slightly herbal and nutty flavours, showing impressive complexity. Drink now or cellar.

> DRY $35 V+

Akarua Bannockburn Central Otago Pinot Noir ★★★★★

Estate-grown, hand-picked from mature vines and aged for 11 months in French oak barriques (27 per cent new), the 2017 vintage (★★★★★) is a bold, finely textured red. Fragrant, mouthfilling and supple, it is crammed with concentrated, ripe plum, cherry and spice flavours, showing great vigour and potential. Best drinking 2021+.

Vintage	17
WR	6
Drink	20-25

DRY $45 AV

Akarua The Siren Bannockburn Central Otago Pinot Noir ★★★★★

The 2016 vintage (★★★★★) of Akarua's top Pinot Noir was estate-grown and selected from the best eight barrels out of 800. Deep ruby, it is a powerful, sturdy, very ripe-tasting wine, lush and smooth, with concentrated plum, cherry and spice flavours, and very gentle tannins. Youthful, with a complex bouquet, it should break into full stride 2021+.

Vintage	16
WR	7
Drink	20-28

DRY $100 AV

Akitu A1 Central Otago Pinot Noir ★★★★★

Estate-grown 380 metres above sea level at Mt Barker, in the Wanaka sub-region, the barrel-aged 2018 vintage (★★★★★) is a very elegant red, full of youthful drive. Ruby-hued, mouthfilling and sweet-fruited, it is silky and savoury, with cherryish, spicy, nutty flavours, showing excellent poise and complexity. Best drinking 2022+.

DRY $59 AV

Akitu A2 Central Otago Pinot Noir ★★★★☆

Grown at high altitude at Mt Barker, in the Wanaka sub-region, the 2018 vintage (★★★★☆) was designed as a 'highly drinkable wine of unthinkable quality'. Matured in French oak casks, it is a bright ruby, attractively scented red, with strong, ripe, cherryish, spicy, nutty flavours, fresh acidity, and loads of drink-young charm. Best drinking 2022+.

DRY $40 AV

Alexander Dusty Road Martinborough Pinot Noir ★★★★☆

Designed for early drinking, but typically age-worthy, this second-tier red consistently offers great value. The powerful, almost Syrah-like 2019 vintage (★★★★★) is an estate-grown, single-vineyard wine, hand-picked and matured for 11 months in French oak barriques (15 per cent new). From a very low-cropping year (frost and drought-affected), it is deeply coloured, with dense cherry, plum and spice flavours, ripe, bold and very youthful. A 'buy now, drink later' proposition, it's well worth cellaring to 2023+.

Vintage	19	18	17	16	15	14
WR	5	6	6	6	6	6
Drink	21-22	20-24	20-23	20-22	20-21	P

DRY $27 V+

Alexander Martinborough Pinot Noir   ★★★★★

Offering top value, the 2018 vintage (★★★★★) was estate-grown in Martinborough, hand-picked and matured for 11 months in French oak barriques (25 per cent new). Deep ruby, it has rich, well-ripened, plummy, spicy, nutty flavours, complex and savoury, and a well-structured, long finish. A powerful young red, still very youthful, it's well worth cellaring to 2023+.

Vintage	18	17	16	15	14
WR	7	7	7	7	7
Drink	22-26	21-25	20-24	20-23	20-22

 DRY $38 V+

Allan Scott [Black Label] Marlborough Pinot Noir   (★★★★)

Offering good value, the 2018 vintage (★★★★) is a fragrant red, hand-picked from mature vines, fermented with indigenous yeasts and barrel-aged (20 per cent new). Ruby-hued, it is mouthfilling and savoury, with ripe-fruit flavours, good complexity, and a smooth, harmonious finish. Best drinking 2021+.

 DRY $22 V+

Amisfield Breakneck Reserve Central Otago Pinot Noir   (★★★★★)

Still very youthful, the 2017 vintage (★★★★★) is 'a selection of our finest barrels'. Hand-picked and matured in French oak barriques, it was bottled unfined and unfiltered. Deep ruby, it is mouthfilling and highly concentrated, with dense, vibrant berry and spice flavours, and a firmly structured finish. Best drinking 2023+.

 DRY $80 AV

Amisfield Central Otago Pinot Noir   ★★★★★

Estate-grown at Pisa, in the Cromwell Basin, the powerful 2017 vintage (★★★★★) was hand-picked, fermented with indigenous yeasts and matured in French oak barriques. Bright ruby, it is mouthfilling, sweet-fruited and savoury, with concentrated cherry, plum and spice flavours, showing good complexity, and a well-structured finish. Still very fresh and youthful, it's well worth cellaring to 2022+.

 DRY $50 AV

Amisfield RKV Reserve Central Otago Pinot Noir   ★★★★★

Estate-grown and hand-picked from selected blocks in the Rocky Knoll Vineyard at Pisa, in the Cromwell Basin, the 2016 vintage (★★★★★) was fermented with indigenous yeasts and matured in French oak barriques. Already very expressive, it is ruby-hued, fragrant and mouthfilling, with cherry, plum, spice and nut flavours, complex, savoury and smooth. A delicious mouthful, it should be at its best 2021+.

DRY $120 AV

Anchorage Family Estate Nelson Pinot Noir ★★☆

The 2019 vintage (★★☆) was French oak-aged for six months. Light ruby, it is fresh and light-bodied, with gentle plum and spice flavours, offering smooth, easy drinking.

DRY $19 –V

Anna's Way Marlborough Pinot Noir ★★★☆

The 2017 vintage (★★★☆) was matured for 10 months in French oak barrels. Lightish in colour, with a hint of development, it is medium-bodied, with gentle, plummy, spicy, slightly nutty flavours, showing some complexity, and a smooth finish. (From Awatere River Wine Co.)

DRY $23 V+

Aotea by Seifried Nelson Pinot Noir (★★★★☆)

The highly attractive 2019 vintage (★★★★☆) was hand-picked, matured in French oak barriques and barrel-selected as Seifried's best Pinot Noir. Full ruby, it is mouthfilling, fleshy, sweet-fruited and supple, with strong, ripe cherry, plum and spice flavours, finely textured and savoury. Best drinking 2022+.

Vintage	19
WR	6
Drink	21-26

DRY $39 V+

Apopo by Stanley Estates Marlborough Pinot Noir (★★★★)

Enjoyable young, the attractive, ruby-hued 2019 vintage (★★★★) is medium-bodied, vibrantly fruity and supple, with fresh, ripe cherry, plum and spice flavours, a touch of complexity and very good depth. Best drinking mid-2021+.

DRY $39 AV

Archangel Central Otago Pinot Noir ★★★★

Estate-grown south of Wanaka, at the northern end of the Cromwell Basin, the 2016 vintage (★★★★) is a single-vineyard red, matured for a year in French oak casks (25 per cent new). Full, bright ruby, it is floral and sweet-fruited, with fine-grained tannins and very satisfying depth of plummy, spicy flavours. A supple, youthful red, it's well worth cellaring to 2021+.

DRY $37 AV

Aronui Single Vineyard Nelson Pinot Noir ★★★★

From Kono (which also owns the Tohu brand), the 2016 vintage (★★★★) was estate-grown at Upper Moutere, hand-picked and French oak-aged. It is light ruby, savoury and sweet-fruited. Made with a gentle touch, it has delicate cherry, plum, spice and nut flavours, velvety tannins, and very good complexity and harmony.

DRY $25 V+

Ashwell Martinborough Pinot Noir ★★★★☆

The youthful 2018 vintage (★★★★☆) was barrel-matured for a year. Full, bright ruby, it's a very age-worthy, full-bodied red, with concentrated, ripe plum and spice flavours, nutty and savoury, and a moderately firm finish. Best drinking 2021+. The 2019 vintage (★★★★☆) is deep ruby, sweet-fruited and savoury. Full-bodied, it has very good concentration of cherry, plum and spice flavours, hints of liquorice and nuts, and impressive complexity. A very age-worthy red, it's well worth cellaring to 2022+.

Vintage	19	18	17
WR	5	6	6
Drink	20-29	20-28	20-27

DRY $40 AV

Askerne Hawke's Bay Pinot Noir ★★★☆

Already drinking well, the 2018 vintage (★★★★) is bargain-priced. Ruby-hued, it is fleshy, with generous, ripe, cherryish, nutty flavours, showing good complexity, and a very harmonious finish. Drink now or cellar.

DRY $23 V+

Astrolabe Comelybank Vineyard Waihopai Valley Marlborough Pinot Noir ★★★★★

The powerful 2019 vintage (★★★★★) was grown in the lower Waihopai Valley, hand-harvested and matured for 10 months in French oak casks (25 per cent new). Boldly coloured, it is a fresh, very youthful, almost Syrah-like red, with dense, plummy, spicy flavours, a hint of liquorice, and obvious potential. Best drinking 2023+.

Vintage	19
WR	7
Drink	20-30

DRY $50 AV

Astrolabe Marlborough Pinot Noir ★★★★

The elegant, youthful 2018 vintage (★★★★) is a regional blend, grown from the Waihopai Valley to the Kekerengu Coast. Matured for 10 months in French oak barriques (25 per cent new), it is bright ruby, scented and supple, with vibrant cherry, plum and spice flavours, showing very good depth, savoury notes adding complexity, and a fresh, finely poised finish.

Vintage	18	17	16
WR	6	7	7
Drink	20-26	20-25	20-24

DRY $35 AV

Astrolabe Sleepers Vineyard Kekerengu Marlborough Pinot Noir ★★★★

The 2019 vintage (★★★★) was grown on the Kekerengu Coast, hand-harvested and matured for 10 months in French oak barrels (25 per cent new). A very distinctive red, it is full-coloured and fragrant, with concentrated, vigorous plum/spice flavours, a strong herbal thread, and fresh acidity.

DRY $50 –V

Astrolabe Valleys Wairau Valley Pinot Noir ★★★☆

Designed as a 'lightly wooded, early release' style, the 2016 vintage (★★★★) is drinking well now. Maturing gracefully, it is lively, with cherry, plum, spice and nut flavours, fresh and savoury, and good complexity. The youthful 2018 vintage (★★★☆) is ruby-hued, with strong cherry, plum and spice flavours, a hint of tamarillo, and fresh acidity. Best drinking mid-2021+.

Vintage	19	18	16
WR	NM	6	6
Drink	NM	20-27	20-23

DRY $27 AV

Astrolabe Wrekin Vineyard Marlborough Pinot Noir ★★★★★

The powerful 2019 vintage (★★★★★) was hand-harvested in Marlborough's upper Brancott Valley and matured for 10 months in French oak barrels (25 per cent new). Boldly coloured, it is mouthfilling, rich and supple, with deep, lush plum, cherry and spice flavours, and a lasting finish. It should flourish for a decade.

DRY $65 AV

Ata Rangi Martinborough Pinot Noir ★★★★★

One of the greatest of all New Zealand wines, this Martinborough red is powerfully built and concentrated, yet seductively fragrant and supple. 'Intense, opulent fruit with power beneath' is founder Clive Paton's goal. 'Complexity comes with time.' The grapes are drawn from numerous sites, including the estate vineyard, planted in 1980, and the vines, up to 39 years old, have a very low average yield of 4.5 tonnes of grapes per hectare. The wine is fermented with indigenous yeasts and maturation is for 11 months in French oak barriques (35 per cent new in 2017). The 2017 vintage (★★★★★) is a very 'complete', highly perfumed wine. Full-coloured, it is savoury and supple, with deep, vigorous plum and spice flavours, seasoned with nutty oak, and a long, finely structured finish. A complex, very age-worthy red, it should be at its best 2022+.

Vintage	17	16	15	14	13	12	11
WR	6	7	7	7	7	7	7
Drink	20-30	20-28	20-27	20-26	20-25	20-24	20-23

DRY $75 AV

🍇🍇🍇

Ataahua Waipara Pinot Noir ★★★★☆

Invitingly perfumed, the 2018 vintage (★★★★☆) is a ruby-hued, medium-bodied North Canterbury red, with moderately youthful, cherryish, spicy flavours. Silky-textured, it has fresh acidity, very good complexity, and lots of early-drinking appeal. The age-worthy 2017 vintage (★★★★) was hand-harvested and barrel-aged for a year. Deep ruby, with a hint of development, it has generous cherry, plum and spice flavours, showing good complexity, and a moderately firm finish. Best drinking 2021+.

DRY $37 V+

Auntsfield Single Vineyard Southern Valleys Marlborough Pinot Noir   ★★★★★

Grown on north-facing slopes at Auntsfield, on the south side of the Wairau Valley, the 2019 vintage (★★★★★) is highly impressive. Boldly coloured, it is a powerful, full-bodied red with dense, ripe plum, cherry and spice flavours, good tannin backbone, and obvious potential for long-term cellaring. Open 2023+.

DRY $45 AV

Aurum Madeleine Organic Central Otago Pinot Noir   ★★★★☆

Named after the winemaker's daughter, the 2016 vintage (★★★★★) was estate-grown at Lowburn, hand-picked, fermented with indigenous yeasts, matured for a year in seasoned French oak casks, and bottled unfined and unfiltered. Full (and not entirely clear) in colour, it is mouthfilling and silky-textured, with deep cherry, plum and spice flavours, supple and savoury, and excellent complexity and harmony. A thought-provoking wine, it should be at its best 2021+. Certified organic.

Vintage	16
WR	6
Drink	22-32

DRY $88 –V

Aurum Mathilde Organic Central Otago Pinot Noir   ★★★★★

Estate-grown at Lowburn, the very age-worthy 2017 vintage (★★★★★) was hand-picked, fermented with indigenous yeasts, matured for a year in French oak casks (20 per cent new), and bottled unfined and unfiltered. Deep ruby, it is mouthfilling, with dense, vibrant, plummy, spicy flavours, still fresh and youthful, and a well-structured, moderately firm finish. Full of potential, it's well worth cellaring to 2022+.

Vintage	17	16
WR	6	6
Drink	20-30	20-26

DRY $55 AV

Aurum Organic Central Otago Pinot Noir   ★★★★☆

Certified organic, the impressive 2018 vintage (★★★★★) was estate-grown and hand-harvested at Lowburn, matured for a year in French oak casks (20 per cent new), and bottled unfined and unfiltered. Deeply coloured, it is fragrant and full-bodied, with concentrated, youthful cherry, plum and spice flavours, savoury notes adding complexity, and a finely structured finish. A very age-worthy red, it should be at its best 2022+.

Vintage	18	17
WR	6	6
Drink	20-30	20-24

DRY $38 V+

Awatere River Marlborough Pinot Noir   ★★★☆

The 2018 vintage (★★★☆) was matured for 11 months in French oak barriques. Ruby-hued, it is a fresh, medium-bodied, supple red, with ripe cherry, plum and spice flavours, hints of herbs and nuts, considerable complexity, and gentle tannins. Best drinking 2021+.

DRY $30 –V

B Martinborough Pinot Noir   (★★★★☆)

'I made this wine for when my darling comes home and says: "Is there a bottle open?",' says winemaker Ben Dugdale. Grown at two sites, the 2016 vintage (★★★★☆) is a mouthfilling, ruby-hued wine with generous cherry, plum, spice and nut flavours, complex and savoury, and some maturity showing. Drink now or cellar.

DRY $30 V+

B Pinot Brothers Bendigo Pinot Noir   (★★★★☆)

The 2018 vintage (★★★★☆) was hand-picked and matured for nine months in seasoned French oak barrels. Deep ruby, it is full-bodied, with strong cherry, plum and spice flavours, showing excellent complexity and harmony. Best drinking 2022+.

DRY $50 –V

B Pinot Brothers Waitaki Pinot Noir   (★★★★★)

The very graceful 2018 vintage (★★★★★) was hand-picked in North Otago and matured for nine months in seasoned French oak barrels. Bright ruby, it is invitingly floral, with vibrant, ripe cherry, plum and spice flavours, complex and supple. Already delicious, it's a wine of substance and charm.

DRY $50 AV

Babich Winemakers' Reserve Marlborough Pinot Noir   ★★★★☆

The 2017 vintage (★★★★☆) was estate-grown in the Cowslip Valley Vineyard, in the Waihopai Valley, and matured for 10 months in barrels (35 per cent new). Full, bright ruby, it is a very graceful, sweet-fruited, savoury and supple red, with cherry, plum and spice flavours, showing good complexity, and a long, harmonious finish. Best drinking 2021+.

Vintage	17
WR	6
Drink	20-24

DRY $45 –V

Baby Doll Marlborough Pinot Noir   ★★☆

The 2019 vintage (★★☆) is deep ruby, with a slightly earthy bouquet. Fresh and berryish, slightly gutsy and firm, it's a solid, youthful red, but lacks real charm. (From Yealands.)

DRY $20 –V

Bald Hills 3 Acres Bannockburn Central Otago Pinot Noir   ★★★★☆

Offering great value, the 2017 vintage (★★★★★) was hand-picked and matured for a year in French oak barriques (28 per cent new). Full-coloured, it is fragrant and mouthfilling, with deep, ripe cherry, plum and spice flavours, refined tannins, and lovely mouthfeel and texture. Savoury and seductive, it's well worth cellaring.

 DRY $32 V+

Bald Hills Bannockburn Single Vineyard Central Otago Pinot Noir   ★★★★☆

Maturing very gracefully, the 2016 vintage (★★★★★) was estate-grown and matured for a year in French oak barriques (33 per cent new). Still unfolding, it is full-bodied and vibrantly fruity, with ripe cherry, plum and spice flavours, nutty, savoury notes adding complexity, fresh acidity, and good tannin backbone. Best drinking 2022+.

 DRY $46 –V

Ballasalla Central Otago Pinot Noir   ★★★★☆

The 2017 vintage (★★★★☆) of this single-vineyard Bendigo red offers fine value. Barrel-aged for 10 months, it is bright ruby, with a fragrant, savoury bouquet. Mouthfilling, it is sweet-fruited, with rich cherry, plum and spice flavours, showing very good complexity and harmony, and a smooth finish. (From Folding Hill.)

 DRY $32 V+

Bannock Brae Central Otago Pinot Noir   ★★★★★

This Bannockburn red is typically outstanding. The 2016 vintage (★★★★☆) is a refined, youthful wine, ruby-hued, with ripe cherry, plum, spice and nut flavours, showing good complexity, and a very harmonious, savoury, lengthy finish. Best drinking mid-2021+.

Vintage	16	15	14	13	12	11
WR	7	7	7	7	NM	7
Drink	20-26	20-26	20-25	20-25	NM	20-25

DRY $60 AV

Bannock Brae Goldfields Central Otago Pinot Noir   ★★★★

The 2017 vintage (★★★★) is deep ruby, with a fresh, fragrant bouquet. Mouthfilling, it is vibrantly fruity, with strong cherry, plum and spice flavours, finely integrated oak and ripe, supple tannins. Best drinking 2021+.

Vintage	17	16	15	14	13	12
WR	7	6	6	7	6	7
Drink	20-25	20-24	20-23	20-23	20-22	20-22

 DRY $35 AV

Bel Echo by Clos Henri Marlborough Pinot Noir   ★★★★

The 2017 vintage (★★★★) was estate-grown on the stonier, less clay-bound soils at Clos Henri, in the Wairau Valley, and matured for a year in old French oak barrels. Ruby-hued, it is mouthfilling and sweet-fruited, with cherry, plum, spice and nut flavours, complex and savoury, and a moderately firm but harmonious finish. Drinking well now, it should be at its best 2021+. Certified organic.

Vintage	17	16	15	14	13
WR	6	6	6	6	6
Drink	20-25	20-25	20-22	P	P

DRY $34 AV

Bell Hill Pinot Noir   ★★★★★

From a small vineyard on a limestone slope at Waikari, inland from Waipara, in North Canterbury, this is a rare, distinguished red. It is typically a generous wine, powerful yet silky, with sweet cherry, plum and spice flavours, complex, very harmonious and graceful. Tasted 'blind' in 2017, the notably powerful 2006 vintage was dark, rich and still in full stride. The most recent vintage I have tasted was the 2011 (★★★★★), in late 2014. Full-coloured, with lovely ripeness and harmony, it was youthful, plummy, spicy and savoury, with excellent complexity, and a very finely textured, long finish.

DRY $125 AV

Bellbird Spring Block Eight Waipara Valley North Canterbury Pinot Noir   (★★★★☆)

Drinking well now, the 2015 vintage (★★★★☆) was matured for a year in French oak barrels (50 per cent new). Ruby-hued, with some development showing, it has a fragrant, savoury bouquet. Mouthfilling, with cherry, plum, spice and nut flavours, it shows excellent complexity, with good tannin backbone.

DRY $45 –V

Bellbird Spring Waipara Valley North Canterbury Pinot Noir   (★★★★)

The 2016 vintage (★★★★) was matured for a year in French oak casks (20 per cent new). Ruby-hued, it is fragrant, with fresh, youthful cherry, plum, spice and nut flavours, showing good complexity. Best drinking 2021+.

DRY $37 AV

Big Sky Te Muna Road Martinborough Pinot Noir   ★★★★★

Offering very good value, the 2018 vintage (★★★★★) was estate-grown and matured in French oak casks (15 per cent new). Full-coloured, it is fragrant, mouthfilling and sweet-fruited, with generous, ripe cherry, plum, spice and nut flavours, good tannin support, and a savoury, finely structured finish. A very age-worthy wine, it's well worth cellaring to mid-2021+.

DRY $40 V+

Bird Big Barrel Marlborough Pinot Noir   ★★★☆

Matured in large, 900-litre barrels, the 2017 vintage (★★★☆) is ruby-hued, with a savoury, slightly earthy bouquet. Full-bodied, it has ripe, slightly spicy and nutty flavours and a fairly firm finish.

DRY $38 –V

Black Cottage Marlborough Pinot Noir   ★★★☆

A very enjoyable drink-young style, the 2018 vintage (★★★☆) is a blend of Wairau Valley (mostly) and Awatere Valley grapes, partly oak-aged. Light ruby, it is medium-bodied, vibrant, sweet-fruited and supple, with gentle cherry, plum and spice flavours, fresh acidity and a touch of complexity. (From Two Rivers of Marlborough.)

DRY $20 V+

Black Cottage Reserve Central Otago Pinot Noir   ★★★☆

Still on sale, the 2016 vintage (★★★★) was aged for 10 months in tanks and seasoned French oak barrels. Deep ruby, it is fragrant, full-bodied, fruit-packed and supple, with generous, ripe plum, red-berry and spice flavours, showing a distinct touch of complexity, and a finely textured finish.

DRY $25 AV

Black Estate Damsteep North Canterbury Pinot Noir   ★★★★★

Certified organic, the 2017 vintage (★★★★☆) was estate-grown in the Damsteep Vineyard, planted in 1999 'at the top of Waipara Valley', fermented with indigenous yeasts, matured for a year in seasoned oak barrels, and bottled unfined and unfiltered. Full-coloured, with a fragrant, savoury bouquet, it is medium-bodied, with youthful, ripe, plummy, spicy flavours, showing excellent complexity, fine-grained tannins and obvious potential; best drinking 2022+. The 2018 vintage (★★★★☆) is a ruby-hued, slightly cloudy wine, full-bodied, with strong, youthful, plummy, spicy flavours, fresh acidity, and a tightly structured finish. Best drinking 2022+.

DRY $45 AV

Black Estate Home North Canterbury Pinot Noir   ★★★★☆

Certified organic, the 2017 vintage (★★★★), estate-grown in the Home Vineyard at Omihi, was hand-picked from vines planted in 1994 and 2011. Fermented with indigenous yeasts, it was matured for a year in seasoned French oak barriques, and bottled unfined and unfiltered. Bright ruby, it is medium-bodied, with moderately concentrated, plummy, spicy, slightly nutty flavours, threaded with fresh acidity, and a lively, finely structured finish. Best drinking 2022+. The 2018 vintage (★★★★☆) is ruby-hued, with a highly fragrant, savoury bouquet. Medium-bodied, it has strong, vibrant, plummy, spicy, nutty flavours, fresh acidity, and excellent complexity. Best drinking 2022+.

DRY $45 –V

Black Estate Netherwood North Canterbury Pinot Noir   ★★★★☆

Certified organic, the characterful 2017 vintage (★★★★☆) was hand-picked from ungrafted vines in the first hill-grown vineyard in North Canterbury, established in 1986. Fermented with indigenous yeasts, it was matured for a year in seasoned oak barrels, and bottled unfined and unfiltered. Full and fairly youthful in colour, it is medium-bodied, with rich, plummy, spicy, slightly herbal and nutty flavours, showing excellent complexity, gentle tannins, and a finely poised, harmonious finish. Best drinking 2022+.

DRY $75 –V

Black Peak Wanaka Central Otago Pinot Noir (★★★★★)

The classy, distinctive 2017 vintage (★★★★★) is deeply coloured, youthful and fruit-packed. A powerful young red, it is mouthfilling, with rich cherry, plum and spice flavours, finely integrated oak, good complexity, and a supple, persistent finish. Already delicious, it should be at its best mid-2021+.

DRY $42 V+

Blackenbrook Family Reserve Nelson Pinot Noir ★★★★☆

The bold 2019 vintage (★★★★★) was estate-grown, hand-harvested and matured for a year in French oak barriques (30 per cent new). Deeply coloured, it is a powerful, sturdy, highly concentrated red, with rich, very youthful plum and spice flavours, oak complexity, and a fairly firm finish. A 'masculine' style of Pinot Noir, it will be long-lived; best drinking 2023+.

Vintage	19
WR	7
Drink	21-30

DRY $43 AV

Blackenbrook Nelson Pinot Noir ★★★★

The powerful, estate-grown 2019 vintage (★★★★☆) was hand-harvested and matured for a year in French oak barrels (13 per cent new). Deeply coloured, it is mouthfilling, with rich, ripe, plummy, spicy flavours, showing good complexity. An almost Syrah-like red, it is still very youthful; best drinking 2022+.

Vintage	19
WR	7
Drink	21-25

DRY $29 V+

Blind River Awatere Valley Marlborough Pinot Noir ★★★★

Retasted in mid-2020, the 2017 vintage (★★★★) was estate-grown in the Awatere Valley. Bright ruby, it is attractively scented, with strong, vibrant, plummy, spicy, slightly nutty flavours, showing good complexity. Still youthful, it's a drink-now or cellaring proposition.

Vintage	17
WR	7
Drink	20-25

DRY $35 AV

Boneline, The, Waimanu Waipara Pinot Noir ★★★★☆

Hand-picked from 'old' vines, the 2016 vintage (★★★★☆) was barrel-matured for a year. Deep ruby, it is full-bodied and concentrated, with strong cherry, plum and spice flavours, nutty, savoury notes adding complexity, finely balanced tannins, and a long, harmonious finish. Drink now or cellar.

DRY $40 AV

Boneline, The, Waipara Wai-Iti Pinot Noir   (★★★★)

Currently open and expressive, the 2017 vintage (★★★★) was hand-picked and given 'judicious' wood handling (one year in barrels, 5 per cent new). Full, bright ruby, it is mouthfilling, supple and savoury, with cherry, plum, spice and nut flavours, showing very good complexity and harmony. Best drinking 2021+.

DRY $40 –V

Brancott Estate Identity Awatere Valley Marlborough Pinot Noir   (★★★☆)

The Identity range was created to celebrate Marlborough's sub-regions. Enjoyable young, the 2017 vintage (★★★☆) is ruby-hued, with generous, plummy, spicy flavours, a hint of herbs, some savoury complexity, and a smooth finish.

DRY $22 V+

Brancott Estate Letter Series 'T' Marlborough Pinot Noir   ★★★★

The 2017 vintage (★★★★) is a savoury red, barrel-aged for nine months. Ruby-hued, it is fragrant and full-bodied, with ripe, plummy, spicy flavours, showing good complexity, and a fairly firm finish. Best drinking 2021+.

DRY $25 V+

Brancott Estate Reflection Limited Edition Marlborough Pinot Noir   (★★★★★)

The 2015 vintage (★★★★★) is Pinot Noir on a grand scale. Hand-picked from 15-year-old vines in the Brancott Vineyard, it was fermented with indigenous yeasts and matured for 18 months in French oak barriques (36 per cent new). Deeply coloured, with a fragrant, slightly earthy bouquet, it is powerful and sturdy (14.4 per cent alcohol), with concentrated cherry, plum, spice and nut flavours, very harmonious, rich and supple. Delicious now, it should break into full stride 2021+.

DRY $80 AV

Brennan B2 Central Otago Pinot Noir   ★★★★

Estate-grown at Gibbston, the 2015 vintage (★★★★☆) is a savoury, finely poised red, drinking well now. Full-coloured, with a hint of development, it is fragrant and vibantly fruity, with ripe cherry, plum and spice flavours, a hint of herbs, good tannin backbone, and excellent depth.

DRY $35 AV

Brennan Gibbston Central Otago Pinot Noir   ★★★★☆

Still on sale, the 2014 vintage (★★★★★) is an impressively fragrant, rich and complex red. Full-coloured, it is mouthfilling, with concentrated, ripe cherry, plum, herb and spice flavours, savoury, nutty notes, and a long, harmonious finish.

DRY $65 –V

Brightside Organic New Zealand Pinot Noir   ★★★

Certified organic, the 2017 vintage (★★★☆) was grown in Nelson. Full, bright ruby, it is mouthfilling and vibrantly fruity, with strong, plummy, spicy flavours, an earthy streak, fresh acidity, and good density. Priced sharply. (From Kaimira Estate.)

DRY $17 V+

Brightwater Vineyards Lord Rutherford Nelson Pinot Noir   ★★★★☆

The 2017 vintage (★★★★☆) was estate-grown, fermented with indigenous yeasts, matured for 11 months in French oak barriques (25 per cent new), and bottled unfined and unfiltered. Fragrant, rich and complex, it is sweet-fruited and vibrant, with deep cherry, plum and spice flavours, fine-grained tannins, and a lengthy finish.

Vintage	17	16	15
WR	7	NM	NM
Drink	20-24	NM	NM

 DRY $50 –V

Brightwater Vineyards Nelson Pinot Noir   ★★★★☆

The 2017 vintage (★★★★) was matured for 11 months in French oak casks (20 per cent new), and bottled unfined and unfiltered. Bright ruby, with mouthfilling body, it is sweet-fruited, with good concentration of cherry, plum and spice flavours, a gentle seasoning of oak adding complexity, and a smooth finish.

Vintage	17	16	15	14	13
WR	6	NM	6	7	6
Drink	20-22	NM	P	P	P

 DRY $40 AV

Brightwater Vineyards Te Kāhu Nelson Pinot Noir   (★★★★☆)

Delicious young, the deeply coloured 2019 vintage (★★★★☆) was French oak-matured for nearly a year. Fragrant, full-bodied and sweet-fruited, it is rich and supple, with ripe plum, cherry and spice flavours, gently seasoned with oak, and a very harmonious finish. Best drinking 2022+.

Vintage	19
WR	6
Drink	21-23

 DRY $28 V+

Bristol Farm Central Otago Pinot Noir   ★★★★☆

Still unfolding, the 2018 vintage (★★★★☆) is a fragrant, single-vineyard red, grown at Bannockburn and matured in French oak casks (22 per cent new). Bright ruby, it is mouthfilling and savoury, with strong, ripe cherry, plum and spice flavours, finely integrated oak and good tannin backbone. Open 2022+. Revealing impressive depth, the 2017 vintage (★★★★★) is a 2:1 blend of Bannockburn and Bendigo grapes, matured for 11 months in French oak casks (15 per cent new). Deep ruby, with a fresh, spicy, floral bouquet, it has concentrated, plummy, spicy, nutty flavours, complex, savoury and lingering. Set for a long life, it's well worth cellaring to 2022+.

DRY $45 –V

Bronte Nelson Pinot Noir ★★★★

From Rimu Grove, the impressive 2019 vintage (★★★★☆) was estate-grown and matured for 11 months in French oak casks. Bright ruby, it is mouthfilling and sweet-fruited, with generous cherry, plum and spice flavours, fresh acidity, savoury notes adding complexity, and ripe, supple tannins. Already drinking well, but very age-worthy, it should be at its best 2022+.

Vintage	19	18	17
WR	7	6	6
Drink	20-30	20-26	20-25

DRY $35 AV

Burn Cottage Burn Cottage Vineyard Central Otago Pinot Noir ★★★★★

Estate-grown in the foothills of the Pisa Range, in the Cromwell Basin, the powerful, youthful 2017 vintage (★★★★★) was hand-harvested and matured in French oak barriques (25 per cent new). Deeply coloured, it is mouthfilling, with notably rich, ripe cherry, plum and spice flavours, finely integrated oak, good tannin backbone, and a well-rounded finish. Best drinking 2022+. Certified organic.

Vintage	17	16	15	14	13	12	11
WR	7	7	6	7	7	7	6
Drink	20-27	20-26	20-25	20-25	20-25	20-21	P

DRY $70 AV

Burn Cottage Moonlight Race Central Otago Pinot Noir ★★★★★

The seductive 2018 vintage (★★★★★) was entirely estate-grown at the company's sites at Lowburn and Bannockburn. Fermented with indigenous yeasts, it was matured in French oak casks (19 per cent new). Perfumed, mouthfilling and supple, it has deep, well-ripened plum, spice and nut flavours, gentle tannins, and a silky-textured finish. A very harmonious red that caresses your mouth, it's already delicious.

DRY $45 AV

Burn Cottage Valli Vineyard Gibbston Central Otago Pinot Noir ★★★★★

Since the debut 2014 vintage (★★★★★), Burn Cottage, based in the Cromwell Basin, has drawn grapes from the more elevated Valli Vineyard, at Gibbston (for their reverse swap, see Valli Burn Cottage Vineyard Central Otago Pinot Noir). Matured in French oak barriques (29 per cent new), the 2017 vintage (★★★★★) is rich and finely textured. From 18-year-old vines, it is deeply coloured and highly fragrant. A powerful red, it has notably dense, plummy, slightly herbal and spicy flavours, youthful vigour, and ripe, supple tannins. Best drinking 2022+.

DRY $70 AV

Burnt Spur Martinborough Pinot Noir ★★★★

The 2016 vintage (★★★★) was French oak-aged for 10 months. Full, bright ruby, it is mouthfilling and sweet-fruited, with generous, ripe cherry, plum and spice flavours, showing good complexity, and supple tannins. Drinking well now, it's priced right.

Vintage	16	
WR	6	
Drink	20-23	DRY $28 V+

Camshorn Waipara Pinot Noir (★★★☆)

Priced right, the deep ruby 2019 vintage (★★★☆) is an easy-drinking, vibrantly fruity red with a slightly spicy bouquet. Full-bodied, it has very good depth of fresh, ripe berry, plum and spice flavours, a touch of complexity and a smooth finish.

DRY $20 V+

Carrick Bannockburn Central Otago Pinot Noir ★★★★★

A regional classic. Certified organic, the very age-worthy 2017 vintage (★★★★★) was estate-grown and matured in French oak barriques. Full-coloured, it is mouthfilling, concentrated, savoury and structured, with ripe cherry, plum, spice and nut flavours, slightly earthy notes adding complexity, real depth through the palate, and a long finish. Best drinking mid-2021+.

Vintage	17	16	DRY $47 AV
WR	7	7	
Drink	21-27	20-26	

Carrick Excelsior Central Otago Pinot Noir ★★★★★

Likely to be long-lived, the very classy 2014 vintage (★★★★★) was harvested from mature, estate-grown vines at Bannockburn. A full-coloured, powerful but approachable wine, it was matured for 16 months in barrels (15 per cent new). It has substantial body, fresh, deep cherry, plum and spice flavours, nutty oak adding complexity, fine-grained tannins and a resounding finish. Best drinking 2021+.

Vintage	14	DRY $95 AV
WR	7	
Drink	20-30	

Carrick The Magnetic Central Otago Pinot Noir (★★★★☆)

Showing good personality, the 2016 vintage (★★★★☆) is based on the Abel clone of Pinot Noir, estate-grown at Bannockburn and matured for 11 months in seasoned oak barrels. Ruby-hued, it is a distinctive wine, with concentrated cherry, plum and spice flavours, a gentle seasoning of oak, good complexity, smooth tannins, and loads of drink-young appeal. Certified organic.

Vintage	16	
WR	6	
Drink	20-23	DRY $48 -V

Carrick Unravelled Central Otago Pinot Noir ★★★★

The 2018 vintage (★★★★) of this organically certified red doesn't claim Bannockburn origin on its labels, but is 'essentially a declassification of wine from the Carrick vineyards'. Full, bright ruby, it has very good depth of vibrant, ripe, plummy, spicy flavours, savoury notes adding complexity, supple tannins, and lots of drink-young appeal.

DRY $29 V+

Catalina Sounds Marlborough Pinot Noir ★★★★

Attractive young, but also worth cellaring, the 2018 vintage (★★★★) was partly estate-grown in the Sound of White Vineyard, in the upper Waihopai Valley. Bright ruby, it has moderately rich cherry, plum, spice and nut flavours, showing good complexity, fresh acidity, and a smooth, harmonious finish.

DRY $30 AV

Catalina Sounds Sound of White Marlborough Pinot Noir ★★★★☆

Estate-grown in the Sound of White Vineyard, in the upper Waihopai Valley, the 2017 vintage (★★★★★) is a very classy red. Deeply coloured, it is mouthfilling, sweet-fruited and savoury, with concentrated, ripe fruit flavours, excellent complexity, and a well-structured, lasting finish. Best drinking 2022+.

DRY $50 –V

Ceres Composition Bannockburn Central Otago Pinot Noir ★★★★☆

Already delicious, the 2018 vintage (★★★★★) is a very harmonious red, grown at two sites and matured for a year in French oak casks (18 per cent new). Deep ruby, it is mouthfilling and sweet-fruited, with generous cherry, plum, spice and nut flavours, showing excellent complexity, finely balanced tannins, and a long finish. Drink now or cellar.

DRY $40 AV

Ceres The Artists Collection Inlet Vineyard Bannockburn
Central Otago Pinot Noir (★★★★★)

Delicious now, the 2016 vintage (★★★★★) is ruby-hued, fragrant and sweet-fruited. Savoury, nutty and complex, it has generous cherry, plum, spice and nut flavours that build well to a powerful finish.

DRY $79 AV

Chard Farm Mason Vineyard Central Otago Pinot Noir ★★★★☆

The elegant 2018 vintage (★★★★☆) is a single-vineyard Parkburn red, matured in French oak casks (20 per cent new). Deep ruby, it is mouthfilling and savoury, with ripe cherry, plum and spice flavours, showing good concentration and complexity, and a supple, finely structured finish. Best drinking 2022+.

Vintage	18
WR	6
Drink	20-26

DRY $81 –V

Chard Farm Mata-Au Central Otago Pinot Noir   ★★★★☆

Chard Farm's 'signature' red is estate-grown at Lowburn and Parkburn, in the Cromwell Basin, and barrel-aged (about 20 per cent new). The youthful 2018 vintage (★★★★☆) is a ruby-hued, mouthfilling, savoury and supple red, with concentrated, ripe cherry, plum, spice and nut flavours, showing good complexity. Best drinking 2022+.

Vintage	19
WR	6
Drink	21-27

DRY $45 –V

Chard Farm River Run Central Otago Pinot Noir   ★★★★

The 2018 vintage (★★★☆) was estate-grown in the Cromwell Basin and at Gibbston, and barrel-aged (15 per cent new). Bright ruby, it is mouthfilling, sweet-fruited and smooth, with good depth of flavour, a touch of complexity, and lots of drink-young charm.

Vintage	18
WR	6
Drink	20-23

DRY $33 AV

Chard Farm The Tiger Lowburn Central Otago Pinot Noir   ★★★★☆

The 2018 vintage (★★★★) is a single-vineyard Lowburn wine, hand-picked and barrel-aged (19 per cent new). Light ruby, it is fragrant and supple, with youthful, moderately concentrated flavours, showing good complexity, and a finely textured, lingering finish.

Vintage	18	17
WR	5	7
Drink	20-26	20-25

DRY $81 –V

Chard Farm The Viper Parkburn Central Otago Pinot Noir   ★★★★☆

The elegant, savoury 2018 vintage (★★★★☆) is a single-vineyard Parkburn red, hand-picked and barrel-aged (20 per cent new). Ruby-hued, it is mouthfilling, with concentrated, ripe cherry, plum and spice flavours, showing good complexity, and a supple, very harmonious finish. Best drinking 2022+.

Vintage	18	17
WR	5	7
Drink	20-26	20-25

DRY $79 –V

Cherry Block Central Otago Pinot Noir   (★★★★)

Priced sharply, the 2019 vintage (★★★★) is a single-vineyard red from Alexandra, matured in tanks (60 per cent) and barrels (40 per cent). Deeply coloured, it is mouthfilling and vibrant, with strong, youthful, plummy, spicy flavours, showing considerable complexity, and supple tannins. Best drinking 2022+. (From Snapper Rock Wines.)

DRY $22 V+

Churton Marlborough Pinot Noir

Estate-grown at an elevated site in the Waihopai Valley, hand-harvested, fermented with indigenous yeasts and matured for 18 months in seasoned French oak barriques, this is 'a delicate, refined' Pinot Noir, according to winemaker Sam Weaver. The ruby-hued 2016 vintage (★★★★☆) is mouthfilling and savoury, with moderately concentrated, ripe cherry, spice and nut flavours, showing excellent complexity and harmony, and a finely textured, lingering finish. Certified organic.

Vintage	16	15	14	13
WR	6	6	NM	7
Drink	20-25	20-27	NM	20-28

DRY $39 V+

Clericus Marlborough Wild Pinot Noir

The 2017 vintage (★★★★☆) of this Wairau Valley red is deep ruby, with a fragrant, savoury, slightly herbal bouquet. Full-bodied, it has concentrated plum, herb and spice flavours, complex and savoury, fine-grained tannins and a lengthy finish. Best drinking 2021+. (From Clark Estate.)

DRY $42 AV

Clos de Ste Anne Naboth's Vineyard Pinot Noir

This Gisborne red from Millton is one of this country's northernmost quality Pinot Noirs. Grown at the hillside Clos de Ste Anne site at Manutuke, it is hand-harvested from vines up to 25 years old, fermented with indigenous yeasts, barrique-aged, and bottled without fining or filtering. Certified biodynamic, the 2015 vintage (★★★★) is ruby-hued, fragrant, mouthfilling and savoury, with ripe, strawberryish, spicy, nutty flavours, gentle acidity, and good complexity and harmony.

DRY $60 –V

Clos Henri Marlborough Pinot Noir

From Henri Bourgeois, a top Loire Valley producer with a site near Renwick, the 2016 vintage (★★★★☆) was hand-picked and matured for a year in French oak casks (25 per cent new). Ruby-hued, with a hint of development, it is fragrant and sweet-fruited, with cherry, spice, herb and nut flavours, complex, savoury and supple. Drinking well now, it's certified organic.

Vintage	16	15
WR	6	7
Drink	20-26	20-26

DRY $45 –V

Clos Henri Petit Clos Marlborough Pinot Noir   ★★★★

Certified organic, the 2019 vintage (★★★★☆) is based on Clos Henri's youngest vines. Estate-grown and hand-harvested in the Wairau Valley, it was matured for 11 months in large (7500-litre) French oak vats. Deep ruby, it is mouthfilling, with very good density of ripe cherry, plum and spice flavours, and fine, supple tannins. Already highly enjoyable, it's also well worth cellaring.

Vintage	19
WR	6
Drink	20-24

 DRY $27 V+

Clos Marguerite Marlborough Pinot Noir   ★★★★

The sturdy, generous 2015 vintage (★★★★☆) of this estate-grown, Awatere Valley red is the finest yet. Hand-harvested, it was matured for a year in French oak barrels (partly new). Full coloured, it is fragrant and mouthfilling, with concentrated, plummy, spicy flavours, fresh acidity and very good complexity. Drink now or cellar.

 DRY $52 –V

Cloudy Bay New Zealand Pinot Noir   ★★★★☆

This consistently classy red is grown at sites on the cooler, more clay-influenced south side of the Wairau Valley, in Marlborough. The 2018 vintage (★★★★☆) was matured in French oak barrels (35 per cent new). Ruby-hued, with a hint of development, it is savoury and sweet-fruited. Already delicious, it has cherry, plum, spice and nut flavours, very supple and harmonious.

Vintage	18	17	16	15	14
WR	6	6	7	7	6
Drink	20-26	20-25	20-26	20-25	20-21

 DRY $41 AV

Cloudy Bay Te Wahi Central Otago Pinot Noir   ★★★★★

The 2017 vintage (★★★★★) was estate-grown in the Calvert Vineyard at Bannockburn and Northburn Vineyard, on the east bank of Lake Dunstan. Fermented with indigenous yeasts, it was matured for a year in French oak barrels (30 per cent new). A powerful, softly seductive red, it is deeply coloured and mouthfilling, concentrated and supple, with rich cherry, plum, spice and nut flavours, youthful, and very harmonious. Best drinking 2022+.

Vintage	17	16	15	14
WR	7	7	7	7
Drink	20-27	20-26	20-25	20-24

 DRY $100 –V

Coal Pit Tiwha Central Otago Pinot Noir ★★★★★

Scented and supple, the 2018 vintage (★★★☆) was estate-grown and hand-picked at Gibbston, and matured for a year in French oak casks (40 per cent new). Ruby-hued, it is a refined, vibrantly fruity wine with ripe cherry, plum and spice flavours, a hint of herbs, good complexity and a smooth finish. Best drinking 2022+.

Vintage	18	17	16	15	14	13
WR	6	7	6	6	7	7
Drink	20-25	20-25	20-23	20-22	20-22	20-21

DRY $57 AV

Coopers Creek Marlborough Pinot Noir ★★★☆

Offering very good value, the 2016 vintage (★★★★) is a fragrant, full-bodied wine. Bright ruby, it is sweet-fruited and savoury, with strong, ripe cherry, plum and spice flavours, showing considerable complexity.

DRY $23 V+

Craft Farm Martinborough Pinot Noir (★★★★)

The 2017 vintage (★★★★) is a single-vineyard red, matured for over a year in French oak casks (50 per cent new). Deep ruby, it is savoury and complex, with ripe plum, herb, spice and nut flavours, showing very good depth and harmony. Best drinking 2021+.

DRY $48 –V

Craggy Range Te Muna Road Vineyard Martinborough Pinot Noir ★★★★★

The impressive 2016 vintage (★★★★★) was estate-grown, hand-picked and matured for nine months in French oak barriques (23 per cent new). Forward in its appeal, it is deep ruby, mouthfilling and sweet-fruited, with concentrated, plummy, spicy, nutty flavours, fine-grained tannins, and excellent complexity and harmony. Drink now or cellar.

DRY $46 AV

Crater Rim, The, Omihi Rise Waipara Pinot Noir (★★★★☆)

The lively 2014 vintage (★★★★☆), tasted in 2019, is a single-vineyard, North Canterbury red. Full and bright in colour, it is mouthfilling, with good concentration of ripe cherry, plum, spice and nut flavours, complex, firm and savoury. Open 2021+.

DRY $32 V+

Crater Rim, The, Rata Vineyard Banks Peninsula Pinot Noir (★★★★☆)

Grown in the Kaituna Valley, on Banks Peninsula, the 2015 vintage (★★★★☆) of this Canterbury wine is ruby-hued, with a fragrant, complex bouquet. Mouthfilling, it is savoury, slightly herbal and nutty, in a firm, concentrated, structured style, well worth cellaring to 2021+.

DRY $39 V+

Dan Stuckman Petite Martinborough Pinot Noir　(★★★★)

From a Waiheke Island-based winemaker, the elegant, youthful 2018 vintage (★★★★) is a single-vineyard red, hand-picked and matured for 11 months in oak barriques (18 per cent new). Ruby-hued, it is a floral, medium-bodied wine with vibrant cherry, plum and spice flavours, showing considerable complexity, and a smooth, lingering finish. Best drinking mid-2021+.

 DRY $30 AV

Dashwood by Vavasour Marlborough Pinot Noir　★★★☆

The 2018 vintage (★★★☆) is bright ruby, fragrant, sweet-fruited and supple. Oak-aged for nine months, it is full-bodied, with very good depth of cherry, plum and spice flavours, a touch of complexity, and lots of drink-young charm.

 DRY $22 V+

Deep Down Marlborough Pinot Noir　(★★★★)

Certified organic, the characterful 2020 vintage (★★★★) was aged briefly in old oak puncheons and bottled 'sulphur-free', as an example of 'hands-off winemaking'. Already highly enjoyable, it is ruby-hued, fresh, vibrant and supple, with strong, plummy, spicy flavours and a well-rounded finish.

Vintage	20
WR	6
Drink	20-22

 DRY $39 AV

Delegat Awatere Valley Pinot Noir　★★★★

Offering great value, the 2017 vintage (★★★★) was estate-grown in Marlborough and matured for a year in French oak barriques (new and one year old). Invitingly scented, it is a ruby-hued, strongly varietal wine, sweet-fruited and finely textured, with youthful, cherryish, plummy flavours, gentle tannins and a smooth finish.

 DRY $25 V+

Deliverance Waipara Pinot Noir　(★★★★☆)

From Greystone, the sturdy, generous 2019 vintage (★★★★☆) was grown at two North Canterbury sites and barrel-aged for nine months. Bright ruby, it is mouthfilling and sweet-fruited, with fresh, deep plum and spice flavours, savoury notes adding complexity, and a moderately firm finish. Full of youthful vigour, it should be at its best 2023+.

 DRY $25 V+

Delta Hatters Hill Marlborough Pinot Noir　★★★★☆

The 2019 vintage (★★★★☆) is a savoury red, grown in the Southern Valleys. Deeply coloured, it is mouthfilling and fruit-packed, with strong berry and spice flavours, showing good complexity, fine-grained tannins and obvious potential. The 2018 vintage (★★★★☆)

is a highly attractive red, matured for 10 months in French oak barriques (30 per cent new). Ruby-hued, it is fragrant, sweet-fruited and savoury, with youthful cherry, plum, spice and nut flavours, showing excellent depth and complexity, and supple tannins. Best drinking 2021+.

Vintage	18	DRY $35 V+
WR	5	
Drink	20-23	

Delta Marlborough Pinot Noir ★★★★

Offering fine value, the 2019 vintage (★★★★) is a single-vineyard red, grown in the Southern Valleys. Half of the blend was matured for 10 months in French oak barriques. Full-coloured, it is mouthfilling and vibrantly fruity, with fresh acidity, strong, ripe cherry, plum and spice flavours, and savoury notes adding complexity. Still very youthful, it's well worth cellaring to 2022+.

Vintage	19	DRY $20 V+
WR	6	
Drink	20-22	

Devil's Staircase Central Otago Pinot Noir ★★★☆

From Rockburn, this skilfully crafted, drink-young charmer is matured in tanks, without oak, 'to retain bright fruit'. Deep ruby, with a fresh, fragrant bouquet, the 2018 vintage (★★★☆) is full-bodied, with ripe plum and spice flavours, gentle tannins, and very good depth. It's enjoyable now.

 DRY $30 –V

Diggers Law Central Otago Pinot Noir (★★★★)

Well worth cellaring, the 2018 vintage (★★★★) is a finely textured red, French oak-aged for nearly a year. Ruby-hued, it is smoothly mouthfilling, with moderately concentrated, ripe cherry, spice and nut flavours, fresh acidity and considerable complexity. Best drinking mid-2021+. (From Bannock Brae.)

 DRY $28 V+

Doctors Flat Central Otago Pinot Noir ★★★★★

The highly age-worthy 2016 vintage (★★★★★) is a single-vineyard red, estate-grown at Bannockburn, matured for a year in French oak barrels (25 per cent new), and bottled without fining or filtering. Deep ruby, it is mouthfilling, savoury and supple, with concentrated, ripe cherry, plum and spice flavours and a finely structured, lasting finish. Best drinking 2021+.

Vintage	16	15	14	13	DRY $47 AV
WR	7	7	7	6	
Drink	20-24	20-23	20-22	20-21	

Doctors', The, Marlborough Pinot Noir (★★)

Crafted as a very low alcohol style (9.5 per cent), the 2018 vintage (★★) is pale ruby, with fresh, light, red-berry and spice flavours. It lacks any real stuffing or richness, but offers smooth, easy drinking. (From Forrest Estate.)

DRY $25 –V

Dog Point Vineyard Marlborough Pinot Noir ★★★★★

This classy, finely structured red is estate-grown on the south side of the Wairau Valley, hand-picked and matured for 18 months in French oak barriques (35 per cent new in 2018). The 2018 vintage (★★★★★) is fragrant, mouthfilling and supple, with rich, vibrant cherry, plum and spice flavours, showing excellent complexity and harmony. Still youthful, it's already delicious and likely to be at its best 2023+. Certified organic.

Vintage	18	17	16	15	14	13	12	11
WR	6	7	7	6	7	7	7	5
Drink	20-27	20-27	20-26	20-25	20-25	20-25	20-24	P

DRY $50 AV

Domain Road Bannockburn Central Otago Pinot Noir ★★★★☆

The 2017 vintage (★★★★☆) is a powerful young red, estate-grown, hand-harvested and matured for 10 months in French oak casks (26 per cent new). Deeply coloured, it is vibrantly fruity, with concentrated cherry, plum and spice flavours, good tannin support, and obvious cellaring potential; open 2021+.

DRY $40 AV

Domain Road Defiance Single Vineyard Central Otago Pinot Noir ★★★★☆

The 2017 vintage (★★★★★) is a powerful, single-vineyard Bannockburn red, hand-picked and matured for 10 months in French oak casks (29 per cent new). Deep and youthful in colour, it is highly fragrant, with dense, youthful cherry, plum and spice flavours, showing excellent vigour, concentration and structure. Best drinking 2022+.

Vintage	17	16
WR	7	6
Drink	20-28	20-26

DRY $65 –V

Domaine-Thomson Explorer Central Otago Pinot Noir ★★★★

Offering top value, the classy 2018 vintage (★★★★☆) was estate-grown at Lowburn, in the Cromwell Basin, and matured for eight months in French oak casks (20 per cent new). Bright ruby, it is fragrant and full-bodied, with strong, ripe, plummy, spicy flavours, showing excellent depth, complexity and harmony. As good as many Central Otago Pinot Noirs priced far higher, it's a 'serious' but very approachable red; best drinking 2021+.

DRY $29 V+

Domaine-Thomson Rows 1–37 Single Clone Central Otago Pinot Noir   ★★★★★

The powerful 2017 vintage (★★★★★) is from a single clone (777) of Pinot Noir, estate-grown at Lowburn. Matured in French oak casks (25 per cent new), it is deep ruby, mouthfilling, savoury and well-structured, with dense, ripe, plummy, spicy flavours, finely integrated oak adding complexity, and a long life ahead. Certified organic.

DRY $75 AV

Domaine-Thomson Surveyor Thomson Central Otago Pinot Noir   ★★★★★

Certified organic, the 2016 vintage (★★★★★) is a fragrant, complex red, estate-grown at Lowburn. Matured in French oak casks (20 per cent new), it is mouthfilling, with strong flavours of cherries, plums, spices and nuts, and a moderately firm finish. A very age-worthy wine, it should be at its best 2021+.

DRY $55 AV

Dry Gully Central Otago Pinot Noir   (★★★★☆)

Offering good value, the 2017 vintage (★★★★☆) of this Alexandra red is deeply coloured, with a fresh, fragrant bouquet. Full-bodied and fruit-packed, it has generous, vibrant, plummy, spicy flavours, nutty, savoury notes adding complexity, and good tannin support. Best drinking 2021+.

DRY $32 V+

Dry River Martinborough Pinot Noir   ★★★★★

Dark and densely flavoured, this Martinborough red ranks among New Zealand's greatest Pinot Noirs. It is grown in three company-owned vineyards – Dry River Estate, Craighall and Lovat – on the Martinborough Terrace, and most of the vines are over 20 years old. Matured for a year in French oak hogsheads (20 to 30 per cent new), it is a slower-developing wine than other New Zealand Pinot Noirs, but matures superbly. The 2018 vintage (★★★★★) is an elegant, very youthful red, deep ruby, with a finely scented bouquet. Full of potential, it has deep cherry, plum and spice flavours, a hint of tamarillo, savoury notes adding complexity, fresh acidity, and a very harmonious, persistent finish. Open 2023+.

Vintage	18	17	16	15	14	13	12	11
WR	7	6	7	7	7	7	6	7
Drink	20-30	20-29	20-29	20-28	20-27	20-27	20-25	20-25

DRY $97 AV

🍇🍇🍇

Dunstan Road Central Otago Pinot Noir   (★★★★)

From a small vineyard near Alexandra, the savoury, tightly structured 2016 vintage (★★★★) was matured for a year in French oak casks. Ruby-hued, it is mouthfilling, with youthful, moderately rich cherry, plum, spice and nut flavours, fresh acidity, finely balanced tannins, and good complexity. Best drinking 2021+.

DRY $35 AV

Dunstan Road Reserve Central Otago Pinot Noir   ★★★★

From a small vineyard at Alexandra, I tasted the 2014 to 2016 vintages in September 2019. The 2014 (★★★★☆), French oak-matured for 18 months, has full, fairly youthful colour and a fragrant, savoury, slightly earthy bouquet. Drinking well now, it is mouthfilling, with generous, ripe cherry, plum and spice flavours, showing good complexity, and a finely textured, very harmonious finish. Surprisingly youthful, the 2015 (★★★☆) is a powerful, fruity wine with moderate complexity and fresh acidity. The 2016 vintage (★★★★) shows good complexity. Ruby-hued, it is moderately youthful, with very good depth of cherry, plum and spice flavours, and a fairly firm finish.

DRY $40 –V

Durvillea by Astrolabe Marlborough Pinot Noir   ★★★☆

Offering great value, the 2018 vintage (★★★☆) is a regional blend, mostly hand-picked and matured in French oak barriques of varying ages. Ruby-hued, it is mouthfilling and supple, with cherry, plum and spice flavours, some savoury notes adding complexity, and lots of drink-young appeal.

Vintage	18
WR	6
Drink	20-24

DRY $20 V+

Eaton Marlborough Pinot Noir   (★★★★)

Grown in the upper Waihopai Valley, the 2018 vintage (★★★★) is a single-vineyard red, hand-picked, matured for 11 months in two oak barrels (one new), and bottled unfined and unfiltered. It has light, slightly developed colour. Fragrant, with a hint of herbs, it is savoury, with moderately concentrated cherry and spice flavours, and nutty notes adding complexity. It's already quite open and expressive.

Vintage	18
WR	6
Drink	20-23

DRY $48 –V

Eight Ranges Central Otago Pinot Noir   ★★★★

Showing good cellaring potential, the 2017 vintage (★★★★☆) is a single-vineyard red, grown at Alexandra and matured in French oak barrels. Deep ruby, it is fragrant, sweet-fruited and fresh, with mouthfilling body, strong, youthful, plummy, spicy flavours, showing excellent concentration and complexity, and a moderately firm finish. Best drinking 2021+. (From Tussock Ridge.)

DRY $38 AV

Eight Ranges Trail Rider Central Otago Pinot Noir   (★★★★)

Delicious young, the 2018 vintage (★★★★) from this Alexandra-based producer was matured in French oak (24 per cent new). Bright ruby, it is fragrant and full-bodied, with ripe cherry, plum and spice flavours, nutty, savoury notes adding complexity, and gentle tannins. An elegant, youthful red, it should be at its best 2021+.

DRY $30 AV

Elder, The, Martinborough Pinot Noir

Bright ruby, the attractively perfumed 2017 vintage (★★★★☆) was estate-grown at Te Muna and aged for 10 months in French oak barrels. Refined and supple, it is medium to full-bodied, with ripe cherry, plum and spice flavours, showing very good depth, savoury and nutty notes adding complexity, balanced acidity, and a long finish. Best drinking 2022+.

DRY $63 –V

Eradus Awatere Valley Marlborough Pinot Noir

A good drink-young style, the 2019 vintage (★★★☆) is boldly fruity, with gentle tannins and strong, vibrant, plummy, spicy flavours.

DRY $22 V+

Esk Valley Marlborough Pinot Noir

Already enjoyable, the fresh, youthful 2019 vintage (★★★★) was grown in the Wairau Valley and matured in French oak barriques. Deep ruby, with a fragrant bouquet, it has concentrated, ripe cherry and plum flavours, gentle tannins and a smooth finish. Best drinking 2022+.

DRY $27 V+

Falconhead Marlborough Pinot Noir ★★★

Estate-grown, the 2019 vintage (★★★) was French oak-matured for a year. Bright ruby, it is full-bodied and smooth, with good depth of plummy, spicy, slightly nutty flavours, showing a touch of complexity, and drink-young appeal.

Vintage	19
WR	6
Drink	21-25

DRY $17 V+

Felton Road Bannockburn Central Otago Pinot Noir ★★★★★

The Bannockburn winery's 'standard' Pinot Noir is a distinguished wine, blended from its four sites in the district. Matured in French oak casks (27 per cent new in 2019), it is fermented with indigenous yeasts and bottled without fining or filtering. Barrel-aged for 13 months, the 2019 vintage (★★★★★) is fragrant, deeply coloured and mouthfilling, with concentrated cherry, plum and spice flavours, gently seasoned with nutty oak, supple tannins, and a finely poised, very harmonious finish. Best drinking 2023+.

Vintage	19	18	17	16	15	14	13	12	11
WR	7	7	7	7	7	7	7	7	7
Drink	20-30	20-29	20-28	20-27	20-26	20-25	20-24	20-26	20-23

DRY $68 AV

Felton Road Block 3 Central Otago Pinot Noir ★★★★★

Grown at Bannockburn, on a north-facing slope 270 metres above sea level, this is a majestic Central Otago wine, among the finest Pinot Noirs in the country. The mature vines are cultivated in front of the winery, in a section of the vineyard where the clay content is relatively high, giving 'dried-herbs and ripe fruit characters'. The wine is matured for about a year in Burgundy oak barrels (30 per cent new in 2019), and bottled without fining or filtration. The 2019 vintage (★★★★★) is a bright ruby, powerful wine, still very youthful, with obvious long-term potential. Sweet-fruited, it has highly concentrated, vibrant cherry and spice flavours, complex and savoury, and a very harmonious finish. A lovely young red, it should be at its best 2024+.

Vintage	19 ·	18	17	16	15	14	13	12	11
WR	7	7	7	7	7	7	7	7	7
Drink	20-35	20-34	20-33	20-32	20-31	20-30	20-24	20-26	20-23

 DRY $109 AV

Felton Road Block 5 Pinot Noir ★★★★★

This is winemaker Blair Walter's favourite Felton Road red. Grown in a 'special' block of The Elms Vineyard at Bannockburn, in Central Otago, it is matured for a year or longer in French oak barriques (16 months in 30 per cent new barrels in 2019), and bottled unfined and unfiltered. The 2019 vintage (★★★★★) is a powerful, notably ripe wine (harbouring 14.5 per cent alcohol). Deep ruby, it is very fleshy and sweet-fruited, with rich, vibrant plum and spice flavours, a vague hint of liquorice, gentle acidity, and loads of drink-young appeal. Best drinking 2023+.

Vintage	19	18	17	16	15	14	13	12	11
WR	7	7	7	6	7	7	7	7	7
Drink	20-35	20-34	20-33	20-30	20-31	20-30	20-27	20-26	20-23

 DRY $109 AV

Felton Road Calvert Pinot Noir ★★★★★

Grown in the Calvert Vineyard at Bannockburn – 1 kilometre east of the winery – matured in French oak barriques (30 per cent new in 2019), and bottled unfined and unfiltered, the 2019 vintage (★★★★★) is already delicious. Deep ruby, it is highly fragrant, mouthfilling and supple, with very generous, well-ripened cherry, plum and spice flavours, vibrant, dense and savoury. Powerful, and sure to be long-lived, it should be at its best 2023+.

Vintage	19	18	17	16	15	14	13	12	11
WR	7	7	7	6	7	7	7	7	7
Drink	20-35	20-34	20-33	20-30	20-31	20-28	20-24	20-26	20-23

 DRY $81 AV

Felton Road Cornish Point Pinot Noir ★★★★★

From the company-owned Cornish Point Vineyard at the eastern end of Bannockburn, 6 kilometres from the winery, this is always one of my favourite Felton Road reds. The 2019 vintage (★★★★★) was matured for 13 months in French oak barriques (30 per cent new), and bottled without fining or filtering. Deeply coloured, it is a fragrant, vibrantly fruity wine with dense, cherryish, plummy, well-spiced flavours, and fine, supple tannins. Combining power and grace, it will be long-lived; best drinking 2023+.

Vintage	19	18	17	16	15	14	13	12	11
WR	7	7	7	7	7	7	7	7	7
Drink	20-34	20-32	20-31	20-30	20-29	20-28	20-24	20-26	20-23

 DRY $81 AV

Flaxmore Moutere Pinot Noir (★★★)

Estate-grown and hand-picked in the Moutere hills, the 2018 vintage (★★★) was oak-aged for nine months. Light ruby, with a hint of development showing, it has fresh tamarillo and spice aromas, leading into a light to medium-bodied red with fresh acidity, a hint of herbs, some savoury complexity, and plenty of flavour. Ready.

Folding Hill Bendigo Central Otago Pinot Noir ★★★★★

Highly refined, the youthful 2016 vintage (★★★★★) was hand-harvested, matured for 10 months in French oak barriques (25 per cent new), and bottled unfined and unfiltered. Attractively perfumed, it is deep ruby, with rich, vibrant cherry, plum, spice and nut flavours, very harmonious and persistent. Best drinking 2021+.

Vintage	16	15
WR	6	7
Drink	20-26	20-27

Folding Hill Orchard Block Bendigo Central Otago Pinot Noir ★★★★☆

The tightly structured, youthful 2015 vintage (★★★★☆) was estate-grown, hand-picked in 'the most sheltered part of the vineyard', matured for 20 months in French oak barrels (partly new), and bottled unfined and unfiltered. Bright ruby, with a highly fragrant, perfumed bouquet, it has strong, ripe cherry, plum, spice and nut flavours, with a firm tannin grip. It needs time; open 2022+.

Vintage	15	14
WR	6	7
Drink	20-26	20-27

Folium Marlborough Pinot Noir ★★★★☆

Estate-grown in the Brancott Valley, the 2018 vintage (★★★★) was matured in French oak casks (10 per cent new). Bright ruby, it is youthful, with moderately concentrated, vibrant cherry, plum and spice flavours, fresh acidity, savoury notes adding complexity, and obvious cellaring potential. Best drinking 2021+.

Vintage	18	17	16
WR	4	5	5
Drink	20-25	20-25	20-25

Folium Reserve Marlborough Pinot Noir ★★★★★

The classy 2017 vintage (★★★★★) of this Brancott Valley red was hand-harvested and matured in French oak casks (33 per cent new). Deep ruby, it is fragrant, generous and savoury, with concentrated cherry, plum and spice flavours, showing good complexity, fresh acidity, and a well-structured, powerful finish. Very age-worthy, it should be at its best 2022+.

Vintage	17	16	15
WR	6	5	6
Drink	20-30	20-30	20-30

Forager North Canterbury Pinot Noir ★★★★☆

This single-vineyard red is grown 40 kilometres inland, at 210 metres above sea level, near Waiau. The 2018 vintage (★★★★☆) is ruby-hued, with a fragrant bouquet and subtle, savoury, complex, nutty flavours, very smooth and lingering. The 2017 vintage (★★★★★) was hand-picked and matured for 15 months in seasoned French oak casks. Fragrant and silky-textured, it is deep ruby, with mouthfilling body, vibrant fruit flavours, lively acidity, and excellent depth. A highly refined, elegant red, it should be at its best 2022+.

 DRY $55 –V

Forrest Marlborough Pinot Noir ★★★★

The 2018 vintage (★★★★) was grown in the Southern Valleys and aged in French oak barrels (20 per cent new). Bright ruby, it is fresh and full-bodied, with youthful cherry, plum and spice flavours, showing good complexity, and a moderately firm finish. Best drinking 2021+.

 DRY $30 AV

Framingham Marlborough Pinot Noir ★★★★

This wine is 'feminine', according to Framingham, meaning it is elegant, rather than powerful. The 2018 vintage (★★★★) is a ruby-hued, full-bodied red, sweet-fruited and supple, with generous cherry, plum and spice flavours, nutty, savoury notes adding complexity, and a smooth, harmonious finish. It's drinking well now.

 DRY $35 AV

Fromm Churton Vineyard Marlborough Pinot Noir ★★★★★

The 2017 vintage (★★★★★) is rare – only five barrels were made. Grown organically in the Churton Vineyard, in the Waihopai Valley, it was hand-picked from east-facing clay slopes, fermented with indigenous yeasts, oak-matured, and bottled unfined and unfiltered. Full, bright ruby, it is fresh and smooth-flowing, with strong, vibrant plum, cherry and spice flavours, and a finely poised, long finish. A generous, savoury, supple red, with a real sense of youthful drive, it should be at its best 2021+.

 DRY $55 AV

Fromm Clayvin Vineyard Pinot Noir ★★★★★

This acclaimed Marlborough red is grown and hand-picked on north-facing clay slopes at Clayvin Vineyard, in the Brancott Valley, fermented with indigenous yeasts, matured in French oak barriques, and bottled without fining or filtering. In its youth, it is more floral and charming than its Fromm Vineyard stablemate. Certified organic, the very youthful, vigorous 2017 vintage (★★★★★) is rare – only eight barrels were produced. Deeply coloured, it is full-bodied and sweet-fruited, with very deep, plummy, spicy flavours, earthy, savoury notes adding complexity, fresh acidity, supple tannins, and a lovely combination of power and grace. Full of potential, it should be at its best 2022+.

Vintage	17	16	15	14	13	12	11
WR	7	7	7	6	7	7	7
Drink	20-29	20-28	20-27	20-25	20-25	20-26	20-23

 DRY $85 AV

Fromm Cuvée 'H' Marlborough Pinot Noir ★★★★★

Certified organic, the 2018 vintage (★★★★★) is labelled in honour of Hätsch Kalberer, Fromm's winemaker since the first vintage in 1992. Designed as 'a mindful blend of what our single-vineyard wines offer as a composite', it is a fragrant, powerful, very age-worthy red, blended from five separately made, single-vineyard wines, matured for 16 to 18 months in French oak casks (less than 10 per cent new). Deep ruby, it is sweet-fruited and savoury, with concentrated, youthful, well-ripened cherry, plum and spice flavours, well-integrated oak, excellent complexity, and a finely structured, very harmonious, lasting finish. Best drinking 2023+.

 DRY $65 AV

Fromm Fromm Vineyard Pinot Noir ★★★★★

Winemaker Hätsch Kalberer describes this Marlborough red as 'not a typical New World style, but the truest expression of terroir you could find'. In the Fromm Vineyard near Renwick, in the heart of the Wairau Valley, many clones of Pinot Noir are close-planted on a flat site with alluvial topsoils overlying layers of clay and free-draining gravels. The wine is fermented with indigenous yeasts, matured for 18 months in Burgundy oak barrels (six in 2017), and bottled unfined and unfiltered. Certified organic, the impressive 2017 vintage (★★★★★) looks set for a very long life. Full-coloured, it is savoury, ripe and finely structured, with deep plum, spice and nut flavours. A more graceful, supple red than some earlier vintages, with power through the palate, it's a top vintage, well worth cellaring.

Vintage	17	16	15	14	13	12	11
WR	7	7	7	6	7	7	6
Drink	20-29	20-28	20-27	20-26	20-26	20-25	20-22

DRY $85 –V

Fromm Marlborough Pinot Noir (★★★★☆)

Certified organic, the 2017 vintage (★★★★☆) is a blend of grapes hand-picked from four vineyards – Quarters, Churton, Yarrum and Fromm – in three districts. Matured for 14 to 16 months in French oak barriques (less than 10 per cent new), it is bright ruby, full-bodied and complex, with concentrated, ripe, youthful, savoury, slightly nutty flavours, and a firmly structured finish. Best drinking 2021+.

DRY $43 AV

Fromm Quarters Vineyard Marlborough Pinot Noir ★★★★★

Certified organic, the rare 2017 vintage (★★★★★) was hand-harvested in the lower Brancott Valley, fermented with indigenous yeasts, and matured in three French oak barriques (yielding a total production of 900 bottles). Full-coloured, it is a classy young red, mouthfilling, rich and finely structured, with dense, berryish, spicy, nutty flavours, complex and persistent. A refined, highly approachable and very harmonious wine, it's a drink-now or cellaring proposition.

Vintage	17	16	15
WR	7	6	7
Drink	20-27	20-25	20-25

DRY $55 AV

Gale Force Marlborough Pinot Noir   (★★★)

Grown in the Wairau Valley, the 2017 vintage (★★★) is bargain-priced. Bright ruby, it is full-bodied and vibrantly fruity, with youthful vigour, good depth of fresh, plummy, slightly herbal flavours, and a touch of complexity. Drink now. (From Clark Estate.)

Gibbston Valley China Terrace Bendigo Central Otago Pinot Noir   ★★★★★

Estate-grown at altitude (320 metres above sea level) in the China Terrace Vineyard, at Bendigo, the graceful 2019 vintage (★★★★★) was hand-picked and matured for 10 months in French oak casks (33 per cent new). Deep ruby, it is mouthfilling, rich and sweet-fruited, with highly concentrated, very youthful cherry, plum and spice flavours, excellent complexity, and ripe, supple tannins. A lovely young red, it's well worth cellaring to 2023+.

Vintage	19
WR	7
Drink	21-30

DRY $68 AV

Gibbston Valley Glenlee Central Otago Pinot Noir   ★★★★★

A single-vineyard red, grown at Gibbston, the refined 2019 vintage (★★★★★) was hand-harvested, fermented with indigenous yeasts and matured for 10 months in French oak barriques (20 per cent new). Bright ruby, it is a very graceful wine, mouthfilling and supple, with vibrant, ripe cherry, plum and spice flavours, showing excellent complexity and depth, fresh acidity and obvious potential; best drinking 2023+.

Vintage	19
WR	7
Drink	21-29

DRY $68 AV

Gibbston Valley Gold River Central Otago Pinot Noir   ★★★★

This is the winery's 'lighter' red, for 'immediate enjoyment'. The 2019 vintage (★★★★) was grown at Gibbston (50 per cent) and Bendigo (50 per cent), hand-picked and matured for nine months in seasoned oak casks. Bright ruby, it is full-bodied and sweet-fruited, with vibrant cherry, plum and spice flavours, fresh and well-rounded. A generous, youthful red, it should be at its best mid-2021+.

Gibbston Valley GV Collection Central Otago Pinot Noir   ★★★★★

Drinking well now, the 2018 vintage (★★★★★) is a blend of Pisa (50 per cent), Bendigo (45 per cent) and Gibbston (5 per cent) grapes, hand-picked and matured for 10 months in French oak casks (20 per cent new). Bright ruby, it is mouthfilling, sweet-fruited and supple, with concentrated cherry, plum and spice flavours, nutty, savoury notes adding complexity, and a rich, smooth finish.

Gibbston Valley Le Maitre Gibbston Central Otago Pinot Noir   ★★★★★

Grown in the Home Block at Gibbston, where the oldest vines were planted in 1983, the 2019 vintage (★★★★★), certified organic, was matured for 10 months in French oak casks (25 per cent new). Bright ruby, with a fragrant, slightly earthy bouquet, it is an elegant, still extremely youthful wine, with rich, vibrant cherry, plum and spice flavours, woven with fresh acidity, and good tannin backbone. Highly refined, with good vigour, complexity and structure, it's well worth cellaring to 2023+.

Vintage	19
WR	7
Drink	21-30

DRY $100 AV

Gibbston Valley Reserve Central Otago Pinot Noir   ★★★★★

At its best, this Central Otago red is mouthfilling and savoury, with superb concentration of sweet-tasting, plummy fruit and lovely harmony. The grapes have been drawn from various sub-regions and vineyards over the years and yields have been very low (under 5 tonnes/hectare). The 2019 vintage (★★★★★) was grown at Pisa and matured for 11 months in French oak barriques (22 per cent new). Deep ruby, it is a powerful red, mouthfilling, sweet-fruited and supple, with deep cherry, plum and spice flavours, a hint of liquorice, and a finely balanced, long finish. Best drinking 2023+.

Vintage	19
WR	7
Drink	21-29

DRY $120 AV

Gibbston Valley School House Central Otago Pinot Noir   ★★★★★

This consistently classy red is estate-grown in the late-ripening School House Vineyard, at Bendigo, an extremely elevated site (up to 420 metres above sea level). The 2019 vintage (★★★★★) was hand-picked and matured for 10 months in French oak casks (25 per cent new). Deep ruby, it is a powerful yet elegant red, with dense cherry, plum and spice flavours, and ripe, supple tannins. Still very youthful, it's well worth cellaring to 2023+. Certified organic.

Vintage	19
WR	7
Drink	21-29

DRY $65 AV

Giesen Single Vineyard Selection Clayvin Marlborough Pinot Noir   ★★★★★

Still on sale, the 2014 vintage (★★★★★) has full, fairly mature colour. Highly fragrant, it is full-bodied and sweet-fruited, with ripe cherry, plum, spice and nut flavours, concentrated, savoury and harmonious. Best drinking 2021+.

DRY $60 AV

Gladstone Vineyard Blair Patrick Single Vineyard Wairarapa Pinot Noir   (★★★★★)

The debut 2018 vintage (★★★★★) was matured for a year in French oak casks (35 per cent new). Deep ruby, it is highly fragrant and very refined, in a savoury, youthful, tight-knit style with impressive complexity, fresh acidity and a long, structured finish. Best drinking 2022+.

Vintage	18
WR	6
Drink	21-30

 DRY $100 –V

Gladstone Vineyard Dakins Road Single Vineyard Wairarapa Pinot Noir   (★★★★★)

Finely scented, the debut 2018 vintage (★★★★★) was matured for a year in French oak casks (35 per cent new). Bright ruby, it is a savoury, youthful, well-structured red, with cherry, plum and spice flavours, showing excellent complexity, and a long life ahead. Best drinking 2021+.

 DRY $80 –V

Gladstone Vineyard Pinot Noir   ★★★★☆

Estate-grown and hand-harvested in the northern Wairarapa, and matured for a year in French oak casks (20 per cent new), the 2018 vintage (★★★★☆) is ruby-hued, scented and supple. A very harmonious red, it has ripe cherry, plum and spice flavours, well-integrated oak, very good complexity, and lots of current-drinking appeal. Best drinking 2021+.

 DRY $45 –V

Gold Digger Central Otago Pinot Noir   ★★★★

The 2018 vintage (★★★★) is a single-vineyard red, hand-picked and matured in French and Hungarian oak casks (14 per cent new). Bright ruby, with a fragrant bouquet, it is mouthfilling and supple, with generous, ripe cherry, plum and spice flavours, showing good complexity. It's drinking well now. (From Maori Point Wines.)

 DRY $30 AV

Goldwater Marlborough Pinot Noir   ★★★☆

Offering excellent value, the 2018 vintage (★★★★) was French oak-matured for nine months. An elegant, full-bodied wine, it is bright ruby, with strong, youthful cherry, plum and spice flavours, fresh acidity, gentle tannins, and good immediacy. Drink now or cellar.

DRY $25 AV

Grasshopper Rock Earnscleugh Vineyard Central Otago Pinot Noir   ★★★★★

Estate-grown in Alexandra, this is typically a top buy. From vines planted in 2003, the graceful 2018 vintage (★★★★☆) was hand-picked and matured for 11 months in French oak barriques (29 per cent new). Bright ruby, it is fragrant, savoury and supple, with youthful, ripe cherry, plum and spice flavours, showing good complexity, and a very harmonious finish.

Vintage	18	17	16	15	14	13
WR	7	7	6	6	6	6
Drink	21-28	21-27	21-26	21-25	21-24	21-23

DRY $40 V+

Grava Martinborough Pinot Noir

The 2018 vintage (★★★★) was grown at a site south of Martinborough township, formerly Hudson Vineyard. Matured in French oak barrels (16 per cent new), it is a gentle, strongly varietal, savoury wine with ripe, cherryish, spicy, slightly nutty flavours, balanced tannins, and considerable complexity. Drink now or cellar.

DRY $45 –V

Green Songs Waipara Valley North Canterbury Pinot Noir   (★★★★)

The 2017 vintage (★★★★) from this Nelson-based producer was grown at Waipara and matured for a year in French oak casks (30 per cent new). Deep ruby, with a fresh bouquet of herbs and spices, it is full-bodied, with very good depth of cherry, plum and spice flavours, savoury, earthy notes adding complexity, and a moderately firm finish.

DRY $40 –V

Greenhough Hope Vineyard Nelson Pinot Noir   ★★★★★

One of Nelson's greatest reds, at its best powerful, rich and long-lived. It is estate-grown and hand-picked on an elevated terrace of the south-eastern Waimea Plains, where the vines, planted in gravelly loam clays, have an average age of over 20 years. Yields are very low – 4 to 5 tonnes of grapes per hectare – and the wine is matured for about a year in French oak barriques (15 per cent new in 2017). Certified organic, the 2017 vintage (★★★★☆) was bottled unfined and unfiltered. Bright ruby, it is mouthfilling, with strong, plummy, spicy flavours, complex and savoury. A youthful, well-structured red with cellaring potential, it should be at its best 2021+.

DRY $46 AV

Greenhough Nelson Pinot Noir   ★★★★

The 2016 vintage (★★★★) was hand-picked in the Home and Morison vineyards at Hope, and matured for a year in French oak barriques and puncheons (15 per cent new). Ruby-hued, it is fresh, with very good depth of plummy, spicy, nutty flavours, savoury and complex, and a moderately firm finish. Best drinking 2021+.

Vintage	16	15	14	13
WR	6	6	7	6
Drink	20-21	20-21	P	P

DRY $30 AV

Greenhough Stone's Throw Nelson Pinot Noir   (★★★★)

From two sites – including the home vineyard – just a 'stone's throw' apart on the Waimea Plains, the debut 2017 vintage (★★★★) was matured for 11 months in French oak barriques (13 per cent new). Deep ruby, it is fragrant, fresh and full-bodied, with good concentration of cherry, plum and spice flavours, fresh and smooth. Best drinking 2021+.

DRY $30 AV

Greyrock New Zealand Pinot Noir   (★★★)

The 2019 vintage (★★★) was grown in Hawke's Bay. Enjoyable young, it is ruby-hued and fragrant, with good body, fresh, generous, berry and spice flavours, gentle tannins, and a smooth finish. (From Sileni.)

Greyrock Te Koru New Zealand Pinot Noir   (★★★)

The 2019 vintage (★★★) was grown in Hawke's Bay. Ruby-hued, it is very smooth, with ripe, berryish, slightly nutty flavours, hints of herbs and spices, youthful vigour and decent depth. Best drinking 2021+. (From Sileni.)

Greystone Thomas Brothers Waipara Valley Pinot Noir   ★★★★★

The 2018 vintage (★★★★☆) was grown in the steep, exposed Brothers Block, hand-harvested, fermented with indigenous yeasts, matured for 15 months in French oak barriques (66 per cent new), and bottled unfined and unfiltered. Ruby-hued, it is very savoury and supple, with fresh, youthful cherry, plum and spice flavours, and nutty, earthy notes adding complexity. Best drinking 2022+. Certified organic.

Vintage	18
WR	7
Drink	20-30

DRY $99 AV

Greystone Vineyard Ferment Pinot Noir   ★★★★☆

This red is estate-grown and hand-picked at Waipara, in North Canterbury, and made by fermenting the grapes in the vineyard, using indigenous yeasts. Matured in old oak barriques the 2018 vintage (★★★★) is a gentle, light ruby red, savoury and supple, with moderately rich, delicate flavours, nutty notes adding complexity, fresh acidity, and good potential.

Vintage	18
WR	6
Drink	20-26

DRY $70 –V

Greystone Waipara Valley North Canterbury Pinot Noir   ★★★★★

Finely perfumed, the 2018 vintage (★★★★☆) is a very graceful, deep ruby red, with ripe cherry, plum and spice flavours, fresh acidity and supple tannins. Strongly varietal and very harmonious, it should be at its best 2021+.

DRY $43 V+

Greywacke Marlborough Pinot Noir ★★★★★

Grown at elevated sites in the Southern Valleys, hand-harvested and matured in French oak barriques (partly new), the 2017 vintage (★★★★★) is deeply coloured, with a fragrant, savoury bouquet. Full-bodied, it is powerful, with very deep cherry, plum and spice flavours, showing excellent complexity, and a finely structured, long finish. Best drinking 2022+. The 2018 vintage (★★★★☆) is highly fragrant, with a savoury, spicy, slightly herbal bouquet. Deep ruby, it is mouthfilling, with deep, youthful plum and spice flavours, nutty and savoury notes adding complexity, fresh acidity, and a moderately firm finish. Best drinking 2022+.

Vintage	18	17	16	15	14	13	12	11
WR	6	6	6	6	6	6	6	6
Drink	20-26	20-25	20-24	20-23	20-22	20-21	20-21	P

Grove Mill Wairau Valley Marlborough Pinot Noir ★★★☆

The easy-drinking 2018 vintage (★★★☆) was matured for 10 months in French oak barriques (20 per cent new). Full, bright ruby, it is mouthfilling and sweet-fruited, with cherry, plum and spice flavours, oak complexity, and a well-rounded finish.

Haha Marlborough Pinot Noir ★★★

The 2019 vintage (★★★☆) is ruby-hued, with a fresh, spicy bouquet. Enjoyable young, it is full-bodied and sweet-fruited, with good depth of vibrant cherry, plum and spice flavours, savoury notes adding a distinct touch of complexity, and a smooth finish. Best drinking mid-2021+.

Hans Herzog Marlborough Pinot Noir Grand Duc ★★★★★

The highly impressive 2015 vintage (★★★★★) was estate-grown in the Wairau Valley, hand-harvested, matured for 22 months in French oak barriques, and bottled unfined and unfiltered. Fragrant and deeply coloured, it is sweet-fruited and complex, with finely balanced tannins, and deep cherry, plum, spice and nut flavours. A powerful, savoury red, it's currently delicious, but should be at its best 2021+. Certified organic.

DRY $69 AV

Hawkshead Central Otago Pinot Noir ★★★☆

The 2019 vintage (★★★☆) was hand-harvested and matured for 10 months in French oak barrels (15 per cent new). Bright ruby, it is freshly scented, medium-bodied and supple, with vibrant cherry, plum, spice and herb flavours, slightly nutty notes, and lively acidity. A graceful red with drink-young charm, it should be at its best 2022+.

Hawkshead Gibbston First Vines Central Otago Pinot Noir   ★★★★☆

Estate-grown at Gibbston, the elegant 2018 vintage (★★★★☆) was matured for eight months in French oak barrels. Ruby-hued, with a floral, ripely scented bouquet, it is mouthfilling and supple, with berry and spice flavours, hints of herbs and nuts, oak complexity and fine-grained tannins. An age-worthy wine, it's already drinking well.

DRY $65 –V

Hunter's Marlborough Pinot Noir   ★★★★

The powerful 2019 vintage (★★★★☆) is the best yet – by far. Hand-harvested at a hillside vineyard in the Omaka Valley, it was matured for a year in French oak barriques (15 per cent new). Deeply coloured, it is mouthfilling, with concentrated, ripe cherry, plum and spice flavours, a hint of liquorice, and obvious potential for cellaring. Still very youthful, it should be at its best 2023+.

DRY $29 V+

Hunter's Offshoot Marlborough Pinot Noir   (★★★★)

A very good, drink-young style, the 2019 vintage (★★★★) was estate-grown and hand-harvested at Rapaura, in the Wairau Valley, and briefly barrel-aged. 'Designed to be drunk now', it is deep ruby, sweet-fruited and supple, with rich cherry, plum and spice flavours. Exuberantly fruity, with gentle tannins, it's a distinctive wine, priced right.

DRY $25 V+

Hunting Lodge, The, Central Otago Pinot Noir   ★★★★☆

The 2018 vintage (★★★★) from this West Auckland-based producer is a graceful, age-worthy red, matured for 10 months in French oak casks (35 per cent new). Bright ruby, it is youthful, with ripe cherry, plum and spice flavours, showing considerable complexity, finely balanced tannins, and a lingering finish. Best drinking 2021+.

DRY $39 AV

Hunting Lodge, The, Expressions Marlborough Pinot Noir   (★★★☆)

Drinking well in its youth, the 2018 vintage (★★★☆) is a light to medium-bodied, elegant Pinot Noir, grown in the Southern Valleys and French oak-aged for 10 months (25 per cent new). Ruby-hued, it is supple, with ripe, cherryish, slightly spicy and nutty flavours, showing a distinct touch of complexity, and good harmony.

DRY $24 V+

Impromptu Central Otago Pinot Noir   ★★★★☆

From Misha's Vineyard, this red is designed as a 'more upfront, sweet-fruited' style than its similarly priced stablemate, Misha's Vineyard Cantata Pinot Noir. The 2019 vintage (★★★★☆) was estate-grown at Bendigo and matured in French oak hogsheads (9 per cent new). Bright ruby, it is fragrant and savoury, with strong, ripe cherry, plum and spice flavours, showing good complexity. Still youthful, it's a very age-worthy wine, likely to be at its best 2022+. Fine value.

Vintage	18	17	16	15	14	13
WR	7	6	7	7	6	6
Drink	20-27	20-26	20-26	20-25	20-24	20-23

DRY $30 V+

Invivo Central Otago Pinot Noir ★★★★

The 2018 vintage (★★★☆) is enjoyable young. Fragrant and savoury, with fullish, slightly developed colour, it is moderately rich, with berryish, spicy, nutty flavours, oak complexity, and a fairly firm finish.

Jackson Estate Homestead Marlborough Pinot Noir ★★★☆

Offering good value, the 2019 vintage (★★★★) was partly barrel-aged. Deep ruby, it is still very youthful, with strong, ripe, cherry and plum flavours, vibrant and smooth. Best drinking 2022+. The 2018 vintage (★★★☆) was also partly barrel-aged. Ruby-hued, it is fragrant, mouthfilling and supple, with good depth of ripe, slightly nutty flavours, in a very easy-drinking style.

Vintage	19	18	17
WR	6	5	4
Drink	20-23	20-22	20-22

Jackson Estate Somerset Single Vineyard Waihopai Valley Marlborough Pinot Noir ★★★★

Delicious now, the 2014 vintage (★★★★★) is a highly fragrant red, hand-harvested, barrel-aged, and bottled unfined and unfiltered. Ruby-hued, with some development showing, it is sweet-fruited, savoury, nutty and silky-textured, with excellent complexity, and a long finish. Drink now to 2022.

Jackson Estate Vintage Widow Marlborough Pinot Noir ★★★★☆

The 2016 vintage (★★★★☆) was hand-harvested in the Southern Valleys and matured in French oak barriques. Bright ruby, it is highly fragrant, sweet-fruited and supple, with strong cherry, plum and spice flavours, showing very good complexity. An elegant, savoury red, it's delicious now, but age-worthy too. The 2017 vintage (★★★★★) was hand-picked from the oldest vines in the Somerset and Gum Emperor vineyards, in the Southern Valleys, and matured for 10 months in French oak barriques. Deep ruby, it is a weighty, very savoury red, with concentrated, ripe cherry, plum and spice flavours, seasoned with nutty oak, excellent complexity and good tannin backbone. Still youthful, it should be at its best 2022+.

Vintage	17
WR	6
Drink	21-25

DRY $45 –V

Johanneshof Maybern Single Vineyard Marlborough Pinot Noir ★★★★

Estate-grown on a steep (30 degrees), north-facing slope at Koromiko, between Picton and Blenheim, the 2016 vintage (★★★★) of this distinctive wine was hand-picked, fermented with indigenous yeasts and barrel-aged. Deep ruby, it is full-bodied, sweet-fruited and moderately firm, with strong plum, spice, herb and nut flavours, oak complexity, and good length.

John Forrest Collection Bannockburn Pinot Noir   ★★★★★

The powerful 2014 vintage (★★★★★) was matured for 15 months in French oak casks (30 per cent new). Deeply coloured, it has dense, very ripe cherry and plum flavours, a hint of liquorice, and good tannin backbone. A bold style, built for the long haul, it should be at its best 2021+.

 DRY $65 AV

John Forrest Collection Waitaki Valley Pinot Noir   ★★★★☆

On sale now, the 2013 vintage (★★★★) is full-coloured, with some development showing, and a fragrant, spicy, slightly leafy bouquet. Showing good concentration, it has plummy, herbal flavours, excellent complexity, and current-drinking appeal.

 DRY $65 –V

Johner Estate Gladstone Pinot Noir   ★★★★

Estate-grown in the northern Wairarapa, matured for a year in French oak barrels (25 per cent new), and bottled unfined and unfiltered, the 2017 vintage (★★★★) is a ruby-hued, full-bodied red, showing good complexity. It is savoury, with generous, plummy, spicy flavours, seasoned with nutty oak, a hint of herbs, and a well-rounded finish. Best drinking 2021+.

Vintage	17
WR	5
Drink	20-25

 DRY $39 AV

Johner Estate Gladstone Reserve Pinot Noir   ★★★★☆

The 2016 vintage (★★★★☆) is a single-vineyard, estate-grown Wairarapa red, hand-harvested from the oldest vines, matured for a year in French oak barrels (80 per cent new), and bottled unfined and unfiltered. Ruby-hued, it is mouthfilling, savoury and supple, with concentrated cherry, plum, spice and nut flavours, showing excellent complexity and harmony.

Vintage	16	15	14
WR	6	7	7
Drink	20-27	20-26	20-25

 DRY $60 –V

Johner Estate Wairarapa Pinot Noir   ★★★☆

Labelled as a 'soft and very approachable' style, the 2017 vintage (★★★☆) was matured for a year in seasoned oak barrels. Ruby-hued, it is fragrant and mouthfilling, with cherryish, spicy, slightly nutty flavours, hints of herbs and tamarillos, considerable complexity, and a smooth finish. Drink now.

Vintage	17
WR	5
Drink	20-22

DRY $26 AV

Judge Rock Alexandra Central Otago Pinot Noir ★★★★☆

Still youthful, the 2017 vintage (★★★★☆) is a highly fragrant red, estate-grown and matured in French oak casks (30 per cent new). Bright ruby, it is medium to full-bodied, with concentrated cherry, plum and spice flavours, complex and savoury, and a well-structured finish. Best drinking 2022+.

DRY $45 –V

Jules Taylor Marlborough Pinot Noir ★★★★☆

The 2019 vintage (★★★★☆) was mostly hand-harvested in the Southern Valleys and partly matured for nine months in French oak barriques. Deep, bright ruby, with a slightly funky bouquet, it is mouthfilling and sweet-fruited, with very good density of plummy, spicy flavours, and savoury notes adding complexity. Approachable young, it should be at its best for drinking 2022+.

Vintage	19	18	17	16	15	14
WR	6	5	6	6	6	6
Drink	20-25	20-23	20-22	20-21	P	P

DRY $33 V+

Jules Taylor OTQ Limited Release Single Vineyard
Marlborough Pinot Noir ★★★★☆

Made 'On The Quiet', the bold 2019 vintage (★★★★★) has a certain 'Wow!' factor. Matured for nine months in French oak barriques, it has dark, purple-flushed colour. Almost Syrah-like, it is packed with plummy, spicy flavours, but retains gracefulness, with fine, supple tannins. Likely to be long-lived, it should be at its best 2023+.

Vintage	19
WR	6
Drink	20-25

DRY $45 –V

Julicher Martinborough Pinot Noir ★★★★☆

Still unfolding, the 2016 vintage (★★★★☆) was estate-grown at Te Muna and matured in French oak casks (30 per cent new). Bright ruby, it is sweet-fruited, savoury and supple, with ripe cherry, plum and spice flavours, showing excellent depth and complexity, and a harmonious, rounded finish. Best drinking 2021+.

DRY $42 AV

Junction Possession Central Hawke's Bay Pinot Noir ★★★☆

The moderately concentrated 2018 vintage (★★★☆) was hand-picked on the Takapau Plains and matured for 18 months in French oak barrels (30 per cent new). Ruby-hued, with a hint of development, it has good depth of cherry, plum and spice flavours, showing considerable complexity, and supple tannins. Drink now or cellar.

DRY $29 AV

Kahurangi Estate Mt Arthur Reserve Nelson Pinot Noir   ★★★★

The powerful 2019 vintage (★★★★☆) was matured for 11 months in French and American oak barriques (partly new). Deep ruby, it is sturdy and sweet-fruited, with generous cherry, plum and spice flavours, a hint of herbs, fresh acidity and finely balanced tannins. A very age-worthy red, it's well worth cellaring to 2022+.

 DRY $32 AV

Kaimira Estate Vintner's Selection Brightwater Pinot Noir   ★★★☆

Certified organic, the youthful 2017 vintage (★★★★) was estate-grown in Nelson and matured for 10 months in French oak barrels (20 per cent new). Deep ruby, with a spicy fragrance, it has strong, fresh, berryish, spicy flavours, showing good complexity, and obvious cellaring potential. Best drinking 2021+.

 DRY $30 –V

Kelly Washington Gibbston Central Otago Pinot Noir   (★★★★★)

From Auckland-based Tamra Kelly (formerly chief winemaker at Yealands Estate), the 2017 vintage (★★★★★) is a powerful, single-vineyard red. Fragrant, sturdy and savoury, with deep, ripe flavours of plums, spices, herbs and nuts, it's already a lovely mouthful, but well worth cellaring.

 DRY $55 AV

Kereru Martinborough Pinot Noir   (★★★★)

Still on sale, the hand-picked, barrel-matured 2014 vintage (★★★★) is bright ruby, with a fragrant bouquet. Drinking well now, it has ripe cherry, plum and spice flavours, showing very good complexity and depth, and a smooth finish. (From Porters Estate.)

 DRY $35 AV

Kina Beach Vineyard Nelson Pinot Noir   ★★★

The 2017 vintage (★★★☆) is a single-vineyard red, barrel-aged. Ruby-hued, with a fragrant, slightly herbal bouquet, it is medium-bodied, with fresh, moderately rich flavours, and savoury, nutty notes adding complexity. Enjoyable now.

Vintage	17
WR	5
Drink	20-24

 DRY $29 –V

Kina Beach Vineyard Nelson Reserve Pinot Noir   ★★★★

Still on sale and maturing well, the vigorous 2013 vintage (★★★★☆) is an estate-grown, oak-aged red, bottled unfined and unfiltered. Full-coloured, it is mouthfilling, with concentrated, ripe plum and spice flavours, and a fairly firm finish. Drink now or cellar.

Vintage	13
WR	7
Drink	20-23

DRY $40 –V

Kina Cliffs Reserve Nelson Pinot Noir   (★★★★☆)

Still unfolding, the 2015 vintage (★★★★☆) was hand-picked and matured for 10 months in French oak casks (50 per cent new). Deep and youthful in colour, with a fresh, spicy bouquet, it is mouthfilling, with concentrated, complex flavours, fairly firm tannins, and a lengthy finish. Best drinking mid-2021+.

 DRY $45 –V

Koha Marlborough Pinot Noir   ★★★

The 2018 vintage (★★☆) has lightish, slightly developed colour. Matured in oak barrels (26 per cent new), it has decent depth of ripe cherry and spice flavours, fresh acidity, earthy notes, and a fairly firm finish. (From te Pā.)

Vintage	18
WR	6
Drink	20-29

 DRY $24 –V

Kōparepare Marlborough Pinot Noir   (★★★)

The 2017 vintage (★★★) is made by Whitehaven for LegaSea, to help fund its work to restore inshore fisheries to abundance. Light ruby, it is a medium-bodied style, with ripe cherry, plum and spice flavours, slightly savoury notes adding complexity, and a well-rounded finish. Priced right.

 DRY $20 AV

Kumeu River Hunting Hill Pinot Noir   ★★★★☆

Grown on the slopes above Mate's Vineyard, directly over the road from the winery at Kumeu, the impressive 2019 vintage (★★★★☆), barrel-matured for a year, is a rare example of classy Pinot Noir from the Auckland region. Already very expressive, it is a deep ruby, sweet-fruited red, with generous, youthful plum, cherry and spice flavours, seasoned with nutty oak, and fine, supple tannins. Best drinking 2023+.

Vintage	19
WR	7
Drink	21-29

 DRY $50 –V

Kumeu River Rays Road Pinot Noir   ★★★★

From the company's elevated, north-facing vineyard in Hawke's Bay, the 2019 vintage (★★★★) was hand-picked and matured for a year in French oak barrels. Deep ruby, it is mouthfilling, with strong, youthful cherry, plum, spice and nut flavours, showing good complexity, and a fairly firm finish. Best drinking 2022+.

Vintage	19	18
WR	7	5
Drink	21-29	20-25

DRY $40 –V

Kumeu Village Pinot Noir ★★★

The 2019 vintage (★★★) was estate-grown in Hawke's Bay and at Kumeu, in West Auckland, and handled without oak barrels. Light ruby, it is full-bodied, with ripe, cherryish, gently spicy flavours, a touch of complexity, and good depth. Priced sharply, it should be at its best for drinking mid-2021+.

 DRY $18 V+

Kuru Kuru Central Otago Pinot Noir ★★★★☆

Still on sale, the 2016 vintage (★★★★) is a blend of Bendigo and Alexandra grapes, French oak-aged for nine months. Ruby-hued, with a hint of development, it is mouthfilling and savoury, with generous, spicy, nutty flavours, balanced tannins, and very good complexity. (From Tarras Vineyards.)

 DRY $40 AV

Lake Chalice The Falcon Marlborough Pinot Noir ★★★☆

Barrel-aged for at least six months, the 2019 vintage (★★★☆) is a bright ruby, mouthfilling red, with good depth of youthful cherry, plum and spice flavours, showing some savoury complexity. Offering good value, it should be at its best 2022+.

 DRY $19 V+

Lake Chalice The Raptor Marlborough Pinot Noir ★★★★

The powerful 2017 vintage (★★★★) was grown in the Eyrie Vineyard, in the lower Waihopai Valley, and barrique-aged for 11 months. Deeply coloured, it is fleshy, with ripe plum/spice flavours, fresh and strong. An age-worthy red, it should be at its best 2021+.

 DRY $23 V+

Last Shepherd, The, Central Otago Pinot Noir ★★★☆

Fresh and supple, the 2018 vintage (★★★☆) is enjoyable now. Bright, light ruby, it is a skilfully balanced red, with moderately concentrated, ripe cherry, plum and spice flavours, gentle tannins and an easy-drinking charm. (From Pernod Ricard NZ.)

 DRY $25 AV

Lawson's Dry Hills Marlborough Pinot Noir ★★★☆

The 2018 vintage (★★★☆) was estate-grown and matured for 10 months in French oak barrels (10 per cent new). Bright ruby, it is mouthfilling, with good depth of cherry, plum, spice and nut flavours, showing considerable complexity, and a moderately firm finish. Best drinking 2021+.

Vintage	18	17
WR	6	6
Drink	20-21	20-21

DRY $25 AV

Lawson's Dry Hills Reserve Marlborough Pinot Noir ★★★★☆

The great-value 2017 vintage (★★★★★) was grown at two sites in the Waihopai Valley and matured in French oak barriques (25 per cent new). Retasted in mid-2020, it is deep ruby, very fragrant, mouthfilling and savoury, with concentrated, plummy, spicy flavours and the structure to mature well. Delicious now, it's also worth cellaring. The 2018 vintage (★★★★) was also grown at two Waihopai Valley sites and matured in French oak barriques (25 per cent new). Bright ruby, it is fresh and youthful, with moderately rich, ripe cherry, plum and spice flavours, showing good complexity. Best drinking 2022+.

Vintage	18	17
WR	6	7
Drink	20-22	20-25

 DRY $30 V+

Lawson's Dry Hills The Pioneer Marlborough Pinot Noir ★★★★☆

Currently on sale, the 2015 vintage (★★★★☆) was grown in the Waihopai Valley and matured for 16 months in French oak barriques (30 per cent new). Deep ruby, it is a powerful, still very youthful and vibrant red, with strong, ripe plum, cherry and spice flavours, seasoned with nutty oak, and good complexity. Best drinking 2022+.

Vintage	15	14	13
WR	7	7	7
Drink	20-25	20-25	20-25

DRY $40 AV

Left Field Marlborough Pinot Noir ★★★☆

Bargain-priced, the 2018 vintage (★★★☆) is a ruby-hued red, lively and supple, with satisfying depth of berryish, spicy flavours, showing some savoury complexity. Ready to roll. (From Te Awa.)

DRY $18 V+

Leveret Estate Marlborough Pinot Noir ★★★☆

French oak-aged for a year, the 2019 vintage (★★★☆) is bright ruby, mouthfilling and youthful, with fresh plum and spice flavours, a hint of herbs, lively acidity and a distinct touch of complexity. Best drinking 2022+.

Vintage	19
WR	7
Drink	21-25

 DRY $25 AV

Lime Rock Kota Central Hawke's Bay Pinot Noir (★★★☆)

Ready to roll, the 2016 vintage (★★★☆) was hand-picked and partly barrel-aged. It has lightish, developed colour and moderately rich flavours, slightly herbal, nutty, savoury and supple.

 DRY $28 AV

Loveblock Central Otago Pinot Noir   ★★★★

Delicious young, the 2019 vintage (★★★★) is a single-vineyard red, hand-picked at Bendigo and partly (50 per cent) barrel-aged. Bright ruby, it is perfumed and supple, with vibrant, ripe, sweet-fruit flavours to the fore, in a very charming style.

Lowburn Ferry Home Block Central Otago Pinot Noir   ★★★★★

The powerful 2017 vintage (★★★★★) is a single-vineyard red, hand-harvested in the Cromwell Basin and matured in French oak barriques (38 per cent new). Deep ruby, with a fragrant, very ripe bouquet, it is highly concentrated, with dense, youthful plum and spice flavours, a hint of liquorice, and fine, supple tannins. Blossoming with age, it should be a 10-year wine.

Vintage	17	16	15	14	13
WR	7	7	7	7	7
Drink	20-25	20-23	20-22	20-21	P

Luna Blue Rock Vineyard Martinborough Pinot Noir   ★★★★☆

From hill-grown vines planted in 1995 and 1996, the 2018 vintage (★★★★☆) was matured for a year in French oak barriques and puncheons (15 per cent new), and bottled unfined and unfiltered. Ruby-hued, it is an attractively perfumed, medium to full-bodied, graceful red with fresh, ripe cherry, plum and spice flavours, savoury notes adding complexity, and a lengthy finish. Well worth cellaring.

Luna Eclipse Martinborough Pinot Noir   ★★★★★

The impressive 2018 vintage (★★★★★) was hand-picked from vines planted on the Martinborough Terrace in 1993, matured for a year in French oak barriques and puncheons (15 per cent new), and bottled unfined and unfiltered. Deep ruby, it is mouthfilling, complex and structured, with deep, ripe, berryish, spicy flavours, hints of liquorice and nuts, and a powerful finish. Full of personality, it should be at its best 2022+.

Luna Martinborough Pinot Noir   ★★★★

Offering great value, the 2018 vintage (★★★★) was grown at two sites (mostly Blue Rock Vineyard) and matured for nine months to a year in French oak barriques and puncheons. Ruby-hued, it is mouthfilling and sweet-fruited, with generous, ripe cherry, plum, spice and nut flavours, oak complexity, and a finely structured finish. Best drinking 2022+.

DRY $24 V+

Mahi Marlborough Pinot Noir ★★★★

The savoury, youthful 2019 vintage (★★★★☆) was hand-harvested at three sites, fermented with indigenous yeasts and aged for 10 months in French oak barrels. Ruby-hued, it is mouthfilling and generous, with a slightly earthy bouquet, concentrated, ripe cherry, plum and spice flavours, showing very good complexity, and a moderately firm finish. Best drinking 2022+.

Vintage	19	18	17
WR	6	6	6
Drink	20-26	20-24	20-24

 DRY $34 AV

Main Divide North Canterbury Pinot Noir ★★★★

A consistently rewarding, great-value red from Pegasus Bay. The 2018 vintage (★★★★) was grown at Waipara and matured for 18 months in French oak barrels. Fragrant and full-bodied, it has excellent depth of ripe cherry, plum and spice flavours, nutty, savoury notes adding complexity, and a smooth finish.

Vintage	18
WR	6
Drink	20-25

 DRY $25 V+

Main Divide Te Hau Reserve North Canterbury Pinot Noir ★★★★☆

A terrific example of a drink-young style, the 2019 vintage (★★★★★) was estate-grown and matured in French oak barriques (30 per cent new). Combining power and grace, it is deep ruby, mouthfilling, sweet-fruited and supple, with dense, ripe flavours, savoury notes adding complexity, and a finely textured, very harmonious finish. (From Pegasus Bay.)

 DRY $33 V+

Maori Point Central Otago Pinot Noir ★★★★☆

This single-vineyard wine is grown at Tarras, in the Cromwell Basin, matured for nearly a year in oak barrels (mostly French, 22 per cent new in 2017), and bottled unfined and unfiltered. The 2017 vintage (★★★★★) is the finest yet. Deep, bright ruby, it is mouthfilling, savoury and supple, with concentrated, ripe cherry, plum and spice flavours, showing good complexity, that build to a finely textured, harmonious finish. Delicious now, it should be at its best 2021+. Fine value.

Vintage	17	16
WR	7	5
Drink	21-25	20-23

 DRY $39 V+

Maori Point Grand Reserve Professors' Block Central Otago Pinot Noir (★★★★☆)

Delicious now, the 2015 vintage (★★★★☆) is a rare, estate-grown red, matured for two years in four French oak barrels (50 per cent new), and bottled unfined and unfiltered. Ruby-hued, it is an elegant, savoury, supple wine, with strong cherry, plum and spice flavours, nutty and complex. Showing some maturity, it's a drink-now or cellaring proposition.

DRY $70 –V

Maori Point Vineyard Reserve Central Otago Pinot Noir   ★★★★★

Still youthful, the very elegant 2016 vintage (★★★★★) was estate-grown at Tarras, hand-harvested, matured for two years in French oak barrels, and bottled unfined and unfiltered. Deep, bright ruby, it has a fragrant, savoury, spicy bouquet. Mouthfilling, it is concentrated and supple, with deep, ripe, plummy, spicy, slightly nutty flavours, showing good complexity, and a finely structured, harmonious finish. Currently delicious, it should be at its best 2022+.

 DRY $64 AV

Margrain Home Block Martinborough Pinot Noir   ★★★★☆

The elegant 2016 vintage (★★★★☆) was harvested from mature vines and matured in French oak barriques. Deeply coloured, it is still youthful, with concentrated, vibrant cherry, plum and spice flavours, a hint of liquorice, savoury notes adding complexity, and good tannin backbone. Well worth cellaring, it should be at its best 2021+.

 DRY $45 –V

Martinborough Vineyard Home Block Pinot Noir   ★★★★★

The elegant, silky-textured 2017 vintage (★★★★★) was matured for a year in French oak casks (23 per cent new). Deep ruby, with a perfumed, savoury bouquet, it is mouthfilling and supple, with excellent weight and concentration of cherry, plum, spice and nut flavours. A refined, complex, very harmonious red, it's delicious now, but well worth cellaring.

Vintage	17	16	15
WR	7	7	7
Drink	20-30	20-31	20-30

 DRY $63 AV

Martinborough Vineyard Marie Zelie Reserve Pinot Noir   ★★★★★

The intriguing 2013 vintage (★★★★★) is the first since 2010. Hand-picked from the oldest vines and matured in French oak barriques, it is all about refinement, rather than sheer power. Light ruby in hue, it is very finely perfumed, with cherry, red-berry and nut flavours, highly complex, very savoury and harmonious. A gentle, persuasive, persistent wine, it's likely to be at its best 2021+.

 DRY $225 –V

Martinborough Vineyard Te Tera Pinot Noir   ★★★★

Te Tera ('The Other') is designed for early drinking, compared to its stablemates. The 2018 vintage (★★★★) was matured for 10 months in French oak barrels (14 per cent new). Bright ruby, it is softly mouthfilling, with ripe cherry, plum and spice flavours, oak complexity, and very gentle tannins. Already highly enjoyable, it's an excellent example of the 'drink-young' style.

Vintage	18	17
WR	7	7
Drink	20-25	20-22

 DRY $30 AV

Matahiwi Estate Holly Wairarapa Pinot Noir ★★★★

The 2019 vintage (★★★★) was barrel-aged. Deep ruby, it is mouthfilling, sweet-fruited and supple, with generous cherry, plum and spice flavours, seasoned with nutty oak, fresh acidity, and considerable complexity. Best drinking 2023+.

Vintage	19	18
WR	6	6
Drink	20-30	22-28

 DRY $40 –V

Matahiwi Estate Wairarapa Pinot Noir ★★★☆

The 2019 vintage (★★★☆) was matured in barrels and tanks. Full-coloured, it is vibrantly fruity, with strong, fresh cherry, plum and spice flavours, and gentle tannins. Still youthful, with drink-young appeal, it should be at its best around 2022.

Vintage	19
WR	6
Drink	20-26

 DRY $30 –V

Matt Connell Bendigo Single Vineyard Central Otago Pinot Noir ★★★★★

The lovely 2017 vintage (★★★★★) was matured for 10 months in French oak barriques (25 per cent new). It's a rare wine – only 820 bottles were produced. Deep ruby, it is full-bodied, concentrated and structured, with rich cherry, plum, spice and nut flavours, showing excellent complexity, and a finely poised, persistent finish. Best drinking 2021+.

DRY $67 AV

Matt Connell Wines Rendition Central Otago Pinot Noir ★★★★★

Mouthfilling, richly flavoured and supple, the 2017 vintage (★★★★★) was grown at Bendigo and Lowburn, hand-harvested, matured for 10 months in French oak barriques (25 per cent new), and bottled unfined and unfiltered. Deep ruby, floral, vibrant and sweet-fruited, it is very finely textured, with concentrated, plummy, spicy flavours, hints of herbs and nuts, and well-integrated oak adding complexity. Delicious young, it's also age-worthy.

DRY $44 V+

Maude Central Otago Pinot Noir ★★★★☆

Enticingly perfumed, the 2018 vintage (★★★★★) is a savoury red, grown at Queensberry and Lowburn, in the Cromwell Basin, and matured for 10 months in French oak barriques (30 per cent new). Bright ruby, it is a very refined, full-bodied wine, with generous cherry, plum, spice and nut flavours, impressive complexity, and ripe, supple tannins. Best drinking 2022. Fine value.

Vintage	18	17	16	15	14
WR	5	7	7	5	7
Drink	20-25	20-30	20-28	20-22	20-28

 DRY $38 V+

Maude Mt Maude Wanaka Reserve EMW Pinot Noir   (★★★★☆)

'EMW' means 'East meets West' – in this case, two blocks in the estate's Mt Maude Vineyard at Wanaka, in Central Otago. Matured in French oak casks (10 per cent new), the 2017 vintage (★★★★☆) is deeply coloured, with a fragrant, slightly herbal bouquet. A very age-worthy, structured red, it is mouthfilling, with berry, herb and spice flavours, showing excellent complexity, and a firm foundation of tannin. Best drinking 2021+.

Maude Mt Maude Wanaka Reserve Kids Block Pinot Noir   (★★★★★)

Invitingly fragrant, the 2016 vintage (★★★★★) is based on estate-grown vines planted in 2000. Matured in French oak casks (30 per cent new), it is still unfolding. Ruby-hued, savoury and mouthfilling, with ripe cherry, plum, spice and nut flavours, finely balanced tannins, and impressive complexity, it should be at its best 2021+.

Maui Waipara Pinot Noir   ★★☆

The 2018 vintage (★★☆) has lightish colour, showing considerable development. It's a full-bodied, slightly rustic and austere wine, with plenty of firm, spicy flavour, but lacks a bit of charm. (From Tiki.)

McArthur Ridge Southern Tor Central Otago Pinot Noir   ★★★★

Grown at Alexandra, the deep ruby 2017 vintage (★★★★) has a fragrant, earthy, slightly herbal bouquet. Full-bodied, it has generous, spicy, slightly nutty flavours, savoury notes adding complexity, and a moderately firm, lingering finish. Best drinking 2021+. Delicious now, the 2016 vintage (★★★★☆) offers top value. Deeply coloured, it is fleshy and supple, with concentrated, ripe, plummy, spicy flavours, fine-grained tannins, and a welcoming fragrance. Drink now or cellar.

ME by Matahiwi Estate Wairarapa Pinot Noir   (★★★★)

The attractive 2019 vintage (★★★★) was matured in tanks and old oak barrels. Deep ruby, it is mouthfilling and fruit-packed, with strong, ripe cherry, plum and spice flavours, fresh, youthful and generous. Best drinking 2022+.

Vintage	19
WR	6
Drink	20-25

DRY $24 V+

Mediator, The, by Urlar Gladstone Pinot Noir   ★★★★

The fragrant 2017 vintage (★★★★) was grown in the northern Wairarapa, hand-picked and matured in French oak casks (15 per cent new). Full, bright ruby, it is scented and supple, with good intensity of ripe cherry, plum and spice flavours. It's drinking well now.

Milcrest Estate Nelson Pinot Noir ★★★

The 2016 vintage (★★★☆) is enjoyable now. Full-coloured, it is fragrant, generous and smooth, with ripe, plummy, slightly savoury flavours.

 DRY $29 –V

Milcrest Estate Reserve Nelson Pinot Noir (★★★★)

Still on sale, the 2014 vintage (★★★★) was grown on the Kina Peninsula and matured for 11 months in French oak barrels. Full-bodied and smooth, it has strong, ripe cherry, plum and spice flavours, nutty and savoury notes adding complexity, and good tannin support. It's enjoyable now.

 DRY $36 AV

Mills Reef Reserve Marlborough Pinot Noir ★★★☆

The powerful 2019 vintage (★★★★) was matured for seven months in French oak casks (23 per cent new). Deep ruby, it is mouthfilling and sweet-fruited, with generous, plummy, spicy flavours, savoury notes adding complexity, and a firm finish. Full of youthful impact, it's worth cellaring to 2022+.

Vintage	19
WR	6
Drink	21-24

 DRY $25 AV

Millton La Cote Gisborne Pinot Noir ★★★★☆

Light ruby, with a fragrant, savoury bouquet, the medium-bodied 2018 vintage (★★★★) was hand-picked, fermented with indigenous yeasts, barrel-aged, and bottled unfined and unfiltered. A delicate, supple red, it is sweet-fruited, with gentle, cherryish, spicy flavours, showing good complexity.

 DRY $35 V+

Misha's Vineyard Cantata Central Otago Pinot Noir ★★★★☆

Designed principally for 'on-premise' sale in restaurants, this label offers consistently good value. Estate-grown at Bendigo, the 2018 vintage (★★★★☆) was fermented with indigenous yeasts and matured in French oak hogsheads (17 per cent new). Bright ruby, with a fragrant, savoury bouquet, it is mouthfilling, with generous, ripe cherry, plum and spice flavours, moderately firm tannins, and good complexity. Already approachable, it should be at its best 2021+.

Vintage	18	17	16	15
WR	7	6	7	7
Drink	20-29	20-28	20-28	20-28

 DRY $30 V+

Misha's Vineyard The High Note Central Otago Pinot Noir ★★★★★

Estate-grown at Bendigo, in the Cromwell Basin, the impressive 2018 vintage (★★★★★) was hand-picked from 15-year-old vines, fermented with indigenous yeasts and matured for a year in French oak hogsheads (37 per cent new). Deep ruby, it is fragrant, very savoury and smooth, with mouthfilling body and concentrated, ripe cherry, plum, spice and nut flavours, showing excellent complexity and harmony. Already approachable, it should break into full stride from 2022 onwards.

Vintage	18	17	16	15	14	13	12	11
WR	7	6	7	7	6	6	7	5
Drink	20-30	20-28	20-29	20-28	20-27	20-26	20-25	20-22

DRY $45 AV

Misha's Vineyard Verismo Central Otago Pinot Noir ★★★★★

This 'reserve style' red is estate-grown at Bendigo and oak-matured longer than its High Note stablemate. On sale now, the 2014 vintage (★★★★★) was harvested at over 24 brix and matured for 18 months in French oak hogsheads (16 per cent new). Full ruby, with some development showing, it has a fragrant, savoury, scented bouquet. Still fresh and vigorous, it is sweet-fruited, with cherry, plum, spice and nut flavours, showing excellent structure, complexity and harmony. Best drinking 2021+.

Vintage	14	13	12	11
WR	6	6	7	5
Drink	20-28	20-27	20-26	20-24

DRY $75 AV

Mission Barrique Reserve Marlborough Pinot Noir ★★★★

The 2019 vintage (★★★★) was estate-grown in the Awatere Valley and French oak-matured. Bright ruby, it is mouthfilling, with strong cherry, plum and spice flavours, showing good complexity, and a moderately firm finish. Still youthful, it should be at its best 2022+.

Vintage	19	18
WR	6	5
Drink	21-29	20-28

DRY $30 AV

Mission Jewelstone Central Otago Pinot Noir (★★★★)

The 2019 vintage (★★★★) was grown in the Cromwell Basin and matured for six months in French oak barrels. Full-coloured, it is sweet-fruited, with good intensity of cherry, plum, spice and nut flavours. Fresh, youthful and supple, it should be at its best 2022+.

DRY $50 –V

Mission Marlborough Pinot Noir (★★★)

Drinking well now, the 2018 vintage (★★★) is a 'fruit-driven' (lightly oaked) style. Light ruby, it is medium-bodied, with good depth of fresh, berryish, slightly spicy flavours, showing a touch of savoury, nutty complexity, and a smooth finish.

DRY $18 V+

Mission Vineyard Selection Marlborough Pinot Noir ★★★☆

Offering good value, the 2019 vintage (★★★☆) was estate-grown in the Awatere Valley. Bright ruby, it is full-bodied, with ripe cherry, plum and spice flavours, showing a distinct touch of complexity, fresh acidity, and good depth. Best drinking mid-2021+.

DRY $22 V+

Momo Organic Marlborough Pinot Noir ★★★★

From Seresin, the 2019 vintage (★★★★) is certified organic. Estate-grown and partly hand-picked in the Raupo Vineyard, in the Omaka Valley, it was matured for nine months in seasoned oak barrels. Bright ruby, it has good density of youthful, ripe plum, cherry and spice flavours, in a 'fruit-driven' style that should repay cellaring to 2022+.

 DRY $25 V+

Mondillo Bella Reserve Central Otago Pinot Noir ★★★★★

The sturdy, lush 2017 vintage (★★★★★) was estate-grown and hand-selected at Bendigo, and matured for 19 months in French oak barriques (one year old). Deeply coloured, it is a powerful red with dense, ripe cherry, plum, spice and nut flavours, gentle acidity, impressive complexity, and a very harmonious, rounded finish. Best drinking 2022+.

 DRY $95 AV

Mondillo Central Otago Pinot Noir ★★★★★

The delicious 2017 vintage (★★★★★) is a rich, savoury, supple Bendigo red, estate-grown and matured for 10 months in French oak barrels (25 per cent new). Deeply coloured, with a fragrant, berryish, spicy bouquet, it is a powerful, sturdy wine, with generous, ripe cherry, plum, spice and nut flavours, finely integrated oak, good complexity, and a well-rounded finish.

Vintage	17	16	15	14	13	12	11
WR	7	7	7	7	7	7	6
Drink	20-23	20-22	20-22	20-22	20-22	P	P

DRY $45 AV

Monowai Upper Reaches Hawke's Bay Pinot Noir (★★★☆)

Still on sale, the 2015 vintage (★★★☆) is a Crownthorpe-grown red, matured for a year in new to two-year-old French oak casks. Ruby-hued, it is lively, with very good depth of plum, berry, spice and nut flavours, fresh acidity, and a fairly firm finish. Ready.

DRY $35 –V

Montana New Zealand Collection Smooth and Velvety Marlborough Pinot Noir (★★☆)

The 2018 vintage (★★☆) is a light-bodied red with slightly earthy aromas, gentle berry, plum and spice flavours, a touch of complexity, fresh acidity, and a smooth finish. Pleasant, easy drinking.

DRY $18 AV

Mount Brown Estates Grand Reserve North Canterbury Pinot Noir   ★★★★

Well worth cellaring, the 2019 vintage (★★★★☆) was estate-grown at Waipara and matured in French oak barriques (25 per cent new). Deep ruby, it is mouthfilling, with rich, plummy, cherryish, gently spicy flavours, fresh acidity, and a finely structured finish. A bold, vibrant young red, it should be at its best 2023+.

Vintage	19
WR	7
Drink	21-28

DRY $29 V+

Mount Brown Estates North Canterbury Pinot Noir   ★★★☆

The good-value 2019 vintage (★★★☆) was matured for 10 months in French oak casks (18 per cent new). Bright ruby, it is freshly scented, with strong cherry, plum and spice flavours, balanced acidity, and plenty of youthful vigour and promise.

Vintage	19	18
WR	7	4
Drink	20-24	20-24

DRY $22 V+

Mount Edward Central Otago Pinot Noir   ★★★★★

Certified organic, the youthful 2017 vintage (★★★★★) of this regional blend was fermented with indigenous yeasts, matured for 11 months in French oak casks (15 per cent new), and bottled unfined and unfiltered. Deeply coloured, it is attractively scented, mouthfilling and supple, with concentrated cherry, plum, spice and herb flavours, smooth and sustained. Already delicious, it should be at its best 2022+.

DRY $49 AV

Mount Edward Morrison Vineyard Central Otago Pinot Noir   (★★★★★)

Still a baby, the 2017 vintage (★★★★★) was hand-picked in the small Morrison Vineyard at Lowburn and matured for 16 months in French oak casks (75 per cent new). Full-coloured, it is a sturdy, powerful red, dense and savoury, with concentrated flavours, a real sense of youthful drive, and a tightly structured finish. Likely to be long-lived, it's well worth cellaring to 2023+. Certified organic.

DRY $75 AV

Mount Edward Muirkirk Vineyard Pinot Noir   (★★★★★)

Grown at Bannockburn, the 2016 vintage (★★★★★) was matured for 16 months in French oak casks (15 per cent new), and bottled without fining or filtration. Mouthfilling, with fullish, slightly developed colour, it is a refined, subtle wine, fragrant, very savoury and complex, with leathery, mushroomy notes, and a smooth, lingering finish. Drink now to 2022. Certified organic.

DRY $75 AV

Mount Riley 17 Valley Marlborough Pinot Noir ★★★★☆

Already delicious, the 2019 vintage (★★★★☆) is a classy wine, priced sharply. Hand-picked and matured for 10 months in French oak casks (partly new), it is deeply coloured, finely scented, rich and supple. Powerful but not heavy, it is sweet-fruited, with strong plum, berry and spice flavours, showing excellent vigour and harmony. Best drinking 2022+.

DRY $35 V+

Mount Riley Limited Release Central Otago Pinot Noir (★★★★)

Already very approachable, the 2019 vintage (★★★★) is an elegant, medium to full-bodied red, hand-picked at Lowburn and matured for 10 months in French oak. Bright ruby, it is vibrant and sweet-fruited, with ripe cherry and spice flavours, showing very good depth, finely integrated oak and gentle tannins. Good value.

DRY $25 V+

Mount Riley Marlborough Pinot Noir ★★★☆

Looking for an excellent, bargain-priced Pinot Noir? Matured for nine months in French oak barriques, the 2019 vintage (★★★★) is deep ruby, fresh and full-bodied, with a strong surge of plummy, slightly spicy flavours, gently seasoned with nutty oak, and a moderately firm finish. Best drinking mid-2021+.

DRY $20 V+

Mountford Liaison North Canterbury Pinot Noir (★★★★★)

Superior to many $45 Pinot Noirs, the 2016 vintage (★★★★★) is full of personality and an irresistible buy. Estate-grown at Waipara, it was hand-picked, mostly from vines planted in 2009, matured in French oak casks, and bottled unfined and unfiltered. Deep ruby, it is highly fragrant, mouthfilling and sweet-fruited, with generous cherry, plum, spice, herb and nut flavours, complex and savoury. A finely structured red, delicious now, it should also be drinking well up to 2023. (From Koyama Wines.)

DRY $28 V+

Moutere Hills Nelson Pinot Noir ★★★★

The 2019 vintage (★★★★) is a single-vineyard red, hand-picked at Upper Moutere and matured for 11 months in French oak. Bright ruby, it is full-bodied and sweet-fruited, with strong, ripe cherry, plum, spice and nut flavours, showing good complexity, fresh acidity, and finely balanced tannins. Best drinking 2022+.

Vintage	19
WR	7
Drink	20-26

DRY $35 AV

Moutere Hills Sarau Reserve Nelson Pinot Noir ★★★★☆

Likely to be long-lived, the 2015 vintage (★★★★☆) is an estate-grown red, hand-harvested at Upper Moutere and matured for 11 months in French oak casks. It has fullish, slightly developed colour. Mouthfilling, it has generous, ripe, plummy, cherryish, spicy flavours, a slightly earthy streak, and the structure and depth to mature well. Best drinking 2021+.

DRY $55 –V

Mt Beautiful North Canterbury Pinot Noir ★★★★

Drinking well in its youth, the 2018 vintage (★★★★) was estate-grown at Cheviot, north of Waipara, and matured in French oak barriques (20 per cent new). Ruby-hued, it is fragrant and savoury, with plummy, spicy, nutty flavours, showing good complexity, and a very harmonious finish. Drink now or cellar.

Vintage	18	17	16	15
WR	6	6	7	6
Drink	20-26	20-25	20-27	20-25

Mt Difficulty Bannockburn Central Otago Pinot Noir ★★★★★

This is one of the region's highest-profile reds. Matured for a year in French oak casks (25 per cent new), the 2017 vintage (★★★★★) is full-coloured and youthful, with fresh, strong cherry, plum and spice flavours, earthy, savoury notes adding complexity, good tannin backbone, and obvious cellaring potential. Best drinking 2021+.

Vintage	17	16	15	14	13
WR	6	6	6	6	6
Drink	20-32	20-28	20-27	20-26	20-25

Mt Difficulty Ghost Town Bendigo Pinot Noir ★★★★★

The youthful 2017 vintage (★★★★★) is a single-vineyard red, grown on Chinaman's Terrace, at Bendigo, and matured for a year in French oak barrels (25 per cent new). An elegant, concentrated wine, bright ruby, it is mouthfilling and vibrantly fruity, with rich, ripe cherry, plum and spice flavours, nutty oak adding complexity, supple tannins, and good cellaring potential. Best drinking 2022+.

Vintage	17
WR	6
Drink	20-32

Mt Difficulty Havoc Farm Gibbston Pinot Noir (★★★★★)

Full of youthful drive, the elegant 2016 vintage (★★★★★) is a single-vineyard red, grown over 400 metres above sea level at Gibbston, and matured for 15 months in French oak casks (27 per cent new). The colour is deep; the bouquet is highly fragrant, with hints of berries and herbs. A classic sub-regional style, it has concentrated, cherryish, plummy, spicy flavours, with a long, finely structured finish. It should blossom with cellaring.

DRY $75 AV

Vintage	16
WR	6
Drink	20-30

Mt Difficulty Long Gully Bannockburn Central Otago Pinot Noir   ★★★★★

From vines planted in 1992, the 2017 vintage (★★★★★) is a single-vineyard red, matured for 15 months in French oak casks (25 per cent new). Deeply coloured, with a fragrant, spicy bouquet, it's a powerful, classy young red, with deep cherry, plum and spice flavours, finely integrated oak, impressive complexity, and a well-structured, long finish. Best drinking 2022+.

Vintage	17
WR	6
Drink	20-32

 DRY $110 AV

Mt Difficulty Mansons Farm Bannockburn Pinot Noir   ★★★★★

Described on the label as 'dark and brooding', the powerful 2016 vintage (★★★★★) was matured for 14 months in French oak barrels (27 per cent new). Bright ruby, it is mouthfilling and savoury, with concentrated, ripe, plummy, spicy, nutty flavours, showing excellent complexity, and a lasting finish. Likely to be long-lived, it should be at its best 2021+.

 DRY $110 AV

Mt Difficulty Packspur Lowburn Valley Pinot Noir   (★★★★★)

From the oldest vineyard at Lowburn, in the Cromwell Basin, the graceful 2017 vintage (★★★★★) was grown at 360 to 380 metres above sea level and matured for 15 months in French oak barrels (25 per cent new). Full, bright ruby, it is an elegant, mouthfilling and supple red, with youthful cherry, plum and spice flavours, woven with fresh acidity, good complexity, and a long, silky-smooth finish.

Vintage	17
WR	5
Drink	20-32

 DRY $75 AV

Mt Difficulty Pipeclay Terrace Bannockburn Pinot Noir   ★★★★★

From vines planted in 1996, the 2017 vintage (★★★★★) was matured for 15 months in French oak barrels (25 per cent new). Deep ruby, it is a mouthfilling, powerful but approachable style, with youthful cherry, plum, spice and nut flavours, savoury notes adding complexity, and a vigorous, lasting finish. Best drinking 2022+.

Vintage	17
WR	6
Drink	20-32

 DRY $110 AV

Mt Difficulty Target Gully Bannockburn Pinot Noir   ★★★★★

The 2016 vintage (★★★★☆), from vines planted in 1994, is a single-vineyard red, matured for 15 months in French oak casks (27 per cent new). Full ruby, it has strong cherry, plum and spice flavours, nutty and savoury, good complexity, and a smooth finish. Fairly forward in its appeal, it's drinking well now.

Vintage	16
WR	5
Drink	20-30

DRY $110 –V

Mt Rosa Central Otago Pinot Noir ★★★★☆

The 2016 vintage (★★★★) is a moderately youthful Gibbston red, matured for 10 months in French oak casks (10 per cent new). Ruby-hued, it is sweet-fruited, with ripe cherry, plum and spice flavours, earthy, savoury notes adding complexity, and a smooth finish. Tasted in September 2019, the 2014 vintage (★★★★☆) has fairly mature colour. Aged for 11 months in French oak casks (10 per cent new), it is developing well. Savoury and complex, with generous cherry, plum, spice and herb flavours, it's probably at its peak.

Vintage	16	14
WR	3	5
Drink	21-24	20-22

DRY $50 –V

Mud House Central Otago Pinot Noir ★★★★

Estate-grown at Bendigo, in the Claim 431 Vineyard, and matured in a mix of tanks and French oak barriques, the 2018 vintage (★★★☆) is a lively red, with very good depth of ripe cherry, plum and spice flavours, showing some savoury complexity.

DRY $20 V+

Muddy Water Waipara Pinot Noir ★★★★☆

Certified organic, the perfumed, good-value 2017 vintage (★★★★★) was harvested principally from vines planted in 1993, hand-picked, matured for 14 months in French oak barriques (30 per cent new), and bottled unfined and unfiltered. Full, bright ruby, it is very savoury, fresh and youthful, with dense, ripe cherry, plum and spice flavours, seasoned with nutty oak, fine-grained tannins, and strong personality. Best drinking 2021+. The 2018 vintage (★★★★☆) was matured for 14 months in French oak barriques (39 per cent new), and bottled unfined and unfiltered. Ruby-hued, it is a floral, supple, youthful red, with complex, savoury, nutty flavours and a lengthy, harmonious finish. Best drinking 2022+. Certified organic.

Vintage	18
WR	7
Drink	20-30

DRY $39 V+

Nanny Goat Vineyard Central Otago Pinot Noir ★★★★

Still youthful, the 2018 vintage (★★★★) is bright ruby, mouthfilling and vibrantly fruity, with strong cherry, plum and spice flavours, oak complexity, and finely balanced tannins. Best drinking 2021+.

DRY $36 AV

Nanny Goat Vineyard Super Nanny Central Otago Pinot Noir (★★★★★)

Deep ruby, the 2018 vintage (★★★★★) has an inviting, savoury fragrance. Mouthfilling, concentrated and supple, it's a powerful, high-impact style, with strong, ripe fruit flavours, savoury notes adding complexity, good supporting tannins, and obvious potential. Best drinking 2021+.

DRY $55 AV

Nautilus Clay Hills Vineyard Marlborough Pinot Noir   ★★★★☆

The delicious 2016 vintage (★★★★★) is a single-vineyard red, grown in the Southern Valleys and matured in French oak casks (33 per cent new). Deep ruby, it is full-bodied and fleshy, with rich, ripe cherry, plum, spice and nut flavours. Finely textured, it's a very harmonious red, well worth cellaring, but already a lovely mouthful.

Vintage	17	16
WR	7	7
Drink	20-27	20-26

 DRY $70 –V

Nautilus Southern Valleys Marlborough Pinot Noir   ★★★★☆

The 2017 vintage (★★★★☆) was matured in French oak barrels (30 per cent new). Deeply coloured, with a fragrant, slightly earthy bouquet, it is mouthfilling and sweet-fruited, with rich cherry, plum and spice flavours and fresh acidity. A powerful, very youthful wine, it should be at its best 2023+. (Note: there is no 2018 vintage – the grapes all went into the company's Opawa Marlborough Pinot Noir.)

Vintage	17	16	15	14
WR	7	6	7	7
Drink	20-27	20-26	20-23	20-22

 DRY $42 AV

Neck of the Woods Gibbston Central Otago Pinot Noir   ★★★★

The youthful 2017 vintage (★★★★) was grown at Gibbston and matured in French oak casks (33 per cent new). Deeply coloured, it has a fragrant, fresh, spicy, slightly leafy bouquet. Full-bodied, with good substance, it has strong, plummy, spicy flavours, fairly firm tannins, and obvious cellaring potential. Best drinking 2021+.

 DRY $37 AV

Neudorf Moutere Pinot Noir   ★★★★★

Typically a very classy Nelson red. It is hand-picked from 'older vines' at Upper Moutere, fermented with indigenous yeasts, matured for 10 to 12 months in French oak barriques (22 per cent new in 2017), and usually bottled without fining or filtering. The full ruby 2017 vintage (★★★★★) has a savoury, complex bouquet. Mouthfilling and supple, it has strong, ripe cherry, plum, spice and nut flavours, showing excellent complexity, gentle acidity, and a velvet-smooth, very harmonious finish. A 'forward' vintage, it's already drinking well. Certified organic.

Vintage	17	16	15	14	13	12	11
WR	6	6	7	6	6	7	6
Drink	20-24	20-23	20-22	20-21	P	20-23	P

 DRY $65 AV

Neudorf Tom's Block Nelson Pinot Noir ★★★★☆

Typically good value, this is an ideal introduction to Neudorf's Pinot Noir style. Grown at three sites at Upper Moutere, the 2017 vintage (★★★★☆) was hand-harvested, matured in French oak barriques (20 per cent new), and bottled without fining or filtration. Ruby-hued, with a fragrant, savoury bouquet, it has youthful cherry, plum and spice flavours, showing excellent complexity, buried tannins, and plenty of personality. Best drinking 2023+.

Vintage	17	16	15	14	13
WR	6	7	7	6	6
Drink	20-24	20-23	20-22	20-21	P

 DRY $33 V+

Nga Waka Martinborough Lease Block Pinot Noir ★★★★★

Offering fine value, the youthful 2018 vintage (★★★★★) is a single-vineyard red, from vines planted in 1999. Barrel-matured and bottled unfined and unfiltered, it is bright ruby, mouthfilling and very savoury, with cherry, plum, spice and nut flavours, complex and finely structured. Best drinking 2022+.

 DRY $40 V+

Nga Waka Martinborough Pinot Noir ★★★★☆

Already drinking well, the 2018 vintage (★★★★☆) was matured for nearly two years in French oak barriques (20 per cent new). Bright ruby, with a scented, savoury bouquet, it is mouthfilling, sweet-fruited and supple, with ripe plum, spice and nut flavours, showing good complexity. Best drinking 2022+. Fine value.

 DRY $33 V+

Nikau Point Reserve Marlborough Pinot Noir ★★★☆

Priced sharply, the 2019 vintage (★★★☆) was estate-grown. Deep ruby, it is mouthfilling and fruit-packed, with lively cherry, plum and spice flavours, fresh and strong, and a smooth finish.

Vintage	19
WR	5
Drink	20-23

 DRY $16 V+

Nobody's Hero Marlborough Pinot Noir (★★★★)

Priced right, the 2019 vintage (★★★★) was grown in the Wairau Valley and matured in French oak barriques. Deep ruby, it is mouthfilling and fruit-packed, with concentrated, ripe, plummy, spicy flavours, a gentle seasoning of oak, and a fairly firm finish. Best drinking 2022+. (From Framingham.)

DRY $25 V+

Nockie's Palette Georgetown Central Otago Pinot Noir   (★★★★☆)

The 2016 vintage (★★★★☆) is a youthful, single-vineyard red, estate-grown at the eastern end of the Kawarau Gorge. Bright ruby, it is fragrant and savoury, with good intensity of ripe plum and spice flavours, oak complexity, fresh acidity, and a long, finely structured finish. Best drinking 2021+.

 DRY $38 V+

Nor'Wester by Greystone North Canterbury Pinot Noir   ★★★★

From vineyards 'scattered across the region', the 2018 vintage (★★★★) was grown at Waipara, fermented with indigenous yeasts and matured for 10 months in French oak barriques. Ruby-hued, it is a mouthfilling, supple wine with moderately concentrated, gentle cherry, plum and spice flavours, nutty, savoury notes adding complexity, and a well-rounded finish. Best drinking mid-2021+.

Vintage	18	17
WR	6	6
Drink	20-29	20-28

 DRY $29 V+

Novum Marlborough Pinot Noir   ★★★★★

The graceful 2019 vintage (★★★★★) is still very youthful. Matured in French oak casks (30 per cent new), it is a bright ruby, medium to full-bodied red, ripely flavoured, savoury and supple. It has good density of cherry, plum and spice flavours, showing impressive complexity, and a finely structured finish. Best drinking 2022+.

 DRY $47 AV

Odyssey Reserve Iliad Marlborough Pinot Noir   ★★★★☆

Still unfolding, the 2017 vintage (★★★★☆) was estate-grown and hand-picked at the top of the Brancott Valley, and matured in French oak casks (30 per cent new). Fragrant, with bright, youthful colour, it is savoury and firmly structured, with concentrated plum, spice and nut flavours, good tannin backbone, and obvious potential; best drinking mid-2021+. Certified organic.

 DRY $32 V+

Ohau Woven Stone Pinot Noir   (★★★☆)

Grown in the Horowhenua, the 2019 vintage (★★★☆) is a ruby-hued, fresh, full-bodied red, with good depth of cherry, plum and spice flavours, a hint of tamarillo, some savoury complexity, fresh acidity, and a smooth finish. Best drinking mid-2021+.

DRY $25 AV

Old Coach Road Nelson Pinot Noir   ★★☆

Barrel-matured for seven months, the 2019 vintage (★★☆) is a bright ruby, full-bodied red with ripe, plummy, slightly spicy flavours, and fresh acidity. Priced right. (From Seifried.)

Vintage	19
WR	6
Drink	20-23

 DRY $14 V+

Old House Vineyards Falcon Hill Nelson Pinot Noir ★★★★☆

The attractively perfumed 2018 vintage (★★★★☆) was hand-picked at Upper Moutere and matured for 11 months in French oak casks (50 per cent new). Deep ruby, it is an elegant red, fresh and supple, with youthful cherry, plum and spice flavours, lively acidity, nutty, savoury notes adding complexity, and a well-rounded finish. Well worth cellaring, it should be at its best 2022+.

Vintage	18	17
WR	6	7
Drink	20-30	20-30

DRY $39 V+

Old House Vineyards Fantail New Zealand Pinot Noir (★★★★)

Estate-grown in Nelson, the 2018 vintage (★★★★) was hand-picked and French oak-aged for 11 months. Bright ruby, it is sweet-fruited, savoury and supple, with ripe cherry, plum and spice flavours, gently seasoned with oak, and lots of drink-young appeal. Best drinking 2021+. Priced sharply.

Vintage	18
WR	6
Drink	20-27

DRY $24 V+

Omeo Hidden Valley Single Vineyard Central Otago Pinot Noir ★★★★☆

The 2017 vintage (★★★★★) is a top buy. A single-vineyard wine, grown at Alexandra, it was matured for 10 months in seasoned French oak casks. Delicious now, it is deep ruby, mouthfilling, sweet-fruited and supple, with strong cherry, plum and spice flavours, a hint of herbs, excellent complexity, and a savoury, finely balanced finish. Still youthful, it should be at its best 2022+.

Vintage	17
WR	6
Drink	20-24

DRY $30 V+

On Giants' Shoulders Martinborough Pinot Noir (★★★★☆)

The finely scented 2018 vintage (★★★★☆) is a single-vineyard, hand-harvested red, matured for a year in French oak casks (20 per cent new). Deep ruby, it is sweet-fruited and complex, with good density of ripe cherry, spice and nut flavours, refined tannins, and obvious potential; best drinking 2022+.

DRY $50 –V

On Giants' Shoulders The Collaborator Martinborough Pinot Noir (★★★★)

The youthful 2018 vintage (★★★★) was hand-picked and matured for a year in French oak casks (33 per cent new). Ruby-hued, with a scented, slightly nutty bouquet, it is medium-bodied and supple, with gentle, ripe cherry, plum and spice flavours, and a finely textured finish. Open 2022+.

DRY $50 –V

On Giants' Shoulders The Guest Martinborough Pinot Noir   (★★★★★)

The classy 2018 vintage (★★★★★) is a rare red – only 263 bottles were made. From vines planted in 1982 (AM 10/5 clone), it was hand-picked, fermented with indigenous yeasts, matured for 18 months in a seasoned French oak puncheon, and bottled unfined and unfiltered. Deep ruby, it is enticingly perfumed, mouthfilling, very savoury and silky, with a lovely spread of youthful cherry, plum, spice and nut flavours, good tannin support, and a long, harmonious finish. Already delicious, it should break into full stride 2023+.

DRY $50 AV

Opawa Marlborough Pinot Noir   ★★★☆

From Nautilus, the 2019 vintage (★★★★) was grown in the Wairau Valley and barrel-matured (12 per cent new). Deep ruby, with a slightly earthy bouquet, it is mouthfilling, with generous, ripe, cherryish, plummy, spicy flavours, and a well-rounded finish. Already drinking well, it should be at its best 2022+.

DRY $28 AV

Ostler Caroline's Waitaki Valley Pinot Noir   ★★★★☆

Estate-grown in North Otago, the impressive 2016 vintage (★★★★☆) is a powerful red, deeply coloured. Full-bodied, it has concentrated, ripe, plummy flavours to the fore, hints of herbs and liquorice, a subtle seasoning of oak, and gentle tannins. Best drinking 2021+.

DRY $59 –V

Oyster Bay Marlborough Pinot Noir   ★★★☆

The 2018 vintage (★★★☆) was grown in the Wairau and Awatere valleys, and French oak-matured for nearly a year. Bright ruby, it is fragrant and softly mouthfilling, with generous cherry, plum and spice flavours, showing some savoury complexity, and lots of drink-young appeal.

DRY $25 AV

Pā Road Marlborough Pinot Noir   ★★★

Offering good value, the 2019 vintage (★★★☆) was partly barrel-aged. Bright ruby, it is fragrant, lively and youthful, with very good depth of ripe, plummy, spicy, slightly nutty flavours, showing a distinct touch of complexity. Best drinking mid-2021+.

DRY $19 AV

Paddy Borthwick Left Hand Wairarapa Pinot Noir   ★★★★☆

Estate-grown at Gladstone, in the northern Wairarapa, this small-volume red (1450 bottles in 2018) gives left-handed winemaker Briony Carnachan the chance to express her 'logical, creative and precise' approach. Bright ruby, the 2018 vintage (★★★★★) is a refined wine, with ripe cherry, plum and spice flavours, showing excellent concentration, and a lingering, silky-smooth finish. A very savoury, harmonious wine, it's already delicious, but well worth cellaring to 2022+.

DRY $55 –V

Paddy Borthwick Right Hand Wairarapa Pinot Noir   ★★★★★

Estate-grown at Gladstone, this small-volume wine (1450 bottles in 2018) is made by Paddy Borthwick, an 'intuitive, impulsive and thoughtful', right-handed vigneron. The 2018 vintage (★★★★★) is deep ruby, with a fragrant, savoury bouquet. A youthful, slightly 'masculine' style, it has concentrated, ripe cherry, plum and spice flavours, complex and savoury, good tannin backbone, and obvious potential for cellaring. Best drinking 2023+.

DRY $55 AV

Paddy Borthwick Wairarapa Pinot Noir   ★★★★

Estate-grown at Gladstone, in the northern Wairarapa, the 2018 vintage (★★★★) is a bright ruby, youthful red, with strong, cherryish, plummy, spicy, slightly nutty flavours, threaded with fresh acidity, and good complexity. Best drinking 2022+.

DRY $35 AV

Palliser Estate Martinborough Pinot Noir   ★★★★★

This is typically an enticingly perfumed, notably elegant and harmonious red. The 2019 vintage (★★★★★) is deep ruby and invitingly scented. Mouthfilling, rich and supple, it is sweet-fruited, with concentrated, plummy, spicy flavours, finely balanced, savoury and complex, and obvious potential for cellaring. Highly refined, it should be at its best 2023+.

DRY $59 AV

Palliser Estate Wharekauhau Vineyard Martinborough Pinot Noir   (★★★★★)

The very age-worthy 2018 vintage (★★★★★) was picked from mature, 20-year-old vines. Deep ruby, with a perfumed, savoury bouquet, it is highly refined and intense, with youthful, ripe cherry, plum and spice flavours, showing excellent complexity, and a finely structured finish. Best drinking 2022+.

DRY $85 AV

Paper Road Wairarapa Pinot Noir   (★★★★)

From Borthwick Vineyard at Gladstone, in the northern Wairarapa, the 2019 vintage (★★★★) offers good value. Already enjoyable, it is bright ruby, sturdy, sweet-fruited and supple, with generous berry, plum and spice flavours, smooth and harmonious. Best drinking mid-2021+.

DRY $25 V+

Pask Instinct Vine Velvet Marlborough Pinot Noir   (★★☆)

The easy-drinking 2018 vintage (★★☆) was matured in seasoned French oak barrels. A light style, it is ruby-hued, with gentle cherry and nut flavours, a touch of tannin, and solid depth. Drink young.

DRY $17 AV

Pegasus Bay North Canterbury Pinot Noir ★★★★★

This is one of North Canterbury's greatest Pinot Noirs, typically very rich in body and flavour. Many of the vines are over 25 years old and the wine is matured for 18 to 22 months in French oak barriques (about 40 per cent new). The 2017 vintage (★★★★★) is full-coloured and finely perfumed. Mouthfilling, sweet-fruited, savoury and supple, it is still youthful, with concentrated, ripe cherry, plum and spice flavours, oak complexity, and a rich, smooth finish. Best drinking 2022+.

Vintage	17
WR	6
Drink	20-29

 DRY $52 AV

Pegasus Bay Prima Donna Pinot Noir ★★★★★

For its top Waipara red, Pegasus Bay wants 'a heavenly voice, a shapely body and a velvety nose'. Based on the oldest vines, it is matured for 15 to 20 months in French oak barriques (50 per cent new). The deeply coloured 2016 vintage (★★★★★) is mouthfilling and sweet-fruited, with vibrant cherry, plum and spice flavours, concentrated, savoury and supple, that build to a powerful finish. It needs time; open 2022+. The 2017 vintage (★★★★★) is deeply coloured, with a highly fragrant, very savoury bouquet. A powerful, weighty red, it is notaby concentrated, with deep, vibrant plum and spice flavours, rich and complex, and finely balanced tannins. Still very youthful, it should be long-lived; open 2023+.

Vintage	17	16	15	14	13	12	11
WR	6	6	6	NM	6	7	6
Drink	20-30	20-30	20-34	NM	20-28	20-28	20-23

 DRY $100 AV

Pencarrow Martinborough Pinot Noir ★★★★

This is Palliser Estate's second-tier label, but in most years it is impressive and offers good value. The 2018 vintage (★★★★) is drinking well now. Ruby-hued, it has ripe cherry, plum and spice flavours, nutty notes adding complexity, and a smooth, very harmonious finish.

 DRY $31 AV

Peregrine Central Otago Pinot Noir ★★★★★

Outstanding in top seasons, this classic red is estate-grown mostly in the Cromwell Basin but also at Gibbston. The refined 2017 vintage (★★★★★) is a very youthful blend of Bendigo, Pisa and Gibbston grapes, matured for 10 months in French oak barrels. Bright ruby, it is mouthfilling, rich and flowing, with strong, lively cherry, plum and spice flavours, a hint of tamarillo, supple tannins, and a very harmonious finish. Best drinking 2023+. Certified organic.

DRY $45 AV

Peregrine Saddleback Central Otago Pinot Noir   ★★★★

The highly approachable 2018 vintage (★★★★) was matured for 10 months in seasoned French oak casks. Bright ruby, it is fragrant and supple, with ripe cherry, plum and spice flavours, showing very good depth, and a distinct touch of complexity. A graceful red, it's a drink-now or cellaring proposition.

DRY $27 V+

Pick & Shovel Reserve Central Otago Pinot Noir   (★★★☆)

A drink-young charmer, the 2018 vintage (★★★☆) is ruby-hued, fresh and very harmonious, with ripe, moderately concentrated flavours, showing some savoury complexity, and a smooth finish.

DRY $28 AV

Pinot 3 The Red Edition   (★★★)

The attractive, non-vintage wine (★★★) I tasted in August 2020 is a blend of Pinot Noir and Pinot Gris, made without oak. Bright, light ruby, it is sweet-fruited, lively and supple, with simple, berryish flavours, and lots of drink-young charm. (From Untitled Wines, based in West Auckland.)

DRY $20 AV

Pinot Naturel by Fromm   ★★★★

Certified organic, the 2018 vintage (★★★★) is an 'uncomplicated' red from Fromm that 'can be drunk young and slightly cooler'. Grown and hand-harvested in Marlborough, it was fermented with indigenous yeasts and bottled without fining or filtering, with 'minimal sulphur at bottling to ensure stability'. Bright ruby, it is a generous, supple red, fresh and lively, with strong, plummy flavours, showing some complexity, and a smooth finish. Delicious young.

DRY $32 AV

Pinot Petit by Untitled Wines   (★★★☆)

The non-vintage wine (★★★☆) I tasted in August 2020 is a highly unusual blend of Pinot Noir and Petit Verdot. Bright ruby, it is a medium-bodied, vibrantly fruity red, with ripe berry and plum flavours, supple tannins, and good depth. Enjoyable young. (From Untitled Wines, based in West Auckland.)

DRY $25 AV

Pisa Range Estate Black Poplar Block Pinot Noir   ★★★★★

Estate-grown at Pisa Flats, north of Cromwell, in Central Otago, this classy, enticingly scented wine is well worth discovering. The 2015 vintage (★★★★★) was picked from the oldest vines and matured for a year in French oak barriques (33 per cent new). A fragrant, powerful red, it is deeply coloured. Robust (15 per cent alcohol), it is youthful, fresh, sweet-fruited and concentrated, with very ripe plum, spice and slight liquorice flavours, and good tannin support. Best drinking 2021+.

Vintage	15	14	13	12	11
WR	7	6	7	6	NM
Drink	20-25	20-26	20-25	20-23	NM

DRY $56 AV

Porters Estate Martinborough Pinot Noir ★★★★

I tasted the 2014, 2015 and 2016 vintages together in August 2019. Hand-picked and matured in French oak barriques (partly new), the 2016 vintage (★★★★) is bright ruby, mouthfilling and spicy, with cherry, plum and nut flavours, a hint of tamarillo, good complexity and a moderately firm finish. My favourite is the 2015 vintage (★★★★☆), a powerful, savoury, deeply coloured wine with concentrated cherry, plum and spice flavours, slightly earthy notes adding complexity, and good cellaring potential. Still unfolding, the 2014 vintage (★★★★) is mouthfilling and generous, earthy and savoury, with good flavour complexity, and the structure to age well.

Vintage	16	15	14
WR	6	6	6
Drink	20-30	20-27	20-22

DRY $45 –V

Porters Reserve Martinborough Pinot Noir (★★★★★)

Still developing, the impressive 2015 vintage (★★★★★) was hand-picked and matured in French oak barriques (partly new). Deep, bright ruby, it is mouthfilling and concentrated, with rich cherry, plum, spice and nut flavours, complex and savoury, and a well-structured, moderately firm finish. Best drinking 2022+.

Vintage	15
WR	7
Drink	20-30

DRY $75 AV

Prophet's Rock Cuvée aux Antipodes Central Otago Pinot Noir ★★★★★

The memorable 2018 vintage (★★★★★) is the first to be labelled as a Pinot Noir (the 2016 and 2017 vintages were listed in the Branded Reds section). Estate-grown at an elevated (320–400 metres above sea level) site at Bendigo, it is deep ruby, with a highly fragrant, savoury bouquet. An authoritative wine, it is weighty, fresh and finely structured, with ripe cherry, plum and spice flavours, showing notable density, complexity and harmony. Built for a long life, it's already delicious.

DRY $120 AV

Prophet's Rock Home Vineyard Central Otago Pinot Noir ★★★★★

This consistently rewarding red is estate-grown at a high-altitude site at Bendigo. Barrel-aged for 17 months and bottled unfiltered, the youthful 2017 vintage (★★★★★) is deeply coloured, with notably concentrated, ripe, plummy, spicy flavours, showing impressive vigour and length. Best drinking 2024+.

DRY $65 AV

Prophet's Rock Infusion Central Otago Pinot Noir   ★★★★

Delicious young, the 2018 vintage (★★★★☆) was estate-grown in the Rocky Point Vineyard at Bendigo. All freshness and suppleness, it was 'made without the normal extraction from the grape skins during fermentation. Instead, the wine was fermented using indigenous wild yeast in old barrels, after being pressed and removed from its skins.' A rosé in all but name, 'best served lightly chilled', it is fresh and crisp, with strong, berryish flavours, and a dry finish. Ready.

DRY $33 AV

Prophet's Rock Retrospect Pinot Noir   ★★★★★

The 2015 vintage (★★★★★) of this Central Otago red was designed to be released at five years old. Estate-grown at Bendigo and barrel-aged, it is a deeply coloured, powerful, savoury red, robust but not heavy, with concentrated, complex cherry, plum and spice flavours, finely integrated oak, fresh acidity, and a well-structured finish. Best drinking 2022+.

DRY $135 –V

Providore First Edition Central Otago Pinot Noir   (★★★★)

Grown mostly at Gibbston and partly oak-aged, the 2018 vintage (★★★★) is bright ruby, floral and boldly fruity, with generous, plummy, slightly spicy flavours, gentle tannins, and lots of drink-young charm.

DRY $25 V+

Pruner's Reward, The, Waipara Valley Pinot Noir   ★★★☆

From Bellbird Spring, the savoury 2016 vintage (★★★★) was matured for a year in French oak casks (15 per cent new). Ruby-hued, with a hint of development, it is drinking well now, with ripe cherry, spice and nut flavours, showing very good vigour, depth and harmony.

DRY $27 AV

Pyramid Valley Angel Flower Pinot Noir   ★★★★☆

Showing some early maturity, the 2016 vintage (★★★★☆) was estate-grown on an elevated, north-facing slope at Waikari, in North Canterbury. Matured for a year in French oak casks (10 per cent new), and bottled unfined and unfiltered, it has a savoury, slightly herbal bouquet. Mouthfilling, it is a very savoury rather than vibrantly fruity wine, spicy, herbal and complex, with fine-grained tannins, and excellent flavour depth and harmony. Best drinking now to 2021.

DRY $125 –V

Pyramid Valley Central Otago Pinot Noir   ★★★★☆

The very youthful 2018 vintage (★★★★★) was estate-grown at Lowburn and matured for 10 months in French oak barriques and cuves (partly new). Bright ruby, it is highly fragrant, with strong, ripe cherry, plum, spice and nut flavours, complex and savoury. Built to last, it's well worth cellaring to 2022+.

DRY $50 –V

Pyramid Valley Earth Smoke Pinot Noir ★★★★★

Estate-grown on an east-facing block at Waikari, in North Canterbury, the 2016 vintage (★★★★★) was matured for a year in French oak barrels (10 per cent new). Full of personality, it has deep, moderately developed colour. Drinking well now, but also worth cellaring, it is mouthfilling, savoury and complex, with spicy, slightly herbal flavours, showing excellent depth and harmony.

 DRY $130 –V

Pyramid Valley North Canterbury Pinot Noir (★★★★☆)

The subtle 2018 vintage (★★★★☆) was 'grower-sourced' (meaning not estate-grown) at Waipara. Ruby-hued, it is a fragrant, savoury, supple red with ripe cherry, plum and spice flavours, showing very good complexity, and a lingering finish. Still youthful, it should be at its best mid-2021+.

 DRY $50 –V

Quartz Reef Bendigo Estate Single Ferment Pinot Noir ★★★★★

Certified organic and biodynamic, the powerful 2018 vintage (★★★★★) is 'a single ferment... personally selected by Rudi Bauer as it best expresses the Bendigo Estate vineyard' in Central Otago. Estate-grown and hand-harvested, it was matured for 15 months in French oak casks, and bottled unfined and unfiltered. Deep ruby, it is an authoritative, concentrated, well-structured red, with obvious potential. Mouthfilling, it has deep, ripe plum, spice and nut flavours, good tannin backbone, notable complexity, and a lasting finish. Best drinking 2023+.

 DRY $85 AV

Quartz Reef Bendigo Estate Single Vineyard Central Otago Pinot Noir ★★★★★

Certified organic and biodynamic, the extremely graceful 2018 vintage (★★★★★) was estate-grown at Bendigo, hand-picked and matured for a year in French oak barriques. Deep ruby, it is sweet-fruited and vibrant, with rich cherry, plum, spice and nut flavours, complex and finely poised, and an enticingly scented bouquet. Best drinking 2022+.

Vintage	18	16	15	14	13
WR	6	6	6	7	7
Drink	20-24	20-21	20-22	P	P

 DRY $49 AV

Rapaura Springs Limestone Terrace Marlborough Pinot Noir ★★★★☆

The 2018 vintage (★★★★) is a single-vineyard, Awatere Valley wine. Matured in French oak casks (32 per cent new), it is a ruby-hued, very graceful red, with cherry, plum and spice flavours, showing good complexity, and gentle tannins. Best drinking 2021+.

Vintage	18
WR	6
Drink	20-25

 DRY $50 –V

Rapaura Springs Reserve Central Otago Pinot Noir ★★★☆

The ruby-hued, vibrant, supple 2018 vintage (★★★☆) was matured in French and Hungarian oak. It has very satisfying depth of fresh, ripe cherry, plum and spice flavours, showing some savoury complexity, and a smooth finish. Best drinking 2021+.

DRY $33 –V

Rapaura Springs Reserve Marlborough Pinot Noir ★★★☆

The 2019 vintage (★★★☆) of this regional blend is bright ruby, with a slightly earthy bouquet. Mouthfilling, it has fresh, strong, youthful cherry, plum and spice flavours, showing considerable complexity, and a moderately firm finish. Best drinking 2022+.

Vintage	19
WR	6
Drink	20-25

DRY $19 V+

Rapaura Springs Rohe Awatere Pinot Noir (★★★☆)

Bright ruby, the 2018 vintage (★★★☆) was grown in the Awatere Valley and matured in French oak casks (38 per cent new). It has gentle cherry, spice and nut flavours, showing good complexity, and a fairly firm finish. Best drinking 2021+.

Vintage	18
WR	6
Drink	20-25

DRY $37 –V

Rapaura Springs Rohe Southern Valleys Marlborough Pinot Noir (★★★★)

Worth cellaring, the 2018 vintage (★★★★) was matured in French oak barrels (56 per cent new). Full, bright ruby, it is fragrant and supple, with ripe cherry, plum and spice flavours, showing very good depth, and gentle tannins. A graceful red, it should be at its best 2021+.

Vintage	18
WR	6
Drink	20-25

DRY $37 AV

Remarkable Bannockburn Central Otago Pinot Noir ★★★☆

I tasted three vintages of this single-vineyard red in August 2020. The 2018 vintage (★★★★), barrel-aged for 10 months, is fragrant, with ripe cherry, plum and spice flavours, showing good complexity, and lots of current-drinking appeal. The deeply coloured, slightly hazy 2017 vintage (★★☆) lacks finesse. Ready now, the 2016 vintage (★★★☆) has plummy, spicy flavours, firm and strong.

DRY $33 –V

Renato Nelson Pinot Noir ★★★★

The 2017 vintage (★★★★) was hand-picked at Kina and aged for 10 months in French oak barriques (25 per cent new). Bright ruby, it is mouthfilling and sweet-fruited, with very good depth of ripe cherry, plum and spice flavours, nutty and savoury notes adding complexity, and a finely textured, very harmonious finish. Good value.

Vintage	17	16	15	14	13
WR	6	5	NM	7	5
Drink	20-23	20-22	NM	20-23	P

 DRY $25 V+

Rimu Grove Nelson Pinot Noir ★★★★☆

Estate-grown near Mapua, on the Nelson coast, this is typically a rich wine with plenty of personality. The 2017 vintage (★★★★), French oak-matured for 11 months, is drinking well now. A 'forward' year, it is mouthfilling and supple, with generous, savoury, nutty flavours, showing good complexity, and gentle tannins.

Vintage	17	16	15	14	13	12	11
WR	7	6	7	7	7	7	7
Drink	20-32	20-30	20-30	20-30	20-30	20-30	20-27

 DRY $52 –V

Rippon Emma's Block Pinot Noir ★★★★★

From an east-facing slope, this Lake Wanaka wine has 'animated femininity', according to winemaker Nick Mills. It is typically matured in French oak barrels (25 per cent new in 2017) for two winters in Central Otago, and bottled unfined and unfiltered. The 2017 vintage (★★★★★) is full-coloured, fragrant and savoury, with an array of cherry, plum, herb and spice flavours, showing impressive complexity and density, and good tannin backbone. Best drinking 2023+.

Vintage	17
WR	7
Drink	20-32

 DRY $105 AV

Rippon 'Rippon' Mature Vine Central Otago Pinot Noir ★★★★★

This Lake Wanaka red has a long, proud history. Estate-grown but not a single-block wine – winemaker Nick Mills views it as 'the farm voice' – it is typically a very elegant, 'feminine' style, rather than a blockbuster. The 2017 vintage (★★★★★) was hand-harvested, fermented with indigenous yeasts, matured over two winters in French oak barrels (25 per cent new), and bottled unfined and unfiltered. Deeply coloured, it is sweet-fruited, savoury and supple, with rich, vibrant cherry, plum and spice flavours, seasoned with nutty oak, fresh acidity, and excellent complexity and harmony. Best drinking 2022+.

Vintage	17
WR	7
Drink	20-32

DRY $65 AV

Rippon Tinker's Field Mature Vine Pinot Noir ★★★★★

Named after Rippon's co-founder, Rolfe Mills ('Tink' to his friends), this exceptional wine is based on 'the oldest vines on the property'. Winemaker Nick Mills describes the typical style as 'unforced masculinity'. Grown on a north-facing slope at Lake Wanaka, in Central Otago, it is matured for 17 months in French oak barriques (25 per cent new in 2017), and bottled without fining or filtering. The 2017 vintage (★★★★★) is a majestic wine. Deeply coloured, it is mouthfilling and very savoury, with dense, ripe cherry, plum and spice flavours, hints of blackcurrant and liquorice, and fairly firm tannins. A riveting red, it should flourish for a decade.

Vintage	17
WR	7
Drink	20-32

DRY $115 AV

Riverby Estate Marlborough Pinot Noir ★★★★

This good-value, single-vineyard red is grown in the heart of the Wairau Valley and French oak-aged for a year (30 per cent new in 2019). The 2019 vintage (★★★★) is a fragrant, softly mouthfilling wine, ruby-hued and sweet-fruited, with very good depth and harmony. Delicious young, it's a drink-now or cellaring proposition.

Vintage	19
WR	7
Drink	21-35

DRY $28 V+

Riverby Estate Reserve Marlborough Pinot Noir ★★★★

The 2015 vintage (★★★★☆) of this single-vineyard, Rapaura red was hand-picked and matured for 15 months in French oak casks (45 per cent new). Ruby-hued, it is mouthfilling, with good concentration of ripe, savoury, nutty, cherryish, plummy flavours, showing good complexity, and a fairly firm finish. Best drinking 2021+.

Vintage	15
WR	6
Drink	20-30

DRY $35 AV

Riwaka River Estate Resurgence Nelson Pinot Noir ★★★★

The 2015 vintage (★★★★) of this single-vineyard red has a fragrant, savoury, slightly herbal bouquet. Deep ruby, it is full-bodied and smooth, with very satisfying depth of cherry, plum, spice and nut flavours, showing good complexity.

DRY $35 AV

Roaring Meg Central Otago Pinot Noir ★★★★

From Mt Difficulty, the 2018 vintage (★★★★) of this highly popular red was hand-picked and matured for nine months in French oak casks (18 per cent new). Full, bright ruby, it is fresh, sweet-fruited, savoury and supple, with good concentration of berry, plum and spice flavours, showing considerable complexity. Enjoyable young, it should be at its best 2021+.

DRY $32 AV

Rock Ferry 3rd Rock Central Otago Pinot Noir   ★★★★★

Estate-grown at a high-altitude site at Bendigo, in the Cromwell Basin, the impressive 2016 vintage (★★★★★) was matured for a year in French oak barriques (25 per cent new). Deep ruby, with a fragrant, spicy, savoury bouquet, it is mouthfilling and sweet-fruited, with concentrated, vibrant cherry, plum and spice flavours, revealing excellent complexity, and good tannin support. A lovely young red, approachable now, it should be at its best 2021+.

DRY $45 AV

Rock Ferry Trig Hill Vineyard Pinot Noir   ★★★★★

The classy, youthful 2016 vintage (★★★★★) was estate-grown, 400 metres above sea level, at Bendigo, in Central Otago, hand-picked and matured for 20 months in French oak barriques (25 per cent new). Deep ruby, it is finely scented and weighty, with deep cherry, plum and spice flavours, oak complexity, and a long, finely structured finish. Best drinking 2022+. Certified organic.

DRY $65 AV

Rock N Pillar Central Otago Pinot Noir   (★★★★)

Enjoyable young but worth cellaring, the 2017 vintage (★★★★) is a single-vineyard Alexandra red. Deeply coloured, with fresh cherry, plum and herb aromas and flavours, gently seasoned with French oak, it is a lively wine, generous and supple. Best drinking 2021+.

DRY $32 AV

Rockburn Central Otago Pinot Noir   ★★★★★

This consistently stylish blend of Cromwell Basin (mostly) and Gibbston grapes typically has concentrated cherry, plum and dried-herb flavours, silky-textured and perfumed. Estate-grown in the Parkburn Vineyard (83 per cent) and Gibbston Valley Back Road Vineyard (17 per cent), the 2019 vintage (★★★★★) was matured for 10 months in French oak casks (33 per cent new). Deep ruby, it is enticingly fragrant, full-bodied and sweet-fruited, with rich fruit flavours, nutty, savoury notes adding complexity, gentle tannins, and a finely poised, harmonious finish.

Vintage	19	18	17	16	15
WR	6	6	6	7	6
Drink	21-28	20-27	20-26	20-27	20-26

DRY $50 AV

Rockburn Eight Barrels Gibbston Vineyard Central Otago Pinot Noir   (★★★★★)

Still a baby, the 2019 vintage (★★★★★) is a single-vineyard red, grown at Gibbston and matured for over a year in French oak casks (75 per cent new). Deep ruby, it is mouthfilling and vibrantly fruity, with concentrated cherry, plum and spice flavours, a hint of herbs, good complexity, fresh acidity, and gentle tannins. A savoury, youthful red with obvious potential, it's well worth cellaring to 2023+.

DRY $96 AV

Rockburn Eleven Barrels Parkburn Vineyard Central Otago Pinot Noir   (★★★★★)

The powerful 2019 vintage (★★★★★) 'truly represents the Pisa sub-region', in the Cromwell Basin. Matured for 14 months in French oak casks (18 per cent new), it is a deep ruby, full-bodied, savoury red, with dense, very ripe cherry, plum and spice flavours, a hint of liquorice, good tannin backbone, and the depth and structure to mature well over the long haul. Best drinking 2024+.

DRY $96 AV

Rockburn Six Barrels Central Otago Pinot Noir   (★★★★★)

Still youthful, the 2017 vintage (★★★★★) is a deeply coloured, single-vineyard red, grown at Gibbston and barrel-aged in French oak (30 per cent new). Lush and silky-textured, it has a fragrant bouquet of fresh herbs and spices. Mouthfilling, with concentrated plum, herb and spice flavours, balanced acidity, gentle tannins, and a finely poised, savoury, lasting finish, it should be at its best from 2022 onwards.

Vintage	17
WR	7
Drink	20-30

DRY $95 AV

Rockburn The Chosen Central Otago Single Vineyard Pinot Noir   (★★★★★)

'Crafted for immediate enjoyment', the 2018 vintage (★★★★★) is a graceful Gibbston red, from a notably early-ripening season. It was matured for 10 months in French oak barrels (15 per cent new). Bright ruby, it is fragrant and softly mouthfilling, with deep, very ripe plum, spice and herb flavours, savoury, nutty notes adding complexity, gentle acidity, and a long, well-rounded finish. Weighty, rich and harmonious, it's already delicious.

Vintage	18
WR	7
Drink	20-23

DRY $65 AV

Rocky Point Central Otago Pinot Noir   ★★★★☆

From Prophet's Rock, the 2019 vintage (★★★★☆) is a youthful, fruit-packed red, hand-harvested at the company's two sites at Bendigo and matured in French oak casks (15 per cent new). Full-coloured, it is mouthfilling, vibrant and supple, with fresh acidity and concentrated, plummy, spicy, slightly nutty flavours. Already highly approachable, it should be at its best from 2022 onwards.

DRY $33 V+

Rongopai Estate Premium Selection Marlborough Pinot Noir   ★★☆

Light, fresh and fruity, the 2017 vintage (★★☆) is a simple style of Pinot Noir, priced accordingly. Enjoyable young, it has cherry, plum and herb flavours, woven with fresh acidity, and a smooth finish. (From Babich.)

DRY $16 AV

Ruru Central Otago Pinot Noir   ★★★☆

The 2019 vintage (★★★☆) is a single-vineyard red, estate-grown at Alexandra and matured in French oak casks (15 per cent new). Ruby-hued, with a fragrant bouquet, it is mouthfilling and supple, with vibrant cherry, plum and spice flavours, an earthy streak, a distinct touch of complexity, and finely balanced tannins. Best drinking mid-2021+.

DRY $27 AV

Ruru Reserve Central Otago Pinot Noir   ★★★☆

The 2019 vintage (★★★) of this single-vineyard Alexandra red was matured in French oak barrels (20 per cent new). Bright ruby, with a slightly rustic bouquet, it has good depth of ripe cherry, plum and spice flavours, an earthy streak, some complexity, and a moderately firm finish. It needs time; open 2022+.

DRY $38 –V

Russian Jack Martinborough Pinot Noir   ★★★

Enjoyable young, the 2018 vintage (★★★) was mostly barrel-aged. Ruby-hued, it is softly mouthfilling, with ripe cherry, plum and spice flavours in a gentle, easy-drinking style. (From Martinborough Vineyard.)

Vintage	18
WR	6
Drink	20-24

DRY $25 –V

Sacred Hill Single Vineyard Marlborough Pinot Noir   (★★☆)

The 2018 vintage (★★☆) was picked with 'a degree of raisining' and matured for 10 months in French oak barrels (25 per cent new). It has light, advanced colour. Softly mouthfilling, with hints of cherries, herbs and spices, showing a touch of complexity, it's a very 'forward' wine, disappointing for the price.

DRY $28 –V

Saint Clair Omaka Reserve Marlborough Pinot Noir   ★★★★☆

This is Saint Clair's top Pinot Noir. Full of youthful promise, the 2019 vintage (★★★★★) is a powerful, single-vineyard red, grown in the Southern Valleys and matured for 11 months in French oak barrels (25 per cent new). Deep ruby, it is mouthfilling and weighty, with concentrated cherry, plum, spice and nut flavours, complex, savoury, and finely structured. Best drinking 2023+.

DRY $46 –V

Saint Clair Origin Marlborough Pinot Noir   ★★★☆

This middle-tier red is partly barrel-aged. The 2019 vintage (★★★) is bright ruby and full-bodied, with strong cherry, plum and spice flavours, an earthy streak, and a fairly firm finish.

DRY $25 AV

Saint Clair Pioneer Block 14 Doctor's Creek Marlborough Pinot Noir ★★★★☆

Still unfolding, the 2019 vintage (★★★★☆) is a full-bodied red, estate-grown at Fairhall, south-west of Blenheim, and matured for 11 months in French oak barrels. Bright ruby, it is savoury, complex and supple, with strong, ripe cherry, spice and nut flavours, fresh acidity, and fine-grained tannins. Best drinking 2022+.

 DRY $40 AV

Saint Clair Pioneer Block 15 Strip Block Marlborough Pinot Noir ★★★★☆

Grown in the lower reaches of the Waihopai Valley and barrel-aged for 10 months, the 2018 vintage (★★★★☆) is an attractively perfumed wine, ruby-hued, savoury and supple. Showing good complexity, it is very harmonious, with silky tannins, and lots of drink-young appeal.

 DRY $40 AV

Saint Clair Pioneer Block 22 Barn Block Marlborough Pinot Noir ★★★★☆

From a relatively warm site at the base of the hills on the south side of the Wairau Valley, the 2018 vintage (★★★★) is an age-worthy red, matured for 10 months in French oak barriques (22 per cent new). Bright ruby, it has strong, ripe cherry, plum and spice flavours, showing good complexity, fresh acidity, and a smooth finish. Best drinking 2022+.

 DRY $40 AV

Saint Clair Pioneer Block 23 Master Block Marlborough Pinot Noir ★★★★☆

Softly seductive, the 2018 vintage (★★★★☆) is a ruby-hued red, grown in Benmorven Vineyard, west of Blenheim. Barrel-aged for 10 months, it is refined and supple, with ripe cherry, plum, spice and nut flavours, good complexity, and a well-rounded finish. Already delicious, it should be at its best 2021+.

 DRY $40 AV

Sanctuary Marlborough Pinot Noir ★★★☆

Ruby-hued, the 2017 vintage (★★★) was matured in an even split of tanks and old French oak barriques. Light and supple, it is sweet-fruited, with fresh cherry and spice flavours, showing a touch of complexity. It's ready to roll.

 DRY $25 AV

Satellite Marlborough Pinot Noir ★★★

From Spy Valley, the 2018 vintage (★★★☆) is drinking well now. Ruby-hued, with a hint of development, it is medium to full-bodied, with good depth of plummy, spicy, slightly nutty flavours, showing a distinct touch of complexity.

DRY $23 AV

Satyr by Sileni Estates Foothills Pinot Noir ★★★★

The 2019 vintage (★★★★) was grown at coastal and elevated, inland sites in Hawke's Bay. Already quite open and expressive, it is ruby-hued, mouthfilling and savoury, with cherry, plum, spice and nut flavours, showing good complexity, and loads of drink-young appeal. A great buy.

 DRY $16 V+

Saving Grace Pinot Noir   (★★★☆)

Attractive young, the 2018 vintage (★★★☆) is a single-vineyard red, grown in North Canterbury, barrel-aged for nine months, and bottled unfined and unfiltered. Ruby-hued, it is medium-bodied, with moderately concentrated, cherryish flavours, showing some savoury complexity, gentle tannins, and a very smooth finish. (From Waipara Hills, this label is mostly for restaurants.)

DRY $25 AV

Scout Lowburn Central Otago Pinot Noir   (★★★★)

The distinctive 2019 vintage (★★★★) is a single-vineyard, Lowburn red, hand-harvested, matured in old oak puncheons, and bottled unfined and unfiltered. Light ruby, it is a fresh, medium-bodied wine, with youthful, ripe, cherryish, slightly nutty flavours. A graceful, gentle, savoury red, it's already enjoyable.

DRY $34 AV

Scout Southern Valleys Marlborough Pinot Noir   (★★★★☆)

The good-value 2019 vintage (★★★★☆) was grown in the hillside Yarrum Vineyard, matured in old French oak barriques and puncheons, and bottled unfined and unfiltered. Bright ruby, it is youthful, with generous, ripe cherry, plum and spice flavours, showing excellent complexity, good tannin backbone, and a smooth finish. Well worth cellaring, it should be at its best 2023+.

DRY $34 V+

Scout Waipara Pinot Noir   (★★★★☆)

The graceful 2019 vintage (★★★★☆) is a single-vineyard red, hand-picked at Omihi, matured in old oak barriques and puncheons, and bottled unfined and unfiltered. Bright ruby, it is a refined, medium to full-bodied red, with youthful, ripe cherry and spice flavours, fresh acidity, and a lengthy finish. Subtle and savoury, it should be at its best 2022+.

DRY $34 V+

Seifried Nelson Pinot Noir   ★★★☆

The 2019 vintage (★★★★) is one of the best yet. From vines over 30 years old, at Brightwater and Rabbit Island, it was matured for eight months in French oak barriques (partly new). Deep ruby, with a slightly earthy fragrance, it is mouthfilling, with concentrated, ripe, plummy, slightly spicy and nutty flavours, and good tannin support. A youthful, generous, firmly structured red, it should be at its best 2022+. Great value.

Vintage	19
WR	6
Drink	20-24

DRY $19 V+

Seresin Leah Marlborough Pinot Noir ★★★★

Certified organic, the 2017 vintage (★★★★☆) was estate-grown in the Raupo Creek Vineyard, in the Omaka Valley, hand-picked and matured for 15 months in French oak barriques (10 per cent new). Deep ruby, it is mouthfilling and savoury, with fresh cherry, plum and spice flavours, nutty and savoury, and good tannin backbone. Well worth cellaring, it should be at its best 2022+. Fine value.

DRY $35 AV

Seresin Noa Marlborough Pinot Noir ★★★★☆

The powerful 2014 vintage (★★★★★) is a single-vineyard red, estate-grown near Renwick, hand-picked, matured for 18 months in French oak barriques (17 per cent new), and bottled unfined and unfiltered. Deep ruby, with some development showing, it has a highly fragrant, savoury bouquet. Weighty, with concentrated, ripe, spicy, nutty flavours, and a firmly structured finish, it's very age-worthy; best drinking now to 2023.

DRY $95 –V

Seresin Rachel Marlborough Pinot Noir ★★★★☆

The 2014 vintage (★★★★☆) was grown mostly in the Raupo Creek Vineyard, in the Omaka Valley, hand-harvested, matured for a year in French oak barriques (7 per cent new), followed by six months aging in oak puncheons, and bottled unfined and unfiltered. It has a fragrant, savoury, spicy bouquet, leading into a mouthfilling, sweet-fruited, complex wine, with fresh acidity, and strong cherry, plum, spice, herb and nut flavours. Best drinking 2022+.

DRY $50 –V

Seresin Raupo Creek Marlborough Pinot Noir ★★★★★

Drinking well now, the 2014 vintage (★★★★★) was estate-grown in the Omaka Valley, hand-picked, matured for 18 months in French oak barriques (13 per cent new), and bottled unfined and unfiltered. Ruby-hued, with some development showing, it is still fresh and vigorous, with cherry, plum, spice and herb flavours, showing excellent complexity, that build well to a finely structured, lasting finish. Best drinking 2021+. Certified organic.

DRY $75 AV

Seresin Sun & Moon Marlborough Pinot Noir ★★★★★

Certified organic, the 2014 vintage (★★★★★) is 'the purest expression of Pinot Noir we can make'. Hand-picked and fermented with indigenous yeasts, it was matured for 18 months in French oak barriques (14 per cent new), and bottled unfined and unfiltered. Full ruby, with a hint of development, it is mouthfilling, very savoury and complex, with highly concentrated cherry, spice and nut flavours, hints of herbs and liquorice, and a well-structured finish. Best drinking 2022+.

DRY $130 –V

Seresin Tatou Marlborough Pinot Noir   ★★★★

The 2014 vintage (★★★★☆) was grown in the Tatou Vineyard, at the western end of the Wairau Valley, hand-picked, matured for 18 months in French oak barriques (14 per cent new), and bottled unfined and unfiltered. Deep ruby, with a hint of development, it is full-bodied, with strong, fresh cherry, plum and spice flavours, hints of herbs and spices, and savoury notes adding complexity. Best drinking 2021+.

DRY $85 –V

Sileni Cellar Selection Hawke's Bay Pinot Noir   ★★★

The easy-drinking 2019 vintage (★★★) has a Beaujolais-like charm. Bright ruby, it is medium-bodied and vibrantly fruity, with lively cherry, plum and spice flavours, fresh and finely balanced.

DRY $19 AV

Sileni Exceptional Selection Hawke's Bay Pinot Noir   ★★★★

The 2017 vintage (★★★☆) has moderately youthful, ruby colour. Matured for nine months in oak barriques (20 per cent new), it is mouthfilling and fleshy, with strong, ripe cherry, plum and spice flavours, hints of liquorice and nutty oak, and a fairly firm finish. The 2016 vintage (★★★★) is full-bodied and sweet-fruited, with generous cherry, plum and spice flavours. Best drinking 2021+.

DRY $70 –V

Sileni Grand Reserve Plateau Hawke's Bay Pinot Noir   ★★★★

Grown in the elevated, inland Plateau Vineyard, the 2018 vintage (★★★★) was barrel-aged. Bright ruby, it is fragrant and supple, with vibrant cherry, plum and spice flavours, showing very good complexity, vigour and depth. Best drinking 2021+.

DRY $32 AV

Sileni Grand Reserve Springstone Hawke's Bay Pinot Noir   ★★★★

Grown in the inland, elevated Mangatahi district, the 2017 vintage (★★★☆) is ruby-hued, with a hint of development. It has strong, ripe cherry, plum, spice and nut flavours, showing good complexity, and a firm, slightly 'grippy' finish.

DRY $32 AV

Sisters Ridge North Canterbury Pinot Noir   (★★★☆)

From Mt Beautiful, the 2017 vintage (★★★☆) was French oak-aged for 10 months. Offering great value, it is a bright ruby, medium-bodied red, with ripe cherry, plum and spice flavours, a hint of herbs, fresh acidity, and some complexity. Drink now.

DRY $19 V+

Smith & Sheth Cru Kawarau Pinot Noir

(★★★★★)

The finely scented, bright ruby 2018 vintage (★★★★★) was hand-picked from 25-year-old vines at Gibbston and matured for 10 months in French oak barriques (28 per cent new). A refined, subtle red, it has deep, ripe cherry, plum, spice and nut flavours, savoury notes adding complexity, supple tannins, and a long, very harmonious finish.

 DRY $50 AV

Snapper Rock Marlborough Pinot Noir

★★★

Made in a 'fruit-driven' style, the 2019 vintage (★★★) is ruby-hued, with good depth of fresh, plummy, spicy flavours, a touch of tannin, and drink-young appeal. Enjoyable now, the 2018 vintage (★★★) is a single-vineyard red, grown at Ward, in the Awatere Valley, and briefly oak-aged. Ruby-hued, with a hint of development, it is medium-bodied, with ripe, berryish, slightly spicy flavours, gentle acidity, and a smooth finish.

 DRY $18 V+

Soho Havana Yarrum Vineyard Marlborough Pinot Noir

★★★★

The 2017 vintage (★★★★) is a mouthfilling, supple red, hand-picked and French oak-matured (25 per cent new). Full, bright ruby, it has ripe, cherryish, plummy, slightly spicy flavours, showing good concentration, nutty, savoury notes adding complexity, and obvious potential. Best drinking 2021+.

 DRY $38 AV

Spinyback New Zealand Pinot Noir

★★★

The 2019 vintage (★★★) from Waimea Estates is a departure from the wines of past years, which were labelled as of Nelson origin. Ruby-hued, it is fresh and lively, with good depth of cherry, plum and spice flavours, in a supple, easy-drinking style.

 DRY $17 V+

Spy Valley Envoy Johnson Vineyard Waihopai Valley Marlborough Pinot Noir

★★★★★

The 2016 vintage (★★★★★) was estate-grown in the Waihopai Valley, hand-harvested and matured in French oak barrels for 18 months. Ruby-hued, it is mouthfilling and supple, with deep, ripe, plummy, spicy flavours, showing excellent complexity, and a long, finely textured finish. A subtle, very age-worthy wine, it should break into full stride 2021+.

Vintage	16	15	14	13	12	11
WR	6	6	6	NM	7	7
Drink	20-25	20-23	P	NM	P	P

DRY $55 AV

Spy Valley Envoy Outpost Vineyard Omaka Valley Marlborough Pinot Noir   ★★★★★

From hill-grown vines in the Omaka Valley, the classy 2015 vintage (★★★★★) was hand-picked, fermented with indigenous yeasts and matured for 16 months in French oak casks. Deeply coloured, it is mouthfilling, sweet-fruited and concentrated, with ripe cherry, plum, spice and nut flavours, complex and savoury, which build to a smooth, lasting finish. A delicious, classy, finely structured red, it should mature gracefully.

Vintage	15	14	13	12	11
WR	6	6	6	7	6
Drink	20-25	P	P	P	P

 DRY $55 AV

Spy Valley Southern Valleys Marlborough Pinot Noir   ★★★★☆

Offering good value, the 2017 vintage (★★★★☆) was estate-grown in the Southern Valleys and matured for 11 months in French oak barrels. Deep ruby, it is fragrant, savoury and supple, with generous cherry, plum, spice and nut flavours, showing excellent complexity and harmony. It's drinking well now.

Vintage	17	16	15	14	13
WR	7	7	6	6	6
Drink	20-24	20-23	20-23	P	P

 DRY $33 V+

Stables Reserve Ngatarawa Hawke's Bay Pinot Noir   ★★★

Priced sharply, the 2018 vintage (★★★☆) is a bright ruby, softly mouthfilling red, savoury and sweet-fruited, with cherry, plum and spice flavours, showing considerable complexity, and a smooth finish. Drink now.

 DRY $20 AV

Staete Landt State of Grace Marlborough Pinot Noir   ★★★★

The age-worthy 2016 vintage (★★★★) was hand-picked at Rapaura, on the north side of the Wairau Valley, and matured in French oak barriques. Bright ruby, it is mouthfilling and savoury, with ripe plum/spice flavours, and a lingering, fairly firm finish. Best drinking 2021+.

Vintage	16
WR	5
Drink	20-25

 DRY $35 AV

Stanley Estates Block 8 Awatere Valley Marlborough Pinot Noir   ★★★★

Well worth cellaring, the youthful 2019 vintage (★★★★) was matured in French oak barriques. Full-coloured, it is mouthfilling, with strong, vibrant cherry, plum and spice flavours, showing considerable complexity. Best drinking 2022+.

Vintage	15
WR	6
Drink	20-24

DRY $25 V+

Starborough Family Estate Marlborough Pinot Noir ★★★★

The 2019 vintage (★★★★) was estate-grown in the Awatere (60 per cent) and Wairau (40 per cent) valleys, and matured in French oak casks (20 per cent new). Bright ruby, it is vibrantly fruity and supple, with generous, ripe cherry, plum and spice flavours, oak complexity, fresh acidity, and good length. Best drinking 2022+.

DRY $28 V+

Stoneleigh Latitude Marlborough Pinot Noir ★★★☆

Celebrating the 'Golden Mile' along Rapaura Road, on the stony north side of the Wairau Valley, the 2019 vintage (★★★☆) is deep ruby, with a slightly earthy bouquet. Mouthfilling, it has good depth of youthful cherry, plum and spice flavours, and a fairly firm finish. Best drinking 2022+. Priced sharply.

DRY $17 V+

Stoneleigh Organic Marlborough Pinot Noir (★★★☆)

Certified organic, the 2019 vintage (★★★☆) is a ruby-hued, fresh, medium-bodied red, with good depth of youthful cherry, plum and spice flavours, earthy notes, and some savoury complexity. Best drinking 2022. Fine value.

DRY $18 V+

Stoneleigh Rapaura Series Marlborough Pinot Noir ★★★★

The powerful 2019 vintage (★★★★☆) is a deeply coloured, single-vineyard red, with a fragrant, ripe, slightly earthy bouquet. Mouthfilling and sweet-fruited, it has rich, youthful cherry, plum and spice flavours, showing very good complexity. Best drinking 2022+. Fine value.

DRY $25 V+

Stoneleigh Wild Valley Marlborough Pinot Noir ★★★☆

Fermented with indigenous ('wild') yeasts, the 2019 vintage (★★★☆) is bright ruby, with fresh, ripe cherry, plum and spice flavours, showing a touch of complexity, and good vigour and depth. Priced sharply.

DRY $17 V+

Sugar Loaf Southern Valleys Marlborough Pinot Noir ★★★★

The 2019 vintage (★★★★☆) was 'sourced entirely from our hillside vineyard in Marlborough's Southern Valleys' and barrel-aged. Deeply coloured, it is mouthfilling, generous and supple, with good density of youthful, ripe, plummy, spicy flavours, savoury notes adding complexity, and a very harmonious finish. Best drinking 2022+. Fine value.

DRY $28 V+

Summerhouse Central Otago Pinot Noir ★★★☆

The 2019 vintage (★★★☆) is bright ruby, fresh and lively, with moderately concentrated cherry, plum and spice flavours, balanced acidity, a touch of complexity, and a smooth finish. Best drinking mid-2021+.

Vintage	19
WR	5
Drink	20-25

 DRY $26 AV

Summerhouse Marlborough Pinot Noir ★★★☆

The 2018 vintage (★★★☆) was matured in French oak barriques (20 per cent new). Bright ruby, it is mouthfilling and sweet-fruited, with very good depth of fresh cherry, plum and spice flavours, showing considerable complexity. Drink now.

Vintage	18
WR	6
Drink	20-25

 DRY $33 –V

Tankersley Estate Central Otago Pinot Noir ★★★★☆

I tasted the 2016 and 2015 vintages in 2020. Grown in the Cromwell Basin and French oak-aged for 18 months, the powerful 2016 vintage (★★★★☆) is full-coloured, ripely scented and sweet-fruited, with generous flavours, a hint of liquorice, fresh acidity, and good complexity. Best drinking 2022+. The 2015 vintage (★★★★★) was French oak-matured for a year. It has full, bright, moderately youthful colour, and a fragrant, spicy, slightly nutty bouquet. Mouthfilling and generous, it is a powerful red, with fresh, ripe plum and spice flavours, vigorous, savoury and structured. Best drinking 2022+.

 DRY $35 V+

Tarras Vineyards Central Otago Pinot Noir ★★★★☆

Estate-grown in The Canyon Vineyard at Bendigo, the 2018 vintage (★★★★☆) is bright ruby, with a fragrant, complex bouquet. A refined, youthful red, it has strong, ripe cherry, plum and spice flavours, seasoned with nutty oak, balanced acidity, and supple tannins. Best drinking 2022+.

DRY $40 AV

Tarras Vineyards The Canyon Single Vineyard Central Otago Pinot Noir ★★★★★

The fragrant, complex 2017 vintage (★★★★★) was estate-grown at Bendigo. Full-coloured, it is rich and savoury, with deep cherry, plum and spice flavours. Still youthful, it is finely structured and well worth cellaring to 2023+.

DRY $65 AV

Tatty Bogler Bannockburn Central Otago Pinot Noir ★★★★

Scented and supple, the 2019 vintage (★★★★) is a finely balanced red, matured for a year in French oak casks (20 per cent new). Ruby-hued, it is strongly varietal, with youthful, ripe cherry, plum and spice flavours, a gentle seasoning of oak, and loads of drink-young appeal.

 DRY $35 AV

Tatty Bogler Waitaki Valley North Otago Pinot Noir ★★★★

From Forrest Estate, the 2016 vintage (★★★★) was matured for 10 months in French oak casks (20 per cent new). It has full, moderately youthful colour and a fragrant, slightly leafy bouquet. Full-bodied, it is vibrantly fruity, with strong plum, spice and herb flavours, fresh acidity, oak complexity and a moderately firm finish. Tasted in 2020, the 2015 vintage (★★★★) has a fragrant, slightly leafy bouquet, leading into a vibrant, supple wine with strongly varietal, moderately concentrated cherry, plum, herb and spice flavours, oak complexity, and fresh acidity. Drink now to 2022.

 DRY $45 –V

Te Awanga Estate Hawke's Bay Pinot Noir (★★★☆)

Still on sale, the 2015 vintage (★★★☆) was oak-matured for six months. Ruby-hued, with some development showing, it is probably at its peak. Full-bodied and savoury, with hints of spices and mushrooms adding complexity, it has very good depth, and a fairly firm finish.

 DRY $25 AV

Te Awanga Estate One Off Red Planet Martinborough Pinot Noir (★★★★)

Drinking well now, the 2016 vintage (★★★★) was barrel-aged for 18 months. Ruby-hued, it is moderately youthful, with mouthfilling body, and cherry, plum, spice and nut flavours, showing good complexity.

 DRY $35 AV

Te Kairanga John Martin Martinborough Pinot Noir ★★★★★

This typically impressive red is based on the 'best vineyard parcels'. The 2017 vintage (★★★★☆) was matured in French oak barrels (25 per cent new). Deep ruby, it is fresh and vibrant, with youthful, cherryish, spicy, nutty flavours, showing good complexity. Savoury and supple, it's well worth cellaring to 2021+.

Vintage	17	16	15	14	13
WR	7	6	7	7	7
Drink	20-27	20-27	20-25	20-25	20-24

 DRY $46 –V

Te Kairanga Martinborough Pinot Noir ★★★★

The 2018 vintage (★★★★) was matured in French oak casks (19 per cent new). Ruby-hued, it is sweet-fruited and supple, in a moderately rich style, with excellent elegance and harmony, and plenty of drink-young charm.

 DRY $30 AV

Te Kairanga Runholder Martinborough Pinot Noir ★★★★☆

Estate-grown and matured in French oak casks (20 per cent new), the 2018 vintage (★★★★☆) is already drinking well. Bright ruby, it is savoury, sweet-fruited and supple, with cherry, spice and nut flavours, good complexity, and excellent depth. Best drinking 2021+.

Vintage	18	17
WR	6	5
Drink	20-25	20-25

DRY $35 V+

Te Kano Central Otago Pinot Noir (★★★★★)

The powerful yet elegant 2017 vintage (★★★★★) was grown at two sites at Bannockburn, French oak-aged for 11 months, and bottled unfined and unfiltered. Deep ruby, it is highly perfumed and full-bodied, with real density of ripe-fruit flavours, oak-derived complexity, and the structure to mature well over the long haul. Best drinking 2021+.

DRY $65 AV

Te Mata Estate Alma Hawke's Bay Pinot Noir ★★★★☆

The highly auspicious 2018 vintage (★★★★★) marked Te Mata's first plunge into the production of top-end Pinot Noir, a variety not commonly linked to Hawke's Bay, but cultivated in the region since the nineteenth century. Estate-grown inland, at the Woodthorpe Terraces Vineyard in the Dartmoor Valley, it was matured in French oak casks (over 50 per cent new). Deeply coloured, it is mouthfilling and savoury, with rich cherry, plum and spice flavours, and fine, supple tannins. A powerful, youthful, dense, well-structured red, it's well worth cellaring to 2022+. The 2019 vintage (★★★★☆), matured for 11 months in French oak barriques (partly new), is a deep ruby, very youthful wine, sweet-fruited, with concentrated cherry, plum and spice flavours, fresh acidity, and obvious potential; best drinking 2023+.

Vintage	19	18
WR	6	6
Drink	20-25	20-29

DRY $60 –V

Te Mata Estate Vineyards Hawke's Bay Pinot Noir ★★★★

The 2019 vintage (★★★★) was matured for 11 months in French oak casks (partly new). Bright ruby, it has generous, ripe cherry, plum and spice flavours, fresh acidity, and savoury, nutty notes adding complexity. Best drinking mid-2021+.

Vintage	19	18
WR	6	6
Drink	20-22	20-22

DRY $30 AV

te Pā Marlborough Pinot Noir ★★★★

Already very approachable, the deep ruby, youthful 2019 vintage (★★★★☆) was matured in French oak barrels (35 per cent new). It has rich, ripe, generous flavours, plummy and spicy, fine-grained tannins, and excellent harmony.

DRY $35 AV

te Pā Reserve Collection Taylor River Marlborough Pinot Noir   (★★★★☆)

The powerful 2017 vintage (★★★★☆) was fully barrel-aged. Bright ruby, it is mouthfilling, with rich, plummy, spicy flavours, woven with fresh acidity, a hint of liquorice, and a well-structured finish. An age-worthy red, it should be at its best 2021+.

DRY $45 –V

Ted by Mount Edward Central Otago Pinot Noir   ★★★★☆

Certified organic, the instantly enjoyable 2018 vintage (★★★★☆) was matured for 11 months in French oak casks (15 per cent new). Ruby-hued, with a fragrant, slightly herbal bouquet, it is mouthfilling and supple, with concentrated, ripe flavours, savoury and nutty notes adding complexity, and loads of drink-young charm.

DRY $35 V+

Terra Sancta Estate Bannockburn Central Otago Pinot Noir   ★★★★☆

The lively, youthful 2017 vintage (★★★★☆) was estate-grown at Bannockburn and matured in French oak barriques (10 per cent new). Deep ruby, with a slightly earthy bouquet, it is fresh and concentrated, with strong, vibrant cherry, plum and spice flavours, good power through the palate, and a well-structured finish. Best drinking 2021+.

Vintage	17	16	15	14	13
WR	7	7	7	7	6
Drink	20-28	20-23	20-26	20-22	P

DRY $35 V+

Terra Sancta Jackson's Block Bannockburn Central Otago Pinot Noir   ★★★★★

Full of personality, the 2018 vintage (★★★★★) of this estate-grown, single-block red was hand-picked, matured in French oak casks (20 per cent new), and bottled unfined and unfiltered. Full, bright ruby, it is a generous wine, fragrant, savoury, ripe and complex, with concentrated cherry, plum and spice flavours, and a well-structured, harmonious, long finish. Very age-worthy, it's well worth cellaring to 2023+.

Vintage	18	17	16	15	14	13	12	11
WR	6	7	7	6	6	5	7	7
Drink	20-30	20-30	20-28	20-25	20-24	P	20-24	P

DRY $52 AV

Terra Sancta Mysterious Diggings Bannockburn Central Otago Pinot Noir   ★★★★

Made for early drinking, the 2019 vintage (★★★☆) was estate-grown and matured in seasoned French oak barrels. Ruby hued, it has good depth of fresh cherry, plum and spice flavours, showing some savoury complexity, and a smooth finish.

Vintage	19	18	17	16	15
WR	6	6	6	7	6
Drink	20-24	20-23	20-21	20-23	P

DRY $27 V+

Terra Sancta Shingle Beach Bannockburn Central Otago Pinot Noir ★★★★☆

The graceful, delicate 2018 vintage (★★★★☆) was estate-grown on the edge of the Kawarau River, hand-picked, and matured in French oak puncheons (20 per cent new). Ruby-hued, it is finely scented and sweet-fruited, with delicate plum, spice and nut flavours, showing excellent complexity, and a long, supple finish. Best drinking 2022+.

Vintage	18
WR	6
Drink	20-30

DRY $45 –V

Terra Sancta Slapjack Block Bannockburn Pinot Noir ★★★★★

From the oldest vines in Bannockburn, planted in 1991, the 2018 vintage (★★★★★) is a ruby-hued, velvety red. Hand-picked and matured in French oak casks (20 per cent new), it was bottled unfined and unfiltered. A very gentle wine, it is mouthfilling, sweet-fruited and supple, with youthful, subtle, delicate cherry and spice flavours, complex and savoury, and a notably harmonious, lasting finish. Best drinking 2022+.

Vintage	18	17	16	15	14	13	12	11
WR	7	7	7	7	7	6	7	7
Drink	20-31	20-30	20-28	20-30	20-25	20-24	20-24	20-25

DRY $83 AV

🍇🍇

Terrace Edge Waipara Valley Pinot Noir ★★★★☆

A consistently attractive red, priced sharply. Certified organic, the 2016 vintage (★★★★☆) was hand-picked, fermented with indigenous yeasts and matured for 11 months in French oak casks (25 per cent new). Bright ruby, it is fragrant, full-bodied, sweet-fruited and savoury, with generous cherry, plum and spice flavours, showing good complexity and harmony. Best drinking 2021+.

Vintage	16
WR	7
Drink	21-26

DRY $30 V+

Thornbury Central Otago Pinot Noir ★★★★

The very youthful 2019 vintage (★★★★☆) is a great buy. Grown at Bendigo, it was hand-picked and matured in French oak barriques (21 per cent new). Deep ruby, it is mouthfilling and sweet-fruited, with strong, vibrant cherry, plum and spice flavours, supple tannins, and a rich, very harmonious finish. Best drinking 2023+. (A complete 'vertical' tasting of all earlier vintages, from 2006 to 2018, held in late 2019, revealed the wine matures very gracefully, typically peaking at 10 years old.)

Vintage	19	18	17	16
WR	5	5	6	6
Drink	20-24	20-23	20-23	20-21

DRY $26 V+

Three Miners Warden's Court Central Otago Pinot Noir   (★★★★)

Showing good potential, the 2017 vintage (★★★★) of this single-vineyard red was grown at Earnscleugh, near Alexandra, and matured for 10 months in French oak barrels (30 per cent new). Deep ruby, it is mouthfilling and fruit-packed, with strong, ripe cherry, plum and spice flavours, fresh acidity, and well-integrated oak adding complexity. An elegant, youthful red, it should be at its best 2021+.

 DRY $38 AV

Three Paddles Martinborough Pinot Noir   ★★★★

From Nga Waka, this second-tier red is a rewarding, drink-young style. The 2017 vintage (★★★★) was French oak-aged for a year (20 per cent new). Fragrant, with a spicy bouquet, it is ruby-hued, with generous, ripe, plummy, spicy flavours, savoury notes adding complexity, and finely balanced tannins. Best drinking 2021+.

Vintage	17	16	15	14	13
WR	6	6	6	7	7
Drink	20-23	20-22	20-22	20-21	P

 DRY $28 V+

Tiki Estate Single Vineyard Waipara Pinot Noir   (★★★★)

Enjoyable now, the 2017 vintage (★★★★) was matured in French oak barriques. Bright ruby, it is fragrant, savoury and supple, with cherry, plum and spice flavours, seasoned with nutty oak, finely balanced tannins, and good complexity. Best drinking 2021+.

Vintage	17
WR	6
Drink	20-21

 DRY $27 V+

Tiki Estate Waipara Pinot Noir   (★★★☆)

Enjoyable young, the 2018 vintage (★★★☆) was barrel-aged. Ruby-hued, it is sweet-fruited and smooth, with gentle cherry, plum, spice and nut flavours, showing some savoury complexity. Best drinking mid-2021+.

Vintage	18
WR	6
Drink	20-21

 DRY $24 V+

Tiki Koro Central Otago Pinot Noir   ★★★★

The youthful 2018 vintage (★★★★) was matured for 10 months in French oak barriques. Bright ruby, it is fresh, vibrantly fruity and supple, with ripe cherry, plum, spice and nut flavours, showing considerable complexity, and obvious cellaring potential. Best drinking 2021+.

Vintage	18
WR	6
Drink	20-21

DRY $35 AV

Tohu Awatere Valley Marlborough Pinot Noir ★★★☆

The 2018 vintage (★★★☆) was grown in the Awatere Valley and matured in French oak barriques (20 per cent new). Light ruby, it is mouthfilling and supple, in a moderately concentrated style with ripe, plummy, spicy, slightly nutty flavours, showing some complexity, and good harmony.

Vintage	18	DRY $25 AV
WR	5	
Drink	20-25	

Tohu Rore Reserve Marlborough Pinot Noir ★★★★

The 2017 vintage (★★★★) is a single-vineyard red, estate-grown in the upper Awatere Valley and matured in French oak barriques. Deeply coloured, it is mouthfilling and very vibrant, with good concentration of ripe cherry, plum and spice flavours. A fruit-packed, supple, age-worthy wine, it should be at its best 2021+.

DRY $35 AV

Tohu Single Vineyard Whenua Awa Awatere Valley
Marlborough Pinot Noir (★★★★☆)

The very age-worthy 2017 vintage (★★★★☆) was estate-grown in the upper Awatere Valley. Deep, bright ruby, it is fragrant and savoury, with concentrated plum, cherry, spice and herb flavours, seasoned with nutty oak, fresh acidity, and very good complexity. Best drinking 2021+.

DRY $42 AV

Tohu Single Vineyard Whenua Matua Upper Moutere Nelson Pinot Noir (★★★★)

The elegant 2017 vintage (★★★★) is ruby-hued, with a fragrant, savoury bouquet. Medium-bodied, it has lots of current-drinking appeal, with ripe cherry, spice and nut flavours, gentle tannins, and a well-rounded, very harmonious finish.

DRY $30 AV

Toi Toi Clutha Central Otago Pinot Noir ★★★☆

Exuberantly fruity, the 2018 vintage (★★★☆) is a good, drink-young style. Deep ruby, it is mouthfilling and supple, with generous, vibrant, plummy, slightly spicy flavours, gentle acidity, and an ultra-smooth finish.

DRY $27 AV

Toi Toi Reserve Central Otago Pinot Noir ★★★☆

The 2018 vintage (★★★★) is a single-vineyard red, hand-picked at Lowburn and matured for 14 months in French oak barrels. Full, bright ruby, it is mouthfilling, sweet-fruited and vibrant, with very youthful cherry, plum and spice flavours, seasoned with oak, considerable complexity, fresh acidity, and lots of youthful vigour. Open 2021+.

DRY $40 –V

Toi Toi Winemakers Selection Central Otago Pinot Noir   (★★★★)

The fragrant, youthful 2018 vintage (★★★★) is deep ruby, with mouthfilling body, strong, ripe, cherryish, gently spicy flavours, savoury notes adding complexity, and a fairly firm finish. Well worth cellaring, it should be at its best 2021+.

 DRY $33 AV

Two Paddocks Central Otago Pinot Noir   ★★★★★

The latest vintages are the best yet. Estate-grown at Earnscleugh (51 per cent), Bannockburn (27 per cent) and Gibbston (22 per cent), and matured for 11 months in French oak barriques (20 per cent), the 2018 vintage (★★★★★) is ruby-hued, fragrant, savoury and supple, with strong, ripe cherry, plum, spice and nut flavours, showing excellent complexity, and a very harmonious, persistent finish. Enjoyable in its youth, it's also well worth cellaring.

 DRY $55 AV

Two Paddocks Picnic Central Otago Pinot Noir   ★★★★

Certified organic, the attractive 2018 vintage (★★★★) is a drink-now or cellaring proposition. Matured for nine months in French oak barriques (5 per cent new), it is ruby-hued, fresh and smooth, with ripe cherry, plum and spice flavours, savoury notes adding complexity, and a finely textured, very harmonious finish.

 DRY $34 AV

Two Paddocks Proprietor's Reserve The First Paddock
Central Otago Pinot Noir   ★★★★★

The highly fragrant 2017 vintage (★★★★★) was estate-grown at Gibbston, hand-harvested from vines planted in 1993, and matured for 11 months in French oak barrels (20 per cent new). Deep ruby, it is an attractively scented, savoury, medium-bodied red, with fresh, youthful cherry, plum and spice flavours, a herbal thread that clearly reflects its Gibbston origin, fresh acidity, and excellent complexity and depth. Best drinking 2022+. Certified organic.

 DRY $85 AV

Two Paddocks Proprietor's Reserve The Fusilier
Bannockburn Vineyard Pinot Noir   ★★★★★

Certified organic, the 2017 vintage (★★★★★) was estate-grown at Bannockburn, hand-picked, fermented with indigenous yeasts and matured for 11 months in French oak barriques (33 per cent new). Deep, bright ruby, it is an attractively perfumed, savoury, medium to full-bodied red, with ripe, plummy, distinctly spicy flavours, earthy, nutty notes adding complexity, fresh acidity, and a long, tightly structured finish. Still youthful, it's well worth cellaring to 2022+.

DRY $85 AV

Two Paddocks Proprietor's Reserve The Last Chance
Earnscleugh Vineyard Pinot Noir   ★★★★★

Estate-grown at Alexandra, in 'possibly the world's most southerly vineyard', the classy 2017 vintage (★★★★★) was hand-picked, fermented with indigenous yeasts and matured for 11 months in French oak barriques (20 per cent new). Deep, bright ruby, it is an invitingly scented, medium to full-bodied red, with lively, ripe, plummy, spicy flavours, savoury and complex, and a tight-knit finish. Still very fresh and youthful, with strong personality, it's well worth cellaring to 2022+. Certified organic.

Two Rivers of Marlborough Tributary Pinot Noir   ★★★★☆

The 2018 vintage (★★★★☆) is a single-vineyard red, hand-picked in the Southern Valleys, matured for 11 months in large, French oak cuves (principally) and seasoned French oak barrels, and bottled unfined and unfiltered. Ruby-hued, it is a strongly varietal wine, full-bodied, sweet-fruited and supple, with vibrant cherry, plum and spice flavours, savoury notes adding complexity, gentle acidity, and lots of early-drinking appeal.

Vintage	18	17	16	15
WR	6	7	6	6
Drink	20-25	20-24	20-23	P

Two Sisters Central Otago Pinot Noir   ★★★★

The 2016 vintage (★★★★☆) is a refined, single-vineyard wine from Lowburn, in the Cromwell Basin. Hand-harvested, fermented with indigenous yeasts and matured in French oak casks (33 per cent new), it is bright ruby, fresh and youthful, in a medium-bodied style, with cherry, plum, spice and nut flavours, showing good complexity, finely balanced tannins, and obvious potential. Best drinking 2021+.

Universe Central Otago Pinot Noir   ★★★☆

The very easy-drinking 2018 vintage (★★★☆), from an Auckland-based producer, was grown in the Alexandra sub-region and French oak-aged. Ruby-hued, it is softly mouthfilling and sweet-fruited, with satisfying depth of fresh cherry, plum and spice flavours, savoury notes adding complexity, gentle tannins, and some cellaring potential; best drinking 2021+.

Urlar Gladstone Pinot Noir   ★★★★☆

Certified organic, this distinctive, savoury red is estate-grown in the northern Wairarapa. The 2017 vintage (★★★★★) was hand-picked, matured for 10 months in French oak barriques (45 per cent new), and bottled unfined and unfiltered. Full, bright ruby, it has a finely scented bouquet. An immediately engaging style, with deep cherry, plum, spice and nut flavours, slightly earthy notes adding complexity, and a softly textured finish, it's full of personality. Best drinking 2021+. (The 2009 vintage, tasted in mid-2020, was probably at its peak, with delicious fragrance, complexity and depth.)

Vintage	17
WR	6
Drink	20-26

DRY $45 –V

Urlar Select Parcels Gladstone Pinot Noir ★★★★★

Certified organic, the lovely 2017 vintage (★★★★★) was estate-grown in the northern Wairarapa, hand-picked and matured in French oak barriques (45 per cent new). A refined wine, it is still youthful. Deeply coloured, it is invitingly scented, very savoury and supple, with concentrated cherry, plum and spice flavours, finely structured and harmonious. Full of aging potential, it should be at its best 2022+.

Vintage	17
WR	6
Drink	20-29

DRY $60 AV

🍇

Valli Bannockburn Vineyard Central Otago Pinot Noir ★★★★★

The delicious 2019 vintage (★★★★★) was hand-harvested, matured in French oak barriques (30 per cent new), and bottled unfined and unfiltered. Fragrant and full-bodied, it is notably refined and harmonious, with concentrated, vibrant, well-ripened cherry, plum and spice flavours, complex, savoury and supple. A very 'complete' wine, it should be at its best 2023+.

Vintage	19	18	17	16	15	14	13	12	11
WR	7	7	6	7	6	7	7	7	6
Drink	22-32	20-30	20-30	20-28	20-27	20-26	20-26	20-25	20-24

DRY $69 AV

🍇🍇

Valli Bendigo Vineyard Central Otago Pinot Noir ★★★★★

The powerful, rich, sweet-fruited 2019 vintage (★★★★★) was hand-picked, matured in French oak barriques (30 per cent new), and bottled unfined and unfiltered. Deep ruby, it is extremely youthful, with a strong surge of vibrant, plummy, spicy flavours, a hint of liquorice, fresh acidity, and good tannin backbone. Best drinking 2023+.

Vintage	19	18	17	16	15	14	13	12	11
WR	6	7	7	7	6	7	7	7	5
Drink	20-30	20-30	20-30	20-26	20-25	20-25	20-25	20-24	20-23

DRY $69 AV

🍇🍇

Valli Burn Cottage Vineyard Central Otago Pinot Noir ★★★★★

The 2019 vintage (★★★★☆) is part of a collaboration between Valli and Burn Cottage, involving access to each other's grapes to explore key aspects of terroir. From vines planted in 2008 near Lowburn, it was matured in French oak barriques (20 per cent new), and bottled unfined and unfiltered. Bright ruby, with a fragrant, slightly earthy bouquet, it is very fresh and youthful, with strong cherry, plum and spice flavours, lively acidity, savoury notes adding complexity, and supple tannins. It needs time; open 2022+.

Vintage	19
WR	6
Drink	21-32

DRY $69 AV

🍇

Valli Gibbston Vineyard Otago Pinot Noir ★★★★★

The stylish 2019 vintage (★★★★★) was hand-picked, matured in French oak barriques (30 per cent new), and bottled unfined and unfiltered. Bright ruby, it is mouthfilling and supple, with vibrant cherry, plum and spice flavours, a hint of herbs, fresh acidity, nutty, savoury notes adding complexity and an inviting fragrance. A very graceful, youthful red, it's well worth cellaring to 2022+.

Vintage	19	18	17	16	15	14	13	12	11
WR	7	7	7	7	7	7	7	6	7
Drink	22-34	20-33	20-32	20-25	20-24	20-25	20-25	20-23	20-24

 DRY $69 AV

Valli Waitaki Vineyard Otago Pinot Noir ★★★★☆

The highly fragrant 2019 vintage (★★★★☆) was hand-harvested, matured in French oak barriques (25 per cent new), and bottled unfined and unfiltered. Bright ruby, it is a stylish, youthful red, with good density of vibrant cherry, spice and herb flavours, a hint of tamarillo, fresh acidity, and supple tannins. A vigorous, complex red, it's well worth cellaring to 2023+.

Vintage	19	18	17	16	15	14	13	12	11
WR	7	7	5	7	6	7	7	7	5
Drink	22-34	20-27	20-26	20-26	20-25	20-25	20-25	20-25	20-23

DRY $79 –V

Vavasour Awatere Valley Marlborough Pinot Noir ★★★★

The youthful 2018 vintage (★★★★) is bright ruby, mouthfilling and supple. Matured for nine months in French oak casks (22 per cent new), it is sweet-fruited and vibrant, with cherryish, plummy, spicy flavours, fresh acidity, and a very harmonious finish. Best drinking 2021+.

Vintage	18	17
WR	6	6
Drink	20-26	20-25

DRY $30 AV

Vavasour Felix's Vineyard Awatere Valley Marlborough Pinot Noir ★★★★☆

From vines planted in 2003 within The Favourite Vineyard, the 2017 vintage (★★★★☆) was matured for 14 months in French oak barriques. Deep and youthful in colour, it is a weighty, bold Pinot Noir, packed with cherryish, plummy, slightly herbal flavours. Still youthful, it's a finely balanced wine, with obvious potential; open 2021+.

Vintage	17
WR	7
Drink	20-30

DRY $41 AV

Vidal Reserve Marlborough Pinot Noir ★★★★

Offering good value, the 2019 vintage (★★★★) was grown in the Wairau Valley and matured for a year in French oak casks (10 per cent new). Deeply coloured, it is full-bodied, with generous, ripe cherry, plum and spice flavours, finely integrated oak adding complexity, and a smooth finish. Best drinking 2022+.

Vintage	19
WR	7
Drink	20-26

 DRY $25 V+

Villa Maria Cellar Selection Marlborough Pinot Noir ★★★★

This is typically one of the country's best-value Pinot Noirs. The graceful 2019 vintage (★★★★) was matured in French oak barriques (15 per cent new). Bright ruby, it is full-bodied and supple, with very good depth of fresh cherry, plum and spice flavours, a slightly earthy streak, and good complexity. Best drinking 2022+.

Vintage	19
WR	6
Drink	20-25

 DRY $25 V+

Villa Maria Private Bin Marlborough Pinot Noir ★★★☆

Offering fine value, the 2019 vintage (★★★☆) was partly barrel-matured. Bright ruby, it is fresh, vibrant and smooth, with mouthfilling body and good depth of ripe-fruit flavours, showing a distinct touch of complexity. A very harmonious wine, it's enjoyable young.

 DRY $18 V+

Villa Maria Reserve Marlborough Pinot Noir ★★★★★

Launched from 2000, this label swiftly won recognition as one of the region's boldest, lushest reds. Grown in the Awatere Valley and the Southern Valleys, it is hand-picked and matured in French oak barriques (22 per cent new in 2019). The 2019 vintage (★★★★★) is a very classy young red. Deeply coloured, it is powerful, concentrated, savoury and complex, with cherry, plum, spice and nut flavours, finely poised, and showing obvious potential for cellaring. Best drinking 2023+.

Vintage	19
WR	6
Drink	20-25

 DRY $50 AV

Villa Maria Single Vineyard Southern Clays Marlborough Pinot Noir ★★★★★

From gentle, north-facing slopes on the south side of the Wairau Valley, the deep ruby 2017 vintage (★★★★☆) was matured in French oak barriques (23 per cent new). A very graceful, fragrant and supple red, it is full-bodied, with vibrant, cherryish, plummy, spicy flavours, showing good complexity, fresh acidity, and a smooth finish. Best drinking 2021+.

Vintage	17
WR	7
Drink	20-25

 DRY $60 AV

Villa Maria Single Vineyard Taylors Pass Marlborough Pinot Noir ★★★★★

Already delicious, the 2018 vintage (★★★★★) was estate-grown in the upper Awatere Valley and matured in French oak barriques (25 per cent new). Ruby-hued, it is finely scented, savoury and supple, with ripe cherry, plum and spice flavours, a hint of herbs, oak complexity, and a silky-textured, lingering finish.

Vintage	18	DRY $60 AV
WR	6	
Drink	20-25	

Volcanic Hills Central Otago Pinot Noir (★★★★)

The 2017 vintage (★★★★) is a vibrant, supple red, French oak-aged for a year. Deep ruby, it has very good vigour and concentration, with cherry, plum and spice flavours, a hint of herbs, savoury notes adding complexity, and a finely balanced finish.

DRY $40 –V

Waimea Nelson Pinot Noir ★★★☆

The 2017 vintage (★★★☆) was estate-grown on the Waimea Plains and barrel-matured for nearly a year. Bright ruby, it is fresh and lively, with good depth of plummy, spicy, slightly nutty flavours, showing a touch of complexity. It's drinking well now.

DRY $25 AV

Wairiki Estate The Redeemer Hawke's Bay Pinot Noir (★★★★)

A top example of the Hawke's Bay regional style, the 2018 vintage (★★★★) is a single-vineyard red, hand-picked at Maraekakaho and matured for 10 months in oak barrels (20 per cent). It has fullish, moderately developed colour, and a fragrant, spicy, slightly nutty bouquet. Already drinking well, it is a characterful wine, mouthfilling and savoury, with cherryish, plummy, spicy flavours, showing good complexity and harmony.

DRY $39 AV

Walnut Block Nutcracker Marlborough Pinot Noir ★★★★

Certified organic, the 2017 vintage (★★★★) was hand-harvested, matured for a year in French oak casks (20 per cent new), and bottled unfined and unfiltered. Deep ruby, it is fragrant, with moderately concentrated, savoury, nutty flavours, showing good complexity, and a fairly firm finish. Best drinking 2021+.

Vintage	17	16	15	DRY $42 –V
WR	7	7	6	
Drink	20-24	20-23	20-22	

Wanaka Village Central Otago Pinot Noir ★★★★☆

From Rippon Vineyard at Wanaka, the 2019 vintage (★★★★☆) is a 'fresh and fun' expression of the estate's mature vines, with no use of oak. A more powerful and far more interesting red than those words normally suggest, it is ruby-hued, with mouthfilling body, deep, youthful cherry, plum and spice flavours, and good tannin support. Best drinking 2022+.

DRY $32 V+

Ward Valley Epicentre Marlborough Pinot Noir   (★★★☆)

Bright ruby, the 2019 vintage (★★★☆) is mouthfilling and vibrant, with strong, ripe cherry, plum and spice flavours, and a moderately firm finish. Best drinking mid-2021+. (From Snapper Rock.)

DRY $22 V+

Ward Valley Mt Victoria Block Marlborough Pinot Noir   ★★★★

Ready to roll, the 2018 vintage (★★★★) is a gentle, sweet-fruited wine, grown in the Awatere Valley and matured for 10 months in French oak barriques. Lightish in colour, it is fragrant, savoury and supple, with cherry, plum, spice and nut flavours, showing very good complexity, and a well-rounded finish. Showing obvious potential, the 2019 vintage (★★★★) was matured for 11 months in French oak barrels. Bright ruby, it is mouthfilling and youthful, with strong, ripe plum and spice flavours, savoury notes adding complexity, and good tannin backbone. Best drinking 2022+. (From Snapper Rock.)

DRY $30 AV

Whitehaven Greg Southern Valleys Single
Vineyard Marlborough Pinot Noir   ★★★★★

The classy 2017 vintage (★★★★★) was hand-harvested, matured for 10 months in French oak barrels, and bottled unfined and unfiltered. Deeply coloured, it is fragrant, full-bodied and supple, in a very savoury style with ripe flavours, showing excellent depth, complexity and harmony, and a long finish. Best drinking 2021+.

DRY $55 AV

Whitehaven Marlborough Pinot Noir   ★★★★

The attractive 2016 vintage (★★★★) is bright ruby, with a fragrant, spicy bouquet. Mouthfilling, sweet-fruited and supple, it is fresh and vibrant, with very good depth, complexity and harmony, and a finely balanced, smooth finish.

DRY $35 AV

Wild Earth Central Otago Pinot Noir   ★★★★★

The 2018 vintage (★★★★☆) is a fragrant, savoury, single-vineyard Bannockburn red, matured for a year in French oak barriques (25 per cent new). Deep ruby, it is well-structured, with fresh, youthful cherry, plum, spice and nut flavours, showing excellent ripeness and complexity. Best drinking 2021+.

DRY $40 V+

Wither Hills Marlborough Pinot Noir   ★★★☆

Priced right, the 2017 vintage (★★★☆) is a bright ruby, fresh, supple red, with moderately rich, cherryish, spicy, slightly nutty flavours, showing some savoury complexity.

DRY $22 V+

Wither Hills Single Vineyard Taylor River Marlborough Pinot Noir   ★★★★

Offering very good value, the 2016 vintage (★★★★☆) is described on the back label as 'masculine, dense, chewy', but is far more approachable than that. Bright ruby, it is fragrant, mouthfilling and sweet-fruited, with generous cherry, plum and spice flavours, very good complexity, and a finely balanced, lingering finish. Maturing gracefully, it should be at its best 2021+.

DRY $28 V+

Wither Hills The Honourable Marlborough Pinot Noir   ★★★★★

Labelled as 'our finest Pinot Noir', the youthful 2018 vintage (★★★★★) is already delicious. Ruby-hued, it is very savoury and supple, with delicious, ripe cherry, plum, spice and nut flavours, and a long, harmonious finish. The 2017 vintage (★★★★★) is ruby-hued, fresh and vigorous, with deep cherry, plum and spice flavours, showing excellent complexity, and a savoury, supple finish. Best drinking 2021+.

DRY $75 AV

Wooing Tree Sandstorm Reserve Single Vineyard
Central Otago Pinot Noir   ★★★★★

Estate-grown at Cromwell, this wine is hand-picked from especially low-yielding vines. Matured for a year in French oak casks (33 per cent new), the 2015 vintage (★★★★☆) is deep ruby, floral, weighty, sweet-fruited and supple. It has strong, cherryish, plummy flavours, complex and savoury, and gentle tannins.

DRY $85 AV

Yealands Estate Single Vineyard Awatere Valley Marlborough Pinot Noir   ★★★★

Estate-grown, the youthful 2019 vintage (★★★★) is a ruby-hued, mouthfilling red with generous plum, cherry and spice flavours, slightly earthy notes, supple tannins, and a finely poised finish. Best drinking 2023+.

DRY $26 V+

Yealands Marlborough Pinot Noir   ★★★☆

Offering very good value, the 2019 vintage (★★★★) is a ruby-hued, full-bodied red with very good depth of ripe, plummy, spicy, slightly earthy and nutty flavours. Finely balanced for early drinking, it is sweet-fruited, with some savoury complexity, and a smooth, very harmonious finish. Drink now or cellar.

DRY $19 V+

Yealands Reserve Awatere Valley Marlborough Pinot Noir   ★★★☆

Estate-grown, the 2018 vintage (★★★☆) is a moderately youthful red, ruby-hued, mouthfilling and sweet-fruited, with fresh cherry, spice and herb flavours, showing good depth, and a smooth finish. The generous 2019 vintage (★★★★) is bright ruby, fragrant and full-bodied, with strong, youthful cherry, plum and spice flavours, oak complexity, and considerable aging potential; best drinking 2022+.

DRY $23 V+

Zephyr Marlborough Pinot Noir   ★★★★☆

Offering fine value, the 2019 vintage (★★★★★) was hand-picked at two sites in the Southern Valleys and matured in French oak casks (15 per cent new). Deep, bright ruby, with a fragrant, fresh bouquet, it is mouthfilling and concentrated, with very generous cherry, plum and spice flavours, supple tannins, and a long, finely balanced finish. Full of youthful vigour, it's well worth cellaring to 2023+.

DRY $33 V+

Pinotage

Popular in New Zealand in the 1960s and 1970s, Pinotage is today overshadowed by more glamorous varieties, with just 19 hectares of bearing vines in 2020. Pinotage now ranks as the country's ninth most extensively planted red-wine variety, behind even Pinot Meunier and Tempranillo.

Pinotage is a cross of the great Burgundian grape, Pinot Noir, and Cinsaut, a heavy-cropping variety popular in the south of France. Cinsaut's typically 'meaty, chunky sort of flavour' (in Jancis Robinson's words) is also characteristic of Pinotage. Valued for its reasonably early-ripening and disease-resistant qualities, and good yields, its plantings are mostly in Gisborne (32 per cent), Auckland (21 per cent), Hawke's Bay (18 per cent) and Northland (16 per cent).

A well-made Pinotage displays a slightly gamey bouquet and a smooth, berryish, peppery palate that can be reminiscent of a southern Rhône. It matures swiftly and usually peaks within two or three years of the vintage.

Karikari Estate Pinotage ★★★★

Estate-grown and hand-harvested on the Karikari Peninsula, in the Far North, the 2016 vintage (★★★☆) was matured for 29 months in French, Hungarian and American oak barrels (30 per cent new). Fullish and now fairly mature in colour, with a slightly rustic bouquet, it is mouthfilling and firm, with ripe, moderately concentrated, spicy, slightly earthy and nutty flavours. A powerful, gutsy red, it's ready to roll.

 DRY $42 –V

Marsden Bay of Islands Pinotage ★★★★

The impressive 2019 vintage (★★★★☆) was hand-harvested and matured in French oak casks (30 per cent new). Full-coloured, it is fragrant, rich and supple, with strong, berryish, spicy flavours, a hint of raisins, slightly gamey notes, good complexity, and a long, harmonious finish. Best drinking 2022+.

 DRY $32 –V

Muddy Water Waipara Pinotage ★★★★★

The 2017 vintage (★★★★★) is a powerful, robust red (15 per cent alcohol), matured for 14 months in French oak barrels (20 per cent new), and bottled unfined and unfiltered. Sturdy, sweet-fruited and firm, it has berryish, spicy flavours, revealing excellent ripeness, complexity and depth. Certified organic.

Vintage	17
WR	6
Drink	20-28

 DRY $65 –V

Sangiovese

Sangiovese, Italy's most extensively planted red-wine variety, is a rarity in New Zealand. Cultivated as a workhorse grape throughout central Italy, in Tuscany it is the foundation of such famous reds as Chianti and Brunello di Montalcino. Here, Sangiovese has sometimes been confused with Montepulciano and its plantings are not expanding. Only 6 hectares of Sangiovese vines were bearing in 2020, mostly in Auckland and Hawke's Bay.

Black Barn Concetta Sangiovese/Montepulciano (★★★★★)

Named after co-founder Concetta Lombardi, the 2015 vintage (★★★★★), now on sale, is an age-worthy, Hawke's Bay blend of Sangiovese (60 per cent) and Montelpulciano (40 per cent), oak-aged for three years. Full-coloured, with a fragrant, fresh, spicy bouquet, it is sturdy, youthful and vibrant, with deep, well-ripened blackcurrant, plum, spice and nut flavours, finely integrated oak, and impressive complexity and harmony.

DRY $85 –V

Te Awanga Estate One Off Silky Smooth Organic Hawke's Bay Sangiovese/Cabernet Sauvignon (★★★★)

The 2018 vintage (★★★★) is a distinctive red, certified organic. Fullish in colour, it is vibrant, berryish, spicy and supple, in a medium to full-bodied style, with fresh, youthful, blackcurrant-like characters, savoury, nutty notes adding complexity, underlying tannins, and good immediacy. Drink now or cellar.

DRY $35 –V

St Laurent

This Austrian variety is known for its deeply coloured, silky-smooth reds. It buds early, so is prone to frost damage, but ripens well ahead of Pinot Noir. Judge Rock imported the vine in 2001, but St Laurent is still extremely rare in New Zealand, with just 1 hectare of bearing vines in 2020, clustered in Waipara, Otago and Marlborough.

Hans Herzog Marlborough St Laurent   ★★★★☆

Certified organic, the 2016 vintage (★★★★☆) was estate-grown in the Wairau Valley, matured for two years in French oak barriques, and bottled unfined and unfiltered. Deeply coloured, it is fragrant, full-bodied and supple, with vibrant blackcurrant and red-berry flavours, gently seasoned with oak, gentle tannins, and loads of current-drinking appeal.

DRY $64 –V

Syrah

Hawke's Bay and the upper North Island (especially Waiheke Island, but also Northland) have a hot, new-ish red-wine variety, attracting growing international acclaim. The classic 'Syrah' of the Rhône Valley, in France, and Australian 'Shiraz' are in fact the same variety. On the rocky, baking slopes of the upper Rhône Valley, and in several Australian states, this noble grape yields red wines renowned for their outstanding depth of cassis, plum and black-pepper flavours.

Syrah was well known in New Zealand a century ago. Government viticulturist S.F. Anderson wrote in 1917 that Shiraz was being 'grown in nearly all our vineyards [but] the trouble with this variety has been an unevenness in ripening its fruit'. For today's winemakers, the problem has not changed: Syrah has never favoured a too-cool growing environment (wines that are not fully ripe show distinct tomato or tamarillo characters). It needs sites that are relatively hot during the day and retain the heat at night, achieving ripeness in Hawke's Bay late in the season, at about the same time as Cabernet Sauvignon. To curb its natural vigour, stony, dry, low-fertility sites or warm hillside sites are crucial.

In 2020 some 443 hectares of Syrah were bearing – a steep rise from 62 hectares in 2000. Syrah is now New Zealand's third most widely planted red-wine variety, behind Pinot Noir and Merlot, but well ahead of Cabernet Sauvignon, Malbec and Cabernet Franc. Over 75 per cent of the vines are in Hawke's Bay, with most of the rest in Auckland and Northland (although there are pockets as far south as Central Otago).

Syrah's potential in this country's warmer vineyard sites is finally being tapped. The top wines possess rich, vibrant blackcurrant, plum and black-pepper flavours, with an enticingly floral bouquet, and are winning growing international applause. Could Syrah replace Bordeaux-style Merlot and Cabernet Sauvignon-based blends over the next decade or two as the principal red-wine style from Hawke's Bay and the upper North Island? Don't rule it out.

Aotea by the Seifried Family Nelson Syrah (★★★★)

The fresh, youthful 2018 vintage (★★★★) was hand-picked and matured for over a year in French oak barriques (partly new). Full-coloured, with a peppery bouquet, it has strong, plummy, spicy, slightly nutty flavours, a hint of tamarillo, oak complexity, savoury notes, and good potential; best drinking 2022+.

Vintage	18
WR	7
Drink	20-27

 DRY $39 –V

Ash Ridge Doppio Chave Syrah ★★★★★

The deeply coloured, youthful 2016 vintage (★★★★★) is based on the Chave clone of Syrah, estate-grown in the Bridge Pa Triangle of Hawke's Bay, barrel-aged, and bottled unfined and unfiltered. A very graceful red, it is perfumed and mouthfilling, but not heavy, with ripe, plummy, spicy flavours, and a long finish. Best drinking 2023+.

DRY $75 AV

Ash Ridge Doppio MS Syrah ★★★★☆

The 2016 vintage (★★★★☆) is based on the MS (Mass Selection) clone of Syrah. Like its Doppio stablemate (see above), it was estate-grown in the Bridge Pa Triangle of Hawke's Bay, barrel-aged, and bottled unfined and unfiltered. Deeply coloured, with a floral, slightly earthy bouquet, it is mouthfilling, with very good intensity of youthful, plummy, spicy flavours, and gentle tannins. Best drinking 2022+.

 DRY $75 –V

Ash Ridge Estate Hawke's Bay Syrah ★★★☆

Estate-grown in the Bridge Pa Triangle, this label is Ash Ridge's top-selling wine. Barrel-aged in French and American oak, the 2017 vintage (★★★) is the only Syrah produced that season. Bright ruby, it is medium-bodied, with fresh, plummy, spicy flavours, a hint of tamarillo, some savoury complexity, and a smooth finish.

DRY $20 AV

Ash Ridge Premium Estate Hawke's Bay Syrah ★★★★☆

The attractive 2016 vintage (★★★★) was matured for 18 months in predominantly French oak casks (15 per cent new). Deep ruby, with a fragrant, peppery bouquet, it is medium to full-bodied, with good density of plummy, spicy flavours, considerable complexity, and supple tannins. Drink now or cellar.

DRY $30 AV

Ash Ridge Reserve Hawke's Bay Syrah ★★★★☆

The very elegant 2016 vintage (★★★★☆) was estate-grown in the Bridge Pa Triangle, barrel-aged, and bottled unfined and unfiltered. Deeply coloured, with a fragrant, peppery bouquet, it is medium to full-bodied, with good intensity of plummy, spicy, peppery flavours, fresh acidity, savoury notes adding complexity, and fine, supple tannins. Best drinking 2021+. (There is no 2017 vintage.)

DRY $50 –V

Askerne Hawke's Bay Syrah ★★★☆

Highly approachable in its youth, but also worth cellaring, the 2018 vintage (★★★★) is a mouthfilling, sweet-fruited red, matured for over a year in French oak casks (38 per cent new). Full-coloured, it has generous, ripe, berryish, spicy flavours, with finely integrated oak adding complexity, and a supple, well-rounded finish.

DRY $24 AV

Awaroa Waiheke Island Syrah ★★★★☆

Fresh and lively, the 2017 vintage (★★★★) is a medium to full-bodied red, hand-harvested and matured for a year in French oak barriques. Fragrant, with hints of spices and olives, it has strong plum and spice flavours, fresh acidity, savoury notes adding complexity, and good potential; best drinking 2022+.

DRY $45 –V

Babich Hawke's Bay Syrah ★★★

An attractive, drink-young style, the 2018 vintage (★★★) is a medium-bodied red, vibrant and supple, with plummy, spicy flavours, fresh acidity, and gentle tannins.

Vintage	18
WR	7
Drink	20-23

DRY $20 –V

Babich Winemakers' Reserve Hawke's Bay Syrah   ★★★★☆

The 2017 vintage (★★★★) is a full-bodied red, grown in the Bridge Pa Triangle and matured for eight months in French oak barrels (25 per cent new). Deep ruby, with a fragrant, peppery bouquet, it has strong, plummy, spicy flavours, showing good complexity, and a backbone of fine-grained tannins. A 'forward' vintage, but also worth cellaring, it should be at its best 2021+.

Vintage	17
WR	5
Drink	20-23

DRY $35 AV

Black Barn Vineyards Hawke's Bay Syrah   (★★★★☆)

Delicious young, but also well worth cellaring, the 2019 vintage (★★★★☆) was hand-picked in the Havelock North hills. Deep ruby, it is fresh and full-bodied, with strong, ripe, plummy, spicy flavours, savoury notes adding complexity, and a well-rounded finish. Best drinking 2022+.

DRY $39 AV

Boulder Bay Syrah   (★★★★☆)

Currently on sale, the 2015 vintage (★★★★☆) was estate-grown on Moturoa Island, in the Bay of Islands. A rare Northland red, it has deep, bright colour, with a fragrant, ripe, spicy bouquet. Fresh and full-bodied, it is sweet-fruited, with strong, plummy, berryish, spicy flavours, a hint of liquorice, good tannin backbone, and a lasting finish. Best drinking 2021+.

DRY $35 AV

Brookfields Back Block Hawke's Bay Syrah   ★★★★☆

Offering great value, the very youthful 2019 vintage (★★★★☆) was grown on a 'north-facing, very hot site' and matured for a year in seasoned French oak casks. It has deep, purple-flushed colour. Fragrant, with strong, ripe, vigorous, plummy, spicy flavours, a hint of liquorice, nutty oak adding complexity, and good tannin backbone, it should be long-lived. Best drinking 2023+.

Vintage	19	18
WR	7	7
Drink	20-26	20-26

DRY $21 V+

Brookfields Hillside Syrah   ★★★★★

This distinguished red is grown on a sheltered, north-facing slope between Maraekakaho and Bridge Pa, in Hawke's Bay (described by winemaker Peter Robertson as 'surreal – a chosen site'), and matured in French and American oak casks (mostly new). The powerful 2018 vintage (★★★★★) is deeply coloured, fragrant and youthful, with ripe, plummy, spicy flavours, showing excellent density. A classy, finely poised red, complex and savoury, it should be very long-lived.

Vintage	16	15	14	13
WR	7	7	7	7
Drink	21-27	20-26	20-25	20-23

DRY $47 AV

Church Road 1 Single Vineyard Gimblett Gravels Syrah ★★★★★

The 2017 vintage (★★★★★) is a very graceful, supple Hawke's Bay red, matured for 18 months in French oak barriques (41 per cent new). From a vintage that yielded no Syrah under the prestige Tom label, it's a beautiful young red, full-coloured and floral, with intense plum and spice flavours, a hint of liquorice, savoury and nutty notes adding complexity, and silky tannins. Best drinking 2022+.

DRY $90 AV

Church Road Grand Reserve Hawke's Bay Syrah ★★★★★

Full of potential, the 2018 vintage (★★★★★) is a deeply coloured, finely structured red, estate-grown principally in the Redstone Vineyard, in the Bridge Pa Triangle, but also in the Gimblett Gravels, and matured for 20 months in French and Hungarian oak barrels (33 per cent new). Mouthfilling, concentrated and complex, it has deep, ripe plum, spice and black-pepper flavours, fresh acidity, and fairly firm tannins. Best drinking 2023+.

DRY $45 AV

Church Road Hawke's Bay Syrah ★★★★

Enjoyable young, the 2018 vintage (★★★★) is a great buy. Grown mostly in the Bridge Pa Triangle, it was matured for a year in Hungarian and French oak casks (20 per cent new). Deeply coloured, it is a fresh, supple, medium to full-bodied red, with strong, vibrant plum, spice and black-pepper flavours, showing considerable complexity, and a fragrant bouquet. Best drinking mid-2021+.

DRY $20 V+

Church Road McDonald Series Hawke's Bay Syrah ★★★★★

Already delicious, the bargain-priced 2019 vintage (★★★★★) is a floral, spicy red, grown in the Gimblett Gravels (principally) and the Bridge Pa Triangle, and matured for 18 months in French and Hungarian oak barrels (22 per cent new). Deeply coloured, it is fragrant, mouthfilling, rich and supple, with deep plum/spice flavours, oak complexity, and a very harmonious, softly textured finish. Best drinking 2022+.

DRY $28 V+

Church Road Tom Syrah ★★★★★

Syrah is the latest addition to Church Road's elite Tom range. Released in late 2019, the third, 2015 vintage (★★★★★) was mostly (82.5 per cent) estate-grown in the Redstone Vineyard, in the Bridge Pa Triangle of Hawke's Bay; 17.5 per cent was grown in the Gimblett Gravels. Matured for 22 months in French oak barrels (42 per cent new), it has deep, bright, purple-flushed colour and a highly fragrant, floral bouquet. A very elegant, supple, youthful and harmonious red, it is densely packed, with concentrated plum, spice and black-pepper flavours, a hint of liquorice, and a long, refined finish. Already dangerously drinkable, it's well worth cellaring to at least 2022.

DRY $220 –V

Clearview Cape Kidnappers Hawke's Bay Syrah   ★★★★

The very charming 2019 vintage (★★★★) was grown at Te Awanga and sites further inland (simply described as State Highway 50). Full-coloured, with a fresh, fragrant, spicy bouquet, it is mouthfilling, vibrant and supple, with ripe blackcurrant, plum and black-pepper flavours, a touch of complexity, and a well-rounded, very harmonious finish. Delicious young.

DRY $27 AV

Clos de Ste Anne The Crucible Syrah   ★★★★★

The 2015 vintage (★★★★★) is impressive. Grown biodynamically in Millton's elevated Clos de Ste Anne Vineyard in Gisborne, it was hand-harvested, co-fermented with Viognier (5 per cent), and matured in large, seasoned French oak casks. Deeply coloured, it is floral and full-bodied, with plum, spice and black-pepper flavours, hints of earth and dark chocolate, and notable depth, complexity and harmony. A very distinctive red, it's delicious now.

DRY $75 AV

Coopers Creek Hawke's Bay Syrah   ★★★☆

With its full, bright colour and plummy, peppery aromas, the 2016 vintage (★★★☆) is a clearly varietal red. Medium-bodied, it is vibrantly fruity, with good depth of spicy flavours and gentle tannins.

DRY $22 AV

Coopers Creek Reserve Hawke's Bay Syrah   ★★★★★

Set for a long life, the 2018 vintage (★★★★★) is a powerful, highly refined red, grown in the Chalk Ridge Vineyard, on the edge of the Havelock North hills. Hand-harvested and matured for a year in French oak casks (45 per cent new), it is dark and invitingly fragrant, with dense, youthful, well-ripened plum, spice and black-pepper flavours, a hint of liquorice, and a very rich, harmonious finish. Open 2023+.

DRY $60 AV

Coopers Creek Select Vineyards Chalk Ridge Hawke's Bay Syrah   ★★★★☆

The good-value 2018 vintage (★★★★☆) is a sturdy, finely structured, highly fragrant red, hand-picked, blended with a splash of Viognier (1.3 per cent) and matured for a year in French oak casks (27 per cent new). It has excellent concentration of plum, spice and black-pepper flavours, showing good complexity, and a lasting finish. Best drinking 2022+.

DRY $28 V+

Craft Farm Hawke's Bay Syrah   ★★★★☆

From a hillside site overlooking Bridge Pa, the 2016 vintage (★★★★☆) is full-coloured, with a fresh, spicy, very varietal bouquet. Mouthfilling and supple, it has excellent depth of plummy, peppery flavours, oak complexity, and a very harmonious, lingering finish. Best drinking 2021+.

DRY $48 –V

Craggy Range Gimblett Gravels Single Vineyard Hawke's Bay Syrah   ★★★★★

This label is overshadowed by the reputation of its stablemate, Le Sol, but proves the power, structure and finesse that can be achieved with Syrah grown in the Gimblett Gravels of Hawke's Bay. The 2016 vintage (★★★★☆) was matured for 16 months in French oak barriques (20 per cent new). Dense and youthful in colour, it has a floral, peppery fragrance. Mouthfilling and vibrant, with good density of plum, spice and black-pepper flavours, fresh and firm, it's a classy red, best cellared to 2021+.

De La Terre Hawke's Bay Syrah   ★★★★

The 2016 vintage (★★★★) was estate-grown at Havelock North and barrel-aged. Full-coloured, it is fragrant and supple, with vibrant, spicy flavours, showing excellent vigour and depth, and a finely balanced, lingering finish.

De La Terre Reserve Hawke's Bay Syrah   ★★★★☆

The 2017 vintage (★★★★☆) was estate-grown at Havelock North and matured for 18 months in French oak barriques (40 per cent new). Full-coloured, with a fragrant bouquet, it is medium-bodied, very fresh and vibrant, with highly concentrated plum and spice flavours, showing a real sense of youthful vigour. Best drinking 2023+.

Vintage	17	16
WR	6	6
Drink	20-30	20-25

Dry River Lovat Vineyard Martinborough Syrah   ★★★★★

The memorable 2016 vintage (★★★★★) is the best yet. Barrel-matured for eight months and bottled unfined and unfiltered, it is an arresting wine, densely coloured and highly fragrant. Bursting with potential, it has exceptional depth of vibrant plum, spice and black-pepper flavours, buried tannins, and a long, lovely finish. It should flourish for a decade or longer. Best drinking 2023+.

DRY $78 AV

Dunleavy The Grafter Single Vineyard Waiheke Island Syrah   ★★★★

The 2017 vintage (★★★★☆) is full-coloured, with a spicy fragrance. A distinctive, youthful wine, it is strongly varietal, with very good depth and complexity, and a savoury, fairly firm finish. Best drinking 2021+.

Elephant Hill Airavata Hawke's Bay Syrah ★★★★★

An emerging star. The classy 2017 vintage (★★★★★) was estate-grown and hand-harvested in the Gimblett Gravels, co-fermented with a splash of Viognier (1 per cent of the blend), and matured for 26 months in French oak casks (52 per cent new). Deeply coloured, it is rich and smooth-flowing, with concentrated plum, spice and nut flavours, a hint of liquorice, excellent complexity, and a long, very harmonious finish. A wine of rare finesse, it should be at its best 2024+.

Elephant Hill Hawke's Bay Syrah ★★★★☆

The 2018 vintage (★★★★☆) was hand-harvested and matured in French oak barriques. Deeply coloured, with a fragrant, spicy, slightly earthy bouquet, it is mouthfilling, with good concentration of plummy, spicy flavours, a hint of liquorice, supple tannins and a very harmonious finish. Best drinking 2023+.

DRY $34 AV

Elephant Hill Reserve Hawke's Bay Syrah ★★★★★

The 2017 vintage (★★★★★) was estate-grown and hand-picked in the Gimblett Gravels, the Bridge Pa Triangle and at Te Awanga, and matured for 20 months in French oak casks (38 per cent new). Full-coloured, it is fresh, mouthfilling, lively and supple, with concentrated, plummy, spicy flavours, finely integrated oak, good complexity, and a well-balanced, lengthy finish. Well worth cellaring.

Elephant Hill Stone Hawke's Bay Syrah (★★★★★)

The 2017 vintage (★★★★★) is a rare red – only 840 bottles were produced. Estate-grown in the Gimblett Gravels and blended with a splash of Viognier (1 per cent), it was matured for two years in French oak casks (40 per cent new). Deeply coloured and fragrant, it is densely packed, with concentrated, plummy, spicy flavours, finely textured and long. Best drinking 2022+.

DRY $75 AV

Esk Valley Hawke's Bay Syrah ★★★★☆

Priced sharply, the 2018 vintage (★★★★☆) was harvested from 12 to 25-year-old vines and matured for 14 months in French oak barriques and puncheons (15 per cent new). Full-coloured, it is vibrantly fruity and supple, in a medium to full-bodied style with concentrated, ripe, plummy, spicy flavours, showing excellent complexity, harmony and length. Delicious young.

Vintage	18
WR	5
Drink	20-25

Esk Valley Winemakers Reserve Gimblett Gravels Hawke's Bay Syrah ★★★★★

The classy 2016 vintage (★★★★★) was grown in the Cornerstone Vineyard, hand-picked, fermented with indigenous yeasts and matured for 17 months in French oak barriques (30 per cent new). Dark and still purple-flushed, with fragrant plum and spice aromas, it is sturdy and well-structured, with concentrated, youthful plum and black-pepper flavours, good tannin backbone, and lovely harmony and length. Best drinking 2022+.

Vintage	16	15	14	13	12	11	10
WR	7	NM	7	7	NM	NM	7
Drink	20-35	NM	20-30	20-25	NM	NM	20-25

DRY $70 AV

Eventide Waiheke Island Syrah (★★★★)

The distinctive 2018 vintage (★★★★) is based principally on Syrah, blended with minor portions of Petit Verdot and Tannat. Full-coloured, it is vibrantly fruity and smooth, with strong, youthful plum and spice flavours, a hint of tamarillo, a gentle seasoning of oak, and plenty of drink-young appeal.

DRY $40 –V

Falconhead Hawke's Bay Syrah ★★★☆

Priced very sharply, the 2018 vintage (★★★☆) was matured for a year in French oak casks (20 per cent new). Ruby-hued, it is medium to full-bodied, with good depth of ripe plum and spice flavours, nutty and savoury notes adding complexity, and finely balanced tannins. Best drinking now to 2022.

Vintage	18
WR	6
Drink	20-25

DRY $17 V+

Fromm La Strada Marlborough Syrah ★★★★☆

A cool-climate, 'fruit-driven' style – with style. The 2016 vintage (★★★★☆), which includes a splash of Viognier, is certified organic. From various sites in the Wairau Valley, it was hand-picked and matured for 16 to 18 months in barriques and puncheons (almost all seasoned, rather than new). It's a very fragrant red, full-bodied, with ripe plum, spice and black-pepper flavours, slightly earthy notes, gentle tannins, and excellent depth and harmony. Best drinking 2021+.

Vintage	16	15	14	13
WR	7	7	7	7
Drink	20-23	20-22	20-21	20-21

DRY $40 –V

Fromm Marlborough Syrah ★★★★

Certified organic, the 2018 vintage (★★★★) is a medium-bodied blend of Syrah (97 per cent) and Viognier (3 per cent), hand-picked and matured for 19 months in French oak barrels (less than 10 per cent new). Full, bright ruby, it is aromatic, with vibrant, plummy, well-spiced flavours, revealing strong varietal character, a subtle seasoning of oak, and a well-structured finish. Best drinking 2022+.

DRY $38 –V

Fromm Syrah Fromm Vineyard ★★★★★

Estate-grown in the Wairau Valley, Marlborough, hand-harvested from mature vines, and co-fermented with a splash of Viognier (2 per cent), the 2016 vintage (★★★★★) is a rare red (only six barrels were produced). Certified organic, it is deeply coloured, mouthfilling and concentrated, with ripe blackcurrant, plum and spice flavours, fine-grained tannins, and a long, finely structured finish. A classy red, it should be very long-lived; best drinking 2021+.

DRY $63 AV

Georges Road Cuvée 43 Waipara Syrah (★★★★)

Estate-grown and hand-harvested, the 2016 vintage (★★★★) was matured for 19 months in French oak casks (33 per cent new). Dark and youthful in colour, it is fragrant and full-bodied, with mouthfilling body and fresh, concentrated flavours, brambly and spicy, with a hint of herbs. Best drinking 2021+.

DRY $50 –V

Greyrock Te Koru Hawke's Bay Syrah (★★★☆)

The 2018 vintage (★★★☆) has bright, fullish colour. A fresh, medium-bodied style, it is youthful, with ripe, moderately concentrated, plummy, spicy flavours, some savoury notes adding complexity, and finely balanced tannins. Best drinking 2021+.

DRY $20 AV

Greystone Waipara Valley North Canterbury Syrah (★★★★☆)

Still youthful, the 2016 vintage (★★★★☆) is a distinctive red, hand-picked, matured for 15 months in seasoned French oak barrels, and bottled unfined and unfiltered. Deeply coloured, it is fragrant and supple, with concentrated flavours of plums and spices, a hint of olives, oak complexity, and fresh acidity. Best drinking 2022+.

Vintage	16
WR	6
Drink	20-30

DRY $61 –V

Haha Hawke's Bay Syrah ★★★☆

Fresh, lively and youthful, the 2019 vintage (★★★☆) is a charming red, blended with a splash of Cabernet Franc. Full-coloured, it has vibrant plum and black-pepper flavours, a hint of liquorice, fresh acidity, and very good depth. Best drinking 2021+.

DRY $25 –V

Hopesgrove Single Vineyard Hawke's Bay Silver Lining Syrah ★★★★★

The 2014 vintage (★★★★★), tasted in mid-2019, was estate-grown, hand-picked and matured for 28 months in French oak casks (66 per cent new). Deeply coloured, with a real sense of youthful potential, it is mouthfilling and supple, with concentrated, plummy, spicy flavours, complex and savoury. Best drinking 2021+.

Vintage	14
WR	6
Drink	20-29

DRY $65 AV

Hopesgrove Single Vineyard Hawke's Bay Syrah   (★★★★☆)

The 2015 vintage (★★★★☆), tasted in mid-2019, was estate-grown, hand-harvested and matured for 20 months in French oak casks (33 per cent new). Full-coloured, with a fragrant, fresh, spicy bouquet, it is an elegant red, with plummy, spicy flavours, showing good concentration and vigour, savoury notes adding complexity, and good aging potential. Best drinking 2021+.

DRY $40 –V

Huntaway Reserve Hawke's Bay Syrah   (★★★☆)

The 2017 vintage (★★★☆) is a barrel-matured, medium to full-bodied red. Fullish in colour, it is distinctly spicy, with good depth of berry/plum flavours, a hint of tamarillo, savoury notes adding complexity, and gentle tannins.

DRY $22 AV

Hunting Lodge, The, Hawke's Bay Syrah   ★★★★☆

Finely crafted for early enjoyment, but also worth cellaring, the 2019 vintage (★★★★☆) was grown in the Bridge Pa Triangle and matured for 14 months in French and American oak casks (40 per cent new). Full-coloured, with a fresh, spicy fragrance, it is full-bodied, vibrantly fruity and smooth, with plummy, spicy, peppery flavours, oak complexity, good tannin support, and a lengthy finish.

DRY $30 AV

John Forrest Collection Gimblett Gravels Hawke's Bay Syrah   ★★★★★

Still on sale, the classy, delicious 2014 vintage (★★★★★) was grown in the Cornerstone Vineyard and matured for 20 months in oak casks (40 per cent new). Boldly coloured, it is a notably powerful, lush wine, with dense, very ripe plum, blackcurrant and liquorice flavours, good tannin backbone and a finely textured, very harmonious finish. Best drinking 2021+.

DRY $80 AV

Johner Estate Reserve Gladstone Syrah   (★★★★☆)

The powerful 2016 vintage (★★★★☆) was barrel-aged for a year (20 per cent new oak), and bottled unfined and unfiltered. Deeply coloured, it has a fragrant bouquet of plums, herbs and liquorice. Bold and youthful, it is concentrated and clearly varietal, with a hint of tamarillo, nutty oak adding complexty, and good tannin backbone. Best 2021+.

Vintage	16	DRY $50 –V
WR	7	
Drink	20-23	

Junction Offside Central Hawke's Bay Syrah   (★★★★☆)

Already delicious, the 2019 vintage (★★★★☆) is a deeply coloured, fragrant red, hand-picked on the Takapau Plains and matured for nine months in French oak barrels (33 per cent new). Full-bodied, with a spicy bouquet, showing good complexity, it has concentrated, plummy, spicy flavours, a hint of liquorice, supple tannins, and excellent harmony. Drink now or cellar.

DRY $35 AV

Karikari Estate Syrah   ★★★★

The powerful 2017 vintage (★★★★☆) was estate-grown on the Karikari Peninsula in Northland, hand-picked and matured for two years in French (mostly) and American oak casks (30 per cent new). Deeply coloured, with a fragrant, spicy, slightly earthy bouquet, it is sturdy, rich and firm, with concentrated, youthful plum and spice flavours, a hint of liquorice, and obvious potential for cellaring. Best drinking 2022+.

La Collina Syrah   ★★★★★

La Collina ('The Hill') is grown at Bilancia's steep, early-ripening site on the northern slopes of Roys Hill, overlooking the Gimblett Gravels, Hawke's Bay, co-fermented with Viognier skins (but not their juice, giving a tiny Viognier component in the final blend), and matured for 20 to 24 months in 85 per cent new (but 'low-impact') French oak barriques. A majestic red, it ranks among the country's very finest Syrahs. The most recent vintage I have tasted is the 2015 (★★★★★). Full-coloured, with a floral, complex bouquet, it is savoury, with strong, ripe, plummy, spicy flavours, fine-grained tannins, and a lasting finish. It should be at its best for drinking from 2021 onwards.

Vintage	15	14	13	12	11	10
WR	7	7	7	NM	NM	7
Drink	20-28	20-27	20-30	NM	NM	20-28

Lake Chalice The Raptor Hawke's Bay Syrah   (★★★★)

The very youthful 2019 vintage (★★★★) was grown in the Gimblett Gravels and partly barrel-aged. Full-coloured, with a fresh, strong, peppery bouquet, it is full-bodied and vibrantly fruity, with a slightly earthy streak, and good intensity of plum, spice and black-pepper flavours. Best drinking 2022+.

Landing [The] Bay of Islands Syrah   ★★★★★

The very age-worthy 2017 vintage (★★★★★) is a classy, coastal Northland red, estate-grown, hand-picked and matured for 18 months in French oak barriques. Deeply coloured, it is full-bodied, with a savoury, spicy fragrance and concentrated blackcurrant, spice and plum flavours, showing excellent structure and complexity. Best drinking 2022+.

Last Shepherd Hawke's Bay Syrah   (★★★)

Attractive young, the 2017 vintage (★★★) is a lively, medium-bodied red. Deeply coloured, it has satisfying depth of berry, plum and spice flavours, woven with fresh acidity, and a smooth finish. (From Pernod-Ricard NZ.)

Leveret Estate Hawke's Bay Syrah ★★★☆

The full-bodied 2016 vintage (★★★☆) is an easy-drinking red, barrel-aged for a year. It has very good depth of plummy, spicy flavours, with nutty, savoury notes adding complexity, and a smooth finish.

DRY $24 AV

Leveret Estate Reserve Hawke's Bay Syrah ★★★★

Still on sale, the 2015 vintage (★★★★) was matured for two years in French oak casks (80 per cent new). Full-coloured, it is mouthfilling, with strong, fresh, plummy, spicy flavours, slightly earthy notes adding complexity, and finely balanced tannins. Best drinking 2021+.

DRY $26 AV

Luna Blue Rock Martinborough Syrah ★★★★☆

One of the most impressive Syrahs yet from anywhere south of Hawke's Bay, the 2018 vintage (★★★★★) was harvested from vines planted in 1997 and 2008 on a 'precipitous, north-facing slope', south of Martinborough. Matured for a year in French oak barriques and puncheons (30 per cent new), it was bottled unfined and unfiltered. Full-coloured, it is a highly fragrant, mouthfilling red with dense, ripe blackcurrant and spice flavours, complex, savoury and finely structured. A very harmonious wine with strong presence and lovely vibrancy, flow and length, it's already delicious, but well worth cellaring.

DRY $50 –V

Maison Noire Home Block Hawke's Bay Syrah (★★★☆)

The 2018 vintage (★★★☆) is a single-vineyard red, hand-harvested at Waimarama from first-crop vines. Ruby-hued, it is medium-bodied, vibrant and supple, with red-berry, plum and spice flavours, fresh acidity, good harmony, and plenty of drink-young charm. Best drinking mid-2021+.

Vintage	18
WR	5
Drink	20-25

DRY $25 –V

Man O' War Dreadnought Waiheke Island Syrah ★★★★★

Estate-grown at the eastern end of the island, the 2017 vintage (★★★★★) was hand-harvested from the 'steepest and most breathtaking hillside Syrah vineyards', and matured in French oak puncheons (32 per cent new). Deeply coloured, with a fragrant, complex, slightly earthy bouquet, it is mouthfilling, with concentrated blackcurrant, plum and spice flavours, showing excellent complexity, supple tannins and a very harmonious finish. Delicious now, it's also well worth cellaring.

DRY $64 AV

Man O' War Waiheke and Ponui Islands Syrah (★★★★☆)

The 2019 vintage (★★★★☆) is already delicious. Matured in seasoned French oak casks, it is full-coloured, with very inviting, fresh, peppery aromas. Mouthfilling and supple, it has good density of ripe, plummy, spicy flavours, with savoury notes adding complexity.

DRY $34 AV

Marsden Bay of Islands Vigot Syrah ★★★★☆

The impressive 2019 vintage (★★★★☆) is a dark Northland red, matured in French oak casks (30 per cent new). Full-bodied, with a floral, spicy bouquet, it has fresh, strong plum and spice flavours, finely integrated oak, a hint of liquorice, good tannin support, and a very finely balanced finish. Best drinking 2023+.

DRY $40 –V

Martinborough Vineyard Martinborough Syrah/Viognier ★★★★

The elegant 2017 vintage (★★★★☆) includes a splash of Viognier (4 per cent). Matured for a year in French oak casks (33 per cent new), it has fullish colour and a fragrant, peppery bouquet. A fresh, medium to full-bodied wine, it has youthful plum, spice and slight tamarillo flavours, showing good complexity, and a long, spicy finish.

Vintage	17	16
WR	7	7
Drink	20-30	20-30

DRY $45 –V

Matahiwi Estate Hawke's Bay Syrah ★★★★

The very easy-drinking 2019 vintage (★★★★) was grown in the Bridge Pa Triangle and partly barrel-aged. Fullish in colour, it is finely textured, with ripe, plummy, spicy, peppery flavours, showing some savoury complexity, gentle tannins, and lots of drink-young appeal.

Vintage	19	18
WR	6	6
Drink	20-26	20-22

DRY $30 –V

Mills Reef Arthur Edmund Gimblett Gravels Syrah (★★★★★)

Still on sale, the debut 2013 vintage (★★★★★), released in 2018, is rare – about 1000 bottles were produced. Deeply coloured and highly fragrant, it was estate-grown at two sites in Mere Road, and matured for 20 months in French and American oak hogsheads (100 per cent new). Highly refined, it is mouthfilling and sweet-fruited, with deep, notably youthful plum and spice flavours, and a long, very smooth-flowing finish. Already approachable, it should be very long-lived; open 2023+.

DRY $350 –V

Mills Reef Elspeth Gimblett Gravels Hawke's Bay Syrah   ★★★★☆

In top vintages, this is one of Hawke's Bay's greatest Syrahs. The 2016 (★★★★☆) was matured for 17 months in French oak casks (5 per cent new). Enjoyable now, it is a graceful, supple red, full-coloured, with a plummy, spicy fragrance and strong plum and black-pepper flavours, in a clearly varietal, elegant style.

Vintage	16
WR	7
Drink	20-24

 DRY $49 –V

Mills Reef Estate Hawke's Bay Syrah   ★★★

A drink-young charmer, the 2018 vintage (★★★) is a single-vineyard red, matured for seven months in French and American oak casks. Bright ruby, it is floral and supple, in a medium-bodied style with ripe, plummy, distinctly spicy flavours, a touch of complexity and gentle tannins.

 DRY $19 AV

Mills Reef Reserve Hawke's Bay Syrah   ★★★★

Fresh and full-bodied, the 2018 vintage (★★★★) is an age-worthy red, matured in American (56 per cent) and French (44 per cent) oak casks (26 per cent new). Retasted in 2020, it is full-coloured, with strong black-pepper and plum aromas and flavours, showing very good complexity, hints of liquorice and dark chocolate, and supple tannins. A very approachable red, it should be at its best mid-2021+.

 DRY $25 AV

Mission Hawke's Bay Syrah   ★★★

The 2019 vintage (★★★) is enjoyable young. Deep ruby, with a fresh, peppery bouquet, it is a medium to full-bodied style, with vibrant, plummy, spicy flavours, fresh acidity, gentle tannins, and a smooth finish.

 DRY $16 V+

Mission Huchet Gimblett Gravels Syrah   ★★★★★

Named in honour of nineteenth-century winemaker Cyprian Huchet, the 2013 vintage (★★★★★) is a powerful red with a fragrant, spicy bouquet. Estate-grown in Mere Road, in the Gimblett Gravels, and French oak-matured for 18 months (33 per cent new), it is deeply coloured, with a fragrant, spicy bouquet. Mouthfilling, it has richly varietal, concentrated blackcurrant, plum and spice flavours, fine-grained tannins, and a very harmonious finish. An elegant red with a long future, it should be at its best 2021+.

Vintage	13	12	11	10
WR	7	NM	NM	6
Drink	20-25	NM	NM	20-23

DRY $130 –V

Mission Jewelstone Hawke's Bay Syrah   ★★★★★

Currently delicious, but also very age-worthy, the 2016 vintage (★★★★★) is a single-vineyard red, estate-grown at Mere Road, in the Gimblett Gravels, and matured for a year in French oak casks (30 per cent new). Deep and youthful in colour, it is floral, concentrated and supple, with rich blackcurrant and spice flavours, savoury, earthy, nutty notes adding complexity, and a smooth, persistent finish. Best drinking 2021+. Certified organic.

Vintage	16	15	14	13
WR	7	7	7	7
Drink	20-31	20-31	20-30	20-30

DRY $50 AV

Mount Riley Marlborough Syrah   (★★★★)

Worth discovering, the 2019 vintage (★★★★) was estate-grown and hand-picked in the 17 Valley Vineyard, and matured for 11 months in French oak barriques. Deeply coloured, it is already highly approachable, with very good density of youthful plum, spice and black-pepper flavours, and supple tannins. Best drinking 2023+. Fine value.

Vintage	19
WR	5
Drink	21-24

DRY $20 V+

Moutere Hills Nelson Syrah   ★★★★

A top example of South Island Syrah, the 2019 vintage (★★★★☆) is a youthful, estate-grown red, matured in French and American oak casks. Full-coloured, it is mouthfilling, vibrant and supple, with blackcurrant, plum and spice flavours, showing excellent ripeness, vigour and depth, and a very harmonious, sustained finish. Best drinking 2022+.

DRY $35 –V

Mt Difficulty Ghost Town Bendigo Central Otago Syrah   (★★★★)

Syrah is a rare beast in Central Otago, but the 2017 vintage (★★★★) of this single-vineyard red is an auspicious debut. Matured for a year in French oak casks (25 per cent new), it is full-coloured and mouthfilling, with generous, youthful plum and spice flavours, a hint of tamarillo, savoury notes adding complexity, and good tannin backbone. Best drinking 2021+.

Vintage	17
WR	5
Drink	20-32

DRY $26 AV

Nikau Point Reserve Hawke's Bay Syrah   ★★☆

The 2018 vintage (★★☆) was French oak-aged for a year. Fullish in colour, it is a decent, slightly rustic red, with ripe berry and spice flavours, a hint of tamarillo, and a fairly firm finish. Priced right.

Vintage	18
WR	6
Drink	20-25

DRY $16 AV

Obsidian Waiheke Island Syrah ★★★★

Fresh and lively, the 2018 vintage (★★★★) is a medium to full-bodied red, matured in French oak barriques. Deep ruby, it has strong, plummy, spicy flavours, oak-derived complexity and a firmly structured finish. Open 2022+.

DRY $34 –V

Paritua Hawke's Bay Syrah ★★★★☆

The refined 2018 vintage (★★★★☆) was matured for 14 months in French oak casks (50 per cent new). Full-coloured, with a plummy, peppery, strongly varietal bouquet, it is still youthful, with excellent freshness, vigour, complexity and depth, and a savoury, very harmonious finish. Best drinking 2023+.

Vintage	18
WR	6
Drink	20-29

DRY $49 –V

Paritua Stone Paddock Hawke's Bay Syrah (★★★☆)

Enjoyable now, the 2018 vintage (★★★☆) was matured for a year in French oak casks (20 per cent new). Full-coloured, with a fresh, spicy bouquet, it is medium to full-bodied, with vibrant, ripe plum, spice and black-pepper flavours, showing some complexity, and fresh acidity. Best drinking mid-2021+.

Vintage	18
WR	6
Drink	20-28

DRY $25 –V

Pask Declaration Hawke's Bay Syrah ★★★★☆

Still very youthful, the 2019 vintage (★★★★☆) was matured in French oak hogsheads (50 per cent new). Full-coloured, it is mouthfilling, with strong plum, spice and black-pepper flavours, nutty and savoury notes adding complexity, and a long, spicy finish. It should be long-lived; best drinking 2023+.

Vintage	19
WR	7
Drink	21-35

DRY $50 –V

Pask Gimblett Gravels Hawke's Bay Syrah ★★★☆

The 2019 vintage (★★★☆) was matured for a year in seasoned French oak casks. Full-coloured, it is a lively, medium-bodied red with strong, youthful plum and spice flavours, fresh acidity, and nutty, savoury notes adding a touch of complexity. Best drinking 2022+.

DRY $22 AV

Passage Rock Reserve Waiheke Island Syrah   ★★★★★

One of Waiheke's most awarded reds. Estate-grown, the 2015 vintage (★★★★★) was matured for a year in French oak barriques (30 per cent new). Deeply coloured, it has a fragrant, spicy, complex bouquet. Sturdy and strongly varietal, it has deep, plummy, peppery flavours, showing excellent complexity, ripe tannins, and a long, savoury finish. Combining power and elegance, it should be at its best 2022+.

Vintage	15
WR	6
Drink	20-25

Passage Rock Waiheke Island Syrah   ★★★★★

This Waiheke Island red is consistently rewarding. The 2017 vintage (★★★★☆) was matured for a year in small French oak barrels (30 per cent new). Full-coloured, fresh and mouthfilling, it is strongly varietal, with a fresh, peppery fragrance. It has good density of plum, spice and black-pepper flavours, seasoned with nutty oak, good complexity, and refined tannins. Best drinking 2021+.

Vintage	17
WR	5
Drink	20-25

Quarter Acre Hawke's Bay Syrah   ★★★★★

From 'hillside and riverbed vineyards', the youthful 2018 vintage (★★★★☆) was hand-picked and matured in French oak barriques. Full-coloured, with a fragrant, peppery bouquet, it is an elegant, strongly varietal red, vibrant and supple, with good concentration of berry, spice and black-pepper flavours, fresh acidity, and obvious cellaring potential. Best drinking 2022+.

DRY $50 AV

Ra Nui Maid's Quarters Marlborough Syrah   (★★★★)

The elegant 2016 vintage (★★★★) is a single-vineyard red, hand-harvested and matured for a year in French oak barriques (20 per cent new). Bright ruby, with a peppery fragrance, it is vibrantly fruity, with good depth of fresh, plummy, spicy flavours, nutty notes adding complexity, and gentle tannins. A distinctly cool-climate style of Syrah, it should be at its best 2021+.

DRY $45 –V

Radburnd Hawke's Bay Syrah   (★★★★★)

The refined 2018 vintage (★★★★★) was grown in the Bridge Pa Triangle and in the Dartmoor Valley, hand-picked, and matured for 18 months in French oak barriques (partly new). Full-coloured, it is mouthfilling, fresh and supple, with strong plum and spice flavours, fresh acidity, and a finely poised finish. A very elegant style, it has obvious cellaring potential; best drinking 2025+.

DRY $85 –V

Redmetal Vineyards Basket Press Bridge Pa Triangle Hawke's Bay Syrah   ★★★★☆

Already very approachable, the estate-grown 2019 vintage (★★★★★) was blended with a splash of Merlot (9 per cent), and matured for nine months in oak barriques (30 per cent new). Deeply coloured, it is full-bodied and sweet-fruited, with fresh, dense plum, spice and black-pepper flavours, rich and flowing, supple tannins, and excellent depth and harmony. Best drinking 2023+.

DRY $45 –V

Redmetal Vineyards Bridge Pa Triangle Hawke's Bay Syrah   ★★★★

Enjoyable young, the 2019 vintage (★★★★) was blended with a small portion of Merlot (7 per cent) and handled without oak. Full-coloured, it is a generous red, with good concentration of fresh, ripe plum and spice flavours, a hint of liquorice, and gentle tannins. Best drinking 2022+.

Vintage	19
WR	6
Drink	21-26

DRY $24 V+

Riverby Estate Marlborough Syrah   (★★★☆)

Still unfolding, the youthful 2019 vintage (★★★☆) was matured for 11 months in oak barrels (30 per cent new). Bright ruby, it is a lively, medium-bodied red, with ripe, plummy, gently spicy flavours, fresh acidity and gentle tannins. Best drinking 2022+.

Vintage	19
WR	6
Drink	21-30

DRY $28 –V

Rogue Vine Mischievous Rogue Bay of Islands Syrah   (★★★★☆)

Already very approachable, the 2019 vintage (★★★★☆) was grown in Northland and French oak-aged. A powerful young red, it has bold, dark colour. Full-bodied and sweet-fruited, with deep, plummy, spicy flavours, a hint of liquorice, and a gentle seasoning of oak adding complexity, it's well worth cellaring to 2022+.

DRY $35 AV

Sacred Hill Deerstalkers Hawke's Bay Syrah   ★★★★★

The mouthfilling, supple 2016 vintage (★★★★★) is an age-worthy red, hand-harvested in the Gimblett Gravels and matured for 16 months in French oak barriques (25 per cent new). Full-coloured, with fresh, concentrated plum and black-pepper flavours, and a hint of liquorice, it shows excellent density and complexity. Still youthful, it's well worth cellaring to 2022+.

Vintage	16	15	14	13	11	10
WR	6	7	7	7	NM	7
Drink	20-30	20-30	20-24	20-22	NM	P

DRY $60 AV

Sacred Hill Single Vineyard Hawke's Bay Syrah   (★★★☆)

Enjoyable in its youth, the 2018 vintage (★★★☆) was estate-grown in the Deerstalkers Vineyard, in the Gimblett Gravels, and matured for eight months in French oak barrels (20 per cent new). Full-coloured, with a fragrant, peppery bouquet, it is mouthfilling and vibrantly fruity, with fresh, plummy, spicy flavours, showing a touch of complexity, very good depth, and a smooth finish. Best drinking 2021+.

DRY $28 –V

Saint Clair James Sinclair Gimblett Gravels Hawke's Bay Syrah   ★★★☆

The 2018 vintage (★★★☆) is full-coloured, with a fresh, spicy bouquet. Medium-bodied, it is vibrantly fruity, with plummy, spicy flavours, showing clear-cut varietal characteristics, a gentle seasoning of oak, and a smooth finish.

DRY $28 –V

Sileni Cellar Selection Hawke's Bay Syrah   ★★★

Enjoyable young, the 2019 vintage (★★★) is full-coloured, with good depth of fresh, plummy, spicy, slightly earthy flavours, and gentle tannins. Best drinking 2021–22.

DRY $20 –V

Sileni Grand Reserve Peak Hawke's Bay Syrah   ★★★★

Already drinking well, the supple 2018 vintage (★★★★☆) is full-coloured, fragrant and finely balanced. It has concentrated plum and black-pepper flavours, showing good complexity, gentle tannins, and a long, spicy finish.

DRY $35 –V

Smith & Sheth Cru Heretaunga Syrah   ★★★★☆

The elegant 2018 vintage (★★★★☆) was grown in the Gimblett Gravels and barrique-aged. Full-coloured, it is a fresh, medium-bodied red, with good intensity of youthful, plummy, spicy flavours, and a long, peppery finish. A refined, supple, youthful wine, it needs time; open 2022+.

DRY $40 –V

Smith & Sheth Cru Omahu Syrah   ★★★★★

The refined, very age-worthy 2018 vintage (★★★★★) was harvested from mature, 20-year-old vines in the Gimblett Gravels and barrique-matured. Deeply coloured, it is fragrant, complex and savoury, with rich, vibrant plum and black-pepper flavours, finely integrated oak, and a well-structured finish. Best drinking 2023+.

DRY $55 AV

Squawking Magpie Gimblett Gravels Hawke's Bay Stoned Crow Syrah   (★★★★★)

Currently on sale, the 2014 vintage (★★★★★) combines power and grace. A dark, single-vineyard red, it was hand-harvested and matured for 20 months in French oak barrels (33 per cent new). Fragrant and finely textured, with blackcurrant, plum and spice flavours, a hint of liquorice, and ripe, supple tannins, it's a vigorous, concentrated wine with a long life ahead.

DRY $50 AV

Squawking Magpie Gimblett Gravels Syrah   (★★★★☆)

The very age-worthy 2017 vintage (★★★★☆) is a single-vineyard red, matured for 15 months in French oak casks (22 per cent new). Full-coloured, it is a strongly varietal, medium to full-bodied red, with concentrated plum, spice and black-pepper flavours, a hint of tamarillo, good tannin backbone, and excellent complexity. Best drinking 2022+.

DRY $34 AV

Stables Ngatarawa Reserve Hawke's Bay Syrah   ★★★★

The 2019 vintage (★★★★) is a great buy. Oak-aged for 10 months, it is full-coloured, very fresh, vibrant and supple, with generous, plummy, spicy flavours, nutty notes adding complexity, and a very harmonious finish. As an affordable, drink-young style, it's hard to beat.

DRY $16 V+

Staete Landt Arie Marlborough Syrah   ★★★★

The 2015 vintage (★★★★☆) was estate-grown at Rapaura, hand-harvested and matured for 17 months in French oak barriques. Full-coloured, it is mouthfilling and flowing, with strong plum and spice flavours, peppery and lingering. Showing good personality, it's currently delicious.

Vintage	15
WR	7
Drink	20-28

DRY $49 –V

Stonecroft Crofters Gimblett Gravels Hawke's Bay Syrah   ★★★★

Certified organic, the highly attractive 2019 vintage (★★★★☆) was grown at two sites and partly barrel-aged. Designed for early consumption, it is deeply coloured and highly fragrant, with ripe plum and spice flavours, showing excellent vibrancy and depth. Medium-bodied, very fresh and supple, it should be at its best mid-2021+.

DRY $25 AV

Stonecroft Gimblett Gravels Hawke's Bay Reserve Syrah   ★★★★★

Certified organic, the very age-worthy 2018 vintage (★★★★★) was hand-picked from vines planted at Roys Hill in 1984 and matured for over 18 months in French oak barriques (30 per cent new). Deeply coloured, it is perfumed and vibrantly fruity, with concentrated blackcurrant and spice flavours, showing good complexity, fresh acidity, and fine, supple tannins. It needs time; open 2023+.

Vintage	18
WR	6
Drink	22-30

DRY $60 AV

🍇🍇🍇

Stonecroft Gimblett Gravels Hawke's Bay Serine Syrah ★★★★

Certified organic, the 2018 vintage (★★★★) was matured for over 18 months in French oak barrels (20 per cent new). Already drinking well, it is full-coloured, with a fragrant, spicy bouquet. Medium to full-bodied, it is strongly varietal and very harmonious, with fresh, plummy, spicy, peppery, slightly nutty flavours, showing good complexity, supple tannins, and a smooth finish. Best drinking 2021+.

Vintage	18
WR	6
Drink	20-25

 DRY $31 –V

Stonecroft Gimblett Gravels Hawke's Bay Undressed Syrah ★★★★

Certified organic, the 'preservative-free' (no added sulphur) 2019 vintage (★★★★) is a single-vineyard red, matured for five months in seasoned French oak barrels. Deeply coloured, with a floral, fresh bouquet, it is medium-bodied and vibrantly fruity, with generous, plummy, spicy flavours and supple tannins. An attractive, drink-young style.

 DRY $31 –V

Stonecroft The Original Gimblett Gravels Hawke's Bay Syrah ★★★★★

Certified organic, the highly refined 2018 vintage (★★★★★) was hand-harvested from a row of vines planted in 1984 and matured in a single new French oak barrel. Only two previous vintages have been made (2009 and 2014). Full-coloured, it is very graceful, with strong, youthful, plummy, spicy flavours, vigorous, finely textured and harmonious. Still a baby, it demands cellaring; open 2023+.

Vintage	18
WR	7
Drink	23-30

 DRY $150 –V

Stonyridge Pilgrim Waiheke Island Syrah/Mourvedre/Viognier/Grenache ★★★★★

This distinguished Rhône-style blend is estate-grown at Onetangi and matured for a year in French oak barriques (30 per cent new in 2015). The most recent vintage I have tasted is the 2015 (★★★★★). Deeply coloured, it is sturdy (14.5 per cent alcohol), vibrantly fruity and supple, with dense plum and spice flavours, complex and savoury, and ripe, supple tannins. Very finely textured and harmonious, it should be at its best 2021+.

Vintage	15
WR	7
Drink	20-25

DRY $95 AV

Te Awa Single Estate Hawke's Bay Syrah ★★★★☆

The 2018 vintage (★★★★) of this Gimblett Gravels red was matured in French oak hogsheads (30 per cent new). Finely balanced, it is full-coloured, mouthfilling and supple, with youthful, ripe, plummy, spicy flavours, a subtle seasoning of oak, and gentle tannins. Drink now or cellar.

Vintage	18	17	16	15	14	13
WR	5	6	7	NM	7	7
Drink	23-28	20-28	20-28	NM	20-24	20-23

 DRY $30 AV

Te Awanga Estate The Loom Reserve Hawke's Bay Syrah ★★★★

From young vines on a north-facing slope near the coast, the impressive 2018 vintage (★★★★☆) is full-coloured and mouthfilling, with concentrated, ripe plum, spice and nut flavours, savoury notes adding complexity, gentle tannins and a supple, finely balanced finish. Already drinking well, it's an age-worthy red, likely to be at its best 2021+.

 DRY $40 –V

Te Mata Estate Bullnose Syrah ★★★★★

Grown traditionally in the Bullnose and Isosceles vineyards, in the Bridge Pa Triangle inland from Hastings, in Hawke's Bay, this classy red is hand-picked and matured for 15 to 16 months in French oak barriques (40 per cent new in 2018). Unlike its Estate Vineyards stablemate (below), it is not blended with Viognier, and the vines for the Bullnose label are cropped lower. The refined, very youthful 2018 vintage (★★★★★) is the first to include Gimblett Gravels grapes (10 per cent of the blend). Deeply coloured, with a highly fragrant, spicy bouquet, it is mouthfilling and supple, with concentrated, ripe plum and black-pepper flavours, good tannin backbone, and a long finish. Already approachable, it should be at its best 2024+. (The debut 1992 vintage, tasted in late 2019, was past its peak, but fragrant, mellow and still offering a lot of pleasure.)

Vintage	18	16	15	14	13	12	11	10
WR	6	6	7	7	7	7	6	7
Drink	20-24	20-24	20-25	20-24	20-23	20-21	P	P

 DRY $75 AV

Te Mata Estate Vineyards Hawke's Bay Syrah ★★★★

The 2019 vintage (★★★★) is highly enjoyable in its youth. Estate-grown in the Woodthorpe Terraces Vineyard and in the Bridge Pa Triangle, it was matured for eight months in French oak barrels (partly new). Full-coloured, it is purple-flushed, fragrant and supple, with generous plum and spice flavours, gentle tannins, and a very harmonious finish. Already delicious, it should be at its best 2022+.

Vintage	19	18
WR	7	6
Drink	20-22	20-21

 DRY $22 V+

Terrace Edge North Canterbury Syrah ★★★★

Grown on a '45-degree north-facing "roasted slope"', the 2018 vintage (★★★★) was matured for over a year in French oak casks (25 per cent new). Full, bright ruby, with a slightly earthy bouquet, it is mouthfilling, with fresh, concentrated plum and spice flavours, a hint of tamarillo, oak complexity, and a firm finish. Best drinking 2022+. Certified organic.

Vintage	18
WR	7
Drink	21-28

 DRY $36 –V

Thomas Waiheke Island Syrah ★★★★

Estate-grown at the Batch winery, the 2018 vintage (★★★★) is a highly drinkable, youthful, supple red, fresh and full-coloured. Medium-bodied, it has vibrant, plummy, spicy flavours, fresh acidity, and savoury, nutty notes adding complexity. Best drinking 2022+.

 DRY $56 –V

Trinity Hill Gimblett Gravels Syrah ★★★★★

The 2018 vintage (★★★★☆) is a very age-worthy, supple, medium-bodied red with a floral, peppery bouquet. Estate-grown, hand-harvested and blended with a splash of Viognier (2 per cent), it was matured for eight months in a mix of French oak barriques and 5000-litre oak ovals. Strongly varietal, it has concentrated, plummy, peppery flavours, gently seasoned with oak, a hint of liquorice, and gentle tannins. Best drinking 2021+.

DRY $40 AV

Trinity Hill Homage Hawke's Bay Syrah ★★★★★

One of the country's most distinguished – and expensive – reds. Still extremely youthful, the 2018 vintage (★★★★★) was estate-grown in the Gimblett Gravels. Dark and purple-flushed, it is notably concentrated, with vibrant, ripe blackcurrant and spice flavours, oak complexity, and a long, peppery finish. Highly fragrant, savoury and structured, it's crying out for time; best drinking 2025+.

Vintage	17	16	15	14	13	12	11	10
WR	7	7	7	7	7	NM	NM	7
Drink	20-29	20-28	20-27	20-25	20-25	NM	NM	20-25

 DRY $145 AV

Trinity Hill L'Eritage Gimblett Gravels Syrah (★★★★★)

The 2018 vintage (★★★★★) is a highly seductive young red, grown at three sites in the Gimblett Gravels, Hawke's Bay, and matured in an even split of new French oak barriques and a large French oak oval. Dark and purple-flushed, it is beautifully fragrant, mouthfilling, rich and supple, with highly concentrated, ripe plum and black-pepper flavours, a hint of liquorice, and impressive harmony and length. Best drinking 2025+.

 DRY $120 AV

Unison Symphony Gimblett Gravels Hawke's Bay Syrah   (★★★★☆)

Still fresh and youthful, the 2014 vintage (★★★★☆) was estate-grown, hand-picked and matured for 20 months in French and American oak barrels. Full-coloured, it is mouthfilling and savoury, with strong, plummy, spicy, nutty flavours, hints of black pepper and liquorice, and good complexity. Best drinking 2023+.

DRY $55 –V

Unison Syrah Rocks Gimblett Gravels Syrah   (★★★★)

Already very enjoyable, the 2018 vintage (★★★★) was barrel-aged for 18 months. Full-coloured, it is fresh and smooth, in an elegant, medium-bodied style with strong, ripe, plummy, spicy flavours, fresh acidity, and considerable complexity. Best drinking 2022+.

$35 –V

Vidal Legacy Hawke's Bay Syrah   ★★★★★

The estate-grown 2016 vintage (★★★★★) was hand-harvested from 18-year-old vines in the Omahu Gravels and Twyford Gravels vineyards, in the Gimblett Gravels, and matured for 20 months in French oak barriques (43 per cent new). Dark and purple-flushed, it is enticingly floral, with lifted plum and black-pepper aromas. Concentrated and vibrantly fruity, it is richly varietal and smoothly textured, with fresh, concentrated plum, berry and pepper flavours, and a long, spicy finish. Best drinking 2021+. Still a baby, the 2018 vintage (★★★★) is a blend of Syrah (97 per cent) and Viognier (3 per cent), matured for 20 months in French oak casks (49 per cent new). Medium to full-bodied, it is a deep ruby, very vibrant red, with strong plum and spice flavours, some earthy, rustic notes and savoury characters adding complexity. Best drinking 2022+.

Vintage	18
WR	7
Drink	20-30

DRY $70 AV

Vidal Reserve Gimblett Gravels Hawke's Bay Syrah   ★★★★

The 2018 vintage (★★★★) is a bright ruby, vibrant red, grown at two sites and matured for a year in French oak barrels (14 per cent new). A refined, medium-bodied wine, it has plummy, spicy, slightly peppery flavours, showing good complexity, finely balanced tannins, and a lingering finish. Best drinking mid-2021+.

Vintage	18	17	16	15	14	13
WR	6	6	7	7	7	7
Drink	20-26	20-22	20-23	20-23	20-23	20-22

DRY $25 AV

Vidal Soler Gimblett Gravels Hawke's Bay Syrah ★★★★☆

The 2018 vintage (★★★★) is a single-vineyard red, blended with a splash of Viognier (2 per cent) and matured for 20 months in French oak barriques (30 per cent new). Full-coloured, it is a medium-bodied style, vibrantly fruity and supple, with good intensity of plummy, peppery flavours, woven with fresh acidity, and lots of youthful vigour. A strongly varietal red, it needs time; open 2022+.

Vintage	18	17
WR	7	6
Drink	20-26	20-22

DRY $35 AV

Villa Maria Cellar Selection Hawke's Bay Syrah ★★★★

The attractive 2019 vintage (★★★★) was matured for a year in French oak barriques (18 per cent new). Grown mostly (80 per cent) in the Gimblett Gravels, it is full-coloured, mouthfilling and supple, with good concentration of ripe plum and spice flavours. A finely crafted red, it's already enjoyable.

Vintage	19	18	17	16	15	14	13
WR	7	7	6	6	7	7	7
Drink	20-26	20-25	20-24	20-23	20-23	20-24	20-22

DRY $25 AV

Villa Maria Private Bin Hawke's Bay Syrah ★★★☆

The 2018 vintage (★★★☆) is a highly approachable red, bright ruby, fresh and smooth. Medium to full-bodied, it has plenty of ripe, plummy, peppery flavour, some savoury notes adding a touch of complexity, and a well-rounded finish.

DRY $20 AV

Villa Maria Reserve Gimblett Gravels Hawke's Bay Syrah ★★★★★

The 2018 vintage (★★★★★) is a classy red, estate-grown at two sites and matured for a year in French oak barriques (30 per cent new). Deeply coloured, with a fragrant bouquet of spices and liquorice, it is mouthfilling and clearly varietal, with dense plum and spice flavours, complex and savoury, and a well-structured, lingering finish. Best drinking 2023+.

DRY $70 AV

Volcanic Hills Hawke's Bay Syrah (★★★☆)

The 2019 vintage (★★★☆) is a single-vineyard red, grown at Maraekakaho and matured for a year in French oak (25 per cent new). Bright ruby, it is a fresh, youthful, medium-bodied wine, vibrantly fruity, with very good depth of plum and spice flavours, a subtle oak influence, and supple tannins. Best drinking mid-2021+.

DRY $28 –V

Waiheke Road Waiheke Island Syrah   (★★★★☆)

Grown at Te Whau Vineyard, the 2017 vintage (★★★★☆) is a fragrant, very age-worthy red. Deeply coloured, it is mouthfilling and well-structured, with youthful, plummy, spicy flavours, fresh acidity, and excellent vigour and depth. Open 2022+. (From Awaroa Winery.)

DRY $45 –V

Watermark Herringbone Hawke's Bay Syrah   (★★★☆)

The 2017 vintage (★★★☆) was hand-picked and matured for 20 months in French oak barrels (20 per cent new). Lightish in colour, with a fresh, peppery bouquet, it is medium-bodied, with spicy flavours, showing some savoury complexity, and lots of drink-young appeal. (From Hopesgrove.)

DRY $25 –V

Wither Hills Hawke's Bay Syrah   (★★★☆)

The easy-drinking 2018 vintage (★★★☆) was 'matured under different oak regimes'. Ruby-hued, it is an attractive, medium-bodied red, with good depth of ripe, plummy, spicy, slightly nutty flavours, and a well-rounded finish. Drink now to 2021.

DRY $22 AV

Tannat

Although extremely rare in New Zealand, Tannat is well known in south-west France, especially as a key ingredient in the dark, firm, tannic reds of Madiran. Tannat is also a star variety in Uruguay, yielding firm, fragrant reds with rich blackberry flavours. According to New Zealand Winegrowers' *Vineyard Register Report 2017–2020*, only 2 hectares of Tannat vines were bearing in 2020, in Northland, Hawke's Bay and Auckland.

Dancing Petrel Paewhenua Island Mangonui Northland Tannat (★★★★★)

Well worth discovering, the powerful, densely packed 2019 vintage (★★★★★) is set for a long life. Hand-picked and matured in French oak casks (30 per cent new), it has bold, dark, purple-flushed colour, loads of plummy, spicy flavour, a hint of liquorice, firm tannin backbone, and obvious potential. Best drinking 2023+.

DRY $45 AV

De La Terre Grande Reserve Hawke's Bay Tannat ★★★★★

The classy 2016 vintage (★★★★★) was grown and hand-picked at Havelock North and matured for 18 months in French oak casks (50 per cent new). Full-coloured, it is mouthfilling, with fresh, concentrated, berryish, plummy, spicy flavours, a hint of liquorice, savoury notes adding complexity, finely balanced tannins, and a long finish. Best drinking 2021+.

Vintage	16
WR	7
Drink	20-40

DRY $65 AV

De La Terre Reserve Hawke's Bay Tannat ★★★★☆

Still very youthful, the 2017 vintage (★★★★☆) was grown and hand-harvested at Havelock North. Matured for 18 months in French oak casks (30 per cent new), it is deeply coloured, fragrant and full-bodied, with strong blackcurrant, plum and spice flavours, woven with fresh acidity. Best drinking 2022+.

Vintage	17
WR	6
Drink	20-30

DRY $45 –V

Tempranillo

The star grape of Rioja, Tempranillo is grown extensively across northern and central Spain, where it yields strawberry, spice and tobacco-flavoured reds, full of personality. Barrel-aged versions mature well, developing great complexity. The great Spanish variety is starting to spread into the New World, but is still rare in New Zealand, with 20 hectares of bearing vines in 2020, mostly in Hawke's Bay (12 hectares) and Marlborough (3 hectares).

Black Barn Vineyards Hawke's Bay Tempranillo (★★★★☆)

Designed for early enjoyment, the attractive 2019 vintage (★★★★☆) was hand-picked at Havelock North and made with 'minimal' use of oak. Full-coloured, it is a fresh, vibrant, medium to full-bodied red with generous, ripe berry, plum and spice flavours, some savoury notes adding complexity, fresh acidity, and a smooth finish. Best drinking mid-2021+.

DRY $39 AV

Brennan Gibbston Central Otago Tempranillo (★★★★☆)

Drinking well in its youth, the impressive 2018 vintage (★★★★☆) is New Zealand's southernmost Tempranillo. Deeply coloured, with a fragrant bouquet, it is mouthfilling, sweet-fruited, savoury and supple, with generous, plummy, berryish flavours, a hint of herbs, and excellent depth, complexity and harmony.

DRY $45 –V

Church Road McDonald Series Hawke's Bay Tempranillo ★★★★☆

The attractive 2018 vintage (★★★★) was estate-grown in the Redstone Vineyard, in the Bridge Pa Triangle, and matured for 14 months in French oak barrels (25 per cent new). Full-coloured, it is fragrant and mouthfilling, with generous plum/spice flavours, fresh and youthful, considerable complexity, and fine-grained tannins. It's already drinking well.

DRY $32 AV

De La Terre Cloud Series Hawke's Bay Tempranillo (★★★★☆)

The youthful 2018 vintage (★★★★☆) was grown at Havelock North and matured for eight months in seasoned French oak casks. Full-coloured, with a fragrant, slightly earthy bouquet, it is mouthfilling and sweet-fruited, with ripe, brambly flavours, fresh acidity, and refined tannins. Best drinking 2022+.

Vintage	18
WR	6
Drink	20-25

DRY $45 –V

Dry River Craighall Vineyard Martinborough Tempranillo ★★★★☆

'In style the wine sits between our Pinot Noir and Syrah,' says Dry River. The highly impressive 2016 vintage (★★★★★) has promisingly deep, purple-flushed colour. Likely to be long-lived, it is mouthfilling, with dense, vibrant, plummy, spicy flavours, a hint of liquorice, a fairly firm finish and a fragrant bouquet. Best drinking 2022+.

DRY $69 –V

Hans Herzog Marlborough Tempranillo ★★★★★

The lovely 2015 vintage (★★★★★) was estate-grown in the Wairau Valley, matured for 30 months in French oak barriques, and bottled unfined and unfiltered. Full-coloured, it is mouthfilling and savoury, with deep blackcurrant, plum and spice flavours, showing excellent ripeness and complexity. Best drinking 2022+. Certified organic.

Vintage	15	14	13	12	11	10
WR	7	7	7	7	7	7
Drink	20-25	20-24	20-23	20-22	20-21	20-22

DRY $53 AV

Marsden Bay of Islands Tempranillo ★★★★

The youthful 2019 vintage (★★★★☆) is a Northland red, matured for a year in French oak barriques (30 per cent new). Full-coloured and mouthfilling, it is vibrant and savoury, with generous blackcurrant, red-berry and spice flavours, oak complexity, and good tannin backbone. Best drinking 2022+.

DRY $30 –V

Obsidian Estate Waiheke Island Tempranillo ★★★★

The quietly classy 2019 vintage (★★★★☆) was matured in French and American oak barriques. Full-coloured, with a fragrant, slightly coconutty bouquet, it is mouthfilling, with ripe plum and spice flavours, complex and savoury, fresh acidity, and good tannin backbone. A youthful, very age-worthy red, it's well worth cellaring to 2022+.

DRY $43 –V

Rock Ferry Trig Hill Vineyard Tempranillo ★★★★☆

Certified organic, the classy 2016 vintage (★★★★★) was estate-grown at Bendigo, in Central Otago, fermented with indigenous yeasts, and matured for 18 months in French oak puncheons (25 per cent new). Powerful but refined, it is deeply coloured and fragrant, with fresh, dense blackcurrant, red-berry, plum and spice flavours, showing good complexity, firm, ripe tannins, and the structure to mature well for many years. Best drinking 2021+.

DRY $40 –V

Te Awa Single Estate Hawke's Bay Tempranillo ★★★★☆

The 2018 vintage (★★★★) is a Gimblett Gravels red, matured in American and French oak barriques (40 per cent new). It has a fragrant, spicy bouquet, leading into a mouthfilling wine with fresh, moderately concentrated berry, plum and spice flavours, showing some savoury complexity, and supple tannins.

Vintage	18
WR	5
Drink	23-28

DRY $30 AV

Trinity Hill Gimblett Gravels Hawke's Bay Tempranillo ★★★★☆

The classy 2017 vintage (★★★★★) was matured for 16 months in American oak barriques (partly new). Full-coloured, with a fragrant, berryish, spicy bouquet, it is mouthfilling, with excellent density of vibrant blackcurrant, plum and spice flavours, earthy, savoury notes adding complexity, good tannin backbone, and a long, spicy finish. Best drinking 2021+.

DRY $40 –V

Yealands Estate Single Vineyard Awatere Valley Marlborough Tempranillo ★★★★

Drinking well in its youth, the 2018 vintage (★★★☆) is an estate-grown red, ruby-hued and vibrantly fruity, with satisfying depth of ripe plum, berry and spice flavours, some savoury notes adding complexity, and a smooth finish.

DRY $26 AV

Zinfandel

In California, where it is extensively planted, Zinfandel produces muscular, heady reds that can approach a dry port style. It is believed to be identical to the Primitivo variety, which yields highly characterful, warm, spicy reds in southern Italy. However, there were only 2 hectares of bearing Zinfandel vines in New Zealand in 2020, clustered in Hawke's Bay, with no expansion projected. Alan Limmer, formerly of Stonecroft winery, in Hawke's Bay, believes 'Zin' has potential here, 'if you can stand the stress of growing a grape that falls apart at the first sign of a dubious weather map!'

Stonecroft Gimblett Gravels Hawke's Bay Zinfandel ★★★★

Certified organic, the 2018 vintage (★★★★) was estate-grown at Roys Hill, hand-picked from vines planted in 1993 and aged for 16 months in seasoned American oak casks. Bright ruby, with a fresh, spicy bouquet, it is a lively, medium-bodied red, with ripe berry, plum and spice flavours, showing some complexity, and supple tannins. Already enjoyable, it's a drink-now or cellaring proposition.

Vintage	18	17
WR	5	6
Drink	20-24	20-23

DRY $31 –V

Zweigelt

Austria's most popular red-wine variety is a crossing of Blaufränkisch and St Laurent. It's a naturally high-yielding variety, but cropped lower can produce appealing, velvety reds, usually at their best when young. Zweigelt is extremely rare in New Zealand, with 3 hectares believed to be planted, mostly in Nelson and Marlborough (but the variety was not listed separately in New Zealand Winegrowers' *Vineyard Register Report 2017–2020*).

Seifried Nelson Zweigelt ★★★

The easy-drinking 2018 vintage (★★☆) was matured for a year in new and seasoned French oak barriques. Light and moderately youthful in colour, it is a pleasant, smooth red, with moderate depth of berryish, slightly spicy and nutty flavours.

DRY $18 AV

Index of Wine Brands

This index should be especially useful when you are visiting wineries as a quick way to find the reviews of each company's range of wines. It also provides links between different wine brands made by the same producer (for example, Allan Scott and Scott Base).

NOTES

NOTES

NOTES

NOTES

NOTES

NOTES

NOTES

NOTES

NOTES